Beyond Principles of Economics

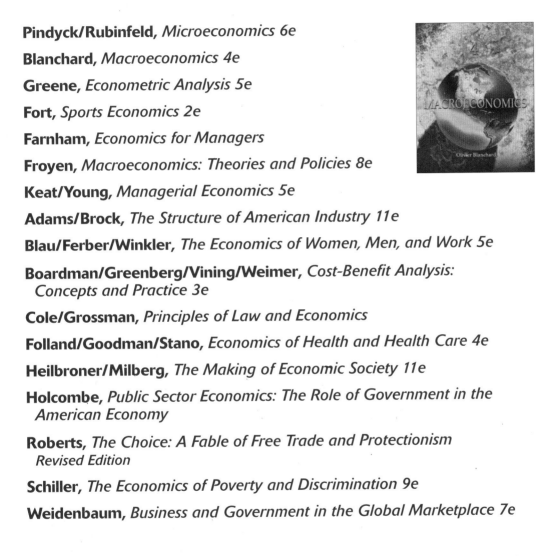

THIRD EDITION

COST-BENEFIT ANALYSIS

Concepts and Practice

Anthony E. Boardman

University of British Columbia

David H. Greenberg

University of Maryland Baltimore County

Aidan R. Vining

Simon Fraser University

David L. Weimer

University of Wisconsin–Madison

PEARSON
Prentice
Hall

Upper Saddle River, New Jersey 07458

Library of Congress Cataloging-in-Publication Data

Cost-benefit analysis: concepts and practice / Anthony
E. Boardman . . . [et al.].—3rd ed.
        p.   cm.
Includes bibliographical references and index.
ISBN 0-13-143583-3 (casebound: alk. paper)
1. Cost effectiveness.   I. Boardman, Anthony E.
HD47.4.C669 2006
658.15'54—dc22

                                              2005023256

Acquisitions Editor: Jon Axelrod
AVP/Executive Editor: David Alexander
VP/Editorial Director: Jeff Shelstad
Product Development Manager: Pamela Hersperger
Project Manager: Francesca Calogero
Editorial Assistant: Michael Dittamo
AVP/Executive Marketing Manager: Sharon Koch
Marketing Assistant: Tina Panagiotou
Senior Managing Editor (Production): Cynthia Regan
Production Editor: Denise Culhane
Permissions Coordinator: Charles Morris
Production Manager: Arnold Vila
Manufacturing Buyer: Michelle Klein
Cover Design: Bruce Kenselaar
Cover Illustration/Photo: Brian Stablyk/Photographers Choice/Getty Images, Inc.
Manager, Multimedia Production: Christy Mahon
Composition: Integra Software Services
Full-Service Project Management: BookMasters, Inc.
Printer/Binder: Hamilton Printing
Typeface: 10/12 Times Ten

Pearson Education LTD.
Pearson Education Singapore, Pte. Ltd
Pearson Education, Canada, Ltd
Pearson Education—Japan

Pearson Education Australia PTY, Limited
Pearson Education North Asia Ltd
Pearson Educación de Mexico, S.A. de C.V.
Pearson Education Malaysia, Pte. Ltd

10 9 8 7 6 5 4
ISBN 0-13-143583-3

To
Barbara, Linda, Melanie, and Ulrike

Brief Contents

Contents

Preface

Collaborative academic projects often take longer than originally anticipated, not just because of the normal delays of coordinating the efforts of busy people, but also because initially modest goals can become more ambitious as participants delve into their subject. We confess to both these sins with respect to preparing the first edition of this text. Our original plans made in 1990 were very modest. We intended to use an expanded version of the chapter on benefit-cost analysis in the text *Policy Analysis: Concepts and Practice* by David Weimer and Aidan Vining as the conceptual foundation for a collection of cases. Our goal was to produce a book that would be conceptually sound, practically oriented, and easily accessible to both students and practitioners. Although our final product was far different in form and content than we initially planned, we believe that our first edition was such a book.

Our plans evolved for a number of reasons. Perhaps most importantly, through our teaching of undergraduate and graduate students as well as our experiences in training government employees, we realized that many topics demanded extended treatment if the essential basics were to be conveyed effectively and if solid foundations were to be laid for further learning of advanced topics. We also decided that fully integrating illustrations and examples with concepts and methods is pedagogically superior to presenting independent cases. The result was a series of chapters that develops conceptual foundations, methods of application, and extensions of cost-benefit analysis through numerous practical examples and illustrations.

Our own use of the book in teaching, as well as comments from other teachers and students, helped us identify several areas for improvement in the second and third editions. In addition to adding new material to each edition, we revised and reorganized a number of chapters to make the presentation clearer and more effective. For example, in preparing the third edition, we essentially rewrote the chapters on the social discount rate and cost-effectiveness analysis and added considerable new material on using shadow prices from secondary sources. We also added a number of exercises based on spreadsheets that are available to instructors.

These improvements were made with our three intended audiences in mind. First, we intend this book for use in courses on public-sector decision-making offered in graduate programs in public policy analysis, public-sector management, urban planning, public administration, business, economics, public health, and environmental studies. Second, we envision it being used at the undergraduate level either as a primary text for a course on cost-benefit analysis or as a supplementary text for economics courses in public finance, public-sector economics, and policy analysis. Third, we intend it to be useful to policy analysts and public managers as a general introduction and practical guide to cost-benefit analysis, as well as a starting point for exploring advanced topics. In order to be appropriate for these diverse audiences, the third edition continues to emphasize clear discussion over formal mathematics, and application over abstract theory. Nevertheless, we think that we cover important, if difficult, conceptual issues in adequate detail both as a framework for thoughtful application and as a basis for further study.

The process of preparing the new edition has been a rewarding one for us. As during preparation of the first two editions, we were forced to think more deeply about some topics that we thought we had already mastered and to develop others with which none of us was very familiar. We did this enjoyably together through numerous exchanges of drafts and during an intensive work session at the University of British Columbia.

FOR INSTRUCTORS

The following supplements are available to adopting instructors. For detailed descriptions, please visit www.prenhall.com/boardman.

Instructor's Resource Center (IRC) online (log in at www.prenhall.com/irc)
Electronic Instructor's Manual
Electronic Solutions Manual

Instructor's Resource Center
Register. Redeem. Log in.

Instructors can access a variety of print, media, and presentation resources available with this text in downloadable, digital format at www.prenhall.com/irc. For most texts, resources are also available for course management platforms such as Blackboard, WebCT, and Course Compass.

It gets better. Once you register, you will not have additional forms to fill out, or multiple usernames and passwords to remember to access new titles or editions. As a registered faculty member, you can log in directly to download resource files and receive immediate access and instructions for installing course management content to your campus server.

Need help? Our dedicated technical support team is ready to assist instructors with questions about the media supplements that accompany this text. Visit 247.prenhall.com for answers to frequently asked questions and toll-free user support phone numbers.

FOR STUDENTS

Visit www.prenhall.com/boardman to access an extended bibliography.

ACKNOWLEDGMENTS

Our project was made more productive and enjoyable by our many colleagues and students who gave us advice, comments, encouragement, or information. We thank here just a few people who were particularly helpful: Marcus Berliant, Edward Bird, James Brander, Eric Hanushek, Robert Havemen, Stanley Engerman, Doug Landin,

Walter Oi, William G. Waters II, and Michael Wolkoff. We thank Roy I. Gobin, George T. Fuller, Ruth Shen, and Larry Karp, who wrote thoughtful reviews of the first edition for the publisher, and Ian Davis, John DeWald, Tim Gindling, and Laurie T. Johnson, who offered valuable comments during preparation of the second edition. Terri Sexton and Nachum Sicherman offered valuable comments during preparation of the third edition. Haynes Goddard kindly provided helpful suggestions for both the second and third editions. We especially thank Mark Moore, whose joint work with us helped us substantially improve our discussion of the social discount rate; Diane Forbes, who helped with the chapter on shadow prices from secondary sources; and Roger Noll, who made extremely valuable suggestions that prompted many substantive revisions to the first edition. Finally, we thank Jennifer Welsch and her team at BookMasters for their excellent editorial work on the third edition. Of course, they are not responsible for any errors that remain.

FEEDBACK

The authors and product team would appreciate hearing from you! Let us know what you think about this textbook by writing to college_economics@prenhall.com. Please include "Feedback about Boardman 3e" in the subject line.

If you have questions related to this product, please contact our customer service department online at 247.prenhall.com.

CHAPTER I

Introduction to Cost-Benefit Analysis

In the Affair of so much Importance to you, wherein you ask my Advice, I cannot for want of sufficient Premises, advise you *what* to determine, but if you please I will tell you *how.* When those difficult Cases occur, they are difficult, chiefly because while we have them under Consideration, all the Reasons *pro and con* are not present to the Mind at the same time; but sometimes one Set present themselves, and at other times another, the first being out of Sight. Hence the various Purposes or Inclinations that alternately prevail, and the Uncertainty that perplexes us.

To get over this, my Way is, to divide half a Sheet of Paper by a Line into two Columns; writing over the one *Pro,* and over the other *Con.* Then during three or four Days Consideration, I put down under the different Heads short Hints of the different Motives, that at different Times occur to me, *for* or *against* the Measure. When I have thus got them all together in one View, I endeavor to estimate their respective Weights; and where I find two, one on each side, that seem equal, I strike them both out. If I find a Reason *pro* equal to some two Reasons *con,* I strike out the three. If I judge some *two* Reasons *con,* equal to some three Reasons *pro,* I strike out the five; and thus proceeding I find at length where the Balance lies; and if after a Day or two of farther consideration, nothing new that is of Importance occurs on either side, I come to a Determination accordingly. And, tho' the Weight of Reasons cannot be taken with the Precision of Algebraic Quantities, yet, when each is thus considered, separately and comparatively, and the whole lies before me, I think I can judge better, and am less liable to make a rash Step; and in fact I have found great Advantage from this kind of Equation, in what may be called *Moral or Prudential Algebra.*

— B. FRANKLIN, LONDON, SEPTEMBER 19, 1772[1]

INDIVIDUAL VERSUS SOCIAL COSTS AND BENEFITS

Benjamin Franklin's advice about how to make a personal decision illustrates many of the features of cost-benefit analysis (CBA). These include a systematic cataloguing of impacts as benefits (pros) and costs (cons), valuing in dollars (assigning weights), and then determining the *net benefits* of the proposal relative to the status quo (net benefits equal benefits minus costs).

When we as individuals talk of costs and benefits, we naturally tend to consider only our *own* costs and benefits, generally choosing among alternative courses of action according to whichever has the largest individual net benefits. Similarly, in evaluating various investment alternatives, a firm tends to consider only those costs (expenditures) and benefits (revenues) that accrue to it. In CBA we try to consider *all of the costs and benefits to society as a whole,* that is, the *social costs* and the *social benefits.* For this reason, some people refer to CBA as *social* cost-benefit analysis.

CBA is a policy assessment method that quantifies in monetary terms the value of all consequences of a policy to all members of society. Throughout this book we use the terms *policy* and *project* interchangeably. More generally, CBA applies to policies, programs, projects, regulations, demonstrations, and other government interventions. The aggregate value of a policy is measured by its net social benefits, sometimes simply referred to as the net benefits. The *net social benefits, NSB,* equal the social benefits, *B,* minus the social costs, *C:*

$$NSB = B - C \qquad\qquad \textbf{(1.1)}$$

Stated at this level of abstraction, it is unlikely that many people would disagree with doing CBA. In practice, however, there are two types of disagreements. First, social critics, including some political economists, philosophers, libertarians, and socialists, have disputed the fundamental utilitarian assumptions of CBA that the sum of individual utilities should be maximized and that it is possible to trade off utility gains for some against utility losses for others. These critics are not prepared to make trade-offs between one person's benefits and another person's costs. Second, participants in the public policy-making process (analysts, bureaucrats, and politicians) may disagree about such practical issues as what impacts will actually occur over time, how to monetize (attach a dollar value to them), and how to make trade-offs between the present and the future.

In this chapter we provide a nontechnical but reasonably comprehensive overview of CBA. Although we introduce a number of key concepts, we do so informally, returning to discuss them thoroughly in subsequent chapters. Therefore, this chapter is best read without great concern about definitions and technical details.

THE PURPOSE AND USES OF CBA

The broad purpose of CBA is to help social decision making. More specifically, the objective is to facilitate more efficient allocation of society's resources. As we will see in Chapter 3, where markets work well, individual self-interest leads to an efficient allocation of resources. Consequently, government analysts and politicians bear the burden of providing a rationale for any governmental interference with private choice. Economists lump these rationales under the general heading of *market failures.* Where markets fail, there is a *prima facie* rationale for government intervention. However, and this is important to emphasize, it is no more than that. One must be able to demonstrate the superior efficiency of a particular intervention relative to the alternatives, including the status quo. For this purpose, analysts use CBA.

There are two major types of cost-benefit analysis. *Ex ante* CBA, which is just standard CBA as the term is commonly used, is conducted while a project or policy is under consideration, before it is started or implemented. *Ex ante* CBA assists in the decision about whether scarce resources should be allocated by government to a specific project or policy. Thus, its contribution to public policy decision making is direct, immediate, and bureau specific. *Ex post* CBA is conducted at the end of a project. At this time, all of the costs are "sunk" in the sense that they have already been given up to do the project. The value of *ex post* analyses is broader but less immediate as they provide information not only about the particular intervention but also about the "class" of such interventions. In other words, they contribute to "learning" by government managers, politicians, and academics about whether particular classes of projects are worthwhile.

Some CBA studies are performed during the course of the life of a project, that is, *in medias res*. Some elements of such studies are similar to an *ex ante* analysis, while others are similar to an *ex post* analysis. Like *ex ante* analyses, *in medias res* analyses have the potential of directly influencing a decision, the continuation of the project. Like *ex post* analyses, they can be based on observation rather than prediction of some costs and benefits. They also provide information that can be used to predict costs and benefits in future *ex ante* analyses.

There is also a fourth type of CBA—one that compares an *ex ante* CBA with an *ex post* (or *in medias res*) CBA *of the same project*. This comparative type of CBA is most useful to policy makers for learning about the efficacy of CBA as a decision-making and evaluative tool. Unfortunately, there are almost no disinterested published examples of this type of CBA.[2] (In Chapter 19 we provide an example of such a comparison.) The paucity of this type of CBA is not as surprising as it may appear because the constituencies for *ex ante* CBA are frequently different from those for *ex post* or *in medias res* CBA.

It is useful to elaborate on the uses of these four types of CBAs. Table 1-1 summarizes the important ways that these four types of cost-benefit analyses aid government decision making.

Project-Specific Decision Making

Ex ante analysis is most useful for deciding whether resources should be allocated to a particular project or program that is under consideration. An *in medias res* analysis of an ongoing project can also be used for decision-making purposes where it is potentially feasible to shift resources to alternative uses. Although such an analysis may lead to discontinuation of service-orientated programs (e.g., government-funded training programs), it will rarely lead to termination of a physical investment project nearing completion, such as a dam or bridge, because a large share of the costs will likely have been incurred, and benefits subsequent to the analysis will usually exceed the remaining costs. However, it can happen. For example, a Canadian Environmental Assessment Panel recommended the decommissioning of a just-completed dam on the basis of an *in medias res* analysis which showed that, with use, future environmental costs would exceed future benefits.[3] Because *ex post* analysis is conducted at the end of

	TABLE 1-1	Value of Different Classes of CBA		

	Class of Analysis			
Value	***Ex Ante***	***In Medias Res***	***Ex Post***	***Ex Ante/Ex Post or Ex Ante/In Medias Res Comparison***
Resource allocation decision for this project.	Yes—helps to select best project or make "go" versus "no-go" decisions, if accurate.	If low sunk costs, can still shift resources. If high sunk costs, usually recommends continuation.	Too late—the project is over.	Same as *in medias res* or *ex post* analysis.
Learning about actual value of specific project.	Poor estimate—high uncertainty about future benefits and costs.	Better—reduced uncertainty.	Excellent—although some errors may remain. May have to wait long for study.	Same as *in medias res* or *ex post* analysis.
Contributing to learning about actual value of similar projects.	Unlikely to add much.	Good—contribution increases as performed later. Need to adjust for uniqueness.	Very useful—although may be some errors and need to adjust for uniqueness. May have to wait long for project completion.	Same as *in medias res* or *ex post* analysis.
Learning about omission, forecasting, measurement and evaluation errors in CBA.	No	No	No	Yes, provides information about these errors and about the accuracy of CBA for similar projects.

Source: Anthony E. Boardman, Wendy L. Mallery, and Aidan R. Vining, "Learning from *Ex Ante/Ex Post* Cost-Benefit Comparisons: The Coquihalla Highway Example," *Socio-Economic Planning Sciences,* 28(2), 1994, 69–84, Table 1, p. 71. Reprinted with kind permission from Elsevier Science Ltd., The Boulevard, Langford Lane, Kidlington OX5 1GB, UK.

the project, it is obviously too late to reverse resource allocation decisions with respect to that particular project.

Learning About the Net Social Benefits of a Specific Project

In the early stages of a project there is considerable uncertainty about its actual impacts and, consequently, about the true net social benefits. As time goes by, more is known about the impacts, and CBA studies conducted later can estimate the net benefits of the project more accurately. In general, *ex post* studies are more accurate than *in medias res* studies, which are more accurate than *ex ante* studies.

Learning About the Potential Benefits of Similar Projects

Ex post analyses provide information not only about a particular policy intervention but, more importantly, about similar interventions as well. They help analysts who are currently conducting *ex ante* CBAs of similar policies. Furthermore, *ex post* analyses (and *in medias res* analyses) potentially contribute to learning by political and bureaucratic decision makers, as well as policy researchers, about whether particular kinds of projects are worthwhile.

The potential for societal learning from *in medias res* and *ex post* analyses depends on the extent to which the particular project being assessed can be replicated or can serve as a generic model for other projects. This is crucial for realistic assessment of the usefulness of CBA.[4] For example, cost-benefit analyses of experiments involving the efficacy of new surgical procedures or new pharmaceutical products usually can be generalized to larger populations. Lessons from many experiments, however, cannot be as easily generalized.[5] For example, if the proposed intervention is several orders of magnitude bigger than the experiment, there may be unknown nonlinear scale effects.[6] Also, if the proposed program has a more extended time frame than the experiment, the incentives for behavioral changes that increase costs or reduce benefits unpredictably may increase.

Learning About the Efficacy of CBA

Comparison of an *ex ante* with either an *in medias res* or an *ex post* analysis is most useful for learning about the value of CBA itself. Most importantly, a comparison CBA provides information about the accuracy of the earlier *ex ante* CBA which, in turn, provides guidance about the accuracy of future *ex ante* analyses. One recent study assesses the accuracy of U.S. regulatory cost estimates (although not of benefits). It finds that in aggregate total costs tend to be overestimated.[7] Information about the predictive ability of CBA is useful for decision-making purposes. Also, comparison studies help analysts understand the reasons for any divergence between predicted and actual benefits or costs. In Chapter 19, we discuss four important potential types of errors: omission errors, forecasting errors, measurement errors, and valuation errors. Understanding the reasons for these errors helps to reduce them in the future.

THE DEMAND FOR CBA

The U.S. federal government first mandated the general use of CBA in Executive Order 12291, issued by President Reagan in early 1981. This order requires a regulatory impact analysis (RIA) for every major regulatory initiative. (An RIA is essentially a cost-benefit analysis that also takes into account distributional and fairness considerations.) President Clinton confirmed the federal government's commitment to CBA in Executive Order 12866 in 1994. Some U.S. federal laws, such as the Unfunded Mandates Reform Act and the Government Performance and Results Act, now specifically mandate some form of *ex ante* analysis.

Nearly all other Western industrialized countries have similar protocols covering broad ranges of programs or specific program areas. For example, Canada's recent Regulatory Policy requires a CBA of regulatory changes.

The demand for *ex post* analysis is generally not so explicit; there are usually no mandatory requirements that it be done. However, on occasion, the U.S. Congress does explicitly mandate *ex post* CBA. The Clean Air Act Amendments (1990), for example, require the Environmental Protection Agency to assess the overall benefits and costs of the first 20 years of the Act. The Small Business Regulatory Enforcement Act (1996) also requires retrospective analysis.

Resource allocation decisions often draw heavily on *ex post* analyses. For example, President Clinton's 1993 State of the Union Address emphasized the relationship between *ex post* analyses of specific Head Start programs (i.e., educational programs for low-income preschool children) and his intention to increase funding and expand the scope of such programs. The U.S. federal government has also explicitly induced a form of *ex post* learning by sponsoring and requiring evaluation of a variety of "pilot tests," "demonstration projects," and "social experiments" including, for example, various welfare reform demonstrations that were conducted by different states during the 1980s and 1990s.[8] Eventually the weight of evidence may lead to a policy change.[9] For example, cost-benefit analyses in the 1960s and 1970s of industry-specific economic regulations showed that the costs of regulation often exceeded the benefits, thereby paving the way for deregulation initiatives in the trucking, airline, and telecommunications industries.[10]

As public officials face citizen resistance to raising taxes or pressure to reduce taxes, they are increasingly forced to ensure that government works more efficiently and effectively. In practice, this provides an impetus toward the increased use of CBA and related methods. Such trends are contemporaneous with greater concern for the environment, which calls for the inclusion of environmental and other social impacts, in addition to government expenditures.

THE COST OF CBA

Although the demand for CBA is increasing, we should keep in mind that it takes many resources (time, skill, and money) to do CBA well, especially where the projects are large, complex, and have unique features. The costs of conducting CBA can be very large. For example, Thomas Hopkins reported in 1992 that a CBA of reducing lead in gasoline cost the Environmental Protection Agency (EPA) roughly $1 million.[11] On average, the EPA spent approximately $700,000 for major CBA projects in the 1980s, that is, for the analysis of projects with compliance cost in excess of $100 million annually.[12] Large-scale evaluations of welfare-to-work programs, of which CBA is one component, often run into millions of dollars.

READERS OF THIS BOOK

This book is primarily for people who want to know how to do CBA. Second, it is for people who want to know how to interpret CBA—in other words, for clients of CBA. Clients can be helped in two ways. In the narrow sense, clients should be well enough informed to judge whether or not a specific CBA has been conducted well. Evidence suggests that U.S. federal agencies, even with extensive budgets, have difficulty performing CBA well. This is certainly also true for other governments with less analytic capacity and smaller budgets. Clients need to be well enough informed to avoid endorsing flawed analysis because, in contrast with the past, there is now a growing trend for oversight agencies and external critics to point out and publicize analytic errors.[13]

In the broad sense, clients may have to evaluate CBA studies well enough to have a sense of the weight of evidence in specific policy areas, such as employment training or environmental regulation. In order to do this well, one has to understand the basic principles of CBA.

THE BASIC STEPS OF CBA: COQUIHALLA HIGHWAY EXAMPLE

CBA may look intimidating and complex. To help make the process of conducting a CBA more manageable, we break it down into nine basic steps, which are listed in Table 1-2. We describe and illustrate these steps using a relatively straightforward example—the construction of a new highway. For each step, we also point out some practical difficulties. The conceptual and practical issues that we broach are the focus of the rest of this book. Do not worry if the concepts are unfamiliar to you; this is a dry run. Subsequent chapters fully explain them.

Imagine that in 1986 a cost-benefit analyst, who works for the Province of British Columbia, Canada, was asked to perform a CBA of a proposed highway between the town of Hope in the south-central part of the Province and Merritt, which is more or less due north of Hope. This highway would be called the Coquihalla Highway. The analyst's CBA is presented in Table 1-3.[14] How did the analyst get these results? What were the difficulties? We will go through the nine steps, one at a time.

1. Specify the set of alternative projects. Step 1 requires the analyst to specify the set of alternative projects. In this example, the provincial government required the analyst to consider only two alternative highways, one with tolls and one without. The provincial department of transportation decided that the toll, if applied, would be $40 for large trucks and $8 for cars. Thus, the analyst has a tractable set of alternatives to analyze.

In practice, however, there are often difficulties even at this stage. For many projects, including this one, the number of potential alternatives is huge. This highway could vary on many dimensions including the following:[15]

Road surface: It could be surfaced in bitumen or concrete.
Routing: It could take different routes.
Size: It could have two, three, four, or six lanes.
Tolls: The tolls could be higher or lower.
Wild animal friendliness: The highway could be built with or without "elk tunnels."
Timing: It could be delayed until a later date.

Changing the highway on just one of these dimensions would generate at least one new alternative. Changing two or three simultaneously would greatly increase the number of alternatives.[16] For example, with four dimensions, each with three possible values, there would be 81 alternatives! Neither decision makers nor analysts can cognitively handle comparisons among such a large number of alternatives. In practice, individuals can only focus on approximately four to seven alternatives, at best.[17] Resource and cognitive constraints mean that analysts typically analyze only a few (less than six) alternatives.

TABLE 1-2	The Major Steps in CBA

1. Specify the set of alternative projects
2. Decide whose benefits and costs count (standing)
3. Catalogue the impacts and select measurement indicators
4. Predict the impacts quantitatively over the life of the project
5. Monetize (attach dollar values to) all impacts
6. Discount benefits and costs to obtain present values
7. Compute the net present value of each alternative
8. Perform sensitivity analysis
9. Make a recommendation

CBA compares the net social benefits of investing resources in a particular potential project with the net social benefits of a hypothetical project that would be displaced if the project under evaluation were to proceed. The displaced hypothetical project is sometimes called the *counter-factual*. Usually, the counter-factual is the status quo, which means there is no change in government policy. In Table 1-3 the analyst compares the net social benefits if the highway were built to the net social benefits under the status quo of the highway not being built.

Sometimes the status quo is not a viable alternative. *If a project would displace a specific alternative rather than a hypothetical one, then it should be evaluated relative to the specific displaced alternative.* Thus, if government has committed

TABLE 1-3 Coquihalla Highway CBA (1986 $ Million)				
	No Tolls		**With Tolls**	
	A **Global** **Perspective**	**B** **Provincial** **Perspective**	**C** **Global** **Perspective**	**D** **Provincial** **Perspective**
Project Benefits:				
Time and Operating Cost Savings	389.8	292.3	290.4	217.8
Horizon Value of Highway	53.3	53.3	53.3	53.3
Safety Benefits (Lives)	36.0	27.0	25.2	18.9
Alternative Routes Benefits	14.6	10.9	9.4	7.1
Toll Revenues	—	—	—	37.4
New Users	0.8	0.6	0.3	0.2
Total Benefits	494.5	384.1	378.6	334.7
Project Costs:				
Construction	338.1	338.1	338.1	338.1
Maintenance	7.6	7.6	7.6	7.6
Toll Collection	—	—	8.4	8.4
Toll Booth Construction	—	—	0.3	0.3
Total Costs	345.7	345.7	354.4	354.4
Net Social Benefits	148.8	38.4	24.2	−19.7

Source: Adapted from Anthony Boardman, Aidan Vining, and W. G. Waters II, "Costs and Benefits through Bureaucratic Lenses: Example of a Highway Project," *Journal of Policy Analysis and Management,* 12(3) 1993, 532–555, Table 1, p. 537.

resources to either a highway project or a rail project, and there is no chance of maintaining the status quo, then the highway project should be compared with the rail project, not the status quo.

This CBA example pertains to a specific highway between Hope and Merritt. There is no attempt to compare this highway project to alternative highway projects in British Columbia, although one could do so. Rarely does the analyst compare a highway project to completely different types of projects, such as health care, antipoverty, or national defense projects. As a practical matter, full optimization is impossible. The limited nature of the comparisons sometimes frustrates politicians and decision makers who imagine that CBA is a *deus ex machina* that will rank *all* policy alternatives. On the other hand, the weight of CBA evidence can and does help in making broad social choices across policy areas.

2. Decide whose benefits and costs count (standing).   Next, the analyst must decide who has standing; that is, whose benefits and costs should be counted. In this example, the analyst's superiors in the provincial government were in a position to decide this, not the analyst. They wanted the analysis done from the provincial perspective, but also asked the analyst to take a global perspective. The provincial perspective measures only the benefits and costs that affect British Columbian residents, including costs and benefits borne by the British Columbian government. The global perspective includes the benefits and costs that affect everyone, irrespective of where they reside. Thus, it includes benefits and costs to Americans, Albertans, and even tourists from the United Kingdom. Combining these two perspectives on standing with the no-tolls and with-tolls alternatives gives the four columns in Table 1-3 labeled A through D.

It is often contentious whether an analysis should be performed from the global, national, state (provincial), or local perspective. While federal governments usually take only national costs and benefits into account, critics argue that many issues should be analyzed from a global perspective. Recent environmental issues that fall into this category include ozone depletion, global climate change, and acid rain. At the other extreme, local governments typically want to consider only benefits and costs to local residents and to ignore costs and benefits that occur in adjacent municipalities or are borne by higher levels of government. Our highway example deals with this issue by analyzing costs and benefits from both the global and the British Columbian perspectives.

3. Catalogue the impacts and select measurement indicators.   Step 3 requires the analyst to list the physical impacts of the alternatives as benefits or costs and to specify the measurement indicators. We use the term *impacts* broadly to include both inputs (required resources) and outputs. For this proposed highway, the anticipated beneficial impacts are time saved and reduced vehicle operating costs for travelers on the new highway ("Time and Operating Cost Savings" in Table 1-3); the value of the highway at the end of the discounting period of 20 years ("Horizon Value of Highway"); accidents avoided (including lives saved) due to drivers switching to the shorter, safer new highway ("Safety Benefits"); reduced congestion on existing alternative routes—the old road ("Alternative Routes Benefits"); revenues collected from tolls ("Toll Revenues"); and benefits accruing to new travelers ("New Users"). The anticipated cost impacts are construction costs ("Construction"), additional maintenance and snow removal ("Maintenance"), toll collection ("Toll Collection"), and toll booth construction and maintenance ("Toll Booth Construction").

Although the list of impacts appears comprehensive, critics might argue that some relevant impacts were omitted. Health impacts from automobile emissions, impacts on the elk population and other wildlife, and changes in scenic beauty were not considered.

From a CBA perspective, analysts are interested only in project impacts that affect the utility of individuals with standing. Impacts that do not have any value to human beings are not counted. (The caveat is that this applies only where human beings have the relevant knowledge and information to make rational valuations.) Politicians often state the purported impacts of projects in very general terms. For example, they might say that a project will promote "community capacity building." Similarly, politicians have a strong tendency to regard "growth" and "regional development" as beneficial impacts. CBA requires analysts to identify explicitly the ways in which the project would make some individuals better off through, for example, improved skills, better education, or higher incomes. Of course, analysts should also include the negative environmental and congestion impacts of growth.

Put another way, in order to treat something as an impact, we have to know there is a cause-and-effect relationship between some physical outcome of the project and the utility of human beings with standing. For some impacts, this relationship is so obvious that we do not think about it explicitly. For example, we do not question the existence of a causal relationship between motor vehicle usage and accidents involving human morbidity and mortality. For other impacts, the causal relationships may not be so obvious. What about the impact of exhaust fumes from vehicle usage of the highway on residents' blood pressure? Or the impact of more airborne lead on blood pressure? Demonstrating such cause-and-effect relationships often requires an extensive review of scientific research.

The identification and cataloguing of some potentially important impact categories may depend upon the state of scientific or social science knowledge concerning the existence of an impact. For example, controversy has surrounded the effect of chlorinated organic compounds in bleached pulp mill effluent on wildlife. Although an earlier Swedish study found such a link, a later Canadian study found none.[18]

Analysts also should be on the lookout for impacts that different groups of people view in opposite ways. Consider, for example, flooded land. Residents of a flood plain generally view floods as a cost because they damage homes, while duck hunters regard them as a benefit because they attract ducks. Even though opposing valuations of the same impact could be aggregated in one category, it is usually more useful to have two impact categories—one for damaged homes and another for recreation benefits.

Specification of impact category measurement indicators usually occurs at the same time as specification of the impact categories. There are no particular difficulties in specifying measurement indicators of each impact category in this illustration. For example, the number of lives saved per year, the number of person-hours of travel time saved, and the dollar value of gasoline saved are reasonably natural indicators. If environmental impacts had been included, then the choice of indicator would have not been so straightforward. For example, the analyst might have to decide whether to use tons of various pollutants or the resultant health effects (e.g., changes in mortality or morbidity).

The choice of measurement indicator depends on data availability and ease of monetization. For example, an analyst may wish to measure the number of crimes avoided due to a policy intervention but may not have any way to estimate this impact. However, the analyst may have access to changes in arrest rates or changes in conviction rates and may be able to use one or both of these surrogates to estimate changes in crime.[19] Bear in mind, however, that all surrogate indicators involve some loss of information. For example, the conviction rate might be increasing while there is no change in the actual crime rate.

4. Predict the impacts quantitatively over the life of the project. The proposed highway project, like almost all projects, has impacts that extend over time. The fourth task is to quantify all impacts for each alternative in each time period. The analyst must make predictions for the no-tolls and with-tolls alternatives, for each year, and for each category of driver (trucks, passenger cars on business, passenger cars on vacation) about

- the number of vehicle-trips on the new highway,
- the number of vehicle-trips on the old roads, and
- the proportion of travelers from British Columbia.

With these estimates, knowing the highway is 195 kilometers long and with other information, the analyst can estimate

- the total vehicle operating costs that users save,
- the number of accidents avoided, and
- the number of lives saved.

For example, the analyst estimated the new highway would save 6.5 lives each year:

Shorter distance:
130 vkm × 0.027 lives lost per vkm   = 3.5 lives/year
Safer (4-lane versus 2-lane):
313 vkm × 0.027 lives lost per vkm × 0.33 = 3.0 lives/year
Total lives saved[20]   = 6.5 lives/year

Lives would be saved for two reasons. First, the new highway will be shorter than existing alternative routes. It is expected that travelers will avoid 130 million vehicle-kilometers (vkm) of driving each year, and evidence suggests that, on average, there are 0.027 deaths per million vehicle-kilometers. The shorter distance is expected, therefore, to save 3.5 lives per year. The new highway is also predicted to be safer per kilometer driven. It is expected that 313 million vehicle-kilometers will be driven each year on the new highway. Based on previous traffic engineering evidence, the analyst estimated that the new highway would lower the fatal accident rate by one-third. Consequently, the new highway is expected to save 3.0 lives per year due to being safer. Combining the two components, 6.5 lives are saved per year.

Now we turn to difficulties of predicting impacts. There is relatively little discussion in the cost-benefit literature of the fact that prediction is both essential and very difficult! Most textbooks focus on theoretical issues, assuming that the relevant market demand and supply curves are known. However, they rarely are.

There are at least three reasons why prediction is often difficult. First, many public policies and programs seek to alter individuals' behavior. But it is often difficult to predict how individuals will respond overall to a change in even a single program parameter. Sometimes the targets of programs respond in unintended and unexpected ways. They may exhibit *compensating behavior* (also described as *offsetting behavior*) that partially or totally negates a predicted positive impact of the project.[21] For example, as automobiles have become intrinsically safer, at least partially because of regulations, drivers have offset these safety enhancements to some extent by engaging in riskier driving behavior.[22] Second, a policy may affect the behavior of third parties in ways that increase or decrease the costs or benefits of the policy. It is often difficult to foresee these *substitution* or *spillover effects.* For example, a law that requires juveniles to wear helmets on bicycles might encourage their parents to also wear helmets (a positive spillover); alternatively, it might lead them to drive their children more and generate more automobile accidents (a negative spillover).[23] Third, prediction may require scientific knowledge that is uncertain. This is illustrated by the current controversy surrounding the burning of fossil fuels, global warming, and the resulting impacts. While the evidence appears to suggest that global warming is a potentially serious problem, some reputable scientists are skeptical of the magnitudes of temperature increases predicted by climate models.[24] The highly publicized controversy surrounding the northern spotted owl also illustrates how widely expert opinions can vary. While some experts see the social costs of logging that eliminates the owl from some areas as relatively minor, Jonathan Rubin and his colleagues have argued the costs may be very large:

> Biologically, the owl is an indicator for old-growth temperate ecosystems: the trees, associated plant communities, and wildlife species that find their optimal habitat in these forests. If the spotted owl cannot survive, its extinction could represent a lack of viability for old-growth habitat itself. Elimination of an ecosystem, itself a unique resource, clearly has greater costs for society than mere extinction of the owl.[25]

Prediction is so important that Chapter 19 is devoted largely to it. As we discuss there, the actual usage levels of the Coquihalla Highway, which was built in 1987, are considerably higher than predicted, but so are the costs. Even this understates the prediction problems as there were errors within benefit categories that did not show up in the aggregate dollar benefit figure because they offset each other. Prediction is especially difficult where projects are unique, have long time horizons, or relationships among variables are complex.

Many of the realities associated with doing steps 3 and 4 are brilliantly summarized by Kenneth Boulding's poem on dam building in the Third World, presented in Exhibit 1-1. Many of his points deal with the omission of impact categories due to misunderstanding or ignorance of cause-and-effect relationships and to prediction errors. He also makes points about the distribution of costs and benefits, which we discuss later.

5. Monetize (attach dollar values to) all impacts.   The analyst next has to monetize each of the impacts. To *monetize* means to value in dollars. In the highway example, the analyst has to monetize each unit of time saved, lives saved, and accidents avoided. For this, the analyst needs the monetary value of an hour saved by each type of traveler, the value of a

---

EXHIBIT 1-1

A BALLAD OF ECOLOGICAL AWARENESS

The cost of building dams is always underestimated,
There's erosion of the delta that the river has created,
There's fertile soil below the dam that's likely to be looted,
And the tangled mat of forest that has got to be uprooted.

There's the breaking up of cultures with old haunts' and habits' loss,
There's the education programme that just doesn't come across,
And the wasted fruits of progress that are seldom much enjoyed
By expelled subsistence farmers who are urban unemployed.

There's disappointing yield of fish, beyond the first explosion;
There's silting up, and drawing down, and watershed erosion.
Above the dam the water's lost by sheer evaporation;
Below, the river scours, and suffers dangerous alteration.

For engineers, however good, are likely to be guilty
Of quietly forgetting that a river can be silty,
While the irrigation people too are frequently forgetting
That water poured upon the land is likely to be wetting.

Then the water in the lake, and what the lake releases,
Is crawling with infected snails and water-borne diseases.
There's a hideous locust breeding ground when water level's low,
And a million ecologic facts we really do not know.

There are benefits, of course, which may be countable, but which
Have a tendency to fall into the pockets of the rich,
While the costs are apt to fall upon the shoulders of the poor.
So cost-benefit analysis is nearly always sure
To justify the building of a solid concrete fact,
While the Ecologic Truth is left behind in the Abstract.

—KENNETH E. BOULDING

Reprinted with the kind permission of Mrs. Boulding.

statistical life saved, and the value of an avoided accident. Ideally, these estimates should be specific to British Columbia in 1986. Some of the dollar values used in this CBA were

- leisure time saved per vehicle (25 percent of gross wage times the average number of passengers) = $6.68 per vehicle-hour,
- business time saved per vehicle = $12 per vehicle-hour,
- truck drivers' time saved per vehicle = $14 per vehicle-hour, and
- value of a life saved = $500,000 per life.

These estimates were based on studies conducted prior to 1986. Recent research suggests the value of a statistical life saved is much higher, as we discuss in Chapter 15.

Sometimes, the most intuitively important impacts are difficult to value in monetary terms. The value of environmental impacts is especially contentious. In CBA, the value of an output is typically measured in terms of "willingness-to-pay." As we discuss in Chapter 4, where markets exist and work well, willingness-to-pay can be determined from the appropriate market demand curve. Naturally, problems arise where markets do not exist or do not work well. Obtaining values for such impact categories can be a life's work. Scholars have spent many person-years trying to determine the appropriate value of a statistical life saved. In practice, most CBA analysts do not reinvent these wheels but instead draw upon previous research: They use "plug in" values whenever possible. Although catalogues of impact values are not comprehensive, considerable progress has been made in this regard as we show in Chapter 15.

If no person is willing to pay for some impact, then that impact would have zero value in a CBA. For example, if construction of a dam would lead to the extermination of a species of small fish, but no one with standing is willing to pay a positive amount to save that species, then the extermination of this fish would have a value of zero in a CBA of the dam.

Some government agencies and critics of CBA are unwilling to attach a monetary value to life or to some other impact. This forces them to use an alternative method of analysis, such as *cost-effectiveness analysis* or *multigoal analysis,* which we discuss in Chapters 2 and 17.

6. Discount benefits and costs to obtain present values.   For a project that has costs or benefits that accrue over extended periods (years), we need a way to aggregate the benefits and costs that arise in different years. In CBA, future benefits and costs are *discounted* relative to present benefits and costs in order to obtain their *present values, PV.* The need to discount arises due to most people's preference to consume now rather than later and, if we consume now, we usually give up resources—there is an opportunity cost. Discounting has nothing to do with inflation per se, although inflation must be taken into account.

A cost or benefit that occurs in year t is converted to its present value by dividing it by $(1 + s)^t$, where s is the social discount rate. Suppose a project has a life of n years and let B_t and C_t denote the benefits and costs in year t, respectively. The present value of the benefits, $PV(B)$, and the present value of the costs, $PV(C)$, of the project are respectively:

$$PV(B) = \sum_{t=0}^{n} \frac{B_t}{(1 + s)^t} \tag{1.2}$$

$$PV(C) = \sum_{t=0}^{n} \frac{C_t}{(1 + s)^t} \tag{1.3}$$

In the highway example the analyst used a real (inflation-adjusted) social discount rate of 7.5 percent.

As we discuss in Chapter 10, the choice of the appropriate social discount rate is contentious. Different theories suggest different values. The value of the social discount rate is thus a good candidate for sensitivity analysis. For government analysts, the discount rate is usually mandated by a government agency with authority (e.g., the Office of Management and Budget, the General Accounting Office, the Ministry of Finance, or the Treasury Board). In many jurisdictions, the specified real (inflation-adjusted) discount rate is mandated to be between 7 and 10 percent. But, as we argue in Chapter 10, these rates are too high. In that chapter, we present the case for a range of rates depending on a few well-defined parameters. Most importantly, if the project does not have impacts beyond 50 years (it is *intragenerational*), then we recommend a social discount rate of 3.5 percent. If the project is *intergenerational*, then we recommend time-declining discount rates, as described in that chapter.[26]

7. Compute the net present value of each alternative.   The *net present value* of an alternative, *NPV*, equals the difference between the present value of the benefits and the present value of the costs:

$$NPV = PV(B) - PV(C) \tag{1.4}$$

The basic decision rule for a single alternative (relative to the status quo) is simple: *adopt the project if its NPV is positive.* In short, the analyst should recommend proceeding with the project if its $NPV = PV(B) - PV(C) > 0$; that is, if $PV(B) > PV(C)$—its benefits exceed its costs.

When there is more than one alternative to the status quo and all the alternatives are mutually exclusive, then the rule is slightly more complicated: *Select the project with the largest NPV.* This rule assumes implicitly that at least one *NPV* is positive. If no *NPV* is positive, then none of the specified alternatives are superior to the status quo, which should remain in place.

Earlier we emphasized the net social benefits of a project. We show in Chapter 6 that the *NPV* of a project or policy is identical to the present value of the net social benefits:

$$NPV = PV(NSB) \tag{1.5}$$

Thus, selecting the project with the largest *NPV* is equivalent to selecting the project with the largest present value of the net social benefits.

In the highway example, project A has a larger *NPV* than project B, and project C has a larger *NPV* than project D. The no-tolls alternatives have higher *NPV*s than the with-tolls alternatives. Thus, if the analyst were confident in the *NPV*s shown in Table 1-3, the analyst should recommend that the highway should be constructed without tolls. However, the *NPV* of the no-tolls alternative is quite small from the provincial perspective, although positive. Earlier, we emphasized that conducting CBA requires prediction and monetization, which are not always completely accurate. It is important to remember that the *NPV*s presented in Table 1-3 are estimates, and that sensitivity analysis should be conducted before making a final recommendation. However, before turning to sensitivity analysis (step 8), we discuss decision making in a bit more detail.

In fact, there is some confusion about the appropriate decision rule. Both the *internal rate of return,* which is discussed in Chapter 6, and the *benefit-cost ratio,* which is discussed in Chapter 2, have also been proposed as decision rules. This is one area

Benefits (B)
Cost (C)

More efficient
resource allocation

Optimum—*most*
efficient resource
allocation

B(Q)

C(Q)

Maximum net
benefits

Q_0 Q_1 Q_2 Q^* Q_3 Output (Q)

Moving from Q_0 toward Q^* increases efficiency; that is: $NPV(Q^*) > NPV(Q_2) > NPV(Q_1) > NPV(Q_0)$

Moving beyond Q^* reduces efficiency, but Q_3 is more efficient than Q_0: $NPV(Q^*) > NPV(Q_3) > NPV(Q_0)$

FIGURE 1-1   CBA Seeks More Efficient Resource Allocation

with more heat than light. The appropriate criterion to use is the *NPV* rule. Other methods sometimes give incorrect answers; the *NPV* rule does not.

An obvious caveat about the *NPV* criterion is that it applies only to the actual alternatives specified. Other alternatives might conceivably be better. While the *NPV* criterion results in a *more efficient* allocation of resources, it does not necessarily recommend *the most efficient* allocation of resources. This point is illustrated in Figure 1-1. Consider a project for which the alternatives vary along an output scale, Q. The benefits and costs associated with alternative scales are represented by the functions $B(Q)$ and $C(Q)$, respectively. The benefits increase as the scale increases, but at a decreasing rate. In contrast, costs increase at an increasing rate. A small-scale project (for example, Q_1) has positive net benefits relative to the status quo, Q_0. As the scale increases, the net benefits increase up to the optimal scale, Q^*.[27] As the scale increases beyond Q^*, the net benefits decrease. Net benefits are positive as long as the benefit curve is above the cost curve, they are zero where the cost curve and benefit curve intersect and are negative for larger-scale projects.

Suppose that the analyst evaluates only two alternative output levels, Q_1 and Q_2, relative to the status quo. Clearly, output level Q_2 is preferred to output level Q_1, which, in turn, is preferred to the status quo, Q_0. The analyst would therefore recommend Q_2. However, as the figure shows, net social benefits are maximized at output level Q^*. This optimal output level was not recommended because it was not among the set evaluated. In this example, use of the *NPV* criterion leads to a more efficient alternative than the status quo, but not to the most efficient alternative.

The analyst may not have included the optimum output level in the set of alternatives for a number of reasons. The optimum output level may not have been known, even approximately, until after the analysis was performed. Cognitive capacity limitations, often summarized as *bounded rationality* problems, may have hindered the analyst from considering the optimal alternative.[28] Additionally, budgetary or political constraints may have limited the range of alternatives considered.

8. Perform sensitivity analysis. As the foregoing discussion emphasizes, there may be considerable uncertainty about both the predicted impacts and the appropriate monetary valuation of each unit of the impact. For example, the analyst may be uncertain about the predicted number of lives saved and about the appropriate dollar value to place on a statistical life saved. The analyst may also be uncertain about the appropriate social discount rate and about the appropriate level of standing. Sensitivity analysis, which we discuss in Chapter 7, attempts to deal with these uncertainties. As shown in Table 1-3, the analyst performed sensitivity analysis on the standing issue by computing the *NPV*s from both the global perspective and the provincial perspective.

There are practical limits to the amount of sensitivity analysis that is feasible. Potentially, every assumption in a CBA can be varied, some infinitely. In practice, one has to use judgment and focus on the potentially most important assumptions. Although this can mean that CBA is vulnerable to the biases of the analyst, carefully thought-out scenarios are usually more informative than a mindless varying of assumptions.

9. Make a recommendation. Generally, the analyst should recommend adoption of the project with the largest *NPV*. In the highway example, three of the alternative projects have positive *NPV*s and one has a negative *NPV*. The latter indicates that from the British Columbian perspective it would be more efficient not to build the Coquihalla highway than to build it and charge tolls. Sometimes the status quo is the best alternative. Here, however, from a global perspective both the with-tolls and no-tolls alternatives are preferable to the status quo. Based on selecting the alternative with the largest *NPV*, the analyst would recommend the selection of A above C, and B above D. In short, the no-tolls alternatives are superior. This result gives a flavor of the possibly counterintuitive recommendations that CBA can support. In this case, tolls lower the *NPV* because they deter people from using the highway, and so fewer people enjoy the benefits.[29]

As we have emphasized, however, the *NPV*s are predicted values. Sensitivity analysis, which we have not shown in detail, might suggest that the alternative with the largest expected *NPV* is not necessarily the best alternative under all circumstances.

Finally, it is important to note that analysts make recommendations, not decisions. CBA concerns how resources *should* be allocated; it is *normative*. It does not claim to be a *positive* (i.e., descriptive) theory of how resource allocation decisions are actually made. Such decisions are made in political and bureaucratic arenas. CBA is only one input to this political decision-making process—one that attempts to push it towards more efficient resource allocation. CBA does not always succeed. Politicians are often reluctant to be upstaged by economic arguments. Indeed, the highway was built with tolls!

BUREAUCRATIC AND POLITICAL "LENSES"[30]

Thus far, we have assumed that CBA is not influenced by bureaucratic or political processes. This approach is reasonable given that CBA concerns how resources should be allocated. In practice, however, CBA frequently gets distorted when bureaucrats or politicians become involved with it. Bureaucrats have a tendency to *see* "costs" and "benefits" differently depending on their position and their agency. Bureaucrats' roles have a strong influence on what they think CBA is, or should be, about. Specifically, their perceptions of what constitutes "benefits" and "costs" are based on whether they are *analysts, spenders,* or *guardians.*[31] These labels are indicative of three different perspectives bureaucrats bring to project evaluation in government. The analysts' perspective is standard CBA, which we have already illustrated in Table 1-3. Guardians and spenders have quite different perspectives.

Most users of CBA have not taken, and will not take, formal courses in cost-benefit analysis. They believe that what they think is CBA is, in fact, CBA, even if it is not. This section describes the perspectives of guardians and spenders, and shows how these perspectives differ from CBA. This helps clarify what CBA actually is, in contrast to what one may think it is. This section also identifies many of the common mistakes in CBA. These mistakes often vary systematically according to one's background and experiences. Even those trained in CBA may modify their orientation toward those of guardians or spenders as a consequence of the immediacy of their daily bureaucratic roles. If you are in a government job, you should make sure you are not unconsciously adopting a guardian or spender perspective. We also hope that by understanding these different perspectives, analysts may be better able to communicate with guardians and spenders, and guardians and spenders may be better able to communicate with each other. Finally, this section helps students understand better why decisions are often not consistent with CBA—they are often made by guardians or spenders, not analysts.

The following bureaucratic lenses are caricatures. In practice, a bureaucrat may not exhibit all of the characteristics associated with a particular lens. From time to time, bureaucrats exhibit schizophrenic tendencies, sometimes adopting one cognitive perspective, sometimes another. Guardians in line agencies are prone to cognitive dissonance because they have dual allegiances. They are likely to be unsure whether they are guardians, spenders, or both. In practice, though, most bureaucrats recognize that they have a tendency to adopt one perspective or another.

Guardians

Guardians are often found in central budgetary agencies, such as the U.S. Office of Management and Budget, and in controllership or accounting functions within line agencies. They tend to have a bottom-line budgetary orientation. Their natural tendency is to equate benefits with revenue inflows to their agency or other governmental coffers (at the same level) and to equate costs with revenue outflows from their agency or other governmental coffers (at the same level). Thus, they engage in *revenue-expenditure analysis.*[32] Guardians have a natural tendency to regard CBA as naive, impractical, and, worst of all in their eyes, a tool whereby spenders can justify whatever it is they want to do.

The conceptual lens of pure guardians can be illustrated by the way they tend to look at the costs and benefits of the Coquihalla Highway. Table 1-4 summarizes how a

TABLE 1-4 Coquihalla Highway from a Provincial Guardian's Perspective (1986 $ Million)		
	No Tolls	*With Tolls*
Revenues ("Benefits"):		
Toll revenues from British Columbia residents	0	112.1
Toll revenues from non-British Columbia residents	0	37.4
	0	149.5
Expenditures ("Costs"):		
Construction	338.1	338.1
Maintenance	7.6	7.6
Toll collection	—	8.4
Toll booth construction	—	0.3
	345.7	354.4
Net Revenue-Expenditure "Benefits"	−345.7	−204.9

Source: Adapted from Anthony Boardman, Aidan Vining, and W. G. Waters II, "Costs and Benefits through Bureaucratic Lenses: Example of a Highway Project," *Journal of Policy Analysis and Management* 12(3) 1993, 532–555, Table 2, p. 539.

provincial-based guardian would evaluate the no-tolls highway alternative and the corresponding with-tolls alternative. These evaluations can be compared to the analyst's evaluations of the no-tolls and with-tolls alternatives that appear in columns B and D of Table 1-3, respectively.

To guardians, all toll revenues are regarded as benefits, whether paid by provincial residents or by nonresidents. Construction costs are a cost, because they require an outlay by the provincial government. Because guardians seek to minimize net budgetary expenditures, their preference, not surprisingly, is for the with-tolls alternative. Indeed, their gut reaction is to consider raising tolls, irrespective of its effect on levels of use or its impact on social benefits.

How does the guardian's perspective differ from CBA? Most importantly, guardians ignore nonfinancial social benefits, in this case $384.1 million for the no-tolls alternative and $297.3 million for the with-tolls alternative. In general, they ignore impacts valued by consumers and producers such as time saved and lives saved. When guardians are in control of a government service, it is easy to understand why one has to wait so long for the service. Neither your time nor anyone else's figures into their calculations. Similarly, guardians tend to ignore nonfinancial social costs, such as congestion and pollution.

In the Coquihalla highway example, all social costs happen to represent governmental budgetary costs, and so there is no difference between the CBA cost figures and the guardians' cost figures. In other situations, however, there might be considerable differences between correct social costs and guardians' costs. Consider, for example, the cost of labor in job-creation programs. Guardians would treat the full financial remuneration to labor as a cost, while CBA analysts would consider only the opportunity cost (such as lost leisure time). Another manifestation of the same mistake concerns the treatment of resources currently owned by the government, such as offices or land. Guardians tend to treat these resources as free because using them for a project does not entail additional budgetary outlay. They ignore the value of these resources in other uses.

Guardians ignore costs not borne by their level of government. Thus, they ignore the loss suffered by British Columbians from paying tolls and treat all toll revenues as a benefit. In CBA tolls are a transfer from travelers to the government: Offsetting costs and benefits result in net benefits of zero. On the other hand, provincial guardians automatically treat subsidies from the federal government as a benefit because they are revenue inflows to their level of government. However, if the federal government has earmarked a certain amount of money to transfer to British Columbia and if funds used for one purpose reduce the amount available for other purposes, then federal funds for this highway should not be treated as a benefit from the provincial perspective.

Finally, guardians generally want to use a high social discount rate. Because of their financial background or their agency's culture, they naturally prefer to use a financial market rate, which is generally higher than the appropriate social discount rate. They also know that using a high discount rate will make it more difficult to justify most projects, because costs usually occur before benefits. Thus, they can limit spenders who, in their view, overestimate benefits, underestimate costs, and generally use money less efficiently than the private sector.

Spenders

Spenders are usually in service or line departments. Some service departments, such as transportation, may be involved with physical projects, while social service departments, such as health, welfare, or education, make human capital investments. Some service departments, such as housing, make both types of expenditures. The views of spenders are somewhat more varied than those of guardians because the constituencies of particular agencies are more varied. Nevertheless, there are several commonalities.

Most importantly, spenders have a natural tendency to regard expenditures on constituents as benefits rather than as costs. For example, they typically see expenditures on labor as a benefit rather than a cost. Spenders regard themselves as builders or professional deliverers of government-mandated services. As spenders focus on providing projects or services to particular groups in society, we characterize them as engaging in *constituency-support analysis*. Table 1-5 summarizes how spenders in the provincial highway department view the no-tolls and with-tolls alternatives.

TABLE 1-5 Coquihalla Highway from a Provincial Spender's Perspective (1986 $ Million)

	No Tolls	*With Tolls*
Constituency "Benefits":		
Project Costs (from CBA)	345.7	354.4
Project Benefits (from CBA)	384.1	334.7
	729.8	689.1
Constituency "Costs":		
Toll Revenues from British Columbia Residents	—	112.1
Net Constituency "Benefits"	729.8	577.0

Source: Adapted from Anthony Boardman, Aidan Vining, and W. G. Waters II, "Costs and Benefits through Bureaucratic Lenses: Example of a Highway Project," *Journal of Policy Analysis and Management* 12(3) 1993, 532–555, Table 3, p. 542.

Spenders treat social benefits and monetary payments received by their constituents (residents of British Columbia in this example) as benefits. Thus, time saved, lives saved, and vehicle operating costs saved by British Columbians are benefits. However, they also treat money received by construction workers who build the highway as a benefit. Thus, spenders think of both project benefits *and* project costs as benefits. With this method of accounting, both the with-tolls and no-tolls highway alternatives generate huge net constituency benefits. In general, spenders tend to support *any* alternative rather than the status quo (no project). Thus, the mistrust of spenders by guardians is perfectly understandable. Guardians and spenders almost always oppose one another.

Spenders view monetary outlays by British Columbian highway users (also their constituents) as costs; for example, they treat tolls paid by British Columbians as costs. Table 1-5 shows that spenders favor the no-tolls alternative primarily because a toll is a cost for some of their constituents. Indeed, spenders normally do not favor user fees, unless their agency keeps the toll revenue within its own budget or the payers are not constituents. If spenders could collect and keep the tolls, then they would face a dilemma: Tolls would reduce constituency benefits, but would increase the agency's budget. Thus, they would face a trade-off between constituency-support maximization and their budget maximization.[33]

In general, as Robert Haveman and others have pointed out, politicians prefer projects that concentrate benefits on particular interest groups and camouflage costs or diffuse them widely over the population.[34] Spenders have similar preferences. They tend to weight each impact category by the strength of the connection that constituents make between the impact and their agency. They focus on impacts for which their constituents will give them a lot of credit, and ignore others. Because people almost always notice expenditures on themselves, such "benefits" are invariably weighted more heavily than social benefits.[35] Thus, for example, construction jobs are more heavily weighted than diffuse social benefits.

Spenders are also similar to politicians in their determination to finish partially completed projects. Congress, for example, decided to complete the Tellico Dam when it was 90 percent complete, even though the incremental costs exceeded the incremental benefits.[36] Presumably, the politicians believed that continuation of the project would bring ongoing political support. Even though sunk costs are, by definition, sunk, and it may not be efficient to finish a partially completed project, spenders tend to believe that there are positive constituency-support benefits from completion of projects.

Spenders treat some inputs as neither benefits nor costs. Currently owned government assets may simply be ignored. In support of the Tellico Dam, for example, the Tennessee Valley Authority (TVA) argued that "since the farm land behind the dam had already been purchased, the value of this land should be considered a sunk cost, even though the land has yet to be flooded and could be resold as farm land if the project was not completed."[37]

Spenders tend to favor large, irreversible, capital-intensive projects, such as urban rail systems, over reversible, less capital intensive projects, such as buses. There are immediate, significant construction job creation benefits. Also, once the infrastructure is in place, it cannot be easily redeployed to other uses, so the system will almost certainly remain in operation and constituents are guaranteed to receive some benefits. Furthermore, the normally lower operating costs for such projects allow for lower prices and relatively high usage levels, thereby further increasing constituency benefits.

The perspective of spenders concerning market efficiency has a bearing on the way they view many aspects of CBA. To spenders, markets are almost always inefficient. Spenders act as if unemployment is high in all labor markets. They believe that unemployment will be reduced by the number of people used on a government project. Even if some workers switch from other employment, these workers' vacated jobs will be filled by unemployed workers. Thus, even if the job created did not go directly to an unemployed worker, there would eventually be a job created somewhere in the economy for an unemployed worker. Spenders do not recognize that project resources are diverted from other potentially productive uses that would also involve the creation of jobs.

Furthermore, spenders believe there are indirect benefits of creating jobs and making other project expenditures, which are called multiplier effects.[38] In the extreme, spenders have a "Midas touch" view of project evaluation: First declare the expenditures (costs) to be a "benefit" and then increase these benefits by a multiplier. As a result, any government project would be seen as producing benefits greater than costs.

Spenders generally favor using a low (even zero) social discount rate. For some, this is because they are not familiar with the concept of discounting. For others, they know this tends to raise the project's *NPV* and, therefore, the probability of its adoption. Other ways spenders generate support for their projects is to choose a poorly performing counterfactual (a straw man), to lowball cost projections, or to overestimate project usage.[39]

CONCLUSION

This chapter provides a broad overview of many of the most important issues in CBA. We deal with these issues in detail in subsequent chapters. At this point, do not worry if you can only see CBA "through the glass, darkly." Do not worry if you cannot entirely follow the highway analysis. Our aim was to give you a taste of the practical realities. We think that it is important to provide readers with a sense of these realities before dealing with the technical issues.

CBA is often taught in a way that is completely divorced from political reality. We wish to avoid this mistake. CBA is a normative tool, not a description of how political and bureaucratic decision makers actually make decisions. Because CBA disregards the demands of politicians, spenders, guardians, and interest groups, it is not surprising that there are tremendous pressures to ignore it or, alternatively, to adapt it to the desires of various constituencies or interest groups. In practice, correct CBA is no more than a voice for rational decision making.

EXERCISES FOR CHAPTER I

1. Imagine that you live in a city that currently does not require bicycle riders to wear helmets. Furthermore, imagine that you enjoy riding your bicycle without wearing a helmet.
   a. From your perspective, what are the major costs and benefits of a proposed city ordinance that would require all bicycle riders to wear helmets?
   b. What are the categories of costs and benefits from society's perspective?
2. The effects of a tariff on imported kumquats can be divided into the following categories: tariff revenues received by the treasury ($8 million), increased use of resources to produce

more kumquats domestically ($6 million), the value of reduced consumption by domestic consumers ($13 million), and increased profits received by domestic kumquat growers ($4 million). A CBA from the national perspective would find costs of the tariff equal to $19 million—the sum of the costs of increased domestic production and forgone domestic consumption ($6 million + $13 million). The increased profits received by domestic kumquat growers and the tariff revenues received by the treasury simply reflect higher prices paid by domestic consumers on the kumquats that they continue to consume and, hence, count as neither benefits nor costs. Thus, the net benefits of the tariff are negative (−$19 million). Consequently, the CBA would recommend against adoption of the tariff.

a. Assuming the agriculture department views kumquat growers as its primary constituency, how would it calculate net benefits if it behaves as if it is a spender?

b. Assuming the treasury department behaves as if it is a guardian, how would it calculate net benefits if it believes that domestic growers pay profit taxes at an average rate of 20 percent?

NOTES

1. "Letter to Joseph Priestley," in *Benjamin Franklin: Representative Selections, with Introduction, Bibliography and Notes,* Frank Luther Mott and Chester E. Jorgenson (New York: American Book Company, 1936), pp. 348–49. We thank Ken MacCrimmon for bringing this quotation to our attention.

2. But see Linda R. Cohen and Roger G. Noll, eds., *The Technology Pork Barrel* (Washington, D.C.: The Brookings Institution, 1991).

3. Federal Environmental Assessment Review Office, Oldman River Dam: Report of the Environmental Assessment Panel, Ottawa, Ontario, May 1992.

4. Of course, other criteria may determine whether evaluative research actually gets used; see the preceding paragraph. For a review of evaluative research utilization in policy analysis, see David H. Greenberg and Marvin B. Mandell, "Research Utilization in Policymaking: A Tale of Two Series of Social Experiments," *Journal of Policy Analysis and Management* 10(4) 1991, 633–656.

5. Robinson G. Hollister, Peter Kemper, and Rebecca A. Maynard, eds., *The National Supported Work Demonstration* (Madison, WI: University of Wisconsin, 1984).

6. See Thomas K. Glennan Jr., "Evaluating Federal Manpower Programs: Notes and Observations," in *Evaluating Social Programs: Theory, Practice and Politics,* Peter H. Rossi and Walter Williams, eds. (New York: Seminar Press, 1972).

7. Winston Harrington, Richard D. Morgenstern, and Peter Nelson, "On the Accuracy of Regulatory Cost Estimates," *Journal of Policy Analysis and Management* 19(2) 2000, 297–322. See also Henry J. Aaron, "Seeing Through the Fog: Policymaking with Uncertain Forecasts," *Journal of Policy Analysis and Management* 19(2) 2000, 193–206.

8. For summaries of the welfare-to-work evaluations, see Daniel Friedlander, David H. Greenberg, and Philip K. Robins, "Evaluating Government Training Programs for the Economically Disadvantaged," *Journal of Economic Literature* 35(4) 1997, 1089–1855; and Karl Ashworth, Andreas Cebulla, David Greenberg, and Robert Walker, "Meta-Evaluation: Discovering What Works Best in Welfare Provision," *Evaluation* 10(2) 2004, 193–216.

9. See Martha Derthick and Paul J. Quirk, *The Politics of Deregulation* (Washington, D.C.: The Brookings Institution, 1985); and Carol H. Weiss, "Evaluation for Decisions: Is Anybody There? Does Anybody Care?" *Evaluation Practice* 9(1) 1988, 5–20.

10. See Robert Hahn and John A. Hird, "The Costs and Benefits of Regulation: Review and Synthesis," *Yale Journal of Regulation* 8(1) 1991, 233–278.

11. Thomas D. Hopkins, "Economic Analysis Requirements as a Tool of Regulatory Reform: Experience in the United States," Statement presented to the Sub-Committee on Regulations and Competitiveness Standing Committee on Finance, House of Commons, Ottawa, September 15, 1992, p. 10.

12. U.S. Environmental Protection Agency, EPA's Use of Benefit-Cost Analysis: 1981–1986, EPA-230-05-87-028, Office of Policy, Planning and Evaluation, August 1987, pp. 1–3.

13. See, for example, General Accounting Office (GAO), *Regulatory Reform: Agencies Could Improve Development, Documentation, and Clarity of Regulatory Economic Analyses,* Report to the Committee on Governmental Affairs, U.S. Senate, GAO/RCED-98-142, May 1998; and Robert W. Hahn, Jason K. Burnett, Yee-Ho I. Chin, Elizabeth A. Mader, and Petrea R. Moyle, "Assessing Regulatory Impact Analyses: The Failure of Agencies to Comply with Executive Order 12,866," *Harvard Journal of Law & Public Policy* 23(3) 2000, 859–885.

14. This example is based on W. G. Waters II and Shane Myers, "Benefit-Cost Analysis of a Toll Highway: British Columbia's Coquihalla," *Journal of Transportation Research Forum* 28(1) 1987, 434–443.

15. In fact, the divided highway was made of concrete with four lanes, and with tunnels for animals to be able to safely reach the other side.

16. In general, if there were n dimensions, each with k possible values, there would be k^n alternatives. For example, if there were three dimensions, each with three possible values, there would be 27 mutually exclusive alternatives.

17. G. A. Miller, "The Magical Number Seven, Plus or Minus Two: Some Limits on Our Capacity for Processing Information," *Psychological Review* 65(1) 1956, 81–97.

18. These studies are discussed by Robert Williamson, "Pulp Cleanup May Be Waste of Money," *Toronto Globe and Mail,* December 23, 1992, pp. A1, A6.

19. Remember that valuation of the impact at step 5 should be consistent with the chosen measurement indicator. For example, the valuation of an arrest should be lower than the valuation of a conviction so that the analyst would obtain similar estimates of the benefits of reduced crime from using either indicator.

20. Of course, some additional deaths will occur as a result of more people traveling by road. This additional cost is netted out against the generated traffic benefits.

21. Sam Peltzman introduced the term compensating behavior in "The Effects of Automobile Safety Regulations," *Journal of Political Economy* 83(4) 1975, 677–725.

22. See, for example, Robert S. Chirinko and Edward P. Harper, "Buckle Up or Slow Down? New Estimates of Offsetting Behavior and Their Implications for Automobile Safety Regulation," *Journal of Policy Analysis and Management* 12(2) 1993, 270–296; and Steven Peterson, George Hoffer, and Edward Millner, "Are Drivers of Air-Bag Equipped Cars More Aggressive? A Test of the Offsetting Behavior Hypothesis," *Journal of Law and Economics* 38(2) 1995, 251–264.

23. In fact, in a recent study Darren Grant and Stephen M. Rutner found no evidence of spillover effects from juvenile helmet laws for bicycles ("The Effect of Bicycle Helmet Legislation on Bicycling Fatalities," *Journal of Policy Analysis and Management* 23(3) 2004, 595–611).

24. For an overview, see Bjørn Lomborg, *The Skeptical Environmentalist: Measuring the Real State of the World* (New York: Cambridge University Press, 2001), 258–324.

25. Jonathan Rubin, Gloria Helfand, and John Loomis, "A Benefit-Cost Analysis of the Northern Spotted Owl," *Journal of Forestry* 89(12) 1991, 25–30, at 26.

26. These values are based on those proposed in a recent article on the social discount rate: Mark A. Moore, Anthony E. Boardman, Aidan R. Vining, David L. Weimer, and David H. Greenberg, "Just Give Me a Number! Practical Values for the Social Discount Rate," *Journal of Policy Analysis and Management* 23(4) 2004, 789–812.

27. Note that at the optimum output level, marginal benefits equal marginal costs: $\dfrac{dB}{dQ} = \dfrac{dC}{dQ}$. One can see that the slope of the benefit curve at Q^* equals the slope of the cost curve at Q^*.

28. For the seminal writing on this topic, see Herbert A. Simon, *Models of Man* (New York: Wiley, 1957). Although this problem is unlikely to be of major importance in situations similar to that depicted in Figure 1-1, cognitive factors become an increasingly important issue when (1) project benefits and costs vary simultaneously on many dimensions, (2) the benefit and cost functions are discontinuous or complex (for example, with interaction terms), or (3) there is uncertainty about the interactions or the functional forms.

29. As we discuss in Chapter 5, tolls on *congested* highways generally increase net social benefits.

30. This section draws heavily upon Anthony Boardman, Aidan Vining, and W. G. Waters II, "Costs and Benefits through Bureaucratic Lenses: Example of a Highway Project," *Journal of Policy Analysis and Management* 12(3) 1993, 532–555.

31. This terminology was introduced by Sanford Borins and David A. Good, "Spenders, Guardians and Policy Analysts: A Game of Budgeting Under the Policy and Expenditure Management System," Toronto, Case Program in Canadian Administration, Institute of Public Administration of Canada, 1987 (revised 1989).

32. Revenue-expenditure analysis is similar to *cash flow analysis* and *budget impact analysis.* Cash flow analysis and budget impact analysis are very helpful for certain purposes, but a problem arises when an analyst does this type of analysis while thinking that she is performing CBA.

33. See, for example, William A. Niskanen, "Bureaucrats and Politicians," *Journal of Law and Economics* 18(3) 1975, 617–643; and André Blais and Stéphane Dion, eds., *The Budget-Maximizing Bureaucrat: Appraisals and Evidence* (Pittsburgh, PA: University of Pittsburgh Press, 1991). For various reasons, senior spenders may be more interested in the discretionary budget or "budget shaping" than in budget maximizing; see Patrick Dunleavy, *Democracy, Bureaucracy and Public Choice* (Englewood Cliffs, NJ: Prentice Hall, 1992). They may, therefore, be willing to support projects that involve considerable "contracting out" and other activities that may not be budget maximizing per se.

34. Robert H. Haveman, "Policy Analysis and the Congress: An Economist's View," *Policy Analysis* 2(2) 1976, 235–250.

35. Barry R. Weingast, et al. refer to this phenomenon as the "Robert Moses effect" after the "famous New Yorker who appreciated it and exploited it so effectively. See Barry R. Weingast, Kenneth A. Shepsle, and Christopher Johnsen, "The Political Economy of Benefits and Costs: A Neoclassical Approach to Distributive Politics," *Journal of Political Economy* 89(4) 1981, 642–664, at 648.

36. R. K. Davis, "Lessons in Politics and Economics from the Snail Darter," in *Environmental Resources and Applied Welfare Economics: Essays in Honor of John V. Krutilla,* Vernon K. Smith, ed. (Washington, D.C.: Resources for the Future, 1988), 211–236.

37. Robert D. Behn, "Policy Analysis and Policy Politics," *Policy Analysis* 7(2) 1981, 199–226, at 213, n. 27.

38. One reason why some bureaucrats attach so much importance to multipliers is because they have a basic grounding in input-output analysis, but they do not clearly understand the fundamental distinction between impact analysis and evaluation analysis; see W. G. Waters II, "Impact Studies and the Evaluation of Public Projects," *Annals of Regional Science* 10(1) 1976, 98–103.

39. See, for example, Bent Flyvbjerg Mette Skamris Holm, and Soren Buhl, "Underestimating Costs in Public Works Projects: Error or Lie?" *Journal of the American Planning Association* 68(3) 2002, 279–293; and Linda R. Cohen and Roger G. Noll, eds., *The Technology Pork Barrel* (Washington, D.C.: The Brookings Institution, 1991).

CHAPTER 2

Conceptual Foundations of Cost-Benefit Analysis

It seems only natural to think about the alternative courses of action we face as individuals in terms of their costs and benefits. Is it appropriate to evaluate public policy alternatives in the same way? The CBA of the highway sketched in Chapter 1 identifies some of the practical difficulties analysts typically encounter in measuring costs and benefits. Yet, even if analysts can measure costs and benefits satisfactorily, evaluating alternatives solely in terms of their net benefits may not always be appropriate. An understanding of the conceptual foundations of CBA provides a basis for determining when CBA can be appropriately used as a decision rule, when it can usefully be part of a broader analysis, and when it should be avoided.

The goal of *allocative,* or *Pareto, efficiency* provides the conceptual basis for CBA. In this chapter we provide a nontechnical introduction to Pareto efficiency. We then explain its relationship to *potential Pareto efficiency,* which provides the practical basis for actually doing CBA. Our exploration of the roles of Pareto efficiency and potential Pareto efficiency in CBA provides a basis for distinguishing it from other analytical frameworks. It also provides a basis for understanding the various philosophical objections commonly made against the use of CBA for decision making.

CBA AS A FRAMEWORK FOR MEASURING EFFICIENCY

CBA can be thought of as providing a framework for measuring efficiency.[1] Though we develop a more formal definition of efficiency in the following section, it can be thought of as a situation in which resources, such as land, labor, and capital, are deployed in their highest valued uses in terms of the goods and services they create. In situations in which analysts care only about efficiency, CBA provides a method for making direct comparisons among alternative policies. Even when goals other than efficiency are important, CBA serves as a yardstick that can be used to provide information about the relative efficiency of alternative policies. Indeed, analysts rarely encounter situations in which efficiency is not one of the relevant goals. Critical evaluation of these assertions requires a more precise definition of efficiency.

Pareto Efficiency

A simple and intuitively appealing definition of efficiency, referred to as *Pareto efficiency,* underlines modern welfare economics and CBA. *An allocation of goods is Pareto efficient if no alternative allocation can make at least one person better off without making anyone else worse off.* An allocation of goods is inefficient, therefore, if an alternative allocation can be found that would make at least one person better off without making anyone else worse off. One would have to be malevolent not to want to achieve Pareto efficiency—why forgo gains to persons that would not inflict losses on others?

Figure 2-1 illustrates the concept of Pareto efficiency in a simple situation involving the allocation of a fixed amount of money between two persons. Imagine that the two persons will receive any total amount of money of up to $100 if they agree on how to split it between themselves. Assume that if they do not agree, then each person receives just $25. The vertical axis measures the amount of money received by person 1, and the horizontal axis measures the amount of money received by person 2. The point labeled $100 on the vertical axis represents the outcome in which person 1 receives the entire $100. Similarly, the point labeled $100 on the horizontal axis represents the outcome in which person 2 receives the entire $100. The line connecting these two extreme points, which we call the *potential Pareto frontier,* represents all the feasible splits between the two persons that allocate the entire $100. Splits involving less than $100 lie within the triangle formed by the potential Pareto frontier and the axes. The one labeled ($25, $25) is such a point. This point represents the status quo in the sense that it gives the amounts the two persons receive if they do not reach an agreement about splitting the $100. The segment of the potential Pareto frontier that gives each person at least as much as the status quo is called the *Pareto frontier.*

The lightly shaded triangle formed by the lines through the status quo point and the Pareto frontier represents all the alternative allocations that would make at least one of the persons better off than the status quo without making the other worse off. The existence of these points, which are feasible alternatives to the status quo that

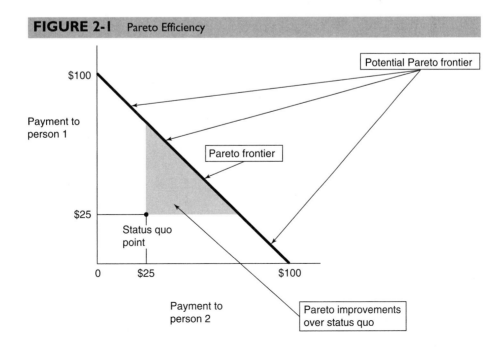

FIGURE 2-1 Pareto Efficiency

make at least one person better off without making the other worse off, means that the status quo is not Pareto efficient. Movement to any one of these points is called a *Pareto improvement.* Any Pareto improvement that does not lie on the potential Pareto frontier would leave open the possibility of further Pareto improvements and thus not provide a Pareto-efficient allocation. Only on the potential Pareto frontier is it impossible to make a feasible reallocation that makes one person better off without making the other person worse off.

It should be clear that the segment of the potential Pareto frontier that guarantees at least $25 to each person represents all the Pareto efficient allocations relative to the status quo. Each of these points makes a Pareto improvement over the status quo and leaves no opportunity for further improvements. The segment of the potential Pareto frontier that represents actual Pareto improvements depends upon the status quo. In other words, implicit in the concept of Pareto efficiency are the initial starting positions of the members of society. We return later to the significance of the difference between the potential and actual Pareto frontiers in our discussion of criticisms of CBA.

Net Benefits and Pareto Efficiency

The link between positive net social benefits (henceforth, net benefits) and Pareto efficiency is straightforward: *If a policy has positive net benefits, then it is possible to find a set of transfers, or "side payments," that makes at least one person better off without making anyone else worse off.* A full understanding of this link requires some reflection on how one measures benefits and costs in CBA. In particular, as illustrated in Figure 2-2, it requires one to consider willingness-to-pay as the method for valuing the outputs of a policy and opportunity cost as the method for valuing the resources required to implement the policy. Though we develop these important concepts more fully in the next three chapters in the context of market exchange, the simple introductions that follow provide the basis for understanding the link between net benefits and Pareto efficiency.

Willingness-to-Pay. Consider a proposed policy that would produce outputs of relevance to three people. Assume that these people make honest revelations of their assessments of the values of the outputs. Through a series of questions, we elicit the payments that each person would have to make or to receive under the policy so that he

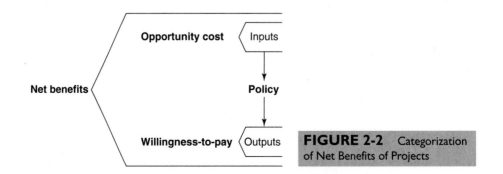

FIGURE 2-2 Categorization of Net Benefits of Projects

would be indifferent between the status quo and the policy with the payments. So, for example, imagine that person 1 honestly reveals that she would be indifferent between the status quo and paying $100 to have the policy implemented. Similarly, person 2 might say that he is indifferent between the status quo and paying $200 to have the policy implemented. These values are the willingness-to-pay of persons 1 and 2 for the policy. Unlike persons 1 and 2, assume that person 3 does not like the impacts of the proposed policy and would have to receive a payment of $250 if the policy were implemented to feel just as well off as he did under the status quo; this $250 is the amount that would have to be given to the person in conjunction with the proposed policy so that he is indifferent between it and the status quo. The negative of this amount ($-$250) would be the willingness-to-pay of person 3 for the policy. As the policy in effect takes something away from person 3, the amount is called the person's *willingness-to-accept.* In this stylized example, the distinction between willingness-to-pay and willingness-to-accept is purely semantic. However, the distinction has substantive importance when one actually seeks to measure willingness-to-pay through survey methods, because, as discussed in Chapters 14 and 17, people often demand larger payments to accept small decrements in some good than they are willing to pay to obtain small increments of exactly the same size. For now, we use willingness-to-pay inclusively, assuming that its elicitation appropriately takes account of whether people perceive policies as giving them something or as taking away something.

The algebraic sum of these willingness-to-pay values is the appropriate measure of the net benefits of the impacts of the policy. In this example, the willingness-to-pay amounts can be divided into $300 of benefits ($100 + $200) accruing to persons 1 and 2 and $250 of costs ($-$250) accruing to person 3. The net benefits are thus positive and equal to $50. If these were the only three persons affected by the policy, and if the policy required no resources to implement, then the $50 would be the appropriate measure of net benefits from the perspective of CBA. Simple implementation of the policy would not be Pareto efficient because person 3 would be made worse off with respect to the status quo.

Yet, we can easily imagine altering the policy so that it would be Pareto efficient. For example, imagine that person 3 receives $75 from person 1 and $175 from person 2 as part of the policy. Now person 1 is better off than the status quo ($100 of benefits minus $75 given to person 3), person 2 is better off ($200 of benefits minus $175 given to person 3), and person 3 is no worse off ($250 of costs from the policy minus $250 of benefits in the form of compensation from persons 1 and 2).

The key point is that if, and only if, the aggregate net benefits of the policy as measured by the willingness-to-pay of all affected individuals are positive, then there exist sets of contributions and payments that would make the policy a Pareto improvement over the status quo.

Opportunity Cost. The implementation of policies almost always requires the use of some inputs that could be used to produce other things of value. For example, implementing a policy to build a bridge across a river would require the use of labor, steel, concrete, construction machinery, and land that could be used to produce other things of value to people. The concept of opportunity cost is used in CBA to place a dollar value on the inputs required to implement policies. *The opportunity cost of using an input to implement a policy is its value in its best alternative use.* Opportunity cost measures the value of what society must forgo to use the input to implement the policy.

Return to the example of the three persons whose aggregate willingness-to-pay for the policy was $50. Imagine that the policy requires inputs that have an opportunity cost of $75. That is, if the policy were implemented, then some other members of society would have to give up goods valued at $75. In this case, the policy does not generate enough net benefits to the three persons to allow them to compensate those who must forgo the $75 of goods—the net benefits to society as a whole are negative $25 ($50 of net benefits to the three persons minus $75 in opportunity costs to the rest of society). Thus, the policy could not be made Pareto efficient because it does not produce enough benefits to permit all those who bear costs to be compensated fully. If the opportunity cost were only $20 instead of $75, then net benefits to society would be $30 and it would be possible to compensate all those who bear costs so that no one is made worse off, and some people are made better off, by the policy. In general, if the net benefits of a policy are positive, then it is potentially Pareto improving.

USING CBA FOR DECISION MAKING

The connection between net benefits and Pareto efficiency should now be clear. *As long as analysts value all impacts in terms of willingness-to-pay and value all required inputs in terms of opportunity costs, then the sign of the net benefits indicates whether it would be possible to compensate those who bear costs sufficiently so that no one is made worse off and at least one person is better off.* Positive net benefits indicate the potential for compensation to make the policy Pareto efficient; negative net benefits indicate the absence of this potential.

One could imagine the following decision rule for CBA: Adopt only policies that are actually Pareto efficient. In other words, only policies that yield positive benefits after providing full compensation to all those who bear costs would be adopted so that there would be no losers, only winners. Although conceptually this is appealing, such a rule would be extremely difficult to apply in practice for a number of reasons. First, it would place great informational burdens on analysts not just to measure aggregate costs and benefits, which can often be inferred from observing prices and quantities in markets, but also to measure costs and benefits for each person, a task that would generally render CBA too costly to use. Second, once the distribution of costs and benefits at the individual level were known, the administrative costs of actually making specific transfers for each government policy would almost certainly be high. Third, it is difficult to operate a practical system of compensation payments that does not distort the investment and work behavior of households. Fourth, the requirement that everyone be fully compensated would create a strong incentive for people to find ways to overstate the costs and understate the benefits that they expect to receive from policies, complicating the already difficult task of inferring how much each person is willing to pay for the outputs produced by the policy. The "actual Pareto efficiency" principle in practice would thus result in society forgoing many policies that offer positive net benefits and the diversion of much effort toward the seeking of unjustified compensation.

Potential Pareto Efficiency

CBA utilizes an alternative decision rule with somewhat less conceptual appeal, but much greater feasibility, than the actual Pareto efficiency rule. It is based on what is known as the *Kaldor-Hicks criterion:* A policy should be adopted if and only if those who will gain could fully compensate those who will lose and still be better off.[2] The Kaldor-Hicks criterion provides the basis for the *potential Pareto efficiency rule,* or, more commonly, the *net benefits criterion: Adopt only policies that have positive net benefits.* As long as net benefits are positive, it is at least possible that losers could be compensated so that the policy potentially could be Pareto improving. In terms of Figure 2-1, any point on the potential Pareto frontier would pass the potential Pareto efficiency rule, while only those points on the potential Pareto frontier that guarantee at least $25 to each person (the heavily shaded segment of the potential Pareto frontier) pass the actual Pareto efficiency rule.

In practice, the assessment of whether particular policies increase efficiency depends on whether they represent *potential Pareto improvements.* That is, do the policies provide sufficient net gains so that all losers could be compensated? Potential Pareto efficiency is achieved only when all potential Pareto improvements have been exhausted.

Several justifications, aside from feasibility, are commonly offered in defense of the potential Pareto efficiency rule. First, by always choosing policies with positive net benefits, society maximizes aggregate wealth. This indirectly helps those who are worse off in society because richer societies have greater capability for helping their poorest members and, if redistribution is a normal good (that is, other things being equal, people want more of it as their wealth increases), members of society have a greater willingness to help.[3] Second, it is likely that different policies will have different sets of winners and losers. Thus, if the rule is consistently applied to government activity, then costs and benefits will tend to average out across people so that each person is likely to realize positive net benefits from the full collection of policies. Third, as we discuss later in this chapter, the rule stands in contrast to the incentives in representative political systems to give too much weight to costs and benefits that accrue to organized groups and too little weight to costs and benefits that accrue to unorganized interests. Its use in public discourse may thereby reduce the chances that Pareto-inefficient policies will be adopted. Fourth, if a more equal distribution of wealth or income is an important goal, then it is possible to address it directly through transfers after a large number of efficiency-enhancing policies have been adopted. In other words, redistribution, at least in theory, can be done "wholesale" with a single redistribution program rather than "retail" in each particular program.

Application of the Decision Rule in Practice

Two polices can be thought of as independent if the adoption of one does not influence the costs and benefits of the other. When all relevant projects are independent, the CBA decision rule is simple: *Adopt all policies that have positive net benefits.* A more general version of the rule applies in situations involving multiple policies that may enhance or interfere with each other: *Choose the combination of policies that maximizes net benefits.* Physical, budgetary, and other constraints may limit the combinations of policies that are feasible.

Consider the list of projects in Table 2-1. Interpret the costs and benefits as being expressed in terms of present values, so that they can be directly compared with dollars of current consumption. Note that projects C and D are shown as synergistic. That is, the net benefits from adopting both together exceed the sum of the net benefits from

TABLE 2-1 Choosing Among Projects: Net Benefits versus Benefit-Cost Ratios

	Costs (millions of dollars)	*Benefits (millions of dollars)*	*Net Benefits (millions of dollars)*	*Benefits/Costs*
No project	0	0	0	–
Project A	1	10	9	10
Project B	10	30	20	3
Project C	4	8	4	2
Project D	3	5	2	1.7
Projects C and D	7	21	14	3
Project E	10	8	−2	0.8

(1) No constraints: Choose A, B, and combination C and D (net benefits equal $43 million).
(2) All projects mutually exclusive: Choose B (net benefits equal $20 million).
(3) Total costs cannot exceed $10 million: Choose A and combination C and D (net benefits equal $23 million).
Source: Adapted from David L. Weimer and Aidan R. Vining, *Policy Analysis: Concepts and Practice,* 4th ed. (Upper Saddle River, NJ: Pearson Prentice Hall, 2005), Figure 16.2.

adopting each one independently. Such might be the case if project C were a dam that created a reservoir that could be used for recreation as well as hydroelectric power and D were a road that increased access to the reservoir. Of course, projects can also interfere with each other; for instance, the dam might reduce the benefits of a downstream recreation project. The important point is that care must be taken to determine interactions among projects so that the combinations of projects providing the greatest net benefits in aggregate can be readily identified.

Suppose we could choose any combination of projects; then we should simply choose all those with positive net benefits—namely, projects A, B, and combination C and D.

Suppose now the policies are mutually exclusive. For example, we cannot drain a swamp to create agricultural land and simultaneously preserve it as a wildlife refuge. When all the available policies are mutually exclusive, efficiency is maximized by choosing the one with the largest net positive benefits—project B, with net benefits of $20 million. Assume, however, that all projects are mutually exclusive, except C and D, which can be built together to obtain synergistic gains. By taking the combination of C and D to be a separate project, we can consider all the projects on the list to be mutually exclusive. Looking down the column labeled "Net Benefits," we see that project B still offers the largest net benefits, and therefore should be the one selected, but the combination of C and D offers the next highest net benefits.

Analysts often compare programs in terms of *benefit-cost ratios.* Note that project B, which offers the largest net benefits, does not have the largest ratio of benefits to costs. Project A has a benefit-cost ratio of 10, while project B has a benefit-cost ratio of only 3. Nevertheless, project B should be selected because it offers larger net benefits than project A. This comparison shows how the benefit-cost ratio can sometimes confuse the choice process when the projects under consideration are of different scale (that is, project B involves substantially higher costs than project A). Furthermore, the benefit-cost ratio is sensitive to whether negative willingness-to-pay (willingness-to-accept) amounts are subtracted from benefits or added to costs. For example, imagine that the cost of $10 million for project B was opportunity costs and the benefits of

$30 million consisted of $40 million for one group and −$10 million for another. Treating the negative willingness-to-pay as a cost rather than as a negative benefit would leave the net benefits unchanged but lower the benefit-cost ratio from 3 to 2. Thus, benefit-cost ratios are subject to manipulation. For these reasons, *we recommend that analysts avoid using benefit-cost ratios and rely instead on net benefits to rank policies.*

Return to Table 2-1 and interpret the listed costs as public expenditures exactly equal to opportunity costs and the listed benefits as the willingness-to-pay values for all project effects. Now assume that, while none of the projects are mutually exclusive in a physical sense, total public expenditures (costs) cannot exceed $10 million because of a budget constraint that is binding for political reasons. If project B is selected, then the budget constraint is met and net benefits of $20 million result. If project A and the combination of projects C and D are selected instead, then the budget constraint is also met, but net benefits of $23 million result. No other feasible combination offers larger net benefits. Thus, under the budget constraint, net benefits are maximized by choosing projects A and the combination of C and D.

FUNDAMENTAL ISSUES RELATED TO WILLINGNESS-TO-PAY

Three sets of fundamental issues arise with respect to the interpretation of willingness-to-pay as a measure of benefits in the assessment of the efficiency of policies. First, a theoretical limitation in the aggregation of willingness-to-pay amounts across individuals opens the possibility that the net benefits criterion will not lead to fully satisfactory rankings of policies. Second, normative issues arise because of the dependence of willingness-to-pay on the distribution of wealth in society. Third, normative issues also arise with respect to the *issue of standing,* which concerns whose willingness-to-pay counts in the aggregation of benefits.

The Theoretical Limitation of Willingness-to-Pay as Basis for Social Orderings

Although using net benefits as a basis for choosing efficient public policies is intuitively appealing, its implementation through the aggregation of the willingness-to-pay amounts of the members of society confronts a fundamental theoretical limitation: Ranking policies in terms of net benefits does not guarantee a transitive social ordering of the policies.

A *transitive* ordering requires that if *X* is preferred to *Y,* and *Y* is preferred to *Z,* then *X* is preferred to *Z.* The logic of transitivity seems so clear that it is usually taken as an axiom of rationality in the preferences of individuals. We would certainly be skeptical about the mental state of someone who tells us she prefers apples to oranges, and she prefers oranges to peaches, but she prefers peaches to apples. This violation of transitivity implies a cyclical, and therefore ambiguous, ordering of the alternatives. Clearly, transitivity is a desirable property of any preference ordering.

If every member of a society has transitive preferences, does it follow that reasonable procedures for aggregating their preferences will always produce a transitive social ordering? An example makes clear that the answer is no. Consider a common aggregation procedure: majority rule voting over pairs of alternatives. Imagine that

TABLE 2-2	Cyclical Social Preferences under Pairwise Majority Rule Voting		
Preference Ordering	*Voter 1*	*Voter 2*	*Voter 3*
First Choice	X	Z	Y
Second Choice	Y	X	Z
Third Choice	Z	Y	X

(1) Pairwise Voting Outcomes: X versus Y, X wins; Y versus Z, Y wins; X versus Z, Z wins.
(2) Implied Social Ordering: X is preferred to Y, Y is preferred to Z, but Z is preferred to X!

society consists of three voters who have preferences over three alternatives, *X, Y,* and *Z,* as displayed in Table 2-2. Specifically, voter 1 prefers *X* to *Y* to *Z,* voter 2 prefers *Z* to *X* to *Y,* and voter 3 prefers *Y* to *Z* to *X.* If the voters express their sincere preferences in each round of voting, then we would find that given the choice between *X* and *Y,* a majority of voters (voters 1 and 2) would vote for *X* because they each prefer it to *Y.* Similarly, given the choice between *Y* and *Z,* a majority would vote for *Y.* Yet in a choice between *X* and *Z,* a majority would vote for *Z.* Thus, the implied social ordering is intransitive because *X* is preferred to *Y, Y* is preferred to *Z,* but *Z* is preferred to *X!*

Is the possibility of obtaining an intransitive social ordering peculiar to the use of pairwise majority rule voting to produce rankings alternatives? Surprisingly, it can result from any rule for creating a social ordering that satisfies certain minimal requirements. We cannot expect any rule for creating a social ranking of policy alternatives to be fully satisfactory. In 1951, Kenneth Arrow proved that any *social choice rule* that satisfies a basic set of fairness conditions can produce an intransitive social ordering.[4] *Arrow's theorem* applies to any rule for choice in which two or more persons must select a policy from among three or more alternatives. It requires any such scheme to satisfy at least the following conditions to be considered fair: First, each person is allowed to have any transitive preferences over the possible policy alternatives (*axiom of unrestricted domain*). Second, if one alternative is unanimously preferred to a second, then the rule for choice will not select the second (*axiom of Pareto choice*). Third, the ranking of any two alternatives should not depend on what other alternatives are available (*axiom of independence*). Fourth, the rule must not allow any one person dictatorial power to impose his or her preferences as the social ordering (*axiom of nondictatorship*). Arrow's theorem states that any fair rule for choice (one that satisfies the four previous axioms) will not guarantee a transitive *social ordering* of policy alternatives. That is, it is possible that individual preferences are such that the social ordering will be cyclical. Thus, unless the net benefit rule, which is a social choice rule, violates one of the axioms, it cannot guarantee a transitive social ordering of policies.

In order to ensure that the use of willingness-to-pay in the implementation of the net benefit rule will produce a transitive social ordering of policies, some restrictions, violating the axiom of unrestricted domain, must be placed on the preferences that individuals are allowed to hold.[5] Economic models commonly assume that individual preferences are represented by utility functions (numerical representations of preference orderings) that exhibit positive but declining marginal utility; that is, other things equal, incremental consumption of any good increases utility but not by as much as the previous incremental unit. Unfortunately, this relatively weak restriction of the domain of preferences (it rules out preferences that cannot be represented by such utility functions) is not enough to guarantee that the net benefit rule based on willingness-to-pay will *always* produce a transitive social ordering. Two additional restrictions are required: (1) The utility functions of individuals must be such that the individual demand curves that they imply can be aggregated into a market demand curve with the sum of individual incomes as an argument, and (2) all individuals must face the same set of prices.[6] The first restriction is quite strong in that it requires each individual's demand for each good to increase linearly with increasing income and have the same rate of increase for each individual. The second restriction, generally satisfied when all goods are traded in markets, may be violated when policies allocate quantities of goods to individuals who cannot resell them in markets.

The necessity of restricting the allowed preferences of individuals to guarantee a transitive social ordering from the use of willingness-to-pay in the implementation of the net benefits criterion makes clear that it is an imperfect criterion for assessing the relative efficiency of alternative policies.[7] Of course, analysts can avoid this theoretical problem by assuming that the preferences of individual consumers conform to restrictive assumptions consistent with the existence of an appropriate aggregate demand function. Alternatively, analysts can avoid it by assuming that policies affect the price of only a single good. Indeed, as discussed in the next three chapters, analysts seeking to estimate willingness-to-pay typically work with an aggregate, or market, demand schedule for a single good, implicitly assuming away price effects in the markets for other goods.

Despite its theoretical imperfection as a measure of efficiency, willingness-to-pay is an intuitively appealing and practical concept for guiding the implementation of the net benefits criterion. As discussed next, however, its dependence on the distribution of wealth raises a serious normative concern about its use.

Dependence of Willingness-to-Pay on the Distribution of Wealth

The willingness of a person to pay to obtain a desired policy impact will tend to be higher the greater the wealth that she or he has available. Consequently, the sum of the willingness of persons to pay, the benefit measure in CBA, depends on their levels of wealth. If the distribution of wealth in society were to be changed, then it would be likely that the sum of individuals' willingness-to-pay amounts would change as well, perhaps altering the ranking of alternative policies in terms of their net benefits.

The dependence of net benefits on the distribution of wealth would not pose a conceptual problem if losers from adopted policies were *actually* compensated so that the adopted polices would produce actual, rather than potential, Pareto improvements. From a utilitarian perspective, Pareto improvement guarantees that the sum of utilities of individuals in society increases. In application of the potential Pareto principle, however, it is possible that an adopted policy could actually lower the sum of utilities if people with different levels of wealth had different *marginal utilities of money*.[8] As an illustration, consider a policy that gives $10 of benefits to a person with high wealth and inflicts $9 of costs on a person with low wealth. If the low-wealth person's marginal utility of money is higher than that of the high-wealth person, then it is possible that the utility loss of the low-wealth person could outweigh the utility gain of the high-wealth person. Thus, while the Pareto principle allows us to avoid interpersonal utility comparisons by guaranteeing increases in aggregate utility for policies with positive net benefits, the potential Pareto principle does not do so.

The implication of the dependence of willingness-to-pay on wealth is that the justification for the potential Pareto principle weakens for policies that concentrate costs and benefits on different wealth groups. Policies with positive net benefits that concentrate costs on low-wealth groups may not increase aggregate utility; moreover, policies with negative net benefits that concentrate benefits on low-wealth groups may not decrease aggregate utility. However, if the potential Pareto principle is consistently applied and adopted policies do not produce consistent losers or winners, then the overall effects of the policies taken together will tend to make everyone better off. Hence, concerns about reductions in aggregate utility would be unfounded.

Critics of CBA sometimes question the validity of the concept of Pareto efficiency itself because it depends on the status quo distribution of wealth. Returning to Figure 2-1, note that the location of the Pareto frontier would change if the location of the status quo point were changed. Some have advocated the formulation of a social welfare function that maps the utility, wealth, or consumption of all individuals in society into an index that ranks alternative distributions of goods.[9] In this broader framework incorporating distributional values, an efficient policy is one that maximizes the value of the social welfare function. But how does society determine the social welfare function? Unfortunately, Arrow's theorem, as well as practical difficulties in obtaining needed information, precludes the formulation of a social welfare function through any fair collective choice procedure.[10] In practice, it must therefore be provided subjectively by the analyst.[11] We believe that it is usually better to keep the subjective distributional values of analysts explicit by comparing policies both in terms of efficiency and the selected distributional criteria, as illustrated in the discussion of multigoal analysis and distributionally weighted CBA later in this chapter. As an alternative, analysts can report net benefits by wealth or income group as well as for society as a whole.

Dependence of Net Benefits on Assumptions About Standing

The question of whose willingness-to-pay should count in the aggregation of net benefits has come to be known as the issue of standing.[12] It has immediate practical importance in at least three contexts: the jurisdictional definition of society, the exclusion of socially unacceptable preferences, and the inclusion of the preferences of future generations. A recognition of social constraints, rights, and duties often helps answer the question of standing.

Jurisdictional Definition of Society.   The most inclusive definition of society encompasses all people, no matter where they live or to which government they owe allegiance. Analysts working for the United Nations or some other international organization might very well adopt such a universalistic, or global, perspective. Yet for purposes of CBA, most analysts define society at the national level. The basis for this restriction in jurisdiction is the notion that the citizens of a country share a common constitution, formal or informal, that sets out fundamental values and rules for making collective choices. In a sense, they consent to being a society. Furthermore, they accept that the citizens of other countries have their own constitutions that make them distinct polities.

The distinction between universal and national jurisdiction becomes relevant in the evaluation of policies whose impacts spill over national borders. For example, if U.S. analysts adopt the national-level jurisdiction as defining society, then they would not attempt to measure the willingness of Canadian residents to pay to avoid pollution originating in the United States that exacerbates acid rain in Canada. Of course, the willingness of U.S. citizens to pay to reduce acid rain in Canada should be included in the CBA, though in practice, it would be very difficult to measure.

As in the highway example discussed in Chapter 1, a similar issue arises with respect to subnational units of government. As an illustration, consider a city that is deciding whether to build a convention center. Assume that a CBA from the national perspective (giving standing to everyone in the country) predicts that the project will generate $1 million in benefits (which all accrue to city residents) and $2 million in costs (which are also borne by city residents), thereby resulting in negative $1 million in net benefits (or $1 million in net costs). Also assume, however, that through an intergovernmental grants program the national government will repay the city's $2 million of costs resulting from this particular project. The grant appears to the city residents as a $2 million benefit offsetting $2 million in local costs. Thus, from the perspective of the city, the convention center generates $1 million in net benefits rather than $1 million in net costs.

One can make an argument that the city should treat its residents as the relevant society and, hence, should not give standing to nonresidents. The city government has a charter to promote the welfare of its residents. The city by itself can do relatively little to affect national policy—even if it does not take advantage of all the opportunities offered by the national government, other cities probably will. Furthermore, analysts who do not adopt the city's perspective, but instead employ only the broader national perspective, risk losing influence, a possibility of special concern to analysts who earn their living by giving advice to the city.

Adopting the subnational perspective, however, makes CBA a less valuable decision rule for public policy. We believe that analysts should generally conduct CBA from at least the national perspective. They may, of course, also conduct a parallel CBA from the subnational perspective as a response to the narrower interests of their clients. If major impacts spill over national borders, then the CBA should be done from the global as well as the national perspective.

Jurisdictional Membership. Deciding the jurisdictional definition of society leaves open a number of questions about who should be counted as members of the jurisdiction. For example, almost all analysts agree that citizens of their country living abroad should have standing. With respect to noncitizens in their country, most analysts would probably give standing to those who were in the country legally. Less consensus exists with respect to the standing of other categories of people: Should illegal aliens have standing? What about the children of illegal aliens?

One source of guidance for answering these types of questions is the system of legally defined rights.[13] For example, a ruling by the courts that the children of illegal aliens are entitled to access publicly funded education might encourage the analyst to give these children standing in CBA. Reliance on legally defined rights to determine standing, however, is not always morally acceptable. It would not have been right to deny standing in CBA to slaves in the antebellum United States, nonwhites in apartheid South Africa, or Jews in Nazi Germany simply because they lacked legal rights. Therefore, legal rights alone cannot fully resolve the issue of standing in CBA. They provide a presumption, but one that analysts may sometimes have an ethical responsibility to challenge. Democratic regimes usually provide mechanisms for challenging such presumptions, but often with personal cost to individual analysts.

One other issue of membership deserves brief mention. CBA is anthropocentric. Only the willingness-to-pay of people counts. Neither flora nor fauna have standing. That is not to say that their "interests" have no representation. Many people are willing to pay to preserve a species, and some are even willing to pay to preserve individual animals or plants. As discussed in Chapter 9, it is conceptually correct within the CBA framework to take account of these willingness-to-pay amounts, though effectively doing so is very often beyond our analytical reach.

Exclusion of Socially Unacceptable Preferences.   People sometimes hold preferences that society seeks to suppress through widely supported legal sanctions. For instance, although some people would be willing to pay for the opportunity to have sexual relations with children, most countries attempt to thwart the expression of such preferences through strict criminal penalties. Should such socially unacceptable preferences be given standing in CBA?

One approach to answering this question adds duties and prohibitions to legal rights as sources of guidance about social values. Together they can be thought of as social constraints that should be taken into account in CBA just as the analyst takes into account physical and budgetary constraints.[14] Clear and widely accepted legal sanctions may help identify preferences that should not have standing.

An important application arises in estimating the net benefits of policies that are intended to reduce the amount of criminal behavior in society. Some analysts count reductions in the monetary returns to crime as a cost borne by criminals, offsetting the benefits of reduced criminal activity enjoyed by their victims.[15] As the returns from crime are illegal and widely viewed as wrong, however, the social constraint perspective argues against treating them in this manner.

The issue of the standing of preferences can be especially difficult for analysts to resolve when they are dealing with foreign cultures. Consider, for instance, the CBA of a program to bring water to poor communities in Haiti.[16] Analysts found that husbands had a negative willingness-to-pay for the time that their wives saved from easier access to water. By contemporary standards in most urban settings, people would generally regard these preferences as unworthy. Yet in the cultural context of rural Haiti at the time, they were consistent with prevailing norms. Should these preferences of husbands have standing? In practice, lack of data to estimate willingness-to-pay amounts for this sort of impact usually spares analysts from having to answer such difficult questions.

Inclusion of the Preferences of Future Generations.   Some policies adopted today, such as the disposal of nuclear wastes or the restoration of wilderness areas, may have impacts on people not yet born. Though we believe that these people should have standing in CBA, there is no way to measure their willingness-to-pay directly because they are not yet here to express it.[17] How serious a problem does this pose for CBA?

The absence of direct measures of the willingness of future generations to pay for policy impacts generally poses few problems for two reasons. First, because few policies involve impacts that appear only in the far future, the willingness-to-pay of people alive today for the effects during their lifetimes can be used to some extent to predict how future generations will value them. Second, as most people alive today care about the well-being of their children, grandchildren, and great-grandchildren, whether or not they have yet been born, they are likely to include the interests of these generations to some extent in their own valuations of impacts. Indeed, because people cannot predict with certainty the place that their future offspring will hold in society, they are likely to take a very broad view of future impacts.

In Chapters 9 and 10, we return to the question of the standing of future generations when we discuss existence value and the social discount rate.

CONCERNS ABOUT THE ROLE OF CBA IN THE POLITICAL PROCESS

The most vocal critics of CBA fear that it subverts democratic values. Some see the monetizing of impacts as a profane attempt to place a price on everything. Others see CBA as undermining democracy. Though these fears are largely unfounded, they deserve explicit consideration by advocates of CBA.

Does CBA Debase the Terms of Public Discourse?

A number of objections have been raised to the effort made in CBA to value all policy impacts in terms of dollars: Pricing goods not normally traded in markets—for

---

EXHIBIT 2-1

Does wealth produce happiness? Surveys conducted within countries consistently find that rich people (say those in the top quarter of the income distribution) on average report being happier than poorer people (say those in the bottom quarter of the income distribution). Yet, if one looks at either of these groups over time, one discovers that its absolute level of happiness is roughly constant despite the fact that economic growth has made it richer. Similarly, comparing the happiness of the rich (or poor) across countries generally shows similar levels of happiness despite substantial differences in the overall levels of wealth between the countries. What explains this puzzle? Richard Layard suggests two psychological effects that move up the norm to which people

compare their own circumstances as societies become wealthier: habituation and rivalry. Habituation involves getting used to things we have—an initial feeling of happiness from acquisition tends to evaporate as we get used to having the good. Rivalry involves comparing one's situation to those in a reference group—happiness depends on relative position.

These phenomena raise concerns about interpreting changes in social surplus as changes in aggregate happiness. A policy that increased everyone's income would certainly pass the net benefits test. Yet extreme habituation might quickly return everyone to their initial levels of utility, or extreme rivalry would result in no utility gains at all because no one's relative position changes!

Source: Adapted from Richard Layard, "Happiness: Has Social Science a Clue?" Lionel Robbins Memorial Lectures, London School of Economics, Lecture 1: Income and Happiness: Rethinking Economic Policy, March 3, 4, and 5, 2003.

example, life itself—decreases their perceived value by implying that they can be compared to goods that are traded in markets; pricing such goods reduces their perceived value by weakening the claim that they should not be for sale in any circumstance; and pricing all goods undercuts the claim that some goods are "priceless."[18] The language and conceptual frameworks that people use almost certainly affect the nature of debate to some extent. It is not clear, however, how influential the technical concepts of economics are in actually shaping public discourse. In any event, the correct interpretation of how nonmarket goods are monetized largely undercuts the charge that CBA debases public discourse.

Consider the issue of the monetization of the value of life. On the surface it may appear that economists are implying that a price can be put on someone's life. A closer look, which we provide in Chapters 13 and 15, indicates that the value of life estimated by economists is a measure of how much people are willing to pay to reduce their risk of death; in other words, it is the value of a *statistical life,* the willingness-to-pay to avoid risks that will result in one less death in a population. Although it may not be appropriate to place a dollar value on the life of any particular person, it is appropriate to use the value of a statistical life in assessing proposed policies that change the risk of death that people face.

Every day people voluntarily make trade-offs between changes in the risk of death and other values: Driving faster to save time increases the risk of being involved in a fatal traffic accident; eating fatty foods is pleasurable but increases the risk of fatal heart disease; skiing is exhilarating but risks fatal injury. Is it profane to take account of these preferences in valuing the impacts of public policies? Most economists would answer no. Indeed, valuing statistical lives seems less profane than attempting to place a dollar value on a specific person by estimating the person's forgone future earnings, the procedure employed by courts in cases of wrongful death.

Does CBA Undermine Democracy?

Some critics of CBA charge that it undermines democracy by imposing a single goal, efficiency, in the assessment of public policies. Their charge would be justified if the appropriate comparison were between a world in which public policy is determined solely through democratic processes that gave equal weight to all interests and a world in which public policy is determined strictly through the application of CBA. But this is an inappropriate comparison for two reasons. First, actual governmental processes fall far short of "ideal democracy." Second, at most, CBA has modest influence in public policy making.[19]

The interests of vocal constituencies, often those who can organize themselves in anticipation of obtaining concentrated benefits or avoiding concentrated costs, typically receive great attention from those in representative governments who wish to be reelected or advance to higher office. Less vocal constituencies usually have their interests represented less well. The interests of many of these less vocal constituencies are often better reflected in CBA. For example, CBA takes account of the individually small, but in aggregate large, costs borne by consumers because of government price-support programs that raise prices to the benefit of a small number of well-organized agricultural producers. But CBA rarely serves as the decisive decision rule for public policy. Indeed, it is difficult to identify important public policies selected *solely* on the basis of CBA.

A realistic assessment of representative democracy and the current influence of CBA should allay concerns that the latter is subverting the former. To the extent it is influential, CBA probably contributes to more democratic public policy by paying attention to diffuse interests typically underrepresented in a representative democracy. It would have to become much more influential before it could possibly be viewed as undermining democratic processes. Despite our hopes that the readers of this book will help make the use of CBA more prevalent, we have no concerns about it being too influential in the near future.

LIMITATIONS OF CBA: OTHER ANALYTICAL APPROACHES

It is important for analysts to realize the limitations of CBA. Two types of circumstances make the net benefits criterion an inappropriate decision rule for public policy. First, technical limitations may make it impossible to quantify and then monetize all relevant impacts as costs and benefits. Second, goals other than efficiency are relevant to the policy. For example, some policies are intended to affect the equality of outcomes or opportunity. Nevertheless, even when the net benefits criterion is not appropriate as a decision rule, CBA usually provides a useful yardstick for comparing alternative policies in terms of efficiency along with other goals.

Technical Limitations to CBA

CBA in its pure form requires that all impacts relevant to efficiency be quantified and made commensurate through monetization. Only when all the costs and benefits are expressed in dollars can the potential Pareto principle be applied through the calculation of net benefits. Limitations in theory, data, or analytical resources, however, may make it impossible for the analyst to measure and value all impacts of a policy as commensurate costs and benefits. Nonetheless, it may still be desirable to do a qualitative cost-benefit analysis or, if all but one important effect can be monetized, to switch from CBA to cost-effectiveness analysis. A brief description of each of these alternative approaches follows.

Qualitative CBA. The advice given by Benjamin Franklin at the beginning of Chapter 1 can be thought of as a prescription for qualitative CBA. In conducting qualitative CBA, the analyst typically monetizes as many of the impacts as possible and then makes qualitative estimates of the relative importance of the remaining costs and benefits. Consider, for instance, a program to plant trees along an urban highway. The cost of the program, which consists only of the expenditures that must be made to hire a contractor to plant and to maintain the trees, can be directly monetized. The benefits, however, include a number of effects that are likely to be difficult to monetize: the visual pleasure the trees give to motorists, the reduction of noise in adjoining neighborhoods, and the filtering of pollutants from the air. With sufficient resources, the analyst would be able to monetize these benefits through a variety of techniques such as surveys of motorists and comparisons with the effects of other noise-reduction programs on property values. But because the program involves relatively small costs, it is unlikely that such efforts would be justified. Instead, a reasonable approach would be to list these benefits with rough estimates of their order of magnitude.

Analysts who lack the time, data, or other resources needed to value all relevant impacts directly may be able to make use of estimates found in other cost-benefit analyses or economic research. For example, most analysts doing CBA do not directly estimate people's willingness-to-pay for reductions in mortality risk. Instead, as discussed in Chapters 12, 13, and 15, they rely on econometric studies investigating how people trade such things as changes in wages for changes in levels of risk.

When possible, analysts should quantify the impacts of the policy; that is, they should estimate the numeric values of the nonmonetized impacts. For example, consider analysis of a proposed regulation to restrict commercial fishing practices so that fewer dolphins will be killed per ton of tuna harvested. The regulation produces a benefit because some people have a positive willingness-to-pay for dolphin deaths avoided. Actually monetizing, that is, measuring the willingness-to-pay, is a difficult task that might not be feasible for the analyst conducting the CBA. Even if monetization is infeasible, however, it is useful to attempt to predict the number of dolphins saved by the regulation. Doing so increases the usefulness of the qualitative CBA for others by conveying the magnitude of the impact of the regulation. Additionally, the client or other users of the analysis may be able to provide estimates of the willingness of people to pay for each dolphin saved so that (fully monetized) CBA becomes feasible.

Analysts often face a more complicated choice than simply whether to quantify a category of costs or benefits. Empirical measures can have varying degrees of accuracy, ranging from precise estimates in which we have great confidence to imprecise estimates in which we have little confidence. The decision to quantify, and with what degree of effort, should reflect the value of the increased precision that can be obtained and the costs of obtaining it. In other words, we should make such decisions within a CBA framework!

Cost-Effectiveness Analysis.   Analysts can often quantify impacts but not monetize them all. If the analysts are unable or unwilling to monetize the major benefit, then cost-effectiveness analysis may be appropriate. Because not all of the impacts can be monetized, it is not possible to estimate net benefits. The analysts can, however, construct a ratio involving the quantitative, but nonmonetized, benefit and the total dollar costs. A comparison allows the analyst to rank policies in terms of the cost-effectiveness criterion. However, unlike the net benefits criterion of CBA, it does not directly allow the analysts to conclude that the highest-ranked policy contributes to greater efficiency.

Return to the qualitative CBA of the fishing regulation discussed earlier. Imagine that, except for the benefit from avoided dolphin deaths, all the impacts could be monetized to a net cost of c dollars. If the number of avoided dolphin deaths were n_d, then the analyst could construct an effectiveness-cost ratio for the regulation, n_d/c, which can be interpreted as the average number of dolphins saved per dollar of cost borne. (Alternatively, the analyst could construct the cost-effectiveness ratio as c/n_d, which can be interpreted as the average dollar cost per dolphin saved.) Now imagine a number of alternative regulations, each of which involves different net costs and a different number of dolphins saved. A cost-effectiveness ratio can be calculated for each of these programs to facilitate comparison across alternative regulations.

Using cost-effectiveness analysis for decision making usually requires that some additional information be brought to bear. If the objective is to save as many dolphins as possible at a net cost of no more than c^*, then the analyst should select the most effective regulation from among those with net costs of less than c^*. Alternatively, if the objective is to save at least n_d^* dolphins, then the analyst should select the regulation with the lowest cost from among those regulations saving at least n_d^*. This is not necessarily the alternative with the best cost-effectiveness ratio. For example, if $n_d^* = 1,000$, one would choose a regulation that saved 1,000 dolphins at a cost of $1 million ($1,000 per dolphin saved) over an alternative regulation that saved 500 dolphins at a cost of $50 thousand ($100 per dolphin saved).

Analysts often encounter situations in which they or their clients are unable or unwilling to monetize impacts such as human lives saved, injuries avoided, and the acres of old-growth forest preserved. Because cost-effectiveness analysis may be useful in these situations, we consider it in greater depth in Chapter 17.

The Relevance of CBA when Goals Other than Efficiency Matter

One goal, efficiency, underlies CBA. The general public, politicians, and even economists, however, very often consider goals reflecting other values to be relevant to the evaluation of public policies proposed to solve social problems. Although efficiency almost always is one of the relevant goals in policy analysis, other goals such as equality of opportunity, equality of outcome, expenditure constraints, political feasibility, and national security, for instance, may be as, or even more, important. Indeed, the spenders and guardians we met in Chapter 1 behave as if they are responding to goals other than efficiency. When goals in addition to efficiency are relevant, as well as when efficiency is the only goal, but relevant impacts cannot be confidently monetized, *multigoal analysis* provides the appropriate framework. In the special case in which efficiency and equality of outcome are the only relevant goals, *distributionally weighted* CBA may be an appropriate technique.

Multigoal Analysis.   The most general analytical framework is multigoal analysis. At the heart of multigoal analysis lies the notion that all policy alternatives should be compared in terms of all the relevant goals. Though multigoal analysis can be prescribed as a number of distinct steps,[20] three of its aspects are especially important. First, the analyst must move from relevant social values to general goals to specific impact categories that can be used as yardsticks for evaluating alternative policies. For example, the value of human dignity may imply a goal of improving equality of opportunity, which might be expressed as quantifiable impacts such as increasing participation in higher education and expanding workforce participation. Second, the analyst must evaluate each alternative policy, including the status quo, with respect to each of the impacts. Third, as no policy alternative is likely to dominate the others in terms of all the goals, the analyst usually can only make a recommendation to adopt one of the alternatives by carefully considering and making a subjective judgment concerning the trade-offs in the achievement of goals it offers relative to the other alternatives.

As a simple example, consider a multigoal analysis of alternative income transfer policies intended to help poor families. The analyst might construct the worksheet shown in Table 2-3 as a checklist for keeping track of the relevant goals. Increasing efficiency and improving the quality of life of poor families are appropriate substantive goals. The former captures the aggregate gain to society from transfers; the latter captures that portion of the gain going to the poorest families. The goal of achieving

TABLE 2-3 Evaluation Matrix Worksheet for Alternative Family Aid Policies

		Policy Alternatives		
Goals	*Impact Categories*	*Policy A (status quo)*	*Policy B*	*Policy C*
Increase efficiency	Increase labor earnings Increase investment in human capital Reduce administrative costs			
Improve quality of life of poorest families	Reduce number of families below poverty line Reduce number of one-parent families Increase educational achievement of family members			
Achieve political feasibility	Maximize probability of adoption of required legislation			

political feasibility might be added to take account of the fact that a consensus on the relative importance of the substantive goals among politicians is unlikely. In this example, it can be thought of as an instrumental goal that is valuable not for its own sake but because it helps achieve the substantive goals. The major efficiency impacts are likely to be work disincentives for the recipients of aid and the real resource costs of administering the aid policy. If both of these impacts could be monetized, then the criterion for measuring efficiency would simply be the sum of the net benefits of these two impacts as measured in CBA. If either one of them could not be monetized, however, then efficiency would be stated in terms of the two impacts. The goal of improving the quality of life of poor families would probably be expressed in terms of such impacts as reducing the number of families below the poverty line, reducing the number of one-parent families, and increasing the educational achievement of family members. The impact associated with the additional goal of political feasibility might be maximizing the probability of passage of legislation required to implement the policy.

Before selecting among the alternative policies, the analyst should fill in all the cells of a matrix like the one shown in Table 2-3. Each cell would contain a prediction of the effect of a particular policy in terms of a particular impact category. By filling in all the cells, the analyst seeks to gain a comprehensive comparison of the alternatives across all the impact categories, and hence across their related goals.

Note that one can think of CBA, qualitative CBA, and cost-effectiveness analysis as special cases of multigoal analysis. In the case of CBA, there is one goal (increase efficiency) with one criterion (maximize net benefits) so that the evaluation matrix has only one row and the choice among alternatives is trivial (simply select the policy with the largest net benefits). In the case of qualitative CBA, there is also one goal, but because all relevant impacts cannot be monetized, it corresponds to several criteria, one for each

EXHIBIT 2-2

A recent study by the Congressional Budget Office to assess three alternatives for reducing U.S. consumption of gasoline listed the following criteria:

This study weighs the relative merits of tightening CAFE standards, raising the federal gasoline tax, and creating a cap-and-trade program against several major criteria:

Cost-Effectiveness. Reducing gasoline consumption would impose costs (both monetary and nonmonetary) on various producers and consumers. A cost-effective policy would keep those costs to a minimum.

Predictability of Gasoline Savings. How reliably would the policy bring about the desired reduction in gasoline consumption?

Effects on Safety. How would the policy alter the number and severity of traffic accidents?

Effects on Other External Costs Related to Driving. Reducing gasoline consumption would affect not only the United States' energy security and carbon emissions but other driving-related external costs (ones whose full weight is borne by society at large rather than by an individual). Those external costs include traffic congestion, the need for highway construction and maintenance, and emissions of air pollutants besides carbon dioxide.

In addition to those factors, the three policy options would have other implications that policymakers may care about—such as their effects on people at different income levels and in different parts of the country and their impact on the amount of revenue collected by the federal government. (Summary, p.1)

One could imagine turning the analysis into a CBA by monetizing the effects on safety and the effects on other external costs related to driving and treating predictability of gasoline savings through sensitivity analysis. As monetizing the distributional concerns would be difficult, a multigoal analysis with the CBA assessing efficiency and a separate treatment of distributional impacts could be useful.

Source: Adapted from Congressional Budget Office, *Reducing Gasoline Consumption: Three Policy Options,* November 2002 *(www.cbo.gov/showdoc.cfm?index = 991&sequence = 0).*

impact. In the case of cost-effectiveness analysis, the goal of efficiency is often combined with some other goal such as satisfying a constraint on monetary costs or achieving some target level of reduction in the quantified but nonmonetized impact.

Distributionally Weighted CBA. If both efficiency and equality of income are relevant goals and their relative importance can be quantified, then distributionally weighted CBA provides an alternative decision rule to the maximization of net benefits. Instead of considering aggregate net benefits as in standard CBA, net benefits are calculated for each of several relevant groups distinguished by income, wealth, or some similar characteristic of relevance to a distributional concern. As discussed in more detail in Chapter 18, the net benefits of each group are multiplied by a weighting factor, selected by the analyst to reflect some distributional goal, and then summed to arrive at a number that can be used to rank alternative policies.

The major problem analysts encounter in doing distributionally weighted CBA is arriving at an appropriate and acceptable set of weights. One general approach, which takes as a desirable social goal increasing equality of wealth, involves making the weights inversely proportional to wealth (or income) to favor policies that tend to equalize wealth (or income) in the population.[21] Another general approach, which takes as a desirable social goal the raising of the position of the least advantaged in society, involves placing a higher weight on the net benefits of those with incomes or wealth below some threshold levels than on those with incomes or wealth above the threshold. As reasonable arguments can be made in support of each of these approaches, the absence of a consensus about appropriate weights is not surprising.[22]

Obviously, developing weights that allow a single quantitative criterion for ranking alternative policies makes the choice among policy alternatives easy. Yet this ease is achieved only by making an assumption that forces efficiency and equality of outcomes to be fully commensurate. Dissatisfaction with the strong assumption required to do this has led a number of analysts to suggest that distributionally weighted CBA should always be done in conjunction with standard CBA to make clearer the efficiency implications of the selected weights.[23] In doing so, the study becomes in effect a multigoal analysis, raising the question of whether an explicit treatment of efficiency and equality as separate goals might not be a more appropriate framework when both efficiency and distributional concerns are important. Cost-effectiveness analysis might also provide a more reasonable approach than distributionally weighted CBA by posing the question in terms of achieving the most desirable redistribution possible for some fixed level of net cost.[24]

CONCLUSION

CBA is a method for determining if proposed policies could potentially be Pareto improving: Positive net benefits make it possible, in the sense of making available resources to compensate those who bear costs so that some people are made better off without making anyone else worse off. Willingness-to-pay and opportunity cost are the guiding principles for measuring costs and benefits. Much of the rest of this book deals with how to make use of the concepts in practice.

Part II sets out the conceptual foundations for CBA in more depth. It begins by reviewing supply and demand analytics (Chapter 3), and then uses these analytics to show how information revealed in markets can be used to estimate willingness-to-pay and opportunity cost (Chapters 4 and 5). Subsequent chapters consider how to take account of policy effects that accrue in different time periods (Chapters 6 and 10) or with uncertainty (Chapters 7 and 8) and impacts on goods that have value beyond their direct use (Chapter 9).

Part III considers empirical approaches for predicting and valuing policy impacts. Three chapters demonstrate estimation methods based on observed behavior. Policy demonstrations sometimes provide information of direct relevance to CBA, especially in terms of predicting policy impacts (Chapter 11). More often, however, analysts face the task of making inferences about demand schedules from data revealed in markets (Chapter 12) or through other behaviors (Chapter 13). In some circumstances, especially those arising in the context of environmental policy, the unavailability of data from observed behavior forces analysts to rely on survey responses as a basis for estimation (Chapter 14). Analysts can often make use of existing research to find values needed to monetize impacts as costs and benefits (Chapter 15), though some special care must be taken in transferring these values to CBAs of policies in developing countries (Chapter 16).

Part IV further develops two of the analytical methods introduced in this chapter that can be used as alternatives to CBA: cost-effectiveness analysis (Chapter 17) and distributionally weighted cost-benefit analysis (Chapter 18). Chapter 19 concludes by investigating the accuracy of and potential sources of errors in CBAs; the main points are illustrated in conjunction with the highway project described in Chapter 1.

EXERCISES FOR CHAPTER 2

1. Many experts claim that, although VHS came to dominate the video recorder market, Betamax was a superior technology. Assume that these experts are correct, so that, all other things equal, a world in which all video recorders were Betamax technology would be Pareto superior to a world in which all video recorders were VHS technology. Yet it seems implausible that a policy that forced a switch in technologies would be even potentially Pareto improving. Explain.

2. Let's explore the concept of willingness-to-pay with a thought experiment. Imagine a specific sporting, entertainment, or cultural event that you would very much like to attend — perhaps a World Cup match, the seventh game of the World Series, a Rolling Stones concert, or a Kathleen Battle performance.
    a. What is the most you would be willing to pay for a ticket to the event?
    b. Imagine that you won a ticket to the event in a lottery. What is the minimum amount of money that you would be willing to accept to give up the ticket?
    c. Imagine that you had an income 50 percent higher than it is now, but that you didn't win a ticket to the event. What is the most you would be willing to pay for a ticket?
    d. Do you know anyone who would sufficiently dislike the event that they would not use a free ticket unless they were paid to do so?
    e. Do your answers suggest any possible generalizations about willingness-to-pay?

3. How closely do government expenditures measure opportunity cost for each of the following program inputs?
    a. Time of jurors in a criminal justice program that requires more trials.
    b. Land to be used for a nuclear waste storage facility that is owned by the government and located on a military base.
    c. Labor for a reforestation program in a small rural community with high unemployment.
    d. Labor of current government employees who are required to administer a new program.
    e. Concrete that was previously poured as part of a bridge foundation.

4. Three mutually exclusive projects are being considered for a remote river valley: Project R, a recreational facility, has estimated benefits of $10 million and costs of $8 million; project F, a forest preserve with some recreational facilities, has estimated benefits of $13 million and costs of $10 million; project W, a wilderness area with restricted public access, has estimated benefits of $5 million and costs of $1 million. In addition, a road could be built for a cost of $4 million that would increase the benefits of project R by $8 million, increase the benefits of project F by $5 million, and reduce the benefits of project W by $1 million. Even in the absence of any of the other projects, the road has estimated benefits of $2 million.
    a. Calculate the benefit-cost ratio and net benefits for each possible alternative to the status quo. Note that there are seven possible alternatives to the status quo: R, F, and W, both with and without the road, and the road alone.
    b. If only one of the seven alternatives can be selected, which should be selected according to the CBA decision rule?

5. An analyst for the U.S. Navy was asked to evaluate alternatives for forward-basing a destroyer flotilla. He decided to do the evaluation as a CBA. The major categories of costs were related to obtaining and maintaining the facilities. The major category of benefit was reduced sailing time to patrol routes. The analyst recommended the forward base with the largest net benefits. The admiral, his client, rejected the recommendation because the CBA did not include the risks to the forward bases from surprise attack and the risks of being unexpectedly ejected from the bases because of changes in political regimes of the host countries. Was the analyst's work wasted?

6. Because of a recent wave of jewelry store robberies, a city increases police surveillance of jewelry stores. The increased surveillance costs the city an extra $500,000 per year, but as a result, the amount of jewelry that is stolen falls. Specifically, without the increase in surveillance, jewelry with a retail value of $1 million would have been stolen. This stolen jewelry would have been fenced by the jewelry thieves for $600,000. What is the net social benefit resulting from the police surveillance program?

7. (Spreadsheet recommended.) Excessive and improper use of antibiotics is contributing to the resistance of many diseases to existing antibiotics. Consider a regulatory program in the United States that would monitor antibiotic prescribing by physicians. Analysts estimate the direct costs of enforcement to be $40 million, the time costs to doctors and health professionals to be $220 million, and the convenience costs to patients to be $180 million (all annually). The annual benefits of the program are estimated to be $350 million in avoided resistance costs in the United States, $70 million in health benefits in the United States from better compliance with prescriptions, and $280 million in avoided resistance costs in the rest of the world. Does the program have positive net benefits from the national perspective? If not, what fraction of benefits accruing in the rest of the world would have to be counted for the program to have positive net benefits?

NOTES

1. Unless otherwise stated, we intend efficiency to mean *allocative efficiency,* as defined in this section. A broader interpretation of efficiency, which we discuss in a later section, is the maximization of a specific social welfare function that explicitly ranks alternative allocations.

2. Nicholas Kaldor, "Welfare Propositions of Economics and Interpersonal Comparisons of Utility," *Economic Journal* 49(195) 1939, 549–552; and John R. Hicks, "The Valuation of the Social Income," *Economica* 7(26) 1940, 105–124. The principle can also be stated as suggested by Hicks: Adopt a policy if and only if it would not be in the self-interest of those who will lose to bribe those who will gain not to adopt it.

3. Those who are worse off in society may or may not have been the ones who have borne the net costs of public policies. This argument thus shifts the focus from fairness with respect to particular policies to the relative position of those in society who are worse off for whatever reason.

4. Kenneth Arrow, *Social Choice and Individual Values,* 2nd ed. (New Haven, CT: Yale University Press, 1963). For a treatment that can be followed with minimal mathematics, see Julian H. Blau, "A Direct Proof of Arrow's Theorem," *Econometrica* 40(1) 1972, 61–67.

5. For an overview, see Charles Blackorby and David Donaldson, "A Review Article: The Case Against the Use of the Sum of Compensating Variation in Cost-Benefit Analysis," *Canadian Journal of Economics* 23(3) 1990, 471–494.

6. Charles Blackorby and David Donaldson, "Consumers' Surpluses and Consistent Cost-Benefit Tests," *Social Choice and Welfare* 1(4) 1985, 251–262.

7. Even if one does not demand that the potential Pareto principle always produce a transitive social ordering of policies, the most commonly used measure of willingness-to-pay, *compensating variation,* can produce what are called *Scitovsky reversals* (Tibor Scitovsky, "A Note on Welfare Propositions in Economics,"

Review of Economic Studies 41(1) 1941, 77–88). Compensating variation, which is discussed in Appendix 4A, is the change in income that would be needed to make the consumer indifferent between the new policy with the income change and the old policy without it. For example, if the price of a good increases, it is the amount of income needed to compensate consumers so that they would be indifferent between the original price and the new price with the compensation. A Scitovsky reversal results when the sum of compensating variations for a group of individuals is positive for a move from one Pareto efficient policy to another *and* is also positive for a move from the new policy back to the original policy! More generally, the sum of compensating variations can be positive for moves among Pareto-efficient allocations, so that it being positive is a necessary but not a sufficient condition for a potential Pareto improvement (Blackorby and Donaldson, "A Review Article: The Case Against the Use of the Sum of Compensating Variation in Cost-Benefit Analysis," 471–494).

8. The marginal utility of money is how much a person's utility changes for a small increase in the person's wealth. Economists generally assume declining marginal utility of money. That is, as a person's wealth increases, each additional dollar produces smaller increases in utility.

9. Abram Bergson [as Burk], "A Reformulation of Certain Aspects of Welfare Economics," *Quarterly Journal of Economics* 52(2) 1938, 310–334.

10. Tibor Scitovsky, "The State of Welfare Economics," *American Economic Review* 51(3) 1951, 301–315; and Kenneth Arrow, *Social Choice and Individual Values,* 2nd ed. (New Haven, CT: Yale University Press, 1963).

11. One could imagine asking a sample of members of society to value alternative states of the world resulting from alternative policies, including the situations of other people. In this way, their willingness-to-pay would include the value they place on the distributional impacts of policies. Unfortunately, implementing such surveys is very difficult.

12. The seminal work is Dale Whittington and Duncan MacRae Jr., "The Issue of Standing in Cost-Benefit Analysis," *Journal of Policy Analysis and Management* 5(4) 1986, 665–682.

13. Richard O. Zerbe Jr., "Comment: Does Benefit-Cost Analysis Stand Alone? Rights and Standing," *Journal of Policy Analysis and Management* 10(1) 1991, 96–105.

14. For a development of the notion of social constraints in CBA, see William N. Trumbull, "Who Has Standing in Cost-Benefit Analysis?" *Journal of Policy Analysis and Management* 9(2) 1990, 201–218; and Richard O. Zerbe Jr., "Is Cost-Benefit Analysis Legal? Three Rules," *Journal of Policy Analysis and Management* 17(3) 1998, 419–456. For a more general treatment of institutional constraints and social welfare, see Daniel W. Bromley, *Economic Interests and Institutions: The Conceptual Foundations of Public Policy* (New York: Basil Blackwell, 1989).

15. David A. Long, Charles D. Mallar, and Craig V. D. Thornton, "Evaluating the Benefits and Costs of the Job Corps," *Journal of Policy Analysis and Management* 1(1) 1981, 55–76.

16. For a discussion of this case from the perspective of a number of issues of standing of preferences, see Duncan MacRae Jr. and Dale Whittington, "Assessing Preferences in Cost-Benefit Analysis: Reflections on Rural Water Supply Evaluation in Haiti," *Journal of Policy Analysis and Management* 7(2) 1988, 246–263.

17. See Daniel W. Bromley, "Entitlements, Missing Markets, and Environmental Uncertainty," *Journal of Environmental Economics and Management* 17(2) 1989, 181–194.

18. Steven Kelman, "Cost-Benefit Analysis: An Ethical Critique," *Regulation* January/February 1981, 33–40.

19. Alan Williams, "Cost-Benefit Analysis: Bastard Science? And/Or Insidious Poison in the Body Politick?" *Journal of Public Economics* 1(2) 1972, 199–226; and Aidan R. Vining and David L. Weimer, "Welfare Economics as the Foundation for Public Policy Analysis: Incomplete and Flawed but Nevertheless Desirable," *Journal of Socio-Economics* 21(1) 1992, 25–37.

20. For a detailed presentation of multigoal analysis, see David L. Weimer and Aidan R. Vining, *Policy Analysis: Concepts and Practice,* 4th ed. (Upper Saddle River, NJ: Pearson Prentice Hall, 2005), Chapter 14.

21. For a demonstration of the application of various measures of vertical and horizontal equality, see Marcus C. Berliant and Robert P. Strauss, "The Horizontal and Vertical Equity Characteristics

of the Federal Individual Income Tax," in *Horizontal Equity, Uncertainty, and Economic Well-Being,* Martin David and Timothy Smeeding, eds. (Chicago: University of Chicago Press, 1985), 179–211.

22. The fact that people routinely donate to charities suggests that, other things equal, most people would be willing to pay something to obtain a distribution of wealth that is more favorable to the currently poor. Ironically, CBA provides a conceptual way to place a dollar value on alternative distributions of wealth: the sum of the willingness of the individual members of society to pay for moving from the status quo distribution of wealth to an alternative one. Unfortunately, it is usually impractical to elicit willingness-to-pay amounts of this sort.

23. For example, Harberger proposes that a dual test be applied: The policy should have positive weighted and unweighted net benefits. Arnold C. Harberger, "On the Use of Distributional Weights in Social Cost-Benefit Analysis," *Journal of Political Economy* 86(2, part 2) 1978, S87–120.

24. For an excellent development of this approach, see Edward M. Gramlich and Michael Wolkoff, "A Procedure for Evaluating Income Distribution Policies," *Journal of Human Resources* 14(3) 1979, 319–350.

CHAPTER 3

Basic Microeconomic Foundations of Cost-Benefit Analysis

Microeconomic theory provides the basic conceptual foundation for CBA. In this chapter, we review the major concepts of microeconomic theory as they apply to the measurement of costs and benefits. Most of these concepts should be at least somewhat familiar from your previous exposure to economics.

For purposes of simplicity, we assume the presence of perfect competition throughout this chapter. Specifically, we assume that there are so many buyers and sellers in each market that no one can individually affect prices, that buyers and sellers can easily enter and exit from each market, that the goods sold in each market are homogeneous (i.e., identical), that there is an absence of transaction costs in buying and selling in each market, that information is perfect, and that private costs and benefits are identical to social costs and benefits (i.e., there are no externalities). Chapter 4 considers how to measure benefits and costs when some of these assumptions do not hold and, consequently, various forms of market failure are present.

DEMAND SCHEDULES

A demand schedule, or demand curve, indicates the quantities of a good that individuals purchase at various prices. A single person has an individual demand schedule; all individuals in a market contribute to the market demand schedule. A standard assumption in economics is that demand schedules slope downward in a graph of price versus quantity demanded. The reasoning behind this assumption and the importance of it for CBA will become clear as we proceed. A downward-sloped demand schedule is illustrated as line *D* in Figure 3-1.

The rationale for the downward slope is based upon the principle of *diminishing marginal utility*; each additional unit of the good is valued slightly less by each consumer than the preceding unit. For that reason, each consumer is willing to pay less for another unit than for the preceding unit. Indeed, at some point, each consumer would be unwilling to pay anything for an additional unit; his or her demand would be sated.

This notion that demand schedules indicate how much people are willing to pay for various quantities of a good is absolutely critical to understanding the role of demand schedules in CBA. The key is the link between demand schedules and willingness-to-pay, a concept that was introduced in Chapter 2. To explore this link, we consider

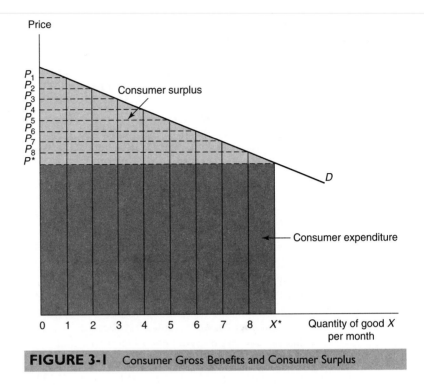

FIGURE 3-1   Consumer Gross Benefits and Consumer Surplus

the market demand schedule for a good, which conveys information about how all the potential consumers of that good in a society value it in aggregate. Figure 3-1 illustrates the demand schedule for good X for these consumers.

Figure 3-1 indicates that there is at least one member of society who is willing to pay a price of P_1 for one unit of good X. Similarly, there is at least one person who would pay a price of P_2 for the second unit of X, and there is someone who would pay P_3 for the third unit of X, and so forth.[1] The message from this exercise should be obvious: The area under the demand schedule—in other words, the sum of all the small rectangles—closely approximates the willingness-to-pay for X by all the members of society. Each additional unit is valued at a price given by the height of the demand schedule; summing these prices over the units corresponds approximately to adding the unit-wide rectangles (the rectangles are approximate because they miss the small triangles at the top of the trapezoids). Thus, the lightly shaded area plus the darkly shaded area in Figure 3-1 approximates society's willingness-to-pay for a given amount of X, specifically for X^* units. To put it just a little differently, the sum of the lightly and darkly shaded areas approximates the total gross benefits society would receive from consuming X^* units of good X.

Of course, under most circumstances, people actually have to pay something to consume good X. Let us assume that the competitive market sets the price of X at P^*. Thus, consumers pay P^*X^*, the darkly shaded area, to the producers of the good. In this case, the net benefits to consumers from consuming X^* units, that is, the gross benefits less the required purchase payments, equal the area below the demand schedule but above the price line. This lightly shaded area is called *consumer surplus*.

Consumer surplus is one of the basic concepts used in CBA to value impacts when demand schedules are known. The reason why consumer surplus is so important to CBA is that, under most circumstances, changes in consumer surplus can appropriately be used as a reasonable approximation of society's willingness-to-pay for a policy change. That is, as stated in Chapter 2, the algebraic sum of willingness-to-pay values is the appropriate measure of the benefits of a policy. In the appendix to this chapter, we examine the circumstances under which changes in consumer surplus do provide close approximations to willingness-to-pay values and the circumstances under which they do not. The major conclusion is that in most instances such approximations are sufficiently accurate for CBA purposes.

Changes in Consumer Surplus

To see how the concept of consumer surplus can be used in CBA, consider a policy that results in a price change. For example, as shown in Figure 3-2(a), a policy that reduces the price of good X from P^* to P_1 would result in a benefit to consumers (that is, an increase in consumer surplus) equal to the area of the shaded trapezoid P^*ABP_1. This benefit results both because consumers gain from paying a lower price for the X^* units they previously purchased and because they gain from the consumption of $X_1 - X^*$ additional units. Similarly, as shown in Figure 3-2(b), a policy that increases the price of good X from P^* to P_2 would impose a "cost" on consumers (a loss in consumer surplus) equal to the area of the shaded trapezoid P_2ABP^*.

If the absolute value of change in the price of X is known and denoted ΔP, the absolute value of the change in the quantity of good X consumed is known and denoted ΔX, and the demand schedule is linear, then the absolute value of the change in consumer surplus, ΔCS, can be readily computed by the following formula for the price decrease shown in Figure 3-2(a):

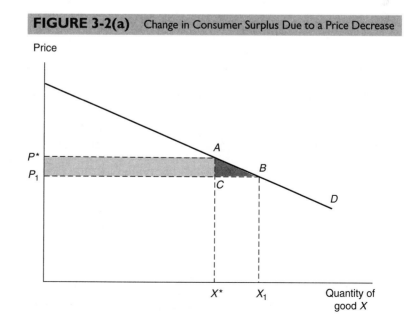

FIGURE 3-2(a) Change in Consumer Surplus Due to a Price Decrease

FIGURE 3-2(b)   Change in Consumer Surplus Due to a Price Increase

$$\Delta CS = \Delta P(X^*) + \tfrac{1}{2}(\Delta X)(\Delta P) \tag{3.1a}$$

and by the following formula for the price increase shown in Figure 3-2(b):

$$\Delta CS = \Delta P(X_2) + \tfrac{1}{2}(\Delta X)(\Delta P) \tag{3.1b}$$

or,

$$\Delta CS = \Delta P(X^*) - \tfrac{1}{2}(\Delta X)(\Delta P) \tag{3.1c}$$

In fact, these formulae provide good approximations to the change in consumer surplus even if the demand curve is not linear. This approximation is discussed further in Chapter 12.

Sometimes after a known price change, the change in quantities consumed, ΔX, is not directly known, but an estimate of the price elasticity of demand is available. The *price elasticity of demand*, ϵ_d, is defined as the percentage change in quantity that results from a 1 percent change in price. Usually it is negative. Defining ΔX and ΔP as the absolute values of the changes in quantities and prices, the absolute value of the price elasticity of demand can be computed as follows:[2]

$$\epsilon_d = (\Delta X/\Delta P)(P^*/X^*) > 0 \tag{3.2}$$

Using the absolute value of the price elasticity of demand, the absolute value of the change in consumer surplus can be computed by using a slight modification of equation (3.1). For the price decrease shown in Figure 3-2(a) it equals:

$$\Delta CS = \Delta P(X^*) + \tfrac{1}{2}[(\Delta X/\Delta P)(P^*/X^*)](\Delta P)(X^*)(\Delta P/P^*)$$
$$= \Delta P(X^*)[1 + \tfrac{1}{2}(\Delta P/P^*)\epsilon_d] \tag{3.3a}$$

For the price increase shown in Figure 3-2(b) it equals:

$$\Delta CS = \Delta P(X^*) - \tfrac{1}{2}[(\Delta X/\Delta P)(P^*/X^*)](\Delta P)(X^*)(\Delta P/P^*)$$
$$= \Delta P(X^*)[1 - \tfrac{1}{2}(\Delta P/P^*)\epsilon_d] \tag{3.3b}$$

Taxes

Now let us assume that the price increase from P^* to P_2 shown in Figure 3-2(b) results from a government-imposed excise tax, where each unit of X has been taxed by an amount equal to the difference between the old and the new price $(P_2 - P^*)$. In this case, the rectangular part of the trapezoid in Figure 3-2(b), P_2ACP^*, represents the tax revenue collected. It can be viewed as a *transfer*—money that is transferred from consumers of X to the government. It is called a transfer because from the perspective of society as a whole its net impact is zero. The transfer of tax revenue imposes a cost on consumers of X, but this cost is offset by an identical benefit received by the government.[3]

The triangular part of the trapezoid, ABC, is a pure cost of the tax, however. That is, consumers lose consumer surplus, but there is no offsetting benefit to some other part of society. This pure loss in consumer surplus is an example of *deadweight loss*.[4] It results from the distortion in economic behavior from the competitive equilibrium. The tax causes some consumers to purchase less output than they would in the absence of the tax because, inclusive of the tax, the price now exceeds those consumers' willingness-to-pay. Those consumers, who in the absence of the tax would collectively have purchased $X^* - X_2$ of the good and received the consumer surplus represented by the triangular area, ABC, lose this consumer surplus.

In general, there will always be a deadweight loss if a government imposes a tax on a good sold in a competitive market. The implications of this for CBA are discussed further in Chapter 4.

Individual versus Market Demand Schedules

One more point regarding demand schedules remains to be discussed: the relationship between the demand schedules of individual consumers in a market and the demand schedule for the entire market. The market demand schedule for a private good is simply the horizontal sum of the individual demand schedules. Individual demand schedules indicate the amount of the good each consumer wants to purchase at each price. By adding together all these quantities at each price, which graphically corresponds to summing the demand schedules for individuals horizontally, the market demand schedule is obtained. This is important for cost-benefit purposes because it implies that a market demand schedule can appropriately be used to measure the effect of a price change on the total consumer surplus of all buyers in the market. In other words, total consumer surplus is the sum of the consumer surpluses of all individual consumers in the market and, consequently, changes in total consumer surplus approximate the sum of all the changes in individual willingness-to-pay values associated with a given price change.

SUPPLY SCHEDULES

Figure 3-3 presents a standard U-shaped *marginal cost curve* for an individual firm. The curve pertains to costs in the short run, when at least one factor of production, for example, capital, is fixed. That is, purchases of the fixed factor have been made previously (it is a "sunk cost") and, hence, additional expenditures on it are not required as output expands. We later consider the long run when all the factors of production are free to vary.

Given at least one fixed factor of production, diminishing returns must eventually occur as output expands and increasing amounts of the variable factors of production, such as labor, are used with the fixed factor(s). This implies that at least part of the marginal cost curve must slope upward, as is shown in the diagram.[5]

It is important to recognize that the upward-sloping segment of the firm's marginal cost curve above the firm's *average variable cost curve, AVC,* corresponds to the firm's supply schedule or supply curve.[6] If the price were lower than the firm's average variable cost, then the firm could not cover its average variable cost and would shut down, rather than produce any output. At a price above average variable cost, however, the upward-sloping segment of the marginal cost curve determines how much output the firm will produce per period at any given price. For example, at a price of P^*, the firm would maximize profit by producing at X^*. If it produced more output than X^*, it would take in less in additional revenue than the additional cost it would incur. If it produced less output than X^*, it would lose more in revenue than it would save in costs.

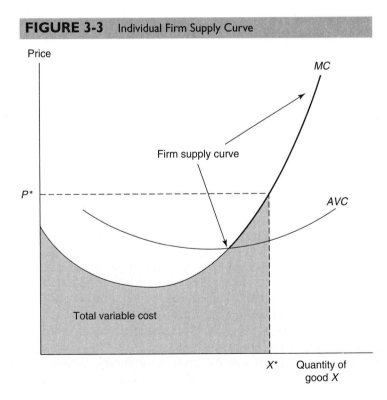

FIGURE 3-3   Individual Firm Supply Curve

Just as the demand schedule indicates the willingness-to-pay for each additional unit of a good consumed, the marginal cost curve indicates the additional cost incurred to produce each additional unit of a good. This means that the area under the marginal cost curve represents the total variable cost of producing a given amount of good X, say X^*.

It is important to emphasize that these variable costs are opportunity costs—the value of what is given up by society to produce X^*—not accounting costs. For example, if the owner of the firm represented in the diagram could earn $80,000 a year working for someone else but actually withdraws a salary of only $50,000 a year from the firm, then it is the $80,000 figure that should be counted as costs incurred by the firm. This amount reflects the value to society of what the owner could produce in alternative employment.

As indicated in Chapter 2, the notion of opportunity cost is critical to CBA. The cost of a policy or project reflects the opportunity costs incurred by various members of society to effect the policy. Consequently, the cost curve in Figure 3-3 should be viewed as drawn under the assumption that the owners of all the resources the firm uses are paid prices equal to the opportunity costs of the resources. In competitive markets they could not receive more, and rather than accept less they would sell to some other firm. For such factors as capital and entrepreneurship, these opportunity costs include a *normal return*[7] because, under perfect competition, these factors would receive such a return in their best alternative use.[8]

Market Supply Schedule

Similar to the case of demand schedules, a market supply schedule can be derived by summing horizontally the individual supply schedules of all the individual firms in a market. These individual supply schedules indicate how much output each firm is willing to sell at each price. Thus, the individual supply schedules provide the information required to determine the total supply available to the market at each price.

A market supply schedule is illustrated in Figure 3-4. As in the case of the marginal cost curves for individual firms, the area under this curve indicates the total variable costs,

FIGURE 3-4   Market Supply Curve

that is, the opportunity costs incurred in producing a given amount of output, say X^*. The area $0abX^*$ is the additional cost of supplying X^*. Put another way, it is the minimum total revenue that firms must receive before they would be willing to produce output X^*.

Producer Surplus

Although area $0abX^*$ is the minimum total revenue that firms in the market represented in Figure 3-4 must receive before they would be willing to produce X^*, at a price of P^*, these firms actually receive total revenues equal to the area represented by the rectangular area $0P^*bX^*$. The difference between this rectangular area and the area under the supply schedule, that is, the area aP^*b, is called *producer surplus*. Thus, in the short run, producer surplus equals the revenues from selling X^* less the variable costs required to produce X^*. Or viewed slightly differently, the sum of total producer surplus and opportunity costs—the sum of areas aP^*b and $0abX^*$—corresponds to total revenues.[9]

Producer surplus is the supply-side equivalent to consumer surplus. Just as changes in prices resulting from government policies have impacts on consumers that can be valued in terms of changes in consumer surplus, price changes also result in impacts on producers that can be valued in terms of changes in producer surplus (or stated slightly differently, as changes in the economic profits of firms in the market). For example, a decrease in price from P^* to P_1 decreases producer surplus (economic profits) by P^*bcP_1 to P_1ca, and an increase in price to P_2 increases producer surplus (economic profits) by P^*bdP_2 to P_2da.[10]

Project Length: Fixed versus Variable Costs

In conducting an actual CBA, the costs considered should be appropriate to the specific policy context. Although we have been emphasizing short-run supply schedules, the appropriate time period for the CBA could correspond to either the short run (where labor is free to vary, but capital is fixed) or the long run (where all inputs can vary). For example, if the government is considering a one-time purchase of concrete to build a road extension, then certain expenditures by firms in the industry from which the government makes the purchase (for instance, the firms' purchase of trucks) may be unaffected. Such costs are best viewed as fixed costs, not variable costs. Thus, they would not be included in the area under the industry's short-run supply schedule and should be ignored in the cost-benefit analysis. On the other hand, if the appropriate time horizon is long or the project is large (for example, the Three Gorges Dam in China), then all the factors of production (such as the number of trucks) are free to vary. The cost of such changes should be included in measuring project costs in a CBA.

Finally, consider a change to an existing program. For example, the government wants to examine the possibility of eliminating price supports in a competitive agricultural market. In this instance, the measured opportunity costs must reflect the value of assets at the time the policy change is made. Some assets may have depreciated in value (for example, although the tractors owned by farmers who would be driven out of business by the fall in prices could be sold, their value would be less than their original purchase price because of depreciation). It is the assets' current economic value that should be considered in the cost-benefit analysis, not their purchase price or their current accounting book value. Other assets may have no remaining value because their costs are *sunk* (barns owned by the farmers who would be driven out of business may have no scrap value) and would, therefore, be ignored in the cost-benefit analysis.

SOCIAL SURPLUS AND ALLOCATIVE EFFICIENCY[11]

The sum of consumer surplus and producer surplus is called *social surplus*. Social surplus is illustrated in Figure 3-5, which depicts both a market demand schedule and a market supply schedule in the same graph. In this graph, which once again is drawn under an assumption of perfect competition, equilibrium occurs at a price of P^* and a quantity of X^*. Social surplus, given this equilibrium, is the large triangular area *abc* between the demand and supply schedules. Viewed slightly differently, social surplus can be defined as the difference between the area under the demand schedule (i.e., the gross benefits received by consumers of output X^*) and the area under the supply schedule (the opportunity cost of the resources required to produce X^* units). If the equilibrium output, X^*, is produced, social surplus—that is, benefits less costs—is maximized.

To reiterate a point made earlier, under well-functioning perfectly competitive markets and in the absence of market failures, the market equilibrium maximizes social surplus. In fact, Pareto efficiency results: It is not possible to make someone better off without making someone else worse off. Indeed, an equilibrium point, such as X^*, is said to be *allocatively efficient* because anything that interferes with the competitive process and causes too few or too many resources to be allocated to the production of a good will reduce social surplus. For example, anything that causes output to be different from this equilibrium level—for instance, to be at either X_1 or X_2—is an economic distortion that shrinks the area of social surplus. Therefore, at least some people will be worse off relative to output level X^*.

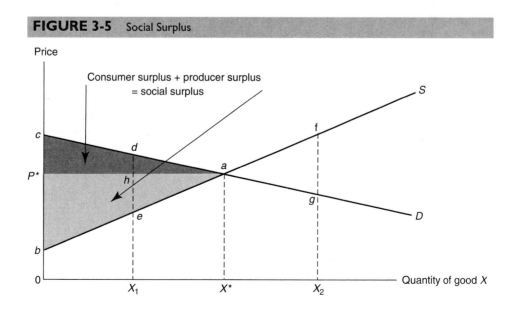

FIGURE 3-5 Social Surplus

The loss in social surplus at X_1 would equal the triangular area *ade*—the area between the demand curve and the supply curve from X_1 to X^*. The loss in social surplus at X_2 would equal the triangular area *afg*—the area between the demand curve and the supply curve from X^* to X_2. These deadweight losses reflect reductions in allocative efficiency. Deadweight losses represent net costs to society because they reduce social surplus relative to what could be attained (at X^*). Thus, any government policy that tends to move the market away from the perfectly competitive equilibrium (e.g., imposition of a tax) imposes a social cost by increasing deadweight loss and reducing social surplus. In contrast, a government policy that moves a distorted market toward the perfectly competitive equilibrium produces social benefits by increasing social surplus and reducing deadweight loss.

For policy purposes, it is important to note the relationship between price and allocative efficiency. Allocative efficiency is maximized in Figure 3-5 at a price of P^* and a quantity of X^*. At the point of equilibrium, *a*, the price paid by consumers equals the marginal cost of producing the good because the supply schedule corresponds to the marginal cost curve. *Allocative efficiency can be obtained only when the price paid by consumers for a good equals the marginal cost to society of producing the good.*[12] This important result can be used to formulate efficient pricing policies.

Distributional Effects Including Government Impacts

This simple model of economic welfare can also be used to examine how the social benefits or costs that result from government policies are distributed among different economic groups in society, including the government. Suppose that initially the perfectly competitive market shown in Figure 3-6 is in equilibrium at a price of P^* and a quantity of X^*. Now suppose that a law is passed guaranteeing sellers a price of P_T.

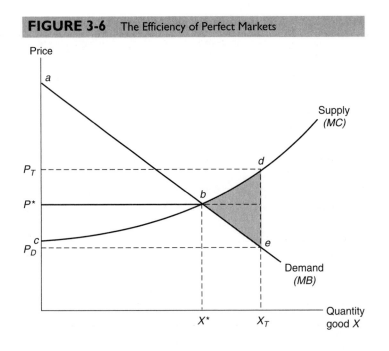

FIGURE 3-6   The Efficiency of Perfect Markets

Such a policy has been utilized in otherwise competitive agricultural markets in the United States, such as those for corn and cotton, and is known as *target pricing*. At a target price of P_T, sellers desire to sell a quantity of X_T. However, buyers are willing to pay a price of only P_D for this quantity, so this becomes the effective market price. Under target pricing, the gap between P_T and P_D is filled by subsidies paid to sellers by the government. As the marginal cost of producing X_T exceeds the willingness of consumers to pay for this quantity of X, a deadweight loss, corresponding to area *bde*, results from the policy. Thus, target pricing with subsidies causes a loss in social surplus by moving the market away from the perfectly competitive equilibrium.

The policy, however, affects buyers, sellers, and taxpayers differently. Because buyers pay a price of only P_D under the policy, total consumer surplus increases from area abP^* to area aeP_D, a gain of P^*beP_D Sellers receive an effective price of P_T, causing total producer surplus to increase from area P^*bc to area P_Tdc, a gain of P_TdbP^*. Taxpayers pay for these benefits to buyers and sellers through government-provided subsidies represented by area P_TdeP_D. Note that these subsidies exceed the combined gains of the buyers and sellers by the area *bde*, the deadweight loss resulting from the policy. While area *bde* represents the net social loss resulting from the policy, the remainder of the subsidies, areas P^*beP_D and P_TdbP^*, represent *transfers* from taxpayers to buyers and to sellers, respectively. While these transfers are a cost to taxpayers, they are benefits to both buyers and sellers in this market. Because the benefits and costs associated with transfers are fully offsetting, they are typically treated in CBA as having no net impact on society.

The proportion of each dollar given up by one group in society (e.g., taxpayers) that as a result of deadweight loss (or administrative costs) does not accrue as transfers to any other group (e.g., consumers or producers) is sometimes called *leakage*. In the target pricing example illustrated in Figure 3-6 (in which administrative costs are ignored), leakage is bde/P_TdeP_D.

EXHIBIT 3-1

The magnitudes of the inefficiencies of agricultural price supports in the United States have at times been very large. For example, Gordon C. Rausser estimated the economic impacts of price support programs for wheat, corn, cotton, peanuts, and dairy products during the mid-1980s. He estimated additional annual costs to consumers of between $3.27 billion and $4.57 billion, annual transfers to producers of between $12.8 billion and $14.9 billion, and annual costs to taxpayers of between $13.5 billion and $15.7 billion. The annual net social cost of these effects

on consumers, producers, and taxpayers was between $1.9 billion and $7.4 billion. That is, the social surplus loss of these policies was several billion dollars annually.

The Federal Agricultural Improvement and Reform Act of 1996, the so-called Freedom to Farm Act, called for phasing out price supports by 2002. Beginning in 1998 with falling world agricultural prices, Congress began reversing the phase-out of price supports. By fiscal year 2001 direct government subsidies to farmers had risen to $20 billion annually.

Sources: Adapted from Gordon C. Rausser, "Predatory Versus Productive Government: The Case of U.S. Agricultural Policies," *Journal of Economic Perspectives* 6(3) 1992, 133–157; and David Orden, "Reform's Stunted Crop: Congress Re-Embraces Agricultural Subsidies," *Regulation* 25(1) 2002, 26–32.

ALTERNATIVE WAYS TO CALCULATE NET SOCIAL BENEFITS

Earlier we mentioned two potential ways to compute social surplus. One way to calculate social surplus is to sum consumer surplus and producer surplus. Thus, for example, the social surplus if the market is at the competitive equilibrium in Figure 3-5 equals area caP^* (consumer surplus) plus area P^*ab (producer surplus), which equals area cab. A second way to calculate social surplus is to subtract the total costs from the total benefits. Thus, for example, social surplus equals area caX^*0 (benefits) minus area baX^*0 (costs), which equals area cab, as before. In summary, assuming no effect on government revenue, the net social benefits of a policy can be computed:

$$NSB = SS = CS + PS, \text{ or} \tag{3.4}$$

$$NSB = B - C \tag{3.5}$$

where SS denotes social surplus, CS denotes consumer surplus, PS denotes producer surplus, B denotes total benefits, and C denotes total costs.

Now consider a change in policy, for example, one that restricts output to X_1 in Figure 3-5. Price might be anywhere on the line de. For expositional convenience suppose the price remains at P^*. The change in social surplus can be computed in two ways. One is to sum the change in consumer surplus and the change in producer surplus. For example, the change in social surplus equals area dah (the change in consumer surplus) plus area hae (the change in producer surplus), which equals area dae. A second way is to compute the change in benefits minus the change in costs. For example, the change in social surplus equals area daX^*X_1 (change in benefits) minus area eaX^*X_1 (change in costs), which also equals area dae. In summary, in the absence of a change in government revenue, the change in the net social benefits of a policy, denoted ΔNSB, can be computed:

$$\Delta NSB = \Delta SS = \Delta CS + \Delta PS, \text{ or} \tag{3.6}$$

$$\Delta NSB = \Delta B - \Delta C \tag{3.7}$$

where $\Delta SS, \Delta CS, \Delta PS, \Delta B,$ and ΔC denote the changes in social surplus, consumer surplus, producer surplus, total benefits, and total costs, respectively.

When a policy change involves changes in net government revenues, these impacts must be included. We need to adjust equation (3.6) thus:

$$\Delta NSB = \Delta SS + \Delta GR, \text{ or} \tag{3.8}$$

$$\Delta NSB = \Delta CS + \Delta PS + \Delta GR \tag{3.9}$$

where ΔGR denotes the change in net government revenues. Notice that equation (3.8) treats changes in government revenue as distinct from changes in social surplus. Although changes in government revenues presumably affect the utility of taxpayers, unlike changes in producer and consumer surplus, they are not represented as gaps between price lines and supply and demand curves.

Equation (3.7) still applies because it follows from equation (3.5). The latter was first introduced in Chapter 1. It includes the benefits and costs to all members of society, including government. Thus, when there are changes in government revenues, we can use equation (3.7) or equation (3.9) to compute the change in net social benefits.

To illustrate, return to Figure 3-6. Suppose that a perfectly competitive market is initially in equilibrium at a price of P^* and a quantity of X^*. Also suppose that a new law is passed that guarantees sellers a price of P_T. Using equation (3.9), the change in net social benefits can be computed as area P^*beP_D (the increase in consumer surplus) plus area P_TdbP^* (the gain in producer surplus) less area P_TdeP_D (the net cost to government), which amounts to a net cost represented by area bde. However, in this particular case, using equation (3.7) to compute the net social benefits is much easier. The change in net social benefits equals area X^*beX_T (the change in benefits) minus area X^*bdX_T (the change in costs), which results in a net cost represented by area bde.

If the analyst simply wants to determine the net social benefits or the change in net social benefits, then using equation (3.5) or (3.7) is often much easier than using equation (3.9). However, if the analyst wants to examine distributional impacts on consumers, producers, and government, then she will use equation (3.9).

CONCLUSIONS

This chapter has reviewed some of the major principles from microeconomics that provide the conceptual foundation for cost-benefit analysis. The key concept is that in conducting a CBA one must estimate the changes in social surplus that result when new policies, programs, or projects are implemented. The chapter, however, mainly focuses on simple changes in prices and tax rates and on markets that are operating under perfect competition. The direction and size of surplus and revenue changes depend on the specific the nature of the policy under consideration and also on the sorts of markets that are affected by the policy. Chapters 4 and 5 make use of the principles reviewed in this chapter to develop measures of benefits and costs that are conceptually appropriate under numerous different circumstances.

Consumer Surplus and Willingness-to-Pay

Earlier in this chapter, we asserted that under most circumstances, estimates of changes in consumer surplus, as measured by demand schedules, can be used in CBA as reasonable approximations of individuals' willingness-to-pay to obtain or to avoid the effects of policy changes. In this appendix, we examine the circumstances under which measured changes in consumer surplus do in fact provide a close approximation to willingness-to-pay and the circumstances under which they do not. For purposes of illustration, we specifically focus on the link between the amount of money a consumer would be willing to pay to avoid a given price increase and estimates based on the demand schedule of the loss in the consumer's surplus resulting from the price increase.

Compensating Variation

The maximum amount of money that consumers would be willing to pay to avoid a price increase is the amount required to return them to the same level of utility they enjoyed prior to the change in price, an amount called *compensating variation*. If the consumers had to spend any more than the value of their compensating variation, then they would be worse off paying to avoid the increase than allowing it to occur. If they could spend any less, then they would be better off paying to avoid the increase, rather than allowing it to occur. Hence, for a loss in consumer surplus resulting from a price increase to equal the consumers' willingness-to-pay to avoid the price increase, it has to correspond exactly to the compensating variation value associated with the price increase.

These assertions are most readily demonstrated by an indifference curve analysis. Such an analysis is presented in Figure 3A-1(a). This diagram represents a consumer who faces a world with only two goods, X and Y. The straight lines in the diagram are budget constraints. The particular budget constraint that the consumer faces depends upon the consumer's income level and on the relative prices of goods X and Y. The greater the consumer's income, the more of X and Y the consumer can afford and, consequently, the greater the distance the budget constraint will be from the origin, 0. Thus, for example, the budget constraint JK represents a higher income level than the budget constraint GI and the budget constraint GH represents a higher income level than the budget constrain LK. The slope of the consumer's budget constraint indicates how many additional units of Y can be obtained if one less unit of X is purchased. Thus, holding everything else constant, the slope of the budget constraint is negative and depends upon the price of X relative to the price of Y. Consequently, if the price of X rises relative to that of Y, the consumer's budget constraint will become more steeply sloped, changing, for example, from budget constraint GH to budget constraint GI. As can be seen, such a change means that a larger number of units of Y can be purchased in exchange for each unit of X that the consumer gives up.

The curved lines in Figure 3A-1(a) are *indifference curves*. All points along a single indifference curve represent combinations of goods X and Y that provide the consumer with equal levels of utility. Thus, the consumer is indifferent between points b and d on U_0 or points a and c on U_1. The further an indifference curve is from the origin, the greater the level of utility. Thus, the consumer would prefer any point on indifference curve U_1 (e.g., point a) to any point on indifference curve U_0 (e.g., point b). This is not surprising in this case because more of both good X and good Y would be consumed at point a than at point b.

The indifference curves in Figure 3A-1(a) are negatively sloped because any movement

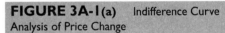

FIGURE 3A-1(a)   Indifference Curve Analysis of Price Change

FIGURE 3A-1(b)   Demand Curve Analysis of Price Change

along an indifference curve definitionally repre-sents a situation whereby an increase in the con-sumption of one good is offset by a sufficient reduction in the consumption of the other good such that the consumer's level of utility is left unchanged.[1] Were the individual to consume either more of both goods or less of both goods, the level of utility would obviously change.

The fact that the indifference curves are convex in shape (i.e., they bend inward toward the origin) reflects diminishing marginal utility—as the consumer consumes more of one good, she becomes increasingly less willing to give up consumption of an additional unit of the other good. For example, the convex shape of indifference curve U_0 implies that at point b the consumer would be willing to give up more units of Y in order to consume one additional unit of X than she would at point d.

Now let us assume that good X in Figure 3A-1(a) is a product on which the consumer spends only a small fraction of her total income, for example, movie tickets, and good Y is a composite good on which the consumer spends the rest of her income. Under these circumstances, good Y is a reasonable approximation of the consumer's total money income. Consequently, the slope of a budget constraint in the figure would indicate the price of good X, that is, the amount of money income (i.e., good Y) the consumer would have to give up to obtain one more unit of X.

Assume that the consumer initially faces budget constraint GH. She will then choose point a on indifference curve U_1. Point a represents an equilibrium because the consumer cannot increase her utility by moving to any alternative point and, hence, has no incentive to do so.[2] Now assume that as a result of a government policy, the price of good X is doubled.[3] This changes the consumer's equilibrium to point b on a more steeply sloped budget constraint, GI, and a lower indifference curve, U_0. Thus, the consumer's consumption of good X falls from X_a to X_b.[4]

If the consumer were paid a lump sum of money sufficient to compensate her entirely for the price increase in X, then this payment would shift the budget constraint in a parallel movement from GI to JK, allowing her to move back to the original indifference curve, U_1. However, the consumer would now choose point c (rather than a) and would consume X_c of the good (rather than X_a). As the vertical distance between the two parallel budget constraints (i.e., the difference between points G and J on the vertical axis) represents the amount of good Y (that is,

money income) that the consumer would have to be paid in order to lose no utility as a result of the price increase, this distance measures the compensating variation associated with the price increase.

As asserted previously, this compensating variation value is the maximum amount that the consumer would be willing to pay to avoid the price increase. To see this, suppose that the price increase occurs and that the consumer is fully compensated for it. Now imagine that if she is willing to pay all the compensation she received—that is, the full value of her compensating variation—the price increase will be revoked. Will she accept or reject this offer? She will, in fact, be indifferent to it. If she accepts the offer, then she will return to her initial equilibrium at point a on indifference curve U_1; if she rejects it, then she will remain at point c, which is also on U_1. Thus, the compensation value represents the maximum amount the consumer would be willing to pay to avoid the price increase. If she could pay a bit less to revoke the price increase, then she would definitely do so. If she had to pay a bit more, then she would prefer to accept the increase.

Income and Substitution Effects

Given the information contained in Figure 3A-1(a), the total effect of the increase in the price of X on the consumer's demand for good X (i.e., the change from X_a to X_b) can be decomposed into two separate effects: a *compensated substitution effect* and an *income effect*.[5] The compensated substitution effect is represented in Figure 3A-1(a) as the change in demand from X_a to X_c. It allows us to examine the effect of a change in the price of X on the demand for X if the individual were exactly compensated for any losses of utility she suffers as a result of the price increase and, as a consequence, remained on indifference curve U_1. The compensated substitution effect always causes the demand for a good to change in the opposite direction from a change in the price of the good. For example, holding the consumer's level of utility constant, an increase in the price of good X causes her to substitute some of the now relatively less expensive good Y for good X. Hence, as shown in the figure, X_c is smaller than X_a.

The income effect is represented in Figure 3A-1(a) as the change in demand from X_c to X_b and results because the increase in the price of good X reduces the consumer's disposable income. If, as the figure implies, X is a *normal good*—that is, if purchases of the good and disposable income are positively related—then the consumer will purchase less of it. Hence, X_b is smaller than X_c. Thus, like the substitution effect, the income effect associated with the price increase will also cause the consumer to reduce her demand for the good.

Demand Schedules

Because the slopes of the budget constraints in Figure 3A-1(a) indicate both the old and the new prices of good X and the points tangent to these budget constraints with indifference curves indicate the amount of the good that the consumer wants at each price, the figure provides information about two points along the consumer's demand schedule for X. Indeed, as we know the quantity of output the consumer would demand after the price increase, both if her utility were held constant and if it were not, we can determine the location of pairs of points along two different demand schedules. These two pairs of points appear in Figure 3A-1(b) as points a' and c' and as points a' and b', respectively. (Ignore the third pair of points, d' and b', for the moment.) We can approximate the demand schedules with straight lines by simply drawing straight lines between the two points in each pair.

The line in Figure 3A-1(b) that connects points a' and b' is a conventional demand schedule of the sort usually emphasized in textbooks. This demand schedule, which is known as a *Marshallian demand schedule*, incorporates both the substitution and income effects associated with changes in the price of good X. Statistical efforts by economists to estimate relations between the price of a good and quantities purchased, which are discussed in Chapter 12, are usually attempts to estimate Marshallian demand schedules empirically, as this work typically involves trying to hold income, other prices, and other factors constant.

The demand schedule in Figure 3A-1(b) that connects points a' and c' keeps utility constant as the price of good X changes and, thus, incorporates only the compensated substitution effect associated with price changes. This demand schedule is sometimes called the *utility compensated* or the *Hicksian compensated variation demand schedule*. Because Hicksian demand schedules are unaffected by income effects, they are usually, as is the case in Figure 3A-1(b), more steeply sloped than Marshallian demand schedules. Unlike Marshallian demand schedules, Hicksian demand schedules usually cannot be directly estimated using statistical techniques. However, it is often possible to indirectly estimate them by first estimating the Marshallian demand schedule and then, in effect, netting out the income effect.[6]

Equivalence of Consumer Surplus and Compensating Variation

Movements up the Hicksian compensated variation demand schedule, for example, from P_a to P_c, are equivalent to allowing the price to increase while compensating the consumer with a lump-sum payment of just sufficient size to permit her to remain on her original indifference curve. This lump-sum payment can be measured graphically as either the vertical distance between the two parallel budget constraints in Figure 3A-1(a) (i.e., as the difference between money income at points G and J) or as the change in consumer surplus indicated by the Hicksian compensated variation demand schedule in Figure 3A-1(b) (the area $P_a a' c' P_c$). Thus, the change in consumer surplus resulting from a price change measured with a Hicksian compensated variation demand schedule exactly equals the consumer's compensating variation; that is, the maximum amount the consumer would be willing to pay to avoid the price increase.

Hence, it is Hicksian compensated variation demand schedules that permit measurement of the compensating variation associated with price changes. To the extent these two demand schedules differ, using a Marshallian compensated variation demand schedule to measure consumer surplus will result in a biased estimate of compensating variation and, therefore, of willingness-to-pay. As can be seen from Figure 3A-1(b), the two alternative demand schedules do produce different measures of consumer surplus, one that differs by the triangular area $a'b'c'$. For a price increase, the change in consumer surplus is smaller if measured with the Marshallian demand schedule than with a Hicksian compensated variation demand schedule; for a price reduction, it is larger.

As previously suggested, the difference between the two types of demand schedules is that the Marshallian schedule incorporates the income effects associated with price changes, as well as the substitution effects, while the Hicksian schedule incorporates only the latter. Thus, the biased estimate of willingness-to-pay that results from using Marshallian rather than Hicksian demand schedules to measure consumer surplus depends upon the size of the income effect associated with a price change. *Usually this income effect and, hence, the bias are small and can be safely ignored in CBA.*[7] This, at least, is the case if the price change is moderate and the good in question accounts for a fairly small part of total consumption. Thus, CBAs of government policies that affect corn, cotton, tobacco, and gasoline prices will generally be little affected by use of Marshallian rather than Hicksian demand schedules. However, *the bias could be of some importance for a CBA of a government policy that would result in large price changes in such consumption goods as housing or automobiles or in large changes in wage rates.* Consequently, except for a few instances when it clearly seems inappropriate to do so, throughout the rest of this book we shall assume that the income effects associated with various policy changes are sufficiently small that consumer surpluses that are measured by using Marshallian demand schedules provide reasonable approximations of willingness-to-pay.

Equivalent Variation as an Alternative to Compensating Variation

In those situations in which the bias should not be ignored, there is an alternative to compensating variation for measuring the welfare effects of price changes that should be used instead because it has more desirable properties: namely, *equivalent variation*.[8]

In terms of Figure 3A-1(a), equivalent variation is the amount of money, GL, that if paid by the consumer would cause her to lose just as much utility as the price increase. If she could pay a bit less, then she would not be as bad off as the price increase makes her. If she had to pay a bit more, then she would be even worse off.

Using the equivalent variation approach, the income effect is represented in Figure 3A-1(a) as the change in demand from X_a to X_d, while the substitution effect is represented as the change in demand from X_d to X_b. Note that, as in the case of the compensating variation approach, both effects that result from the price increase cause the quantity of the good demanded to fall as long as the good is a normal good. Also note that the compensating variation approach measures the substitution effect by holding utility constant at its level *before* the price change was made, while the equivalent variation approach measures the substitution effect holding utility constant *after* the price change. In both cases, however, a Hicksian demand curve can be derived because, holding utility constant, the old and the new prices of good X and the quantity demanded at both prices are all known. Thus, the Hicksian compensated variation demand curve is represented in Figure 3A-1(b) by the line that connects points a' and c' and the Hicksian equivalent variation demand curve is represented by the line that connects points d' and b'. Neither of the Hicksian demand schedules are affected by income effects; hence, they are more steeply sloped than the Marshallian demand schedule. Compensating variation is represented in Figure 3A-1(b) by the area $P_a a' c' P_c$ and equivalent variation by the area $P_a d' b' P_c$.

As indicated by Figure 3A-1(b), the compensating variation that results from the price increase is larger than the change in consumer surplus measured with the Marshallian demand schedule (by the triangular area $a'b'c'$), while the resulting equivalent variation is smaller (by area $b'd'a'$). The opposite would be true in the case of a price decrease. The size of these differences, as previously discussed, depends on the size of the income effect resulting from the change in prices. If they are large, then it is equivalent variation that should ideally be used to measure the change in welfare resulting from a price change, rather than either Marshallian consumer surplus or compensating variation. This is often, but not always, possible if a measure of Marshallian consumer surplus is available.[9]

EXERCISES FOR CHAPTER 3

1. A person's demand for gizmos is given by the following equation:

$$q = 6 - 0.5p + 0.0002I$$

   where q is the quantity demanded at price p when the person's income is I.
   Assume initially that the person's income is \$40,000.
   a. At what price will demand fall to zero? (This is sometimes called the choke price because it is the price that chokes off demand.)
   b. If the market price for gizmos is \$10, how many will be demanded?
   c. At a price of \$10, what is the price elasticity of demand for gizmos?
   d. At a price of \$10, what is the consumer surplus?
   e. If price rises to \$12, how much consumer surplus is lost?
   f. If income were \$60,000, what would be the consumer surplus loss from a price rise from \$10 to \$12?

2. At the current market equilibrium, the price of a good equals \$40 and the quantity equals 10 units. At this equilibrium, the price elasticity of supply is 2.0. Assume that the supply schedule is linear.
   a. Use the price elasticity and market equilibrium to find the supply schedule. (Hint: the supply schedule has the following form: $q = a + (\Delta q/\Delta p)p$. First, find the value of $\Delta q/\Delta p$; then, find the value of a.)
   b. Calculate the producer surplus in the market.
   c. Imagine that a policy results in the price falling from \$40 to \$30. By how much does producer surplus fall?
   d. What fraction of the lost producer surplus is due to the reduction in the quantity supplied and what fraction is due to the fall in price received per unit sold?

3. (This question pertains to the Appendix; instructor-provided spreadsheet recommended.) Imagine a person's utility function over two goods, X and Y, where Y represents dollars. Specifically, assume a Cobb-Douglas utility function:

$$U(X,Y) = X^a\, Y^{(1-a)}$$

   where $0 < a < 1$.

Let the person's budget be B. The feasible amounts of consumption must satisfy the following equation:

$$B = pX + Y$$

where p is the unit price of X and the price of Y is set to 1.

Solving the budget constraint for Y and substituting into the utility function yields:

$$U = X^a (B-pX)^{(1-a)}$$

Using calculus, it can be shown that utility is maximized by choosing:

$$X = aB/p$$

Also, it can be shown that the area under the Marshallian demand curve for a price increase from p to q yielding a change in consumption of X from x_p to x_q is given by:

$$\Delta CS = [aB\ln(x_q) - px_q] - [aB\ln(x_p) - px_p] - (q - p)x_q$$

When $B = 100$, $a = 0.5$, and $p = .2$, $X = 250$ maximizes utility, which equals 111.80. If price is raised to $p = .3$, X falls to 204.12.

a. Increase B until the utility raises to its initial level. The increase in B needed to return utility to its level before the price increase is the compensating variation for the price increase. (It can be found by guessing values until utility reaches its original level.)

b. Compare ΔCS, as measured with the Marshallian demand curve, to the compensating variation.

NOTES

1. Note that viewed in this fashion, the relation depicted in Figure 3-1 is called an *inverse demand curve*; that is, price is viewed as a function of quantity, rather than the other way around, as is more ordinarily the case. One can envision deriving an inverse demand curve through an auction in which bids are taken on the first unit of a good offered for sale, then on the second unit, then the third unit, and so forth, with successively lower bids obtained for each additional unit of the good that is offered. This kind of auction is called a Dutch auction. Although now done electronically, in years past it was common in Holland to have a mechanical "clock" with hands that started at the bid made on the previous unit and swept through successively lower bids until stopped by an individual who wished to make a bid.

2. This is an approximation of the absolute value of the price elasticity. More accurately,

$\epsilon_d = (dQ/dP)(P^*/X^*) < 0$. If the absolute value of ϵ_d is greater than 1 and, hence, the percentage change in quantity demanded is greater than the percentage change in price, then demand is said to be *elastic*. On the other hand, if the absolute value of ϵ_d is less than 1 and, hence, the percentage change in quantity demanded is smaller than the percentage change in price, then demand is said to be *inelastic*. If the value approaches infinity (i.e., the demand schedule is horizontal), then demand is said to be *perfectly elastic*, while if the value is 0 (the demand schedule is vertical), then demand is said to be *completely inelastic*. The use of elasticity estimates in conducting CBAs is further described in Chapter 12.

3. The government is not, of course, the ultimate beneficiary of the tax revenues. This depends on the projects and programs that are funded by the tax revenues.

4. Deadweight loss (*DWL*) may be defined more formally in terms of Figures 3-2(a) and (b) as follows:

$$DWL = \int_{x^*}^{x_1} (MSB - MSC)dx, \qquad \text{if } x^* < x_1$$

$$DWL = \int_{x_2}^{x^*} (MSB - MSC)dx, \qquad \text{if } x_2 < x^*$$

where *MSB* is marginal social benefits and *MSC* is marginal social costs.

When the elasticity of demand (ϵ_d) is known, the change in deadweight loss resulting from a price change—for example, one imposed by a tax—can be computed by using the formula:

$$\Delta DWL = -\tfrac{1}{2} P^* X^* (\Delta P/P^*)^2 \epsilon_d$$

Notice that this formula is similar to equation (3.3).

5. Over longer periods of time, fewer factors of production are fixed so that supply schedules tend to be flatter.
6. In the absence of perfect competition (e.g., in the case of monopoly), the upward-sloping segment of a firm's marginal cost curve is not its supply schedule. This point is further discussed in Chapter 4.
7. By normal return, we simply mean the market price or rate of return that each unit of a resource commands under perfect competition.
8. Thus, because we are presently assuming the existence of perfect competition and well-functioning markets, social opportunity costs, as we have defined them, correspond to private economic

costs. In the absence of perfect competition (or, if externalities exist), private economic costs may differ from the costs that using resources imposes on society. These latter costs, *social opportunity costs*, are the relevant cost measure for purposes of CBA. The use of shadow pricing to obtain appropriate measures of social opportunity costs when markets are distorted is discussed in Chapter 4.

9. To determine profits, fixed costs need to be included in the calculation, that is, revenues – fixed costs – variable costs = economic profits.
10. The longer the time period being considered in cost-benefit analysis, the flatter the market supply schedule (i.e., more elastic) is likely to be, both because more of the factors of production are free to vary and because firms can enter and exit from the market. Consequently, the larger will be the impacts of price increases on producer surplus and the smaller will be the impacts of price decreases.
11. For a recent and very accessible discussion of the topics covered in this section and elsewhere in this chapter and a history of the development of the concept of consumer surplus, see James R. Hines Jr., "Three Sides of Harberger Triangles," *Journal of Economic Perspectives* 13(2) 1999, 167–188.
12. In this discussion, we are assuming perfect competition and, hence, that marginal private costs equal marginal social costs. In Chapter 4, we consider situations where marginal private costs do not equal marginal social costs—for example, when externalities exist.

Appendix Notes

1. The slope of an indifference curve is called the marginal rate of substitution, where the marginal rate of substitution $\dfrac{dX}{dP}\Big|_{\overline{U}} < 0$ and $\overline{U}$ indicates that utility is being held constant.
2. At equilibrium, the marginal rate of substitution will equal the ratio of the price of good X to the price of good Y.
3. Thus, in Figure 3A.1(a), $0I = 1/20H$ or $I = 1/2H$.
4. Depending on the slopes of the indifference curves, the consumption of good Y could either increase or decrease. As shown in Figure 3A.1(a), it slightly decreases in this particular example.

5. In calculus notation, this decomposition can be represented as follows:

$$\frac{dX}{dP} = \frac{dX}{dP}\Big|_{\overline{U}} - X \frac{dX}{dP}\Big|_{\overline{P}}$$

This equation is known as the *Slutsky equation*. The first term to the right of the equal sign is the substitution effect, where utility is held constant. The second term is the income effect, where prices are held constant, and X is the amount of the good consumed prior to the price change.

6. One way of doing this first requires obtaining estimates of the relation between quantity purchased and prices and the relation between quantity purchased and income and then (as implied by the preceding note) using the Slutsky equation to derive the income-compensated (rather than the utility-compensated) relation between prices and quantity purchased. In practice, however, it is not always feasible to estimate the relation between quantity purchased and income and, hence, to use the Slutsky equation.

7. For analyses of the size of the bias, see Ian J. Irvine and William A. Sims, "Measuring Consumer Surplus with Unknown Hicksian Demands," *American Economic Review* 88(1) 1998, 314–322; Robin W. Boadway and Neil Bruce, *Welfare Economics* (Oxford, UK: Basil Blackwell Ltd., 1984), 216–219; Julian M. Alston and Douglas M. Larson, "Hicksian vs. Marshallian Welfare Measures: Why Do We Do What We Do?" *American Journal of Agricultural Economics* 75(3) 1993, 764–769; Jerry A. Hausman, "Exact Consumer's Surplus and Deadweight Loss," *American Economic Review* 71(4) 1981, 662–676; and Robert D. Willig, "Consumer's Surplus Without Apology," *American Economic Review* 66(4) 1979, 589–597.

8. Specifically, using compensating variation is only theoretically correct if consumers have homothetic preferences (i.e., the slopes of all indifferent curves are constant along any ray from the origin), which implies that each good in a consumer's utility function has an income elasticity of one. Equivalent variation does not require a similarly restrictive assumption. See George W. McKenzie, *Measuring Economic Welfare: New Methods* (New York: Cambridge University Press, 1983). Also see Marco Becht, "The Theory and Estimation of Individual and Social Welfare Measures," *Journal of Economic Surveys* 9(1) 1995, 53–87; and the references therein.

   Although equivalent variation is an appropriate measure of the welfare change resulting from a price increase or decrease, it has been argued that either compensating surplus or equivalent surplus is more appropriately used when the quantity of a good, rather than its price, increases or decreases. In this appendix, we focus on price rather than quantity changes. For a discussion of when each of the welfare change measures is most appropriately used, as well as a useful graphical presentation of each, see V. Kerry Smith and William H. Desvousges, *Measuring Water Quality Benefits* (Boston: Kluwer-Nijhoff Publishing, 1986), Chapter 2.

9. A fairly simple procedure for using the Slutsky equation to approximate the Hicksian measures of consumer surplus is described by Irvine and Sims ("Measuring Consumer Surplus . . . "). Also, see note 6.

CHAPTER 4

Valuing Benefits and Costs in Primary Markets

A cost-benefit analysis of a change in government policy sums all the benefits resulting from the policy and subtracts all the associated costs. Doing this requires that the values of all these benefits and costs are measured in monetary terms. Although this is often difficult to accomplish in practice, as suggested in Chapter 1, in principle it would be relatively straightforward to accomplish if all the changes in consumer and producer surplus resulting from a change in government policy, as well as the policy's effects on government revenues, could be determined. Under most circumstances, as indicated in Chapter 3, it is changes in these values that provide conceptually correct measures of the monetary value of a government policy's benefits and costs. Because these values are measured in dollars they can be summed.

This chapter and the next illustrate how changes in consumer surplus, producer surplus, and government revenues could be readily estimated if all the pertinent market demand and supply schedules were known. This chapter focuses on demand and supply schedules in *primary markets*, while Chapter 5 examines demand and supply schedules in *secondary markets*. Primary markets refer to markets that are directly affected by a policy or project; for example, if a city builds a new subway system, the primary markets are the market for public transportation and the market for materials used to build the subway. Secondary markets are markets that are indirectly affected—for example, the market for gasoline if some commuters switch from driving to riding the new subway.

The chapter begins with a brief discussion of why real CBA studies often fail to use conceptually correct measures of benefits and costs and what the implications are of this. We then examine how the effects of government policies in primary markets can be valued. In doing so, we emphasize the concept of willingness-to-pay and, thus, demand schedules and consumer surplus. We next describe the valuation of resources purchased in primary markets as inputs for government projects, stressing the concept of opportunity costs and, hence, the use of supply schedules and producer surplus. Following this, we discuss costs that result from the need to raise tax revenues to pay for government projects.

This chapter also provides brief explanations of common types of market failures including monopoly, externalities, information asymmetries, public goods, and addictive goods. The reason for discussing market failures is that their presence provides the *prima facie* rationale for most, although not all, proposed government interventions that are assessed through CBA. If markets worked perfectly, then Pareto efficiency would be obtained without government intervention: A set of prices would arise that distributes

Current situation: A market is currently functioning without government intervention *and* there is evidence of market failure.

Conclusion: It is worth considering potential government interventions that might increase net social benifits.

CBA analytic task: Given the presence of market failure, assess whether the benefits of a proposed government policy exceed the costs of the policy *and* the cost of market failure.

Rationales for CBA

Current situation: The government has intervened and there is currently no functioning market, *but* there is evidence of government failure.

Conclusion: The current government intervention is not optimal—the current policy is either redundant or replaceable by a potentially more efficient government policy.

CBA analytic task: Given the presence of government failure, assess whether either:

The benefits of eliminating the current government policy exceed the costs of eliminating the policy (i.e., whether, on balance, it is preferable to return to an operational market).

OR

The benefits of replacing the existing government policy with some other government intervention exceed the cost of replacement (i.e., whether some other government policy would increase net social benefits).

FIGURE 4-1   How to Consider Market and Government Failure in CBA

resources to firms and goods to individuals in such a way that it would not be possible to find a reallocation that would make at least one person better off without also making at least one other person worse off. Indeed, doing so could not pass a cost-benefit test. It is only when markets fail that grounds exist for government interventions. However, no more than a *prima facie* case exists. It is up to CBA to demonstrate that a specific intervention is worthwhile. CBA may also be needed to assess existing government policies. In this case, the analyst is essentially attempting to determine whether the current policy is inefficient and, therefore, exhibits "government failure."[1]

Figure 4-1 summarizes the analytic steps to follow depending on whether the analyst observes market failure, government failure, or both.

PRACTICAL VERSUS CONCEPTUALLY CORRECT MEASURES OF BENEFITS AND COSTS

In most CBAs, the measures of benefits and costs actually used differ somewhat from the conceptually correct measures. One purpose of examining the conceptually correct measures of the benefits and costs of a government policy is so they can serve as a benchmark against which the measures used in actual CBAs can be compared. So that we can focus on this objective in this and the next chapter, we ignore the problems inherent in actually deriving demand and supply schedules needed to measure benefits and costs, an issue we take up in detail in Part III. Instead, we focus on how the conceptually correct measures of benefits and costs would be obtained if the necessary schedules were known.

Before turning to the conceptually correct measures, it is helpful to examine why they often differ from the measures used in actual CBAs. A fundamental reason is that it is often convenient to use observed prices in valuing benefits and costs. However, as illustrated later in this chapter, whenever a government policy involves the production of a public good, or an externality or monopoly power is present, market prices may not provide good indicators of the social value of benefits and costs. There are other situations in which a market price does not even exist. For example, persons entering a U.S. National Park pay a fee, but this fee is set by the National Park Service, not by the market. Consequently, it is unlikely that it bears a strong relation to the value of the benefits visitors actually receive from visiting the parks. Thus, a continuum exists. At one end of this continuum are values that can be measured in terms of prices that are set in well-functioning, competitive markets. At the other end is the complete absence of markets that can be used to value benefits and costs resulting from a government policy.

When observed prices fail to reflect the social value of a good accurately or observed prices do not exist, an approach called *shadow pricing* is often used to measure benefits and costs. That is, analysts adjust observed prices or assign values when appropriate observed prices do not exist, thereby finding in "the shadows" needed values that are not readily observable. They attempt to come as close as possible to measuring the value that those receiving benefits from a government project place on them or the lost value to those who incur costs. For example, prices charged by paper factories may understate the true social cost of paper if the production process generates pollution. Given such circumstances, an analyst conducting a CBA may adjust the market price upward to account for the negative externality resulting from the pollution. Another important example of shadow pricing is the considerable effort that economists have put into attempting to place an appropriate value or price on human life. Similarly, economists have also put much work into trying to determine the social value of recreational areas such as public parks.

We indicate many other situations in this chapter when shadow pricing is required and at several junctures suggest approaches that can be taken toward obtaining shadow prices. In Chapters 13–16, we describe additional techniques that are used to obtain shadow prices for purposes of CBA.

Although numerous shadow pricing techniques exist, it is still frequently the case that the measures of benefits and costs used in actual studies differ from their conceptually correct counterparts. There are several reasons for this:

1. As discussed in Chapter 19, errors are sometimes made in CBA. In some instances, for example, the distinction between the measure being used and the conceptually correct measure is sufficiently subtle that it is inadvertently overlooked. In such instances, those conducting the study may be unaware that their results are incorrect and thus do not attempt to use appropriate shadow pricing techniques.
2. It is often difficult to derive an appropriate shadow price. In some studies, consequently, the difference between the actual and the correct measure may be potentially serious, but it is technically infeasible or beyond the time and resources available to those conducting the study to do much about it. In the most extreme

instances, even determining the conceptually correct measures of value is so complex and daunting as to put it beyond the grasp of analysts. Even when shadow prices are used, the resulting measures of benefits and costs may vary from their conceptually correct counterparts. When this is the case, it is at least incumbent upon those conducting the study to point out why and how the study results may be biased.

3. There may be reason to think that the differences between the actual and the correct measures are sufficiently minor such that the study results are not much affected. In such instances, shadow pricing may not be necessary.

VALUING OUTCOMES: WILLINGNESS-TO-PAY

The valuation of policy outcomes should be based on the concept of willingness-to-pay: *Benefits are the sums of the maximum amounts people would be willing to pay to gain outcomes that they view as desirable; costs are the sums of the maximum amounts that people would be willing to pay to avoid outcomes they view as undesirable.*[2] Estimating changes in social surpluses that occur in relevant markets enables us to take account of these costs and benefits. In the discussion that follows, we distinguish between changes in surplus that take place in efficient markets and those that occur in inefficient or distorted markets where market or government failures are found. This discussion also focuses on *gross benefits*, rather than *net benefits*, because it usually ignores the inputs the government must purchase to carry out policies. Measurement of the social cost of these resources is discussed in the following section. Net benefits would be obtained by subtracting these costs from gross benefits.

Valuing Benefits in Efficient Markets

Valuation of gross benefits is relatively straightforward when a policy affects the supply schedules of goods in efficient markets. Under these circumstances, the rule is as follows: *The gross social benefits of a policy equal the net government revenue generated by the policy plus the resulting change in social surplus.* We examine two common situations where this rule is applicable. First, we consider policies that directly affect the quantity of a good available to consumers. For example, a publicly operated childcare center shifts the supply schedule to the right, as it results in more child care being offered to consumers at each price. This often (but not always) reduces prices, resulting in benefits to consumers. Second, we consider policies that shift the supply schedule down by altering the price or availability of some input used to produce the good. An example is deepening a harbor so that it accommodates larger, more efficient ships, thus reducing the cost of transporting bulk commodities to and from the port for shipping companies. This results in direct reductions in costs to producers.

Direct Increases in Supply Available to Consumers Figure 4-2 shows the gross benefits that result when a project directly increases the available supply of a good in a well-functioning market, but the increase is so small that the price of the good is unaffected. If the government sells the additional units of the good at the market price, then it may be treated like other competitors in an efficient market. Hence, as shown in the figure, it faces a horizontal demand schedule, D, for the good at the market price, P_0. If the project directly adds a quantity, q', to the market, then the supply schedule as seen by consumers

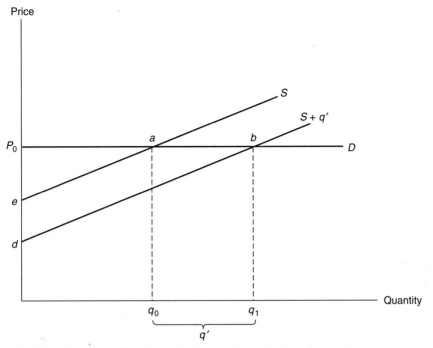

Price

P_0

a b D

S

$S + q'$

e

d

q_0 q_1

q'

Quantity

Social surplus change (ignoring costs of project inputs to the government):

Project (a): Direct increase in supply of q'— gain of project revenue equal to area of rectangle q_0abq_1
Project (b): Supply schedule shift through cost reduction for producers — gain of trapezoid $abde$

FIGURE 4-2   Measuring Benefits in an Efficient Market with No Price Effects

shifts from S to $S + q'$.[3] Because the demand schedule is horizontal, the price of the good and, hence, social surplus are unaffected by the shift in the supply schedule. However, if consumers purchase the additional units of the good, the government receives revenue equal to P_0 times q', the area of rectangle q_0abq_1. The rectangle q_0abq_1 also, of course, represents a cost to those consumers who purchase the good. This "cost," however, is exactly offset by benefits that these persons enjoy in consuming the good and, consequently, can be ignored in our analysis. Therefore the revenues received by the government are the only gross benefits that accrue from the project selling q' units in the market. The project does not provide net benefits to consumers.

If the government adds a sufficiently large quantity of a good to a market so that the price of the good is reduced, however, then consumers will benefit. Figure 4-3 illustrates this possibility by showing a downward-sloping demand schedule, D. The intersection of the demand schedule and the supply schedule, S, indicates the equilibrium price, P_0, prior to the project. The equilibrium price of the good falls to P_1 after the government provides the q' units of the good. This time, because of the reduction in the price facing consumers, there is a change in social surplus. If consumers pay for the additional units of the good from the project at the new market price, then the gain in consumer surplus corresponds to the area of trapezoid P_0abP_1. Because private-sector suppliers continue to operate on the original supply schedule, S, they suffer a loss of producer surplus equal

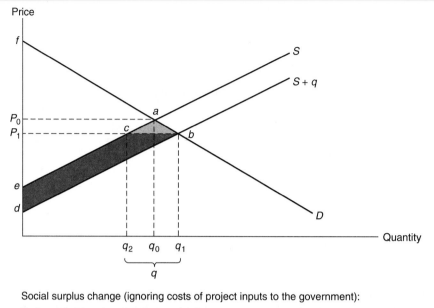

Social surplus change (ignoring costs of project inputs to the government):

Project (a): Direct increase in supply of *q* —gain of triangle *abc* plus project revenue equal
to area of rectangle q_2cbq_1

Project (b): Supply schedule shift through cost reductions for producers—gain of trapezoid *abde*

FIGURE 4-3 Measuring Benefits in an Efficient Market

to the area of trapezoid P_0acP_1. Thus, the gain in social surplus among private actors equals the area of triangle *abc*, which is lightly shaded. In addition, the government receives revenues from the project equal to the area of rectangle q_2cbq_1. The sum of project revenues and the gain in social surplus in the market equals area q_2cabq_1, which is the total gross benefits from the project selling q' units in the market.

What benefits would accrue if q' units of the good were instead distributed free to selected consumers? If the price of the good does not change, as in the situation depicted in Figure 4-2, then the answer is straightforward: As a result of receiving q' units of the good free, consumers gain surplus equal to the area of rectangle q_0abq_1, an area that exactly corresponds to the revenues that would have accrued had the project's output been sold.

The answer is more complex if the q' units of the good are distributed free, but the increase in supply causes its price to fall. This situation is shown in Figure 4-3. Under these circumstances, if the q' units are given only to those consumers who would have valued these units at P_1 or higher, then the project's gross benefit measure is again exactly the same as it would have been had the output been sold. As before, the reduction in price from P_0 to P_1 results in an increase in social surplus equal to area *abc*. With free distribution, however, no revenue accrues to the project. Instead, as a result of receiving q' units of the good free, consumers enjoy an additional surplus equal to the area of rectangle q_2cbq_1. Thus, total gross benefits from the project once again equal the area of trapezoid q_2cabq_1.

It is more likely, however, that if q' units of the good are distributed for free, some would go to consumers who are located below point *b* on the market demand schedule shown in Figure 4-3. In other words, some units would be distributed to some consumers in greater quantities than they would have purchased at price P_1. If these consumers keep the excess units, then area q_2cabq_1 overestimates the project's benefit because these persons value their marginal consumption of these units at less than P_1. Area q_2cabq_1 approximates project benefits, however, if recipients of the excess units sell them to others who would have been willing to buy them at a price of P_1 (provided the transaction costs associated with the sale of the excess units are zero).

Suppose, for example, that a project provides previously stockpiled gasoline free to low-income consumers during an oil supply disruption (an in-kind subsidy). Some low-income households will find themselves with more gasoline than they would have purchased on their own at price P_1; therefore, they will try to sell the excess. Doing so will be relatively easy if access to the stockpiled gasoline is provided through legally transferable coupons; it would obviously be more difficult if the gasoline had to be physically taken away by the low-income households. If the gasoline coupons could be costlessly traded among consumers, then we would expect the outcome to be identical to one in which the gasoline is sold in the market and the revenue given directly to low-income consumers.

Reductions in Costs to Producers   We now turn to a different type of public-sector project: one, such as harbor deepening, that lowers the private sector's cost of supplying a market. Figure 4-3 can again be used to analyze this situation. In this case, however, the supply schedule shifts to $S + q'$, not because the project directly supplies q' to the market, but rather because reductions in marginal costs allow private-sector firms to offer q' additional units profitably at each price.[4] As in the case of direct supply of q', the new equilibrium price is P_1. Thus, the gain in consumer surplus corresponds to the area of trapezoid P_0abP_1. The change in producer surplus corresponds to the difference in the areas of triangle P_0ae (the producer surplus with supply schedule S) and triangle P_1bd (the producer surplus with supply schedule $S + q'$). Area P_1ce is common to the two triangles and therefore cancels. Hence, producers enjoy a net gain in surplus equal to area $ecbd$ minus area P_0acP_1. Adding this gain to the gain in consumer surplus, area P_0abP_1, means that the gain in social surplus resulting from the project equals the area of trapezoid $abde$. (That is, area $ecbd$ + area P_0abP_1 – area P_0acP_1 = area $ecbd$ + area abc = area $abde$.[5]) Because no project revenue is generated, area $abde$ alone is the gross benefit of the project. Notice that because we once again ignore expenditures the government incurs in purchasing inputs needed to undertake the project, we are again measuring gross benefits rather than net benefits.

Valuing Benefits in Distorted Markets

If market or government failures distort the relevant product market, then project benefits should continue to be measured as changes in social surplus resulting from the project plus net government revenues generated by the project. However, complications arise in determining the correct social surplus changes. We illustrate these complications by examining five different types of market failures: monopoly, information asymmetry, externalities, public goods, and addictive goods. We do not attempt to provide a comprehensive discussion of market failures in this chapter, just an overview. For a comprehensive discussion, we recommend a recent book by David Weimer and Aidan Vining, which is cited in the first endnote.[6]

Monopoly.   It is useful to examine monopoly first because it is an excellent example of a topic discussed in Chapter 3: a deviation from the competitive equilibrium that results in a deadweight loss and, hence, reduces social surplus.[7] One key to understanding monopoly is to recognize that because, by definition, a monopolist is the only firm in its market, it views the market demand curve as the demand schedule for its output.

Because market demand schedules slope downward, if the monopolist sells all its output at the same price, then it can sell an additional unit of output only by reducing the price on every unit it sells. Consequently, the monopolist's marginal revenue—the additional revenue it receives for each additional unit of output it sells—is less than the selling price of that output. For example, if a monopolist could sell four units of output at a price of $10 but must reduce its price to $9 in order to sell five units, its revenue would increase from $40 to $45 as a result of selling the fifth unit. Therefore, the $5 in marginal revenue it receives from the fifth unit is less than the $9 selling price of the unit. Thus, as shown in Figure 4-4, the monopolist's marginal revenue curve, denoted MR, is located below its demand schedule, denoted AR.[8]

Given this situation, the monopolist would maximize profit by producing at Q_m, where its marginal cost equals its marginal revenue.[9] The price it can charge is determined by the demand schedule it faces. At the output level Q_m it would set its price equal to P_m.

As in the competitive market case, the social surplus generated by the output produced and sold by the monopolist is represented graphically by the area between the demand schedule and the marginal cost curve that is to the left of the intersection of the marginal revenue and marginal cost curves. The social surplus above the price line (i.e., the consumer surplus) is captured by buyers; the social surplus below the price line (the producer surplus) is captured by the monopolist.

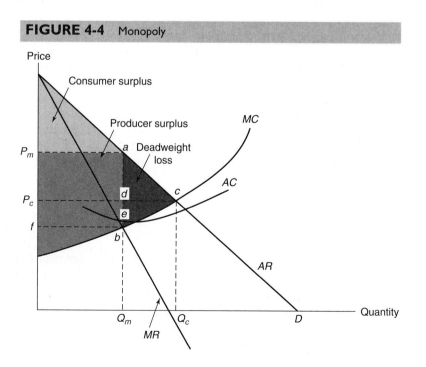

FIGURE 4-4   Monopoly

Although the term monopolist is sometimes used pejoratively, in a CBA any increase in producer surplus received by a monopolist that results from a government policy is counted as a benefit of the policy. The rationale is that owners of monopolies, like consumers and the owners of competitive firms, are part of society; therefore, benefits accruing to them "count."[10]

Notice that, unlike the perfectly competitive case, social surplus is not maximized if the monopolist is left to its own devices. This is because the monopolist does not produce at the "competitive level," Q_c, where the marginal cost curve intersects the demand schedule, and does not charge the competitive price, P_c. This lost social surplus, which is represented in Figure 4-4 by the triangular area abc, is the deadweight loss that results from monopolistic behavior. Were it possible for the government to break the monopoly represented in Figure 4-4 into a large number of competing firms so that a competitive outcome resulted,[11] two things would happen: First, the deadweight loss would disappear and social surplus would increase by the area abc. In CBA, this is counted as a benefit of the government's actions. Second, because the competitive price, P_c, is less than the monopolistic price, P_m, consumers would capture that part of the monopolist's producer surplus that is represented by the rectangular area $P_m a d P_c$. In CBA, this is viewed as a transfer.

Natural Monopoly So far, we have been focusing on a general form of monopoly. We now turn to a specific type of monopoly: *natural monopoly*. The essential characteristic of a natural monopoly is that its fixed costs are very large relative to its variable costs; public utilities, roads, and bridges all provide good examples. As shown in Figure 4-5, these large fixed costs cause average costs to be very large at low levels of output and, as the fixed component of costs is spread over increasing units of output, they continue to fall over a large range of output. This, in turn, means that over this wide range of output,

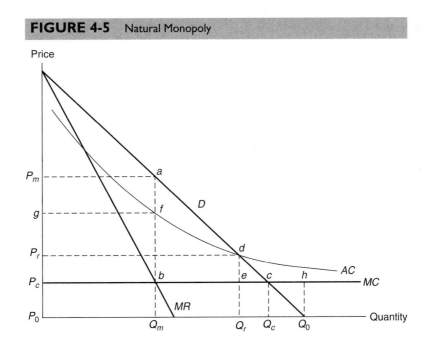

FIGURE 4-5 Natural Monopoly

average costs will exceed marginal costs. Indeed, in Figure 4-5, average costs exceed marginal costs over what we shall term the *relevant range of output*, which is the range between the first unit of output and the amount consumers would demand at a zero price, Q_0.

In principle, marginal costs could be rising or falling over the relevant output range, but for the sake of simplicity, we have drawn the marginal cost curve as horizontal. The important point is that the marginal cost curve is below the average cost curve over the relevant range, so that it pulls average cost down as output increases. Hence, average costs continue to fall over the relevant range of output. As a result, one firm, a natural monopoly, can provide a given amount of output at a lower average cost than could two or more firms.

In these circumstances, it is reasonable for the government to permit a monopoly to exist. If it does, however, it must decide whether to regulate the monopoly, and if it regulates it, what type of policies to invoke. To make our discussion of these policies as concrete as possible, we will assume that the natural monopoly represented in Figure 4-5 is a road and that output is the number of cars that travel the road. Although most roads are built under government contract and operated by the government, they could instead be built and operated by private-sector firms under various regulatory frameworks. In fact, several roads have been built by private companies or public-private partnerships over the past 200 years.[12]

The government could follow one of four policies. The first is simply to allow the road-operating authority, whether a private-sector firm or a government agency, to maximize profits. As discussed previously, profits are maximized at output Q_m, where marginal cost equals marginal revenue. The road-operating authority could obtain this output level by charging a toll (i.e., a price) set at P_m. However, under this policy, output is restricted below the competitive level of Q_c, and willingness-to-pay, P_m, exceeds marginal costs, P_c. This results in a deadweight loss equal to area *abc*. The policy is also unattractive politically because it typically permits substantial monopoly profits, corresponding to area $P_m afg$.

An alternative policy that is often used in regulating natural monopolies is to require the road-operating authority to set its price at P_r, where the average cost curve crosses the demand schedule. This policy eliminates monopoly profits by transferring social surplus from the road-operating authority to persons using the road. It also expands output, increasing social surplus and reducing deadweight loss from area *abc* to area *dec*. Thus, as compared to allowing the road-operating authority to maximize profits, society receives a benefit from the policy that corresponds to area *adeb*. But deadweight loss is not completely eliminated. In other words, society could potentially benefit still further if output could be expanded.

The third policy alternative does this by requiring the road construction and operating authority to set its price at P_c, where the marginal cost curve intersects the demand schedule—in other words, by requiring competitive market pricing. This completely eliminates the deadweight loss, thereby maximizing net social benefits. But a problem exists with this policy: Price is below average costs; hence, revenues no longer cover costs. As a result, tax money must be used to subsidize the road construction and operating authority.

The fourth policy alternative is the one most often used in the case of roads: to allow free access, or in other words, to charge a zero price. In this case, output would expand to Q_0, the point at which the demand schedule intersects the horizontal axis. The problem with this policy is that output expands to a level at which marginal costs exceed willingness-to-pay (WTP). This results in a deadweight loss equal to the triangular area chQ_0, a social cost of making the road free. Moreover, because no tolls are collected directly from road users, the entire construction and operating costs of the road must be paid through government subsidies obtained from taxes.

Information Asymmetry   The term *information asymmetry* implies that information about a product or a job may not be equal on both sides of a market. For example, sellers may have more information concerning how well made or safe a product is than buyers, doctors may know more about needed care than patients, or employers may know more about job-related health risks than their workers.

The implications of information asymmetry are easy to show in a diagram. To do this, we focus on the case in which sellers of a product have more information than buyers. Such a situation is represented in Figure 4-6, which shows two demand schedules. One of these schedules, D_i, represents how many units of the product buyers would desire if they had full information concerning it, while the other demand schedule, D_u, indicates how many units they actually desire, given their lack of full information.[13] In other words, the two demand schedules represent, respectively, consumers' WTP with and without full information concerning the product. They indicate that if buyers had full information, their WTP would be lower.[14]

Figure 4-6 shows that there are two effects of information asymmetry. First, by raising the price and the amount of the good purchased, information asymmetry increases producer surplus and reduces consumer surplus, resulting in a transfer from consumers to sellers. This transfer is shown by the trapezoidal area $P_u acP_i$. Second, by increasing the amount of the good sold relative to the full information case, information asymmetry results in a deadweight loss, which is shown as the triangular area *abc*.

FIGURE 4-6   Information Asymmetry

These two effects, especially the second one, suggest a rationale for the government to intervene by providing the missing information. If the government does this effectively, society will benefit because deadweight loss is reduced. In addition, there will be a transfer of surplus (back) from sellers to buyers. However, there are also costs associated with the government obtaining and disseminating information. These costs, which do not explicitly appear in the diagram, may be sizable.[15] Hence, for a government information program to have positive net benefits, and not just positive gross benefits, the deadweight loss associated with the lack of information in the absence of government intervention must usually be substantial.

It is useful to discuss the circumstances under which information asymmetry is sufficiently important that the benefits from government intervention are likely to exceed the costs. This largely depends upon two factors: first, the ease with which consumers can obtain the information for themselves; and second, whether third parties that could provide the missing information are likely to arise through market forces. To discuss these factors, it is helpful to distinguish among three types of products: (1) search goods, (2) experience goods, and (3) post-experience goods.[16]

Search goods are products with characteristics that consumers can learn about by examining them prior to purchasing them. For example, a student who needs a notebook for a class can go to the bookstore and easily learn pretty much everything he or she wants to know about the characteristics of alternative notebooks. Under such circumstances, information asymmetry is unlikely to be serious.

Experience goods are products about which consumers can obtain full knowledge, but only after purchasing and experiencing them. Examples are tickets to a movie, a meal at a new restaurant, a new television set, and a house. At least to a degree, information asymmetry concerning many such products takes care of itself. For example, once consumers have been to a restaurant, they acquire some information concerning the expected quality of the meal should they eat there again. Warranties, which are typically provided for televisions and many other major consumer durables, serve a similar purpose. In addition, market demand for information about experience goods often prompts third parties to provide information for a fee. This reduces information asymmetry. For example, newspaper reviews provide information about movies and restaurants; in the United States, *Consumer Reports* provides information about many goods; and inspection services examine houses for perspective buyers.

In the case of *post-experience goods*, consumption does not necessarily reveal information to consumers. Government intervention to reduce information asymmetry associated with post-experience goods is most likely to be efficiency-enhancing because learning through individual action does not always occur. Examples of this situation include adverse health effects associated with a prescription drug and a new automobile with a defective part. Employee exposure to an unhealthy chemical at work is similar. In these cases, information asymmetry may persist for long periods of time, even after the health of some people has been ruined. Moreover, because the needed information is often expensive to gather and individuals may be unwilling to pay for it, third parties may not provide the necessary information. Under these circumstances, there may be a strong rationale for government intervention.

Externalities   An *externality* is an effect that production or consumption has on third parties—people not involved in the production or consumption of the good. It is a by-product of production or consumption for which there is no market. Indeed, externalities are sometimes referred to as the problem of "missing markets." Examples include pollution caused by a factory and the pleasure derived from a neighbor's beautiful garden. Externalities may occur for a wide variety of reasons. For example, some result because a particular type of manufacturing technology is used (e.g., air pollution caused by smokestack industry). Others arise because of interdependencies (or synergies) between producers and consumers or different groups of producers (e.g., beekeepers who unintentionally provide pollination services for nearby fruit growers). Still other externalities occur because of networks (e.g., the larger the number of persons who purchase a particular type of automobile, the greater the number of qualified service garages available to each owner). Because the number of externalities is enormous, a careful CBA should first be conducted before the government intervenes to correct any specific externality.[17]

We first examine a negative externality (i.e., one that imposes social costs) and then a positive externality (i.e., one that produces benefits). Figure 4-7 illustrates a market in which the production process results in a negative externality, such as air or water pollution. The supply schedule, S^*, reflects only the private marginal costs incurred by the suppliers of the good, while the second supply schedule, $S^\#$, incorporates the costs that the negative externality imposes on third parties, as well as the private marginal costs incurred by suppliers. The vertical distance between these two curves, measured over the quantity of the good purchased, can be viewed as the amount those subjected to the negative externality would be willing to pay to avoid it. In other words, it represents the costs imposed by the externality on third parties. The length of this distance depends in part upon whether the market somehow compensates third parties for the negative externality. For example, it would be smaller if homeowners were able to purchase their houses at lower prices because of pollution in their neighborhood than if they were not.

FIGURE 4-7 Negative Externality

Figure 4-7 indicates that, if left to its own devices, the market sets too low a price for the good ($P^* < P^\#$) because it fails to take account of the cost to third parties of producing the good. As a result, too much output is produced ($Q^* > Q^\#$). This causes deadweight loss, which is represented by the shaded triangular area labeled C. This deadweight loss reflects the fact that for each unit of additional output produced in excess of $Q^\#$, marginal social costs (shown by the supply schedule $S^\#$) increasingly exceed marginal social benefits (shown by the demand schedule D).

The standard technique for reducing deadweight loss resulting from negative externalities is to impose taxes.[18] For example, the suppliers of the good represented in Figure 4-7 could be required to pay a tax, t, on each unit they sell, with the tax set equal to the difference between marginal social costs and marginal social benefits (shown in the figure as the vertical distance at Q^* between the two supply schedules). As production costs would now include the tax, the supply schedule of sellers, S^*, would shift upward to $S^\#$. Consequently, the price paid by consumers would increase from P^* to $P^\#$, the net price received by producers would fall from P^* to $P^\# - t$, and output produced and sold would fall from Q^* to $Q^\#$. Note that pollution associated with the good would be reduced, but not completely eliminated, because the good would continue to be produced, although in smaller amounts.[19]

Figure 4-7 implies that the benefits and costs of the government's tax policy are distributed unequally among different groups in the economy. These are displayed in the following social accounting ledger.

	Benefits	*Costs*
Consumers of good		$A + B$
Producers of good		$E + F$
Third parties	$B + C + F$	
Government revenue	$A + E$	
Social benefit	C	

Because the policy causes consumers to pay a higher price for less of the good, they lose surplus equal to areas A and B. Similarly, because the tax causes producers to sell less of the good but increases their production costs, they lose producer surplus equal to areas E and F. On the other hand, because of the reduction in production of the good and, hence, in pollution, third parties receive benefits from the policy equal to areas B, C, and F. Finally, the government receives tax revenues equal to areas A and E. Because areas A, B, E, and F represent transfers from one group to another, only area C can be counted as a gain to society as a whole from the tax policy. This area corresponds to the deadweight loss eliminated by the tax policy. To compute the *net* social benefit of the tax, the cost of administering it would have to be subtracted from the reduction in deadweight loss.

Now let us look at an example of a positive externality, a program that subsidizes the purchase of rodent extermination services in a poor neighborhood. One mechanism for doing this is to provide residents with vouchers that are worth a certain number of dollars, v, for each unit of extermination services they purchase. After subtracting the face value of these vouchers from what they charge neighborhood residents for their services, exterminators would then be reimbursed the face value of the voucher by the government.

By increasing the use of extermination services, such a program may result in a positive externality: The fewer the rodents in the neighborhood, the easier it is for residents in adjoining neighborhoods to control their own rodent populations. This situation is illustrated in Figure 4-8, where the market demand schedule, D_M, is shown as understating the social demand schedule, D_S. The area between these two demand schedules represents the WTP for the extermination voucher program by residents of adjoining neighborhoods, assuming they had knowledge of the potential benefits from the program to them. Thus, the market equilibrium price, P_0, and quantity, q_0, are both too low from the social perspective, resulting in deadweight loss equal to $C + F + H$.

What are the social benefits of a program that distributes vouchers worth $\$v$ per unit of extermination service to the residents of a poor neighborhood? As implied by Figure 4-8, when the vouchers become available, residents of the poor neighborhood face a supply schedule that is below the original market supply schedule, S, by $\$v$. As a consequence of a voucher-induced shift in the supply schedule, neighborhood residents increase their purchases of extermination services from q_0 to q_1, paying an effective price of P_1. Consumers in the targeted neighborhood enjoy a surplus gain equal to the area of trapezoid $B + E$; producers, who now receive a higher supply price of $P_1 + v$, enjoy a surplus gain equal to the area of trapezoid $A + C$; and people in the surrounding neighborhoods, who enjoy the positive externality, gain surplus equal to the area of

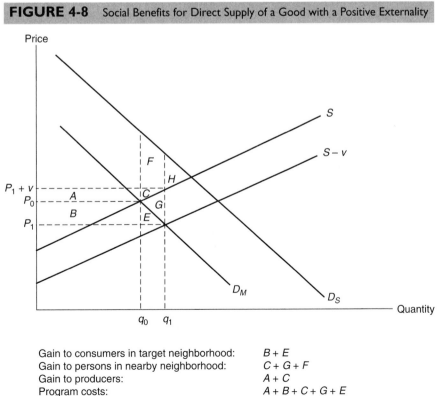

FIGURE 4-8 Social Benefits for Direct Supply of a Good with a Positive Externality

Gain to consumers in target neighborhood:	$B + E$
Gain to persons in nearby neighborhood:	$C + G + F$
Gain to producers:	$A + C$
Program costs:	$A + B + C + G + E$
Net benefits:	$C + F$

parallelogram $C + G + F$, the area between the market and social demand schedules over the increase in consumption. The program must pay out v times q_1 in subsidies, which equals the area of rectangle $A + B + C + G + E$. Subtracting this program cost from the gains in social surplus in the market yields gross program benefits: the area of trapezoid $C + F$.[20] This benefit results because the program succeeds in eliminating part (although not all) of the deadweight loss in the market for extermination services.

Public Goods   Once produced, public goods—for example, flood control projects or national defense—are available for everyone. No one can or, indeed, should be excluded from enjoying their benefits. In this sense, public goods may be regarded as a special type of positive externality. Similar to other positive externalities, private markets, if left to their own devices, tend to produce less public goods than is socially optimal. Pure public goods have two key characteristics: They are nonexcludable and they are nonrivalrous.

A good is nonexcludable if it is impossible, or at least highly impractical, for one person to prevent others from consuming it.[21] If it is supplied to one consumer, it is available for all consumers, a phenomenon sometimes called *jointness in supply*. For example, it would be very difficult for a user of the light emitted from a particular streetlight to prevent others from using that light. In contrast, most private goods are excludable. For instance, a purchaser of a hamburger can exclude others from taking a bite unless overcome by physical force.

The reason nonexcludability causes market failure is easy to see. Once a nonexcludable good such as street lighting or national defense exists, it is available for everyone to use. Because there is no way to exclude people from its use, a *free-rider problem* results. As a consequence, there is not sufficient incentive for the private sector to provide it. Usually it must be publicly provided, if it is going to be provided at all.

Nonrivalry implies that one person's consumption of a good does not prevent someone else from also consuming it; consequently, more than one person can obtain benefits from a given level of supply at the same time. For example, one person's use of a streetlight to help him see at night does not diminish the ability of another person to use the same light. But if one person eats a hamburger, another cannot consume the same hamburger. The hamburger is rivalrous; a streetlight is nonrivalrous. Thus, unlike the hamburger, even if it were feasible to exclude a second person from using street lighting, it would be inefficient to do so because the marginal cost of supplying lighting to the second person is zero.

The reason nonrivalry causes market failure can be examined by contrasting how a *total marginal benefit curve*, a curve that reflects the incremental benefits to consumers from each additional unit of a good that is available for their consumption, is derived for a rivalrous good with how such a curve is derived for a nonrivalrous good. To do this graphically as simply as possible, we assume that there are only two potential consumers of each of the two goods. Thus, Figure 4-9 displays two graphs: one for the rivalrous good (hamburger) and one for the nonrivalrous good (streetlight). Each graph contains three curves: a demand schedule representing consumer A's WTP (d_A), a demand schedule representing consumer B's WTP (d_B), and a total marginal benefit (MB) curve, which is derived from the demand schedules for the two consumers.

The total marginal benefit curve for the rivalrous good is equivalent to a market demand schedule. To derive this curve, the two demand schedules for individual consumers are summed horizontally. For example, at a price of P^*, consumer A would want to consume q_1 and consumer B would want q_2 of the good. Total market demand for the good at a price of P^* is equal to $q_1 + q_2$, a total of Q^*. Thus, WTP for (or equivalently,

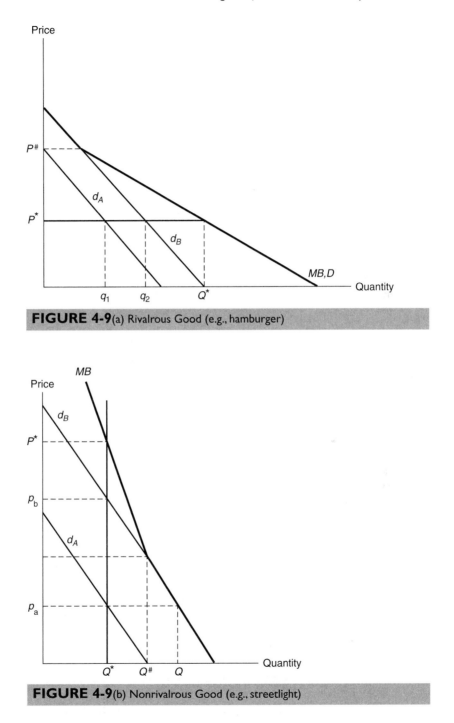

FIGURE 4-9(a) Rivalrous Good (e.g., hamburger)

FIGURE 4-9(b) Nonrivalrous Good (e.g., streetlight)

marginal benefits from) the last unit of the total of Q^* units consumed is P^*. Notice that until the price falls below $P^\#$, the marginal benefit curve would correspond to B's demand schedule because A would not demand any of the good.

In contrast, the total marginal benefit curve for the nonrivalrous good is derived by adding the demand schedules for individual consumers vertically rather than horizontally. At an output level of Q^*, for example, total WTP (i.e., the total marginal benefits from the last unit of the good that is made available) is equal to $p_a + p_b$ or P^*. Notice that at output levels above $Q^\#$, consumer A's WTP falls to zero and, consequently, the marginal benefit curve corresponds to consumer B's demand schedule.

The reason the demand schedules for individual consumers must be summed horizontally in the presence of rivalry and vertically in its absence can be clarified through use of a numerical example. If at a price of $2 consumer B wanted to buy two hamburgers and consumer A one hamburger, then total demand would equal three hamburgers—the horizontal sum of demands at a particular price. But if at a price of $1,000, B wanted two streetlights on the block on which he and A both lived, but A wanted only one, then two streetlights would completely satisfy the demands of both. Thus, the total demand for a nonrivalrous good cannot be determined by summing the quantity of the good each consumer desires at a given price. It must be determined instead by summing each consumer's WTP for a given quantity of the good. Hence, although A and B have a different WTP for the two streetlights, their total WTP for the two streetlights can be determined by adding A's WTP for two lights to B's.

The distinction between how the total demand for rivalrous and nonrivalrous goods is determined has an important implication. In the case of the rivalrous good, consumers will reveal to the market how much they want. For example, if the price of hamburgers is set at P^*, consumer A will actually purchase q_1 of the good and consumer B will actually purchase q_2. But in the case of a nonrivalrous good, no market mechanism exists that causes consumers to reveal how many units they would purchase at different prices. For example, if the price of streetlight is at p_b, consumer B would be willing to purchase Q^* of the good. But if B did that, A would not purchase any because, as a result of B's purchase, he could consume all he wanted. In other words, A would free ride on B. Because of this free-rider problem, B might refuse to make any purchase until A agreed to make some sort of contribution.[22]

When only a small group of people is involved, they may be able to work out the free-rider problems caused by the nonexcludability and nonrivalry of public goods through negotiations. For example, a neighborhood association might make arrangements for installing and paying for streetlights. But too much or too little of the good may be produced. For example, if consumers A and B are to be charged for streetlights on the basis of their WTP, each will probably try to convince the other that they place a low value on streetlights regardless of how they actually value them. It is therefore difficult to determine where the total marginal benefit curve for a public good is located, even if only a small group of people is involved. When a large group of people share a good that is nonexcludable and nonrivalrous, such as national defense, negotiations become impractical. Consequently, if the good is going to be produced at all, the government must almost certainly intervene by either producing the good itself or subsidizing its production.

Because streetlighting is both nonrivalrous in consumption and nonexcludable, it is close to being a pure public good. Other goods may be either nonrivalrous or nonexcludable, but not both. For example, an uncrowded road is essentially nonrivalrous in nature. One person's use of it does not keep another from using it.

Yet, it is excludable. Individuals could be required to pay a toll to use it. Thus, it is sometimes called a *toll good*.[23] Fish in international waters provide an example of a good that is rivalrous but nonexcludable. Fish and fishers move around so it is difficult to preclude fishers from catching a particular type of fish, for example, tuna. But if a fisher catches a tuna, then that tuna is no longer available to other fishers. This type of good is called an *open access resource*.[24] Goods that are either nonrivalrous or nonexcludable, but not both, do not exhibit all of the characteristics of public goods, but do exhibit some of these characteristics. However, for the sake of brevity, we have focused on pure public goods, which are both nonrivalrous and nonexcludable. Examples of goods that are close to being pure public goods are streetlights, flood control, national defense, and crime deterrence resulting from police patrolling the streets.

As suggested by the preceding analysis, because of both nonrivalry and nonexcludability, actual markets for pure public goods are unlikely to exist. However, marginal benefit and marginal cost curves, which are analogous to market demand and supply schedules, do exist. We have already shown how to derive a marginal benefit curve for a public good. And, as in the case of a private good, the marginal cost curve for a public good simply reflects the costs of producing each incremental unit of the good. Social welfare is maximized when marginal benefits equal marginal costs, while deadweight loss results at either smaller or larger output amounts. However, because of the absence of a true market, little or none of a pure public good would be produced without government intervention, or at least some sort of negotiation process. Thus, in the absence of government intervention or negotiations, society would forgo social surplus resulting from consumption of the good. Even if the government does intervene or negotiations do take place, there is nonetheless no guarantee that output of the good will be at the point where marginal benefits equal marginal costs because the marginal benefit curve for a pure public good is inherently unknowable. As a consequence, too much or too little of it may be produced. However, as described in Chapter 14, techniques exist that can be used to obtain information about WTP for public goods.

Intrapersonal Externalities: Consumption under Addiction   For some people, the consumption of a particular good today increases their demand for its consumption in the future. For example, exposure to classical music during childhood may contribute to a demand for such music in adulthood. Economic models of addictive goods assume that the amount demanded at any time depends on the amount of previous consumption. *Rational addiction* occurs when consumers fully take account of the future effects of their current consumption.[25] If current consumption is myopic or fails to take account of future risks, then addiction is not rational. For example, some children may fail to anticipate the consequences of tobacco addiction during their adulthood or some adults may fail to anticipate the risk that their casual gambling may become a disruptive compulsion. Such cases involve *negative intrapersonal externalities*—harm imposed by current consumers on their future selves.

The presence of negative intrapersonal externalities brings into question the appropriateness of using changes in social surplus measured under market demand schedules as the basis for assessing the benefits of alternative policies. On the one hand, the demand schedule reveals the marginal willingness of the market to pay for additional units of the good. On the other hand, the satisfaction from addictive consumption may not actually make consumers better off—it avoids the pain of abstinence but does not provide as much happiness as would alternative consumption in a nonaddicted state. The stated desire and costly efforts made by many adult smokers to quit smoking suggests that they perceive benefits from ending their addiction. In other words, they wish they had not been addicted by their younger selves.

A plausible approach to measuring consumer surplus in the presence of undesirable addiction involves assessing consumer surplus using unaddicted demand schedules.[26] Figure 4-10 illustrates the approach taking as an example addicted, or so-called problem, gamblers. It shows two demand schedules: D_A, the demand schedule for gambling in the presence of the addiction, and D_R, the demand schedule for the same group of addicted gamblers if they were instead like the majority of recreational gamblers who enjoy gambling but do not have a strong compulsion to gamble that leads them to regret their gambling behaviors. The quantity of gambling demanded by these addicted gamblers at price P is Q_A. If they were not addicted, however, then they would consume only Q_R at that price. Q_A minus Q_R is the excess consumption due to the addiction. Consumption up to level Q_R involves a positive consumer surplus of PaP_C. The consumption from Q_R to Q_A involves expenditures of Q_RabQ_A but consumer value equal to only Q_RacQ_A as measured under their recreational demand schedule, resulting in a loss equal to area abc. Overall, participation in this market by these addicted gamblers yields consumer surplus equal to $PaP_C - abc$. If a policy resulted in these addicted gamblers becoming unaddicted recreational gamblers, then a surplus gain of abc would result.

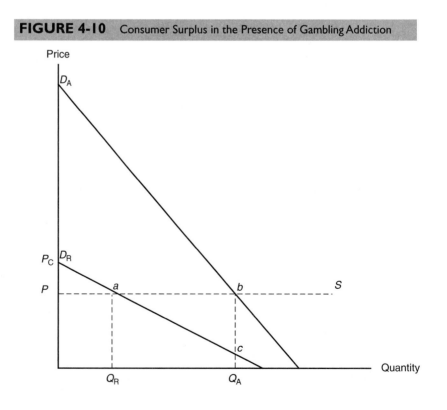

FIGURE 4-10   Consumer Surplus in the Presence of Gambling Addiction

The Australian Productivity Commission applied this approach to estimate consumer surplus losses and gains from the Australian gambling industry. It estimated a consumer surplus gain for recreational gamblers (97.9% of all gamblers) to be between AU$2.7 billion and AU$4.5 billion annually but a consumer surplus loss of almost AU$2.7 billion annually for problem gamblers (2.1% of all gamblers).[27]

VALUING INPUTS: OPPORTUNITY COSTS

Public policies usually require resources (i.e., inputs) that could be used to produce other goods or services instead. Public works projects such as dams, bridges, highways, and subway systems, for example, require labor, materials, land, and equipment. Similarly, social service programs typically require professional employees, computers, telephones, and office space; wilderness preserves, recreation areas, and parks require at least land. Once resources are devoted to these purposes, they obviously are no longer available to produce other goods and services. Almost all public policies incur opportunity costs. Conceptually, these costs equal the value of the goods and services that would have been produced had the resources used in carrying them out been used instead in the best alternative way. These opportunity costs, as seen in Chapter 3, are represented by areas under supply schedules. These areas are the theoretically appropriate measures of the costs of the inputs.

As a practical matter, the most obvious and natural way to measure the value of the resources used by a project is simply as the direct budgetary outlay needed to purchase them. Under certain circumstances, the direct budgetary outlay is also identical to the conceptually appropriate opportunity cost measure, but under other circumstances, it is not. To determine when it is and is not permissible to use budgetary outlays, we compare the conceptually appropriate measure of costs with the direct budgetary outlay measure of costs in three alternative market situations: (1) when the market for a resource is efficient (i.e., there are no market failures) and purchases of the resource for the project will have a negligible effect on the price of the resource; (2) when the market for the resource is efficient, but purchases for the project will have a noticeable effect on prices; and (3) when the market for the resource is inefficient (i.e., there is a market failure). As will be seen, in the first of these situations, budgetary expenditures usually accurately measure project opportunity costs; in the second situation, budgetary outlays often only slightly overstate project opportunity costs; and in the third situation, expenditures may substantially overstate or understate project opportunity costs.

Before beginning, it may be helpful to make a general point concerning opportunity costs: The relevant determination is what must be given up today and in the future, *not* what has already been given up. The latter costs are *sunk* and, unlike variable costs, are not represented by the areas under supply schedules. In CBA, the extent to which costs are sunk depends importantly on whether an *ex ante*, *ex post*, or *in medias res* analysis is being conducted. For instance, suppose that you are asked to evaluate a decision to complete a bridge after construction has already begun. What is the opportunity cost of the steel and concrete that is already in place? It is not the original expenditure made to purchase them. Rather, it is the value of these materials in their current best alternative use. This value is most likely measured by the maximum amount for which the steel and concrete could be sold as scrap. Conceivably, the cost of scrapping the materials may exceed their value in any alternative use so salvaging them would not be justified. Indeed, if salvage is still necessary, perhaps for environmental or other reasons, then the opportunity cost of the materials will be negative (and thus counted as a benefit, an avoided cost) when calculating the net gains of continuing construction. In situations where resources that have already been purchased have exactly zero scrap value (the case of labor already expended, for instance), the costs are entirely sunk and are not relevant to decisions concerning future actions.

Measuring Opportunity Costs in Efficient Markets with Negligible Price Effects

Perfectly Elastic Supply Schedules   An example of this is when a government agency running a training program for unemployed workers purchases pencils for trainees. Assuming an absence of failures in the market for pencils, and that the agency buys only a small proportion of the total pencils sold in the market, the agency is realistically viewed as facing a horizontal supply schedule for pencils. Thus, the agency's purchases will have a negligible effect on the price of pencils; it can purchase additional pencils at the price they would have cost in the absence of the training program.

This situation is depicted in Figure 4-11. If a project purchases q' units of the input factor represented in the diagram (e.g., pencils), the demand schedule, D, would shift horizontally to the right by q'. As implied by the horizontal supply schedule, marginal costs remain unchanged and, hence, the price remains at P_0. The area under the supply

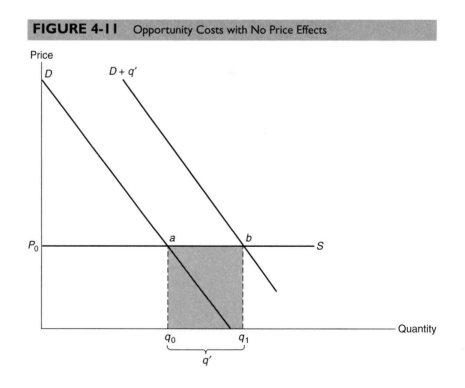

FIGURE 4-11   Opportunity Costs with No Price Effects

schedule represents the opportunity cost of the factor and P_0 is the opportunity cost of one additional unit of the factor. Consequently, the opportunity cost to society of the q' additional units of the factor needed by the project is simply the original price of the factor times the number of units purchased (i.e., P_0 times q'). In Figure 4-11, this is represented by the shaded rectangle abq_1q_0. Thus, the amount that the agency must pay to purchase additional pencils equals the opportunity cost of the resources used to produce them. In other words, if the q' units of the factor were not used for purposes of the project, then P_0 times q' worth of goods could be produced elsewhere in the economy.

What is important about the situation just described is that the social cost of the units of the factor needed by the project, the shaded rectangular area in Figure 4-11, is identical to the budgetary outlay required to purchase the units; both are equal to P_0 times q'. Because most factors have neither steeply rising nor declining marginal cost curves, *it is often reasonable to presume that expenditures required for project inputs equal their social costs*. This is the case when the quantity of the resource purchased makes only a small addition to the total demand for the resource, and where, in addition, there is no reason to suspect the existence of significant market failures.

Perfectly Inelastic Supply Schedules   In contrast to pencils, let us now examine a government purchase of a parcel of land for a park. We assume that, unlike the pencils, the quantity of land in a specified area is fixed at A acres. Thus, the government faces a vertical rather than horizontal supply schedule. In addition, we assume that if the government does not purchase the land, it will be sold in one-acre parcels to private buyers who will build houses on it.

This situation is represented in Figure 4-12, where S is the supply schedule and D the private-sector demand schedule. If the owners of the land sell it in the private market, they receive the amount represented by the rectangle $PbA0$. Now let us assume that the government secures all A units of the land at the market price through its eminent domain powers, paying owners the market price of P. Thus, the government's budgetary cost is represented in Figure 4-12 by area $PbA0$.

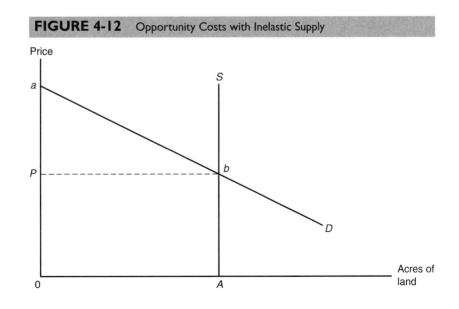

FIGURE 4-12   Opportunity Costs with Inelastic Supply

Here, however, the government's budgetary outlay understates the opportunity cost of removing the land from the private sector. The reason is that the potential private buyers of the land lose consumer surplus (triangle *aPb* in Figure 4-12) as a result of the government taking away their opportunity to purchase land, a real loss that is not included in the government's purchase price. The full cost of the land if it is purchased by the government is represented in Figure 4-12 by all of the area under the demand schedule to the left of the vertical supply schedule, area *abA*0, not only the rectangular area below the price line.[28]

Measuring Opportunity Costs in Efficient Markets with Noticeable Price Effects

It is possible that even when a resource required by a project is purchased in an essentially efficient market, such a large quantity is required that its price is bid up. This could occur, for example, if the construction of a very large dam requires massive amounts of concrete. In such a situation, the project should be viewed as facing an upward-sloping supply schedule for the resource input. Such a supply schedule is illustrated in Figure 4-13. In this example, project purchases of q' units of the resource would shift the demand schedule, D, to the right. Because the supply schedule, S, is upward sloping, the equilibrium price rises from P_0 to P_1, indicating that the large purchase causes the marginal cost of the resource to rise. The price increase causes the original buyers in the market to decrease their purchases from q_0 to q_2. However, total purchases, including those made by the project, expand from q_0 to q_1. Thus, the q' units of the resource purchased by the project come from two distinct sources: (1) units bid away from their previous buyers, and (2) additional units sold in the market.

Total project expenditures on the resource are equal to P_1 times q'. In Figure 4-13, these expenditures are represented by areas $B + C + G + E + F$, which together form

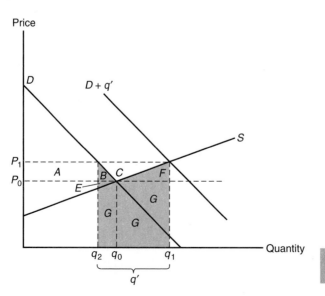

FIGURE 4-13   Opportunity Costs with Price Effects

a rectangle. Unlike the case where the price of the resource does not change, however, this expenditure does not correspond to the opportunity cost of using q' units of the resource. The price change must be taken into account in computing the opportunity cost. In doing this, the general rule is that *opportunity cost equals expenditure less (plus) any increase (decrease) in social surplus occurring in the factor market.* In other words, budgetary outlays on a resource do not equal opportunity costs when the outlays cause a change in social surplus in the market for the resource.

To understand why, first look at the areas labeled A and B in Figure 4-13. These two areas represent a decrease in the consumer surplus of the original buyers because of the price increase. However, sellers gain more in producer surplus as a result of the price increase than the original buyers lose—a gain represented by areas $A + B + C$. Part of the gain in producer surplus, the area represented by $A + B$, merely offsets the loss in consumer surplus and, hence, is a transfer from buyers to sellers. However, area C represents a gain in social surplus that partially offsets the social cost resulting from increased government expenditure on the resource.[29] To measure the social cost of the project's purchase of the resource, this net gain in social surplus must be subtracted from the project's total budgetary outlay on the resource, areas $B + C + G + E + F$. Thus, the net social cost of the project's purchase of q' units of the resource is represented by areas $B + G + E + F$. The effects of the purchase are summarized in the following accounting ledger.

	Benefits	*Costs*
Original buyers		$A + B$
Sellers	$A + B + C$	
Project expenditures		$B + C + G + E + F$
Net social cost		$B + G + E + F$

The basic point is that when prices change the budgetary outlay does not equal the social cost. In the example shown in Figure 4-13, they differ by area C. As an examination of the figure suggests, however, unless the rise in prices is quite substantial, this area will be small relative to total budgetary cost. This suggests that in many instances budgetary outlay will provide a good approximation of true social cost.

If the price of an input does go up substantially, however, then the budgetary cost must be adjusted for CBA purposes. If the demand and supply schedules are linear (or can be reasonably assumed to be approximately linear), then the amount of this adjustment, which is the area represented by C, can be readily calculated. It equals the amount of the factor purchased for the project, q', multiplied by $\frac{1}{2}(P_1 - P_0)$, half the difference between the new and the old prices.[30] The opportunity cost of purchasing the resource for the project can also be computed directly by multiplying the amount purchased by the average of the new and old prices, $\frac{1}{2}(P_1 + P_0)(q')$.[31] The average of the new and old prices is a shadow price; it reflects the social opportunity cost of purchasing the resource more accurately than either the old price or the new price alone.

It is useful to recognize that the social cost of using a resource for a project or program does not necessarily depend upon the mechanism that a government uses to obtain it. Suppose, for example, that instead of paying the market price for q' units of the resource represented in Figure 4-13, the government instead first orders supplying firms to increase their prices to the original buyers in the market from P_0 to P_1, thereby causing sales to these buyers to fall from q_0 to q_2. Next suppose that the government orders these firms to supply q' units to the government at the additional cost required to produce them. The social surplus loss resulting from the price increase to the original buyers is area $B + E$, which is the deadweight loss attributable to the increase. The social opportunity cost of producing the additional q' units of the resource for the government, which in this case corresponds to the government's budgetary expenditure, is the trapezoidal area $G + F$. Thus, the total social cost that results from the government's directive is $B + G + E + F$. This social cost is exactly the same as the social cost that results when the government purchases the resource in the same manner as any other buyer in the market. Notice, however, that this time the government's budgetary outlay, $G + F$, is smaller, rather than larger, than the social opportunity cost of using the resource.

Measuring Costs in Inefficient Markets

As indicated in Chapter 3, in an efficient market, price equals marginal social cost. Whenever price does not equal marginal social cost, allocative inefficiency results. A variety of circumstances can lead to inefficiency: absence of a working market, market failures (e.g., public goods, externalities, natural monopolies, markets with few sellers, and information asymmetries), and distortions due to government interventions (such as taxes, subsidies, regulations, price ceilings, and price floors). Any of these distortions can arise in factor markets, complicating the estimation of opportunity cost.

Because of space limitations, it is possible to examine only three distortions here. First, we consider the situation in which the government purchases an input at a price below the factor's opportunity cost. Second, we examine the case in which the government hires from a market in which there is unemployed labor. Third, we explore the situation in which the government purchases inputs for a project from a monopolist. In each of these situations, shadow pricing is needed to measure accurately the opportunity cost of the input.

Purchases at Below Opportunity Costs   Consider a proposal to establish more courts so that more criminal trials can be held. Budgetary costs include the salaries of judges and court attendants, rent for courtrooms and offices, and perhaps expenditures for additional correctional facilities (because the greater availability of trial capacity leads to more imprisonment). For these factors, budgetary costs may correspond well to social opportunity costs. However, the budget may also include payments to jurors, payments that typically just cover commuting expenses. If any compensation is paid to jurors for their time, then it is usually set at a nominal *per diem* not related to the value of their time as reflected, perhaps, by their wage rates. Thus, budgetary outlay to jurors almost certainly understates the opportunity cost of jurors' time. Consequently, some form of shadow pricing is necessary. A better estimate of jurors' opportunity cost is, for example, their commuting expenses plus the number of juror-hours times either the average or the median pretax hourly wage rate for the locality. The commuting expenses estimate should include the actual resource costs of transporting jurors to the court, not just out-of-pocket expenses. The hourly pretax wage rate times the hours spent on jury duty provides a measure of the value of goods forgone because of lost labor, although several criticisms of it are discussed in Chapter 13.

Hiring Unemployed Labor   We have stressed that assessing opportunity costs in the presence of market failures or government interventions requires a careful accounting of social surplus changes. Analysis of the opportunity cost of workers hired for a government project who would otherwise be unemployed illustrates the kind of effort that is required.

Let us examine the opportunity costs of labor in a market in which minimum wage laws, union bargaining power, or some other factor creates a wage floor that keeps the wage rate above the market-clearing level and, consequently, there is unemployed labor.[32] Notice that we are focusing here on a very specific form of unemployment: that which occurs when the number of workers who desire jobs at the wage paid in a particular labor market exceed the number of workers employers are willing to hire at that wage. Workers who are unemployed for this reason are sometimes said to be *in surplus*. We focus on surplus workers so that we can examine their opportunity costs when they are hired for a government project. This issue is of particular importance because there are government projects that are specifically designed to put surplus workers to work and numerous other projects that are likely to hire such workers. Of course, there are other forms of unemployment than the type considered here. For example, some persons are briefly unemployed while they move from one job to another.

Before discussing how the opportunity cost of surplus labor might be measured, it may be useful to consider more explicitly the extent to which the labor hired to work on a government project reduces the number of unemployed workers.[33] Consider, for example, a project that hires 100 workers. How many fewer workers will be unemployed as a result? In considering this question, it is important to recognize that the project does not have to hire directly from the ranks of the unemployed. Even if the project hires 100 previously employed persons, this will result in 100 job vacancies, some of which may be filled by the unemployed. If the unemployment rate for the type of workers hired for the project (as determined by their occupation and geographic location) is very high (say, over 10 or 15%), the number of unemployed workers may fall by nearly 100. But if the unemployment rate for the workers is low (say, below 5%), most of the measured unemployed are probably between jobs rather than in surplus. As a consequence, the project is likely to cause little reduction in the number of persons who are unemployed. Instead the project will draw its workforce from those employed elsewhere or out of the labor force. At rates of unemployment between 5 and 10 percent, the reduction in the number of unemployed persons will probably be well under 100 but substantially above zero.

Figure 4-14 depicts a situation in which a government project reduces unemployment. In this figure, the pre-project demand schedule for labor, D, and the supply schedule for labor, S, intersect at P_e, the equilibrium price in the absence of the wage floor, P_m. At the wage floor, L_s, workers desire employment, but only L_d workers are demanded so that $L_s - L_d$ workers are unemployed. Now imagine that L' workers are hired for a government project at a wage of P_m. This shifts the demand schedule to the right by L'. As long as L' is less than the number of unemployed laborers, the price remains at the floor.

We now consider five alternative measures of the social cost of hiring the L' unemployed workers. All five of these measures are subject to criticism. Indeed, it is not obvious that, as a practical matter, it is possible to obtain an accurate value of the social cost of hiring the unemployed. However, some of the alternative measures described here are far better approximations of the true social cost than others.

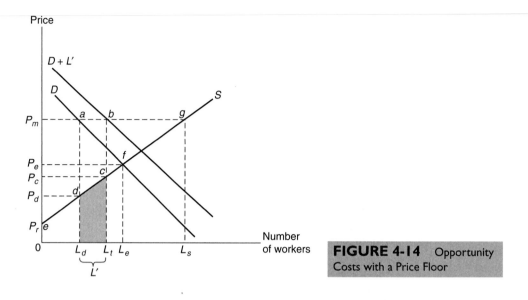

FIGURE 4-14 Opportunity Costs with a Price Floor

1. **Measure A.** It is sometimes suggested that because the unemployed are not working, there are zero opportunity costs in putting them to work. This treats the unemployed, however, as if their time is valueless. This is clearly inappropriate on two grounds. First, many unemployed persons are in fact engaged in productive enterprises such as job search, child care, and home improvements. Second, even if they were completely at leisure, leisure itself has value to those who are enjoying it. Consequently, few, if any, unemployed persons are willing to work at a zero wage. Indeed, the supply schedule in Figure 4-14 represents the value that various individuals, both those who are employed and those who are unemployed, place on their time when they are not employed. For example, an individual located at point f would only be willing to accept employment at a price of P_e or greater. Thus, P_e provides a measure of the value that this person places on his or her time. In other words, his or her opportunity cost of giving up leisure time to work is P_e. Similarly, individuals located on the supply schedule at points c and d value their time at P_c and P_d, respectively. No individual is willing to work at a price below P_r, and, as P_r has a positive value, Figure 4-14 implies that the opportunity cost of hiring the unemployed must be above zero.

2. **Measure B.** Figure 4-14 indicates that total budgetary expenditure on labor for this project is P_m times L', which equals the area of rectangle abL_tL_d. This budgetary outlay for labor, however, is likely to overstate substantially the true social cost of hiring workers for the project. As implied by the supply schedule in Figure 4-14, although employed workers are paid a price of P_m, most would be willing to work for less. This difference between the value they place on their time, as indicated by the supply schedule, and P_m, the price they are actually paid while employed, is producer (i.e., worker) surplus, which may be viewed as a transfer to the workers from the government agency hiring them. To obtain a measure of the social cost of hiring workers for the project, this producer surplus must be subtracted from the budgetary expenditure on labor. Measure B fails to do this.

3. **Measure C.** As the project expands employment in the market represented by Figure 4-14 from L_d to L_t, one might assume that the trapezoid *abcd* represents producer surplus enjoyed by the newly hired. Given this assumption, one would subtract area *abcd* from area abL_tL_d to obtain a measure of the social cost of hiring workers for the project. Thus, the social cost would be measured as the shaded trapezoid cdL_dL_t, the area under the supply schedule between L_d and L_t. This shaded area would equal the opportunity cost of the newly hired workers— that is, the value of the time they give up when they go to work.

4. **Measure D.** One shortcoming of measure C is that it is implicitly based on an assumption that all the unemployed persons hired for the project value their time at less than P_c and at greater than P_d. In other words, this approach assumes that these workers are all located between points *c* and *d* on the supply schedule. However, there is no basis for such an assumption. Indeed, it is quite likely that some of the hired unemployed persons value their time at well above P_c and that others value their time at well under P_d. In fact, the figure implies that unemployed persons who value their time as low as P_r and as high as P_m would be willing to work on the project because the project would pay them a price of P_m. Thus, perhaps, a better assumption is that the unemployed persons who would actually get hired for the project are distributed more or less equally along the supply schedule between points *e* and *g*, rather than being confined between points *d* and *c*. This assumption implies that the unemployed persons who are hired for the project value their time by no more than P_m, by no less than P_r, and, on average, by $\frac{1}{2} (P_m + P_r)$. Thus, the social cost of hiring L' workers for the project would be computed as equal to $\frac{1}{2} (P_m + P_r)(L')$.

5. **Measure E.** One practical problem with using measure D in an actual CBA is that the value of P_r, the lowest price at which any worker represented in Figure 4-14 would be willing to accept employment, is unlikely to be known. Given this, some assumption about the value of P_r must be made. One possible, and perhaps not unreasonable, assumption is that the supply schedule passes through the origin and, hence, the value of P_r equals zero. The fact that the probabilities of illness, divorce, and suicide all increase with unemployment, while job skills deteriorate, suggest that P_r could, in practice, be very low for at least some unemployed persons. If we once again assume that the unemployed persons who are hired for the project are distributed more or less equally along the supply schedule between the point at which it intersects the vertical axis and point *g*, then this implies that the unemployed persons who are hired for the project value their time by no more than P_m, by no less than zero, and, on average, by $\frac{1}{2} (P_m + 0) = \frac{1}{2} P_m$. Hence, the social cost of hiring workers for the project would be computed as $\frac{1}{2} P_m (L')$. Note that the estimate provided by this computation is equal to half the government's budgetary outlay. While this cost estimate would be smaller and almost certainly less accurate than that computed using measure D, it is usually easier to obtain.

Given our preceding argument that nonwork time has a positive value, measure E is probably best viewed as providing an easily obtainable lower-bound estimate of the true project social costs for labor, while the project budgetary cost for labor, measure B, provides an upper-bound estimate.

Purchases from a Monopoly We now turn to a final example of measuring the social cost of project or program purchases in an inefficient market—the purchase of an input supplied by a monopoly. In this circumstance, a government agency's budgetary outlay overstates the true social costs resulting from the purchase. This overstatement occurs because the price of the input exceeds the social cost of producing it. As a consequence, a substantial share of the revenues a monopolist receives are transfers or *monopoly rents*. Thus, in principle, a CBA should not use the budgetary outlay as a measure of social cost.

Figure 4-15 illustrates a government agency's purchase of an input from a monopoly. Prior to the purchase, the input is produced at level Q_1, where the monopolist's marginal cost and marginal revenue curves intersect. The price at Q_1, as determined by the demand schedule, is P_1. Now, as a result of the agency's purchase of Q' units, the monopolist's demand schedule and the marginal revenue curve shift to the right. The price of the input increases to P_2 and the quantity sold increases to Q_2. At the new higher price, the agency purchases a quantity equal to the distance between Q_3 and Q_2, while the original buyers in the market reduce the quantity they purchase by an amount equal to the distance between Q_1 and Q_3.

As in our previous examples, the direct budgetary cost of the agency's purchase equals the price times the quantity purchased: $P_2(Q_2 - Q_3)$. In Figure 4-15, this is represented by the rectangle between Q_3 and Q_2 and bounded by P_2 (i.e., areas $A + C + G + E$). However, these budgetary costs overstate the true social cost. To find the true social cost of the agency's purchase, one must examine the effects of the purchase on the monopolist and the original buyers of the input, as well as on the agency's revenues.

Because the monopolist sells more of the input at higher prices, its producer surplus increases. This increase has two parts: (1) that resulting from the higher price the monopolist now receives for the units that it previously sold (which is represented in Figure 4-15 by areas $B + C + E$), and (2) that resulting from the additional units that

FIGURE 4-15 Opportunity Costs When Buying from a Monopoly

the monopolist now sells (area G). Thus, as can be seen from the figure, part of the cost to the agency, areas $C + G + E$, is a transfer to the monopolist.

Original buyers in the market are clearly worse off as a result of the agency's purchase because they now have to pay a higher price for the input. In measuring their loss of consumer surplus, it is the original demand schedule that is pertinent because this is the schedule that reflects the original buyers' willingness-to-pay for the input. Thus, the total loss in consumer surplus by the original buyers, all of which is a transfer to the monopolist, is equal to areas $B + C$.

The following distributional accounting ledger summarizes the effects of the purchase.

	Benefits	Costs
Original buyers		$B + C$
Monopolistic seller	$B + C + G + E$	
Project expenditures		$A + C + G + E$
Net social cost		$A + C$

The major conclusion of this analysis is that in the case of input purchases from a monopolist, budgetary expenditures are larger than the social costs. The reason is that the price the monopoly charges exceeds the marginal cost of producing the input. Consequently, in conducting a CBA, the government's budgetary cost should, in principle, be adjusted downward through shadow pricing. In practice, however, the error that would result from using the unadjusted budgetary expenditures would often not be very large. As an examination of Figure 4-15 suggests, the size of the bias, areas $G + E$, depends on the extent to which the price the monopoly charges exceeds its marginal costs—in other words, on how much monopoly power it actually has. This, in turn, depends on how steeply sloped the demand schedule is. Thus, before an analyst develops shadow prices, a sometimes difficult undertaking, he or she should ask whether it is really necessary to do so.

The General Rule Other market distortions also affect opportunity costs in predictable ways. It is useful to summarize the direction of the bias created by some of these distortions. In factor markets in which supply is taxed, direct expenditure outlays overestimate opportunity cost; in factor markets in which supply is subsidized, expenditures underestimate opportunity cost. In factor markets exhibiting positive externalities of supply, expenditures overestimate opportunity cost; in factor markets exhibiting negative externalities of supply, expenditures underestimate opportunity costs. To determine opportunity costs in such cases, apply the rule: Opportunity cost equals direct expenditures on the factor minus (plus) gains (losses) in social surplus occurring in the factor market.

PROJECT EFFECTS ON GOVERNMENT REVENUES AND TAXES

As illustrated in this chapter, government projects affect government revenues in a wide variety of ways. In principle, by affecting government revenues, these projects either require taxes to increase or allow them to decrease.

In Chapter 3, we indicated that a tax on a good, such as an excise tax, usually results in deadweight loss. Taxes on individuals also generally result in a deadweight loss. In general, social surplus may be lost in taxing consumers, individuals, or producers and transferring the proceeds to the government. Consequently, a project that is funded through additional taxes will generally increase deadweight loss, while a project that increases government revenues and thereby allows reductions in taxes will generally decrease deadweight loss. Although these changes in deadweight loss are often ignored in conducting CBAs, they should not be.

Because there are numerous sources of deadweight loss in addition to taxes, economists refer to the deadweight loss that results specifically from a tax as *excess burden* and the change in deadweight loss resulting from raising an additional dollar of tax revenue as the *marginal excess tax burden* (METB). Estimates of the METB under different types of taxes are presented in Chapter 15. The size of the METB is usually measured as a percentage of the additional tax dollars collected as a result of an increase in tax rates. As will be seen in Chapter 15, this percentage is positive and substantial for most types of taxes, although it is larger for some types of taxes than others. It depends on the magnitude of the behavioral response to a change in taxes, for example, the extent to which consumer purchases change due to an excise tax or the change in work hours due to a tax on earnings. Exhibit 4-1 presents a hypothetical, but not implausible, illustration of computing the average social cost of taxing higher-income households and redistributing the money to lower-income households. In this illustration, it costs, on average, $1.63 to transfer each dollar.

As suggested earlier in this chapter, taxes may increase social surplus. For example, if prior to being taxed a good was overconsumed due to a negative externality, then the introduction of a tax could increase efficiency by reducing the overconsumption. In this case the METB would be negative.[34] Generally, however, the METB is positive: The social cost of raising a dollar of revenue through a tax is usually larger than a dollar.

In principle, if a government project is funded through additional taxes that increase excess burden, then this increase should be counted as part of the social cost of the project.[35] Symmetrically, project revenues that allow the government to reduce taxes and thereby reduce excess burden provide a social benefit. Specifically, *project expenditures and project revenues that affect the government's financial position should be translated into social costs and benefits by multiplying them by the marginal excess tax burden.* Thus, to correctly estimate the change in net social benefits that results from a project that affects government revenues, equation (3.9) from Chapter 3 must be modified to the following:

$$\Delta NSB = \Delta CS + \Delta PS + [(1 + \text{METB}) \times \Delta GR] \qquad (4.1)$$

To be more specific, in conducting a CBA, an analyst should first take account of all project costs and benefits, exclusive of effects on the marginal excess burden. Some of these costs and benefits will likely result in decrements and increments to the government's financial position. The analyst should compute the additional costs and benefits that result from these changes in the government's financial position by multiplying them by the estimated value of the METB. For purposes of doing this, it is useful to distinguish among five categories of project costs and benefits. First, *project costs that represent expenditures on the project by the government should be multiplied by the*

The following table, which was adopted with modifications from a study by Edgar Browning, is based on a hypothetical society with only five households. The idea is to tax everyone to obtain $1,350 in additional revenue and then distribute this equally to everyone. The net effect, as shown in column 6, is a total transfer of $270 from the two richest households to the two poorest households. As shown in column 8, the real incomes of the two poorest households increase by $240 in aggregate, whereas the real incomes of the three richest households decrease by $390. Thus, it costs society $390/$240 = $1.63 in lost income for every dollar transferred, ignoring administrative costs.

The Marginal Cost of Redistribution

Household (1)	Initial (Gross) Earnings (2)	Net Change in Earnings (3)	Additional Tax Revenue* (4)	Transfer (5)	Net Transfer (6)	Change in Disposable Income (7)	Change in Real Income (8)
A	10,000	−25	90	270	180	155	170
B	20,000	−50	180	270	90	40	70
C	30,000	−75	270	270	0	−75	−30
D	40,000	−100	360	270	−90	−190	−130
E	50,000	−125	450	270	−180	−305	−230
Total	150,000	−375	1,350	1,350	0	−375	−150

*These figures are rounded to the nearest $10.

Source: Adapted from Edgar K. Browning, "The Marginal Cost of Redistribution," *Public Finance Quarterly* 21(1) 1993, 3–32, Table 1 at p. 5. Reprinted by permission of Sage Publications, Inc.

For purposes of the illustration, it is assumed that all households initially work 2,000 hours a year and face a marginal tax rate of 40 percent. Thus, as indicated in column 2, the gross before-tax hourly wage rate of household A is $5 ($10,000/2,000), but its after-tax net wage rate is only $3 ($5 × 0.6). The gross and net hourly wage rates for the remaining four households may be similarly computed. It is further assumed that the compensated labor supply elasticity for all households is 0.15, a value that is consistent with empirical estimates presented in Chapter 11. In other words, it is assumed that a 1 percent change in net wages, holding income constant, will cause households to change their hours worked by 0.15 percent.

Suppose now that the government introduces a separate income tax of 1 percent that increases each household's marginal tax rate from 40 to 41 percent. This reduces each household's net after-tax wage rate by 1.67 percent (i.e., 0.01/0.60 = 0.0167). As a consequence, hours worked fall by 0.25 percent ($0.15 × 0.0167 = 0.0025$), or 5 hours per year. Hence, as shown in column 3, earnings also fall by 0.25 percent.

Net additional tax revenue is given in column 4. For example, household A initially paid taxes of $4,000 ($10,000 × 0.4), while after the new income tax, it paid taxes of about $4,090 ($9,975 × 0.41), an increase of approximately $90. The total of $1,350 in additional tax revenue is divided equally and $270 is distributed to each household. The net transfer (column 5 − column 4) is given in column 6.

Column 7 presents the total change in disposable income, which is obtained by adding

(Continued)

(Continued)

columns 3 and 6. The net incomes of the three richest households have been reduced by $570 in aggregate, while the net incomes of the two poorest families have been increased by a total of only $195. But all families are now working less and enjoying more leisure. Assuming that the value of additional leisure equals the after-tax net wage rate, household A receives a leisure gain valued at $15 ($3 × 5 hours), household B receives a leisure gain valued at $30 ($6 × 5 hours), and so forth. The total change in real income (including the value of the gain in leisure) is given in column 8. The real incomes of households A and B increase by $240 in aggregate, while the incomes of households C, D, and E decrease by $390.

METB. Second, *project benefits that accrue as revenue to the government should also be multiplied by the METB.* Third, *costs that accrue as losses in social surplus exclusive of government expenditures should **not** be multiplied by the METB.* Fourth, *benefits that accrue as gains in social surplus exclusive of government revenue should **not** be multiplied by the METB.* Fifth, *transfers, which otherwise either would not be recorded as costs and benefits or would be recorded as exactly offsetting costs and benefits, should be recorded and multiplied by the METB if they represent increments or decrements to government cash flow.* In other words, project-specific taxes or subsidies must be multiplied by METB; they do not "cancel out." Thus, care should be taken to enumerate all costs and benefits, including transfers.

CONCLUSIONS

This chapter has shown that the benefits and costs associated with government programs and projects are appropriately determined by valuing the resulting changes in net government revenue flows, producer surplus, and consumer surplus. Even when the relevant demand and supply schedules are known, great care must be exercised in order to measure the changes appropriately, especially when the relevant markets are distorted. Two types of relevant markets were considered: the market in which the policy intervention takes place and factor markets where the government purchases the inputs required by the program or project. These markets, primary markets, are the ones that are directly affected by a particular policy. Markets that are indirectly affected—secondary markets—are the focus of the following chapter.

EXERCISES FOR CHAPTER 4

1. Consider a low-wage labor market. Workers in this market are not presently covered by the minimum wage, but the government is considering implementing such legislation. If implemented, this law would require employers in the market to pay workers a $5 hourly wage. Suppose all workers in the market are equally productive, the current market-clearing wage rate is $4 per hour, and that at this market-clearing wage there are 600 employed workers. Further suppose that under the minimum wage legislation, only 500 workers would be employed and 300 workers would be unemployed. Finally, assume that the market demand and supply schedules are linear and that the market reservation wage, the lowest wage at which any worker in the market would be willing to work, is $1.

   Compute the dollar value of the impact of the policy on employers, workers, and society as a whole.

2. Suppose the government is considering an increase in the toll on a certain stretch of highway from $.40 to $.50. At present, 50,000 cars per week use that highway stretch; after the toll is imposed, it is projected that only 40,000 cars per week will use the highway stretch.
    a. Assuming that the marginal cost of highway use is constant (i.e., the supply schedule is horizontal) and equal to $.40 per car, what is the net cost to society attributable to the increase in the toll? (Hint: The toll increase will cause the supply schedule, not the demand schedule, to shift.)
    b. Because of the reduced use of the highway, the government would reduce its purchases of concrete from 20,000 tons per year to 19,000 tons per year. Thus, if the price of concrete were $25 per ton, the government's cost savings would be $25,000. However, the government's reduced demand for concrete causes its market price to fall from $25 to $24.50 per ton. Moreover, because of this reduction in price, the purchases of concrete by nongovernment buyers increase by 300 tons per year. Assuming that the factor market for concrete is competitive, can the government's savings of $25,000 be appropriately used as the measure of the social value of the cost savings that result from the government purchasing less concrete? Or would shadow pricing be necessary?

3. A country imports 3 billion barrels of crude oil per year and domestically produces another 3 billion barrels of crude oil per year. The world price of crude oil is $18 per barrel. Assuming linear schedules, economists estimate the price elasticity of domestic supply to be 0.25 and the price elasticity of domestic demand to be 0.1 at the current equilibrium.
    a. Consider the changes in social surplus that would result from imposition of a $6 per barrel import fee on crude oil that would involve annual administrative costs of $50 million. Assume that the world price will not change as a result of the country imposing the import fee, but that the domestic price will increase by $6 per barrel. Also assume that only producers, consumers, and taxpayers within the country have standing. Determine the quantity consumed, the quantity produced domestically, and the quantity imported after the imposition of the import fee. Then estimate the annual social net benefits of the import fee.
    b. Economists have estimated that the marginal excess burden of taxation in the country is 0.25. Reestimate the social net benefits assuming that 20 percent of the increase in producer surplus is realized as tax revenue under the existing tax system. In answering this question, assume that increases in tax revenues less the cost of administrating the import fee are used to reduce domestic taxes.
    c. The reduction in the country's demand for imports may affect the world price of crude oil. Assuming that the import fee reduces the world price from $18 to $16 per barrel, and thus, the after-tax domestic price is $16 + $6 = $22 per barrel, a net increase in domestic price of $4 per barrel, repeat the analysis done in parts a and b.

4. (Spreadsheet required.) A proposed government project in a rural area with 100 unemployed persons would require the hiring of 20 workers. The project would offer wages of $12 per hour. Imagine that the reservation wages of the 100 unemployed fall between $2 and $20.
    a. Estimate the opportunity cost of the labor required for the project assuming that the government makes random offers to the 100 unemployed until 20 of them accept jobs. (First, generate a list of the reservation prices of 100 persons according to the formula $2 + $18u where u is a random variable distributed uniformly [0,1]. Second, work down the list to identify the first 20 workers with reservation wages less than $12. Third, sum the reservation wages of these 20 workers to get the opportunity cost of the labor used for the project.)
    b. Estimate the opportunity cost of the labor required for the project assuming that the government can identify and hire the 20 unemployed with the lowest reservation wages.
    c. Repeat part a 15 times to get a distribution for the opportunity cost and compute its standard deviation.

NOTES

1. For a detailed examination of government failures, see David L. Weimer and Aidan R. Vining, *Policy Analysis: Concepts and Practice*, 4th ed. (Upper Saddle River, NJ: Pearson Prentice Hall, 2005), Chapter 8, 156–191.

2. As mentioned in Chapter 1, sometimes in a CBA a policy outcome that people would be willing to pay to avoid is referred to as a negative benefit, rather than as a cost. These two terms can be viewed as equivalent.

3. A change in price only causes a movement along the supply schedule, a change in quantity supplied. But a project that provides more of a good increases the supply of the good, resulting in a shift of the supply schedule.

4. This assumes, of course, that the market is sufficiently competitive and the firms in it are sufficiently efficient that all of the cost savings are passed on to consumers in the form of a price decrease.

5. An alternative method of measuring the gain in social surplus is simply to compare total social surplus with and without the project. In the absence of the project, total social surplus would be represented by the triangular area *fae*, while in the presence of the project, total social surplus would be represented by the triangular area *fbd*. Subtracting the smaller triangle from the larger triangle, we again find that the net gain in social surplus equals the trapezoidal area *abde*.

6. For a theoretical treatment of externalities, public goods, and club goods, see Richard Corres and Todd Sandler, *The Theory of Externalities, Public Goods and Club Goods* (New York: Cambridge University Press, 1986).

7. There are, of course, other types of markets in which individual firms have market power—for example, those characterized by oligopoly or monopolistic competition. We focus on markets characterized by monopoly, and especially natural monopoly, because government intervention is most likely to occur in these markets.

8. If the demand schedule is linear, the marginal revenue curve will also be linear and will be located halfway between the demand schedule and the vertical axis. That is, given a linear demand curve, $p = a - bq$,

$$TR = p \times q = (a - bq)q = aq - bq^2$$

Therefore, marginal revenue = $dTR/dq = a - 2bq$. Hence, the slope of the marginal revenue curve ($-2b$) is twice the size of the slope of the demand curve ($-b$).

9. To maximize its profit (π), the monopolist would produce where the difference between total revenues (TR) and total costs (TC) are as large as possible. That is, where $\pi = TR - TC$ is at a maximum. At this point, $d\pi/dQ = dTR/dQ - dTC/dQ = 0$. Hence, $MR = MC$. However, while quantity is determined by the intersection of the monopolist's marginal cost and marginal revenue curves, price is not. Thus, unlike a perfectly competitive firm's marginal cost curve, a monopolist's marginal cost curve cannot be interpreted as its supply schedule.

10. Of course, foreign-owned firms, regardless of whether they are competitive or monopolistic, usually would not be given standing. Therefore, their benefits would not be counted in a CBA.

11. There are, of course, alternative policies that the government might adopt in response to the monopoly. For example, it might tax the monopolist's profits, regulate the prices the monopolist charges, or operate the monopoly as a state-owned enterprise.

12. For a survey of recent infrastructure public-private partnerships (P3s) in the United States and Canada, see Anthony E. Boardman, Finn Poschmann, and Aidan R. Vining, "North American Infrastructure P3s: Examples and Lessons Learned," in Carsten Greve and Graeme Hodge, eds., *The Challenge of Public-Private Partnerships: Learning from International Experience* (Cheltenham, UK: Edward Elgar, forthcoming). This article discusses a number of road projects including the Dulles Greenway in Virginia, Highway 407 outside Toronto, and the Confederation Bridge that links Prince Edward Island to the mainland of Canada.

13. In principle, it is possible that D_u could be to the left of D_i, rather than to the right of it as shown in Figure 4-6. This would occur if instead of desiring more of the product in the absence of information concerning it than they would with the information, consumers desire less of it. In practice,

however, such situations are unlikely to continue for long because strong incentives would exist for sellers to eliminate such information asymmetry by providing buyers with the needed information, thereby increasing their demand for the product. But when the actual demand schedule is to the right of the fully informed demand schedule, the incentive, in contrast, is for sellers to withhold the information.

14. The two demand schedules are drawn closer together at high prices rather than at low prices to imply that at higher prices buyers would go to more trouble to obtain additional information about the product than they would at lower prices. Whether or not this is actually the case, however, is not essential to the analysis.

15. This is discussed more fully in Aidan R. Vining and David L. Weimer, "Information Asymmetry Favoring Sellers: A Policy Framework," *Policy Sciences* 21(4) 1988, 281–303.

16. For a more extensive discussion of these three types of products, see Vining and Weimer, "Information Asymmetry Favoring Sellers: A Policy Framework."

17. For an entertaining discussion of possible misuses of the term "externality" and when intervention may or may not be appropriate for correcting externalities, see Virginia Postrel, "External Cost: The Dangers of Calling Everything Pollution," *Reason*, 1999.

18. This tax can be levied either in the traditional manner—that is, on the good itself—or, alternatively, by the government issuing transferable permits that, in effect, tax effluents emitted by firms, rather than the goods they produce. Under the latter approach, which is currently being used in the United States to control sulphur dioxide emissions, firms that have found ways to control their pollution relatively inexpensively can sell their permits to pollute to firms for which pollution control would be relatively more costly. In principle, the advantage of this approach is that a market is established that places responsibility for pollution control on those firms that can do it most efficiently. For a detailed description and critique of the permit approach, see Karl Hausker, "The Politics and Economics of Auction Design in the Market for Sulfer Dioxide Pollution," *Journal of Policy Analysis and Management* 11(4) 1992, 553–572.

19. Indeed, when, as in the case illustrated in Figure 4-7, the tax is levied on the good, there is no special incentive for firms to reduce the amount of pollution resulting from their production process. However, when the effluent itself is taxed—for example, through use of the transferable pollution permits discussed in the previous footnote—such incentives do exist.

20. In this example, gross program benefits only differ from net program costs by the administrative costs required to operate the program. Also notice that in the context of the example the rule that gross project benefits equal changes in social surplus plus net revenues generated by the project continues to hold once it is recognized that in this instance net revenues are actually negative.

21. When it is feasible to do so, private firms attempt to make nonexcludable goods excludable. One example of this is scramblers used by certain television cable networks.

22. The free-rider problem is also closely linked to difficulties in remedying problems resulting from externalities. For example, because clean air is both nonrivalrous and nonexcludable, in the absence of government intervention, limited incentive for the private sector to produce clean air by reducing air pollution exists.

23. In some circumstances, toll goods may be provided by clubs, which are voluntary organizations that are capable of excluding nonmembers from consuming goods provided by the club, including those that are nonrivalrous. See James M. Buchanan, "An Economic Theory of Clubs," *Economica* 32(1) 1965, 1–14; and Richard Cornes and Todd Sandler, *The Theory of Externalities, Public Goods, and Club Goods* (New York: Cambridge University Press, 1986).

24. Open access implies that anyone who has the physical capability to use units of the good may do so. When the set of possible users of the good is restricted, then the good is considered a *common property resource*. For example, fish in international waters are an open access good, while fish in coastal waters may be available only to denizens of the country enforcing sovereignty over the waters and are thus a common property good. Common property resources are similar to open access goods except that the set of potential users is clearly defined. For an extensive discussion of such goods, see Weimer and Vining,

Policy Analysis: Concepts and Practice, 4th ed., 85–91. Two additional publications that focus on common property resource goods are Elinor Ostrom, *Governing the Commons* (New York: Cambridge University Press, 1990); and Glenn Stevenson, *Common Property Economics* (New York: Cambridge University Press, 1991). Although economists tend to use the terms interchangeably, the distinction between open access goods and common property resources is worth making because restriction of the set of possible users seems to be a prerequisite for self-regulation that may emerge to limit the extent of overconsumption. See Elinor Ostrom, *Governing the Commons: The Evolution of Institutions for Collective Action.*

25. Gary S. Becker and Kevin M. Murphy, "A Theory of Rational Addiction," *Journal of Political Economy* 96(4) 1988, 675–700.

26. Independent developments of this approach can be found in Fritz L. Laux, "Addiction as a Market Failure: Using Rational Addiction Results to Justify Tobacco Regulation," *Journal of Health Economics* 19(4) 2000, 421–437; and Australian Productivity Commission, *Australia's Gambling Industries*, Inquiry Report No. 10, 26 1999, Appendix C, 11–13. Available at *www.pc.gov.au/ inquiry/gambling/finalreport/index.html.*

27. Australian Productivity Commission, *Australia's Gambling Industries*, Chapter 5, p. 24.

28. If the government were to purchase only a small part of the fixed supply of land on the open market, its budgetary outlay would very closely approximate the opportunity cost of removing the land from the private sector. In this case, the government's entry into the market would bid up the price of the land slightly, crowding potential private-sector land buyers who are just to the left of point *b* on the demand schedule out of the market. These buyers would lose a negligible amount of surplus. In addition, those private-sector buyers who remain in the market would pay a slightly higher price. Hence, surplus would be transferred between these buyers and the sellers of the land.

29. There is a natural tendency for those who are promoting a particular government project (e.g., a dam or a recreational area) to emphasize the potential benefits to those who must supply resources to the project. Our analysis suggests that in well-functioning markets these benefits only occur if the price of these resources increases, and even then, part of the benefits to the suppliers of the resources is offset by increases in costs to the original buyers of the resources. Note, however, that the analysis is based on the assumption that the resources used in the project would be fully employed even in the absence of the project. As will be seen later in this chapter, if this assumption does not hold, additional project benefits can then accrue to suppliers of resources.

30. This formula is based on a bit of geometry. The triangular area C equals one-half the rectangular area from which it is formed, $B + C + F$. Thus, area C is equivalent to $\frac{1}{2}(P_1 - P_0)(q')$.

31. This amount is derived as follows:

$$P_1 q' - \tfrac{1}{2}(P_1 - P_0)q' = \tfrac{1}{2}(P_0 + P_1)(q').$$

32. For a discussion of various forms of wage rigidity that result in unemployment, see Ronald G. Ehrenberg and Robert S. Smith, *Modern Labor Economics: Theory and Public Policy*, 7th ed. (Reading, MA: Addison Wesley Longman, Inc., 2000), Chapter 15.

33. For more detailed discussions of these issues, see Robert H. Haveman, "Evaluating Public Expenditure Under Conditions of Unemployment," in *Public Expenditure and Policy Analysis*, 3rd ed., Robert H. Haveman and Julius Margolis, eds. (Boston: Houghton Mifflin Company, 1983), 167–182; and E. J. Mishan, *Cost-Benefit Analysis*, 4th ed. (London: Unwin Hyman, 1988), 325–329.

34. More generally, the efficiency implications of interventions depend on the distortions already in the market. For example, Charles Ballard demonstrates that when labor markets for low-income groups are distorted by high effective marginal tax rates, redistributing through wage subsidies can actually result in efficiency gains. Charles L. Ballard, "The Marginal Efficiency Cost of Redistribution," *American Economic Review* 78(5) 1988, 1019–1033.

35. Louis Kaplow ("On the (Ir)Relevance of Distortion and Labor Supply Distortion to Government Policy," *Journal of Economic Perspectives*, [18]4 2004, 159–175) has recently argued against taking account of excess burden in CBA. However, his analysis rests on the very strong assumption that the individuals who pay

taxes for a good or service provided by the government are identical to the individuals who benefit from the policy and the benefits received by each taxpayer are proportional to their contribution through taxes. To illustrate the implications of this assumption, consider an individual whose taxes are increased by $100 to help the government purchase a new aircraft carrier. If this individual's surplus also increases by $100 as a result of purchasing the aircraft carrier, Kaplow suggests that, on net, the individual's surplus does not change. Thus, Kaplow argues that, under these circumstances, excess burden can be ignored. Kaplow further argues that if the benefits were $110 instead of $100, excess burden can still be ignored, but the purchase would pass the cost-benefit test because (given the proportionality assumption above) benefits would exceed costs for all taxpayers who contributed to the purchase. Although Kaplow recognizes that his assumption that the benefits of a government project accrue to the same persons that incur the taxes needed to pay for the project is a very strong assumption, he seems to suggest that the assumption should be made because it greatly simplifies CBA. We believe that the assumption is so far out of accord with actual government policies (for example, consider a program such as the one described in Exhibit 4-1 that taxes the wealthy to increase the income of the poor) that making it would result in substantial errors in CBA. Moreover, even if the assumption were to hold, a $100 increase in taxes would increase excess burden because it would distort the trade-off between work and leisure. It is not at all evident that a $100 increase in surplus that results from the government's purchase of an aircraft carrier would correct this distortion.

CHAPTER 5

Valuing Benefits and Costs in Secondary Markets

In conducting CBAs of government policies, there is a natural tendency to list as many effects of the policies as one's imagination permits. For example, an improvement in public transportation in a particular city may increase bus usage and reduce car usage. It may also reduce downtown pollution and congestion. In addition, it may reduce the demand for automobile repairs, parking places, and gasoline.

To assess these effects, one must first determine which occur in primary markets and which occur in secondary markets. Primary markets refer to markets that are directly affected by a policy, while secondary markets are markets that are indirectly affected. The changes in bus and car usage previously mentioned clearly occur in the primary market for public transportation. The reductions in pollution and congestion also can be thought of as occurring in the primary market for public transportation, though these particular impacts are in the external, or missing, part of that market. Any effect that occurs in a primary market should be accounted for in a CBA. On the other hand, effects on the demand for auto repairs, parking places, and gasoline occur in secondary markets and, as will be seen, often can (and indeed should) be ignored in conducting CBA. This last group of effects are often referred to as *secondary, second-round, spillover, side, pecuniary*, or *indirect effects*.

While Chapter 4 examined the benefits and costs of government policies that occur in primary markets, this chapter focuses on policy impacts in secondary markets. As in Chapter 4, we distinguish between efficient and distorted markets. In addition, the chapter takes a brief look at the special implications of secondary market effects for local communities, as the benefits of such effects are often touted by advocates of local infrastructure projects such as sports stadiums and convention centers.

VALUING BENEFITS AND COSTS IN EFFICIENT SECONDARY MARKETS

Complements and Substitutes

Secondary market effects result because government policies affect the prices of goods in primary markets, and this, in turn, noticeably affects the demand for other goods. These latter goods are referred to as *complements* and *substitutes*.

Consider the following example. Stocking a lake near a city with fish lowers the effective price of access to fishing grounds for the city's residents. They not only fish more often, but they also demand more bait and fishing equipment. We say that access to fishing grounds and fishing equipment are complements because a decrease (increase) in the price of one will result in an increase (decrease) in the demand for the other. In contrast, fishing is a substitute for golfing because as the price of fishing goes down (up), the demand for golfing goes down (up).

If government policies affect the demand for goods in secondary markets, then prices in these secondary markets may or may not change as a result. We first discuss the simpler situation in which prices do not change. We then analyze the more complex situation in which prices do change in secondary markets.

Efficient Secondary Market Effects without Price Changes

Because most goods have substantial numbers of complements and substitutes, many government projects cause effects in large numbers of secondary markets. Accounting for all these effects would impose an enormous burden on analysts. Fortunately, however, such effects can often be ignored in CBA without substantially biasing the estimates of net benefits. When can we ignore secondary market effects? *We can, and indeed, should ignore impacts in undistorted secondary markets as long as changes in social surplus in the primary market resulting from a government project are measured **and** prices in the secondary markets do not change.* The reason for this is that in the absence of price adjustments in secondary markets in response to price changes in primary markets, impacts are typically fully measured as surplus changes in primary markets. Measuring the same effects in both markets will, therefore, result in double counting. Thus, for example, if prices of fishing equipment do not change, then the increased consumption of fishing equipment is not relevant to the CBA of a project that increases access to fishing grounds.

A closer look at the fishing example should make the rule for the treatment of secondary markets clearer. For simplicity, we assume that the price of fishing equals the marginal social cost of fishing and that marginal social costs are constant. This, in turn, implies that no producer surplus or externalities exist in the primary market (e.g., highway congestion does not result because of increased travel to the newly stocked lake).

Figure 5-1(a) shows the market for "fishing days." Prior to the stocking of the nearby lake, the effective price of a day of fishing (largely the time costs of travel) was P_{F_0}, the travel cost to a lake much further away. Once fishing is available at the nearby lake, the effective price falls to P_{F_1} and, as a consequence, the number of days spent fishing by local residents rises from q_{F_0} to q_{F_1}. The resulting increase in social surplus equals the area of trapezoid $P_{F_0}abP_{F_1}$, the gain in consumer surplus. We measure this gain in consumer surplus using the demand schedule for fishing, D_F. As is customary in textbooks, this demand schedule should be viewed as the relation between price and quantity that would exist in the primary market if the prices of all secondary goods were held constant. Later we discuss the importance of this assumption.

Now consider the market for fishing equipment. The decline in the effective price of fishing days shifts the demand schedule for fishing equipment from D_{E_0} to D_{E_1} as shown in Figure 5-1(b). If the supply schedule is perfectly elastic, which is likely when the local market accounts for only a small fraction of regional or national demand, then the shift in demand will not increase the price of fishing equipment.

Does this shift in demand for fishing equipment represent a change in consumer welfare that should be counted in a CBA of the fish-stocking project? In other words, should the gap between the old and new demand schedules that is above the price line be

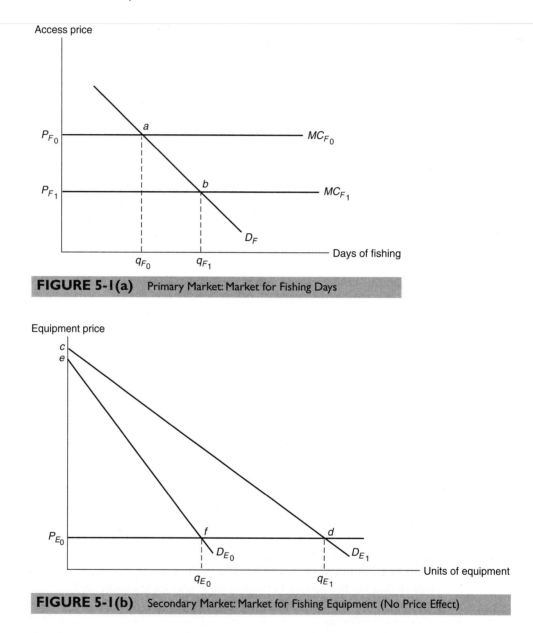

FIGURE 5-1(a)   Primary Market: Market for Fishing Days

FIGURE 5-1(b)   Secondary Market: Market for Fishing Equipment (No Price Effect)

counted as an additional increase in consumer surplus? It is tempting to treat the increase in consumer surplus from efP_{E_0} to cdP_{E_0} in panel (b) as an additional increase in social benefits that should be added to $P_{F_0}abP_{F_1}$ in panel (a), but this should *not* be done. As discussed next, doing so would result in double counting. As long as price does not change in the equipment market as a result of stocking the lake, the social surplus change in the fishing market measures the entire benefit from the stocking project.

To see this, first consider fishers who already own all the fishing equipment they need at the time the lake is stocked and, hence, presently contribute no demand to the market for fishing equipment. The value that these persons place on their existing fish-ing equipment will tend to increase as a result of stocking the nearby lake. However, because they are not in the market for new fishing equipment, the gap between the old and new demand schedules for new fishing equipment does not reflect this increase. Of course, these persons' willingness-to-pay for fishing days will presumably be higher than it otherwise would have been as a result of the fact that they will not have to make further expenditures for fishing equipment. But any additional increase in consumer surplus that these fishers enjoy as a result of already owning fishing equipment at the time the nearby lake is stocked will already be reflected by the primary market demand schedule for fishing days, which will be further to the right than it otherwise would be. It cannot show up in the secondary market for fishing equipment.

Now consider individuals who do not own fishing equipment at the time the lake is stocked but are now induced to make such purchases. The gap between the two demand schedules in Figure 5-1(b) accurately reveals the increased value that these persons place on fishing equipment. That is, these people are now willing to pay more for fishing equipment, and indeed they will buy more fishing equipment. It is the only way they can fully realize surplus gains from the stocking project. But this expenditure is not an additional benefit from the stocking project. Just like the fishers who already own fishing equipment, the increase in consumer surplus that these persons receive from the stocking project is fully reflected by the primary market demand schedule for fishing days. This includes any consumer surplus that they receive from their purchases of fishing equipment. Thus, counting the gap between the two demand schedules in panel (b) as benefits and also counting the increase in consumer surplus shown in panel (a) as benefits would result in counting the same benefits twice.

Persons who do not own fishing equipment at the time the lake is stocked would be even better off if, like the current owners of fishing equipment, they did not have to buy new equipment in order to take advantage of the newly stocked lake. Thus, every-thing else being equal, willingness-to-pay for fishing days is presumably greater among those who already own fishing equipment than among those who must purchase it. The increase in consumer surplus that results from the stocking project for both groups, even if different from one another, will be fully reflected in the primary market demand schedule for fishing days.

It is important to stress that secondary market effects can be ignored only if social surplus in the primary market is measured directly. As discussed in greater detail in Chapter 13, in situations in which cost-benefit analysts are unable to measure social sur-plus changes in primary markets, they may infer them instead from the demand shifts in secondary markets. For example, imagine that analysts have no information about the demand schedule for fishing days, but they do know how the demand schedule for fish-ing equipment will change. With no direct measure of the benefits from stocking the lake, they might take the difference between the social surplus in the fishing equipment market after the project (based on demand schedule D_{E_1}) and the social surplus in the equipment market prior to the project (based on demand schedule D_{E_0}). They would then apply some scaling factor to correct for the underestimation that results from the fact that not all the consumer surplus from fishing will be reflected in the equipment market. (Because some fishers will use old equipment and collect their own bait, their surplus will not appear in the equipment market. Moreover, equipment and bait com-prise only some of the inputs to fishing.)

Efficient Secondary Market Effects with Price Changes[1]

The situation is more complex when the supply schedule in the secondary market is upward sloping. To see this, we examine the effect of stocking the lake on the demand for golfing. In Figure 5-2, panel (a) once again shows the demand for fishing days, while panel (b) now shows the demand for golfing days. As before, the reduction in the price of fishing

FIGURE 5-2(a)   Primary Market: Market for Fishing Days

FIGURE 5-2(b)   Secondary Market: Market for Golfing Days (Price Effects)

days from P_{F_0} to P_{F_1} as a result of stocking the lake causes an increase in social surplus equal to the area $P_{F_0}abP_{F_1}$ (for the moment ignore demand schedules D_{F_1} and D^*).

As fishing and golf are presumed to be substitutes, a reduction in the price of fishing days from P_{F_0} to P_{F_1} would cause the demand for golfing to fall. Thus, the demand schedule for golfing in panel (b) would shift to the left from D_{G_0} to D_{G_1}. As previously emphasized, by itself this shift does not represent a change in consumer surplus that is not already fully accounted for in measuring the change in consumer surplus in the primary market. Golfers are obviously not made worse off by stocking the lake, although some may now place a lower valuation on golf. Instead, by itself, the shift in demand merely indicates that in the absence of golf, the consumer surplus gains from stocking the lake would have been even larger. The existence of golf is reflected in the location of D_{F_0}, the demand schedule for fishing days, which is farther to the left than it would have been if golf were not available as a substitute for fishing.

The shift of demand from D_{G_0} to D_{G_1}, however, causes the fees for golf course use to fall from P_{G_0} to P_{G_1}. This, in turn, results in an increase in consumer surplus, one represented by the area $P_{G_0}efP_{G_1}$, which has not previously been taken into account. In addition, the fall in golfing fees also causes a reduction in producer surplus equal to area $P_{G_0}gfP_{G_1}$. As the reduction in producer surplus exceeds the increase in consumer surplus, a net loss in social surplus equal to the area of triangle *efg* results.[2]

Should this loss in social surplus in the golfing market be subtracted from the social surplus gain in the fishing market in measuring net gains from the project? It is frequently unnecessary to do so. The reason is that the increase in consumer surplus gain in the fishing market is often likely, in practice, to be measured as the area $P_{F_0}acP_{F_1}$ rather than as the area $P_{F_0}abP_{F_1}$. If measured in this way, the increase in consumer surplus in the fishing market would be understated by the triangular area *abc*, but this triangle closely approximates triangle *efg*, the net loss in social surplus in the golfing market.

To see why the consumer surplus gain in the fishing market is often, in practice, measured as the area $P_{F_0}acP_{F_1}$ rather than as the area $P_{F_0}abP_{F_1}$, one must recognize that our fishing story does not end with the shift in the demand schedule in the secondary market. If golf and fishing are substitutes, the reduction in golf course fees will cause people to switch from fishing to golf, and the demand for fishing days will fall. This is shown in panel (a) as a leftward shift in the demand schedule for fishing days from D_{F_0} to D_{F_1}. By itself, this shift does not cause any further changes in social surplus; because we have assumed that the supply of fishing days is perfectly elastic, prices in the market for fishing days are unaffected. Note, however, that by drawing a line between the original and the final equilibrium points in panel (a) of Figure 5-2—that is, between points a and c—one can derive a special type of demand schedule, D^*.

This demand schedule, which is sometimes called an *observed* or *equilibrium demand schedule*,[3] indicates what the demand for fishing days will be once prices in other markets, including the market for golfing days, have fully adjusted to the change in prices in the market for fishing days. Thus, D^* differs from the demand schedules D_{F_0} and D_{F_1}, which, as mentioned earlier, indicate the number of fishing days demanded at each price for fishing days, *holding the prices of all other goods constant*. As it is frequently difficult statistically to hold the prices of secondary goods constant while measuring the relation between price and quantity demanded in a primary market, empirically estimated demand schedules—the ones actually observed and available for use in a CBA—often more closely resemble equilibrium demand schedules such as D^* than "textbook-style" demand schedules such as D_{F_0} and D_{F_1}.[4]

Thus, the equilibrium demand schedule, D^*, is the one that is likely to be used in practice to obtain a measure of the increase in social surplus resulting from the reduction in the price of fishing days. However, the resulting measure, $P_{F_0}acP_{F_1}$, understates the true measure of the gain in social surplus in the primary market, $P_{F_0}abP_{F_1}$, by the triangular area *abc*. But, as previously suggested, area *abc* provides a good approximation of area *efg* in panel (b),[5] the area that should be subtracted from area $P_{F_0}abP_{F_1}$ to obtain an accurate measure of the overall net gains from stocking the lake. In other words, area *abc* represents part of the benefits from the fish-stocking project and area *efg* an approximately offsetting cost of the project. Hence, by using the equilibrium demand schedule to measure the change in social surplus, we incorporate social surplus changes that occur in the market for golfing days, as well as those that occur in the market for fishing days. We do not have to obtain separate measures of the surplus changes that occur in secondary markets.[6]

This is important because it illustrates an important general point: By using an equilibrium demand schedule for the primary market—the type of demand schedule that is often empirically estimated, and thus available—one can capture the effects of policy interventions in both the primary market in which they were initiated *and* in all secondary markets. Thus, we can restate our earlier rule concerning project impacts in secondary markets: *We should ignore effects in undistorted secondary markets, regardless of whether there are price changes, if we are measuring benefits in the primary market using empirically measured demand schedules that do not hold prices in secondary markets constant.* Some interesting implications of this rule are illustrated in Exhibit 5-1, where an equilibrium demand schedule is used in assessing the effects of a policy that restrained automobile imports.

EXHIBIT 5-1

In 1981, under strong pressure from the Reagan administration and the U.S. Congress, the Japanese government agreed to limit the number of automobiles shipped to the United States. This so-called voluntary export restraint agreement (VERA) was motivated by the notion that, because Japanese imports were substitutes for U.S.-produced automobiles, a reduction in the number of imports would increase the sales of domestically produced cars.

A CBA of the VERA for automobiles, as well as other similar import restraint agreements, can be conducted with the aid of the model illustrated in the figures that appear in this exhibit. In this model, the U.S. market for cars imported from Japan is viewed as the primary market, as it is the market where the policy action was directed, while the market for U.S.-produced automobiles is viewed as the secondary market. In the figures, D_J and S_J represent the demand and supply schedules for Japanese imports in the absence of the VERA, while D_{US} and S_{US} represent their counterparts in the market for domestically produced automobiles. Thus, in the absence of the VERA, Q_J cars would have been imported from Japan to the United States and sold at price P_J, while Q_{US} domestically produced autos would have been purchased at price P_{US}. The figures reflect the fact that in 1981 Japanese imports were considerably less expensive, on average, than their U.S. counterparts. The flat supply schedule for Japanese automobiles is based on the assumption that the Japanese were willing to supply as many cars as U.S. consumers were willing to purchase at a price of P_J.

The VERA set a ceiling on the number of cars the Japanese could export to the United States at Q'_J, thereby substantially reducing the number of Japanese automobiles available to U.S. consumers. Thus, the new supply schedule

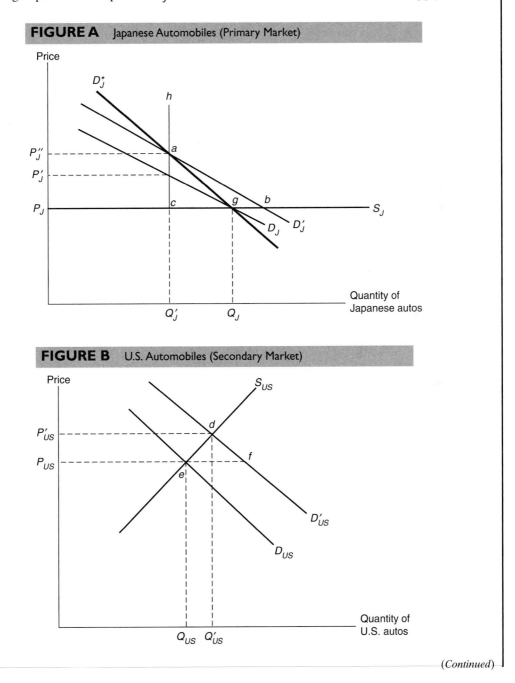

FIGURE A Japanese Automobiles (Primary Market)

FIGURE B U.S. Automobiles (Secondary Market)

(*Continued*)

(Continued)

for Japanese imports corresponded to $P_j ch$. As a result, the price of Japanese imports increased to P_J'. Because imported automobiles and domestic automobiles are substitutes, the higher price of Japanese automobiles caused an upward shift in the demand for domestic automobiles to D_{US}', increasing their price to P_{US}' and their quantity to Q_{US}'. The increased price of domestic autos, in turn, caused the demand schedule for Japanese imports to shift to D_J', prompting an additional increase in their price to P_J''.

It can be seen that the VERA resulted in deadweight loss equal to the triangular area *abc*. In addition, because of the higher prices paid for Japanese automobiles, Japanese automobile producers received a transfer from U.S. consumers corresponding to the rectangular area $P_J'' ac P_J$. Based on information about the prices and sales of imported and domestic automobiles under the VERA and empirical estimates of the slopes of the relevant supply and demand schedules, David G. Tarr and Morris E. Morkre calculated that in 1981 the deadweight loss equaled $155 million and the transfer equaled $753 million. If Japanese automobile producers are not given standing, and the very nature of the VERA suggests that they should not be, the sum of these two figures, $908 million, was the total social cost of the VERA in 1981. Similar costs also occurred in each of the following years until 1985, when the policy was dropped.

Tarr and Morkre used an estimate of the equilibrium demand schedule, D_J^*, to compute the value of the deadweight loss resulting from the VERA. Thus, their estimate corresponded to *agc*. As pointed out in the text, by using the equilibrium demand schedule, we need focus only on the primary market to determine the effects of a policy on social surplus. By doing this, however, we ignore the domestic beneficiaries of the VERA—U.S. auto producers and workers. Indeed, producer surplus in the market for U.S. automobiles, the secondary market in our analysis, increased by area $P_{US}' de P_{US}$. This increase, however, was more than offset by the decrease in consumer surplus that occurred in the secondary market, area $P_{US}' df P_{US}$. (As suggested in the text, the difference between the increase in producer surplus and the decrease in consumer surplus in the secondary market, area *def*, is taken into account by using the equilibrium demand schedule to measure the VERA's impacts in the primary market.) Thus, although U.S. auto producers gained surplus, a VERA policy must decrease overall domestic social surplus. In fact, as pointed out by Jose A. Gomez-Ibanez, Robert A. Leone, and Stephen A. O'Connell, over the long run a VERA can hurt domestic auto producers and workers by, for example, encouraging Japanese producers to circumvent limits on the number of imports by selling high-price rather than low-price autos and by setting up production plants in the United States.

Sources: Adapted from David G. Tarr and Morris E. Morkre, "Aggregate Costs to the United States of Tariffs and Quotas on Imports: General Tariff Cuts and Removal of Quotas on Automobiles, Steel, Sugar, and Textiles" (Washington, D.C.: Bureau of Economics Staff Report to the Federal Trade Commission, 1984), 54–74; and Jose A. Gomez-Ibanez, Robert A. Leone, and Stephen A. O'Connell, "Restraining Auto Imports: Does Anyone Win?" *Journal of Policy Analysis and Management* 2(2) 1983, 196-219.

VALUING BENEFITS AND COSTS IN DISTORTED SECONDARY MARKETS

Unfortunately, use of equilibrium demand schedules in primary markets misses part of the effects that occur in distorted secondary markets—that is, in secondary markets in which prices do not equal social marginal costs. To see why, examine Figure 5-3, a slightly

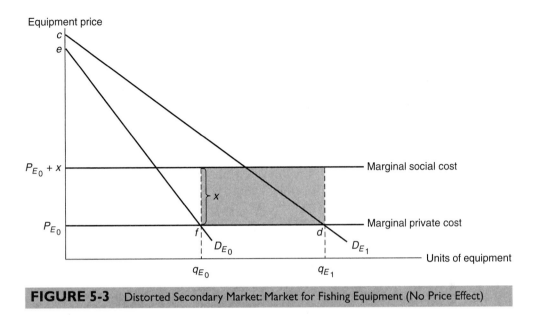

FIGURE 5-3 Distorted Secondary Market: Market for Fishing Equipment (No Price Effect)

altered version of panel (b) of Figure 5-1. This new figure is based on the assumption that because of negative externalities the market price of fishing equipment, P_{E_0}, underestimates the marginal social cost by x cents. (Think of the equipment as lead sinkers, some of which eventually end up in the lake, where they poison ducks and other wildlife. The x cents would then represent the value of the expected loss of wildlife from the sale of another sinker.) In this case, the expansion of consumption involves a social surplus loss equal to x times $q_{E_1} - q_{E_0}$, which is represented in Figure 5-3 by the shaded rectangle. This loss, which is not reflected at all by market demand or supply schedules in the fishing market, should be subtracted from the benefits occurring in that market in order to obtain an accurate measure of net gains from the program.

Another type of distortion in secondary markets is imposed by the presence of taxes. For example, Figure 5-4 illustrates local produce markets for beef and chicken, which are substitutes for one another. For simplicity, the supply schedules in both markets are assumed to be perfectly elastic. In the absence of any taxes on these products, the price of beef (the primary good) would be P_B and the price of chicken (the secondary good) would be P_C.

For purposes of our illustration, let us assume that chicken is currently subject to a tax of t_C cents per pound, but beef is not presently taxed. Given this situation, the existing demand schedules for beef and chicken are represented by D_{B_0} and D_{C_0}, respectively. As panel (b) of Figure 5-4 indicates, the tax on chicken provides the government with revenue equal to area T but reduces consumer surplus by areas $T + U$. Thus, the tax on chicken results in deadweight loss equal to the triangular area U.

Now assume that the government is considering imposing a tax of t_B cents per pound on beef. As indicated in panel (a), if the new tax is adopted, the government will collect revenue represented by area A, but consumers of beef will lose surplus equal to the areas $A + B$. Consequently, imposition of the new tax will result in deadweight loss in the beef market equal to area B.

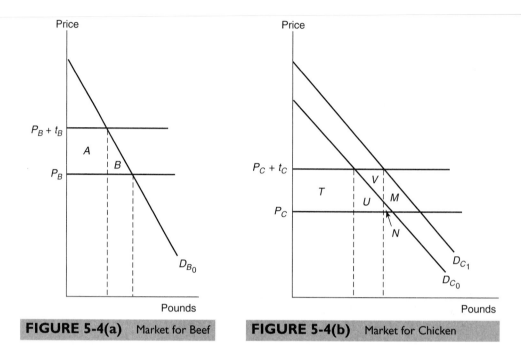

FIGURE 5-4(a) Market for Beef

FIGURE 5-4(b) Market for Chicken

The increase in the market price of beef shifts the demand schedule for chicken, a substitute, from D_{C_0} to D_{C_1}. For reasons discussed previously, this shift does not represent a change in consumer surplus. Indeed, the deadweight loss in the market for chicken remains the same, although it does shift from area U to areas $M + N$. However, the shift does cause an increase in the sale of chickens, as consumers substitute chicken for beef, resulting in an increase in tax revenues collected by the government. This increase, which is represented in panel (b) by area $U + V$, is a benefit from the tax imposed on beef that could conceivably more than offset the deadweight loss occurring in the beef market. The various effects of the tax on beef are summarized in the following social accounting ledger.

	Benefits	*Costs*
Consumers	—	$A + B$
Government revenue	$A + U + V$	—
Social benefit and costs	$U + V$	B

Notice that while *all* of the change in consumer surplus takes place in the primary market, increases in tax revenues occur in both markets.

The important lesson from this illustration is that, unlike situations in which there are no distortions in secondary markets, benefits and costs of a policy intervention cannot be fully measured by observing only the effects that occur in primary markets. Effects that occur in distorted secondary markets should, in principle, be valued separately. Yet, in practice, it may be very difficult to do so. Estimation problems usually preclude accurate measurement of welfare changes that occur in secondary markets. Estimating own-price effects (how quantity demanded changes as the price of the good changes) is often difficult; estimating cross-price effects (how the quantity demanded of good Y changes as the price of good Z changes) is more difficult yet. Consequently, we are rarely very confident of predictions of demand shifts in secondary markets. Moreover, when secondary markets are distorted, it is also difficult to measure the size of the distortions. (Recall the x-cent loss of wildlife from the sale of another sinker. How is the value of x to be estimated?) But such measures are usually needed if program effects in distorted secondary markets are to be taken into account.

Fortunately, price changes in most secondary markets are likely to be small. Most pairs of goods are neither strong complements nor strong substitutes. Hence, large price changes in the primary markets are usually necessary to produce noticeable demand shifts in the secondary markets. Thus, even when secondary markets are distorted, ignoring these markets may result in relatively little bias to CBA.

INDIRECT EFFECTS OF INFRASTRUCTURE PROJECTS

Public infrastructure projects that improve transportation or communications, for example, road building or harbor deepening, may substantially reduce the cost of production in some industries. These reductions in costs may have indirect effects in markets for consumption goods by reducing the prices at which the goods are sold. These indirect effects are similar but not quite the same as the secondary market effects that are the main topic of this chapter. In the case of secondary markets, a government policy influences prices in a primary market, which in turn influences demand in secondary markets in which goods that are complements of or substitutes for the primary market good are sold. In the case of an indirect effect, a government infrastructure project reduces the production costs of firms by reducing their expenditures on various inputs, and this direct effect of the project causes indirect effects by reducing prices in markets in which the goods produced by the firms are sold.

Although the two situations differ, both raise a similar question: Can the change in social surplus that results from the government's policy be adequately measured by focusing on the market in which the intervention takes place? In both cases the answer is similar: It can if the markets that are indirectly affected are not seriously distorted.

We have already demonstrated this point when secondary market effects occur. To illustrate this in the case of indirect effects that result from public expenditures on infrastructure improvement, consider the harbor-deepening project that was discussed in the Chapter 4. The direct effect of the project on shippers that use the harbor is a gain in surplus that is represented by area P_0abP_1 in Figure 4-3. However, the shippers do not necessarily keep this entire gain. Competitive pressures will likely result in firms paying lower prices for productive inputs that are shipped through the harbor. This, in turn, will cause cost curves in the markets in which these firms sell their goods to shift downward and to the right. If prices in these markets fall as a result, then consumer surplus will increase.

In competitive markets for these goods, this indirect gain in consumer surplus is already captured by the direct surplus gain represented by area P_0abP_1 in Figure 4-3.[7]

The reason is that some of the surplus gains initially enjoyed by shippers are ultimately passed on to the buyers of consumption goods through the reductions in the prices of these goods. If markets where the indirect effects occur are distorted, however, then some of the changes in surplus in these markets may not be captured by surplus changes in the market where the direct effects take place. For example, the price reductions may engender increases in sales in markets with both positive and negative externalities. If so, third parties will enjoy an increase in surplus when positive externalities are present and will suffer a decrease in surplus when negative externalities exist. These changes are not reflected by the direct changes in surplus.

SECONDARY MARKET EFFECTS FROM THE PERSPECTIVE OF LOCAL COMMUNITIES

Advocates of localized recreational facilities—for example, advocates of new sports stadiums, museums, and parks—frequently contend that major benefits will occur in secondary markets. For example, they predict that the demand for the services of local restaurants, hotels, and other businesses will increase. In addition, they often claim that such projects result in *multiplier effects*; that is, as purchases from nearby businesses increase, these businesses will, in turn, also spend their newly gained revenues nearby, and this, in turn, will generate still more revenues that will be spent locally, and so forth.

As long as secondary markets in a community are not distorted, one should be very cautious in counting revenues from local projects that are generated by secondary market effects and multiplier effects as project benefits. There are several reasons for exercising this caution.

First, absent market distortions, these revenues are relevant only when standing is restricted to some group smaller than society as a whole, such as to residents of a specific geographic area. As discussed in this chapter, when society is broadly defined, such claims cannot be justified unless the secondary market is distorted. For example, in evaluating the fish-stocking project from the narrow perspective of the local county, one might count as a benefit increases in revenues received by local businesses resulting from nonresidents buying fishing equipment in the county or frequenting local hotels or restaurants. From the broader social or national perspective, however, these expenditures simply represent a transfer from nonresidents to residents because they occur only as a result of consumers shifting their spending from one geographic area to another.

Second, when standing is restricted to residents of a local community, any social surplus gains that accrue to nonresidents as a result of a local project can no longer be counted as project benefits. For example, surplus gains enjoyed by sports team fans or owners who reside outside the community no longer count. Thus, the case for a local project could actually be stronger if standing is not restricted to the local community than if it is.

Third, as indicated earlier in this chapter, even if the demand for local product and services increases as a result of a local project, suppliers do not receive increases in surplus unless prices increase. Even when prices do increase, the resulting increase in producer surplus is at least partially offset because consumers who are residents of the local community must now pay more for goods and services and, as a result, lose consumer surplus. However, some residents may value the growth that occurs in the local economy in and of itself. Moreover, expansions in local businesses may provide some opportunities for taking advantage of economies of scale and, therefore, could produce benefits in the form of lower production costs.

Fourth, localized multiplier effects generally tend to be relatively small because local businesses are often owned by nonresidents. Moreover, many of the purchases by local businesses are made outside the local area. Thus, expenditures made within a local area readily dissipate elsewhere, and this becomes increasingly true as standing is restricted to a smaller geographic area.

It is only when secondary markets are distorted that effects in these markets can potentially generate important benefits for the community. However, negative impacts can also occur, such as increases in pollution and congestion that result when nonresidents use local roads to reach a recreational facility. Local projects are most likely to generate significant positive benefits in secondary markets when local rates of unemployment are high or other local resources are idle and substantial barriers to resource mobility exist. Under such circumstances, increases in demand in secondary markets and the multiplier effects that accompany these demand increases could significantly reduce levels of unemployment and increase the utilization of other idle resources such as empty buildings. The utilization of idle resources such as empty buildings has very low opportunity costs, and as discussed in Chapter 4, large increases in surplus accrue to many unemployed workers when they are hired. However, as also pointed out in Chapter 4, it is only when the rate of unemployment is fairly high that a substantial fraction of those hired are likely to be drawn from the ranks of the unemployed.

CONCLUSION

Most of the key concepts from Chapters 4 and 5 are summarized in Table 5-1. As the table indicates, changes in social surplus serve as the basis for measuring the costs and benefits of policies. The concept of opportunity cost helps us value the inputs that policies divert from other uses; the concept of willingness-to-pay helps us value policy outputs. The key to valuing outputs is to identify the primary markets in which they occur. When the outputs are not traded in organized markets, ingenuity is often needed to infer supply and demand schedules (remember the market for "fishing days"). For this purpose, various shadow pricing techniques, such as those discussed in Part III of this book, are often needed. Costs and benefits that occur in undistorted secondary markets are typically very difficult to value, but generally need not and, indeed, should not be added to costs and benefits that are measured in primary markets. Doing so will usually result in double counting.

The rules that appear in Table 5-1 cannot be used without first determining the type of market in which the various potential impacts of a project or program occur—primary, secondary, or factor market—and then determining whether the market is efficient or inefficient. In practice, this is sometimes difficult. To illustrate the sorts of judgments that must be made in practice, we conclude by listing selected impacts of a hypothetical street-widening project that would substantially increase traffic along the route and ask the reader to consider what type of market each occurs in and, hence, whether each should be included in an *ex-ante* cost-benefit analysis of the project. Our own judgment concerning each, which is based on the assumption that surplus gains by

TABLE 5-1 Rules for Measuring Social Benefits and Costs of Government Interventions

Type of Intervention	Efficient Markets	Inefficient Markets
Purchases from factor markets. (Concept: value costs as the opportunity cost of the purchased resources.)	If supply schedule is flat, value cost as direct budgetary expenditure. (Example: purchase of materials from a competitive national market.) If supply schedule is not flat, value cost as direct budgetary expenditure less (plus) any increase (decrease) in social surplus in market. (Example: purchases of materials from a competitive local market.)	Value costs as direct budgetary expenditure less (plus) any increase (decrease) in social surplus in market. (Examples: hiring unemployed labor; purchases of materials from a monopoly.)
Changes in costs to consumers or producers in primary markets. (Concept: value benefits as willingness-to-pay for the change and costs as willingness-to-pay to avoid the change.)	Value change as net change in social (i.e., consumer and producer) surplus plus (less) any increase (decrease) in government revenues. (Example: government provision of goods and services to consumers or producers.)	Value change as net change in social (i.e., consumer, producer, and third-party) (less) increase (decrease) in government revenues. (Example: tax or subsidy in market with externality.)
Changes in quantities exchanged in secondary markets as a result of government intervention in primary or factor markets. (Concept: commodities exchanged in secondary markets are typically complements of or substitutes for commodities exchanged in primary markets; most impacts in secondary markets can be valued in primary markets.)	If prices do not change in secondary market, ignore secondary market impacts. If prices do change, but benefits in primary market are measured using a demand schedule with other market prices held constant, then social surplus changes in the secondary market will always represent reductions in social surplus that should be subtracted from changes in the primary market. But if benefits in the primary market are measured using a demand schedule that does not hold other prices constant, ignore secondary market impacts. (Example: price changes in primary market cause demand schedule shifts in competitive secondary market.)	Costs or benefits resulting directly from increases in the size of the distortion should, in principle, be measured. Other impacts in secondary market should be ignored if prices do not change. (Example: price changes in primary market causes the demand schedule to shift in a secondary market with externality.)

These rules pertain only to measuring impacts of government interventions on society as a whole. Issues concerning standing are ignored in the rules.

those who drive on the street are measured using an equilibrium demand schedule for trips, appears in Exhibit 5-2.

1. The increased traffic would cause vibrations that crack the walls of adjacent houses.
2. Profits of gasoline at filling stations that are located along the route would increase.
3. The property values of these stations would also increase.
4. Traffic on adjacent streets would decline. Therefore, the remaining motorists would experience quicker and cheaper journeys.
5. Air pollution along the route would increase.
6. The increased auto traffic would require the city to hire three more police officers to enforce traffic regulations.
7. The greater number of motorists would lead to an increased number of traffic violations, and the resulting fines would mean that the city receives increased revenue.
8. Fewer people would ride buses; as a consequence the bus company would lay off 10 bus drivers.
9. Widening the road would necessitate cutting down a number of trees. These trees would then be sold to a nearby sawmill.

EXHIBIT 5-2

1. The cracked walls in houses that would result from the increased traffic are a negative externality. Although the externality would occur in the secondary market for housing, it should be taken into account in the study.

2. The increased purchases of gasoline would occur in a secondary market. If this market is not seriously distorted (e.g., by externalities or monopoly power), then the increase in gasoline purchases should be ignored because any effects on surplus will be captured by measuring surplus in the primary market. (Notice, however, that doing this neglects the fact that it is the owners of the filling stations, rather than automobile drivers, who receive the increase in surplus from increased purchases of gasoline; it also ignores the possibility that filling station owners who are located on other streets may face reductions in surplus.)

3. The property market is also a secondary market. Hence, these effects should be ignored.

4. The decrease in traffic on adjacent streets can be viewed as a reduction in a negative externality—congestion—that distorts a secondary market (the adjacent streets are presumably substitutes for the street that would be widened). This is a real benefit that should be taken into account.

5. Air pollution is a negative externality that distorts the primary market. Hence, it should be taken account of in the CBA.

6. The hiring of three additional police officers would take place in a factor market for labor and can be viewed as a direct cost of the project.

7. The increase in traffic fines would simply be a transfer between motorists and the city and, except for their distributional implications, can be ignored by the CBA.

8. The 10 laid off bus drivers would lose their jobs because the demand schedule in the secondary market for public transportation would shift to the left. Unless this market or the factor markets that serve this market are distorted, the shift in demand can be ignored in the CBA. Examples of such distortions are the loss of monopoly profits by the bus company or the inability of the bus drivers to find new jobs because of high rates of unemployment. Otherwise, the bus drivers would simply find new jobs at a similar level of compensation, implying that widening

(Continued)

(*Continued*)

the road would have no effect on the social value of the output they produce.

9. The benefits and costs of cutting down the trees and selling them to a sawmill can be assessed independently of the street-widening project. If the benefits from cutting down the trees exceed the costs, then the trees should be cut regardless of whether the street-widening project is undertaken. However, if the costs exceed the benefits, then the costs and benefits of cutting the trees should be included in the CBA of the street-widening project.

EXERCISES FOR CHAPTER 5

1. Recall exercise 2 from Chapter 4 in which an increase in the toll on a highway from $.40 to $.50 would reduce use of the highway by 10,000 cars per week.
   a. Because of the reduced use of the highway, demand in the secondary market for subway rides increases. Assuming that the price of subway rides is set equal to the marginal cost of operating the subway and marginal costs are constant (i.e., the supply schedule is horizontal), and no externalities result from the reduced use of the highway and the increased use of the subway, are there additional costs or benefits due to the increased demand for subway rides? Why or why not?
   b. Because of the reduced use of the highway, demand in the secondary market for gasoline falls by 30,000 gallons per year. There is a stiff tax on gasoline, one that existed prior to the new toll. Assuming that the marginal cost of producing gasoline is $1 per gallon, that these marginal costs are constant (i.e., the supply schedule is horizontal), that no externalities result from the consumption of gasoline, and that the gasoline tax adds 30 percent to the supply price, are there any additional costs or benefits due to this shift? If so, how large are they?

2. Recall exercise 3 from Chapter 4 in which a country imposes an import fee on the crude oil it imports. Assume that prior to the imposition of the import fee, the country annually consumed 900 million short tons of coal, all domestically mined, at a price of $22 per short ton. How would the CBA of the import fee change if, after imposition of the import fee, the following circumstances are assumed to result from energy consumers switching from crude oil to coal?
   a. Annual consumption of coal rises by 40 million short tons, but the price of coal remains unchanged.
   b. Annual consumption of coal rises by 40 million short tons and the price of coal rises to $23 per short ton. In answering this question, assume that the prices of other goods, including coal, were not held constant in estimating the demand schedule for crude oil.
   c. Annual consumption of coal rises by 40 million short tons and the price of coal rises to $23 per short ton. In answering this question, assume that the prices of other goods, including coal, were held constant in estimating the demand schedule for crude oil. Also assume that the demand schedule for coal is completely inelastic.
   d. The market price of coal underestimates its marginal social cost by $5 per short ton because the coal mined in the country has a high sulphur content that produces smog when burned. In answering this question, assume that the annual consumption of coal rises by 40 million short tons, but the price of coal remains unchanged.

3. Recall exercise 3 from Chapter 4 in which a country imposes an import fee on the crude oil it imports. Imagine that all the crude oil imports to the country are made by ships owned by its nationals. The Association of Petroleum Shippers argues that the reduction

in imports resulting from the import fee will drive down the price of shipping services and thereby inflict a loss on them. The Committee for Energy Independence, which favors the import fee, argues that the reduction in shipping prices will benefit consumers of shipping services. Which argument is correct? In preparing an answer, make the following assumptions: The import fee will reduce the quantity of imported crude oil from 3 billion to 2.5 billion barrels per year; the reduction in barrels shipped will drive per-barrel shipping costs down from $1 per barrel to $.75 per barrel; and the elasticity of demand in the shipping market at the new equilibrium ($.75, 2.5 billion barrels) is –0.3. Also assume that the shipping market is undistorted and that the prices of other goods, including shipping services, were held constant in estimating the demand schedule for crude oil.

4. (Instructor-provided spreadsheet required.) Consider an individual's utility function over two goods, q_m and q_s, where m indicates the primary market in which a policy will have its effect and s is a related secondary market:

$$U = q_m + \alpha q_s - (\beta_m q_m^2 + \gamma q_m q_s + \beta_s q_s^2)$$

where α, β_m, β_s, and γ are parameters such that $\beta_m > 0$, and $\beta_s > 0$, $\beta_m < (1 - \gamma q_s)/2q_m$, $\beta_s < (1 - \gamma q_m)/2q_s$, and $\gamma < p_m \beta_s/p_s + p_s \beta_m/p_m$. For purposes of this exercise, assume that $\alpha = 1$, $\beta_m = 0.01$, $\beta_s = 0.01$, and $\gamma = -0.015$. Also assume that the person has a budget of $30,000 and the price of q_m, p_m, is $100 and the price of q_s, p_s, is $100. Imagine that the policy under consideration would reduce p_m to $90.

The provided spreadsheet has two models. Model 1 assumes that the price in the secondary market does not change in response to a price change in the primary market. That is, p_s equals $100 both before and after the reduction in p_m. Step 1 solves for the quantities that maximize utility under the initial p_m. Step 2 solves for the quantities that maximize utility under the new p_m. Step 3 requires you to make guesses of the new budget level that would return the person to her original level of utility prior to the price reduction—keep guessing until you find the correct budget. (You may wish to use the Tools|Goal Seek function on the spreadsheet instead of engaging in interative interative guessing.) Step 4 calculates the compensating variation as the difference between the original budget and the new budget. Step 5 calculates the change in the consumer surplus in the primary market.

Model 2 assumes that $p_s = a + bq_s$. Assume that $b = 0.25$ and a is set so that at the quantity demanded in step 2 of model 1, $p_s = 100$. As no analytical solution for the quantities before the price change exists, step 1 requires you to make guesses of the marginal utility of money until you find the one that satisfies the budget constraint for the initial p_m. Step 2 repeats this process for the new value of p_m. Step 3 requires you to guess both a new budget to return the person to the initial level of utility and a marginal utility of money that satisfies the new budget constraint. A block explains how to use the Tools|Goal Seek function to find the marginal utility consistent with your guess of the new budget needed to return utility to its original level. Step 4 calculates the compensating variation. Step 5 calculates the change in the consumer surplus in the primary market and bounds on the change in consumer surplus in the secondary market.

Use these models to investigate how well the change in social surplus in the primary market approximates compensating variation. Note that as utility depends on consumption of only these two goods, there are substantial income effects. That is, a price reduction in either of the goods substantially increases the individual's real income. Getting started: The values in the spreadsheet are set up for a reduction in p_m from $100 to $95. Begin by changing the new primary market price to $90 and resolving the models.

NOTES

1. For a helpful analysis that uses a somewhat different approach than the one presented in this section but reaches very similar conclusions, see Herbert Mohring, "Maximizing, Measuring, and Not Double Counting Transportation-Improvement Benefits: A Primer on Closed- and Open-Economy Cost-Benefit Analysis," *Transportation Research* 27(6) 1993, 413–424.

2. As advocates of a policy often claim benefits in secondary markets, it is ironic that demand shifts in undistorted secondary markets that cause price changes always involve losses in social surplus. This can be seen by using panel (b) in Figure 5-2 to illustrate the case of an outward shift in demand in a secondary market, as well as the case of an inward shift in demand. Simply take D_{G_1} as the original demand schedule and D_{G_0} as the post-project demand schedule. Using the post-project demand schedule for measuring social surplus changes, we see that the price increase from P_{G_1} to P_{G_0} results in a producer surplus increase equal to the area of trapezoid $P_{G_1}fgP_{G_0}$ and a consumer surplus loss equal to the area of $P_{G_1}hgP_{G_0}$ so that social surplus falls by the area of triangle *fgh*.

3. See Richard E. Just, Darrell L. Hueth, and Andrew Schmitz, *Applied Welfare Economics and Public Policy* (Englewood Cliffs, NJ: Prentice Hall, 1982), Chapter 9.

4. For greater detail concerning this point, see Just, Hueth, and Schmitz, *Applied Welfare Economics and Public Policy*, 200–213.

5. Indeed, under certain assumptions, areas *abc* and *efg* will almost exactly equal one another. The most important of these assumptions is that the price changes in the two markets represented in Figure 5-2 are small and that no income effects result from these price changes. If there are no income effects, there will be symmetry in substitution between the two goods. In other words, their cross-substitution effects will be equal. That is, $\partial q_F / \partial P_G = \partial q_G / \partial P_F$. Given this equality, $\Delta P_F \Delta q_F \approx \Delta P_G \Delta q_G$. Hence, area *abc* approximately equals area *efg*. Typically, income effects do occur as a result of price changes, but as discussed in Appendix 3A, these effects tend to be small for most goods. Consequently, one would anticipate that area *abc* would generally closely approximate area *efg*.

6. Separate measures would have to be obtained, however, to examine how benefits and costs were distributed among various groups. For example, area *abc* is a gain to consumers, while area *efg* is a loss to producers. To the extent these two areas are equal, they represent a transfer of surplus from producers to consumers. In addition, surplus corresponding to area $P_{G_0}efP_{G_1}$ is also transferred from producers to consumers.

7. For a formal demonstration of this assertion, see Jan Rouwendal, "Indirect Welfare Effects of Price Changes and Cost-Benefit Analysis," unpublished paper (Amsterdam: Tinbergen Institute, 2002).

CHAPTER 6

Discounting Benefits and Costs in Future Time Periods

Both private and public decisions can have important consequences that extend over time. When consumers buy houses, automobiles, or education, they generally expect to derive benefits and incur costs over a number of years. When the government builds a dam, subsidizes job training, regulates carbon dioxide emissions, or leases the outer continental shelf for oil exploration, it sets in motion impacts that extend over many years. Often analysts have to compare projects with benefits and costs that arise in different time periods. Formally, they have to make intertemporal (across time) comparisons. To do this, analysts *discount* future costs and benefits so that all costs and benefits are in a common metric—the present value. Thus, they can measure and compare the net social benefits of each policy alternative using the *net present value* criterion.

This chapter deals with the practical issues one must know in order to compute the net present value of a project (or policy).[1] It assumes that the *social discount rate*, the rate at which analysts should discount the future benefits and costs of a project, is known. As we discuss in Chapter 10, some controversy remains over the appropriate social discount rate. Nonetheless, in practice, oversight agencies, such as the Office of Management and Budget in the United States, Her Majesty's Treasury in the United Kingdom, or the Treasury Board in Canada, often specify the rate that analysts should use.

The sections of this chapter cover the following topics: the basics of discounting, compounding and discounting over multiple years, the timing of benefits and costs, long-lived projects and calculating horizon values, comparing projects with different time frames, real versus nominal dollars, relative price changes, and sensitivity analysis in discounting. Appendix 6A presents some shortcut methods for calculating the present value of annuities and perpetuities. The topics covered in this chapter are essentially uncontroversial. Readers who are familiar with the time value of money and capital budgeting techniques may want to skip this chapter.

THE BASICS OF DISCOUNTING

Projects with Lives of One Year

Technically speaking, discounting takes place over *periods* rather than years. However, because the period of discounting is a year in almost all public-sector applications, and it is easier to think of years rather than periods, we generally use the term years. In this section we consider projects that last for exactly one year. In the following section we consider projects that last for longer than one year.

Suppose a city government has the opportunity to buy a parcel of land for $10 million. It knows that if it buys the land, then the land will be sold for $11 million one year from now. Should the city buy the land now?

Before proceeding, it is worth noting that it is often useful to lay out the annual benefits and costs of a project on a *time line*, as shown in Figure 6-1. The horizontal axis represents time measured in years. Benefits appear above the time line and costs are below it. Although a time line might seem unnecessary for this simple example, this tool clarifies the timing of the benefits and costs of a project when timing is in doubt or the project is more complicated.

To decide whether to buy the land, the city should compare the project, which has a cost of $10 million now and a benefit of $11 million in one year, to the most likely alternative—in this case, the *status quo* (not buy the land). There are three ways to do this, each of which gives the same answer.

Future Value Analysis This method compares what the city will receive in the future if it invests in the project with what it will receive in the future if it invests the money in the best alternative. Suppose that if the city does not buy the land, it will invest the money in Treasury bills (T-bills) at an interest rate of 7 percent.[2] If it invests in T-bills, then it will have $10.7 million in one year—the principal amount of $10 million plus interest of $700,000. This amount, $10.7 million, is called the *future value, FV,* of the T-bills because it represents the amount the city will have in a future period if it buys the T-bills. The city can compare this future value with the future value it will receive if it invests in the land, $11 million, and choose the alternative that has the highest future value. In this example, the city should buy the land.

In general, the future value in one year of some amount X is given by the following formula:

$$FV = X(1 + i) \tag{6.1}$$

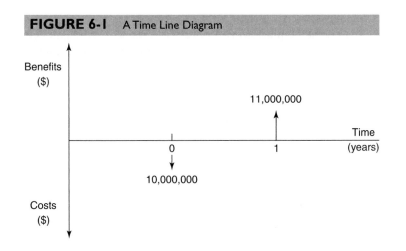

FIGURE 6-1   A Time Line Diagram

Benefits ($)

11,000,000

Time (years)

0   1

10,000,000

Costs ($)

where i is the annual rate of interest. The idea of future value is intuitively appealing for anyone who has ever had a savings account. For example, if one invests $1,000 in a savings account at 5 percent, one will have $1,000(1 + 0.05) = $1,050 in a year. The future value is also called the *compound value*. Equation (6.1) illustrates the basic idea of *simple compounding*.

Note that interest rates are often stated as percentages, such as 5 percent. This corresponds to an interest rate, i, equal to 0.05.

Present Value Analysis We now switch from compounding to discounting and from future values to present values. Present value analysis compares the current equivalent value of investing in the project with the current equivalent value of investing in the best alternative project, given prevailing interest rates. The current equivalent value of an amount that will be received in the future is called its *present value, PV*. For example, the present value of buying the land that will be worth $11 million in one year's time, given that the city can invest money at 7 percent, is found by setting $FV = \$11,000,000$, $X = PV$, and $i = 0.07$ in equation (6.1):

$$PV(1 + 0.07) = \$11,000,000$$

Solving this equation for PV gives:

$$PV = \frac{\$11,000,000}{1.07} = \$10,280,374$$

In contrast, the present value of the best available alternative, buying the T-bills now, is $10 million.[3] Comparing these two present values shows that the city will be $280,374 better off in present value terms if it buys the land.

In general, if the prevailing interest rate is i, then the present value of an amount received in one year, Y, is given by:

$$PV = \frac{Y}{1 + i} \tag{6.2}$$

The process of calculating the present value of a future amount is called *discounting*. Comparing equations (6.1) and (6.2) shows that discounting is the opposite of compounding.[4] As is evident from equation (6.2), the present value of a future amount decreases as the interest rate increases.

Net Present Value Analysis This method calculates the present values of all the benefits and costs of a project, including the initial investment, and sums them to obtain the *net present value, NPV*, of the project. For the land purchase example, the *NPV* is the difference between the present value of the land if the city buys it and the current cost of the land:

$$NPV = \$10,280,374 - \$10,000,000 = \$280,374$$

These calculations are represented graphically on a time line in Figure 6-2. As the *NPV* of buying the land is positive, the city should buy the land. The city will be $280,374 better off in present value terms if it invests in this project.

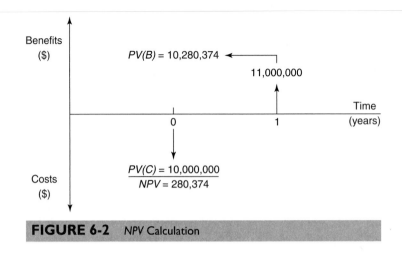

Benefits
($)

PV(B) = 10,280,374

11,000,000

Time
(years)

0

1

PV(C) = 10,000,000
NPV = 280,374

Costs
($)

FIGURE 6-2 *NPV Calculation*

By definition, the *NPV* of a project equals the difference between the present value of the benefits, *PV(B)*, and the present value of the costs, *PV(C)*:

$$NPV = PV(B) - PV(C) \tag{6.3}$$

As discussed in Chapter 1, the *NPV* method provides a simple criterion for deciding whether to undertake a project. If the *NPV* of a project is positive, then one should proceed with it; if the *NPV* is negative, then one should not. The positive *NPV* decision rule assumes implicitly that no other alternative with a higher *NPV* exists. *If there are multiple, mutually exclusive alternatives, then one should select the alternative with the highest* NPV.

The foregoing example assumes that the city has $10 million available that could be used either to buy the land or to invest at interest rate *i*. Sometimes analysts calculate *NPV*s of projects for which the government does not have all the cash immediately available and has to borrow some funds. *Implicitly, analysts assume that the government can borrow or lend funds at the same interest rate* i. *Under this assumption it does not matter whether the government currently has the money or not: The* NPV *rule still holds.* In Chapter 10 we discuss how the source of funding for a project may affect the choice of the discount rate. However, even in these situations, analysts should select the project with the largest *NPV*.

COMPOUNDING AND DISCOUNTING OVER MULTIPLE YEARS

We now generalize these results across many years. Again, we first discuss future values, then present values, and finally net present values.

Future Value over Multiple Years Suppose that the city could invest the $10 million for five years with interest at 7 percent per annum, compounded annually. Using equation (6.1), at the end of the first year the city would have $10 million × 1.07 = $10.7 million. Again using equation (6.1), at the end of the second year the city would have $10.7 million × 1.07 = $11.449 million. Notice that the interest in the second year, $0.749

TABLE 6-1	Investment of $10 Million with Interest Compounded Annually at 7 Percent		
Year	*Beginning of Year Balance ($ millions)*	*Annual Interest ($ millions)*	*End of Year Balance ($ millions)*
1	10.000	0.700	10.700
2	10.700	0.749	11.449
3	11.449	0.801	12.250
4	12.250	0.858	13.108
5	13.108	0.918	14.026

million, is more than the interest in the first year, $0.700 million. In the second and subsequent years, interest is earned on the principal amount *and* on the interest that has been reinvested (*interest on the interest*). Interest on reinvested interest is called *compound interest*. This process is called *compounding interest*. Table 6-1 illustrates that when interest is compounded, the compound value can grow quickly. For example, at an interest rate of 7 percent, the original capital amount increases by more than 40 percent after only five years. During this five-year period, the total interest earned is $4.026 million.

There is an important distinction between compound interest and *simple interest*. With simple interest, interest is paid only on the original principal amount (i.e., not on reinvested interest). Using simple interest, after five years the total interest would amount to only $3.5 million. This is $0.526 million less than if interest had been compounded, a considerable amount given the original principal amount of $10 million. Over longer periods (10 years or more) the divergence between compound interest and simple interest becomes quite large. This gap increases with time, thereby lending credence to the adage of many pension funds sales agents who exhort young adults "to invest early and leave it there."

In general, if an amount, denoted by X, is invested for n years and interest is compounded annually at i percent per annum, then the future value is:[5]

$$FV = X(1 + i)^n \qquad \qquad \textbf{(6.4)}$$

For example, if $10 million is invested for four years with interest compounded annually at 7 percent, then the future value is:

$$FV = \$10(1 + 0.07)^4 = \$13.108 \text{ million}$$

The term $(1 + i)^n$, which gives the future value of $1 in n years at annual interest rate i, compounded annually, is called the *compound interest factor*. In this example, the compound interest factor is 1.3108. Most finance textbooks include an appendix of compound interest factors. Many pocket calculators have this function, as do most computer spreadsheet programs.[6]

Present Value over Multiple Years   Now consider present values, which require discounting rather than compounding. Suppose that a government agency wants to undertake an organizational restructuring in three years that is expected to cost $100,000 at that time. If interest rates are 6 percent, then the amount needed now to yield $100,000 in three years, denoted by PV, can be found by substituting into equation (6.4):

$$PV (1 + 0.06)^3 = \$100,000.$$

Solving this equation for PV gives:

$$PV = \frac{\$100,000}{(1 + 0.06)^3} = \frac{\$100,000}{1.19102} = \$83,962$$

Consequently, the government agency would need $83,962 now to have $100,000 in three years.

In general, the present value of an amount received in n years, denoted Y, with interest compounded annually at rate i is:

$$PV = \frac{Y}{(1 + i)^n} \tag{6.5}$$

The term $1/(1 + i)^n$ is called the *present value factor,* or the *discount factor.* It equals the present value of $1 received in n years when the interest rate is i, compounded annually. For example, the present value factor in the foregoing example equals $1/(1 + .06)^3 = 0.8396$. Again, these factors are available in most finance textbooks, on calculators, and in computer spreadsheet programs.

If a project yields benefits in many periods, then we can compute the present value of the whole stream by adding the present values of the benefits received in each period. Specifically, if B_t denotes the benefits received in period t for $t = 0,1,\ldots,n$, then the present value of the stream of benefits, denoted $PV(B)$, is:

$$PV(B) = \frac{B_0}{(1 + i)^0} + \frac{B_1}{(1 + i)^1} + \cdots + \frac{B_{n-1}}{(1 + i)^{n-1}} + \frac{B_n}{(1 + i)^n}$$

$$PV(B) = \sum_{t=0}^{n} \frac{B_t}{(1 + i)^t} \tag{6.6}$$

Similarly, if C_t denotes the costs incurred in period t for $t = 0, 1,\ldots,n$, then the present value of a stream of costs, denoted $PV(C)$, is:

$$PV(C) = \sum_{t=0}^{n} \frac{C_t}{(1 + i)^t} \tag{6.7}$$

To illustrate the use of equation (6.6), consider a government agency that has to choose between two alternative projects. Project I yields a benefit of $10,500 four years from now, whereas project II yields $5,500 four years from now and an additional

$5,400 five years from now. Assume the interest rate is 8 percent. Which is the better project? The present values of the projects follow:

$$PV(\text{I}) = \frac{\$10,500}{(1 + 0.08)^4} = \$7.718$$

$$PV(\text{II}) = \frac{\$5,500}{(1 + 0.08)^4} + \frac{\$5,400}{(1 + 0.08)^5} = \$4,043 + \$3,675 = \$7,718$$

In this example, the present values of the two projects happen to be identical. Thus, one would be indifferent between them. Time lines for these two projects are show in Figure 6-3.

Net Present Value of a Project   We have now introduced all of the material on basic discounting needed for CBA. As discussed earlier, the *NPV* of a project is the difference between the present value of the benefits and the present value of the costs, as represented in equation (6.3). Substituting equations (6.6) and (6.7) into equation (6.3) gives the following useful expression:

$$NPV = \sum_{t=0}^{n} \frac{B_t}{(1 + i)^t} - \sum_{t=0}^{n} \frac{C_t}{(1 + i)^t} \qquad \textbf{(6.8)}$$

FIGURE 6-3   Comparing Project I and Project II

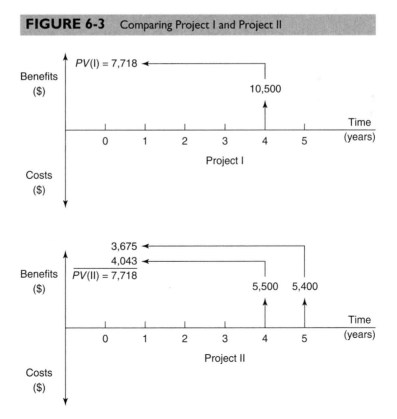

To illustrate the mechanics of computing the *NPV* of a project using this formula, suppose a district library is considering purchasing a new information system that will give users access to a number of online databases for five years. The benefits of this system are estimated to be $100,000 per annum, including both cost savings to the library and user benefits. The information system costs $325,000 to purchase and set up initially, and $20,000 to operate and maintain each year. After five years, the system will be dismantled and sold, resulting in a net cash inflow of $20,000. Such amounts that arise at the end of a project are sometimes referred to as the *terminal value* or *liquidation value*. Assume the appropriate discount rate is 7 percent and there are no other costs or benefits.

A time line for this project is shown in Figure 6-4. It shows the timing of each bene-fit and cost, their present values, the present value of all the benefits, the present value of all the costs, and the *NPV* of the project. The present value of the benefits is $424,280; the present value of the costs is $407,004; and the *NPV* of the project is $17,276. As the *NPV* is positive, the library should purchase the new information system.

An alternative way to compute the *NPV* of a project is to compute the present value of the annual *net (social) benefits*. Let $NB_t = B_t - C_t$ denote the annual net bene-fits that arise in year t $(t = 0, 1, 2, \ldots, n)$. It follows from equation (6.8) that the NPV *of a project equals the present value of the net benefits:*[7]

$$NPV = \sum_{t=0}^{n} \frac{NB_t}{(1 + i)^t} \qquad (6.9)$$

FIGURE 6-4 Time Line of the Benefits and Costs of the Library Information System

TABLE 6-2   The Net Present Value of the Library Information System

Year	Event	Annual Benefits	Annual Costs	Annual Net Benefits
0	Purchase and install	0	325,000	−325,000
1	Annual benefits and costs	100,000	20,000	80,000
2	Annual benefits and costs	100,000	20,000	80,000
3	Annual benefits and costs	100,000	20,000	80,000
4	Annual benefits and costs	100,000	20,000	80,000
5	Annual benefits and costs	100,000	20,000	80,000
5	Liquidation	20,000	0	20,000
	PV	$424,280	$407,004	$17,276

To illustrate that equation (6.9) and equation (6.8) produce the same *NPV*, Table 6-2 contains the annual benefits, annual costs, and annual net benefits of the library information system project. Using equation (6.9), the present value of the net benefits of the project is $17,276, as shown in the last column of Table 6-2. This is the same value as the *NPV* obtained earlier by taking the difference between the present value of the benefits and the present value of the costs.

In many respects, tables and time lines are interchangeable. For comparison purposes a time line using net benefits appears in Figure 6-5. Tables and time lines present key information succinctly and facilitate computation of project *NPV*s. Neither is necessary. Analysts can experiment with them and use them whenever they are helpful. For complicated projects it is often useful to start with a time line to

FIGURE 6-5   Time Line of the Net Social Benefits of the Library Information System

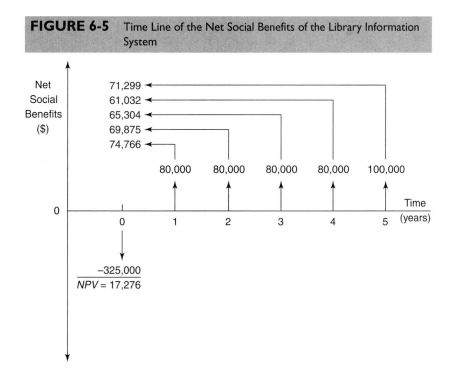

indicate precisely when impacts occur and then enter the data into a spreadsheet to compute the *PV*s and *NPV*s.

Two special situations are worth discussing briefly. In some projects all of the costs occur at the beginning ($t = 0$) and only benefits occur in the ensuing years ($t = 1, 2, \ldots, n$). In this situation, equation (6.8) simplifies to:

$$NPV = \sum_{t=0}^{n} \frac{B_t}{(1 + i)^t} - C_0$$

In some projects, benefits or costs occur indefinitely. For such projects we replace n in equation (6.8) or (6.9) with infinity, ∞. Alternatively, we discount benefits and costs over some finite discounting period and then estimate separately the present value of subsequent net benefits—the horizon value. Estimation of horizon values is discussed later in this chapter.

Continuous Compounding   Throughout this chapter we assume that interest is compounded once per period, with a period being a year. In practice, interest on mortgages, savings accounts, and other investments is often compounded more than once per period. It may be compounded semiannually, monthly, or even daily. Sometimes, interest is compounded continuously.[8] In general, the present value of a future amount declines as the frequency of discounting increases. However, the difference between assuming interest is compounded once per period and assuming it is compounded continuously is not great. For example, under the assumption of continuous compounding, the *PV* of the benefits of the library information system would be $421,374, the *PV* of the costs would be $406,456, and the *NPV* would be $14,918.

TIMING OF BENEFITS AND COSTS

The compounding and discounting formulae presented so far assume that all benefits and costs occur at the end of each period (year). Impacts are assumed to arise immediately ($t = 0$), or at the end of the first year ($t = 1$), or at the end of the second year ($t = 2$), and so on. For many projects this is a reasonable assumption. Furthermore, when most of the costs occur early in the project and most of the benefits occur late in the project, this assumption is conservative in the sense that the *NPV*s are lower than they would be if they were computed under alternative assumptions.

To illustrate this point, reconsider the library information system example, but now assume that the annual benefits of $100,000 all occur at the beginning of each year instead of at the end of each year, and assume the timing of all other benefits and costs is unchanged. A time line under these assumptions is given in Figure 6-6. The present value of the benefits increases by $28,702 from $424,280 to $452,982, and the *NPV* of the project increases by $28,702 from $17,276 to $45,978, more than two and one-half times the *NPV* calculated previously. Clearly, the *NPV* of a project can vary considerably according to the assumption made about the timing of benefits or costs.

When costs or benefits occur over the course of a year, a more appropriate approach is to treat them as if they accrued in the middle of that year. So, for instance, if the $100,000 in benefits and $20,000 in operating costs were distributed throughout each of

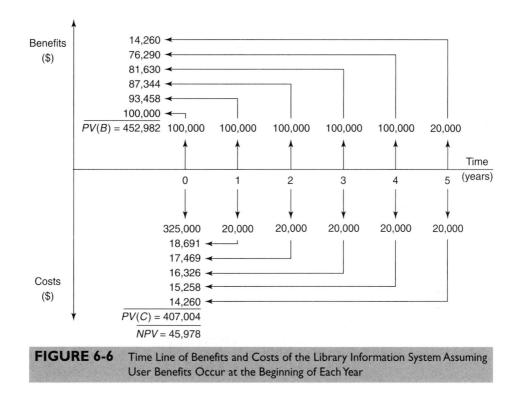

FIGURE 6-6 Time Line of Benefits and Costs of the Library Information System Assuming User Benefits Occur at the Beginning of Each Year

the five years of the library project, one would discount these benefits and costs at times $t = 0.5, 1.5, 2.5, 3.5,$ and 4.5. If, as before, the installation costs of \$325,000 occurred at the beginning of the first year of the project ($t = 0$) and the liquidation benefit of \$20,000 arose at the end of the fifth year ($t = 5$), then the *NPV* of the project would be \$28,562.

LONG-LIVED PROJECTS AND HORIZON VALUES

Earlier we stated that analysts should discount benefits and costs using equation (6.8) or, equivalently, equation (6.9). These equations imply that all of the impacts attributable to the project occur during the first *n* years. Subsequent benefits and costs are assumed to equal zero.

Even though a project may be finished from an engineering or administrative perspective after a relatively short period of time, the benefits (and some costs) may continue to flow from the project for many years. In England, for example, cars travel on roads that were laid out by the Romans more than 18 centuries ago. The Great Wall of China continues to generate tourism benefits even though it was built to discourage particularly unwelcome "visitors" many centuries ago. The same issue also arises in human capital investment programs, especially training and health programs. For example, preschool training programs may benefit participants throughout their entire lives, years after they participated in the program; some benefits may even accrue to their children. All of these impacts should be included in a CBA. In practice, it is often not clear how to handle costs and benefits that arise far in the future.

One option is to estimate the benefits and costs (or the net benefits) in each and every period and to calculate the *NPV* using the following formula:

$$NPV = \sum_{t=0}^{\infty} \frac{NB_t}{(1+i)^t} \qquad (6.10)$$

It is practical to use this method if it is reasonable to assume that the net benefits are constant or grow or decline at a constant rate; see Appendix 6A. But these assumptions may not be appropriate. Furthermore, as analysts are likely to be more confident about predicting the "near future" than the "far future," it is often useful to distinguish between them.

An alternative approach computes the net present value of the project as the sum of the present value of the net benefits throughout a *relatively* short discounting period (often the *useful life* of the project) plus the present value of the horizon value—the value of the project at the end of the discounting period (horizon):

$$NPV = \sum_{t=0}^{k} \frac{NB_t}{(1+i)^t} + PV(H_k) \qquad (6.11)$$

Thus, analysts distinguish between "near future" impacts (during the first k periods) and "far future" impacts (in all subsequent periods). The latter are reduced to a single number, the present value of the horizon value, denoted $PV(H_k)$. The *horizon value* reflects the value *at the end of the discounting horizon* of all subsequent benefits and costs.[9]

When using horizon values, the length of the discounting period, k, is arbitrary in theory.[10] In practice, the discounting period is usually determined by the nature of each project. For example, it is common to use a 20-year discounting period for highways because they tend to last about 20 years before they require major repairs. Sometimes the discounting period ends when the intervention ends and the remaining assets are liquidated. For this reason, the horizon value is sometimes referred to as the terminal value. Notice that many short projects have horizon values. For example, the library information project had an horizon value even though it lasted only five years. Some projects have negative horizon values. For example, there may be costs associated with decommissioning a site used for a World Exposition, the Olympic Games, or the production of nuclear power.

Alternative Methods for Estimating Horizon Values

A variety of methods exist for estimating horizon values. One method is based on simple projections, another uses scrap values or liquidation values, a third uses (economic) depreciated values, a fourth is based on initial construction costs, and a fifth assumes the horizon value is zero. Analysts may try to check their results by calculating the horizon value in several different ways. Because of uncertainty concerning the actual magnitude of the horizon value, *sensitivity analysis* is often conducted by selecting alternative horizon values and seeing how this affects the findings.

Horizon Value Based on Simple Projections   One theoretically appropriate method estimates the horizon value based on simple extrapolations of benefits and costs (or net benefits). This is similar to estimating equation (6.10) directly, but it distinguishes between the "near future" and the "far future." Consider, for example, the construction of a new dike and suppose the annual net benefits have been calculated for the first 35 years. It is necessary to estimate the horizon value after 35 years. One possibility is to make an assumption about the growth in future net benefits. Suppose analysts expect net benefits will be $1 million in the thirty-sixth year and will grow at 1.5 percent per annum indefinitely. Using equation (6A.7) in Appendix 6A, the formula for the present value of a perpetuity that grows at a constant rate, and an interest rate of 8 percent, the horizon value of the project at the end of the *thirty-fifth year* is $1/(0.080 − 0.015) million = $15.38 million. The present value of this horizon value is $1.04 million.

For many government projects, especially training programs, it is reasonable to assume that the annual net benefits decay at a constant rate after some date. In this case equation (6A.7) can be used with a negative growth rate.

There is strong evidence that, for medium- to long-term periods, simple forecasting models predict better than more complicated models. Thus, this method may estimate the *NPV* of the project at least as well as more complicated direct estimation of equation (6.10).

Horizon Value Based on Salvage Value or Liquidation Value   For some projects, the terminal value (also called scrap value, residual value, liquidation value, or salvage value) of the plant and equipment may be used as the horizon value. For example, a school board may buy some buses, operate them for a specific period of time, and then sell them at their market value. This liquidation value may be used as the horizon value.

This method is appropriate in CBA when no other social costs or benefits arise beyond the discounting period, when there is a well-functioning market in which to value the asset, and when the market value reflects the asset's social value (e.g., no negative externalities). For example, the library information system example assumes that $20,000 (plus dismantling costs) is an accurate measure of the net social benefits of the equipment at liquidation. However, if the equipment would be used in schools where its social value (less new setup costs) would be more than $20,000 (plus dismantling costs), then a higher horizon value should be used.

In practice, it is difficult to determine the liquidation value of some assets. Clearly, there is no market for used highways and, even if there were, the market value would probably not reflect the discounted value of future net social benefits.

Estimating Horizon Value Based on Depreciated Value   The third method recognizes that the current value of an asset equals the present value of its future net benefits. However, instead of estimating the stream of future benefits and costs, this method estimates the value of an asset by subtracting its depreciation from its initial value, where its depreciation is calculated based on empirical market studies of similar assets.

The value of most assets declines at a geometric rate; that is, the value in each year is a constant proportion of the value in the previous year. The rate of depreciation varies between 0 and 1. It is high for assets with short lives, such as tires, motor vehicles, and medical equipment, and is low for assets with long lives, such as steam turbines, warehouses, railroad structures, and water systems. A recent study by Barbara Fraumeni describes the methodology used by the Bureau of Economic Analysis (BEA) for calculating depreciation and presents a comprehensive summary of the depreciation rates and service lives of many assets.[11]

It is important to emphasize that we are referring to real (i.e., economic) depreciation, not accounting depreciation. There may be a huge difference. Economic depreciation concerns the decline in the economic value of an asset over time. In contrast, accounting depreciation, also called capital cost allowance, is often largely determined by tax or reporting requirements. Tax authorities may allow companies to take 100 percent depreciation in one year, in which case a company can write off 100 percent of the cost of an investment, even though the investment itself may yield benefits that extend over decades. Thus, the depreciated accounting value may bear no relationship to the reduced usefulness or the amount of wear and tear of an asset. *Accounting depreciation should never be included as a cost (expense) in CBA.*

Using the economic depreciated value for the horizon value is appropriate when estimating the liquidation value of a specific asset is difficult, but one knows the depreciation rate of similar assets. Of course, one should make adjustments where appropriate. For example, if the asset will be used more heavily or maintained more poorly than normal, then one should raise the depreciation rate. As noted previously, one should ensure that the depreciated value reflects the anticipated future use of the asset. For example, an aircraft may have a fairly high depreciated value, but if it is in mothballs and nobody will fly it, then the social benefits may be much less, possibly zero.

Estimating Horizon Value Based on the Initial Construction Cost   This method estimates the horizon value as a fraction of the initial construction cost. In the highway example in Chapter 1, for example, the horizon value of the highway was assumed to equal 75 percent of the initial construction cost: $0.75 \times \$338.1$ million = $\$253.58$ million.[12] The 75 percent figure is quite arbitrary. It may bear no relationship to the future net social benefits. Thus this method, while simple, is not intuitively appealing.

Setting the Horizon Value Equal to Zero   A final method chooses a fairly long discounting period and ignores subsequent benefits and costs. In effect, this is a special case of the first method we discussed—it is equivalent to assuming that after k periods the net benefits in each subsequent period are zero. This is often a reasonable assumption in private-sector decision making because project evaluation requires only the consideration of private benefits and costs that may approach zero fairly quickly. The social impacts of government projects, however, may last many years. Analysts may omit important benefits or costs if they use a time horizon that is too short.

Reprise of Horizon Values

The analyst must decide on both the discounting period and the method for calculating the horizon value. *We suggest analysts discount over the useful life of the project and estimate the horizon value on the basis of simple projections, if plausible assumptions can be made.* The other methods for computing horizon values are more difficult in practice or are more ad hoc. *Consequently, one should usually perform sensitivity analysis on the horizon value.*

The length of the discounting period and the method for calculating the horizon value may be interdependent. If, for example, the analyst is going to assume the horizon value is zero, then he or she should use a relatively long discounting period. If the analyst is using one of the other methods, then it makes sense to discount over the project's useful life. For physical projects, estimates of useful life are usually provided by engineers.

COMPARING PROJECTS WITH DIFFERENT TIME FRAMES

Projects with different time frames are not directly comparable. In effect, projects should always be compared over the same discounting period so that they have the same opportunity to accumulate costs and benefits.

Lack of Comparability between Projects with Different Time Frames

Suppose a government-owned electric utility company is considering two alternative proposals for new sources of energy. One is a major hydroelectric dam (*HED*), which would last 75 years; the other is a cogeneration plant (*CGP*), which would last 15 years. After considering all relevant social benefits and costs, and assuming a discount rate of 8 percent, the *NPV* of the 75-year hydroelectric project is $30 million and the *NPV* of the 15-year cogeneration project is $24 million. Is the hydroelectric project preferable simply because it has the larger *NPV*? The answer is no. These projects are not commensurable because they have different life spans. The cogeneration project could be "rolled over" five times within the life of the hydro project.

There are two methods for evaluating projects with different time frames: rolling over the shorter project method and the *equivalent annual net benefit method*. They always lead to the same conclusion, as we now illustrate.

Rolling Over the Shorter Project Method

Suppose that the utility decides to build the cogeneration power plant. Further suppose that in 15 years it builds a new cogeneration plant; in 30 years it builds another new cogeneration plant; and it builds again in years 45 and 60. If so, the length of these five sequential cogeneration plants will be the same as the length of the hydroelectric project. This makes the projects comparable.[13]

The *NPV* of five back-to-back cogeneration power plants is:

$$NPV(5CGP) = \$24,000,000 + \frac{\$24,000,000}{(1+0.08)^{15}} + \frac{\$24,000,000}{(1+0.08)^{30}}$$

$$+ \frac{\$24,000,000}{(1+0.08)^{45}} + \frac{\$24,000,000}{(1+.008)^{60}} = \$34.94 \text{ million}^{[14]}$$

As this *NPV* is higher than the *NPV* of the hydroelectric project, the utility should build the cogeneration plant.

Equivalent Annual Net Benefit Method

An often easier way to compare projects of unequal lengths is the *equivalent annual net benefit (EANB) method*. The *EANB* of a project equals its *NPV* divided by the *annuity factor* that has the same term and discount rate as the project (i.e., the present value of an annuity of $1 per year for the life of the project, discounted at the rate used to calculate the *NPV*):

$$EANB = \frac{NPV}{a_i^n} \qquad (6.12)$$

where a_i^n is the annuity factor, defined by equation (6A.2). The *EANB* is the amount which, if received each year for the life of the project, would have the same *NPV* as the project. For example, the *EANB*s for the hydroelectric and the cogeneration projects equal:[15]

$$EANB(HED) = \$30/12.461 = \$2.407$$
$$EANB(CGP) = \$24/8.559 = \$2.804$$

The *EANB* of the cogeneration project is $2.804 million, which implies that this project is equivalent to an annuity of $2.804 million per year for 15 years. In contrast, the net benefit of the hydroelectric alternative is equivalent to an annuity of $2.407 million per year for 75 years. If one could continuously replace each project at the end of its life with a similar project, then the cogeneration project would yield net annual bene-fits equivalent to $2.804 million per year indefinitely and the hydroelectric project would yield annual net benefits equivalent to $2.407 million per year indefinitely. Consequently, the cogeneration alternative is preferable, assuming replacement of both types of plant is possible at the end of their useful lives.

An Additional Advantage of the Cogeneration Project

In fact, if the utility chooses the cogeneration project at the beginning, then it may not be desirable to replace it with an identical cogeneration plant in 15 years. At that time a more efficient alternative may be available. In contrast, if the utility builds the hydroelec-tric project, then it is probably locked in for 75 years. Thus, the cogeneration project has an additional benefit because of its flexibility in allowing the introduction of more efficient technology if it becomes available during the 75-year period. Chapter 7 discusses such benefits, called quasi-option value, in more depth. Here it is sufficient to recognize that the shorter project has an additional benefit that is not incorporated in the *EANB*.

INFLATION AND REAL VERSUS NOMINAL DOLLARS

Conventional private-sector financial analysis measures revenues, expenditures, net income, assets, liabilities, and cash flows in terms of historical monetary units. Such units are referred to as *nominal dollars* (sometimes called *current dollars*). However, if you have ever listened to an older person reminisce, then you probably know that a dollar purchased more in 1970 than it does now—"a dollar's not worth a dollar anymore!" For example, nominal per capita disposable personal income in the United States was approximately seven and one-half times higher in 2002 than in 1970 ($27,170 versus $3,591), but you could not buy seven and one-half times as many goods and services on an average disposable income in 2002 as you could on an average disposable income in 1970. The purchasing power of a dollar declines with price inflation. In order to control for the declining purchasing power of a dollar due to inflation, we convert nominal dollars to *real dollars* (sometimes called *constant dollars*).

To obtain real, or constant, dollar measures, analysts adjust for inflation. In effect, analysts *deflate* dollars to account for higher prices. The two most commonly proposed *deflators* are based on the consumer price index (CPI) and the gross national product (GNP). The CPI is based on a basket of consumer goods and attempts to measure the cost of living. In contrast, the GNP is much broader, reflecting the price of all goods and services in the economy. It is reasonable to argue that the choice of whether to use the CPI or the GNP depends on whether the impacts of a project are concentrated on consumers or are much broader. In practice, however, most CBA studies use the CPI deflator.

The CPI deflator is expressed as the ratio of the cost of purchasing a standard basket of market goods in a particular year to the cost of purchasing the same (or very similar) basket of goods in some base year, multiplied by 100. The CPI for the United States since 1970 is shown in Table 6-3.[16] Currently, the base year in the United States is 1982–1984; thus, for the period 1982–1984, the CPI = 100. The CPI for 1970 was 38.8, which implies that the price of a basket of goods in 1970 was only 38.8 percent of the price of a similar basket of goods in 1982–1984. Similarly, the CPI for 2002 of 179.9 implies that the price of a basket of goods in 2002 was 79.9 percent higher than the price of a similar basket in 1982–1984. Thus, the price of a basket of goods was 179.9/38.8 = 4.64 times higher in 2002 than in 1970. Consequently, returning to our example, a person with an average disposable income of $3,591 in 1970 would be able to purchase in 2002 the same (or similar) basket of goods as a person on an income of $3,591 × 4.64 = $16,662. Because the average disposable income was $27,170 in 2002, we can conclude that effective (i.e., real) average disposable incomes increased by ($27,170 − $16,662)/$16,662 = 0.63, or 63 percent from 1970 to 2002.

In order to convert amounts measured in nominal dollars for some year into amounts measured in real dollars for the base year (1982–1984), we simply divide by the CPI for that

TABLE 6-3   The U.S. Consumer Price Index (CPI)
All items
1982–1984 = 100

Year	CPI	%	Year	CPI	%
1970	38.8	5.7	1988	118.3	4.1
1971	40.5	4.4	1989	124.0	4.8
1972	41.8	3.2	1990	130.7	5.4
1973	44.4	6.2	1991	136.2	4.2
1974	49.3	11.0	1992	140.3	3.0
1975	53.8	9.1	1993	144.5	3.0
1976	56.9	5.8	1994	148.2	2.6
1977	60.6	6.5	1995	152.4	2.8
1978	65.2	7.6	1996	156.9	3.0
1979	72.6	11.3	1997	160.5	2.3
1980	82.4	13.5	1998	163.0	1.6
1981	90.9	10.3	1999	166.6	2.2
1982	96.5	6.2	2000	172.2	3.4
1983	99.6	3.2	2001	177.1	2.8
1984	103.9	4.3	2002	179.9	1.6
1985	107.6	3.6	2003	184.0	2.3
1986	109.6	1.9	2004	188.9	2.7
1987	113.6	3.6			

Source: ftp://ftp.bls.gov/pub/special.requests/cpi/cpiai.txt.

year (divided by 100). For example, the average real income of people in 1970 measured in 1982–1984 dollars was $3,591/0.388 = $9,255, and the average real income of people in 2002 measured in 1982–1984 dollars was $27,170/1.799 = $15,103, an increase of 63 percent.

To convert these amounts from base year dollars to, say, 2003 dollars, they are multiplied by the CPI for 2003, which is 184.0 (divided by 100):

$$($3,591/0.388) \times 1.84 = $17,029, \text{ and}$$
$$($27,170/1.799) \times 1.84 = $27,789$$

Thus, the average real disposable incomes of people in 1970 and 2003, expressed in 2003 dollars, were $17,029 and $27,789, respectively. More generally, as the preceding example illustrates, to convert amounts expressed in year *a* nominal dollars into amounts expressed in year *b* real dollars, the year *a* dollar amounts are divided by the CPI for year *a* and multiplied by the CPI for year *b*.

Problems with the CPI

Although the CPI is the most widely used measure of inflation, it has historically overstated the rate of increase in the cost of living. In the mid-1990s, a commission set up by the Senate Finance Committee and chaired by Michael Boskin estimated that in the United States the CPI overestimated the increase in the cost of living by about 1 percentage point per annum, with a range between 0.8 percentage points and 1.6 percentage points.[17] As a result, people receiving entitlements with increases linked to the CPI were, in effect, receiving more than was necessary to keep their purchasing power constant.

There are four main reasons for the upward bias in the CPI.[18] The first is the commodity substitution effect. The basic problem is that the CPI does not accurately reflect consumers' current purchases of goods.[19] When the price of a good rises, consumers change their spending patterns and buy similar, but less expensive, products. As this switch to less expensive goods is not immediately picked up by the CPI, the cost of living is overestimated.[20] A second, related problem is the new goods problem. For example, when pharmaceutical patents expire, some consumers switch to new generic drugs, which are often as effective as patented drugs but are considerably less expensive. These generic drugs did not exist earlier and so were not included in the base basket of goods. A third problem is the quality improvement effect. The CPI does not reflect changes in product quality, such as more safe and reliable cars, or improvements in the quality of living due to new products, such as iPods or PDAs. A fourth problem is called the discount stores effect. In practice, the CPI tends to be measured by sampling products in the same stores over time. While government statisticians are visiting the same older, relatively expensive stores, consumers are switching to newer, cheaper discount stores.

Economists and statisticians are correcting these problems. In the United States, the CPI underwent some major revisions in 1998 that reduced the bias to about 0.65 percent per annum.[21] Nonetheless, we suggest that, when using historical CPI data for the United States, *analysts should convert amounts measured in nominal dollars to amounts measured in real dollars in two ways: using the official CPI as suggested earlier in this section and using a price deflator that increases at one percentage point per annum less than the CPI for years prior to 1998 and at one-half a percentage point per annum less than the CPI for subsequent years.* For example, someone with an income of $100,000 in 1994 would have a real income in 2003 dollars of $124,157 using the official CPI, but an income of $114,115 using a price deflator that increases at one percentage point per annum less than the CPI prior to 1998 and at one-half a percentage point less than the CPI subsequently.

The bias in the CPI is probably not as large in other countries. For example, Allan Crawford estimates that it was about one-half a percentage point per annum in 1998 in Canada.[22] One reason why it was lower in Canada than the United States is that the base basket of goods was updated every 4 years in Canada versus approximately every 10 years in the United States. Also, the CPI in Canada attaches a much lower weight to medical services.

Analyzing Future Benefits and Costs in CBA

Analysts may project benefits and costs in either real dollars or nominal dollars. Also, they may use a real interest rate or a nominal interest rate. Care must be taken to ensure that the units of measurement of benefits and costs are consistent with the units of measurement of the discount rate. *If benefits and costs are measured in nominal dollars, then the analyst should use a nominal discount rate; if benefits and costs are measured in real dollars, then the analyst should use a real discount rate.* Both methods result in the same numerical answer.[23]

In the private sector, it is more natural to work in nominal dollars. Interest rates and other market data are expressed in nominal dollars; *pro forma* income and cash flow projections make more sense in nominal dollars; and the tax system is based on nominal amounts. However, for analysis of public policy projects, *it is usually easier and more intuitively appealing to express all benefits and costs in real dollars and to discount using a real discount rate.* Returning to our library example, it makes more sense to think about the current and future annual benefits in terms of cost savings to the library at today's prices and to think about user benefits in terms of the number of hours of use at today's value per hour than it does to think about these benefits in terms of future prices or values. If one expects user benefits will actually increase over time, for example, due to more people using the system or because each person uses it more often, then the projected real annual benefits will increase. This would be clear if annual benefits and costs were in real dollars. If, alternatively, the annual benefits were expressed in nominal dollars, then it might not be immediately obvious whether increases were due to increases in real benefits or were due to inflation.

If the analyst prefers to work in real dollars, but benefits, costs, or the interest rate are expressed in nominal dollars, then the amounts in nominal dollars must be converted to real dollars. *To convert future benefits and costs from nominal dollars to real dollars, we use the formula for computing present values, equation (6.5), but discount at rate* m, *where m is the expected rate of inflation during the project:*[24]

$$Real\ cost\ or\ benefit_t = \frac{Nominal\ cost\ or\ benefit_t}{(1 + m)^t}$$

To convert a nominal interest rate, i, *to a real interest rate,* r, *with an expected inflation rate,* m, *we use the following equation:*[25]

$$r = \frac{i - m}{1 + m} \tag{6.13}$$

For example, if the nominal interest rate is 10 percent and inflationary expectations are 4 percent, then the real interest rate is $[(.10–.04)/1.04] \times 100 = 5.77$ percent. If expected inflation is quite low (m is small), the real interest rate *approximately* equals the nominal interest rate minus the expected rate of inflation: $r \cong i - m$. For example, if the nominal interest rate is 10 percent and inflationary expectations are 4 percent, then the real interest rate is approximately 6 percent.

In order to convert benefits or costs from real dollars to nominal dollars, analysts can use the formula for computing future values, equation (6.4), but compound at the expected rate of inflation. To convert a real interest rate to a nominal interest rate, solve equation (6.13) for i.

Estimates of Expected Inflation

Moving from nominal interest to real interest rates or from nominal dollars to real dollars, or vice versa, requires an estimate of the *expected* rate of inflation *during the life of the proposed project.* Analysts often use the current CPI as an estimate of future inflation. However, this estimate will be too low when inflation is increasing and too high when inflation is decreasing. It would be better to use one of a number of widely available forecasts, although these are often only available as one-year or two-year forecasts.[26]

Inflation forecasts are available from reputable investment firms, branches of the federal government, a Federal Reserve Bank, or the Organisation for Economic Co-Operation and Development (OECD). Each week the *Economist* presents recent changes in consumer prices and producer prices in many countries. Every month it surveys forecasters (mainly bankers) and summarizes their consumer price increase expectations for the current year and the following year in most major developed countries.

Three easily accessible survey measures of inflationary expectations are available in the United States: the Livingston survey of professional economists, the Michigan survey of households, and the Survey of Professional Forecasters (SPF).[27] Lloyd Thomas has compared the one-year predictive performance of these surveys and two simple naive alternatives, one using the latest 12-month CPI figure and the other based on the Fisher model of interest rates, equation (6.13).[28] He finds that the surveys perform better than the naive models, with the *median* household forecasts performing best. He notes that the forecasts of professional economists have improved over time and he suggests that the SPF is likely to become increasingly popular. Of particular interest, SPF respondents have been asked to provide 10-year-ahead inflation forecasts of the CPI since 1991.

A Practical Example of Handling Inflation: Garbage Trucks

A practical example illustrates the basic issues in handling inflation and moving from market interest rates, which are nominal rates, to real interest rates. Consider a city that uses a rural landfill to dispose of solid refuse. By adding large trucks to the refuse fleet, the city would save $100,000 in disposal costs during the first year and equivalent amounts in each successive year. The trucks would be purchased today for $500,000 and would be sold after four years when the city will open a resource recovery plant that will obviate the need for landfill disposal. The real liquidation value of the trucks (i.e., the current market value of four-year-old trucks of the same type and quality as the city would buy) is $200,000. The city can currently borrow money at a market interest rate of 10 percent. Analysts generally expect that inflation will be 4 percent during the next four years. Should the city buy the trucks? As usual, the answer should be yes if the *NPV* is positive. Is it?

Using Real Dollars

The annual benefits and costs in real dollars are given in column 3 of Table 6-4. It is assumed that the annual savings are the same in real terms each year. This assumption is based on several implicit assumptions, for example, that the amount of vehicle operating maintenance does not change over the period and, if the city does not buy the larger trucks, it will not have to pay for overtime. Furthermore, it implicitly assumes that the *relative valuations* (prices) of wages, gasoline, and other components that figure into the benefit calculations do not change over time.

As benefits and costs are expressed in real dollars, we need to use a real discount rate. As the market interest rate is 10 percent and inflationary expectations are 4 percent, the real interest rate is approximately 6 percent. More precisely, using equation (6.13), the real interest rate is 5.77 percent.[29] Applying this real discount rate to the real annual benefits and costs yields an *NPV* equal to $8,155. Thus, as long as no alternative equipment configuration offers a greater *NPV*, the city should purchase the larger trucks.

Using Nominal Dollars

If analysts take the market interest rate facing the city as the appropriate discount rate, which is a nominal rate, then they must predict future costs and benefits in nominal dollars. To convert amounts in real dollars to nominal dollars, simply inflate them by the expected rate of inflation, *m*. The right-hand column of Table 6-4 shows the anticipated benefits and costs of this project in nominal dollars, assuming a 4 percent annual inflation rate. As mentioned earlier, this example assumes that wage rates, gasoline prices, and other prices that figure into the benefit calculations increase at the same rate as the general price level. Notice that the city expects to receive $233,972 when it sells the trucks at the end of the fourth year. This is called the *nominal liquidation value* of the trucks.

Discounting the benefits and costs measured in nominal dollars using a nominal (market) interest rate of 10 percent gives an *NPV* of the project equal to $8,155, as shown in Table 6-4. Thus, the two methods give exactly the same answer.

TABLE 6-4   The Net Preset Value of Investment in New Garbage Trucks

Year	Event	Annual Benefits and Costs (in real dollars)	Annual Benefits and Costs (in nominal dollars)
0	Purchase	−500,000	−500,000
1	Annual savings	100,000	104,000
2	Annual savings	100,000	108,160
3	Annual savings	100,000	112,486
4	Annual savings	100,000	116,986
4	Liquidation	200,000	233,972
	NPV	8,155[a]	8,155[b]

[a] *Using a real discount rate of 5.769231 percent.*
[b] *Using a nominal discount rate of 10 percent.*

RELATIVE PRICE CHANGES

The preceding section discusses how to handle general price increases due to inflation. It assumes relative prices do not change. This section discusses how to handle relative price changes.

The importance of relative price changes is illustrated by a CBA of a development project in British Columbia to supply coal to Japanese customers.[30] Consider Table 6-5. The second, third, and fourth columns contain the proposed project's benefits, costs, and net benefits, respectively, according to a CBA prepared by the provincial government of British Columbia (roughly equivalent to a state government in the United States).[31] Overall, the net benefits were estimated to be $330 million. The main beneficiaries of this project were expected to be the Canadian National Railway (CNR), which was the state-owned railway company at that time, and the Canadian federal government, which would receive corporate taxes. Here corporate taxes and royalties are a benefit to government but a cost to industry; thus, they are a transfer and they "net out."[32] The British Columbian government was also expected to benefit

TABLE 6-5 CBA of North East Coal Development Project

	Benefits ($ million)	Costs ($ million)	Net Benefits Base Case ($ million)	90% Base Price ($ million)	90% Base Price and Quantity ($ million)
Mining Sector	3,316	3,260*	56	−146	−240
Transport Sector					
Trucking	33	33	0	0	0
Canadian National Railway	504	358	146	146	121
B.C. Railway	216	202	15	15	6
Port Terminal	135	150	−15	−15	−23
Analysis and Survey	11	11	0	0	0
British Columbia**					
Royalties	77	0	77	69	62
Corporate Taxes	154	0	154	125	107
Producer Surplus (Labor)	25	0	25	25	25
Environment	10	5	5	5	5
Highways***	0	88	−88	−88	−88
Tumbler Ridge Branchline	91	267	−176	−176	−185
Canada					
Corporate Taxes	132	0	132	107	92
Highways, Port Navigation	0	26	−26	−26	−26
Producer Surplus (Labor)	25	0	25	25	25
Totals	4,729	4,400	330	66	−119

* Includes taxes and royalties.
** Excluding impacts included elsewhere.
*** Highways, electric power, townsite.
Source: Based on W. G. Waters II, "A Reanalysis of the North East Coal Development," (undated), Tables 2 & 3. All figures in millions of 1980 dollars, assuming a 10 percent real discount rate with the discounting period ending in 2003 and no terminal value.

from royalties and higher corporate taxes, but it would pay for the Tumbler Ridge Branchline, an extension of the provincially owned railway system to the North East Coal Development Project. The mining sector would benefit in terms of increased profits (producer surplus). Also, this project was expected to create jobs for unemployed workers in British Columbia and the rest of Canada. The present value of the producer surplus to labor was estimated to be $25 million. Notice that this analysis does not include any consumer surplus because it was conducted from the perspective of British Columbia and all of the coal would be exported.

The fifth column contains the expected net benefits to each sector if the price of coal were to fall to 90 percent of the base price. Under this assumption, the aggregate net benefits would fall by $264 million from $330 million to $66 million, a substantial change. The sixth column contains the expected net benefits to each sector if the price of coal were to fall to 90 percent of the base price and Japanese customers were to cut back their purchases of coal to 90 percent of their expected orders. Under this assumption, the overall net benefits would fall by $449 million from $330 million to –$119 million.[33] Thus, fairly small changes in relative prices and quantities purchased would have a huge impact on the *NPV* of this project.

In this example the benefits and costs were broken down by sector to illustrate the distributional impacts. The main anticipated "winners" were the CNR and the federal government of Canada. If the price of coal fell by 10 percent, then the mining sector would lose money. Also, the residents of British Columbia would switch from being marginal "winners" to marginal "losers," largely because royalties and corporate taxes would decrease while the costs of highways and the Tumbler Ridge Branchline would be fixed. If the price and quantity levels were to fall to 90 percent of the anticipated levels, then the mining sector would lose badly.

SENSITIVITY ANALYSIS IN DISCOUNTING

This chapter assumes that the rate that should be used to discount future benefits and costs is known. However, for reasons discussed in Chapter 10, there are significant differences of opinion about the correct social discount rate. Also, for reasons discussed earlier in this chapter, there may be considerable uncertainty about the magnitude of the horizon value. Because the discount rate and the horizon value often determine the sign of the *NPV* and, therefore, whether a project should be adopted, analysts frequently conduct sensitivity analyses with respect to these two parameters.

Varying the Discount Rate and the Horizon Value

As discussed more fully in Chapter 7, the most straightforward way to perform sensitivity analysis is to vary each parameter about which there is uncertainty and recalculate the *NPV*. This is easy to do on a spreadsheet. If the policy recommendations are robust (i.e., the *NPV* remains either positive or negative) under all plausible values of the parameters, we can have greater confidence that the recommendations are valid.

Figure 6-7 plots the *NPV* of the library project against the discount rate for two different horizon values, one of $20,000 and the other $0. As the discount rate increases, the *NPV* of the project decreases. This common pattern arises for investment projects whose costs occur early and whose benefits occur late. Using a higher discount

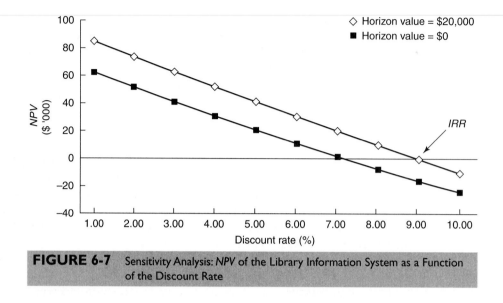

FIGURE 6-7   Sensitivity Analysis: *NPV* of the Library Information System as a Function of the Discount Rate

rate results in a lower *NPV* because the future benefits are discounted more than are the more immediate costs.

The top curve corresponds to a horizon value of $20,000. The *NPV* equals $17,276 if the discount rate equals 7 percent. The *breakeven* discount rate is 8.9 percent, which can be read off the graph where the *NPV* = 0 or found exactly by trial and error.[34] As long as the horizon value equals $20,000 and the appropriate discount rate is less than 8.9 percent, the project offers a positive *NPV* and should be adopted; if the appropriate discount rate is more than 8.9 percent, then the project has a negative *NPV* and should not be adopted.

If the horizon value equals zero, then the curve shifts down by the discounted value of $20,000. As this value decreases as the discount rate increases, the curve shifts down less for high interest rates than for low interest rates. Thus, it is flatter than the curve with a horizon value of $20,000. Although the *NPV* is smaller at every interest rate, it is still positive as long as the discount rate is less than 7.35 percent. Most analysts agree that the appropriate real social discount rate is less than 7.35 percent. (See Chapter 10.) Consequently, we can be reasonably confident that if the project goes ahead it will have a positive *NPV*.

Of course, we could also compute the *breakeven horizon value*—the horizon value at which the *NPV* equals zero. Assuming the appropriate discount rate is 7 percent, the project would break even if the present value of the horizon value were − $3,016 and, therefore, if the horizon value were −$4,230. This implies the city would just break even on the project if it *cost* $4,230 to dismantle the project at the end.

The Internal Rate of Return

The discount rate at which the *NPV* is zero is also called the *internal rate of return (IRR)*. The *IRR* of the library information system project is 8.9 percent, which implies that it is equivalent to a project of similar size that provides annual benefits equal to 8.9 percent of the original amount for five years (the length of the project) and returns all of the initial invested capital at the end of the fifth year.

The *IRR* can be used to express the decision rule for selecting projects *when there is only one alternative to the status quo*. If the *IRR* of a project is greater than the appropriate social discount rate, then one should proceed with the project; if the *IRR* is less than the appropriate social discount rate, then one should not proceed with it. In this example, the library should proceed with the project because the *IRR* of 8.9 percent is greater than the appropriate social discount rate of 7 percent. The basic idea, which we discuss in depth in Chapter 10, is that society should only invest in projects that earn a higher return than could be earned by investing the resources elsewhere. In other words, the appropriate discount rate should reflect the opportunity cost of the funds.

There are, however, a number of potential problems with using the *IRR* for decision making. First, it may not be unique; that is, there may be more than one discount rate at which the *NPV* is zero. This problem only arises when annual net benefits change more than once from positive to negative (or vice versa) during the discounting period. Second, *IRR*s are percentages (i.e., ratios), not dollar values. Therefore, they should not be used to select one project from a group of mutually exclusive projects that differ in size. This scale problem always arises with the use of ratios, including benefit-cost ratios, cost-effectiveness ratios, and *IRR*s. Nonetheless, if it is unique, the *IRR* conveys useful information to decision makers or other analysts who want to know how sensitive the results are to the discount rate.[35]

CONCLUSION

This chapter presents the main issues concerning the mechanics of discounting in CBA. It assumes that the appropriate discount rate is known. In fact, determination of the appropriate discount rate to use in CBA is a highly contentious issue, which we discuss in Chapter 10.

APPENDIX 6A

Shortcut Methods for Calculating the Present Value of Annuities and Perpetuities

In many practical situations the benefits or costs of a project can be treated as annuities or perpetuities. If so, there are some relatively easy ways to calculate the present values.

An *annuity* is an equal, fixed amount received (or paid) each year for a number of years. A *perpetuity* is an annuity that continues indefinitely. Suppose, for example, that in order to finance a new state highway, a state government issues $100 million worth of 30-year bonds with an interest rate of 7 percent paid annually. The annual interest payments of $70,000 are an annuity. If at the end of *each* 30-year period the state government refinances the debt by issuing another 30-year bond that also has an interest rate of 7 percent, then the annual interest payments of $70,000 would continue indefinitely, which is a perpetuity. Sometimes an annuity or perpetuity grows or declines at a constant rate. In any of these situations, using equation (6.6) or (6.7), the method described in the main body of this chapter to compute the present value, can be extremely time consuming. Fortunately, some simple formulas enable analysts to compute present values easily.

Present Value of an Annuity

The library information system problem contains two annuities: the annual benefits of $100,000 per year for five years, which we refer to as annuity A1, and the annual costs of $20,000 per year for five years, which we refer to as annuity A2. From Figure 6-4 we see that the present value of A1 is $410,020 and the present value of A2 is $82,004. But there is an easier way to obtain the present values.

Using equation (6.6), the present value of an annuity of A per annum (with payments received at the end of each year) for n years with interest at i percent is given by:

$$PV = \sum_{t=1}^{n} \frac{A}{(1+i)^t}$$

This is the sum of n terms of a geometric series with the common ratio equal to $1/(1+i)$. Consequently,

$$PV = Aa_i^n \tag{6A.1}$$

where

$$a_i^n = \frac{1-(1+i)^{-n}}{i} \tag{6A.2}$$

The term a_i^n, which equals the present value of an annuity of $1 per year for n years when the interest rate is i, is called an *annuity factor*. Tables of annuity factors are contained in most finance textbooks and are also built into many calculators and computer spreadsheets.

Returning to our library example, the present value of annuity A1 computed using equations (6A.1) and (6A.2) is:

$$PV(A1) = \$100,000 \times \frac{1-(1+0.07)^{-5}}{0.07}$$
$$PV(A1) = \$100,000 \times 4.1002$$
$$PV(A1) = \$410,020$$

Similarly,

$$PV(A2) = \$20,000 \times 4.1002 = \$82,004$$

Although this example dealt with only a five-year annuity, it is easy to compute the present value of annuities that extend over much longer periods.

When working with annuities it is important to get the timing of the cash flows exactly right. Equation (6A.1) assumes that the benefits or costs occur at the end of each period (year), with the first payment occurring one year from now. This type of annuity is called an *ordinary annuity*. Care is required when the annuity payments start immediately or when they begin more than one year from now.

An *annuity due* is an annuity with payments that occur at the beginning of each period (year). Many spreadsheets allow one to compute the present values of ordinary annuities and of annuities due. If the spreadsheet (or calculator) computes only ordinary annuities, then one can calculate the *PV* of an annuity due for *n* years by computing the *PV* of an ordinary annuity for *n*–1 years and adding the value of the initial payment or receipt made today.

A *deferred annuity* is an annuity whose first payment is deferred until after the first year. Suppose, for example, a government agency is considering refinancing some of its debt. Currently, it is scheduled to make debt payments of $150,000 per year for seven years with the first payment in three years. Assuming interest rates are 8 percent, what is the present value of this obligation? A time line for this problem is shown in Figure 6A-1. The first step is to treat the seven annual payments as an ordinary annuity and compute its present value using equations (6A.1) and (6A.2) or a calculator. The *PV* of the annuity is $780,956. The second and most important step is to recognize that this amount is the value of an ordinary annuity *in two years' time*—one year before the first payments. The third and final step is to discount the $780,956 back two years to obtain the present value of $669,543.

It is informative to note how the present value of an annuity varies with time and the interest rate. *The present value of an annuity decreases as the interest rate increases, and vice versa.* This is a partial explanation for why bond prices rise as interest rates fall, as they did in the United States between 1988 and 1993.

Another important observation is that when there is a relatively constant annuity stream, *annuity payments received after about the twentieth year add little to the present value when interest rates are 10 percent or higher.* Thus, private companies are often reluctant to make very long-term investments such as reforestation.

Present Value of a Perpetuity

A *perpetuity* is an annuity that continues indefinitely. Taking the limit of equation (6A.2) as *n* goes to infinity, the annuity factor reduces to 1/*i*, if *i* > 0. Consequently, the present value of an

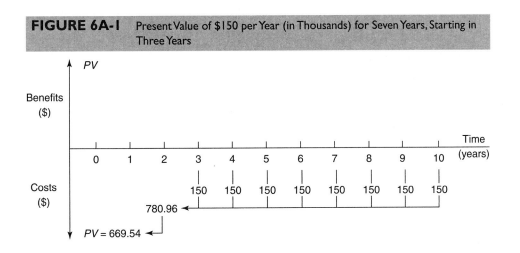

FIGURE 6A-1 Present Value of $150 per Year (in Thousands) for Seven Years, Starting in Three Years

amount, denoted by A, received (at the end of) each year in perpetuity is given by:

$$PV = \frac{A}{i} \quad \text{if } i > 0 \quad \textbf{(6A.3)}$$

To provide some intuition for this formula, suppose that a municipality has an endowment of $10 million. If interest rates are 6 percent, then this endowment will provide annual interest payments of $600,000 indefinitely. More generally, if the municipality has an endowment of X and if the interest rate is i, then the perpetual annual income from the endowment, denoted by A, is given by $A = iX$. Rearranging this equation, the present value of the perpetual annuity is given by $X = A/i$, which is equation (6A.3).

Equation (6A.3) is easy to apply. For example, the present value of a perpetuity of $150,000 per year when interest rates are 8 percent is:

$$PV = \frac{\$150,000}{0.08} = \$1,875,000$$

When interest rates are 10 percent, the present value of a perpetuity is especially easy to calculate: it simply equals the perpetuity multiplied by 10. For example, the present value of a perpetuity of $150,000 per year is $1,500,000 when interest rates are 10 percent.

The Present Value of an Annuity that Grows or Declines at a Constant Rate

Sometimes a project's benefits (or costs) grow at a constant rate. Let B_t denote the annual benefits in year t. If the annual benefits grow at a constant rate, g, then the benefits in year t will be:

$$B_t = B_{t-1}(1 + g) = B_1 (1 + g)^{t-1} \quad t = 2, \ldots, n \tag{6A.4}$$

Under these circumstances, and if $i > g$, then the present value of the total benefits—the stream over n years—can be shown to be:[1]

$$PV(B) = \frac{B_1}{(1 + g)} a^n_{i_0} \tag{6A.5}$$

where $a^n_{i_0}$ is defined by equation (6A.2) and:

$$i_0 = \frac{i - g}{1 + g} \tag{6A.6}$$

Comparing equation (6A.1) with (6A.5) shows that the PV of a benefit stream that starts at B_1 in year 1 and grows at a constant rate g for $n - 1$ additional years, when the interest rate is i, equals the PV of an annuity of $B_1/(1 + g)$ for n years when the interest rate is i_0, where i_0 is given by equation (6A.6).

To illustrate how to calculate the present value of a stream of benefits that grows at a constant rate, return again to the library example. Suppose we now assume that, due to increased use, annual benefits grow at 2 percent per annum *after the first year* (and, as before, $i = 0.07$). From equation (6A.5), the present value of the stream of benefits equals the present value of an annuity of $100,000/1.02 = $98,039 per annum for five years, discounted at the following rate:

$$i_0 = \frac{i - g}{1 + g} = \frac{0.07 - 0.02}{1.02} = 0.049$$

which amounts to $425,636.[2] In contrast, when the annual benefits are constant ($100,000), the present value equals $410,020, a difference of $15,614. This increase would be carried straight to the bottom line because the NPV would also increase by $15,614; in fact, the NPV almost doubles from $17,276 to $32,890. This example illustrates that even quite small growth rates can have large impacts on NPVs.

If the growth rate is small, then $B_1/(1 + g) \cong B_1$ and $i_0 \cong i - g$. Therefore, from equation (6A.5), the present value of a benefits stream that starts at B_1 and grows at rate g for $n-1$ additional years approximately equals the present value of an annuity of B_1 for n years discounted at rate $i - g$. This approximation makes it clear that when benefits grow at a positive rate, the annuity is discounted at a lower rate, which will yield a higher *PV*. On the other hand, if the benefits are declining at a constant rate, then the annuity is discounted at a higher rate, which will yield a lower *PV*.

To illustrate this approximation, note that the present value of a stream of benefits that starts at $100,000 per year and grows at 2 percent per annum for four additional years with $i = 0.07$ is approximately equal to the present value of an annuity of $100,000 per year for five years discounted at $i - g = 5$ percent, which equals $432,948.[3] This value is slightly higher than the correct amount of $425,634, but it is within 2 percent of the right answer and it is easier to calculate.

Equation (6A.5) only holds if the interest rate exceeds the growth rate: $i > g$. If $i \leq g$, then it should not be used. Importantly, though, it can always be used if g is negative, that is, if benefits decline at a constant rate. Of course, equation (6A.5) pertains to costs that change at a constant rate as well as to benefits that change at a constant rate.

Present Value of Benefits (or Costs) that Grow or Decline at a Constant Rate in Perpetuity

If the initial benefits, B_1, grow indefinitely at a constant rate g and if the interest rate equals i, then the *PV* of the benefits is found by taking the limit of equation (6A.5) as n goes to infinity, which gives:

$$PV(B) = \frac{B_1}{i - g} \quad \text{if } i > g \qquad \textbf{(6A.7)}$$

Some finance students may recognize this model as the Gordon growth model, which is also called the dividend growth model. This model can be used to value a stock that yields a constant flow of dividends that grow at a constant rate.[4] As before, this formula holds only if $i > g$.

EXERCISES FOR CHAPTER 6

1. A highway department is considering building a temporary bridge to cut travel time during the three years it will take to build a permanent bridge. The temporary bridge can be put up in a few weeks at a cost of $740,000. At the end of three years, it would be removed and the steel would be sold for scrap. The real net *costs* of this would be $81,000. Based on estimated time savings and wage rates, fuel savings, and reductions in risks of accidents, department analysts predict that the benefits in real dollars would be $275,000 during the first year, $295,000 during the second year, and $315,000 during the third year. Departmental regulations require use of a real discount rate of 5 percent.
   a. Calculate the present value of net benefits assuming that the benefits are realized at the end of each of the three years.
   b. Calculate the present value of net benefits assuming that the benefits are realized at the beginning of each of the three years.
   c. Calculate the present value of net benefits assuming that the benefits are realized in the middle of each of the three years.
   d. Calculate the present value of net benefits assuming that half of each year's benefits are realized at the beginning of the year and the other half at the end of the year.
   e. Does the temporary bridge pass the net benefits test?
2. A government data processing center has been plagued in recent years by complaints from employees of back pain. Consultants have estimated that upgrading office furniture at a net cost of $425,000 would reduce the incidence and severity of back injuries each year, allowing the center to avoid medical care that currently costs $68,000 each year. They estimate that the new furniture would also provide yearly benefits of avoided losses in work time and employee comfort worth $18,000. The furniture would have a useful life of five years, after

which it would have a positive salvage value equal to 10 percent of its initial net cost. The consultants made their estimates of avoided costs assuming that they would be treated as occurring at the beginning of each year.

In its investment decisions, the center uses a nominal discount rate of 9.5 percent and an assumed general inflation rate of 3 percent. It expects the inflation rate for medical care will run between 3 and 5 percent but is uncertain as to the exact rate. In other words, it is uncertain as to whether the cost of medical care will inflate at the same rate as other prices or rise 2 percent faster. Should the center purchase the new furniture?

3. A town's recreation department is trying to decide how to use a piece of land. One option is to put up basketball courts with an expected life of 8 years. Another is to install a swimming pool with an expected life of 24 years. The basketball courts would cost $180,000 to construct and yield net benefits of $40,000 at the end of each of the 8 years. The swimming pool would cost $2.25 million to construct and yield net benefits of $170,000 at the end of each of the 24 years. Each project is assumed to have zero salvage value at the end of its life. Using a real discount rate of 4 percent, which project offers larger net benefits?

4. The environmental protection agency of a county would like to preserve a piece of land as a wilderness area. The current owner has offered to lease the land to the county for 20 years in return for a lump-sum payment of $1.1 million, which would be paid at the beginning of the 20-year period. The agency has estimated that the land would generate $110,000 per year in benefits to hunters, bird watchers, and hikers. Assume that the lease price represents the social opportunity cost of the land and that the appropriate real discount rate is 5 percent.

   a. Assuming that the yearly benefits, which are measured in real dollars, accrue at the end of each of the 20 years, calculate the net benefits of leasing the land.

   b. Some analysts in the agency argue that the annual real benefits are likely to grow at a rate of 2 percent per year due to increasing population and county income. Recalculate the net benefits assuming that they are correct.

5. Imagine that the current owner of the land in the previous exercise was willing to sell the land for $2 million. Assuming this amount equaled the social opportunity cost of the land, calculate the net benefits if the county were to purchase the land as a permanent wildlife refuge. In making these calculations, first assume a zero annual growth rate in the $110,000 of annual real benefits; then assume that these benefits grow at a rate of 2 percent per year.

6. (Spreadsheet required.) New City is considering building a recreation center. The estimated construction cost is $12 million with annual staffing and maintenance costs of $750,000 over the 20-year life of the project. At the end of the life of the project, New City expects to be able to sell the land for $4 million, though the amount could be as low as $2 million and as high as $5 million. Analysts estimate the first-year benefits (accruing at the end of the year of the first year) to be $1.2 million. They expect the annual benefit to grow in real terms due to increases in population and income. Their prediction is a growth rate of 4 percent, but it could be as low as 1 percent and as high as 6 percent. Analysts estimate the real discount rate for New City to be 6 percent, though they acknowledge that it could be a percentage point higher or lower.

   a. Calculate the present value of net benefits for the project using the analysts' predictions.

   b. Investigate the sensitivity of the present value of net benefits to alternative predictions within the ranges given by the analysts.

NOTES

1. Parts of this chapter draw on Anthony E. Boardman and David H. Greenberg, "Discounting and the Social Discount Rate," in Fred Thompson and Mark T. Green, eds., *Handbook of Public Finance* (New York: Marcel Dekker, 1998), 269–318.

2. T-bill is an abbreviation of Treasury bill. A T-bill is a short-term bond issued by the Treasury

Department of the U.S. government. Usually, the minimum size is $100,000. A T-bill yields an interest rate that is slightly higher than the rate of interest offered by banks on personal savings accounts. Some banks offer a "T-bill account," which enables customers with less than $100,000 (but more than some specified minimum) to earn almost the same rate as that given on T-bills.

3. $PV = \$10,280,374/1.07 = \$10,000,000$.

4. The following equation summarizes the relationship between discounting and compounding for projects of one year's duration:

$$PV = \frac{FV}{1+i}$$

where PV is the present value and FV is the future value.

5. Consider the future value in two years. At the end of the first year, one would have $FV = X(1+i)$. At the end of the second year, one would have $FV = [X(1+i)](1+i) = X(1+I)^2$, and so on.

6. One should be aware, however, that different sources may give slightly different answers due to rounding error. For example, the more accurate answer to the foregoing question, without rounding, is $13,107,960. In practice, rounding errors are not material. In cases when a table or calculator is unavailable, there is a handy rule for computing approximate future values called the "rule of 72." Capital roughly doubles when the interest rate (expressed in percentage points) times the number of years equals seventy two: $100 \times i \times n = 72$. For example, if the interest rate is 8 percent, then your capital doubles in $72/8 = 9$ years. Similarly, in order to double your capital in 10 years, you need an interest rate of at least $72/10 = 7.2$ percent.

7. $$NPV = \sum_{t=0}^{n} \frac{B_i}{(1+i)^t} - \sum_{t=0}^{n} \frac{C_t}{(1+i)^t}$$
$$= \sum_{t=0}^{n} \frac{B_t - C_t}{(1+i)^t} = \sum_{t=0}^{n} \frac{NB_t}{(1+i)^t}$$

8. If interest is compounded continuously, then the present value of $\$Y$ received in n years time with interest rate i is given by:

$$PV = \frac{Y}{e^{in}}$$

where, $e = \lim_{n\to\infty}\left(1 + \frac{1}{n}\right)^n$ is the base of the natural logarithm, which equals 2.71828 to five decimal places. For example, the present value of $100,000 received in five years with interest at 7 percent, compounded continuously, is:

$$PV = \frac{\$100,000}{e^{0.07\times5}} = \frac{\$100,000}{1.419} = \$70,469$$

9. Comparing equations (6.11) with equation (6.9) implies:

$$PV(H_k) = NPV - \sum_{t=0}^{k} \frac{NB_t}{(1+i)^t} = \sum_{t=k+1}^{n} \frac{NB_t}{(1+i)^t}$$

10. For example,

$$NPV = \sum_{t=0}^{20} \frac{NB_t}{(1+i)^t} + PV(H_{20})$$
$$= \sum_{t=0}^{30} \frac{NB_t}{(1+i)^t} + PV(H_{30})$$

11. Barbara M. Fraumeni, "The Measurement of Depreciation in the U.S. National Income and Product Accounts," *Survey of Current Business* 77(7) 1997, 7–23. This article extends Charles R. Hulten, "The Measurement of Capital," in Ernst R. Berndt and Jack E. Triplett, eds., *Fifty Years of Economic Measurement: The Jubilee of the Conference on Research in Income and Wealth* (Chicago, IL: The University of Chicago Press, 1990), 119–152.

12. This is the value 20 years after the highway was completed, which was 21.5 years after the decision to build the highway in 1986. Consequently, according to the method, the present value of the horizon value was $53.3 million.

13. If project A were two-thirds the length of project B, then the analyst should compare three project As back-to-back with two project Bs back-to-back.

14. The difference between the *NPV* of five back-to-back cogeneration plants and the *NPV* of only one cogeneration plant is $10.94 million.

In effect, we would have arrived at the same figure if we had evaluated building only one cogeneration plant, but assigned a horizon value with a present value of $10.94 million to this project.

15. The annuity factor for the hydroelectric project is the present value of an annuity of $1 per year for 75 years using an interest rate of 8 percent which, using equation (6A.2) or a calculator, equals 12.461. Similarly, the annuity factor for the cogeneration project equals the present value of $1 per annum for 15 years at an interest rate of 10 percent.

16. The most recent CPI figures for the United States as well as CPI figures back to 1913 are available from the Bureau of Labor Statistics at its Web site: *www.bls.gov*. The most recent CPI figures for Canada are available from Statistics Canada at its Web site *www.statcan.ca*. For long-term historical Canadian data, see F. H. Leacy, ed., *Historical Statistics of Canada* (Ottawa, Ontario: Statistics Canada, 1983).

17. See Michael J. Boskin, Ellen R. Dulberger, Robert J. Gordon, Zvi Griliches, and Dale W. Jorgenson, *Toward a More Accurate Measure of the Cost of Living*, Final Report to the Senate Finance Committee from the Advisory Committee to Study the Consumer Price Index (Washington, D.C.: Senate Finance Committee, 1996). In Canada, the CPI was overestimated by about 0.7 percentage points per annum.

18. For more detail see Brent R. Moulton, "Bias in the Consumer Price Index: What Is the Evidence?" *Journal of Economic Perspectives* 10(4) 1996, 159–177; and Allan Crawford, "Measurement Biases in the Canadian CPI: An Update," *Bank of Canada Review* Spring 1998, 39–56.

19. For practical reasons the CPI is a Laspeyres index, which uses the quantities of each good consumed in a previous period to compute expenditures in the current period.

20. See Zvi Griliches and Iain Cockburn, "Generics and New Goods in Pharmaceutical Price Indexes," *American Economic Review* 84(5) 1994, 1213–1232.

21. For more information about the CPI revisions see *www.bls.gov/cpi/*.

22. See Allan Crawford, "Measurement Biases in the Canadian CPI: An Update."

23. Recall that the *NPV* for a project is given by equation (6.8), and suppose that these benefits,

B_t, and costs, C_t, are in nominal dollars and i is the nominal interest rate. Let b_t denote real benefits, c_t denote real costs, and suppose the rate of inflation is m, then, using equation (6.4), $B_t = b_t(1 + m)^t$ and $C_t = c_t(1 + m)^t$. Consequently,

$$NPV = \sum_{t=0}^{n} \frac{B_t - C_t}{(1+i)^t} = \sum_{t=0}^{n} \frac{(b_t - c_t)(1+m)^t}{(1+i)^t}$$

Now, to simplify, set $1/(1 + r) = (1 + m)/(1 + i)$, which gives:

$$NPV = \sum_{t=0}^{n} \frac{b_t - c_t}{(1+r)^t}$$

As we discuss later, we can interpret r as the real interest rate.

24. The expected CPI in t periods in the future equals $(1 + m)^t$ times the current CPI. Therefore, dividing the future amounts measured in nominal dollars by $(1 + m)^t$, in accordance with equation (6.5), is exactly the same as the method implied at the end of the previous section for converting amounts expressed in year b dollars into amounts expressed in year a dollars, namely, dividing by the expected CPI in t periods in the future and multiplying by the CPI for the current year.

25. This relationship is known as the Fisher effect. For derivation of this expression, note that $1 invested today at a nominal interest rate of i yields $(1 + i)$ one year later. However, with an inflation rate of m during the year, $(1 + i)$ one year from now buys only as much as $(1 + i)/(1 + m)$ does today. The real interest rate, r, is therefore defined by $(1 + r) = (1 + i)/(1 + m)$. Rearranging this expression, gives equation (6.13).

Alternatively, suppose that we invest $1 for a year, the real rate of return is r and the rate of inflation during the year is m, then the we would have $(1 + r)(1 + m)$ in a year. Thus, the nominal rate of return i is:

$$i = (1 + r)(1 + m) - 1, \text{ or}$$
$$(1 + i) = (1 + r)(1 + m)$$

Rearranging this expression also gives equation (6.13).

26. An alternative procedure draws on the Fisher model and assumes the real yield on bonds of a particular duration is constant over time. Specifically, this estimate of expected inflation during the life of the project equals the current yield on bonds that have the same term as the project minus the historical real yield on bonds of this term. For example, if the life of the project is 20 years, if the yield on bonds that mature in 20 years is currently 10 percent, and if 20-year bonds typically yield a real return of 2 percent, then the expected annual rate of inflation over this period is about 8 percent. If the life of the project is only 3 years, if the yield on bonds that mature in 3 years is 9 percent, and if the historical real yield on bonds that mature in 3 years is 1.5 percent, then the expected annual rate of inflation over the next 3 years is about 7.5 percent. Notice that in this example, the market expects inflation will be higher in years 4 through 20 than in the first three years. For historical nominal and real returns on stocks, corporate bonds, government bonds, and Treasury bills, see Ibbotson Associates, *Stocks, Bonds and Inflation: 1989 Yearbook* (Chicago: Ibbotson Associates, 1989), and their more recent publications.

27. For more information about the Livingston survey and the SPF see the Web site of the Federal Reserve Bank of Philadelphia at *www.phil.frb.org*. For more information about the Michigan survey of households see the Institute for Social Research's Survey of Consumer Attitudes Web site at *www.isr.umich.edu*.

28. Lloyd B. Thomas Jr., "Survey Measures of Expected U.S. Inflation," *Journal of Economic Perspectives* 13(4) 1999, 125–144.

29. From equation (6.13), $r = (0.10 - 0.04)/(1 + 0.04) = 5.77$ percent. More accurately, the real discount rate is 5.769231 percent, which is the rate used in the *NPV* calculations in this example in order to ensure that the results for the real and nominal methods are identical.

30. An initial study was prepared by the government of British Columbia, "A Benefit-Cost Analysis of the North East Coal Development," (Victoria, B. C.: Ministry of Industry and Small Business, 1982). Subsequent analysis was conducted by W. G. Waters II, "A Reanalysis of the North East Coal Development" (working paper, University of British Columbia, undated).

31. The initial study made shadow price adjustments for foreign exchange earnings. These are excluded from Table 6-5 because, according to Bill Waters, the author of the reanalysis, they are probably inappropriate.

32. Like many studies, this study ignores the marginal excess tax burden.

33. This scenario of declining prices and declining quantities sold is quite plausible for this project. The major Japanese customers were simultaneously encouraging development of Australian and other sources. If these alternative sources came online at the same time, there would be a worldwide excess supply, internationally determined coal prices would fall, and demand for B.C. coal would fall.

34. By definition, the breakeven discount rate can be found by setting the left-hand side of equations (6.8) or (6.9) equal to zero and solving for *i*. In practice, this can be quite difficult. Usually, trial and error is a lot easier. Spreadsheet programs allow trial and error to be done quite easily.

35. If expenditures equal social costs and if the total amount of expenditures is constrained, then ranking projects on the basis of the *IRR* criterion may maximize the total *NPV*s. For example, if three projects cost a *total* of $1 billion and, in addition, each has a higher *IRR* than a fourth project that costs $1 billion by itself, then the first three projects will also have a larger *combined NPV* than the *NPV* of the fourth project. In effect, the *IRR* provides an estimate of the average annual net benefit per unit of (constrained) expenditure. Problems with ranking project in terms of their *IRR*s only arise when the total expenditure on the projects with the highest *IRR*s does not exactly equal the total amount available. Even if the first, second, and third projects have higher *IRR*s than the fourth project, the fourth project *may* still have a higher *NPV* than the three smaller projects combined if its total cost is larger (but still no more than $1 billion). In any constrained project choice setting, the optimal set of projects can always be found by using linear programming.

APPENDIX NOTES

1. $PV(B) = \sum_{t=1}^{n} \dfrac{B_1(1 + g)^{t-1}}{(1 + i)^t} = \sum_{t=1}^{n} \dfrac{B_1}{(1 + g)}\left(\dfrac{1 + g}{1 + i}\right)^t$

Setting $i_0 = (i - g)/(1 + g)$ implies $1/(1 + i_0) = (1 + g)/(1 + i)$. Therefore,

$PV(B) = \sum_{t=1}^{n} \dfrac{B_1}{(1 + g)}\left(\dfrac{1}{(1 + i_0)^t}\right) = \dfrac{B_1}{(1 + g)}\, a_{\overline{i_0}}^{n}$

2. Alternatively, substituting equation (6A.2) into equation (6A.5) gives the following formula for computing the *PV* of the benefits:

$PV(B) = \dfrac{B_1}{(1 + g)}\left(\dfrac{1-(1 + i_0)^{-n}}{i_0}\right)$

Therefore, for this example:

$PV(B) = \dfrac{\$100,000}{(1 + 0.02)} \times \dfrac{1 - (1 - 0.049)^{-5}}{0.049}$

$= \$98,039 \times 4.3415 = \$425,636$

3. That is:

$PV(B) = \sum_{t=1}^{n} \dfrac{B_1}{(1 + i - g)^t} = \sum_{t=1}^{5} \dfrac{\$100,000}{(1 + 0.07 - 0.05)^t}$

$= \$432,948$

4. See M. Gordon, *The Investment, Financing and Valuation of the Corporation* (Homewood, IL: Richard D. Irwin, 1962), 46–47.

CHAPTER 7

Dealing with Uncertainty: Expected Values, Sensitivity Analysis, and the Value of Information

Cost-benefit analysis often requires us to predict the future. Whether it is desirable to begin a project depends on what we expect will happen after we have begun. But, as mere mortals, we rarely are able to make precise predictions about the future. Indeed, in many situations analysts can be certain that circumstances largely beyond their clients' control, such as epidemics, floods, bumper crops, or fluctuations in international oil prices, will greatly affect the benefits and costs that would be realized from proposed policies. How can analysts reasonably take account of these uncertainties in CBA?

In this chapter, we consider three topics relevant to uncertainty: *expected value* as a measure reflecting risks, *sensitivity analysis* as a way of investigating the robustness of net benefit estimates to different resolutions of uncertainty, and the *value of information* as a benefit category for CBA and as a guide for allocating analytical effort. Expected values take account of the dependence of benefits and costs on the occurrence of specific contingencies, or "states of the world" to which analysts are able to assign probabilities of occurrence. Sensitivity analysis is a way of acknowledging uncertainty about the values of important parameters in our predictions—it should be a component of almost any CBA. When analysts have opportunities for gaining additional information about costs or benefits, they may be able to value the information by explicitly modeling the uncertainty inherent in their decisions. A particular type of information value, called *quasi-option value*, is relevant when assessing currently available alternatives that have different implications for learning about the future.

EXPECTED VALUE ANALYSIS

One can imagine several types of uncertainty about the future. At the most profound level, one might not be able to specify the full range of relevant circumstances that may occur. Indeed, the human and natural worlds are so complex that one cannot hope to anticipate every possible future circumstance. Yet, in many situations of relevance to one's daily life and public policy, it is reasonable to characterize the future in terms of a number of distinct contingencies. For example, in deciding whether to take an umbrella to work, one might reasonably divide the future into two contingencies: Either it will or will not rain sufficiently to make the umbrella useful. Of course, other relevant contingencies can be imagined as well—it will be a dry day, but one may or may not be the victim of an attempted mugging in which the umbrella would prove valuable in self-defense! Yet if these additional contingencies are very unlikely, it is often reasonable to leave them out of one's model of the future. Modeling the future as a set of relevant contingencies involves yet another narrowing of uncertainty: How likely are each of the contingencies? If one is willing to assign probabilities of occurrence to each of the contingencies, then uncertainty about the future becomes a problem of dealing with risk. In relatively simple situations, risk can be readily incorporated into CBA through expected value analysis.

Contingencies and Their Probabilities

Modeling uncertainty as risk begins with the specification of a set of *contingencies* that, within the simplified model of the world being employed, are *exhaustive* and *mutually exclusive*. Contingencies can be thought of as possible events, outcomes, or states of the world such that one and only one of the relevant set of possibilities will actually occur. What makes a set of contingencies the basis of an appropriate model for conducting a CBA of a policy?

One important consideration is that the contingencies capture the full range of likely variation in net benefits of the policy. For example, in evaluating an oil stockpile for use in the event of an oil price shock sometime in the future, one would want to consider at least two contingencies: There never will be an oil price shock (a situation in which the policy is likely to result in net losses), and there will be a major price shock (a situation in which the policy is likely to result in net gains).

Another consideration is how well the contingencies represent the possible outcomes between the extremes. In some circumstances, the possible contingencies can be listed exhaustively so that they are fully representative. More often, however, they sample an infinite number of possibilities. In these circumstances, each contingency can be thought of as a *scenario*, which is just a description of a possible future. Do the specified contingencies provide a sufficient variety of scenarios to convey the possible futures adequately? If so, then the contingencies are representative.

Figure 7-1 illustrates the representation of a continuous scale with discrete contingencies. The horizontal axis gives the number of inches of summer rainfall in an agricultural region. The vertical axis gives the net benefits of a water storage system, which increase as the amount of rainfall decreases. Imagine that an analyst represents uncertainty about rainfall with only two contingencies: "excessive" and "deficient." The excessive contingency assumes 22 inches of rainfall, which would yield zero net benefits from the storage system. The deficient contingency assumes zero inches of rainfall, which would yield $4.4 million in net benefits. If the relationship between rainfall and net benefits follows the straight line labeled *A*, and all the rainfall amounts between 0 and 22 are equally likely, then the average of net benefits over the full continuous range would be $2.2 million. If the analyst assumed that each of the contingencies were equally likely, then the average over the two contingencies would also be $2.2 million, so that using two scenarios would be adequately representative.[1]

Now imagine that the net benefits follow the curved line labeled *B*. Again assuming that all rainfall amounts between 0 and 22 inches are equally likely, the average of net benefits over the full continuous range would only be about $1.1 million, so that using only two contingencies would grossly overestimate the average net benefits from the storage system.[2] Adding "normal" as a contingency that assumes 11 inches of rainfall and averaging net benefits over all three contingencies yields net benefits of $1.6 million, which is more

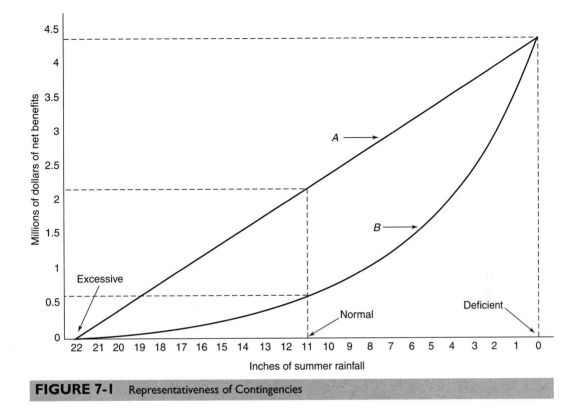

FIGURE 7-1 Representativeness of Contingencies

representative than the average calculated with two contingencies but still considerably larger than the $1.1 million calculated over the full continuous range. Even more contingencies are desirable. For example, moving to five equally spaced contingencies gives an average of $1.3 million, which is much closer to the average over the continuous range.[3]

Once we have specified a tractable but representative set of contingencies, the next task is to assign probabilities of occurrence to each of them. To be consistent with the logical requirement that the contingencies taken together are exhaustive and mutually exclusive, the probabilities that we assign must each be nonnegative and sum to exactly 1. Thus, if there are three contingencies, C_1, C_2, and C_3, we must assign corresponding probabilities p_1, p_2, and p_3 such that $p_1 + p_2 + p_3 = 1$.

The probabilities may be based solely on historically observed frequencies; on subjective assessments by clients, analysts, or other experts based on a variety of information and theory; or on both. For example, return to the contingencies in Figure 7-1: agriculturally "excessive," "normal," and "deficient" precipitation in a river valley for which a water storage system has been proposed. The national weather service may be able to provide data on average annual rainfall over the last century that allows an analyst to estimate the probabilities of the three levels of precipitation from their historical frequencies. If such data were not available, then the analyst would have to base the probabilities on expert opinion, comparison with similar valleys in the region for which

---

EXHIBIT 7-1

Being explicit about contingencies, their probabilities, and their consequences can help structure complex decision problems. Consider the following letter that President Abraham Lincoln wrote to Major General George B. McClellan on February 3, 1862:

My dear Sir:

You and I have distinct, and different plans for a movement of the Army of the Potomac—yours to be down the Chesapeake, up the Rappahannock to Urbana, and across land to the terminus of the Railroad on the York River—, mine to move directly to a point on the Railroad South West of Manassas.

If you will give me satisfactory answers to the following questions, I shall gladly yield my plan to yours.

First. Does not your plan involve a greatly larger expenditure of time and money than mine?

Second. Wherein is a victory more certain by your plan than mine?

Third. Wherein is a victory more valuable by your plan than mine?

Fourth. In fact, would it not be less valuable, in this, that it would break no great line of the enemy's communications, while mine would?

Fifth. In case of disaster, would not a safe retreat be more difficult by your plan than by mine?

Yours truly, Abraham Lincoln

Source: John G. Nicolay and John Hay, eds., *Abraham Lincoln: Complete Works, Volume Two* (New York: The Century Company, 1894), 120.

---

data are available, or some other subjective assessment. As such subjective assessments are rarely made with great confidence, it is especially important to investigate the sensitivity of the results to the particular probabilities chosen.

Calculating the Expected Value of Net Benefits

The specification of contingencies and their respective probabilities allows us to calculate the *expected net benefits* of a policy. We do so by first predicting the net benefits of the policy under each contingency and then taking the weighted average of these net benefits over all the contingencies, where the weights are the respective probabilities that the contingencies occur. Specifically, for n contingencies, let B_i be the benefits under contingency i, C_i be the costs under contingency i, and p_i be the probability of contingency i occurring. Then the expected net benefits, $E[NB]$, are given by the formula:

$$E[NB] = p_i\,(B_i - C_i) + \ldots + p_n\,(B_n - C_n) \tag{7.1}$$

which is just the expected value of net benefits over the n possible outcomes.[4]

When facing complicated risk problems, analysts often find it useful to model them as *games against nature*. A game against nature assumes that nature will randomly, and nonstrategically, select a particular state of the world. The random selection of a state of the world is according to assumed probabilities. The selection is nonstrategic in the sense that nature does not alter the probabilities of the states of the world in response to the action selected by the analysts. A game against nature in *normal form* has the following elements: *states of nature* and their *probabilities of occurrence*, *actions* available to the decision maker facing nature, and *payoffs* to the decision maker under each combination of state of nature and action.

EXHIBIT 7-2

In their evaluation of alternative government oil stockpiling programs in the early 1980s, Glen Sweetnam and colleagues at the U.S. Department of Energy modeled the uncertainty surrounding oil market conditions with five contingencies: *slack market*—oil purchases for the U.S. stockpile of up to 1.5 million barrels per day (mmb/d) could be made without affecting the world oil price; *tight market*—oil purchases increase the world price at the rate of $3.60 per mmb/d; *minor disruption*—loss of 1.5 mmb/d to the world market (e.g., caused by a revolution in an oil-exporting country); *moderate disruption*—loss of 6.0 mmb/d to the world market (e.g., caused by a limited war in the Persian Gulf); *major disruption*—loss of 12.0 mmb/d to the world market (e.g., caused by a major war in the Persian Gulf). For each of the 24 years of their planning horizon, they assumed that the probabilities of each of the contingencies occurring depended only on the contingency that occurred in the previous year. For each year, they calculated the social surplus in the U.S. oil market conditional on each of the five market contingencies and change in the size of the stockpile.

The model they constructed allowed them to answer the following questions: For any current market condition and stockpile size, what change in stockpile size maximizes the present value of expected net benefits? How much storage capacity should be constructed? How fast should it be added? The model and the answers it provided were influential in policy debates concerning expansion of the U.S. stockpile, the Strategic Petroleum Reserve.

Sources: Adapted from Glen Sweetnam, "Stockpile Policies for Coping with Oil-Supply Disruptions," in George Horwich and Edward J. Mitchell, eds., *Policies for Coping with Oil-Supply Disruptions* (Washington, D.C.: American Enterprise Institute for Public Policy Research, 1982), 82–96. On the role of the model in the policy-making process, see Hank C. Jenkins-Smith and David L. Weimer, "Analysis as Retrograde Action: The Case of Strategic Petroleum Reserves," *Public Administration Review* 45(4) 1985, 485–494.

Table 7-1 shows the analysis of alternatives for planetary defense against asteroid collisions as a game against nature in normal form. It considers three possible states of nature over the next 100 years: exposure of Earth to collision with an asteroid larger than one kilometer in diameter, which would have enough kinetic energy to have severe regional or even global effects on society (10 on the Torino Scale); exposure of Earth to collision with an asteroid smaller than one kilometer but larger than 20 meters in diameter, which would have severe local or regional effects on society (8 or 9 on the Torino Scale); and no exposure of Earth to an asteroid larger than 20 meters in diameter. The game shows three actions: build a forward-based asteroid defense, which would station nuclear devices sufficiently deep in space to give a good possibility of their timely use in diverting asteroids from collision courses with Earth; build a near-Earth asteroid defense, which would be less expensive but not as effective as the forward-based defense; and build no asteroid defense.

Although actually estimating the payoffs for this game would be a monumental and controversial analytical task, Table 7-1 displays some hypothetical figures. The payoffs, shown as the present value of net costs over the next century, range from $30 trillion (Earth is exposed to a collision with an asteroid larger than one kilometer in diameter in the absence of any asteroid defense) to $0 (Earth is not exposed to collision with an asteroid larger than 20 meters and no defense system is built). Note that

TABLE 7-1 A Game against Nature: Expected Values of Asteroid Defense Alternatives

State of Nature	Exposure to a Collision with an Asteroid Larger Than One Kilometer in Diameter	Exposure to a Collision with an Asteroid between 20 Meters and 1 Kilometer in Diameter	No Exposure to Collision with an Asteroid Larger Than 20 Meters in Diameter	
Probabilities of states of nature (over next century)	.001	.004	.995	
Actions (alternatives)	Payoffs (net costs in billions of 2000 dollars)			Expected Value
Forward-based asteroid defense	5,060	1,060	60	69
Near-Earth asteroid defense	10,020	2,020	20	**38**
No asteroid defense	30,000	6,000	0	54

Choose near-Earth asteroid defense: Expected net cost = $38 billion.

estimating the costs of a collision between Earth and an asteroid would itself involve expected value calculations that take account of size, composition, and point of impact of the asteroid. The $30 trillion figure is a bit larger than the world's annual sum of gross domestic products.

The last column of Table 7-1 shows expected values for each of the three alternatives. The expected value for each alternative is calculated by summing the products of its payoff conditional on states of nature with the probabilities of those states. For example, the expected value of payoffs (present value of net costs) for no asteroid defense is:

$$(0.001)(\$30,000 \text{ billion}) + (0.004)(\$6,000 \text{ billion}) + (0.995)(\$0) = \$54 \text{ billion}$$

Similar calculations yield $69 billion for forward-based asteroid defense and $38 billion for near-Earth asteroid defense. As the maximization of expected net benefits is equivalent to minimizing expected net costs, the most efficient alternative is near-Earth asteroid defense. Alternatively, one could think of near-Earth asteroid defense as offering expected net benefits of $16 billion relative to no defense ($54 billion in expected net costs minus $38 billion in expected net costs equals $16 billion in expected net benefits), while forward-based asteroid defense offers negative $15 billion in expected net benefits relative to no defense ($54 billion in expected net costs minus $69 billion in expected net costs equals negative $15 billion in expected net benefits).

In CBA, it is common practice to treat expected values as if they were certain amounts. For example, imagine that a perfect asteroid defense system would have a present value cost of $100 billion under each of the states of nature. In this case, assuming accurate prediction of costs, the $100 billion *would be certain* because it does not depend on which state of nature actually results. CBA generally treats a certain amount such as this as fully commensurate with expected values, even though the latter will not actually result in its expected value. In other words, although the expected net cost of no asteroid defense is $54 billion, assuming an accurate prediction of payoffs, the actually realized net cost will be $30 trillion, $6 trillion, or $0. If the perfect defense system cost $54 billion, then CBA would rank it and no defense as equally efficient.

Treating expected values as if they were certain amounts implies that the person making the comparison has preferences that are *risk neutral*. A person has risk neutral preferences when he or she is indifferent between certain amounts and lotteries with the same expected payoff. A person is *risk averse* if he or she prefers the certain amount and is *risk seeking* if he or she prefers the lottery. Buying insurance, which offers a lower expected payoff than the certain premium charged, indicates risk aversion; buying a lottery ticket, which offers a lower expected value than its price, indicates risk seeking.

Chapter 8 considers the appropriateness of treating expected values and certain equivalents as commensurate (e.g., risk neutrality). It explains that doing so is not conceptually correct in measuring willingness-to-pay in circumstances in which individuals face uncertainty. Nevertheless, it argues that, in practice, *treating expected values and certain amounts as commensurate is generally reasonable when either the pooling of risk over the collection of policies, or the pooling of risk over the collection of persons affected by a policy, will make the actually realized values of costs and benefits close to their expected values.* For example, a policy that affects the probability of highway accidents involves reasonable pooling of risk across many drivers (some will have accidents, others will not) so that realized values will be close to expected values. In contrast, a policy that affects the risk of asteroid collision does not involve pooling across individuals (either everyone suffers from the global harm if there is a collision or no one does if there is no collision), so that the realized value of costs may be very far from their expected value. As discussed in Chapter 8, such unpooled risk may require an adjustment to expected benefits called *option value.*

Decision Trees and Expected Net Benefits

The basic procedure for expected value analysis, taking weighted averages over contingencies, can be directly extended to situations in which costs and benefits accrue over multiple years, as long as the risks in each year are independent of the realizations of risks in previous years. Consider, for example, a CBA of a dam with a 20-year life. Assume that the costs and benefits of the dam depend only on the contingencies of below-average rainfall and above-average rainfall in the current year. Additionally, if the analyst is willing to make the plausible assumption that the amount of rainfall in any year does not depend on the rainfall in previous years, then the analyst can simply calculate the present value of expected net benefits for each year and calculate the present value of this stream of net benefits in the usual way.

The basic expected value procedure cannot be so directly applied when either the net benefits accruing under contingencies or the probabilities of the contingencies depend on the contingencies that have previously occurred. For example, above-average rainfall in one year may make the irrigation benefits of a dam less in the next year because of accumulated ground water. In the case of a policy to reduce the costs of earthquakes, the probability of a major earthquake may change each year depending on the mix of earthquakes that occurred in the previous year.

Such situations require a more flexible framework for handling risk than basic expected value analysis. *Decision analysis* provides the needed framework.[5] Though it takes us too far afield to present decision analysis in any depth here, we sketch its general approach and present simple illustrations that demonstrate its usefulness in CBA. A number of book-length treatments of decision analysis are available for those who wish to pursue this topic in more depth.[6]

Decision analysis can be thought of as a *sequential, or extended form, game* against nature. It proceeds in two basic stages. First, one specifies the logical structure of the decision problem in terms of sequences of decisions and realizations of contingencies using a diagram, called a *decision tree*, that links an initial decision (the trunk) to final outcomes (branches). Second, using *backward induction*, one works from final outcomes back to the initial decision, calculating expected values of net benefits across contingencies and pruning dominated branches (i.e., eliminating branches with lower expected values of net benefits).

Consider a vaccination program against a particular type of influenza that involves various costs.[7] The costs of the program result from immunization expenditures and possible adverse side effects; the benefits consist of the adverse health effects that are avoided if an epidemic occurs. This flu may infect a population over the next two years before sufficient immunity develops worldwide to stop its spread. Figure 7-2 presents a simple decision tree for a CBA of this vaccination program. The tree should be read from left to right to follow the sequence of decisions, denoted by □, and random selections of contingencies, denoted by ○. The tree begins with a decision node, the square labeled 0 at the extreme left. The upper bough represents the decision to implement the vaccination program this year; the lower bough represents the decision not to implement the program this year.

FIGURE 7-2 Decision Tree for Vaccination Program Analysis

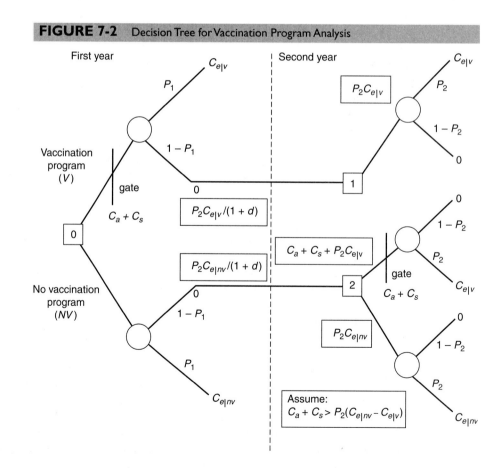

Upper Bough: The Vaccination Program   Follow the upper bough first. If the program is implemented, then it will involve direct administrative costs, C_a, and the costs of adverse side effects, such as contracting the influenza from the vaccine itself, suffered by those who are vaccinated, C_s. Note that C_s, like most of the other costs in this example, is itself an expected cost based on the probability of the side effect, the cost to persons suffering the side effect, and the number of persons vaccinated. The solid vertical line on the bough can be thought of as a toll gate at which point the program costs, $C_a + C_s$, are incurred. A chance node, represented by a circle, appears next. Either the influenza infects the population (the upper branch, which occurs with probability P_1 and results in costs $C_{e|v}$, where the subscript should be read as "epidemic occurs given that the vaccination program has been implemented"), or the influenza does not infect the population (the lower branch, which occurs with probability $1 - P_1$ and results in zero costs at that time). If the influenza does occur, then the population will be immune in the next year. Thus, the upper branch does not continue. If the influenza does not occur, then there is still a possibility that it might occur in the next year. Therefore, the lower branch continues to the second year, where the square labeled 1 notes the beginning of the second year. It leads directly to another chance node that specifies the two contingencies in the second year: The influenza infects the population (the upper subbranch, which occurs with probability P_2 and results in costs $C_{e|v}$), or the influenza does not infect the population (the lower subbranch, which occurs with probability $1 - P_2$ and results in zero costs).[8] We assume that P_2 is known at the time of the initial decision.[9]

Lower Bough: No Vaccination Program   We now return to the initial decision node and follow the lower bough representing no vaccination program in the first year. Initially there is no cost associated with this decision. A chance node follows with two branches: Either the influenza infects the population (the lower branch, which occurs with probability P_1 and results in costs $C_{e|nv}$), or the influenza does not infect the population (the upper branch, which occurs with probability $1 - P_1$ and results in zero costs).[10] If the influenza does occur, then there is no need to consider the next year. If it does not occur, then the tree continues to decision node 2: Either implement the vaccination program in the second year (the upper subbranch crossing the gate where program costs $C_a + C_s$ are incurred) or do not implement it (the lower subbranch).

   If the program is implemented, then a chance node occurs: The influenza infects the population (the lower twig, which occurs with probability P_2 and results in costs $C_{e|v}$), or the influenza does not infect the population (the upper twig, which occurs with probability $1 - P_2$ and results in zero costs). We complete the tree by considering the parallel chance node following the decision not to implement the program in the second year: The influenza infects the population (the lower twig, which occurs with probability P_2 and results in costs $C_{e|nv}$), or the influenza does not infect the population (the upper twig, which occurs with probability $1 - P_2$ and results in zero costs).

Solving the Decision Tree   To solve the decision problem, we work from right to left, replacing chance nodes with their expected costs and pruning off parallel nodes that are dominated. Consider the chance node following decision node 1. Its expected cost, calculated by the expression $P_2 C_{e|v} + (1 - P_2)0$, equals $P_2 C_{e|v}$.

   Now consider the chance nodes following decision node 2. The lower chance node, following a decision not to implement the vaccination program, has an expected cost of

$P_2C_{e|nv}$. The upper chance node has an expected cost of $P_2C_{e|v}$, to which must be added the certain payment of program costs so that the full expected cost of implementing the vaccination program in the second year is $C_a + C_s + P_2C_{e|v}$. We can now compare the expected cost of the two possible decisions at node 2: $P_2C_{e|nv}$ versus $C_a + C_s + P_2C_{e|v}$. To illustrate, assume that program costs are greater than the expected cost reduction from the vaccine, that is, $C_a + C_s > P_2(C_{e|nv} - C_{e|v})$, then $P_2C_{e|nv}$ is smaller than $C_a + C_s + P_2C_{e|v}$ so that not implementing the program dominates implementing it. (If this were not the case, then the lower branch would be unequivocally dominated by the upper branch.[11]) We can now prune off the upper subbranch. If we reach decision node 2, then we know that we can obtain expected second-year costs of $P_2C_{e|nv}$.

At decision node 0 the expected costs of implementing the vaccination program (i.e., following the upper bough) consist of direct costs plus the expected costs of the following chance node, which now has the payoffs $C_{e|v}$ if there is an epidemic and the discounted expected value of node 1, $P_2C_{e|v}/(1 + d)$ if there is not an epidemic. Note that because this latter cost occurs in the second year, it is discounted using rate d. Thus, the present value of expected costs from implementing the vaccination program is given by:

$$E[C_v] = C_a + C_s + P_1C_{e|v} + (1 - P_1)P_2C_{e|v}/(1 + d) \qquad (7.2)$$

where the last term incorporates the expected costs from the second year.

The expected costs of not implementing the vaccination program are calculated in the same way: The payoff if there is not an epidemic becomes the discounted expected costs from decision node 2, $P_2C_{e|nv}/(1 + d)$; the payoff if there is an epidemic is still $C_{e|nv}$. Therefore, the expression:

$$E[C_{nv}] = P_1C_{e|nv} + (1 - P_1)P_2C_{e|nv}/(1 + d) \qquad (7.3)$$

gives the present value of expected costs of not implementing the program.

The final step is to compare the present values of expected costs for the two possible decisions at node 0. We prune the bough with the larger present value of expected costs. The remaining bough is the optimal decision.

As an illustration, suppose that we have gathered data suggesting the following values for parameters in the decision tree: $P_1 = .4$, $P_2 = .2$, $d = .05$, $C_{e|v} = .5C_{e|nv}$ (the vaccination program cuts the costs of influenza by half), $C_a = .1C_{e|nv}$ (the vaccination costs 10 percent of the costs of the influenza), and $C_s = .01C_{e|nv}$ (the side-effect costs are 1 percent of the costs of the influenza). For these values, $E[C_v] = .367C_{e|nv}$ and $E[C_{nv}] = .514C_{e|nv}$. Therefore, the vaccination program should be implemented in the first year because $E[C_v] < E[C_{nv}]$.

Calculating Expected Net Benefits of the Vaccination Program   Returning explicitly to CBA, we can recognize the benefits of the vaccination program as the costs it avoids. Thus, the present value of expected net benefits of the vaccination program is simply $E[C_{nv}] - E[C_v]$, which in the numerical illustration presented in the preceding paragraph equals $0.147C_{e|nv}$. In Chapter 8, we return to the question of the appropriateness of expected net benefits as a generalization of net benefits in CBA.

Extending Decision Analysis   Decision analysis can be applied to both public- and private-sector issues, and it can be used to structure much more complicated analyses than the CBA of the vaccination program. Straightforward extensions include more than two alternatives at decision nodes, more than two contingencies at chance nodes, more than two periods of time, and different probabilities of events in different periods. For example, analyses of the U.S. oil stockpiling program typically involve trees so large that they can only be fully represented and solved by computers.[12] Even in less complex situations, however, decision analysis can be very helpful in showing how risk should be incorporated into the calculation of expected net benefits.

SENSITIVITY ANALYSIS

Whether or not we structure a CBA explicitly in terms of contingencies and their probabilities, we always face some uncertainty about the magnitude of the impacts we predict and the values we assign to them. Our basic analysis usually submerges this uncertainty by using our most plausible estimates of these unknown quantities. These estimates comprise what is called the *base case*. The purpose of sensitivity analysis is to acknowledge the underlying uncertainty. In particular, it should convey how sensitive predicted net benefits are to changes in assumptions. If the sign of net benefits does not change when we consider the range of reasonable assumptions, then our results are robust and we can have greater confidence in them.

Large numbers of unknown quantities, the usual situation in CBA, make the brute force approach of looking at all combinations of assumptions unfeasible. For example, the vaccination program analysis, which we further develop in the next section, involves 17 different uncertain numerical assumptions. If we looked at just three different values for each assumption, there would still be over 129 million different combinations of assumptions to consider.[13] Even if we could compute net benefits for all these combinations, we would still face the daunting task of sorting through the results and communicating them in an effective way.

Instead, we illustrate three more manageable approaches to doing sensitivity analysis. First, we demonstrate *partial sensitivity analysis*: How do net benefits change as we vary a single assumption while holding all others constant? Partial sensitivity is most appropriately applied to what the analyst believes to be the most important and uncertain assumptions. It can be used to find the values of numerical assumptions at which net benefits equal zero, or just break even. Second, we consider *worst- and best-case analysis*: Does any combination of reasonable assumptions reverse the sign of net benefits? Analysts are generally most concerned about situations in which their most plausible estimates yield positive net benefits, but they want to know what would happen in a worst case involving the least favorable, or most conservative, assumptions. Third, we present *Monte Carlo sensitivity analysis*: What distribution of net benefits results from treating the numerical values of key assumptions as draws from probability distributions? The mean and variance, or spread, of the distribution of net benefits convey information about the riskiness of the project.

A Closer Look at the Vaccination Program Analysis

We illustrate these techniques by considering a more detailed specification of the costs relevant to the decision analysis of the hypothetical vaccination program presented in Figure 7-2. This program would vaccinate some residents of a county against a possible influenza epidemic.[14]

Consider the following general description of the program. Through an advertising and outreach effort by its Department of Health, the county expects to be able to recruit a large fraction of older residents in poor health who are at high mortality risk from influenza, and a much smaller fraction of the general population, for vaccination. As the vaccine is based on a live virus, some fraction of those vaccinated will suffer an adverse reaction that, in effect, converts them to high-risk status and gives them influenza, a cost included in C_s. As the vaccine does not always confer immunity, often because it is not given sufficiently in advance of the exposure to the influenza virus, its effectiveness rate is less than 100 percent. Everyone who contracts the influenza must be confined to bed rest for a number of days. Analysts can value this loss as the average number of hours of work lost times the average wage rate for the county, although this procedure might overestimate the opportunity costs of time for older persons and underestimate the cost of the unpleasantness of the influenza symptoms for both younger and older persons. They can place a dollar value on the deaths caused by the influenza by multiplying the number of expected deaths times the dollar value of life. The various numerical assumptions for the analysis appear in Table 7-2. Notice, for example, that the base case value used for each saved life is $3 million. That is, it is assumed that people make decisions about how much value they place on changes in risks of death as if they valued their lives at $3 million.

The benefits of vaccination arise through two impacts. First, those effectively vaccinated are immune to the influenza. Thus, the program targets persons with high mortality risk because they benefit most from immunity. Second, through what is known as the *herd immunity* effect, a positive externality, vaccinated persons reduce the risks of infection to those not vaccinated—this is the reason why some low-risk persons are recruited for vaccination to increase the total fraction of the population that is vaccinated.[15] These two effects cause the expected costs of the epidemic with vaccination, $C_{e|v}$, to be less than the expected costs of the epidemic without the vaccination program, $C_{e|nv}$.

Table 7-3 relates the specific numerical assumptions in Table 7-2 to the parameters in Figure 7-2. From Table 7-3, we see that the direct program costs, C_a, depend on the overhead (i.e., fixed) costs, o, and cost per vaccination, q, times the number of vaccinations given $(V_h + V_l)$. The costs of side effects, C_s, depend on the adverse reaction rate, α, the number vaccinated, and the cost per high-risk infection, $wt + m_h L$, where wt is the opportunity cost of lost labor and $m_h L$ is the cost of loss of life. The epidemic's costs without the vaccination program, $C_{e|nv}$, depend on the infection rate, i, the number of high-risk susceptibles, rN, the number of low-risk susceptibles, $(1 - r)N$, and the costs per high- and low-risk infections. Finally, the cost of the epidemic with the vaccination program, $C_{e|v}$, depends on the postvaccination infection rate, $i - \theta ve$, the number of high-risk individuals remaining susceptible, $rN - eV_h$, the number of low-risk individuals remaining susceptible, $(1 - r)N - eV_l$, and the costs per low- and high-risk infections. Working through these formulas yields expected net benefits equal to $7.718 million (see Table 7-3) for the base-case assumptions presented in Table 7-2.

Partial Sensitivity Analysis   An important assumption in the analysis is the probability that the epidemic occurs. In the base case, we assumed that the probability of the epidemic in the next year, given no epidemic in the current year, p_2, is one-half the probability of the epidemic in the current year, p_1. To investigate the relationship between net benefits and the probability of epidemic, we vary p_1 (and, hence, p_2) holding all other base-case values

TABLE 7-2 Base-Case Values for Vaccination Program CBA

Parameter	Value [Range]	Comments
County Population (N)	380,000	Total population in the county
Fraction High Risk (r)	.06 [.04, .08]	One-half population over age 64
Low-Risk Vaccination Rate (v_l)	.05 [.03, .07]	Fraction of low-risk persons vaccinated
High-Risk Vaccination Rate (v_h)	.60 [.40,.80]	Fraction of high-risk persons vaccinated
Adverse Reaction Rate (α)	.03 [.01, .05]	Fraction vaccinated who become high risk
Low-Risk Mortality Rate (m_l)	.00005 [.000025, .000075]	Mortality rate for low-risk infected
High-Risk Mortality Rate (m_h)	.001 [.0005, .002]	Mortality rate for high-risk infected
Herd Immunity Effect (θ)	1.0 [.5, 1.0]	Fraction of effectively vaccinated who contribute to herd immunity effect
Vaccine Effectiveness Rate (e)	.75 [.65, .85]	Fraction of vaccinated who develop immunity
Hours Lost (t)	24 [18, 30]	Average number of work hours lost to illness
Infection Rate (i)	.25 [.20, .30]	Infection rate without vaccine
First-Year Epidemic Probability (p_1)	.40	Chance of epidemic in current year
Second-Year Epidemic Probability (p_2)	.20	Chance of epidemic next year
Vaccine Dose Price (q)	$9/dose	Price per dose of vaccine
Overhead Cost (o)	$120,000	Costs not dependent on number vaccinated
Opportunity Cost of Time (w)	$12/hour	Average wage rate in the county
Value of Life (L)	$3,000,000	Assumed value of life
Discount Rate (d)	.05	Real discount rate
Number High-Risk Vaccinations (V_h)	13,680	High-risk persons vaccinated: $v_h rN$
Number Low-Risk Vaccinations (V_l)	17,860	Low-risk persons vaccinated: $v_l(1-r)N$
Fraction Vaccinated (v)	.083	Fraction of total population vaccinated: $rv_h + v_l(1-r)$

constant. Specifically, we vary p_1 from 0 to 0.5 by increments of 0.05. We thereby isolate the marginal partial effect of changes in probability on net benefits.

The results of this procedure are displayed as the line labeled $L = \$3$ million in Figure 7-3. This label reminds us of another base-case assumption, the value of life equals $3 million, which we vary next. Because the equations underlying the calculation of net benefits were embedded in a spreadsheet on a personal computer, it was easy to generate the points needed to draw this line by simply changing the values of p_1 and recording the corresponding net benefits.

As expected, this line is upward sloping: The higher the probability of the epidemic, the larger the net benefits of the vaccination program. Note that for values of p_1

TABLE 7-3   Formulas for Calculating the Net Benefits of Vaccination Program

Variable	Value (millions of dollars)	Formula
C_a	0.404	$o + (V_h + V_l)q$
C_s	3.111	$\alpha(V_h + V_l)(wt + m_h L)$
$C_{e|nv}$	57.855	$i[rN(wt + m_h L) + (1 - r)N(wt + m_l L)]$
$C_{e|v}$	36.014	$(i - \theta v e)\{(rN - eV_h)(wt + m_h L) + [(1 - r)N - eV_l](wt + m_l L)\}$
EC_v	22.036	$C_a + C_s + p_1 C_{e|v} + (1 - p_1)p_2 C_{e|v}/(1 + d)$
EC_{nv}	29.754	$p_1 C_{e|nv} + (1 - p_1)p_2 C_{e|nv}/(1 + d)$
$E[NB]$	7.718	$EC_{nv} - EC_v$

less than about .11, net benefits become negative (i.e., it lies below the solid horizontal line). In other words, if we think that the probability of the epidemic in the current year is less than .11, and we are willing to accept the other base-case assumptions, then we should not implement the program. The probability at which net benefits switch sign is called the *breakeven value*. Finding and reporting breakeven values for various parameters is often a useful way to convey their importance.

The line labeled $L = \$1$ million repeats the procedure changing the base-case assumption of the value of life from \$3 million per life to \$1 million per life.[16] The graph thus conveys information about the impact of changes in two assumptions: Each line individually gives the marginal impact of epidemic probability; looking across lines conveys information about the impact of changes in the assumed value of life. As this illustration suggests, we can easily consider the sensitivity of net benefits to changing two assumptions at the same time by constructing families of curves in a two-dimensional graph. Although

FIGURE 7-3   Expected Net Benefits of Vaccination

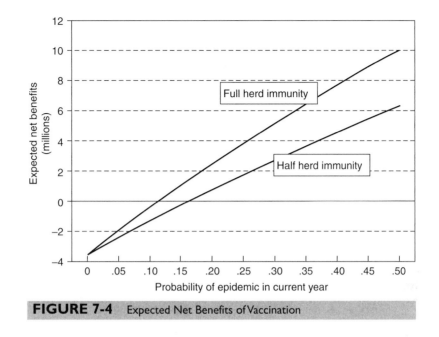

FIGURE 7-4 Expected Net Benefits of Vaccination

computers make it feasible to produce graphs that appear three-dimensional, the added information that these graphs convey is sometimes difficult to interpret.

Figure 7-4 considers one more example of partial sensitivity analysis. It repeats the investigation of the marginal impact of epidemic probability on net benefits for two different assumptions about the size of the herd immunity effect, θ. The upper curve is for the base case that assumes a full herd immunity effect ($\theta = 1$). The lower curve assumes that only one half of the effect occurs ($\theta = .5$), perhaps because the population does not mix sufficiently uniformly for the simple model of herd immunity assumed in the base case to apply. (Both cases return to the base-case assumption of $3 million per life saved.) Note that the breakeven probability rises to over 0.15 for the weaker herd immunity effect. Of course, we could instead give primary focus to the herd immunity effect by graphing net benefits against the size of the herd immunity effect, holding epidemic probability constant.

A thorough investigation of sensitivity ideally considers the partial marginal impacts of changes in each of the important assumptions. However, there is a "chicken and egg" problem: Identifying the important assumptions often cannot be done before actually doing the sensitivity analysis because importance depends on the marginal response of net benefits to changes in assumptions, as well as the plausible range of the assumptions. In the analysis of the vaccination program, for example, partial sensitivity analysis might well be warranted for most of the assumptions presented in Table 7-2.

Worst- and Best-Case Analysis The base-case assumptions, which generally assign the most plausible numerical values to unknown parameters, produce an estimate of net benefits that we think is most representative. In the vaccination program example, these assumptions yield fairly large positive net benefits. We can put a plausible lower bound on net benefits by considering the least favorable of the *plausible range* of values for each of the assumptions. In this way, we can calculate a pessimistic prediction of net benefits. Also, we can calculate an optimistic prediction of net benefits by using the most favorable assumptions. As we discuss later in the chapter, information usually has value in decision making to the extent it can potentially lead us to make a different choice. Therefore, worst-case analysis is generally most valuable when the expected net benefits are positive; best-case analysis is generally most valuable when the expected net benefits are negative. It should be kept in mind, however, that if the ranges are plausible, then the probability of actually realizing net benefits as extreme as either the worst or the best case gets very small as the number of parameters gets large.

Worst-case analysis acknowledges that society, or specific decision makers, may be risk averse. That is, they often care not just about expected net benefits, the appropriate consideration in most cases, but also about the possible "downside." Furthermore, as we point out in Chapters 1 and 19, there are often cognitive limitations and bureaucratic incentives to generate optimistic forecasts. Worst-case analysis provides a useful check against these biases.

As a demonstration of worst-case analysis, we take the lower end of each of the ranges presented in Table 7-2 for r, v_l, v_h, m_l, m_h, θ, e, t, and i, and the higher end of the range for α. For example, we assume that r, the fraction of the population at high mortality risk, equals .04 rather than the base-case value of .06. (For the time being, we keep p_1, p_2, q, o, w, L, and d at their base-case values.) With worst-case assumptions, net benefits fall to $0.101 million. Though still positive, this more conservative estimate is almost two orders of magnitude (10^2) less than under the base-case assumptions.

Return to the question of the sensitivity of net benefits to the probability of epidemic. The breakeven probability rises from about 11 percent under the base-case assumptions to almost 37 percent under the more conservative worst-case assumptions. In other words, expected net benefits would no longer be positive if we assessed the probability of an epidemic to be only slightly less likely than 0.4, the assumed value under the base case.

Care must be taken in determining which are the most conservative assumptions. Under the base-case assumptions, for example, net benefits increase as our assumed value of life increases. Under the conservative assumptions, however, net benefits decrease as the value of life increases. This reversal in the direction of the marginal impact of the value of life occurs because the higher rate of adverse reactions, α, under the conservative case is sufficiently large so that the expected number of deaths is greater with the vaccination program (1.8 deaths) than without it (1.7 deaths).

More generally, caution is warranted when net benefits are a nonlinear function of a parameter. In such cases, the value of the parameter that either minimizes or maximizes net benefits may not be at the extreme of its plausible range. Close inspection of partial sensitivity graphs generally gives a good indication of the general nature of the relationship, though these graphs can sometimes be misleading because they depend on the particular assumed values of all other parameters. A more systematic approach is to inspect the functional form of the model used to calculate net benefits. When a nonlinear relationship is present, extreme values of assumptions may not necessarily result in extreme values of net benefits. Indeed, inspection of Table 7-3 indicates that net benefits are a quadratic function of vaccination rates v_l and v_h because they depend on $C_{e|v}$, which involves the product of direct effects and the herd effect. Under the base-case assumptions, for instance, net benefits would be maximized if all high-risk persons were vaccinated and 46 percent of low-risk persons were vaccinated. As these rates are well above those that could realistically be obtained by the program, we can reasonably treat the upper and lower bounds of vaccination rates as corresponding to extreme values of net benefits.

If the base-case assumptions generate negative net benefits, then it would have been reasonable to see if more optimistic, or best-case, assumptions produce positive net benefits. If the best-case prediction of net benefits is still negative, then we can be very certain that the policy should not be adopted. If it is positive, then we may want to see if combinations of somewhat less optimistic assumptions can also sustain positive net benefits.

Monte Carlo Sensitivity Analysis   Partial- and extreme-case sensitivity analyses have two major limitations. First, they may not take account of all the available information about assumed values of parameters. In particular, if we believe that values near the base-case assumptions are more likely to occur than values near the extremes of their plausible ranges, then the worst and best cases are highly unlikely to occur because they require the joint occurrence of a large number of independent low-probability events. Second, these techniques do not directly provide information about the variance, or spread, of the statistical distribution of realized net benefits. If we cannot distinguish between two policies in terms of expected values of net benefits, then we may be more confident in recommending the one with the smaller variance because it has a higher probability of producing realized net benefits near the expected value.

Monte Carlo analysis provides a way of overcoming these problems. The name suggests the casinos of that famous gambling resort. It is apt because the essence of the approach is playing games of chance many times to elicit a distribution of outcomes. Monte Carlo analysis has played an important role for many years in the investigation of statistical estimators whose properties cannot be adequately determined through mathematical techniques alone. The falling opportunity cost of computing, especially the greater availability of flexible spreadsheet software for microcomputers, makes Monte Carlo analysis feasible for most practicing policy analysts. As it is a method that effectively takes account of uncertainty about assumed parameters in complex analyses, it should be in every analyst's tool kit.

The basic steps for doing Monte Carlo analysis are as follows. First, specify probability distributions for all the important uncertain quantitative assumptions. For the Monte Carlo analysis of the vaccine program, we focus on the ten parameters with expressed ranges in Table 7-2. If we do not have theory or empirical evidence that suggests a particular distribution, then it is sometimes reasonable to specify a uniform distribution over the range. That is, we assume that any value between the upper and lower bound of plausible values is equally likely. For example, we assume that the distribution of the fraction of the population at risk, r, is uniformly distributed between .04 and .08. Often, though, we believe that values near the most plausible estimate should be given more weight. For example, assume that analysts believe that hours lost due to influenza follow a normal distribution. They could then center it at the best estimate of 24 hours and set the standard deviation at 3.06 so that there is only a 5 percent chance of values falling outside the plausible range of 18 to 30 hours. (See Appendix 7A for a brief discussion of working with probability distributions on spreadsheets.) As discussed in Chapter 12, analysts can sometimes estimate unknown parameters statistically using regression analysis. They might then wish to use their 95 percent confidence intervals as their ranges. Commonly used regression models allow analysts to approximate the distribution of an unknown parameter as normal with mean and standard deviation given by their empirical estimates.

EXHIBIT 7-3

Influenza vaccination programs are usually targeted to those in high-risk groups, such as infants, the elderly, and people with compromised immune systems. Is vaccination of healthy workers cost-beneficial? Kristin L. Nichols attempts to answer this question with a cost-benefit analysis. Benefits of vaccination include avoided lost work days, hospitalizations, and deaths. Costs include the costs of the vaccination and lost work days, hospitalizations, and deaths from side effects. She employed Monte Carlo analysis to estimate net benefits. Noting that previous studies reported that managers generally took fewer sick days than other personnel, she built a negative correlation between sick days and wage rate, two of the important parameters, into the Monte Carlo trials. She

estimated the mean value of net benefits to be $13.66 (1998 dollars) with a 95 percent confidence interval ranging from $32.97 in positive net benefits to $2.18 in negative net benefits. In order to assess the relative importance of various assumed parameters to net benefits, she regressed the net benefits from each trial on the randomly drawn values of the parameters. Net benefits were most sensitive to the illness rate, the work absenteeism rate due to influenza, and the hourly wages. In addition, a poor match between the vaccine and the circulating virus strain gave negative net benefits. Not surprisingly, the 95 percent confidence interval from the Monte Carlo analysis was much tighter than the best/worst-case range of positive net benefits of $174.32 to negative net benefits of $21.27.

Source: Adapted from Kristin L. Nichol, "Cost-Benefit Analysis of a Strategy to Vaccinate Healthy Working Adults Against Influenza," *Archives of Internal Medicine* 161(5) 2001, 749–759.

Second, we execute a trial by taking a random draw from the distribution for each parameter to arrive at a set of specific values for computing realized net benefits. For example, in the case of the vaccination program analysis, analysts have to determine which contingencies occur in each of the two periods. To determine if an epidemic occurs in the current year, they take a draw from a Bernoulli distribution with probability p_1 of yielding "epidemic" and $(1 - p_1)$ of yielding "no epidemic." That is, it is as if we were to flip a coin that has a probability of p_1 of landing with "epidemic" face up. Although not all computer spreadsheets allow users to take draws directly from a Bernoulli distribution, almost all spreadsheets allow users to take draws from random variables uniformly distributed between 0 and 1—a draw from the uniform distribution produces an outcome within this range that is as likely to occur as any other outcome in the range. Thus there is a p_1 probability of a value between zero and p_1 occurring. To implement a draw from a Bernoulli distribution that has a probability of p_1 of yielding "epidemic," one simply compares the draw from the uniform distribution to p_1: If the random draw from the uniform distribution is smaller (larger) than p_1, then assume that an epidemic does (not) occur in the current year; if an epidemic does not occur in the current year, then follow a similar procedure to determine if an epidemic occurs in the second year. Three mutually exclusive realizations of net benefits are possible:

Epidemic in neither year: $NB = -(C_a + C_s)$
Epidemic in current year: $NB = -(C_a + C_s) + (C_{e|nv} - C_{e|v})$
Epidemic in next year: $NB = -(C_a + C_s) + (C_{e|nv} - C_{e|v})/(1 + d)$

where the value of *NB* depends on the particular values of the parameters drawn for this trial.

Note that these estimates of *NB* no longer involve expectations with respect to the contingencies of epidemics, though the cost estimates themselves are expected values. For each random draw, only one combination of contingencies can actually occur. (The epidemic poses a collective risk to the population, while the costs result from the realizations of independent risks to individuals in the population.)

Third, we repeat the trial described in the second step many times to produce a large number of realizations of net benefits. The average of the trials provides an estimate of the expected value of net benefits. An approximation of the probability distribution of net benefits can be obtained by breaking the range of realized net benefits into a number of equal increments and counting the frequency with which trials fall into each one. The resulting *histogram* of these counts provides a picture of the distribution. The more trials that go into the histogram, the more likely it is that the resulting picture gives a good representation of the distribution of net benefits. Underlying this faith is the law of large numbers, which tells us that, as the number of trials approaches infinity, the frequencies will converge to the true underlying probabilities.

Figure 7-5 presents a histogram of 1,000 replications of random draws from the bracketed assumptions in Table 7-2. The assumed distributions are all uniform except that for hours lost, *w*, which follows a normal distribution, and whether or not the epidemic occurs, which, although a Bernoulli distribution, is implemented with the readily available uniform distribution. The height of each bar is proportional to the number of trials that had net benefits falling in the corresponding increment.

The average of net benefits over the 1,000 trials is $5.48 million. This differs from our base-case calculation of $7.72 million because the base-case value of the herd immunity

FIGURE 7-5 Histogram of Realized Net Benefits

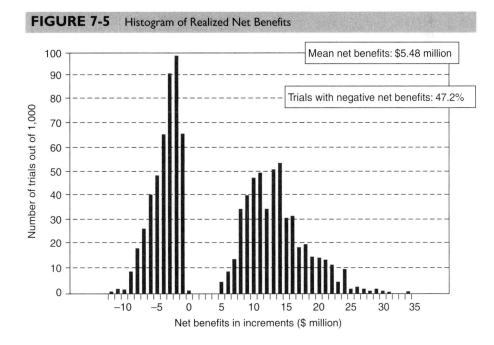

factor, θ, was set at 1 rather than at the middle of the plausible range. Repeating the Monte Carlo procedure with the herd immunity factor set to 1 yields an average of realized net benefits of $7.47 million, which is almost identical to the base-case calculation of expected net benefits.[17]

The histogram provides a visual display of the entire distribution of net benefits so that its spread and symmetry can be easily discerned. The trials themselves can be used to calculate directly the sample variance, standard deviation, and other summary statistics describing net benefits.

The most striking feature of the histogram is that it portrays a bimodal distribution. If an epidemic occurs in either year, then the vaccination program has positive net benefits and it is as if we are drawing only from the right-most hump of the distribution. If an epidemic occurs in neither year, then the vaccination program has negative net benefits and it is as if we are drawing from the left-most hump of the distribution. The assumed probabilities of epidemic in the two years lead us to expect positive net benefits 52 percent of the time $[p_1 + (1 - p_1) p_2]$, which is close to the 52.8 percent of trials with positive net benefits in the Monte Carlo analysis.

The Monte Carlo results presented in Figure 7-5 treated several parameters as if they were certain. Most importantly, they treated the values of time and life as certain. As suggested in Chapter 15, we are in fact uncertain about these values. One approach would be to repeat the Monte Carlo analysis treating these parameters as random variables as well. In effect, we would be mixing uncertainty about predicted effects with uncertainty over how we value those effects. In some situations, this may be appropriate, but here it would probably be clearer to distinguish between these two types of uncertainty. To take account of our uncertainty about how we should value effects, we can simply repeat the original Monte Carlo analysis for a number of combinations of fixed values of time and life. Our results would be a collection of histograms like Figure 7-5 that would provide the basis for assessing how sensitive our assessment of net benefits is to changes in these critical values.

INFORMATION AND QUASI-OPTION VALUE

The various analytical techniques developed in the previous sections provide a basis for assessing uncertainty about information (assumed or measured parameters) in CBA. In this section we demonstrate the use of games against nature to place value on information itself. We use the normal form to illustrate the basic concepts. We then use decision trees to explicate a particular information value, the quasi-option value, that arises in the context of delaying irreversible decisions to allow time for the gathering or revelation of information about the future.

Introduction to the Value of Information

The value of information in the context of a game against nature answers the following question: By how much would the information increase the expected value of playing the game? As an example of how to answer this question, return to the asteroid defense game presented in Table 7-1. Imagine that scientists have proposed developing a detection device that would allow them to determine with certainty whether the Earth would be exposed to a collision with a large asteroid (diameter greater than one kilometer) in the next 100 years. What is the maximum investment that should be made to develop this device?

EXHIBIT 7-4

Research and development projects typically have very uncertain costs and benefits when they are initiated. Based on an assessment of detailed case studies of six research and development projects (Supersonic Transport, Applications Technology Satellite Program, Space Shuttle, Clinch River Breeder Reactor, Synthetics Fuels from Coal, and Photovoltaics Commercialization), Cohen and Noll concluded: "The final success of a program usually hinges on a few key technical objectives and baseline economic assumptions about demand or the cost of alternative technologies, or both. The results of the research that addressed the key technical issues, and realizations a few years after that program was started of the key unknown economic parameters, typically made the likely success of a project very clear" (p. 82).

For example, Susan Edelman prepared CBAs of the supersonic transport project with the information that would have been available to conscientious analysts in each of a number of years. She reports that the plausible range of benefit-cost ratios fell from 1.97 to 4.97 in 1963 to 1.32 to 1.84 in 1971. They declined as it became clear that either higher operating costs or reduced loads would result from failures to achieve technical objectives and that operations over land would likely be restricted to reduce the impacts of sonic booms on people (pp. 112–121).

Source: Adapted from Linda R. Cohen and Roger G. Noll, eds., *The Technology Pork Barrel* (Washington, D.C.: The Brookings Institution, 1991).

If the device were to be built, then it would tell us which of two possible futures were true: First, with a probability of .001, it would tell us that there would be a collision with a large asteroid. Second, with a probability of .999, it would tell us that there would be no collision with a large asteroid. Each of these two futures implies a different game against nature. These are shown in Table 7-4.

Game One, shown on the left side of Table 7-4, results if the detection device indicates that the Earth will be exposed to collision with a large asteroid. Not surprisingly, in this game the best action is to choose forward-based asteroid defense, which has the smallest net costs of the three actions ($5,060 billion). Game Two, shown on the right side of Table 7-4, results if the detection device indicates that the Earth will not be exposed to collision with a large asteroid. As exposure to collision with a large asteroid is ruled out, the probabilities of the other two possible states of nature are adjusted upward so that they sum to 1 (.004004 and .995996). In this game, the best action is to choose no asteroid defense, which has the smallest net costs of the three actions ($24.02 billion).

Prior to developing the detection device, we do not know which of these two games it will give us to play. We do know, however, that it will indicate Game One with probability .001 and Game Two with probability .999. Thus we can compute an expected net cost over the two games as (.001)($5,060 billion) + (.999)($24.02 billion) = $29.06 billion. In order to place a value on the information provided by the device, we compare the expected net cost of the optimal choice in the game without it ($38 billion as shown in Table 7-1) with the expected net cost resulting from optimal choices in the games with it ($29.06 billion). The difference between these net costs ($38 billion – $29.06 billion) equals $8.94 billion, which is the value of the information provided by

TABLE 7-4 Reformulated Games against Nature: Value of Device for Detecting Large Asteroids

State of Nature	Game One p = .001 Exposure to a Collision with an Asteroid Larger Than 1 Kilometer in Diameter	Game Two p = .999 Exposure to a Collision with an Asteroid between 20 Meters and 1 Kilometer in Diameter	No Exposure to Collision with an Asteroid Larger Than 20 Meters in Diameter
Probabilities of states of nature (over next century)	1	.004004	.995996

Actions (alternatives)	Payoffs (net costs in billions of 2000 dollars)	Expected Value	Payoffs (net costs in billions of 2000 dollars)		Expected Value
Forward-based asteroid defense	5,060	**5,060**	1,060	60	64.01
Near-Earth asteroid defense	10,020	10,020	2,020	20	28.01
No asteroid defense	30,000	30,000	6,000	0	**24.02**

Game One: Choose forward-based asteroid defense: Expected net cost = $5,060 billion.
Game Two: Choose no asteroid defense: Expected net cost = $24.02 billion.
Expected net cost of decision with detection device: (.001)($5,060 billion) + (.999)($24.02 billion) = $29.06.
Value of information provided by detection device: $38 billion − $29.06 billion = $8.94 billion.

the device. Consequently, as long as the detection device cost less than $8.94 billion, it would be efficient to develop it.

Note that the value of the information derives from the fact that it leads to different optimal decisions. The optimal choice without the device is near-Earth asteroid defense. The optimal choice with the device is either forward-based asteroid defense if collision exposure is confirmed or no asteroid defense if the absence of collision exposure is confirmed.

In practice, analysts rarely face choices requiring them to value perfect information of the sort provided by the asteroid detection device. They do, however, routinely face choices involving the allocation of resources—time, energy, budgets—toward reducing uncertainty in the values of the many parameters used to calculate net benefits. For example, a statistical estimate based on a random sample of size 600 will be much more precise than one based on a sample of 300. How can the analyst determine if the investment in the larger sample size is worthwhile?

In a CBA involving many assumed parameters, Monte Carlo analysis may provide especially useful information. For example, suppose an agency is deciding whether it is worthwhile to invest analytical resources in conducting a study that would reduce the estimate of the variance of hours lost from the influenza described in the previous section. One could replicate the analysis presented in Figure 7-5 with a smaller assumed variance of hours lost and compare the resulting distribution of net benefits to that resulting with the larger variance. A necessary condition for the investment of analytical resources to be worthwhile is a meaningful change in the distribution of realized net benefits.

Quasi-Option Value

It may be wise to delay a decision if better information relevant to the decision will become available in the future. This is especially the case when the costs of returning to the status quo once a project has begun are so large that the decision is effectively irreversible. For example, consider the decision of whether to develop a virgin wilderness area. We may be fairly certain about the costs and benefits of development to the current generation. We may be very uncertain of the opportunity cost to future generations of losing the virgin wilderness, however. If information will become available over time that will reduce our uncertainty about how future generations will value the wilderness area, then it may be desirable to delay a decision about irreversible development so that we have the opportunity to incorporate the new information into our decision. The expected value of information gained by delaying an irreversible decision is called *quasi-option value*.[18]

Quasi-option value can be quantified by explicitly formulating a multiperiod decision problem that allows for the revelation of information about the value of options in later periods.[19] Although some environmental analysts see quasi-option value as a distinct benefit category for policies that preserve unique assets such as wilderness areas, scenic views, and animal species, it is more appropriately thought of as a correction to the calculation of expected net benefits through an inappropriate one-period decision problem. As the calculation of quasi-option value itself requires specification of the proper decision problem, *whenever quasi-option value can be quantified, the correct expected net benefits can and should be calculated directly*.

As background for an illustration of quasi-option value, Table 7-5 sets out the parameters for a CBA of alternatives for use of a wilderness area. The value of net benefits from full development (*FD*) and limited development (*LD*) are measured relative to no development (*ND*) for two contingencies. Under the contingency labeled "Low Value," which will occur with a probability p, future generations place the same value as current generations on preservation of the wilderness area. Under the contingency labeled "High Value," which will occur with a probability $1 - p$, future generations place a much higher value than current generations on preservation of the wilderness area. If the Low Value contingency occurs, then *FD* yields a positive present value of net benefits equal to B_F and *LD* yields a positive present value of net benefits equal to B_L. That is, after

TABLE 7-5 Benefits and Costs of Alternative Development Policies Assuming No Learning

	Preservation Contingencies	
	Low Value	*High Value*
Full development (*FD*)	B_F	$-C_F$
Limited development (*LD*)	B_L	$-C_L$
No development (*ND*)	0	0
Probability of contingency	p	$1 - p$

Expected value of full development:	$E[FD] = pB_F - (1 - p)C_F$
Expected value of limited development:	$E[LD] = pB_L - (1 - p)C_L$
Expected value of no development:	$E[ND] = 0$
Adopt full development if:	$pB_F - (1 - p)C_F > pB_L - (1 - p)C_L$ and $pB_F - (1 - p)C_F > 0$

taking account of all costs and benefits, the present value of net benefits for *FD* and *LD* are the positive amounts B_F and B_L, respectively. If instead the High Value contingency occurs, then *FD* yields a negative present value of net benefits equal to $-C_F$ and *LD* yields a negative present value of net benefits equal to $-C_L$, where C_F and C_L are net costs and therefore signed negative to be the present value of net benefits. Assume that $B_F > B_L > 0$ and $C_F > C_L > 0$ so that *FD* yields greater net benefits under the Low Value contingency and greater net costs under the High Value contingency than *LD*.

Imagine that we conduct a CBA assuming that no learning will occur over time. That is, we assume that no useful information will be revealed in future periods. The expected net benefits of *FD* equal $pB_F - (1 - p)C_F$; the expected net benefits of *LD* equal $pB_L - (1 - p)C_L$; and the expected net benefits of *ND* equal 0. We would simply choose the alternative with the largest expected net benefits.

Now consider the case of *exogenous learning*. That is, we assume that after the first period we discover with certainty which of the two contingencies will occur. Our learning is exogenous in the sense that the information is revealed to us no matter what actions we take.

Figure 7-6 presents a decision tree for the case of exogenous learning. The square box at the extreme left-hand side of the figure represents our initial decision. If we

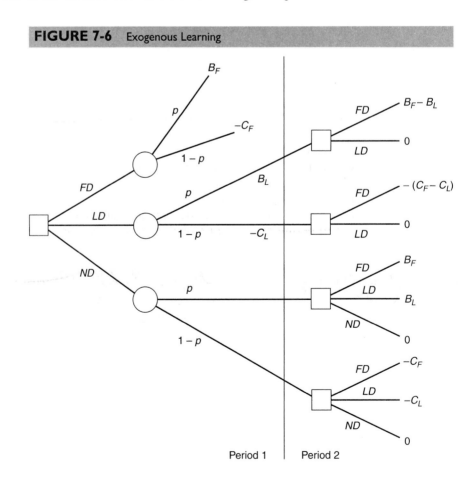

FIGURE 7-6   Exogenous Learning

select *FD*, then we have the same expected value as in the case of no learning—we have made an irreversible decision and, hence, learning has no value because we have no decision left to make in period 2. If we select either *LD* or *ND* in the first period, then we do have a decision left to make in period 2 after we know which contingency has occurred. The expected values of the *LD* and *ND* decisions in period 1 can be found by the method of backward induction introduced in the vaccine example developed earlier in the chapter.

Consider *LD* first. If the Low Value contingency is revealed at the beginning of period 2, then the optimal decision will be to complete the development to obtain net benefits $B_F - B_L$. The present value of this amount is obtained by discounting at rate d. It is then added to B_L, the period 1 net benefits, to obtain the net benefits of *LD* conditional on the Low Value contingency occurring. If the High Value contingency is revealed at the beginning of period 2, then the optimal decision is to forgo further development so that the net benefits conditional on the High Value contingency occurring consist only of the $-C_L$ realized in period 1. Multiplying these conditional net benefits by their respective probabilities yields the expected net benefits for limited development in period 1 of $p[B_L + (B_F - B_L)/(1 + d)] - (1 - p)C_L$. Note that it differs from the expected value in the no-learning case by the expected net benefits of the period 2 option, $p(B_F - B_L)/(1 + d)$, which is the quasi-option value of *LD*.

Next consider the decision *ND* in period 1. If the Low Value contingency is revealed at the beginning of period 2, then the optimal decision is *FD*, which has a present value of $B_F/(1 + d)$. If the High Value contingency is revealed at the beginning of period 2, then the optimal decision is *ND*, which has a present value of 0. Consequently, the expected net benefits from choosing *ND* in period 1 are $pB_F/(1 + d)$, which equal the quasi-option value of *ND*.

The middle column of Table 7-6 summarizes the expected values of the period 1 alternatives for the case of exogenous learning.

Figure 7-7 presents a decision tree for the case of endogenous learning. Unlike the case of exogenous learning, information is generated only from development itself. For example, the value placed on preservation by future generations may depend on the risk that development poses to a species of bird that feeds in the wilderness area during its migration. The effect of limited development on the species may provide enough information to permit a reliable prediction of the effect of full development. If no

TABLE 7-6 Expected Values for Decision Problems: Quasi-Option Values (QOV) Measured Relative to No Learning Case

	No Learning	*Exogenous Learning*	*Endogenous Learning*
$E[FD]$	$pB_F - (1 - p)C_F$	$pB_F - (1 - p)C_F$ $QOV = 0$	$pB_F - (1 - p)C_F$ $QOV = 0$
$E[LD]$	$pB_L - (1 - p)C_L$	$p[B_L + (B_F - B_L)/(1 + d)]$ $- (1 - p)C_L$ $QOV = p(B_F - B_L)/(1 + d)$	$p[B_L + (B_F - B_L)/(1 + d)]$ $- (1 - p)C_L$ $QOV = p(B_F - B_L)/(1 + d)$
$E[ND]$	0	$pB_F(1 + d)$ $QOV = pB_F/(1 + d)$	0 $QOV = 0$

FIGURE 7-7 Endogenous Learning

development is undertaken, then no new information will be available at the beginning of the second period. If full development is undertaken, then new information will be generated but there will be no decision for it to affect.

As shown in the last column of Table 7-6, the expected net benefits for the *FD* and *LD* alternatives in the case of endogenous learning are identical to those for the case of exogenous learning. The expected net benefits of *ND* are zero, however, because there will be no new information to alter the decision not to develop in the future.

Table 7-7 compares the different learning cases for a specific set of parameter values. If we specify the decision problem as one of no learning, then *FD* has the largest expected net benefits. Imagine that instead we specify the decision problem as the exogenous learning case. Now *ND* has the largest expected net benefits. Furthermore, relative to the case of no learning, the quasi-option value of *ND* is $46.3 million (46.30 – 0) and the quasi-option value of *LD* is $23.15 million (28.15 – 5). Now imagine that we specify

TABLE 7-7 Numerical Illustration of Quasi-Option Value ($ million)

Assumptions:

$B_F = 100$ $B_L = 50$ $p = .5$	$C_F = 80$ $C_L = 40$ $d = .08$	No Learning	Exogenous Learning	Endogenous Learning
$E[FD]$		10.00	10.00	10.00
$E[LD]$		5.00	28.15	28.15
$E[ND]$		0.00	46.30	0.00

the decision problem as the case of endogenous learning. *LD* has the largest expected net benefits. Relative to the case of no learning, the quasi-option value of *LD* is $23.15 million (28.15 – 5) and the quasi-option value of *ND* is 0 (0 – 0).

This simple numerical illustration conforms to the common wisdom about quasi-option value: *It tends to be large for no development in cases of exogenous learning and large for limited development in cases of endogenous learning.* It is important to keep in mind, however, that the illustration is based on very stylized models of learning. Differently specified models could yield different rankings and different quasi-option values for the alternatives. Even with this simple model, different numerical assumptions could lead to different rankings of alternatives.

Note that our numerical estimates of quasi-option values in the illustration depend on expected values calculated by comparing what was assumed to be the correct two-period decision problem to a one-period decision problem that incorrectly fails to take account of learning. Of course, if we knew the correct decision problem, then there would be no need to concern ourselves with quasi-option value as a separate benefit category because solving the decision problem would lead to the appropriate calculations of expected net benefits.

Quasi-Option Value and the Option Value Multiple

Economists have developed an investment theory based on models of investment projects that have three characteristics: First, they are irreversible in the sense that they involve large initial costs that cannot be recovered if they are abandoned. Second, they can be delayed. And third, information about their likely consequences will be revealed during the delay.[20] Of course, these are just the characteristics that make quasi-option value relevant. The innovative contribution of the new investment theory is that it links very general assumptions about the nature of uncertainty in project benefits to appropriate adjustments in net benefits based on the discount rate.

The approach is best illustrated with a specific example.[21] First, consider a project that requires an irreversible initial investment of C and that yields current benefits of B_0. Assume further that benefits are expected to grow over time (e.g., because of increases in population or wealth), so that the benefits at any time t in the future are given by $B_t = B_0 e^{gt}$, where g is the rate of growth of benefits.[22] As shown in Chapter 6, if there is an infinite time horizon, then the stream of benefits has a present value of $B_0/(i - g)$ where i is the discount rate. Thus, the present value of net benefits will be positive if $B_0/(i - g) > C$, or $B_0 > (i - g)C$.

Now imagine that the future benefits of this project are not certain—in addition to the underlying growth trend, they include a random component. By making some specific assumptions about the nature of the random component, it is possible to show that the proper decision rule is to implement the project *now* only if $B_0 > OVM(i - g)C$, where *OVM* is called the *option value multiple*.[23] *OVM* is always greater than 1, therefore this decision rule will reject immediate adoption of some projects that have positive net benefits. As annual benefits have both an upward trend and a random component, they may turn out in some year in the future to be sufficiently large so that a project that was initially rejected under the stringent *OVM* decision rule can later pass it and appropriately be adopted.

Table 7-8 shows *OVM*s for assumed values of g, i, and σ, the annual standard deviation of benefits, for a specific model of future benefits.[24] For example, the *OVM*

TABLE 7-8 Option Value Multiples for Specific Growth Rates (g), Standard Deviations (σ), and Discount Rates (i)[a]

	i = 0.04					i = 0.07				
g/σ	0.05	0.10	0.15	0.20	0.25	0.05	0.10	0.15	0.20	0.25
0.000	1.19	1.42	1.69	2.00	2.36	1.14	1.31	1.49	1.70	1.93
0.005	1.30	1.55	1.84	2.19	2.60	1.19	1.36	1.56	1.78	2.03
0.010	1.46	1.73	2.06	2.46	2.92	1.27	1.44	1.64	1.88	2.14
0.015	1.72	2.00	2.38	2.84	3.38	1.36	1.53	1.75	2.00	2.28
0.020	2.12	2.43	2.86	3.14	4.07	1.48	1.65	1.88	2.15	2.45
0.025	2.80	3.15	3.69	4.39	5.24	1.63	1.80	2.04	2.33	2.67
0.030	4.01	4.64	5.38	6.37	7.60	1.82	2.00	2.26	2.57	2.93
0.035	8.28	9.12	10.48	12.40	14.70	2.07	2.26	2.53	2.88	3.28

[a] *Assumes geometric Brownian motion with drift:* $dB = gBdt + \sigma B\epsilon_t (dt)^{1/2}$ *where B is benefits, dB is the differential of benefits, dt is the differential of time, and ϵ_t is a normally distributed random variable with mean zero and unit variance.*

entry for a zero growth rate, a discount rate of .04, and an annual standard deviation of .05 is 1.19. Under these assumptions, the magnitude of observed annual benefits must be 19 percent larger than under the standard net benefits rule to justify the project. Note that these *OVM* values are for a specific model of future benefits; other plausible models could produce different *OVM* values.

Three patterns emerge from inspection of Table 7-8. First, looking down the columns, it is clear that the *OVM* is larger for higher growth rates in benefits. Higher growth rates have the effect of reducing the opportunity cost of delaying the project. With a positive growth rate the present value of benefits falls less over time than the present value of costs, reducing the cost of delay. Second, looking across the rows for a particular discount rate, the *OVM* is larger for larger standard deviations in annual benefits. Greater uncertainty makes the information about the magnitude of benefits revealed through delaying the project more valuable. Third, the *OVM* is smaller for higher discount rates. Higher discount rates raise the cost of forgoing immediate benefits.

Unless analysts face a problem for which one of the particular models, such as the one underlying Table 7-8, that have already been analyzed is appropriate, they must use quite demanding analytical techniques to find the *OVM*. Additionally, they must make estimates of the parameters of the model, a task for which little information is likely to be available. Consequently, they are unlikely to be able to make confident assessments about the appropriate *OVM*. Nevertheless, the concept of *OVM* urges caution in applying the standard net benefits test to projects involving large irreversible investments and the potential for learning about future benefits through delay.

Quasi-Option Value in Practice

How should we treat quasi-option value in practice? Two heuristics seem warranted. First, *quantitative quasi-option values should be based on an explicit decision problem that structures the calculation of the expected net benefits.* An explicit decision problem focuses attention on the key assumptions that determine the magnitude of quasi-option value. It also makes it unnecessary to consider quasi-option value as a distinct benefit category. Second, *when insufficient knowledge is available to formulate a decision problem for explicitly calculating the magnitude of quasi-option value or, alternatively, the* OVM, *it should be discussed as a possible source of bias rather than added as an arbitrary quantitative adjustment to expected net benefits.* As with other biases, one can ask the question: How big would quasi-option value have to be to affect the ranking of policies?

CONCLUSION

Uncertainty is inherent to some degree in every CBA. Through expected value analysis, we attempt to average over the possible contingencies to arrive at expected net benefits as a plausible prediction of net benefits. In situations not explicitly involving risk, we often assume parameter values that are more appropriately thought of as draws from probability distributions rather than as certainties. The purpose of sensitivity analysis is to determine how net benefits change if these parameters deviate from their assumed values. Partial sensitivity analysis, the most commonly used approach, focuses attention on the consequences of alternative assumptions about key parameters. Extreme-case analysis examines whether combinations of plausible assumptions exist that reverse the sign of net benefits. Monte Carlo analysis attempts to estimate the distribution of net benefits by explicitly treating assumed parameter values as random variables. It is especially useful when the risk of the policy is of particular concern and the parameters have nonuniform distributions or the formula for the calculation of net benefits involves the parameters in other than simple sums. While the nature of the policy under consideration and the resources available to the analysts attempting to estimate its benefits and costs determine the appropriate form of sensitivity analysis, every CBA should be subjected to tests of its sensitivity to the assumptions it employs.

Explicit decision analysis frameworks, including games against nature in both normal and extensive form, provide a basis for assessing the value of information in risky circumstances. It allows an explicit calculation of quasi-option value, which is sometimes treated as a separate benefit category in CBAs. Quasi-option values take account of the value of being able to act upon future information. As solving a correctly specified decision problem naturally incorporates quasi-option values, they need not be treated as distinct benefits. Quantitative claims about quasi-option values should be based on an explicit decision problem.

APPENDIX 7A

Doing Monte Carlo Sensitivity Analysis with a Simple Spreadsheet

Spreadsheets greatly reduce the labor needed to conduct sensitivity analysis. Usually the calculation of net benefits can be organized so that partial sensitivity analysis can be done by simply changing the value of a single spreadsheet cell. Although specialized software is available for doing Monte Carlo analysis, such as Crystal Ball (Decisioneering, Inc.) for use with Excel and DATA (TreeAge, Inc.) for decision analysis, with a bit of effort it can be done with any simple spreadsheet that provides a random number generator.

Generating Random Variables

Most spreadsheets provide a function for generating random variables that are distributed uniformly from 0 to 1. [In Excel, the function is RAND(); in Quattro Pro, the function is @RAND.] To generate uniform random variables with other ranges, one simply multiplies the draw from the random variable uniformly distributed from 0 to 1 by the desired range and then adds the minimum value. So, for example, to get the appropriate random variable for the fraction of high-risk persons in the population, r in Table 7-2, use the following formula: $.04 + (.08 - .04)z$ where z is the uniform random variable with range 0 to 1.

Some other distributions can be generated directly from the uniform distribution. For example, to obtain draws from an exponential distribution, one would simply take the natural logarithm of the uniformly distributed random variable and multiply it by the negative of the desired expected value of the exponential distribution. The most useful distribution, the normal, can also be generated in most spreadsheets by combining functions for the inverse of the cumulative normal distribution and the uniform

distribution. [In Excel, the formula for generating a draw from a standard normal distribution is NORMSINV(RAND()) and the formula for Quattro Pro is @NORMSINV(@RAND).]

The standardized normal distribution can be given any expected value and variance through simple transformations: Add a constant equal to the desired expected value and multiply by the square root of the desired variance. A range of 3.92 standard deviations includes 95 percent of the area of the normal distribution. To get the random variable we used in the Monte Carlo analysis for hours lost, t in Table 7-2, we added 24 to the standardized normal and multiplied it by $(30 - 18)/3.92$ so that there was only a 5 percent chance that a value of t would be generated outside the range 18 to 30.

Most books on mathematical statistics indicate how random variables distributed as chi-square, Student's t, F, and multivariate normal can be generated using combinations of normally distributed random variables. Similarly, the gamma distribution and the discrete Poisson distribution can be generated from exponential distributions. Discussion of these methods here would take us too far afield.

Steps in Monte Carlo Sensitivity Analysis

Once procedures have been developed for generating appropriately distributed random variables, doing Monte Carlo analysis is straightforward, although, depending on the capabilities of the spreadsheet and the hardware upon which it operates, perhaps somewhat tedious. A simple approach follows.

First, construct a row of appropriate random variables and the formulas that use them to compute net benefits. The last cell in the row should contain net benefits.

Second, copy the entire row a number of times so that the last column of the resulting block contains different realizations of net benefits. Most spreadsheet and hardware arrangements should be able to handle blocks of more than 1,000 rows without memory or time problems.

Third, analyze the accumulated realizations in the last column along the lines of Figure 7-5, calculating the mean and standard deviation, and plotting as a histogram.

EXERCISES FOR CHAPTER 7

1. The initial cost of constructing a permanent dam (i.e., a dam that is expected to last forever) is $425 million. The annual net benefits will depend on the amount of rainfall: $18 million in a "dry" year, $29 million in a "wet" year, and $52 million in a "flood" year. Meteorological records indicate that over the last 100 years there have been 86 "dry" years, 12 "wet" years, and 2 "flood" years. Assume the annual benefits, measured in real dollars, begin to accrue at the end of the first year. Using the meteorological records as a basis for prediction, what are the net benefits of the dam if the real discount rate is 5 percent?

2. Use several alternative discount rate values to investigate the sensitivity of the present value of net benefits of the dam in exercise 1 to the assumed value of the real discount rate.

3. The prevalence of a disease among a certain population is .40. That is, there is a 40 percent chance that a person randomly selected from the population will have the disease. An imperfect test that costs $250 is available to help identify those who have the disease before actual symptoms appear. Those who have the disease have a 90 percent chance of a positive test result; those who do not have the disease have a 5 percent chance of a positive test. Treatment of the disease before the appearance of symptoms costs $2,000 and inflicts additional costs of $200 on those who do not actually have the disease. Treatment of the disease after symptoms have appeared costs $10,000.

The government is considering the following possible strategies with respect to the disease:

S1. Do not test and do not treat early.
S2. Do not test and treat early.
S3. Test and treat early if positive and do not treat early if negative.

Find the treatment/testing strategy that has the lowest expected costs for a member of the population.

In doing this exercise, the following notation may be helpful: Let D indicate presence of the disease, ND absence of the disease, T a positive test result, and NT a negative test result. Thus, we have the following information:

$$P(D) = .40, \text{ which implies } P(ND) = .60$$
$$P(T|D) = .90, \text{ which implies } P(NT|D) = .10$$
$$P(T|ND) = .05, \text{ which implies } P(NT|ND) = .95$$

This information allows calculation of some other useful probabilities:

$$P(T) = P(T|D)P(D) + P(T|ND)P(ND) = .39 \text{ and } P(NT) = .61$$
$$P(D|T) = P(T|D)P(D)/P(T) = .92 \text{ and } P(ND|T) = .08$$
$$P(D|NT) = P(NT|D)P(D)/P(NT) = .07 \text{ and } P(ND|NT) = .93$$

4. In exercise 3 the optimal strategy involved testing. Does testing remain optimal if the prevalence of the disease in the population is only .05? Does your answer suggest any general principle?

5. (Use of a spreadsheet recommended for parts a through e and necessary for part f.) A town with a population of 164,250 persons who live in 39,050 households is considering introducing a recycling program that would require residents to separate paper from their household waste so that it can be sold rather than buried in a landfill like the rest of the town's waste. Two major benefits are anticipated: revenue from the sale of waste paper and avoided tipping fees (the fee that the town pays the owners of landfills to bury its waste). Aside from the capital costs of specialized collection equipment, household containers, and a sorting facility, the program would involve higher collection costs, inconvenience costs for households, and disposal costs for paper that is collected but not sold. The planning period for the project has been set at eight years, the expected life of the specialized equipment.

    The following information has been collected by the town's sanitation department:

    Waste Quantities: Residents currently generate 3.6 pounds of waste per person per day. Over the last 20 years, the daily per capita amount has grown by about 0.02 pounds per year. Small or no increases in the last few years, however, raise the possibility that levels realized in the future will fall short of the trend.

    Capital Costs: The program would require an initial capital investment of $1,688,000. Based on current resale values, the scrap value of the capital at the end of eight years is expected to be 20 percent of its initial cost.

    Annual Costs: The department estimates that the separate collection of paper will add an average of $6/ton to the cost of collecting household waste. Each ton of paper collected and not sold would cost $4 to return to the landfill.

    Savings and Revenues: Under a long-term contract, tipping fees are currently $45 per ton with annual increases equal to the rate of inflation. The current local market price for recycled paper is $22 per ton but has fluctuated in recent years between a low of $12 per ton and a high of $32 per ton.

    Paper Recovery: The fraction of household waste made up of paper has remained fairly steady in recent years at 32 percent. Based on the experience of similar programs in other towns, it is estimated that between 60 and 80 percent of paper included in the program will be separated from other waste and 80 percent of the paper that is separated will be suitable for sale, with the remaining 20 percent of the collected paper returned to the waste stream for landfilling.

    Household Separation Costs: The sanitation department recognized the possibility that the necessity of separating paper from the waste stream and storing it might impose costs on households. An average of 10 minutes per week per household of additional disposal time would probably be needed. A recent survey by the local newspaper, however, found that 80 percent of respondents considered the inconvenience of the program negligible. Therefore, the department decided to assume that household separation costs would be zero.

    Discount Rate: The sanitation department has been instructed by the budget office to discount at the town's real borrowing rate of 6 percent. It has also been instructed to assume that annual net benefits accrue at the end of each of the eight years of the program.

    a. Calculate an estimate of the present value of net benefits for the program.
    b. How large would annual household separation costs have to be per household to make the present value of net benefits fall to zero?
    c. Assuming that household separation costs are zero, conduct a worst-case analysis with respect to the growth in the quantity of waste, the price of scrap paper, and the percentage of paper diverted from the waste stream.
    d. Under the worst-case assumptions of part c, how large would the average yearly household separation costs have to be to make the present value of net benefits fall to zero?

    e.   Investigate the sensitivity of the present value of net benefits to the price of scrap paper.

    f.   Implement a Monte Carlo analysis of the present value of net benefits of the program.

6.   Imagine that, with a discount rate of 5 percent, the net present value of a hydroelectric plant with a life of 70 years is $25.73 million and that the net present value of a thermal electric plant with a life of 35 years is $18.77 million. Rolling the thermal plant over twice to match the life of the hydroelectric plant thus has a net present value of ($18.77 million) + ($18.77 million)/$(1 + 0.05)^{35}$ = $22.17 million.

        Now assume that at the end of the first 35 years, there will be an improved second 35-year plant. Specifically, there is a 30 percent chance that an advanced solar or nuclear alternative will be available that will increase the net benefits by a factor of three, a 60 percent chance that a major improvement in thermal technology will increase net benefits by 50 percent, and a 10 percent chance that more modest improvements in thermal technology will increase net benefits by 10 percent.

    a.   Should the hydroelectric or thermal plant be built today?

    b.   What is the quasi-option value of the thermal plant?

NOTES

1. A more realistic assumption (e.g., rainfall amounts closer to the center of the range are more likely) would not change this equality as long as the probability density function of rainfall is symmetric around 11 inches.

2. Assuming that rainfall is distributed uniformly over the range, the expected value of net benefits is simply the area under curve *B* from 22 inches to 0 inches. See note 4 on how to calculate this area for any distribution of rainfall.

3. The representativeness is very sensitive to the particular shape of the probability density function of rainfall. The use of two contingencies would be even less representative if amounts of rainfall near 11 inches were more likely than more extreme amounts.

4. In the case of a continuous underlying dimension, such as price, the expected value of net benefits is calculated using integration, the continuous analog of addition. Let $NB(x)$ be the net benefits given some particular value of x, the underlying dimension. Let $f(x)$ be the probability density function over x. Then,

$$E[NB] = \int NB(x)f(x)dx$$

where the integration is over the range of x.

5. The term *decision analysis* was originally used to include both choice under risk (statistical decision analysis) and games against strategic opponents (game theory). Now it is commonly used to refer only to the former.

6. We recommend Howard Raiffa, *Decision Analysis: Introductory Lectures on Choices under Uncertainty* (Reading, MA: Addison-Wesley, 1969); Morris H. DeGroot, *Optimal Statistical Decisions* (New York: McGraw-Hill, 1970); Robert L. Winkler, *Introduction to Bayesian Inference and Decision* (New York: Holt, Rinehart and Winston, 1972); and Robert D. Behn and James W. Vaupel, *Quick Analysis for Busy Decision Makers* (New York: Basic Books, 1982) as general introductions. For more direct application to CBA, see Miley W. Merkhofer, *Decision Science and Social Risk Management: A Comparative Evaluation of Cost-Benefit Analysis, Decision Analysis, and Other Formal Decision-Aiding Approaches* (Boston: D. Reidel Publishing Company, 1987).

7. This example is hypothetical, although concern about influenza epidemics has been the subject of public policy debate. See, for example, Richard E. Neustadt and Harvey V. Fineberg, *The Swine Flu Affair: Decision-Making on a Slippery Disease* (Washington, D.C.: U.S. Government Printing Office, 1978); and David S. Fedson, "The Influenza Vaccination Demonstration Project: An Expanded Policy Goal," *Infection Control and Hospital Epidemiology* 11(7) 1990, 357–361.

8. Note that in this example the probability of an epidemic in the second year is conditional on whether an epidemic occurred in the first year. If an epidemic has occurred in the first year, then the population gains immunity and there is zero

probability of an epidemic in the second year. If an epidemic has not occurred, then there is some probability, p_2, that one will occur in the second year.

9. Instead, we might have allowed the estimate of P_2 to be adjusted after information was revealed, or gathered, during the first year. If this were the case, then we might use *Bayes' theorem* to update the initial beliefs about P_2 in the face of the new information. Bayes' theorem provides a rule for updating subjective probability estimates on the basis of new information. Let A and B be events. A basic axiom of probability theory is that:

$$P(A \text{ and } B) = P(A|B)P(B) = P(B|A)P(A)$$

where $P(A \text{ and } B)$ is the probability of both A and B occurring, $P(A)$ is the probability of A occurring, $P(B)$ is the probability of B occurring, $P(A|B)$ is the conditional probability that A occurs given that B has occurred, and $P(B|A)$ is the conditional probability of B occurring given that A has occurred. It follows directly from the axioms that:

$$P(A|B) = P(B|A)P(A)/P(B)$$

which is the simplest statement of Bayes' rule.

Its application is quite common in diagnostic tests. For example, we may know the frequency of a disease in the population, $P(A)$, the probability that a test will yield a positive result if randomly given to a member of the population, $P(B)$, and the conditional probability that, given the disease, the test will be positive, $P(B|A)$. We would thus be able to calculate, $P(A|B)$, the conditional probability that someone with a positive test has the disease.

Discussions of Bayes' rule can be found in almost any introductory text on probability and statistics. For a more advanced treatment, see S. James Press, *Bayesian Statistics: Principles, Models, and Applications* (New York: John Wiley and Sons, 1989).

10. Note the assumption that the probability of the influenza reaching the population, p_1, is independent of whether or not this particular population is vaccinated. This would not be a reasonable assumption if the vaccination were to be part of a national program that reduced the chances that

the influenza would reach this population from some other vaccinated population.

11. In this particular problem, it will never make sense to wait until the second year to implement the program if it is going to be implemented at all. If, however, the risk of side effects were expected to fall in the second year, say, because a better vaccine would be available, then delay could be optimal. In terms of the decision tree, we could easily model this alternative scenario by using different values of C_s in the current and next years.

12. For a discussion of the application of decision analysis to the stockpiling problem, see David L. Weimer and Aidan R. Vining, *Policy Analysis: Concepts and Practice*, 4th ed. (Upper Saddle River, NJ: Pearson Prentice Hall, 2005), Chapter 17.

13. Calculating the number of combinations: $3^{17} = 129,140,163$.

14. For examples of CBA applied to hepatitis vaccine programs, see Josephine A. Mauskopf, Cathy J. Bradley, and Michael T. French, "Benefit-Cost Analysis of Hepatitis B Vaccine Programs for Occupationally Exposed Workers," *Journal of Occupational Medicine* 33(6) 1991, 691–698; Gary M. Ginsberg and Daniel Shouval, "Cost-Benefit Analysis of a Nationwide Neonatal Inoculation Programme against Hepatitis B in an Area of Intermediate Endemicity," *Journal of Epidemiology and Community Health* 46(6) 1992, 587–594; and Murray Krahn and Allan S. Detsky, "Should Canada and the United States Universally Vaccinate Infants against Hepatitis B?' *Medical Decision Making* 13(1) 1993, 4–20.

15. Call the basic reproductive rate of the infection R_0. That is, each primary infection exposes R_0 individuals to infection. If i is the fraction of the population no longer susceptible to infection because of previous infection, then the actual reproductive rate is $R = R_0(1 - i - v)$, where v is the fraction of the population effectively vaccinated. If R falls below 1, then the infection dies out because, on average, each infection generates less than one new infection. Assuming that the population is homogeneous with respect to susceptibility to infection and that infected and noninfected individuals uniformly mix in the population, a rough estimate of the ultimate i for the population is given by the formula $i = 1 - (1/R_0) - v$ where $1 - 1/R_0$ is the estimate of the infection rate in the absence of the vaccine.

For an overview, see Roy M. Anderson and Robert M. May, "Modern Vaccines: Immunisation and Herd Immunity," *The Lancet* 8690(March) 1990, 641–645; and Joseph W. G. Smith, "Vaccination Strategy," in Philip Selby, ed., *Influenza, Virus, Vaccines, and Strategy* (New York: Academic Press, 1976), 271–294.

16. The $L = \$3$ million and $L = \$1$ million lines cross because lives are at risk both from the vaccination side effects and from the epidemic. At low probabilities of epidemic, the expected number of lives saved from vaccination is negative so that net benefits are higher for lower values of life. At higher probabilities of epidemic, the expected number of lives saved is positive so that net benefits are higher for higher values of life.

17. In general, if the calculation of net benefits involves sums of random variables, using their expected values yields the expected value of net benefits. If the calculation involves sums and products of random variables, then using their expected values yields the expected value of net benefits only if the random variables are uncorrelated. In the Monte Carlo approach, correlations among variables can be taken into account by drawing parameter values from either multivariate or conditional distributions rather than from independent univariate distributions as in this example. Finally, if the calculation involves ratios of random variables, then even independence (i.e., an absence of correlations) does not guarantee that using their expected values will yield the correct expected value of net benefits. In this latter situation, the Monte Carlo approach is especially valuable because it provides a way of estimating the correct expected net benefits.

18. The concept of quasi-option value was introduced by Kenneth J. Arrow and Anthony C. Fisher, "Environmental Preservation, Uncertainty, and Irreversibility," *Quarterly Journal of Economics* 88(2) 1974, 312–319.

19. Jon M. Conrad, "Quasi-Option Value and the Expected Value of Information," *Quarterly Journal of Economics* 44(4) 1980, 813–820; and Anthony C. Fisher and W. Michael Hanemann, "Quasi-Option Value: Some Misconceptions Dispelled," *Journal of Environmental Economics and Management* 14(2) 1987, 183–190.

20. For overviews, see Robert S. Pindyck, "Irreversibility, Uncertainty, and Investment," *Journal of Economic Literature* 29(3) 1991, 1110–1148; Avinash Dixit and Robert Pindyck, *Investment Under Uncertainty* (Princeton, NJ: Princeton University Press, 1994); and Gilbert E. Metcalf and Donald Rosenthal, "The 'New' View of Investment Decisions and Public Policy Analysis: An Application to Green Lights and Cold Refrigerators," *Journal of Policy Analysis and Management* 14(4) 1995, 517–531.

21. This example is based on Anthony Edward Boardman and David H. Greenberg, "Discounting and the Social Discount Rate," in Fred Thompson and Mark T. Green, eds., *Handbook of Public Finance* (New York: Marcel Dekker, 1998), 269–318.

22. More generally, the same analysis follows if B_t is interpreted as net benefits in time t exclusive of the initial sunk cost C.

23. The assumption, common in models of the prices of securities, is that benefits follow a geometric Brownian motion with drift. This implies future benefits are distributed according to a lognormal distribution with an expected value growing at the trend rate g.

24. Assuming geometric Brownian motion with drift, $OVM = \beta/(\beta - 1)$ where:

$$\beta = .5 - g/\sigma^2 + \sqrt{(g/\sigma^2 - .5)^2 + 2i/\sigma^2}$$

and σ^2 is the variance of the random component.

CHAPTER 8

Option Price and Option Value

In the actual practice of CBA in circumstances involving significant risks, analysts almost always apply the Kaldor-Hicks criterion to expected net benefits. They typically estimate changes in social surplus conditional on particular contingencies occurring, and then they compute an expected value over the contingencies as demonstrated in Chapter 7. Economists, however, now generally consider *option price*, the amount that individuals are willing to pay for policies prior to the realization of contingencies, to be the theoretically correct measure of willingness-to-pay in circumstances of uncertainty. Whereas social surplus can be thought of as an *ex post* measure of welfare change in the sense that individuals value policies as if contingencies have already occurred, option price is an *ex ante* welfare measure in the sense that consumers value policies without knowing which contingency will actually occur. These measures generally differ from one another. In this chapter, we consider the implications of the common use of expected social surplus, rather than option price, as the method for measuring benefits.

The central concern of this chapter is the conceptually correct measure of willingness-to-pay in circumstances in which individuals face uncertainty. Individuals may face uncertainties about their demand for a good, the supply of a good, or both. With respect to demand, one may be uncertain about one's future income, utility function (tastes), and the prices of other goods. For example, one's utility from skiing may depend on the sturdiness of one's knees, a physical condition that cannot be predicted with certainty. With respect to supply, one may be uncertain about the future quantity, quality, or price of a good. For example, the increase in the quality of fishing that will result from restocking a lake with game fish depends on such circumstances as weather and spills of toxic chemicals, and thus is uncertain to some degree.

In contrast to Chapter 7, we limit our attention to uncertainties of direct relevance to individuals. We ignore uncertainties that are not of direct individual relevance, but instead arise because analysts must make predictions about the future to estimate measures of willingness-to-pay. In the context of the CBA of the vaccination program discussed in Chapter 7, for example, the probability of epidemic, the probability an unvaccinated individual will be infected, the probability a vaccinated individual will be infected, and the probability a vaccinated individual will suffer a side effect are exactly the types of uncertainties considered in this chapter. The analyst's uncertainties about the magnitude of these probabilities, the appropriate shadow price of time, or the number of people who will choose to be vaccinated were adequately addressed in the discussion of sensitivity analysis presented in Chapter 7. Although these analytical uncertainties are usually of greatest practical concern in CBA, we seek here to provide the conceptual foundation required for understanding the appropriate measure of costs and benefits when individuals face significant uncertainties. We are especially interested in how to assess government policies that increase or reduce the uncertainties that individuals face.

This chapter has three major sections. The first introduces option price and clarifies its relationship to expected surplus. The second section introduces the concept of *option value*, the difference between option price and expected surplus, and reviews the theoretical literature that attempts to determine its sign. Although sometimes thought of as a conceptually distinct category of benefits, option value is actually an adjustment to measured benefits to account for the fact that they are usually measured in terms of expected surplus rather than in terms of option price. The third section provides a general assessment of the appropriateness of the use of expected surplus as a proxy for option price.

EX ANTE WILLINGNESS-TO-PAY: OPTION PRICE[1]

Viewing benefits (or costs) in terms of the willingness of individuals to pay to obtain desirable (or avoid undesirable) policy impacts provides a clear perspective on the appropriateness of treating expected net benefits as if they were certain amounts. By identifying the conceptually correct method for valuing uncertain costs and benefits, we can better understand the circumstances under which the use of expected net benefits is more or less appropriate.

There is now a near consensus among economists that the conceptually correct way to value the benefits of a policy in circumstances involving risk is to sum the *ex ante* amounts that the individuals affected by the policy would be willing to pay to obtain it.[2] To see this, imagine that each person, knowing the probabilities of each of the contingencies that would occur under the policy, would give a truthful answer to the following question: *Prior to knowing which contingency will actually occur, what is the maximum amount that you would be willing to pay to obtain the policy?* Each individual's answer to this question is what economists call the person's *option price* for the policy. If we think of the policy as a lottery having probabilities of various payoffs to the person, then the individual's option price is a *certainty equivalent* of the lottery—that is, an amount the person would pay for a ticket without knowing the payoff (or contingency) that is actually realized. (It is called a certainty equivalent because the amount paid for a lottery ticket is certain even if the payoff is not.)

By summing the option prices of all persons, we obtain the aggregate benefits of the policy, which can then be compared to its opportunity cost in the usual way. If the opportunity cost is not dependent on which contingency actually occurs, then we have fully taken account of risk by comparing the aggregate willingness-to-pay, which is independent of the contingency that actually occurs, with the certain opportunity cost.

Illustrations of Option Price

To illustrate the concept of option price, return to the asteroid defense policies set out in Table 7-1 in the previous chapter. Assume that the United Nations wishes to evaluate forward-based asteroid defense from the perspective of humankind. Analysts might employ a contingent valuation survey of the sort described in Chapter 14. It would require surveyors to explain to each person (or more likely to a representative of each household) the possible contingencies (exposure to collision with an asteroid larger than one kilometer diameter, exposure to collision with an asteroid between 20 meters and one kilometer in diameter, and no exposure to collision with an asteroid larger than 20 meters in diameter), the probabilities of each contingency, and the consequences to the Earth under each contingency with and without forward-based asteroid defense. Each person would then be asked questions to elicit the maximum amount that he or she would be willing to pay to have forward-based asteroid defense. These amounts would be summed over all earthlings to arrive at the social benefits of forward-based asteroid defense. As this sum represents aggregate willingness-to-pay before people know which contingency occurs, and therefore is the willingness-to-pay irrespective of which one actually occurs, it can be thought of as a certainty equivalent. Let us assume that the social net benefits, the sum of individual option prices, equaled $100 billion. The net benefits of forward-based asteroid defense would then be calculated as this amount minus the certain program costs of $60 billion, or $40 billion.

Recall that in actual CBA, analysts more commonly measure benefits by first estimating the social surplus under each contingency and then taking the expected value of these amounts using the probabilities of the contingencies. For example, the information in Table 7-1 indicates that the expected benefits of forward-based asteroid defense relative to no program to be –$15 billion. (The expected value of net costs of no program, $54 billion, minus the expected value of net costs of forward-based asteroid defense, $69 billion.) Thus, in this example, the expected surplus would underestimate net benefits by $55 billion ($40 billion minus –$15 billion). This difference between option price and expected surplus is the option value of forward-based asteroid defense. In this case, the option value can be thought of as an additional "insurance benefit" of the program. It is the maximum amount beyond expected benefits that individuals are willing to pay to have the defense program available to reduce the risk of the catastrophic consequences that would result from an undefended collision with a large asteroid.

In general, how does this expected surplus measure compare to the option price? Assuming that individuals are risk averse, *expected surplus can either underestimate or overestimate option price depending on the sources of risk*. For an individual who is risk averse and whose utility function depends only on income, expected surplus will underestimate option price for policies that reduce income risk and overestimate option price for policies that increase income risk. In order to understand how these possibilities can arise, it is necessary to look more carefully at the relationship between option price and expected surplus from the perspective of an individual consumer. The following diagrammatic expositions illustrate cases where option price exceeds expected surplus (a temporary dam) and expected surplus exceeds option price (a bridge).

Table 8-1 shows the contingent payoffs for building a temporary dam that provides water for irrigation. With or without the dam, the farmer can be viewed as facing two contingencies: It rains a lot or it does not rain very much. If it is wet, then he will always produce more crops than if it is dry. Without the dam, the farmer would receive an income of $100 if it rains a lot and only $50 if it does not rain very much. As a result of the dam, his income will increase by $50 if it is dry but by only $10 if it is wet. These $50 and $10 figures are the surplus that the farmer receives from the dam under each contingency. In expected value terms, assuming that the dry and wet contingencies

TABLE 8-1 Example of a Risk-Reducing Project

| | Policy | | |
| | Dam | No Dam | Probability of Contingency |
Contingency			
Wet	110	100	.5
Dry	100	50	.5
Expected value	105	75	
Variance	25	625	

Surplus point:	$U(110 - S_w) = U(100)$ implies $S_w = 10$
	$U(100 - S_d) = U(50)$ implies $S_d = 50$
Expected surplus:	$E(S) = .5S_w + .5S_d = 30$
Expected utility of no dam:	$EU = .5U(100) + .5U(50)$
Willingness-to-pay locus:	(δ_w, δ_d) such that
	$.5U(110 - \delta_w) + .5U(100 - \delta_d) = EU$
Option price:	$.5U(110 - OP) + .5U(100 - OP) = EU$
	$EU = 4.26$ and $OP = 34.2$
	for $U(c) = \ln(c)$, where c is net income
Comparison:	$OP > E(S)$

are equally likely, this surplus equals $30. This $30 expected surplus figure corresponds to the measure of benefits that is used in CBA when option price is not estimated.[3]

Notice that this example assumes that the dam will store water that can be used for irrigation purposes if it is dry. Consequently, the dam will do more for the farmer if it turns out to be dry than if it turns out to be wet. As a result, his income depends much less on which contingency actually occurs once the dam is built than it did without the dam. In other words, the dam reduces the income risk faced by the farmer by reducing the variation in his income. A useful summary measure of this reduction in income risk is provided by the effect of the dam on the variance of the farmer's income, which is $625 without the dam but only $25 with the dam.[4]

To determine the farmer's benefits from the dam, we first calculate his expected utility, *EU*, without the dam. We then find his option price, which is the maximum amount he would be willing to pay for the dam or, equivalently, the amount that gives him the same expected utility as he would have without the dam. To compute these amounts, we need to know the farmer's utility function. Normally, we would not have this information, which is why, in practice, expected surplus rather than option price is normally used to determine net benefits. For purposes of our illustration, however, we assume that the farmer's utility is given by the natural log of his income as shown in Table 8-1.

The curved line in Figure 8-1 shows this utility function. In the absence of a dam, the farmer realizes income of $50 dollars if it is dry and $100 if it is wet. Because the probabilities of wet and dry are each one-half, the expected utility without the dam can be found as the point midway between the utilities of these no-dam incomes. The point on the vertical axis labeled $EU = 4.26$ is exactly *a* units of utility away from each of the contingent utilities. As it is midway between them, it equals the expected utility. If the dam is built, then the farmer receives an income of $100 if it is dry and $110 if it

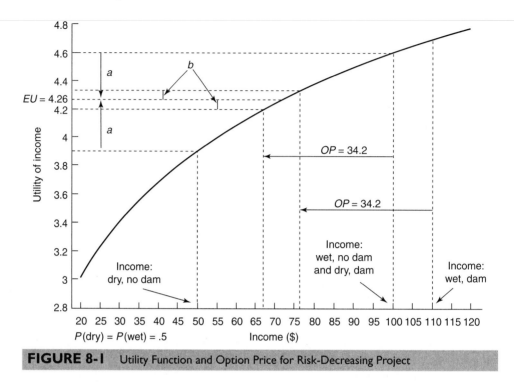

FIGURE 8-1 Utility Function and Option Price for Risk-Decreasing Project

is wet. The option price for the dam is the maximum amount of income the farmer would be willing to give up to have the dam—in other words, the amount that would allow him to obtain the same expected utility with the dam as he would obtain without it. The arrows marked $OP = 34.2$ shift the contingent incomes with the dam by subtracting $34.20 from each so that the net contingent incomes are $65.80 and $75.80. The utilities of these net incomes are each *b* units of utility away from 4.26 so that their expected utility equals the expected utility of no dam. Thus, either no dam or a dam with a certain payment of $34.20 gives the farmer the same expected utility.

The farmer's option price for the dam of $34.20 exceeds his expected surplus of $30. Thus, if the opportunity cost of the project were $32 and the farmer were the only beneficiary, then the common practice of using expected surplus would result in rejecting building the dam when, in fact, the option price indicates that building the dam would increase the farmer's utility.

Figure 8-2 provides an alternative graphical representation of the relationship between expected surplus and option price for the farmer. The vertical axis indicates the farmer's willingness-to-pay amounts if it is dry; the horizontal axis represents his willingness-to-pay amounts if it is wet. Thus, point A represents his surplus under each contingency.

There is a slightly different way to view point A. Imagine that before the government will build the dam the farmer would be required to sign a contract, Contract A, that stipulates that he will pay the government an amount equal to X_w if it turns out to be wet and an amount equal to X_d if it turns out to be dry. This is called a *contingent contract* because its terms depend on events that will not be known until sometime

FIGURE 8-2 Risk-Reducing Project: Expected Surplus and Option Price

in the future. Although the government is unlikely to require a contingent contract in practice, it is a useful device for thinking about how much the farmer values the dam or, in other words, his benefits from the dam. These benefits correspond to the maximum value that the government could assign to $\$X_w$ and $\$X_d$ and still get the farmer to sign Contract A, $10 and $50, respectively. The farmer would be willing to sign at these amounts because he would be exactly back to the situation he faced without the dam, when his income equaled $100 if it rained and $50 if it was dry. In other words, $10 and $50 are his maximum willingness-to-pay under Contract A.

Notice that because the $10 payment if it is wet and the $50 payment if it is dry put the farmer back to where he would be without the dam, they measure the surplus he receives because the dam increases his income but not the utility he receives because the dam reduces the income risk he faces. If the farmer makes these payments, then his income variability would be exactly what it was without the dam. To examine the change in income risk resulting from the dam, imagine now that the government is also willing to let the farmer choose an alternative contract, Contract B, that allows him to pay the same amount, $30, regardless of which contingency actually occurs. If the government does this, then the expected value of the payment it will receive would be equal under the two contracts. However, Contract B would place the farmer on a line that bisects the origin of Figure 8-2. This line is called the *certainty line* because payment amounts along it are the same regardless of which contingency actually occurs. Thus, any point along this line, including B, represents a certainty equivalent.

The certainty line intersects another line. This one passes through the surplus point, but every point along it has the same expected value. For example, in the case of our illustration, the expected value would always be equal to $30 along this line. This line is called the *fair bet line*. To see why, imagine flipping a coin. A payoff of $10 if you get heads and $50 if you get tails would have exactly the same expected value as $20 if you get heads and $40 if you get tails. Thus, the slope of the fair bet line, –1, is equal to the negative of the ratio of the probabilities of the contingencies. As one moves along the fair bet line toward the certainty line, the expected value always remains the same, but the variation in income decreases. Finally, at point *B* on the certainty line, the payoff is equal regardless of which contingency, heads or tails, actually occurs.[5] In our example, this payoff is $30.

We now return to our farmer and the dam and ask whether he would be indifferent between signing Contract *A,* under which he must pay $10 if it is wet and $50 if it is dry, and Contract *B,* under which he must pay $30 regardless of whether it is wet or dry, noting that the expected value of his income would be equal under the two contracts. To answer this, we look at what his income would be under the two contracts:

Contingency	Probability	Income under Contract A	Income under Contract B
Wet	.5	$100	$80
Dry	.5	$50	$70
EV		$75	$75

Although the expected value of income under the two contracts would be identical, the variation in income between the two contingencies is obviously much less under Contract *B.* Thus, by comparing Contracts *A* and *B,* we can examine the effect of the dam on the risk facing the farmer, while holding the expected value of his income constant. If the farmer is risk averse and, hence, would prefer a more stable to a less stable income from year to year, then he will not be indifferent between the two contracts but will prefer *B* to *A* because he will face less risk with *B* than with *A.*

Now, recall that at point *A* in Figure 8-2 the farmer was willing to sign a contract that would require him to pay $10 if it is wet and $50 if it is dry and that the expected value of these payments was $30. Because the farmer prefers point *B* to point *A,* this suggests that in order to reach the certainty line, the farmer would be willing to sign a contract requiring him to pay a certainty equivalent greater than $30. The maximum such amount that he would pay is represented by point *C* in Figure 8-2, a point that is farther northeast along the certainty line than point *B.* Point *C* represents the farmer's option price, the maximum amount that he would be willing to pay for *both* the increase in expected income and the reduction in income risk resulting from the dam. In other words, it incorporates the full value of the dam to the farmer. Conceptually, it is the correct measure of benefits that the farmer would receive from the dam. But in CBAs, it is point *B,* the expected value of the surpluses resulting from the dam, that is typically measured. While point *B* captures the effect of the dam on expected income, it does not incorporate the effect of the dam on income variability or risk.

Although the farmer would prefer point *B* to point *A,* he would be indifferent between points *A* and *C.* Indeed, a curve drawn between these points is very similar to an indifference curve. This curve, the *willingness-to-pay locus,*[6] shows all of the combinations of contingent payments for the dam that give the farmer the same expected utility with the dam as without it.[7] It is based on knowledge of the probabilities of the contingencies prior to knowing which one will actually occur.

TABLE 8-2 Example of a Risk-Increasing Project

| | Policy | | Probability of Contingency |
Contingency	Bridge	No Bridge	
No earthquake	200	100	.8
Earthquake	100	80	.2
Expected value	180	96	
Variance	1600	64	

Surplus point: $U(200 - S_n) = U(100)$ so $S_n = 100$
$U(100 - S_e) = U(80)$ so $S_e = 20$

Expected surplus: $E(S) = .8S_n + .2S_e = 84$

Expected utility of no bridge: $EU = .8U(100) + .2U(80)$

Willingness-to-pay locus: (δ_n, δ_e) such that
$.8U(200 - \delta_n) + .2U(100 - \delta_e) = EU$

Option price: $.8U(200 - OP) + .2U(100 - OP) = EU$
$EU = 4.56$ and $OP = 71.1$
for $U(c) = \ln(c)$, where c is net income

Comparison: $OP < E(S)$

If the cost of the project does not depend on the contingency that occurs, then it would also be represented as a point on the certainty line. If the option price lies farther to the northeast along the certainty line than does the cost, then the project would increase the farmer's welfare.

Table 8-2 describes a policy involving constructing a bridge in an area where the probability of an earthquake is 20 percent. The bridge would increase the expected value of income that the individual described in the table receives, but at the same time, it would make her income more dependent on whether or not a quake actually occurs. In other words, the bridge increases the income risk facing the individual. Consequently, as shown in the table, the expected surplus of $84 exceeds the option price of $71.10. Thus, if the opportunity cost of the bridge were a certain $75 and the person were the only beneficiary, then the option price indicates that building it would reduce her expected utility if she actually had to pay the opportunity cost of its construction. Hence, the bridge should not be built even though the expected surplus from building it is positive.

This situation is illustrated in Figure 8-3. The bridge can be viewed as initially placing the individual at point D. Once again, we can imagine the government requiring the individual to sign a contingent contract, Contract D. In this case, the individual would be willing to pay up to $100 in the event that there is not a quake but only $20 if there is a quake. By signing such a contract, she would be no worse off than she was without the bridge.

We have taken account of the fact that the bridge would increase expected surplus but not the fact that it would also affect income risk. Thus, as before, we imagine that the government is also willing to sign a different contract, Contract E, as long as the expected value of the payments continues to equal $84, their expected value under Contract D.

FIGURE 8-3 Risk-Increasing Project: Expected Surplus and Option Price

Which contract would she prefer? If she is risk averse, she would prefer Contract *D* to Contract *E* because, in the following table even though the expected value of her income is identical under the two contracts, her income would be subject to less risk:

Contingency	Income under Probability	Income under Contract D	Contract E
No quake	.8	$100	$116
Quake	.2	$80	$16
EV		$96	$96

Because a risk-averse individual would prefer Contract *D* to Contract *E*, her willingness-to-pay locus for the bridge would be below her fair bet line. Consequently, her option price, which is represented by point *F*, is less than $84. As in the previous illustration, the individual would be indifferent between points *D* and *F*, but not between points *D* and *E*.

Is Option Price the Best Measure of Benefits?

The illustrations previously described demonstrate that, in general, option price does not equal expected surplus in circumstances of uncertainty. In the first illustration, option price was larger than the expected value; in the second illustration, it was smaller. We have implicitly taken option price to be the correct benefit measure. Is this generally the case? The answer to this question requires a clearer specification of the institutional environment of policy choice.

The key consideration concerns the availability of insurance against the risks in question. *If complete and actuarially fair insurance is unavailable against the relevant risks, then option price is the conceptually correct measure of benefits.* Insurance is complete if individuals can purchase sufficient coverage to eliminate their risks entirely. It is actuarially fair if its price depends only on the true probabilities of the relevant contingencies. In the case of two contingencies, with the probability of contingency 1 equal to p and the probability of contingency 2 equal to $1 - p$, actuarially fair insurance would allow the individual to trade contingent income in contingency 1 for contingent income in contingency 2 at a price of $p/(1 - p)$. For example, if p equals .2, then the price of insurance equals .25 (.2/.8), so that to increase income in contingency 1 by $100, the individual would have to give up $25 in contingency 2. Graphically, the availability of actuarially fair insurance means that individuals could move along the fair bet lines toward the certainty lines shown in Figures 8-2 and 8-3 through purchases of insurance.

Complete and actuarially fair insurance is rarely available in the real world.[8] The problem of *moral hazard*, the changes in risk-related behavior of insurees induced by insurance coverage, encourages profit-maximizing insurers to limit coverage through copayments.[9] Insurers may be unwilling to provide full insurance against losses to unique assets that cannot be easily valued in markets.[10] *Adverse selection* occurs when insurees have better information about their true risks than do insurers. Adverse selection may result in either the combining of low- and high-risk persons in the same price pool or the limiting of the extent of coverage to induce high risks to reveal themselves.[11] The pooling of high- and low-risk persons implies that at least one of the groups receives an actuarially unfair price; limiting available coverage to high-risk persons means that complete insurance is unavailable. Routine administrative costs, as well as efforts to control moral hazard and adverse selection, inflate prices above the actuarially fair levels. Limited pools of insurees or uncertainty about the magnitudes of risks may require a further increment in prices to reduce the risk of bankruptcy.[12] Finally, some risks are so highly correlated across individuals that risk pooling does not sufficiently reduce aggregate risk to allow actuarially fair prices.[13] In order to manage the risk of going bankrupt, insurers facing correlated risks must charge an amount above the actuarially fair price to build a financial cushion or buy reinsurance to guard against the possibility of having to pay off on many losses at the same time.

Imagine that, despite these practical limitations, complete and actuarially fair insurance were available for the risk in question. It would then be possible for the sponsor of the project to trade the contingent surplus amounts for a certain payment by purchasing sufficient insurance to move along the fair bet line, which represents actuarially fair insurance, to the certainty line. In this way, a certain payment corresponding to the expected surplus could be achieved. For example, returning to Figure 8-3, the project sponsor could guarantee a certain payment of $84, which is larger than the option price of $71.10. Notice, however, that if the option price exceeds the expected surplus (the situation illustrated in Figure 8-2), then the latter will understate the conceptually correct measure of project benefits even if complete and actuarially fair insurance can be purchased. In general, therefore, *if complete and actuarially fair insurance is available, then the larger of option price or expected surplus is the appropriate measure of benefits.*

This generalization ignores one additional institutional constraint: It is not practical to specify contingency-specific payments that would move an individual from his or her contingent surplus point to other points on his or her willingness-to-pay locus. The impracticality may arise from a lack of either information about the shape of the entire willingness-to-pay locus or the administrative capacity to write and execute contingent contracts through taxes and subsidies whose magnitudes depend on the occurrence of events. Yet, if such contracts were administratively feasible *and* the analyst knew the entire willingness-to-pay locus, then the policy could be designed with optimal contingent payments so that the person's post-payment contingent surpluses would have the greatest expected value, which could then be realized with certainty through insurance purchases.

Figure 8-4 illustrates this possibility. In the absence of payments, the person realizes either S_1 or S_2 depending on which contingency occurs. If, in addition to the direct effects of the policy, the person were given a payment equal to $FB_1 - S_1$ if contingency 1 occurred or paid a fee of $S_2 - FB_2$ if contingency 2 occurred, then the person's post-payment contingent surpluses would be given by point FB^*. Because FB^* is the point of tangency between the willingness-to-pay locus and a fair bet line, it has the largest expected value of any point on the willingness-to-pay locus. Starting at this point, complete and actuarially fair insurance would allow the policy sponsors to move along the fair bet line to the certainty line. The resulting certain payment, $E(FB^*)$ would be the maximum certain amount of benefit produced by the payment-adjusted policy.[14]

Thus, *in the exceedingly unlikely circumstance that optimal contingent payments are feasible **and** complete and actuarially fair insurance is available, the expected value of*

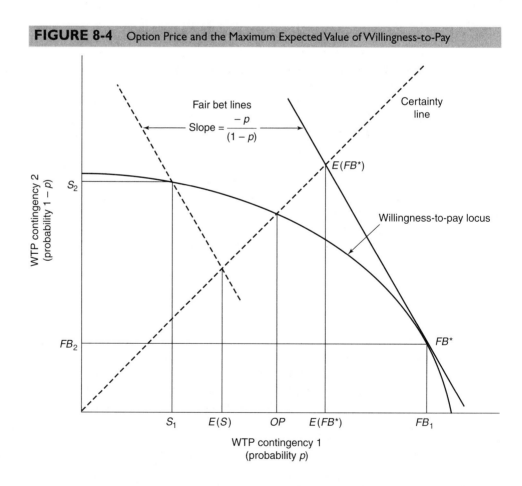

FIGURE 8-4   Option Price and the Maximum Expected Value of Willingness-to-Pay

the point on the willingness-to-pay locus that is just tangent to the fair bet line is the appropriate measure of benefits.

In summary, if the policy under consideration involves costs that are certain and complete and actuarially fair insurance is unavailable, then option price is the appropriate measure of benefits because it allows us to compare certain willingness-to-pay amounts with certain costs. In practice, however, option prices are difficult to measure. Indeed, as will be evident from the discussion of option values in the next section, very specific assumptions about the nature of risks must be made to be able to determine whether option price is larger or smaller than the commonly measured expected surplus.

DETERMINING THE BIAS IN EXPECTED SURPLUS: SIGNING OPTION VALUE

Early attempts to apply CBA to recreational resources such as national parks raised uneasiness about the appropriateness of expected surplus as a benefit measure. In a seminal article dealing with the issue, Burton Weisbrod pointed out that estimates of the benefits of preserving a national park based solely on the benefits accruing to actual visitors do not capture its value to those who anticipate visiting it sometime in the future but actually never do.[15] He argued that these nonvisitors would be willing to pay something to preserve the option of visiting. He called this amount *option value*, which has been interpreted by many as a separate benefit category of relevance to valuing assets, such as natural resources, that offer opportunities for future consumption.

Yet CBA requires a more precise definition of option value.[16] The key to formulating it lies in the recognition that option price fully measures a person's *ex ante* willingness-to-pay for a policy in the presence of uncertainty about the benefits that will accrue *ex post*. The uncertainty may arise from a variety of sources, including not only uncertainty about the demand the person will actually have for the goods produced by the policy if it is implemented (Weisbrod's point), but also uncertainty about the quantities, qualities, and prices of the goods, as well as the prices of other goods. Because, even with such uncertainties, it is a full measure of willingness-to-pay, option price includes option value.

It is now standard to define *option value* as the difference between option price and expected surplus:

$$OV \equiv OP - E[S] \qquad (8.1)$$

where OV is option value, OP is the option price, and $E[S]$ is expected surplus. For example, the option value for the dam presented in Table 8-1 is $4.20, the option price of $34.20 minus the expected surplus of $30. The option value of the bridge presented in Table 8-2 is −$12.90, the option price of $71.10 minus the expected surplus of $84.

Rearranging the equation defining option value gives the practical interpretation of option value as an adjustment to expected surplus required to make it equal to option price:

$$OP = E[S] + OV \qquad (8.2)$$

where the left-hand side is the certain amount a person is willing to pay, the conceptually correct measure of benefits, and the right-hand side consists of expected surplus, which is what is typically measurable, and option value, which is the amount that would have to be added to expected surplus to make it equal to option price. Though it may seem natural to interpret option value as a distinct benefit category, it is probably better to interpret it as the bias in estimated benefits resulting from measurement by expected surplus rather than option price. Unfortunately, either interpretation requires caution because the sign, let alone the magnitude, of option value is often difficult to determine.

Determining the Sign of Option Value

The sign of option value may be positive or negative, depending on a variety of assumptions concerning the source and nature of risk, the characteristics of the policy being analyzed, and the underlying structure of individual utility. With only a few exceptions, the sign of option value has proven to be theoretically ambiguous. This raises the issue of the usefulness of the concept of option value for even determining the direction of bias when expected surplus is used as an approximation of option price.

The earliest studies (see Appendix 8A) attempted to determine the sign of option price when the change in the price or quantity of the good being valued is certain but the demand for the good is uncertain. For example, in the earliest effort to sign option value, Charles J. Cicchetti and A. Myrick Freeman III assumed that there is some probability that a person will have positive demand for the good.[17] Their conclusion that option price is always positive when demand is uncertain was later contradicted by Richard Schmalensee, who showed that the sign was ambiguous under general assumptions.[18]

Subsequent efforts to sign option value without making specific assumptions about individuals' utility functions have produced an unequivocal result only with respect to uncertainty in income. Specifically, in valuing a certain change in the price or quantity of a normal good (quantity demanded increases with increases in income), option value will be negative for a risk-averse person with uncertain income because the change in price or quantity of the good accentuates the income uncertainty. Conversely, in valuing a certain change in the price or quantity of an inferior good (quantity demanded decreases with increases in income), option value will be positive for a risk-averse person. As CBA typically involves valuing normal goods, this general result cautions against the tendency to think of option value as a positive adjustment to expected surplus.

On the other hand, with the imposition of a variety of different restrictive assumptions, it appears that for risk-averse persons uncertainty about the quantity, quality, or

---

EXHIBIT 8-1

In 1980 Richard G. Walsh, John B. Loomis, and Richard A. Gillman combined survey and recreational use data in an effort to estimate the willingness of Colorado households to pay for increments of land designated for wilderness. They estimated that residents of the state were willing to pay a total of $41.6 million annually for 2.6 million acres. Approximately $6.0 million, or almost 15 percent, of this total was option value.

Source: Adapted from Richard G. Walsh, John B. Loomis, and Richard A. Gillman, "Valuing Option, Existence, and Bequest Demands for Wilderness," *Land Economics* 60(1) 1984, 14–29.

price of a normal good (supply-side uncertainty) will usually result in a positive option value. For example, Douglas M. Larson and Paul R. Flacco show that if the demand for a normal (inferior) good is linear, semilog, or loglinear in price, then option price is positive (negative) for uncertainty in the price or quality of the good being valued.[19] They also show that uncertainty about the prices of other goods and tastes—demand-side uncertainty—similarly yields positive (negative) option values for normal (inferior) goods for these demand functions.[20]

Overall, the theoretical studies of option value suggest the following general heuristic: *With risk-averse individuals and normal (inferior) goods, treat option value as negative (positive) for income uncertainty, positive (negative) for other demand-side uncertainties, and generally positive (negative) for supply-side uncertainties.* Of course, the assumed sign of option value should be consistent with the specific assumptions employed. So, for example, if the empirically estimated demand for a normal good employs a loglinear functional form with a positive income elasticity, then option value would be negative for income uncertainty, positive for other demand-side uncertainties, and positive for supply-side uncertainties.

It should not be surprising that in view of the difficulty in establishing the sign of option value, even less progress has been made in putting bounds on its size relative to expected surplus. Calculations by V. Kerry Smith suggest that the size of option value relative to expected surplus is likely to be greater for assets that have less perfect substitutes.[21] Larson and Flacco derived expressions for option value for the specific demand functions that they investigated, but the implementation of these expressions is computationally very difficult.[22] Consequently, it is generally not possible to quantify option value using the information from which estimates of expected surplus are typically made.

RATIONALES FOR EXPECTED SURPLUS AS A PRACTICAL BENEFIT MEASURE

Although option price is generally the conceptually correct measure of benefits in circumstances of uncertainty, analysts most often estimate benefits in terms of expected surpluses. As indicated in the preceding discussion of option value, determining even the sign of the bias that results from the use of expected surplus rather than option price is not always possible. In this section we consider the reasonableness of expected surplus as a practical benefit measure.

We present two arguments often made in defense of the use of expected surplus. One argument is based on the consideration of benefits at the aggregate social level. Another argument applies at the level of the individual policy when people face independent risks so that realized net benefits are likely to be close to expected net benefits. We consider each of these arguments in turn.

Expected Values and Aggregate Social Benefits

If society were risk neutral, then choosing policies that individually maximized expected net benefits would be efficient in the sense of maximizing the expected value of society's entire portfolio of policies.[23] If we assume that projects spread costs and benefits broadly over a large population, then the effect of any particular project on the net income of any person is likely to be small. Even if people are risk averse, their preferences can be reasonably approximated as being risk neutral for such small changes in income. Therefore, aggregation of individual preferences would lead to risk neutrality at the social level so that expected surplus would be an appropriate measure of benefits.[24]

The variable magnitudes and uneven distribution of costs and benefits that often arise from public policies undercut this line of argument, however. Policies of great import may involve large costs and benefits that remain significant at the individual level, even when spread over a large population. Policies that are targeted at specific groups, such as the unemployed, or at geographical regions often impose substantial costs on and produce substantial benefits for specific individuals. Thus, because social risk neutrality is a questionable assumption, this aggregate-level argument for the use of expected surplus is weak.

A related line of argument is based on the assumption that society holds a fully diversified portfolio of policies that allows it to self-insure against the risk of any particular project. In other words, society is able to pool risk across projects so that it effectively has complete and actuarially fair insurance. (As previously noted, insurance is complete if it is available against all risks; it is actuarially fair if it is offered at a premium equal to the expected values of the risks.) As discussed earlier, with the availability of such insurance, the larger of option price and expected surplus is the appropriate benefit measure. Thus, benefits would always be at least as large as expected surplus so that any project with positive expected net benefits would be potentially Pareto improving. Of course, the comparison of mutually exclusive policies in terms of expected surpluses could be misleading if any of the projects have option prices larger than expected surpluses.

It is worth noting that this version of the argument does not rely on the collection of policies effectively averaging costs and benefits across individuals as does the first version of the argument. Rather, it relies on an averaging of aggregate net benefits across policies so that the potential Pareto criterion can be met overall, if not at the level of the individual project.

The weakness of this argument is that diversification does not eliminate all risk. A portfolio of policies as broad as even the whole stock market would still involve some systematic risk. For example, imagine adding independent policies with positive expected net benefits to the portfolio. Although the variance of the average net benefits of the policies would approach zero, the variance in total net benefits would actually increase. The variance in total net benefits means that society cannot guarantee that it will realize the total expected value of net benefits. As diversification does not permit fully effective self-insurance, it does not provide a fully satisfactory rationale for the practical use of expected net benefits.

Expected Values and Pooling Risks across Individuals: Collective and Individual Risk

We next consider the possibility of risk pooling at the level of the individual policy. It is important to make a distinction between collective risk and individual risk.

By *collective risk*, we simply mean that the same contingency will result for all individuals in society. For example, in the context of doing a CBA for a nuclear power plant, the contingencies might be "no accident" and "nuclear accident"—everyone in the geographic area experiences the same realized contingency. The actual realized net benefits can differ substantially from the expected net benefits because all individuals share either the favorable or the unfavorable outcome, rather than the weighted average of the two. In such circumstances, the world does not offer us a "middle" outcome corresponding to the expected value. Realized net benefits will, therefore, differ substantially from expected net benefits.

In contrast, consider the case of a large number of individuals who have identical preferences and who face the same probabilities of realizing each of the contingencies, but the contingency that each individual realizes is independent of the contingency realized by any other individual. This is a case of *individual risk*. This might occur, for instance, in the context of evaluating an automobile safety device using a model of traffic accidents in which there is some probability that a driver will have a potentially fatal accident for each mile driven. Multiplying the expected net benefits for one individual by the number of individuals yields a measure of total expected net benefits for the policy that can appropriately be treated as approximately certain. The reason is that in circumstances of individual risk with large numbers of individuals exposed to the risk, the proportion of individuals realizing each contingency approximates the probability associated with that contingency. In other words, the averaging process tends to produce realizations of total net benefits close to those calculated by the expected value procedure.

This averaging is analytically equivalent to the availability of actuarially fair insurance—it effectively translates, through a movement along a fair bet line, any contingent surplus point to a point on the certainty line. Thus, *in cases of individual risk, the larger of option price and expected surplus is the appropriate benefit measure.* As with complete diversification, the use of expected surplus as a benefit measure would guarantee that adopted policies were potentially Pareto improving but would not necessarily lead to the adoption of the most efficient policies in comparisons of mutually exclusive alternatives.

Reprise: Expected Surplus as a Practical Measure

How reasonable is the use of expected surplus as a practical benefit measure? Although social risk neutrality argues for expected surplus as the correct benefit measure, its underlying assumptions are not plausible. Somewhat more plausibly, diversification across policies argues for expected surplus as a conservative measure of benefits. That is, benefits can be no smaller than expected surplus. The pooling of individual risks among those affected by a policy argues convincingly for treatment of expected surplus as a conservative measure of benefits. Overall, these arguments suggest that when neither option prices nor option values can be estimated, and risks are individual rather than collective, analysts can reasonably use expected surplus as an approximate measure of benefits. When dealing with cases involving collective risk, they should take special care to consider the potential bias in this approach.

CONCLUSION

We rarely have much opportunity to infer option prices directly from observable behavior, though insurance premiums and self-protection investments may convey some useful information about people's willingness-to-pay for reductions in risk. Contingent valuation surveys provide an alternative approach for directly eliciting option prices through structured conversations with respondents, but they are prone to the problems we discuss in Chapter 14. Consequently, we often have no alternative but to predict policy effects under the specified contingencies, value them with shadow price estimates from observed market behavior, and calculate expected net benefits. In cases of individual risk, it is unlikely that this procedure will result in an overestimation of net benefits. In cases of collective risk, however, these expected net benefits may either understate or overstate the conceptually correct benefits based on option price by an amount called the option value. Unfortunately, confidently signing, let alone quantifying, option price is often not possible.

APPENDIX 8A

Signing Option Value

The following table shows the progression of theoretical investigations of the sign of option value.

Study	*Assumptions and Conclusions*	*Comments*
Douglas M. Larson and Paul R. Flacco, "Measuring Option Prices from Market Behavior," *Journal of Environmental Economics and Management* 22(2) 1992, 178–198.	(1) Linear, semilog, or loglinear demand functions; uncertainty in own-price, other prices, quality, or tastes: Option value positive for normal goods; option price negative for inferior goods. (2) Linear demand, uncertainty about income, normal or inferior goods: Option value is zero. (3) Semilog or loglinear demand; uncertainty about income; normal or inferior goods: Option value is negative.	Assumption of specific functional forms for demand allow signing of option value for nonincome uncertainty. Linear demand implies risk neutrality; semilog and loglinear demands imply risk aversion for normal goods and risk seeking for inferior goods.
Richard C. Hartman and Mark L. Plummer, "Option Value under Income and Price Uncertainty," *Journal of Environmental Economics and Management* 14(3) 1987, 212–225.	(1) Uncertainty in income: Option value is negative for normal goods. (2) Uncertainty in own-price and other prices: Sign of option value is ambiguous.	General in the sense that preferences may depend on contingencies.
Mark L. Plummer and Richard C. Hartman, "Option Value: A General Approach," *Economic Inquiry* 24(3) 1986, 455–471.	(1) Uncertainty in income and risk aversion: Option value is negative for normal goods. (2) Uncertainty in quality and risk aversion: Option value is positive for normal goods. (3) Uncertainty in tastes and risk aversion: Option value ambiguous for more than two contingencies.	Sign of option value for uncertain parameter depends on signs of the changes in surplus and marginal utility with respect to the parameter.
A. Myrick Freeman III, "The Sign and Size of Option Value," *Land Economics* 60(1) 1984, 1–13.	(1) Uncertainty in demand due to exogenous factors and risk aversion: Option value is positive. (2) If probability of demand is low, expected consumer surplus is large, and person is highly risk averse, then option value may be large.	Depends on assumption that marginal utilities and attitudes toward risk independent of exogenous factors; demonstrated for only two contingencies.
Richard C. Bishop, "Option Value: An Exposition and Extension," *Land Economics* 58(1) 1982, 1–15.	(1) Uncertainty in demand: Sign of option value is ambiguous.	Supply-side case demonstrated for only two contingencies.

(Continued)

(Continued)

	(2) Uncertainty in supply (price uncertainty): Option value is positive.	
Richard Schmalensee, "Option Demand and Consumer's Surplus: Valuing Price Changes under Uncertainty," *American Economic Review* 62(5) 1972, 813–824.	Uncertainty in demand: Sign of option value is ambiguous.	Sign depends on risk aversion and whether surplus is measured by equivalent or compensating variation.
Charles J. Cicchetti and A. Myrick Freeman III, "Option Demand and Consumer Surplus: Further Comment," *Quarterly Journal of Economics* 85(3) 1971, 528–539.	Uncertainty in demand: Option value is positive.	Overly strong assumptions imply the same utility results under each contingency.

EXERCISES FOR CHAPTER 8

1. A large rural county is considering establishing a medical transport unit that would use helicopters to fly emergency medical cases to hospitals. Analysts have attempted to estimate the benefits from establishing the unit in two ways. First, they surveyed a random sample of residents to find out how much they would be willing to pay each year for the unit. Based on responses from the sample, the analysts estimated a total willingness-to-pay of $8.5 million per year. Second, the analysts estimated the dollar value of the improvements in health outcomes and avoided medical costs of users of the unit to be $6.2 million per year.

   Taking the analysts' estimates at face value, specify the following:

   a. The aggregate of individuals' annual option prices for the unit.
   b. The annual total expected gain in social surplus from use of the unit.
   c. The annual aggregate option value for the unit.

2. Imagine that we want to value a cultural festival from the point of view of a risk-averse person. The person's utility is given by $U(I)$ where $I is her income. She has a 50 percent chance of being able to get vacation time to attend the festival. If she gets the vacation time, then she would be willing to pay up to $S to attend the festival. If she does not get the vacation time, then she is unwilling to pay anything for the festival.

   a. What is her expected surplus if the cultural festival takes place?
   b. Write an expression for her expected utility if the festival does not take place.
   c. Write an expression incorporating her option price, OP, for the festival if the festival takes place. (To do this, equate her expected utility if the festival takes place to her expected utility if the festival does not take place. Also, assume that if the festival does take place, then she makes a payment of OP whether or not she is able to attend the festival.)
   d. Manipulate the expression for option price to show that the option price must be smaller than her expected surplus. (In doing this, begin by substituting $0.5S - e$ for OP in the equation derived in part c. Also keep in mind that because the person is risk averse, her marginal utility declines with income.)
   e. Does this exercise suggest any generalizations about the benefits of recreational programs when individuals are uncertain as to whether they will be able to participate in them?

3. (Spreadsheet required.) Imagine that a rancher would have an income of $80,000 if his county remains free from a cattle parasite but only $50,000 if the county is exposed to the

parasite. Further imagine that a county program to limit the impact of exposure to the parasite would reduce his income to $76,000 if the county remains free of the parasite but increase it to $70,000 if the county is exposed to the parasite. Assume that there is a 60 percent chance of exposure to the parasite and that the rancher's utility is the natural logarithm of his income. What is the rancher's option price for the county program? (Set up the appropriate equation and solve through iterative guessing.)

NOTES

1. Our discussion in this section is based on Daniel A. Graham, "Cost-Benefit Analysis Under Uncertainty," *American Economic Review* 71(4) 1981, 715–725; V. Kerry Smith, "Uncertainty, Benefit-Cost Analysis, and the Treatment of Option Value," *Journal of Environmental Economics and Management* 14(3) 1987, 283–292; and Charles E. Meier and Alan Randall, "Use Value Under Uncertainty: Is There a 'Correct' Measure'?" *Land Economics* 67(4) 1991, 379–389. The latter is the best overview of this topic despite a pedagogically relevant typographical error (the slope of the fair bet line is misstated in several diagrams).

2. Measuring benefits by persons' *ex ante* willingness-to-pay assumes that they correctly assess and process risks. Lack of information about risks, or biases in processing the information, muddies the comparison between this approach and the expectational approach if the latter involves more accurate risk assessments. For overviews, see Colin F. Camerer and Howard Kunreuther, "Decision Processes for Low Probability Risks: Policy Implications," *Journal of Policy Analysis and Management* 8(4) 1989, 565–592, and W. Kip Viscusi, *Fatal Trade-offs: Public and Private Responsibilities for Risk* (New York: Oxford University Press, 1992).

3. Formally, let m_i be the person's wealth under contingency i and let Z be an indicator of whether or not the policy under consideration is adopted ($Z = 0$ if not adopted; $Z = 1$ if adopted). The person's utility under contingency i can be written as $U(m_i, Z)$. The person's surplus (willingness-to-pay) for the project given that contingency i occurs, S_i, satisfies the equation:

$$U(m_i - S_i, 1) = U(m_i, 0)$$

The expected value of the person's contingent surpluses is $E(S) = p_1 S_1 + p_2 S_2$ in the case of two contingencies with probabilities p_1 and p_2, respectively.

4. Variance is defined as: $\text{Var}[X] = E\{(X - E[X])^2\}$. For a discrete random variable with possible outcomes $x_i, i = 1, 2, \ldots n,$

$$E[X] = \Sigma x_i p(x_i) \text{ and } \text{Var}[X] = \Sigma(x_i - E[X])^2 p(x_i)$$

where $p(x_i)$ is the probability of the ith outcome occurring.

In the case of the payoffs from the dam given in Table 8-1:

$$E[X] = (.5)(F110) + (.5)(100) = 105$$
$$\text{and } \text{Var}[X] = (.5)(110 - 105)^2 + (.5)(100 - 105)^2$$
$$= 25$$

5. The intersection of the fair bet line and the certainty line corresponds to the solution of the following equations:

$$E(S) = p_1 x_1 + p_2 x_2 \text{ (expected value line)}$$
$$x_1 = x_2 \text{ (certainty line)}$$
$$p_1 = 1 - p_2$$

where x_1 defines the location of points on the vertical axis and x_2 defines the location of points on the horizontal axis. Solving these equations gives $E(S) = x$, where x is the point of intersection.

6. Two aspects of the relation among the fair bet line, the certainty line, and the willingness-to-pay locus are worth noting. First, if insurance were available in unlimited quantity at an actuarially fair price, then the person could actually move from any point on the willingness-to-pay locus along the fair bet line to the certainty line by buying insurance.

The near consensus that option price is the appropriate benefit measure is based on the reasonable assumption that complete and actuarially fair insurance markets generally do not exist in the real world. Second, a fair bet line can be drawn through any point. Thus, for example, if we wanted to know which point on the willingness-to-pay locus has the largest expected value, then we would find the point that is just tangent to a fair bet line.

7. Continuing with the notation from note 3, points on the willingness-to-pay locus, (w_1, w_2), satisfy the following equation:

$$p_1 U_1(m_1 - w_1, 1) + p_2 U_2(m_2 - w_2, 1) = EU$$

where $EU = p_1 U_1(m_1, 0) + p_2 U_2(m_2, 0)$ is the person's expected utility without the project.

8. For a general introduction to the theory of insurance, see Isaac Ehrlich and Gary S. Becker, "Market Insurance, Self-Insurance, and Self-Protection," *Journal of Political Economy* 80(4) 1972, 663–648.

9. Mark V. Pauly, "The Economics of Moral Hazard: Comment," *American Economic Review* 58(3) 1968, 531–537.

10. Philip J. Cook and Daniel A. Graham, "The Demand for Insurance and Protection: The Case of Irreplaceable Commodities," *Quarterly Journal of Economics* 91(1) 1977, 141–156.

11. One way to get high-risk persons to reveal themselves is to offer two insurance options: one that gives full coverage at a premium that is actuarially fair for high risks and another that gives only limited coverage at a premium that is actuarially fair for low risks. If the level of coverage under the latter option is sufficiently low, then high risks will be better off revealing themselves to get the full coverage. The result is a so-called *separating equilibrium* in which both risk groups honestly reveal themselves. The information is gained, however, at the cost of limiting coverage to low-risk persons. See Michael Rothschild and Joseph Stiglitz, "Equilibrium in Competitive Insurance Markets: An Essay on the Economics of Imperfect Information," *Quarterly Journal of Economics* 90(4) 1976, 629–650. An extension of the Rothschild-Stiglitz model, which incorporates contracting costs, allows for the possibility that low-risk persons receive more favorable

coverage. See Joseph P. Newhouse, "Reimbursing Health Plans and Health Providers: Efficiency in Production Versus Selection," *Journal of Economic Literature* 34(3) 1996, 1236–1263.

12. J. David Cummins, "Statistical and Financial Models of Insurance Pricing and the Insurance Firm," *Journal of Risk and Insurance* 58(2) 1991, 261–301.

13. Jack Hirshleifer and John G. Riley, *The Analytics of Uncertainty and Information* (New York: Cambridge University Press, 1992).

14. The difference between $E[FB^*]$ and $E[S]$ is called the *option premium*. Unlike option value, it is always nonnegative. See Dennis C. Cory and Bonnie Colby Saliba, "Requiem for Option Value," *Land Economics* 63(1) 1987, 1–10. Unfortunately, the extreme assumptions of complete and actuarially fair insurance, knowledge of the entire willingness-to-pay locus, and the feasibility of contingent-specific payments give the notion of option premium little practical relevance to CBA.

15. Burton A. Weisbrod, "Collective Consumption Services of Individual Consumption Goods," *Quarterly Journal of Economics* 78(3) 1964, 71–77.

16. The possibility of double counting benefits with this formulation was soon pointed out by Millard F. Long, "Collective-Consumption Services of Individual-Consumption Goods," *Quarterly Journal of Economics* 81(2) 1967, 351–352.

17. Charles J. Cicchetti and A. Myrick Freeman III, "Option Demand and Consumer Surplus: Further Comment," *Quarterly Journal of Economics* 85(3) 1971, 528–539.

18. Richard Schmalensee, "Option Demand and Consumer's Surplus: Valuing Price Changes under Uncertainty," *American Economic Review* 62(5) 1972, 813–824. Robert Anderson later showed that the contradictory results arose because of additional assumptions made by Cicchetti and Freeman that had the unattractive consequence of guaranteeing the option buyer a certain utility level no matter which contingency arose. Robert J. Anderson Jr., "A Note on Option Value and the Expected Value of Consumer's Surplus," *Journal of Environmental Economics and Management* 8(2) 1981, 187–191.

19. Douglas M. Larson and Paul R. Flacco, "Measuring Option Prices from Market Behavior," *Journal of Environmental Economics and Management* 22(2) 1992, 178–198.

20. Larson and Flacco, "Measuring Option Prices from Market Behavior." As discussed in Chapter 12, empirical estimation of demand equations usually involves at least income and own-price as explanatory variables for quantity. If the sign of the estimated coefficient of income is positive (negative), then the good is normal (inferior).

21. V. Kerry Smith, "A Bound for Option Value," *Land Economics* 60(3) 1984, 292–296.

22. Their expressions require not only estimates of the parameters of the demand equations, but also fairly complicated expectations over the parameters that are treated as uncertain.

23. To say that society is risk neutral implies that there is a social welfare function that ranks alternative distributions of goods among individuals.

That is, it gives a "score" to each possible distribution such that a distribution with a higher score is preferred by society to a distribution with a lower score. Aggregation of individual preferences, however, cannot guarantee a social welfare function that satisfies minimally desirable properties as noted in Chapter 2. Again, see Tibor Scitovsky, "The State of Welfare Economics," *American Economic Review* 51(3) 1951, 301–315. More generally, see Kenneth J. Arrow, *Social Choice and Individual Values*, 2nd ed. (New Haven, CT: Yale University Press, 1963).

24. Kenneth J. Arrow and Robert C. Lind, "Uncertainty and the Evaluation of Public Investment Decisions," *American Economic Review* 60(3) 1970, 364–378.

CHAPTER 9

Existence Value

Within the CBA framework, people's willingness-to-pay for a policy change comprehensively measures its social benefits. Though analysts sometimes elicit willingness-to-pay amounts through contingent valuation surveys (see Chapter 14), they prefer to make inferences about them from observations of people's behaviors where possible (see Chapters 11, 12, and 13). The behaviors usually involve changes in consumption of a good whose price or quantity is affected by the policy change, or changes in consumption of substitutes for, or complements of, the good—observed responses to price changes permit inferences about demand curves that, in turn, allow willingness-to-pay to be estimated. For many, perhaps most, applications of CBA, analysts can reasonably assume that social surplus changes estimated on the basis of observable changes in the consumption or prices of goods conceptually capture the entire willingness-to-pay. Yet in some applications of CBA, especially those involving changes in unique natural resources, people may be willing to pay for the existence of goods that they themselves will never "consume." Correctly conceptualizing and measuring such *existence values* poses a difficult challenge to the application of CBA.

In this chapter, we consider existence value as a category of benefit. It is often lumped together with option value and quasi-option value under the heading of *nonuse* or *passive use* benefits. As discussed in Chapters 7 and 8, however, option and quasi-option values are better thought of as adjustments to standard benefit measures to take account of various aspects of uncertainty rather than as distinct categories of benefits. In contrast, existence value is a meaningful benefit category, though one that poses problems of definition. After framing existence value as a benefit category, we discuss the theoretical and empirical problems analysts face in measuring it.

ACTIVE AND PASSIVE USE VALUE

The notion that people may place a value on the very existence of "unique phenomena of nature" that they neither visit, nor ever anticipate visiting, was introduced into the CBA literature almost 30 years ago by John V. Krutilla.[1] Consider, for example, a wilderness area that provides habitat for rare game animals. Hunters might be willing to pay to preserve the wilderness area because it either lowers the price or increases the quality of hunting. Naturalists might be willing to pay to preserve the area because it provides a desirable area for hiking or bird watching. Nearby residents may be willing to pay to preserve the area because it provides scenic beauty and prevents commercial development that they find undesirable. People who enjoy nature films may be willing to pay to preserve the area because it provides a unique setting for filming rare species. All of these people value the area because they make use of it in some way. Yet one can imagine that some other people might be willing to pay to preserve the area even though they do not use it in any of these ways. In commonly used terminology, this latter group of people is said to derive *nonuse value* from the wilderness area.

While most economists accept the general idea that people may derive value from mere knowledge of the existence of unique assets such as scenic wilderness, animal species, or works of art, clearly defining nonuse value is a complicated issue and there is not yet a clear consensus on its precise meaning.

One complication is the difficulty of drawing a sharp line between use and nonuse. In terms of standard consumer theory, any good that a person values is an argument in his or her utility function. The good need not involve any observable activity by the person to secure its value. The quantity of a pure public good such as national defense, for instance, is "consumed" by individuals, however passively. Existence value can also be thought of as a pure public good.[2] It is nonrivalrous—the value one person derives from it does not diminish the values derived by others. It is nonexcludable—no one can be excluded from deriving value from the quantity of the good, which is provided commonly to all. Viewed as a public good, it seems more appropriate to describe existence value as *passive use* rather than nonuse.

Yet, how passive must the "consumption" be in order to distinguish use from nonuse? It is probably safe to say that merely thinking about the good does not constitute use as the term is commonly understood. What about discussing the good with other people? Consumption now involves observable behavior, the consumption of a complementary good, time, but most economists would probably consider it nonuse. Consuming films and photo books based on the good, however, probably crosses the line between use and nonuse because it leaves a behavioral trace in the markets for these complementary goods. These distinctions hinge not just on the intrinsic attributes of the good, but also on our ability to observe and value behavior. Thus, in actual application, distinguishing between use and nonuse is not just a purely conceptual issue.

A second complication, which we consider in more detail in Appendix 9A, arises because individuals derive both use and nonuse value from an asset in many contexts. A person's willingness-to-pay for preservation of the wilderness area may be motivated by the anticipation of hunting *and* the pleasure of knowing that future generations will be able to enjoy it as well. While the person's total willingness-to-pay, or as it is often called in this context *total economic value*, is conceptually clear, the division between these two categories of value is ambiguous because the order of valuation is generally relevant. One ordering in this case is to elicit first the person's willingness-to-pay for use and then, taking this amount as actually paid, to elicit the person's willingness-to-pay for nonuse. The other possible ordering is to elicit first the person's willingness-to-pay for nonuse and then, taking this amount as actually paid, elicit the person's willingness-to-pay for use. The orderings should yield the same total willingness-to-pay, but they probably will yield different values for use and nonuse. Obviously, the ordering problem blurs the boundary between use and nonuse.

A third complication has to do with differences in the way quantity changes affect use and nonuse benefits. In general, nonuse benefits tend to be less quantity sensitive than use benefits. For example, consider a species of mammal that will remain viable as long as its population numbers more than 20 thousand. Someone may very well have a nonuse value for the existence of this species that is the same for populations of 25 thousand and 25 million because either level of population is large enough to avoid extinction. Hikers who wish to see this species in its natural habitat, however, may have a use value that is substantially higher for larger populations because the larger population offers a greater likelihood of an encounter with the species.

Finally, the nonuse category raises issues of motivation that are typically avoided by economists. If nonuse does not leave a behavioral trace, then its value can normally only be discovered empirically through stated rather than revealed preferences, in other words, by contingent valuation surveys, which are discussed in Chapter 14. Sometimes economists may be able to find behavior traces outside of normal market transactions. For example, especially at the local level, binding referenda on the provision of public goods are sometimes held. By relating percentages of affirmative votes to district-level property values or incomes, it may be possible to make inferences about willingness-to-pay. Nonetheless, most empirical estimates of nonuse values rely on stated rather than revealed preferences.

A theory about the motivations behind nonuse value can help guide the formulation and interpretation of questions for eliciting stated preferences. For example, a possible motivation for nonuse value is altruism toward either current people or future generations. Yet, it makes a difference whether the altruism is either individualistic or paternalistic. A concern about the general utility levels of others can be described as *individualistic altruism*; a concern about the consumption of specific goods by others is *paternalistic altruism*. For example, giving money to homeless alcoholics is consistent with individualistic altruism, while contributing to a program that gives them only meals is consistent with paternalistic altruism. If the analyst believes that individualistic altruism is the motivation for existence value, then it is important that respondents be given sufficient context to understand the implications of provision of the good on the overall wealth of others. Because the targets of altruism generally bear some share of the costs of the provided goods, individualistic altruism generally results in lower existence values than paternalistic altruism.[3] For example, altruism might motivate someone to want to bequeath the current world climate to subsequent generations. If the altruism is paternalistic rather than altruistic, then, in determining willingness-to-pay for current policies, the person ignores the possibility that members of future generations might prefer some climate change and a higher endowment of capital to no climate change and a lower endowment of capital.

With these caveats in mind, we present Table 9-1 as a way of thinking about existence value as a benefit category within the broader framework of benefit categories.[4]

Consider first benefits that arise from active use of a good. The most obvious benefit category is *rivalrous consumption* of goods, such as trees for wood products, water for irrigation, and grasslands for cattle grazing. As markets usually exist for rivalrous goods, they are the category most amenable to valuation through the estimation of demand schedules and consumer surplus.

The other use categories are for nonrivalrous goods. Those consumed onsite, such as hiking and bird watching that do not interfere with other users or uses, are labeled *direct nonrivalrous consumption*. Though rarely traded in markets, such goods often can be valued by observing the travel and time costs people are willing to bear to

TABLE 9-1	Taxonomy of Benefits: Possible Partitioning of Willingness-to-Pay	
Type of Use	*Benefit Category*	*Example*
Active use	Rivalrous consumption	Logging of old-growth forest
	Nonrivalrous consumption: direct	Hiking in wilderness
	Nonrivalrous consumption: indirect	Watching a film of wilderness area
Passive use (nonuse)	Option value	Possibility of visiting wilderness area in the future
	Pure existence value: good has intrinsic value	Perceived value of natural order
	Altruistic existence value: gift to current generation	Others hiking in wilderness
	Altruistic existence value: bequest to future generation	Future others hiking in wilderness

consume them. (See Chapter 13.) In alternative taxonomies of benefits, this category is sometimes labeled *nondestructive consumption.*

Indirect nonrivalrous consumption takes place offsite. For example, a person may derive value from watching a film about wildlife in a particular wilderness area. Expenditures of time and money on offsite nonrivalrous consumption provide some information for estimating its value, though much less reliably than for the other use categories.

Consider next passive use benefits. Four categories can be distinguished in terms of motivation. The first category, *option value*, was discussed in Chapter 7. It is the amount that someone is willing to pay to keep open the option of use, active or passive, in the future. It is passive in the sense that it would not be fully captured by estimates of willingness-to-pay based on observations of active use.

The second category, *pure existence value*, arises because people believe the good has intrinsic value apart from its use. For example, some people might be willing to pay to preserve a wilderness area because they think that it is right that some natural habitats exist for rare animal species.

The remaining two categories are based on altruism. Some people may be willing to pay to preserve a wilderness area, for example, because they get pleasure from knowing that it is used by others. Generally, the motivation for such *altruistic existence value* is paternalistic in the sense that it is driven by the desire for others to consume this particular good, rather than by the desire to increase their consumption overall. It may be based on the belief that exposure to nature, art, or historical sites is intrinsically good or perhaps on the desire to share with others a type of experience one has found to be emotionally enriching. When the altruism is directed toward future generations, the good is said to have a *bequest value*. People get pleasure from knowing that those not yet born will be able to use (and not use!) the good. Just as people often wish to leave their children a share of the wealth they have accumulated, they may want to bequeath them access to unique goods as well.

The distribution of benefits across these categories obviously depends on the specific attributes of the project being evaluated. By their very nature, projects involving the conservation of wilderness areas are likely to derive a high fraction of their benefits from nonuse values. For example, based on survey data, K. G. Willis estimated existence values for three nature sites of special scientific interest in Great Britain.[5] Consumer surplus associated with use of the sites appeared to account for only about 10 to 12 percent of people's total willingness-to-pay. Option value accounted for a comparable percentage. The remaining portion of willingness-to-pay consisted of existence (pure and bequest) value. Only if the nonuse benefits were included did conservation of these areas appear to have positive net benefits.

THE MEASUREMENT OF EXISTENCE VALUE

Despite the difficulty economists have in clearly defining existence value as a benefit category, few economists would deny that sometimes people are willing to pay a total amount for the preservation of assets that exceeds their willingness-to-pay for their use or anticipated possible future use. Yet, some economists believe that the method of measurement currently available, the contingent value survey, lacks sufficient reliability for existence values to be reasonably included in CBA. Because we consider contingent valuation in detail in Chapter 14, our discussion here raises only the general issues most relevant to the measurement of existence value.

Directly Eliciting Total Economic Value

One way to avoid some of the conceptual problems in defining existence value is to measure willingness-to-pay for a policy change holistically rather than disaggregating it into component parts. In the context of contingent valuation, the analyst poses questions aimed at getting respondents to state their willingness-to-pay amounts based on consideration of *all* their possible motivations for valuing policy changes. The total economic value revealed through this *structured conversation* is each respondent's benefit from the policy change.

The viability of this approach obviously depends on the analyst's ability to structure a meaningful conversation. The analyst must convey a full description of the policy effect being valued. Considerably more context must be provided in the valuation of effects on passive than active use. People typically know their own current levels of use as a starting point for valuing marginal changes. They are less likely to know the total stock of a good that has nonuse value to them. Yet their valuation of marginal changes in the good is likely to depend on how much they think is currently available. For example, people who think that a particular species lives only in one particular wilderness area are likely to place a much higher value on the preservation of that area than if they knew that the species lived in several other already protected areas. Indeed, one can imagine that, given enough information and time for reflection, some people may place a zero or negative value on the existence of more of some good when its quantity is above some threshold. One may place a negative value on policies that increase the number of deer in an area, for instance, if their number is already so large as to threaten the survival of other species.

Existence value based on altruism poses special problems. When individuals are concerned only about their own consumption, it is reasonable to separate costs from benefits.

EXHIBIT 9-1

Public opinion and economic analysis frequently conflict in the evaluation of public subsidies for the construction and operation of stadiums for professional sports teams. Valid CBAs of sports stadiums based only on use benefits almost never find positive social net benefits, especially if done from the national perspective. One possible exception is the baseball stadium built for the Baltimore Orioles at Camden Yards, which appears to have increased average attendance

from 30 thousand to 45 thousand per game. Further, approximately 70 percent of the increase in attendance consists of residents from outside Maryland, suggesting the possibility of positive net benefits if the CBA is done from a state rather than a national perspective.

Bruce W. Hamilton and Peter Kahn conducted a detailed CBA from the perspective of the residents of Maryland. They reported the following annual benefits and costs:

Annual Benefits:		$3.36 million
Job creation	$0.48 million	
Out-of-stadium incremental taxes	$1.25 million	
Incremental admission tax	$1.20 million	
Sales tax on incremental stadium spending	$0.43 million	
Annual Costs:		$14.00 million
Annual Net Benefits:		−$10.64 million

The net cost of the stadium to Maryland taxpayers is $10.64 million per year, which is equivalent to about $14.20 per Baltimore household per year. Hamilton and Kahn note that building the stadium was probably necessary to keep the Orioles from eventually moving to another city, and that citizens of Maryland, even if they never attend Orioles games, may place a value on the stadium

because they get pleasure from simply having the Orioles in Baltimore. Hamilton and Kahn call these values "public consumption benefits," which can be thought of as passive use benefits, consisting of some combination of option value and existence value. Only if the annual value of public consumption benefits exceed $10.64 million would Oriole Park at Camden Yards pass the net benefits test.

Source: Adapted from Bruce W. Hamilton and Peter Kahn, "Baltimore's Camden Yards Ballparks," in Roger G. Noll and Andrew Zimbalist, eds., *Sports, Jobs, and Taxes: The Economic Impact of Sports Teams and Stadiums* (Washington, D.C.: The Brookings Institution, 1997), 245–281. Corrections to original provided by Bruce W. Hamilton.

Each can be estimated separately and combined to find net benefits. Altruistic values, however, may depend on the distribution of both costs and benefits. Respondents thus need to know who is likely to use the good being valued and who is likely to bear the costs of preserving it. Failure to include the latter may inflate existence values if it leads to respondents not taking into account all the effects on others.

    Let us assume that these concerns, along with the more general problems of contingent valuation discussed in Chapter 14, are adequately addressed so that analysts can be confident that they have correctly elicited individuals' total economic value for the policy change under consideration. If their sample of respondents included all the people with standing, then these total valuations would suffice for completing the CBA. Often, however, analysts wish to combine benefits estimated from behavioral data with existence value estimates from a relatively small sample drawn from people with standing. As already noted, partitioning respondents' total willingness-to-pay into use and nonuse values is sensitive to the ordering of categories. If nonuse values from the sample are to be added to use values estimated by other methods to get total benefits, then it is important that questions be asked so as to elicit nonuse values after respondents have considered and reported their use values.

In contrast to use, nonuse does not occur in easily defined geographic markets. Aggregate existence values are very sensitive to the geographic assumptions made in extrapolating from survey samples to the population with standing.[6] People appear to place a higher existence value on resources in closer proximity.[7] Using average existence values estimated from local samples to obtain aggregate existence values for a more geographically extensive population may be inappropriate. Indeed, the question of geographic extrapolation appears to be one of the most controversial aspects of the use of existence values in damage assessment cases.[8]

As a final point, note that as long as the conversation leads respondents to consider all the sources of uncertainty relevant to their valuation of the policy change, their total willingness-to-pay amount is an option price. It is thus fully inclusive of option value so that no adjustments for uncertainty are required.

Behavioral Traces of Existence Value?

Many economists would be more comfortable measuring existence value through the observation of related behavior. As a pure public good, however, its behavioral trace is likely to be so weak that considerable ingenuity will be required to find ways of measuring it through nonconversational methods. Nevertheless, the history of the development of increasingly sophisticated methods for measuring benefits offers some hope that a way will be found.

Bruce Madariaga and Kenneth McConnell suggest one line of investigation.[9] They note that people are willing to pay to join such organizations as the Nature Conservancy and the Audubon Society. Some part of their membership fees can be thought of as voluntary contributions for a public good, the preservation of wilderness areas. Ways of making inferences about existence values from the patterns of contributions to such organizations have yet to be developed. Doing so is complicated by the problem of *free riding*—some who benefit from the public good will not voluntarily contribute to its provision.

More sophisticated models of individual utility may also provide some leverage on the measurement of existence value. Douglas Larson notes that public goods are sometimes complements of, or substitutes for, private goods.[10] If investigators are willing to impose assumptions about the form of the demand for market goods and the nature of the complementarity between market goods and existence values, then they may be able to make inferences about the magnitudes of the existence values from observation of the consumption of the market goods. Larson also suggests that explicitly treating time as a constraint in utility maximization may open up possibilities for measurement based on people's allocations of time. For example, the time people spend watching films or reading books about habitats of endangered species might, with sufficient cleverness, provide a basis for estimating their existence values for the habitats.

Should Existence Value Be Included in CBA?

A growing number of efforts to estimate existence values through surveys can be found in the literature.[11] The particular estimates are often controversial. More generally, the desirability of the effort to incorporate existence values has been debated.[12]

Should existence values be used in CBA? The answer requires a balancing of conceptual and practical concerns. On the one hand, recognizing existence values as pure public goods argues for their inclusion. On the other hand, given the current state of practice, estimates of existence values are very uncertain. This trade-off suggests the following heuristic: *Although existence values for unique and long-lived assets should be estimated whenever possible, costs and benefits should be presented with and without their inclusion to make clear how they affect net benefits.* When existence values for such assets cannot be measured, analysts should supplement CBA with discussion of their possible significance for the sign of net benefits.

CONCLUSION

As CBA is increasingly applied to environmental policies, concern about existence values among analysts will almost certainly grow. Unless methods of measurement improve substantially, however, deciding when and how to include existence values in CBA will continue to be difficult. By being aware of the limitations of these methods, analysts can be better producers and consumers of CBA.

APPENDIX 9A

Expenditure Functions and the Partitioning of Benefits

Policies that have multiple effects pose conceptual problems for the aggregation of benefits. In most situations, we approximate willingness-to-pay by summing the changes in social surplus associated with each of the effects. In general, however, this procedure tends to overestimate total economic value. In this appendix, we introduce some notation for formally representing the measurement of utility changes from policies with multiple effects with expenditure functions, an analytical approach commonly used in more theoretical treatments of social welfare.[1] A stylized numerical example follows to show the ambiguity in the partitioning of benefits among the various effects.

Imagine that a person has a budget B and also has a utility function U that depends on the quantities of goods $X_1, X_2, \ldots, X_n$. Assume that the prices of these goods are $p_1, p_2, \ldots, p_n$, respectively. The problem facing the consumer is to choose the quantities of the goods that maximize U such that $p_1 X_1 + p_2 X_2 + \ldots + p_n X_n \leq B$. Let U^* be the maximum utility that the person can obtain given B and the prices of the goods. We can construct an expenditure function, $e(p_1, p_2, \ldots, p_n; U^*)$, which is defined as the minimum dollar amount of budget necessary to obtain utility U^* at the given prices. Obviously, for the original set of prices that we used to find U^*, $e(p_1, p_2, \ldots, p_n; U^*) = B$.

Assume that we instituted a policy that *increased* the price of the first good from p_1 to q_1. Associated with this new price is the expenditure function $e(q_1, p_2, \ldots, p_n; U^*) = B'$, where B' is greater than B because the person must be given more budget to keep the utility equal to U^* in the face of the higher price. A measure of the consumer surplus loss from the price increase is given by:

$$e(q_1, p_2, \ldots, p_n; U^*) - e(p_1, p_2, \ldots, p_n; U^*)$$

which equals $B' - B$. This amount equals the compensating variation for the price change as discussed in the appendix to Chapter 3.[2]

Imagine now that X_1 and X_2 are goods, perhaps existence value and hiking, provided to the person by a particular wilderness area. How would we use the expenditure function to value the wilderness area, given the original budget and set of prices?

We want to know how much compensation we would have to give to the person to restore his or her utility level to U^* after making X_1 and X_2 equal zero. In terms of the expenditure function, we do this by setting p_1 and p_2 sufficiently high so that the person's demand for X_1 and X_2 is "choked off" at zero quantities. Assume that p_{1c} and p_{2c} choke off demand. To get the total economic value (TEV) of the wilderness area to the individual, we calculate how much additional budget we would have to give the person to return him or her to the original utility level:

$$TEV = e(p_{1c}, p_{2c}, \ldots, p_n; U^*) - e(p_1, p_2, \ldots, p_n; U^*)$$

which is an unambiguous and correct measure of the person's willingness-to-pay for the wilderness area.

Now consider how we might partition TEV into its two components associated with X_1 and X_2. One way would be to first value X_1 and then X_2. We can express this by adding and subtracting $e(p_1, p_{2c}, \ldots, p_n; U^*)$ to the equation for TEV to get the following equation:

$$TEV = [e(p_{1c}, p_{2c}, \ldots, p_n; U^*) - e(p_1, p_{2c}, \ldots, p_n; U^*)] + [e(p_1, p_{2c}, \ldots, p_n; U^*) - e(p_1, p_2, \ldots, p_n; U^*)]$$

where the first line represents the willingness-to-pay to obtain X_1 at price p_1 and the second line represents the willingness-to-pay to obtain subsequently X_2 at price p_2.

The other possible partition is to first restore X_2 at price p_2 and then restore X_1 at price p_1. It is expressed by the following equation:

$$
\begin{aligned}
TEV = &[e(p_{1c}, p_{2c}, \ldots, p_n; U^*) \\
&- e(p_{1c}, p_2, \ldots, p_n; U^*)] \\
&+ [e(p_{1c}, p_2, \ldots, p_n; U^*) \\
&- e(p_1, p_2, \ldots, p_n; U^*)]
\end{aligned}
$$

where the first line represents the willingness-to-pay to obtain X_2 at price p_2 and the second line represents the willingness-to-pay to subsequently obtain X_1 at price p_1.

These alternative partitionings generally will not yield the same willingness-to-pay amounts for X_1 and X_2. Typically, the willingness-to-pay for a good will be greater if the good is introduced in the partitioning sequence earlier rather than later. The rough intuition behind this result is that a good will be relatively less valuable at the margin if it is added to an already full bundle of goods.

If one can measure TEV directly, then this ambiguity in partitioning is of little concern.[3] In most circumstances, however, analysts attempt to construct TEV from independent estimates of separate benefit categories. In terms of expenditure functions, what is commonly done can be expressed as follows:

$$
\begin{aligned}
TB = &[e(p_{1c}, p_{2c}, \ldots, p_n; U^*) \\
&- e(p_1, p_{2c}, \ldots, p_n; U^*)] \\
&+ [e(p_{1c}, p_{2c}, \ldots, p_n; U^*) \\
&- e(p_{1c}, p_2, \ldots, p_n; U^*)]
\end{aligned}
$$

where the first line is the compensating variation for making only X_1 available, the second line is the compensating variation for making only X_2 available, and TB is the total estimated benefits. In general, TB does not equal TEV. TB systematically overestimates TEV. The overestimation tends to increase as the number of benefit components increases.[4]

We next illustrate these concepts with the stylized numerical example presented in Table 9A.1. The model assumes that the person's utility, U, depends on three goods: E, the size of the wilderness area (existence); X, a particular use of the wilderness area such as hiking; and Z, a composite good that represents all goods other than E and X. It also depends on the parameter Q, an index of the quality of the wilderness area. The person has a budget of $B = 100$ and faces prices for $E, X,$ and Z of $p_e = \$.50, p_x = \$1,$ and $p_z = \$2$, respectively.[5] The quantities of $E, X,$ and Z that maximize utility for the parameter values listed in the table can be found through numerical methods to be $E = 9.89$, $X = 30.90$, and $Z = 32.08$.[6] The utility from this combination of goods, U^*, equals 38.93.

The expenditure function follows directly. Obviously, the budget that gives $U^* = 38.93$ is just the budget of $100 in the optimization. Therefore, we can write the expenditure function for the initial position as:

$$
\begin{aligned}
e(p_e = 0.5, p_x = 1, p_z = 2; Q = 1; \\
U^* = 38.93) = 100
\end{aligned}
$$

Before illustrating the partitioning problem, it may be helpful to consider how expenditure functions can be used to find compensating variations for independent policy effects. Consider, for instance, how one can find the compensating variation for a reduction in the price of X from $1 to $.50. The procedure involves finding the expenditure function:

$$
\begin{aligned}
e(p_e = 0.5, p_x = 0.5, p_z = 2; \\
Q = 1; U^* = 38.93) = 63.25
\end{aligned}
$$

by asking what budget amount would allow the person to obtain the original utility at the lower price. The compensating variation for the price reduction is just the difference between the values of the expenditure function with the lower price, $63.25, and the value of the original expenditure function, $100. That is, the person would be indifferent between facing the original price of $1 with a budget of $100 and facing the

TABLE 9A-I	An Illustration of the Benefits Partitioning Problem
Utility function	$U(E, X, Z; Q) = QE^\gamma + QX^\beta + Z^\theta$ where E is the quantity of wilderness that exists, X is the use level of the wilderness, Z is a market good, and Q is an index of quality of the wilderness
Budget constraint	$B = p_e E + p_x X + p_z Z$ where B is the available budget, and p_e, p_x, and p_z are the respective prices of E, X, and Z
Optimization problem	Maximize $L = U + \lambda [B - p_e E - p_x X - p_z Z]$ where λ is the marginal utility of money
Numerical assumptions	$Q = 1; \gamma = 0.5; \beta = 0.75; q = 0.9; p_e = 0.5; p_x = 1;$ $p_z = 2; B = 100$
Solution values	$E = 9.89; X = 30.90; Z = 32.08; \lambda = .318$ $U(9.89, 30.90, 32.08; 1) = 38.93 = U^*$ $e(p_e, p_x, p_z; Q; U^*) = e(0.5, 1, 2; 1; 38.93) = 100$
Expenditure functions	Wilderness area not available: $e(\infty, \infty, 2; 1; 38.93) = 116.95$ Wilderness existence, no use: $e(0.5, \infty, 2; 1; 38.93) = 111.42$ Wilderness use only: $e(\infty, 1, 2; 1; 38.93) = 105.04$
Existence-use partition *TEV = 16.95*	Existence value $= e(\infty, \infty, 2; 1; 38.93) - e(0.5, \infty, 2; 1; 38.93)$ $= 116.95 - 111.42 = 5.53$ Use value $= e(0.5, \infty, 2; 1; 38.93) - e(0.5, 1, 2; 1; 38.93)$ $= 111.42 - 100 = 11.42$
Use-existence partition *TEV = 16.95*	Use value $= e(\infty, \infty, 2; 1; 38.93) - e(\infty, 1, 2; 1; 38.93)$ $= 116.95 - 105.04 = 11.91$ Existence value $= e(\infty, 1, 2; 1; 38.93) - e(0.5, 1, 2; 1; 38.93)$ $= 105.04 - 100 = 5.04$
Independent summation *TB= 17.44*	Existence value $= e(\infty, \infty, 2; 1; 38.93) - e(0.5, \infty, 2; 1; 38.93)$ $= 116.95 - 111.42 = 5.53$ Use value $= e(\infty, \infty, 2; 1; 38.93) - e(\infty, 1, 2; 1; 38.93)$ $= 116.95 - 105.04 = 11.91$

reduced price of \$.50 with a budget of \$63.25. Therefore, the willingness-to-pay for the price reduction is the difference between \$100 and \$63.25, or \$36.75.

Now consider how one could value a policy that would increase the quality index, Q, by 10 percent. The expenditure function for the quality improvement relative to the initial position is:

$$e(p_e = 0.5, p_x = 1, p_z = 2; Q = 1.1;$$
$$U^* = 38.93) = 94.45$$

which indicates that the compensating variation for the quality improvement is –\$5.55

(\$94.45 – \$100), indicating that the original utility could be obtained with a smaller budget.

Returning to the initial position, let us now consider the total value of wilderness, *TEV*, and the two ways of partitioning it between existence and use. We choke off consumption of E and X by setting their prices at infinity. This yields the expenditure function:

$$e(p_e = \infty, p_x = \infty, p_z = 2; Q = 1;$$
$$U^* = 38.93) = 116.95$$

which implies that the wilderness area has a total value of \$16.95 (\$116.95 – \$100). If we partition first by existence and then by use, we calculate:

$$e(p_e = 0.5, p_x = \infty, p_z = 2;$$
$$Q = 1; U^* = 38.93) = 111.42$$

which implies an existence value of $5.53 ($116.95 – $111.42) and a use value of $11.42 ($111.42 – $100).[7] If instead we partition first by use and then by existence, we calculate:

$$e(p_e = \infty, p_x = 1, p_z = 2; Q = 1;$$
$$U^* = 38.93) = 105.04$$

which implies a use value of $11.91 ($116.95 – $105.04) and an existence value of $5.04 ($105.04 – $100).[8] Thus, we see that the sequence

of valuation makes a difference: Existence value and use value are each larger when they are valued first rather than second.[9]

Finally, consider the independent summation of benefits. Existence is valued as in the existence-use sequence and use is valued as in the use-existence sequence. Thus, we would estimate the total economic value of the wilderness to be $17.44 ($5.53 + $11.91), which exceeds the correct compensating variation by $.49 ($17.44 – $16.95).

In summary, the partitioning of benefits between existence and use is conceptually ambiguous when the same individuals derive both values from a policy change. More generally, policies that affect people's utilities in multiple ways are prone to overestimation of willingness-to-pay when each effect is valued independently as a separate benefit category.

EXERCISES FOR CHAPTER 9

1. Imagine a wilderness area of 200 square miles in the Rocky Mountains. How would you expect each of the following factors to affect people's total willingness-to-pay for its preservation?
   a. The size of the total wilderness area still remaining in the Rocky Mountains
   b. The presence of rare species in this particular area
   c. The level of national wealth
2. An analyst wishing to estimate the benefits of preserving a wetland has combined information obtained from two methods. First, she surveyed those who visited the wetland—fishers, duck hunters, and bird watchers—to determine their willingness-to-pay for these uses. Second, she surveyed a sample of residents throughout the state about their willingness-to-pay to preserve the wetland. This second survey focused exclusively on nonuse values of the wetland. She then added her estimate of use benefits to her estimate of nonuse benefits to get an estimate of the total economic value of preservation of the wetland. Is this a reasonable approach? (Note: In responding to this question assume that there was virtually no overlap in the persons contacted in the two surveys.)

NOTES

1. John V. Krutilla, "Conservation Reconsidered," *American Economic Review* 57(4) 1967, 777–786 at 784.
2. Charles Plourde, "Conservation of Extinguishable Species," *Natural Resources Journal* 15(4) 1975, 791–797.
3. Bruce Madariaga and Kenneth E. McConnell, "Exploring Existence Value," *Water Resources Research* 23(5) 1987, 936–942.

4. For an alternative framework, see R. Kerry Turner, Jouni Paavola, Philip Cooper, Stephen Farber, Valma Jessamy, and Stavros Georgiou, "Valuing Nature: Lessons Learned and Future Research Directions," *Ecological Economics* 46(3) 2003, 493–510 at 495 (Table 1).
5. K. G. Willis, "Valuing Non-Market Wildlife Commodities: An Evaluation and Comparison

of Benefits and Costs," *Applied Economics* 22(1) 1990, 12–30.

6. For an overview, see V. Kerry Smith, "Nonmarket Valuation of Environmental Resources," *Land Economics* 69(1) 1993, 1–26.

7. Ronald J. Sutherland and Richard G. Walsh, "The Effect of Distance on the Preservation Value of Water Quality," *Land Economics* 61(3) 1985, 281–291; and Ian J. Bateman and Ian H. Langford, "Non-Users' Willingness to Pay for a National Park: An Application and Critique of the Contingent Valuation Method," *Regional Studies* 31(6) 1997, 571–582.

8. Raymond J. Kopp and V. Kerry Smith, "Benefit Estimation Goes to Court: The Case of Natural Resource Damage Assessment," *Journal of Policy Analysis and Management* 8(4) 1989, 593–612.

9. Bruce Madariaga and Kenneth E. McConnell, "Exploring Existence Value," *Water Resources Research* 23(5) 1987, 936–942.

10. Douglas M. Larson, "On Measuring Existence Value," *Land Economics* 69(1) 1992, 116–122.

11. See, for example, David S. Brookshire, Larry S. Eubanks, and Alan Randall, "Estimating Option Prices and Existence Values for Wildlife Resources," *Land Economics* 59(1) 1983, 1–15; Richard G. Walsh, John B. Loomis, and Richard

A. Gillman, "Valuing Option, Existence, and Bequest Demands for Wilderness," *Land Economics* 60(1) 1984, 14–29; Kevin J. Boyle and Richard C. Bishop, "Valuing Wildlife in Benefit-Cost Analysis: A Case Study Involving Endangered Species," *Water Resources Research* 23(5) 1987, 943–950; K. G. Willis, "Valuing Non-Market Wildlife Commodities: An Evaluation and Comparison of Benefits and Costs," *Applied Economics* 22(1) 1990, 13–30; Thomas H. Stevens, Jaime Echeverria, Ronald J. Glass, Tim Hager, and Thomas A. More, "Measuring the Existence Value of Wildlife: What Do CVM Estimates Really Show?" *Land Economics* 67(4) 1991, 390–400; and John B. Loomis and Douglas S. White, "Economic Benefits of Rare and Endangered Species: Summary and Meta-Analysis," *Ecological Economics* 18(3) 1996, 197–206.

12. See, for example, Donald H. Rosenthal and Robert H. Nelson, "Why Existence Value Should Not Be Used in Cost-Benefit Analysis," *Journal of Policy Analysis and Management* 11(1) 1992, 116–122; and Raymond J. Kopp, "Why Existence Value Should Be Used in Cost-Benefit Analysis," *Journal of Policy Analysis and Management* 11(1) 1992, 123–130.

APPENDIX NOTES

1. A more formal treatment can be found in Alan Randall, "Total and Nonuse Values," in John B. Braden and Charles D. Kolstad, eds., *Measuring the Demand for Environmental Quality* (New York: North-Holland, 1991), 303–321. The original analysis of the importance of the sequence of valuation can be found in J. R. Hicks, *A Revision of Demand Theory* (Oxford, UK: Clarendon Press, 1956), 169–179.

2. Though we use compensating variation as a measure of the dollar value of utility here because we find it most intuitive (as discussed in the appendix to Chapter 3), equivalent variation, which measures welfare changes relative to the utility level after the price change, is generally considered a superior money metric for utility because it provides an unambiguous ordinal measure for ranking price changes.

   If $U\sim$ is the utility after the price change, then the equivalent variation is:

$$e(q_1, p_2, \ldots, p_n; U\sim) - e(p_1, p_2, \ldots, p_n; U\sim)$$

where $e(q_1, p_2, \ldots, p_n; U\sim) = B$.

Compensating and equivalent variation typically differ by a small amount due to income effects. In the case of quantity changes of public goods, however, the size of their difference also depends on the availability of close substitutes for the public good. See W. Michael Hanemann, "Willingness-To-Pay and Willingness-To-Accept: How Much Can They Differ?" *American Economic Review* 81(3) 1991, 635–647.

3. Of course, the value of *TEV* will depend on whether it is measured in terms of compensating variation or equivalent variation.

4. John P. Hoehn and Alan Randall, "Too Many Proposals Pass the Benefit Cost Test," *American Economic Review* 79(3) 1989, 544–551.

5. If E is a public good, then we would interpret p_e as the tax per unit of E that the person pays.

As everyone would have to consume the same quantity, the person would not be able to choose the value of E so that the optimization of utility would be over only X and Z.

6. The partial derivatives of L with respect to E, X, Z, and λ give four equations in four unknowns. Although these *first-order conditions* cannot be solved analytically, they can be rearranged so that E, X, and Z are each expressed as a function of λ and parameters. A solution can be found by guessing values of λ until a value is found that implies values of E, X, and Z that satisfy the budget constraint.

7. If we assume that E is fixed at its initial level, the more realistic case in evaluating an existing wilderness area, then the existence value equals only $5.47. It is smaller than in the example because the person does not have the opportunity to purchase more E when X is not available. This assumption changes neither the *TEV* nor the existence value as estimated by the use-existence partition.

8. It may seem strange to partition in this way because one would normally think of existence as being a prerequisite for use. Some types of uses, however, could be provided without maintaining existence value. For example, through stocking it may be possible to provide game fishing without preserving a stream in its natural form.

9. Using equivalent variation rather than compensating variation as the consumer surplus measure leads to the following:

$$e(p_e = \infty, p_x = \infty, p_z = 2; Q = 1; U\!\sim = 33.81) = 100.00$$
$$e(p_e = 0.5, p_x = 1, p_z = 2; Q = 1; U\!\sim = 33.81) = 84.10$$
$$e(p_e = \infty, p_x = 1, p_z = 2; Q = 1; U\!\sim = 33.81) = 89.00$$
$$e(p_e = 0.5, p_x = \infty, p_z = 2; Q = 1; U\!\sim = 33.81) = 94.68$$

$$TEV_{ev} = 100.00 - 84.10 = 15.90$$

Existence-use partition: existence value $= 100.00 - 94.68 = 5.32$
                           use value $= 94.68 - 84.10 = 10.58$

Use-existence partition: use value $= 100.00 - 89.00 = 11.00$
                           existence value $= 89.00 - 84.10 = 4.90$

Independent summation: existence value $= 100.00 - 94.68 = 5.32$
                           use value $= 100.00 - 89.00 = 11.00$

$$TB_{ev} = 16.32$$

CHAPTER 10

The Social Discount Rate[1]

When evaluating government policies or projects, analysts must decide on the appropriate weights to apply to policy impacts that occur in different years. Given these weights, denoted by w_t, and estimates of the real annual net social benefits, NB_t, the estimated net present value of *(NPV)* a project is given by[2]:

$$NPV = \sum_{t=0}^{n} w_t NB_t \qquad \textbf{(10.1)}$$

In effect, the weights make costs, benefits, or net benefits that occur in the future commenserable with (i.e., comparable to) costs, benefits, or net benefits realized by society today so that we can aggregate them to obtain a single measure of the value of a project, the *NPV*. This chapter deals with theoretical issues pertaining to the selection of an appropriate *set of weights* to use in equation (10.1). Sometimes these weights are referred to as *social discount factors*. Selecting the appropriate set of weights (social discount factors) is equivalent to selecting the *real* social discount rate (SDR).

It is possible to do CBA without knowing the theoretical issues pertaining to the choice of the social discount rate. Indeed, as we discuss near the end of this chapter, government departments usually use prescribed discount rates. Many branches of the U.S. government use a (real) discount rate of 7 percent, whereas in Canada many federal departments use 10 percent and many provincial departments use 8 percent. Over the past few years, there has been a trend toward using lower rates in the United States. The British Treasury has just recommended using a real rate of 3.5 percent. Although a particular government or branch of government may prescribe a particular rate, and you might therefore be able to compute the *NPV*, without a strong conceptual foundation, you would not be able to give advice or answer questions about the choice of the discount rate you were using.

Discounting reflects the generally accepted idea that real resources available at some future date are worth less today than the same amount available right now. This is because, through investment, a given amount of resources that is currently available can be transformed into a greater amount of resources in the future. Discounting is also needed because people prefer to consume a given amount of resources now rather than in the future. For these two reasons it is generally accepted that the social discount factors decline over time; specifically, $0 < w_n \leq w_{n-1} \leq \ldots \leq w_1 \leq w_0 = 1$. However, there is not so much agreement about the specific values of the weights.

Equation (10.1) is a more general version of equations (6.8) and (6.9), the formulas for calculating the *NPV* of a project which were introduced in Chapter 6. These equations are equivalent if:

$$w_t = \frac{1}{(1+i)^t} \tag{10.2}$$

which implies $w_t = \dfrac{w_{t-1}}{(1+i)}$, where $i \geq 0$. Thus, they are equivalent if the weights in one period are proportional to the weights in the previous period and this relationship is constant over time. Put another way, they are equivalent if the weights (social discount factors) decline at a constant rate, i, where i is the real social discount rate. Later in this chapter we relax this assumption and discuss situations in which it might be reasonable to assume that the weights do not decline at a constant rate. If so, there would not be a single SDR that applies to all benefits and costs in all periods.

It is generally accepted that society's choices, including the choice of weights, should be based on individuals' choices. But there are three fundamental unresolved issues. The first issue is whether market interest rates can be used to represent how individuals weight future consumption relative to present consumption. The second issue is whether the individuals in society should include individuals from unborn future generations in addition to individuals who are alive today. The third issue is whether society attaches the same value to a unit of investment as to a unit of consumption.

Different views on these issues lead to the choice of a different discount rate (or set of rates). Some views depend on the specifics of a particular project, such as how it is financed, whether it has long-term environmental or health impacts, and whether costs and benefits affect consumption or investment. Although some rates are more applicable than others in particular situations, there is still considerable disagreement about the most appropriate discount rate in any given set of circumstances.

The next section of this chapter shows that the choice of the SDR does matter: Different social discount rates lead to different policy recommendations. We then discuss the theory behind the SDR using a simple two-period model. In a perfectly competitive capital market, the choice of social discount rate would be obvious. However, in the absence of perfect markets, there are a number of plausible discount rates, including those inferred from market-based behavior and those derived from a very different method known as the "optimal growth rate approach." We discuss the merits of different market-based rates, the circumstances under which each is most applicable, and provide our best judgment about their specific values. The next issue concerns the different treatment of impacts that affect investment or consumption. This leads to a discussion of the shadow price of capital method. Although much of the discussion focuses on market rates, we believe that the SDR should not be based on market rates but on the optimal growth rate model. Hence, the following section provides our reasons for rejecting the use of market rates. It discusses the optimal growth rate model and presents a numerical estimate of the SDR based on this method. The final major issue concerns intergenerational discounting. Again, we discuss the main issues and present our recommended estimates. Finally, we contrast our guidelines with actual practice.

One issue that invariably arises in the discussion of social discount rates is the treatment of risk and uncertainty. One approach is to add a risk premium to the discount rate to reflect the risk. We do not favor this approach. In our view, the best way to handle risk is to use certainty equivalents, as discussed in Chapter 8. Thus, throughout this chapter, we assume that benefits and costs are measured in terms of certainty equivalents.[3] The key issue is to determine the rate at which analysts should discount certainty equivalents.

DOES THE CHOICE OF DISCOUNT RATE MATTER?

The choice of SDR is one of the most important topics in CBA. As Robert Lind points out, the SDR "has critical implications for the federal budget, for regional development, for technological choices, for the environment, and for the size of government."[4]

To see how the value of the SDR can change the ranking of projects, consider a government agency that has only $100,000 to spend on one of three potential projects. The annual net benefits of these projects are shown in Table 10-1. Choosing the lower discount rate (2 percent) would favor project C, while the higher discount rate (10 percent) would favor project B. Thus, the choice of project depends crucially on the choice of discount rate.

Generally, a low discount rate favors projects with the highest total benefits, irrespective of when they occur, because all of the social discount factors are close to 1. Increasing the discount rate applies smaller weights to benefits (or costs) that occur further in the future and therefore weakens the case for projects with benefits that are back-end loaded (such as project C) and strengthens the case for projects with benefits that are front-end loaded (such as project B).

TABLE 10-1	Annual Net Benefits and Net Present Values for Three Alternative Projects		
Year	*Project A*	*Project B*	*Project C*
0	−80,000	−80,000	−80,000
1	25,000	80,000	0
2	25,000	10,000	0
3	25,000	10,000	0
4	25,000	10,000	0
5	25,000	10,000	140,000
NPV $(i = 2\%)$	37,836	35,762	46,802
NPV $(i = 10\%)$	14,770	21,544	6,929

THE THEORY BEHIND THE APPROPRIATE SOCIAL DISCOUNT RATE

To understand the theoretical foundation of discounting, we must recognize that it is rooted in the preferences of individuals. As individuals, we tend to prefer to consume immediate benefits to those occurring in the future. We also face an opportunity cost of forgone interest when we spend dollars today rather than invest them for future use. These two considerations of importance to private decision making, the *marginal rate of time preference* and the *marginal rate of return on private investment*, also provide a basis for deciding how costs and benefits realized by society in the future should be discounted.

This section first introduces the concept of individual marginal rate of time preference. We then show that in a simple two-period model with perfect markets, every individual's marginal rate of time preference will equal the market interest rate. In this case the choice of the social discount rate is obvious. We then generalize the model to a small, isolated country and introduce production. The main results still hold in perfect markets: The social marginal rate of time preference, the rate of return on investment, and the market interest rate would all be equal. Again, the choice of social discount rate would be obvious. Then we indicate that, due to taxes, risk, and transaction costs, the three rates of interest are unlikely to be equal in a real economy. In this circumstance, the choice of social discount rate is not clear. Finally, we examine the optimal growth rate model. This model results in a different value of the SDR. It is important both in short-term projects and in long-lived projects due to practical problems that occur in basing the value of the SDR on market interest rates (which we discuss later).

An Individual's Marginal Rate of Time Preference

Most of us would be unwilling to lend someone $100 today in return for a promise of payment of $100 in a year's time, even if there were no inflation. We generally value $100 today more than the promise of $100 next year in real terms even if we are certain that the promise will be carried out. Perhaps $90 is the most that we would be willing to lend today in return for a promise of payment of $100 in a year's time. Economists refer to our preference to consume sooner rather than later as *time preference*. The rate at which an individual makes marginal trade-offs is called an individual's *marginal rate of time preference* (MRTP).

The concept of time preference can be easily understood in the context of borrowing and lending. Imagine that you are a graduate student who will receive a stipend of $5,000 this year and $9,000 next year. Your rich uncle offers to give you some money and asks if you would rather have $1,000 this year or $1,200 next year. Suppose that you are indifferent between the gifts; that is, you are just willing to sacrifice $200 additional consumption next year in order to consume the extra $1,000 this year rather than next year.[5] In this case, you would have an MRTP of 20 percent. Put another way, the MRTP tells us that you require 20 percent more next year in order to decrease your current consumption by a small amount.

Absent a rich uncle, you might be able to consume more today through borrowing. Although most banks may not be interested in lending you money because they fear you may not pay them back, let us assume that your local credit union will lend money to you at an annual interest rate of 10 percent. That is, you can borrow $1,000 if you promise to pay back this amount plus $100 in interest next year. If you were willing to give up $200 to get an additional $1,000 immediately from your uncle, then you would surely take advantage of the loan that requires you to give up only $100 in consumption next year in order to consume $1,000 more this year. Once you take out the loan, you will have $6,000 to spend this year and $7,900 to spend next year. Now that you have reduced the gap between what you have to spend this year relative to next year, you probably have an MRTP of less than 20 percent. After taking out the loan you may now, if given the choice, prefer a gift of $1,200 next year over a gift of $1,000 this year. If so, this indicates your MRTP is now less than 20 percent. This example illustrates that your MRTP changes as you shift consumption from one year to another year.

Equality of Discount Rates in Perfect Markets

As long as you can borrow as much as you like, you can shift consumption from the future to the present until your MRTP falls to the rate of interest you must pay. If banks offer a rate of interest in excess of your MRTP, then you will happily save now and defer some consumption to the future. For example, if you are indifferent between an additional $1,000 today and an additional $1,050 next year but can deposit $1,000 for one year to obtain an additional $1,060 next year, then you would want to make the deposit. Only when the rate of interest you earn just equals your MRTP will you be indifferent between spending and depositing an additional dollar.

It is easy to show that in a perfectly competitive capital market, the MRTP equals the market interest rate. Suppose that a consumer's utility is a function of consumption over two years: C_1 denotes consumption in this year (year 1) and C_2 denotes consumption in next year (year 2). The consumer maximizes his or her utility, denoted by $U(C_1, C_2)$, subject to a budget constraint in which T denotes the present value of (total) income over the two years and i denotes the market interest rate:

$$\text{Max } U(C_1, C_2) \tag{10.3}$$

$$\text{s.t } C_1 + \frac{C_2}{1 + i} = T \tag{10.4}$$

This problem is represented in Figure 10-1. The curves labeled U^1 and U^2 are *indifference curves*. They represent the individual's preferences over combinations of current and future consumption. Each curve represents combinations of current and future consumption that provide the individual with the same level of utility. Thus, the individual is indifferent between any two points on an indifference curve.[6] All points on the curve U^2 are preferred to all points on the curve U^1; that is, the preference directions are north and east.

The slope of each indifference curve is negative, reflecting the fact that consumers require more consumption in the next period in order to give up consumption in this period. If you are indifferent between an additional $1,000 today and an additional $1,050 next year, for example, then the slope of your indifference curve equals $-1,050/1,000 = -1.05$. The (absolute value of the) slope of the indifference curve measures the rate at which an individual is indifferent between substituting current consumption C_1 for future consumption C_2 and is called the consumer's *marginal rate of substitution* (MRS) between consumption this year and consumption next year.[7] Note that, in this example, the individual wants 5 percent more next year in order to

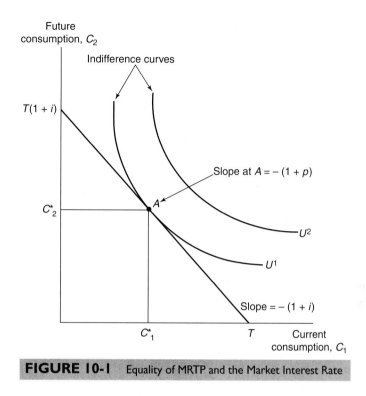

FIGURE 10-1 Equality of MRTP and the Market Interest Rate

defer consumption—the marginal rate of time preference equals 0.05. In general, if you require $1 + p$ more units in the future in order to give up one unit of current consumption, then the slope of the indifference curve is $-(1 + p)$; your marginal rate of substitution is $1 + p$; and your marginal rate of time preference is p. In the relevant range, $p > 0$ and the slope of the indifference curve is greater than 1 in absolute value.

As consumption in the current period increases, the indifference curve becomes flatter, indicating that the consumer requires relatively smaller additional amounts of future consumption in order to forgo a given amount of current consumption. Put another way, as current consumption increases, the consumer's marginal rate of substitution and the consumer's marginal rate of time preference decrease.

The utility maximization problem supposes that the individual receives all of his or her income in the first period and can invest all or part of it at interest rate i.[8] Thus, the individual could spend all of his or her income in year 1, which means $C_1 = T$ and $C_2 = 0$; the individual could spend all of it in year 2, in which case $C_1 = 0$ and $C_2 = (1 + i)T$; or he or she could consume at any other point on the budget constraint represented by the straight line with slope $-(1 + i)$. Each additional unit of consumption in period 1 costs $(1 + i)$ units of consumption in period 2 and each additional unit of consumption in period 2 costs $1/(1 + i)$ units of consumption in period 1.

To determine the optimal consumption levels, we find the point at which the budget constraint is tangential to an indifference curve. This occurs at point A in Figure 10-1 where the optimal consumption levels are denoted C_1^* and C_2^*. At this point the slope of the indifference curve, $-(1 + p)$, equals the slope of the budget constraint.

Rewriting the budget constraint, equation (10.4), thus:

$$C_2 = T(1 + i) - (1 + i)C_1 \qquad \text{(10.5)}$$

shows that the slope of the budget constraint equals $-(1 + i)$.[9] Thus at the optimum consumption level, point A, $p = i$, that is, the market interest rate equals the consumer's MRTP.[10]

This result holds generally for people without extreme preferences over consumption in the two periods.[11] Thus, *every* individual has an MRTP equal to the market interest rate. Because all consumers face the same market interest rate in an economy with a perfect capital market, all consumers have the same MRTP. Thus everyone is willing to trade current and future consumption at the same rate. Because this rate equals the market interest rate, it is natural to interpret the market interest rate as the social discount rate. Later we discuss the appropriateness of interpreting market interest rates as social discount rates when markets are not perfect.

A Simple Two-Period Model with Production

We now present a more general two-period model that pertains to a group of individuals in a hypothetical country. We assume that this country does not trade with other counties. Moreover, as before, we ignore taxes and transaction costs associated with making loans (although we later come back to them). Consequently, anyone who wants a loan can borrow the desired amount at the market interest rate. In addition, except when explicitly indicated otherwise, we ignore market failures such as externalities and information asymmetry, which could cause private and social discount rates to diverge from one another.

The economy of this hypothetical country is depicted in Figure 10-2. The horizontal axis indicates consumption during the current period and the vertical axis indicates consumption during the future period. The major difference between this model and the previous model is that this model incorporates production. The curve labeled *CPF* is a consumption possibility frontier that represents all the combinations of current and future consumption that are feasible if the economy utilizes its resources efficiently.

Suppose that at the beginning of the first period, the country has T units worth of resources, which can be allocated between current consumption and investment. As before, there are two extremes. At one extreme, which is represented by point T on the horizontal axis, society could consume all T units in the current period, invest none, and therefore have no future consumption. At the other extreme, society could consume no units in the current period, invest all T units, and consume S units in the future period, which is represented by point S on the vertical axis. Note that $S > T$, which implies a positive rate of return on all resources invested in the current period.

Point X represents a more realistic intermediate position where current consumption equals C_t^* and future consumption equals C_{t+1}^*. At this point society would relinquish for investment $I_t = T - C_t^*$ units of potential consumption in the current period. In the future period it would consume $C_{t+1}^* = I_t + R$ units, where I_t represents the amount invested in the first period and R represents the return on this investment. Future consumption can be partitioned into two components by drawing a 45° line from point T to the line between X and C_t^* on Figure 10-2. The lower segment corresponds to I_t and the upper segment corresponds to R.

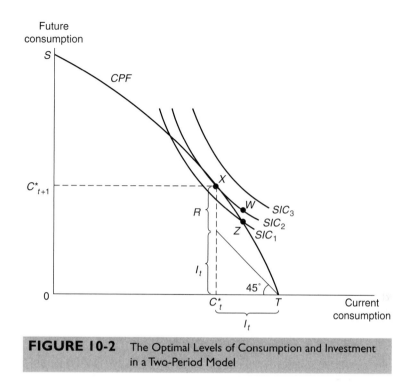

FIGURE 10-2   The Optimal Levels of Consumption and Investment in a Two-Period Model

This model pertains to a country with a portfolio of investment projects. The investment, I_t, can be thought of as a number of smaller investments that sum to I_t. The average rate of return on these investments, which we denote as r, equals R/I_t. This is higher than the marginal return on (a small) investment at X, denoted r_x. To see this, note that when viewed from below, the *CPF* curve is concave (i.e., it bows outward). This implies that as the economy moves along its *CPF* curve from T toward S and more resources are invested in the current period, equal increments in investments engender successively smaller increases in future consumption; in short, it assumes the best investments are made first.

The set of three curves labeled *SIC* in Figure 10-2 are social indifference curves. Each curve represents a combination of current and future consumption that provides society with an equal level of utility. For example, society is indifferent between points X and W on SIC_2. The negative slope of the *SIC*s implies that society is only willing to give up some units of current consumption in order to increase future consumption. The *social marginal rate of time preference* (SMRTP) is the *extra* amount of future consumption that society requires as compensation for giving up one unit of current consumption. Suppose that society requires at least $1 + p_x$ units in the future to give up one unit of current consumption at X, then the SMRTP at X equals p_x and the slope of SIC_2 at X is $-(1 + p_x)$.

The First-Best Solution in the Two-Period Model

Society would, of course, desire to reach the highest possible indifference curve. As can be seen in Figure 10-2, this curve is SIC_2 given an initial endowment of T units and the

CPF. Although SIC_3 is preferable to SIC_2, the country's resources are insufficient to reach SIC_3. Indeed, the economy can only reach SIC_2 at a single point, X. At X, SIC_2 and the *CPF* curve are tangential and their slopes are equal. Consequently, at point X:

$$1 + p_x = 1 + r_x, \text{ or } p_x = r_x$$

Accordingly, were the economy to operate at point X, the SMRTP would equal the marginal rate of return on investment. Furthermore, these rates would equal the economy-wide market rate of interest, denoted by i. In addition, if the rates of interest for borrowing and lending were equal and available to all individuals (i.e., a perfect capital market existed), then everyone would have the same marginal rate of time preference, which would also equal the economy-wide market interest rate. As all of these rates would be equal, the choice of SDR at X would be both obvious and unambiguous. Point X is, therefore, the "first-best" solution.

To see why everybody would have the same MRTP, suppose that an individual initially had a MRTP in excess of i; that is, she wanted to consume more now. This person could borrow at i, a lower rate than she is willing to pay, and thereby increase her current consumption at the expense of her future consumption. This increase in current consumption would increase the relative value of future consumption, causing her MRTP to decline until it eventually equaled i. Analogously, another individual with an MRTP below i would willingly postpone some current consumption in exchange for increased future consumption. By doing so his MRTP would rise until it equaled i. Thus, at X every individual would have the same MRTP, which equals i.

Real Economies: Problems with the Two-Period Model

Point X in Figure 10-2 is the socially optimal point under the assumptions previously discussed. However, real economies are unable to operate at point X. An actual economy with taxes and transaction costs would be more likely to function at point Z, which is a "second-best" outcome. Here, society would underinvest (actual investment $< I_t$); it would only be able to reach SIC_1, not SIC_2. Furthermore, the marginal return on investment would exceed the marginal rate of time preference $(r_z > p_z)$.[12]

To illustrate the wedge between p_z and r_z, consider a firm that could earn a one-year rate of return of 6 percent on an investment of $100, provided by a shareholder. In the presence of taxes and transaction costs, not all of the $6 earned by the firm would be returned to the shareholder. If the firm faced a corporate tax rate of 40 percent, then it would pay $2.40 to the government and give only $3.60 to the shareholder. But a shareholder facing a personal income tax rate of 30 percent would have to pay $1.08 of the $3.60 to the government. Further, imagine that the shareholder faced transaction costs (searching for the investment opportunity, gathering information about its risks, taking steps to reduce the risk, etc.) of $0.52. The return actually realized by the shareholder would be $2 ($6 – $2.40 – $1.08 – $0.52). Thus, the 6 percent rate of return on the investment would only elicit an investment from an individual with an MRTP of 2 percent or less.

Because different individuals and different corporations have different preferences, face different tax rates, and the transactions costs associated with investments vary across investment projects and across individuals, numerous values exist for both the marginal rate of time preference and the marginal rate of return on investment. Thus, there is no obvious choice for the SDR that can be derived from these values.

An Infinite-Period Model: Discounting Using the Optimal Growth Rate

A number of years ago, Frank Ramsey suggested a different approach and proposed a model with an indefinite number of future periods.[13] For reasons that will be discussed later, this model is sometimes known as the "optimal growth rate method." In this model, the economy consists of a single, representative individual (society) who obtains utility from consumption. Society (i.e., the representative individual) discounts future consumption for two reasons. First, society is impatient and prefers to consume more now than in the future, *ceteris paribus*. Second, there is economic growth.

To begin, suppose there are only two periods and there is no growth. Further imagine that the *CPF* is symmetric, as shown in Figure 10-3, and the maximum society could consume in the future equals the amount of goods available for current consumption, that is, $OS = OT$. In this situation, society would discount the utility derived from its consumption of future goods using a "pure" rate of time preference, denoted by d. Because society is impatient, in the absence of taxes and transaction costs, current consumption would exceed future consumption, such as at point X, which is below the 45° line.

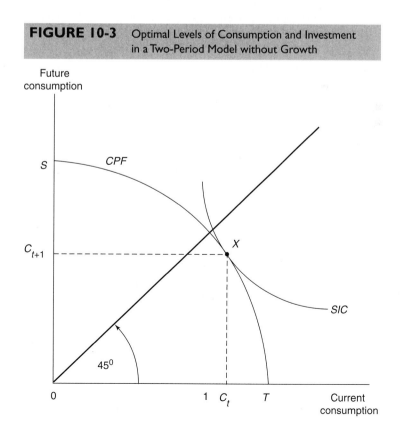

FIGURE 10-3 Optimal Levels of Consumption and Investment in a Two-Period Model without Growth

It may seem reasonable for society to discount consumption next year relative to consumption this year because of pure time preference or impatience. However, when applied over the long term to projects with intergenerational impacts, this would be equivalent to treating the utility of future generations as less valuable to social welfare than the utility of the current generation; society would be giving more weight to the current generation. Ramsey himself found this to be morally objectionable and argued that d should be zero.

Now suppose that there is economic growth. With growth and declining marginal utility of consumption, society can "spread out" consumption, recognizing that it will have greater consumption possibilities in the future. In these circumstances, the value of the social marginal rate of time preference if society were at the optimal point, which was previously denoted as p_x, consists of the sum of two components: one reflecting impatience and the other reflecting growth. Specifically, p_x equals the pure rate of time preference, d, plus a term equal to the long-run rate of growth in per capita consumption, g, multiplied by a constant, e:

$$p_x = d + ge \tag{10.6}$$

where $d, g, e > 0$.

This model assumes that due to ongoing economic growth, society will consistently enjoy higher per capita consumption in the future than it does today. Consequently, as a result of declining marginal utility of consumption, societal welfare would increase if consumption were "smoothed out" (more equal) over time. Put another way, the future should have a lower weight than the present. The rate at which the weights decline across time should be proportional to the growth rate of per capita consumption: the higher the growth rate, the higher the SDR.[14] The parameter e is an elasticity that measures how fast the social marginal utility of consumption falls as per capita consumption rises. Setting e equal to zero implies no discounting of future consumption: Society treats each unit of consumption received in the future as identical to a unit of consumption in the present, signifying a complete lack of concern for intergenerational inequality. As e approaches infinity, society completely discounts each unit of consumption received in the (richer) future, signifying an overwhelming desire to equalize per capita consumption over time. When e equals one, the relative weight on society's consumption in each time period equals the inverse of its relative per capita consumption. Thus, a 10 percent reduction in consumption today, for example, from \$40,000 to \$36,000, is an acceptable trade-off for a 10 percent increase in consumption at a richer, future time, for example, from \$80,000 to \$88,000. Society weighs the loss of \$1 of consumption today as twice as important as a gain of \$1 to its future self, because the future society is twice as rich.

Ramsey also shows that on the optimal growth path of the economy, the value of the marginal rate of return on investment must equal the value of the SMRTP. Thus:

$$r_x = p_x = d + ge \tag{10.7}$$

Here, the x subscript indicates that this result holds for the first-best, or optimal, growth path.

DERIVING THE SOCIAL DISCOUNT RATE FROM THE MARKET: FOUR ALTERNATIVES

This section discusses four potential social discount rates that are derived from rates observable in markets. The first uses a value based on the marginal rate of return on private-sector investments, r_z. The second uses a value equal to the social marginal rate of time preference, p_z. The third uses a value equal to the government's real borrowing rate, i. The fourth uses a weighted average of p_z, r_z, and i, where the weights reflect the amount of the project's resources that are financed by consumption, investment, and foreign borrowing, respectively. In this section, we continue to use the subscript z on p and r to emphasize that we are discussing an economy that is at a point such as Z in Figure 10-2 (rather than at X) and, as a consequence, the marginal rate of time preference is not equal to the marginal rate of return on investment.

All four of these rates presume that resources used for a public project should return more than they would if they remained in the private sector.[15] If the benefits of the project would exceed the opportunity cost of the resources, then it should be undertaken; otherwise, it should not. This is essentially the CBA compensation test: Is it better to invest in a project or to invest at a market rate of interest and then use the returns to compensate the potential beneficiaries of the project?[16]

In determining these market-based rates one must grapple with three issues: What is the most appropriate asset for which to compute a nominal yield? How should expected inflation be measured?[17] Over what time period should the expected real yield be estimated?

Using the Marginal Rate of Return on Private Investment

The argument for using the marginal rate of return on private investment as the social discount rate is that before the government takes resources out of the private sector, it should be able to demonstrate that society will receive a greater return in the public sector than it would have received had the resources remained in the private sector. Therefore, the return on the government project should exceed r_z, the marginal return on private investment.

The most compelling case for the use of r_z was made in an influential article by Arnold Harberger.[18] Harberger analyzed a closed domestic market for investment and savings, such as the one presented in Figure 10-4. In the absence of taxes and government borrowing, the demand curve for investment funds by private-sector borrowers is represented by D_0 and the supply curve of funds from lenders (or savers) is represented by S_0.

Now consider the introduction of a corporate income tax and a personal income tax. The tax on corporate profits would shift the demand curve down to D_1 because part of the returns from investments must now be paid to the government, whereas the tax on interest income would shift the supply curve up to S_S because part of the interest on savings must now be paid to the government. Thus, both taxes would reduce investment.

Given the initial demand and supply curves and these taxes, the market-clearing interest rate would be i. That is, investors would pay an interest rate of i to borrow

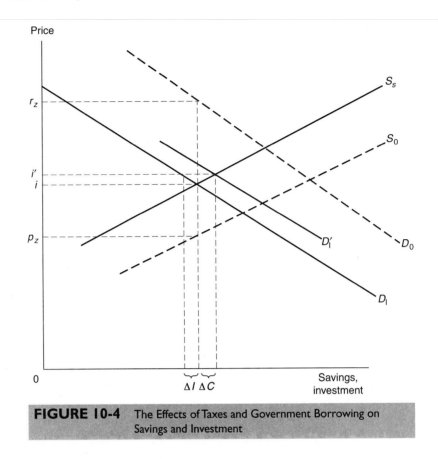

FIGURE 10-4   The Effects of Taxes and Government Borrowing on Savings and Investment

funds, and savers would receive an interest rate of i prior to paying taxes. However, the marginal rate of return on investment before taxes (i.e., the opportunity cost of forgone private-sector investment) would be r_z, with the gap between r_z and i representing taxes paid by investors. The opportunity cost of forgone consumption or, equivalently, the marginal rate of time preference, p_z, would equal the marginal return on savings after taxes (i.e., there would be a gap between p_z and i representing taxes paid by savers on interest income). Thus, as previously discussed, taxes would cause r_z to exceed p_z.

Now consider the effects of a government project that is financed entirely by borrowing in a closed, domestic financial market. Suppose the demand for funds for the new project shifts the market demand curve up to D_I'. The market rate of interest would rise from i to i'. Private-sector investment would fall by ΔI, and private-sector savings would increase by ΔC. Because the increase in private-sector savings would exactly equal the decrease in private-sector consumption, the project would "crowd out" both investment (by ΔI) and consumption (by ΔC).

Harberger suggests that the social discount rate should be obtained by weighting r_z and p_z by the respective size of the relative contributions that investment and consumption would make toward funding the project. That is, he suggests that the social discount rate, SDR, should be computed as follows:

$$SDR = ar_z + bp_z \qquad (10.8)$$

where $a = \Delta I/(\Delta I + \Delta C)$ and $b = (1 - a) = \Delta C/(\Delta I + \Delta C)$.

Finally, Harberger asserts that savings are not very responsive to changes in interest rates. Some empirical evidence supports this assertion, implying that the S_S curve is close to vertical and, as a consequence, ΔC is close to zero.[19] This, in turn, suggests that the value of the parameter a is close to 1 and the value of b is close to 0. In other words, almost all of the resources for public-sector investment would be obtained by crowding out private-sector investment. Harberger, therefore, argues that the marginal rate of return on investment, r_z, is a good approximation of the social discount rate.

Numerical Values of r_z   Probably the best proxy for the *marginal* rate of return on private investment, r_z, is the real, before-tax rate of return on corporate bonds, although some analysts argue for an average return that also includes the rate of return on equities.

There are four reasons for using a bond rate rather than a measure of the average return on equities. The first is that doing so avoids the problem of having to estimate the effective marginal corporate tax rate. Because a firm can deduct the interest it pays to its bondholders before calculating its taxable income, it will equate (on the margin) its expected before-tax return on an investment with the before-tax rate it must pay on its bonds. So the real bond yield is a good direct proxy for r_z. Second, the measure should proxy the marginal pretax return on private investment. Using a measure based on average returns to equities would lead to too high a rate, as the return on a marginal investment is lower than the average return. In the bond market, the interest rate represents the marginal borrower's willingness-to-pay, and this should proxy the return on the marginal investment. Third, bond yields are available contemporaneously, while the average return on equities must be calculated by looking back over a historical period (and will vary greatly according to the period chosen). Finally, returns to equity investments contain a risk premium for holding equities, typically measured as the difference between the observed *ex post* real return to a diversified equity portfolio and the real return to a (default-risk free) government bond.[20]

Two possible candidates to serve as a proxy for r_z are the monthly average of the real yields on Moody's AAA-rated corporate bonds and the real, average monthly yield on all Moody's rated corporate bonds. The expected, real yield on Moody's AAA bonds using the one-year ahead inflation forecasts fluctuated between 3 and 4 percent for much of the post-war period, with a similar pattern in the U.S. Treasury series. Recently, it has varied between 4 and 5 percent. The series for all-rated corporate bonds exhibits a similar pattern, with real returns about nearly half a percentage point higher than the AAA bonds. On balance, 4.5 percent appears to be a reasonable estimate.

Criticisms of the Calculation and Use of r_z   Several factors suggest that use of an SDR of 4.5 percent is too high. Some of these criticisms pertain to the estimation of r_z while others pertain to the strong assumptions made by Harberger. First, private-sector rates of return may be pushed upward by market distortions caused by negative externalities and market prices that exceed social marginal cost.[21] Second, this measure of the marginal rate of return on private investment incorporates a small default risk premium, but it is likely that the government has lower risk as it holds a broader portfolio of projects than any private agent does and, consequently, pays a lower interest rate than private borrowers.[22] This lower rate is the appropriate one to use in discounting public investments.[23] Third, the project might be financed by taxes, rather than by loans, in which case consumption is more likely to be crowded out than investment. The reason is that most taxes are collected from individuals through income, payroll, and consumption taxes, which mainly affect consumption, especially if savings rates are fairly low. Fourth, the project may be partially financed by foreigners. Fifth, there may not be a fixed pool of investment so that government investment replaces private investment dollar-for-dollar. Indeed, government infrastructure projects can raise the private return to capital.[24] If the economy is not fully employing all its resources, then complete crowding out is unlikely. For all these reasons, using values of the SDR in the range of 4 to 5 percent, as suggested here, should be viewed as close to the upper limit of the SDR.

Using the Social Marginal Rate of Time Preference

Many analysts hold that the SDR should be thought of as the rate at which individuals in society are willing to postpone a small amount of current consumption in exchange for additional future consumption (and vice versa). In principle, p_z represents this rate. Another way to justify using this rate is to assume that a project is financed entirely by domestic taxes and to assume that taxes reduce consumption but not investment. Then, it is appropriate to set $a = 0$ and $b = 1$ in equation (10.8), yielding a SDR equal to p_z.

Numerical Values of p_z In practice, the best return that many people can earn in exchange for postponing consumption is the real, after-tax return on savings. This provides a potential way to estimate p_z. As discussed earlier in this chapter, it is appropriate to discount at a risk-free rate. Thus, an obvious candidate for the p_z is the return to holding government bonds, the class of assets that have the lowest risk.[25]

We consider two possible candidates to proxy p_z: the average monthly yield on one-year U.S. government Treasury notes and that on medium-term (10-year) Treasury bonds. Historical monthly series on these are available from 1953 through 2002.[26] The return on medium-term bonds generally exceeds that on the one-year notes. One-year notes are better matched to available measures of expected inflation, but medium-term bonds may give a better idea of the rates at which consumer/savers are willing to postpone consumption for future net benefits.

The nominal, pretax average monthly yields on bonds must be converted to real, after-tax rates by adjusting for taxes and inflation. In practice, it is difficult to know exactly what effective tax rate faces the marginal saver. John Shoven and Michael Topper argue that the personal tax rate on savings in the United States is 30 percent, which we use in our calculations.[27]

To measure the rate of inflation that consumer/savers expected while holding these assets, we use the implicit forecasts for one-year ahead inflation in the Livingston survey,[28] available biannually from 1947 through 2002.[29] We also use the explicit ten-year ahead inflation forecasts available in the biannual survey from June 1991. We match the monthly yields on one-year and ten-year Treasuries (for each June and December from 1953 to 2002) to the implicit one-year ahead inflation forecasts, and we match the June and December returns on ten-year Treasuries with the explicit ten-year ahead inflation forecasts from 1991 to 2002. Using an effective marginal tax rate of 30 percent, we then calculate three sets of biannual estimates (for June and December) of the real, after-tax return to savings, our proxy for the p_z—one for the one-year notes using the one-year ahead inflation forecasts, one for the ten-year bonds using the one-year ahead inflation forecasts, and one for the ten-year bonds using the ten-year ahead inflation forecasts.

The historical series for ten-year Treasuries, using the one-year ahead forecasts for inflation, results in real, expected after-tax savings rates that typically fluctuate between 1 and 2 percent, although there were periods (when inflation was poorly forecast as it rose in the 1970s and fell in the 1980s) during which these rates actually became negative (the 1970s) and then rose dramatically to over 4 percent (the early 1980s). The average rate for the period 1953 through 2002 is 1.3 percent. The series for one-year Treasuries exhibits a similar pattern, with slightly lower real, after-tax returns. The most recent five-year, moving averages for these two series are 1.3 percent and 0.6 percent, respectively. Using ten-year bonds and the explicit, ten-year ahead inflation forecasts for the period 1991 through 2002, we find that real, after-tax returns averaged 1.2 percent, with a range between 0.3 and 2.0 percent. The most recent five-year, moving average is 1.1 percent.

These estimates of the p_z are not that far apart. The real, after-tax returns to ten-year Treasury bonds, which employ recent, explicit ten-year ahead inflation forecasts, probably provide the best estimate. Given this estimate, tempered with the longer-term historical results, we recommend estimating p_z at 1.5 percent, with sensitivity analysis at 1.0 percent and 2.0 percent (approximately plus or minus one standard deviation, given the most recent measures of volatility).

Criticisms of the Calculation and Use of p_z There are three main criticisms pertaining to the computation and use of p_z. First, individuals differ in preferences and opportunities:[30] While some are saving, others are borrowing. At the margin some save by reducing their debt. Because consumer borrowing rates exceed savings rates and because reducing some debt is not taxed, consumers who save by reducing their debt earn a much higher real, after-tax return than other savers. For example, the real after-tax return of paying down one's mortgage is about 3 percent.[31] Some people who save by paying down the balance on their credit cards earn very high returns, often higher than 15 percent. It is not obvious how to aggregate these different individual marginal rates of time preference into a single, social marginal rate of time preference. Second, many individuals simultaneously pay down mortgages, buy government and corporate bonds and stocks for retirement, and sometimes even borrow on their credit cards at very high interest rates.[32] Such behavior makes it unclear whether each individual has a single marginal rate of time preference, a point we return to later. A recent study of retirement offers of annuities or lump-sum payments made to U.S. military personnel finds implied rates of time preference averaging over 25 percent! These varied between 0 and 30 percent by age, race, number of children, education, and rank.[33] Third, as $p_z < r_z$, this method may justify very long-term investments that provide low returns at the expense of higher-return private projects, thereby harming efficiency.

Using the Government's Borrowing Rate

Many economists argue that the government should discount projects using its long-term borrowing rate, i, because this rate reflects the actual cost of financing the (marginal) project. In some cases, it is possible to achieve an actual Pareto improvement for society by borrowing at this rate. Suppose, for example, a project can be financed at a rate of i, and it has a rate of return of y. If y exceeds i and all the funds are borrowed from abroad so that no domestic consumption or private-sector investment is crowded out, then the government may be able to tax the beneficiaries in order to raise the funds needed to pay back its foreign debt (plus interest), and the beneficiaries may still be better off.

Numerical Values of i   To calculate a specific value of the government's borrowing rate, i, we begin with the average monthly yield on 10-year U.S. Treasury bonds for the period April 1953 to December 2001, which was 6.71 percent. Using the actual percentage change in the Consumer Price Index (specifically, the CPI-U for All Items) for this period of 3.89 percent as the expected rate of inflation, we obtain a real return on bonds equal to $(.0671 - .0389)/(1 + .0389) = 2.71$ percent. Correcting for the upward bias in the historical CPI suggests that the real rate of return on these bonds equaled 3.71 percent,[34] with a plausible range for sensitivity analysis of 3 to 5 percent.

Criticisms of the Calculation and Use of i   One criticism of using i as the social discount rate is that a project will produce an actual Pareto improvement only if the beneficiaries alone pay the taxes needed to retire the government loan. In practice, this is unlikely, especially if the project benefits are increases in nonmarket goods or services.[35] Some funding would inevitably come at the expense of the consumption or investment of others.

The other major criticism is that the United States cannot borrow or lend at an unchanging real interest rate. An increase in government borrowing will raise domestic real interest rates and crowd out some investment and (a bit of) consumption, as well as reduce exports relative to imports.[36]

Using the Weighted Average Approach

Proponents of r_z as the social discount rate assume that resources for government investment come from borrowing that crowds out domestic investment dollar for dollar. Advocates of p_z assume that resources come from taxes that crowd out current domestic consumption dollar for dollar. Others argue that foreign borrowing is another potential source of the resources.[37] Thus, government projects do not necessarily crowd out domestic private consumption or investment on a dollar-for-dollar basis. Financing may potentially come from a variety of sources.

Some economists have proposed that the social discount rate should be calculated in terms of the social opportunity cost of the required resources with weights based on the relative contributions of the different sources of the resources.[38] If a is the proportion of the project's resources that crowd out private domestic investment, b is the proportion of the resources that displace domestic consumption, and $1 - a - b$ is the proportion of the resources that are financed by borrowing from foreigners, then the weighted social opportunity cost of capital (WSOC) method computes the social discount rate as the weighted average of these rates:

$$\text{WSOC} = ar_z + bp_z + (1 - a - b)i \qquad \text{(10.9)}$$

As $p_z < i < r_z$, it follows that $p_z < \text{WSOC} < r_z$. Obviously, the previous methods are special cases of this more general approach.

Numerical Values of WSOC   As previously discussed, reasonable historical U.S. estimates for r_z, p_z and i are 4.5 percent, 1.5 percent, and 3.7 percent, respectively. Estimates of a, b, and, hence, $(1 - a - b)$ are harder to obtain. Their values are highly dependent on how the specific project being considered is financed. As a general rule, deficit-financed projects are most likely to displace investment, as the increased demand for loanable funds raises interest rates, given the supply of savings, and crowds out private investment. Consumption is much less likely to be reduced because, as previously suggested, the balance of the evidence suggests it is not very responsive to changes in the market interest rate.[39] Thus, a and $(1 - a - b)$ are likely to be relatively large and b would be small. On the other hand, tax financing is much less likely to displace investment. Taxes reduce consumers' disposable incomes and most disposable income is consumed rather than saved.[40] Hence, b would be large, a small, and $(1 - a - b)$ would probably equal 0. Consequently, if a project is financed through taxes, the value of WSOC would be similar to that of p_z, 1.5 percent, although perhaps a bit larger. If the project was deficit financed, however, then the value of WSOC would be similar to that of r_z (4.5 percent) or i (3.7 percent). The relative sizes of a and $(1 - a - b)$ would not matter very much because r_z and i are similar in size.[41]

How can one determine the financing source? At least until the last few years, Congress and the public have usually viewed new federal expenditures as necessitating additional taxes and reductions in expenditures as allowing tax reductions. Almost all state and local governments are subject to requirements that they run balanced budgets. Thus, it seems appropriate in most circumstances to assume that a project is tax financed.[42] However, if a specific state or municipal bond issue finances a project, then obviously debt financing should be assumed.

Criticisms of the Calculation and Use of the WSOC   Most of the criticisms pertaining to the use of p_z, r_z, or i as the social discount rate also apply to the WSOC. There is, however, one other consideration. The previous approaches each resulted in a single social discount rate. In contrast, the value of WSOC depends on the sources of a project's resources. In practice, governments prefer a single social discount rate because of the difficulty of monitoring assumptions about the sources of resources required for specific projects and of explaining why different discount rates are used on different projects.

THE SHADOW PRICE OF CAPITAL

As previously discussed, a case can be made for using each of four alternative market-based social discount rates: p_z, r_z, i, and the WSOC. Because these rates differ from one another, they will produce varying estimates of the *NPV* of a given project. Thus, whether a particular project has a positive *NPV* may depend on the choice among these alternative rates. The shadow price of capital approach to social discounting provides a strong theoretical justification for choosing p_z as the social discount rate over the other three market-based rates. However, as will be seen, the value of r_z (but not i or WSOC) also remains highly relevant.

If all the resources used in a project displace current consumption and all the benefits produce additions to future consumption, then the social discount rate should reflect social choices in trading present consumption for future consumption and p_z

would be the natural choice for the discount rate. However, any proposed project could produce costs and benefits in the form of changes in consumption *or* investment or both. Due to market distortions, as previously discussed, the rate at which individuals are willing to trade present for future consumption, p_z, differs from the rate of return on private investment, r_z. Thus, flows of investment should be treated differently from flows of consumption. The shadow price of capital method entails distinguishing between project impacts that affect investment and those that affect consumption. Changes in investment are weighted by a parameter, which is greater than 1, called *the shadow price of capital* and denoted by θ. This parameter converts investment gains or losses into *consumption equivalents*. These consumption equivalents, like consumption flows themselves, are then discounted at p_z.[43]

This method has strong theoretical appeal, but it is somewhat difficult to use in practice. Although there seems to be a growing consensus that it is better to use it than not use it, there are few examples of it actually being used to evaluate public sector projects.

The shadow price of capital method requires that discounting be done in four steps. First, the costs and benefits in each period are divided into those that directly affect consumption and those that directly affect investment. Second, flows into and out of investment are multiplied by the shadow price of capital, θ, to convert them into consumption equivalents. The term "shadow" emphasizes that the price of capital cannot be directly observed in a market but must be inferred. Third, changes in consumption are added to changes in consumption equivalents. Fourth, the resultant consumption equivalents and the original consumption flows are discounted at p_z, which reflects how society values the cost of postponing consumption.

Consumption and investment are treated differently because consumption provides an immediate benefit while investment generates a stream of benefits that occur in future periods. To see this, suppose a dollar is invested in the private sector for an indefinite period. Suppose also that it earns a return of r_z each period and this return is consumed each period, while the original dollar is reinvested. Thus, r_z is consumed each period in perpetuity. To obtain the present value of this consumption stream we discount the amounts received each period at p_z. Using the formula for the present value of a perpetuity, which is discussed in Chapter 6, this reduces to:

$$\theta = \frac{r_z}{p_z} \tag{10.10}$$

As previously indicated, the parameter θ is the shadow price of capital. Because r_z is greater than p_z, equation (10.10) implies that its value is greater than 1. *Thus, displaced investment is more costly to society than displaced consumption.*[44] The shadow price of capital represents the present value of the consumption resulting from investing one dollar in the private sector (under the preceding assumptions). By multiplying flows into and out of private-sector investment by θ, we convert them into their consumption equivalents.

To explore the shadow price approach a bit further, suppose that a project yields real annual benefits of B per year indefinitely. If all of these benefits are consumed as they arise, then the present value of this perpetual consumption flow discounted at p_z is B/p_z.

Now consider two extreme cases. If the project's capital cost, C, is paid in year 0 and all these funds are raised from consumption, then the *NPV* rule implies the project should be undertaken if $B/p_z > C$. Thus, in this extreme situation, the shadow price of capital method is equivalent to discounting benefits and costs at the SMRTP.

Next suppose instead that all the costs, which still occur in year 0, displace private investment. Under this assumption, the *NPV* rule implies the project should be undertaken if $B/p_z > \theta C = (r_z/p_z)C$ or, equivalently, if $B/r_z > C$. This condition is equivalent to discounting the benefits and costs at the rate of return on private investment, as suggested by Harberger.

The expression for the shadow price of capital in equation (10.10) is based on several simplifying assumptions. One is that the investment will not depreciate. Another is that the entire return from the investment will be consumed when it occurs. More likely, some of the return will be consumed when it is generated and some will be reinvested. Consideration of these possibilities leads to a more general expression for the shadow price of capital:

$$\theta = \frac{(r_z + \delta)(1 - f)}{p_z - r_z f + \delta(1 - f)} \qquad \textbf{(10.11)}$$

where δ is the depreciation rate of the capital invested; f is the fraction of the gross return that is reinvested; and, as before, p_z is the SMRTP and r_z is the net return on capital after depreciation.[45] Note that in the absence of reinvestment and depreciation (i.e., if $f = 0$ and $\delta = 0$) this formula reduces to our initial expression for θ in equation (10.10).

Numerical Values of θ

To apply equation (10.11), we need values for p_z, r_z, f, and δ. We have already discussed p_z and r_z; thus, we need consider only f and δ. To obtain a value for δ, the depreciation rate of capital, we rely on work by Charles Hulten and Frank Wykoff, who found that the annual depreciation rate for manufacturing equipment was 13.3 percent and for structures used in manufacturing was 3.4 percent.[46] Weighting these rates by the relative proportions of equipment (67 percent) and structures (33 percent) in U.S. capital stock (figures that are available from the *United States Statistical Abstracts*) gives an average annual depreciation rate of $[0.67 \times 0.133 + 0.33 \times 0.034] = 10.0$ percent.[47]

The gross investment rate (the ratio of real gross fixed investment to real GDP) provides a rough estimate of f, the fraction of the gross return that is reinvested. It averaged 13.0 percent for 1947–2002, based on quarterly real GDP data with a range between 10.6 and 18.5 percent. Over the last economic cycle (roughly 1991–2001) the gross investment rate averaged 15.5 percent, while the most recent five-year average was 17.6 percent. The ratio peaked in the second quarter of 2000 and has fallen subsequently but remains above the long-run historical average. This suggests that an average rate of approximately 17 percent is likely in the future, and we choose it as our central estimate of f.

We can now estimate θ using equation (10.11). Our central estimates of p_z is 1.5 percent, r_z is 4.5 percent, δ is 10 percent, and f is 17 percent yield an estimate of $\theta = 1.33$, implying that one dollar of private-sector investment would produce a stream of consumption benefits with an *NPV* equal to $1.33. Using equation (10.10) instead of equation (10.11), our estimate of θ would be 3.0. Earlier, we suggested using a range for r_z of 4.0 to 5.0 percent and a range for p_z of 1.0 to 2.0 percent. Using different combinations of these values, with $f = 17$ percent and $\delta = 10$ percent, results in values for θ of between 1.21 and 1.47. For sensitivity analysis, the larger of these values should be used with $p_z = 1.0$ percent and the smaller with $p_z = 2.0$ percent.

Using the Shadow Price of Capital

To apply the shadow price of capital, one must first determine when and by how much investment is likely to be displaced or augmented. As previously suggested, it seems reasonable under most circumstances to assume that a project is tax financed and, consequently, that it is mostly consumption, rather than investment, that is displaced. In this case, an analyst may proceed by discounting at p_z without using the shadow price of capital. However, as previously mentioned, a project that is financed by state or municipal bond issues is obviously debt financed. If a closed economy is assumed (no possibility of foreign borrowing), then we may assume that the initial costs of the project are raised at the expense of domestic investment, and these should be valued in consumption equivalents using the shadow price of capital before discounting at p_z.

Even if there is deficit financing, in an open economy the government can borrow from abroad at the market interest rate. Increased borrowing may raise interest rates, but this in turn appreciates the exchange rate (under a flexible exchange rate regime) and thus crowds out net exports as well as investment. If the supply of loanable funds from abroad is very responsive to the interest rate, then very little domestic investment is crowded out.[48] Unfortunately, there is very little evidence on how responsive the supply of foreign funds is to the interest rate. For a small project, the analyst can probably reasonably assume that the effect on interest rates, the exchange rate, and the trade deficit is quite small. Hence, discounting in an open economy can use p_z, ignoring the shadow price of capital.[49]

In summary, if a project is strictly tax financed, if the supply of foreign funds is extremely responsive to the interest rate, if the project is quite small, or if the percentage of costs and benefits that comes from investment is the same in every period, then the analyst may simply discount at p_z without using the shadow price of capital. This is likely to approximate the situation in many practical circumstances. However, if the project is deficit financed and the supply of savings and foreign funds are both assumed to be very unresponsive to the interest rate, then the displaced (or augmented) investment flows should be converted to their consumption equivalents using θ before discounting at p_z.

To illustrate, consider a project to improve the physical plant of a city's schools that is financed by a bond issue of $3 million. We assume that the bonds would be purchased solely by city citizens and would be paid for by local residents at 4 percent (real) interest through five equal annual installments of $673,854. Benefits from the project are estimated to be $700,000 a year over a five-year period and $0 thereafter. Following Harberger, we assume that the entire amount borrowed, which would be repaid over five-years, would displace private-sector investment.[50]

Given that the loan is repaid over five years at 4 percent interest, the equal annual installments are $673,854. For the first year, $120,000 ($0.04 \times 3,000,000$) is interest on the loan and $553,854 (673,854 − 120,000) is repayment of principal. Consequently, at the end of the first year, immediately after the first annual payment, the loan balance equals $2,446,146 (3,000,000 − 553,854). Extending this logic to the second and subsequent years, it follows that $576,008 (673,854 − .04 × 2,446,146) is paid toward the capital portion of the loan at the end of the second year, and $599,048, $623,010, and $648,080 are paid toward the loan at the end of years 3, 4, and 5, respectively. By the end of the fifth year the loan is completely paid off (553,854 + 576,008 + 599,048 + 623,010 + 648,080 = 3,000,000). Again following Harberger, we assume that the full amount of each of the loan principal repayments goes toward increasing investment.

The first year's interest on the loan is $120,000 as just discussed. For years 2, 3, 4 and 5, the interest equals $97,846, $74,806, $50,844, and $25,923, respectively. We assume that these amounts are entirely consumed, rather than reinvested.

In summary, under these assumptions, the net changes in investment each year, ΔI_t, are:

$$\Delta I_0 = -\$3,000,000, \Delta I_1 = \$553,854, \Delta I_2 = \$576,008, \Delta I_3 = \$599,048, \Delta I_4 = \$623,010,$$
$$\Delta I_5 = \$648,080.$$

There are three types of changes in consumption: the project benefits of $700,000 per year during each of the five years, the $673,854 loan repayment during each year, and the interest on the loan, which varies each year. Thus, the net changes in consumption, ΔC_t, are:

$$\Delta C_0 = \$0,$$
$$\Delta C_1 = \$700,000 - \$673,854 + \$120,000 = \$146,146,$$
$$\Delta C_2 = \$700,000 - \$673,854 + \$97,846 = \$123,992,$$
$$\Delta C_3 = \$700,000 - \$673,854 + \$74,806 = \$100,952,$$
$$\Delta C_4 = \$700,000 - \$673,854 + \$50,844 = \$76,146$$
$$\Delta C_5 = \$700,000 - \$673,854 + \$25,923 = \$52,146.$$

Using $p_z = 1.5$ as the discount rate, the present value of the changes in consumption is $481,031 and the total present value of the changes in investment is −$134,571. With shadow pricing, the latter figure would be multiplied by $\theta = 1.33$ to convert it to its consumption equivalent and, hence, would equal −$178,979. Thus, with shadow pricing, the project's *NPV* would be $302,052 ($481,031 − $178,979). If shadow pricing were ignored, the *NPV* would increase to $346,460 ($481,031 − $134,571).

Criticisms of Calculation and Use of θ

The shadow price of capital method accounts for increases and displacement of private investment and consumption in a theoretically appropriate fashion, which is an important advantage over other methods. Nonetheless, one can raise several objections. First, as opposed to just choosing a discount rate and using it in the *NPV* formula, it is difficult to explain to policy makers how the *NPV* calculations are made, let alone why. Second, the information requirements are more substantial than for the other discounting approaches. Third, as the previous example suggests, judgment plays an important role, especially in deciding how to allocate benefits and costs between investment and consumption. Hence, the procedure might be manipulated to meet political objectives, although this objection is not unique to the shadow price approach. Whatever method of discounting is used, assumptions must be made and costs and benefits must be estimated. These assumptions and estimates involve judgment and can potentially be manipulated for political or other purposes.[51] Finally, as the *NPV* depends on θ, which in turn depends on r_z and p_z, the results are subject to the criticisms that pertain to the calculation of these parameters.

USING THE OPTIMAL GROWTH RATE APPROACH TO DISCOUNTING

Problems with Using a Market Rate of Interest as the SDR

The optimal growth rate approach to discounting, which was discussed early in the chapter, rejects the notion that social choices should reflect individual preferences as inferred from market interest rates. One reason for rejecting the use of market interest rates is that capital markets are not perfect and individual consumers do not behave as assumed by the standard economic model of intertemporal choice. There are four strands of evidence to support this assertion. First, not only do borrowing and lending rates differ due to taxes and transactions costs, but some individuals are screened out of legitimate credit markets altogether due to informational asymmetries. Hence, individuals differ in both their rates of time preference and in their opportunities: While some are saving at low rates, others are borrowing at higher rates, and still others are borrowing from loan sharks.

Second, many individuals simultaneously lend and borrow: They pay down mortgages, buy government and corporate bonds and stocks for retirement, and borrow on their credit cards.[52] In view of such behavior, it is unreasonable to assume that these individuals are equating their marginal rates of time preference with a single market interest rate.[53]

Third, individual preferences do not appear to be time consistent. For example, individual rates of time preference and implied discount rates appear to decline over the horizon to which they are applied.[54] This implies that choices made at one time may be overturned later even if no new information becomes available, a phenomenon known as time inconsistency. This is problematic as projects that appear socially valuable at the time of an initial decision may later appear to be a mistake, even though nothing has changed except the passage of time.

Fourth, there is a strand of evidence demonstrating that the framing of intertemporal choice affects individuals' implicit rates of time preference. Thus, individuals use different rates to discount large amounts versus small amounts, losses versus gains, choices involving the near future as against choices farther out in time, and choices between speeding up versus delaying consumption.[55] As previously mentioned, depending on the choice being made and the individual making it, one can infer the marginal rate of time preference is anywhere from 0 to 30 percent.[56] These four strands of behavioral evidence severely weaken the case for deriving the social discount rate from observations on individual intertemporal choices in markets.

The Optimal Growth Rate as an Alternative to Market Rates of Interest

Even if individual behavior does not indicate consistent, well-behaved intertemporal choices over public and private goods, society may wish to make public investments as though it does. The optimal growth rate approach to discounting assumes that policy makers use a well-behaved social welfare function that describes the values society places on different amounts of per capita consumption, both public and private, over time. Policy makers choose the amount of public investment in order to maximize the well-being of society now and in the future.

Equation (10.6), which was presented earlier and is restated here for the reader's convenience, implies that the social discount rate that is based on the optimal growth rate approach method, p_x, is the sum of two elements:

$$p_x = d + ge$$

As previously discussed, the first term, d, reflects purely a preference for well-being in the present over the future (i.e., impatience), regardless of economic growth. The second term reflects consumption discounting—a preference for more equality in per capita consumption over time than would otherwise occur. It is the product of two parameters: the growth rate of per capita consumption, g, and the absolute value of the rate at which the marginal value of that consumption decreases as per capita consumption increases, e.

A final reason for rejecting methods based on market interest rates is that these rates only reflect the preferences of individuals currently alive. This is especially problematic when a project's effects span generations. Many critics of using p_z as the social discount rate argue that members of the current generation fail to account appropriately for the effects of long-term projects on the welfare of future generations.[57] So using p_x instead may be recommended when a project's effects are likely to be intergenerational. However, very long-term investments also raise other concerns that we discuss later in the chapter.

Numerical Values of p_x

To estimate p_x by the optimal growth rate method, we need estimates of the elasticity of the social marginal utility of consumption with respect to per capita consumption, e, the utility discount rate, d, and the growth rate in per capita consumption, g.

Using annualized per capita quarterly data on real consumption expenditures for 1947–2002, we estimate that the average growth rate of consumption per head in the United States was 2.3 percent per annum.[58] It is difficult to predict the future long-run growth rate, especially as recent historical growth rates have varied substantially. Given this, we recommend using $g = 2.3$ percent, with sensitivity analysis at 2.0 and 2.5 percent.

Robert Brent suggests that e should be between 0 and 1, with 0.5 as a benchmark.[59] Kenneth Arrow and his colleagues argue that individuals reveal their own values of e by their risk taking and intertemporal choice behavior; they suggest that individual elasticities of marginal utility of consumption lie between 1 and 2.[60] Thus, the recently proposed values for e vary between 0 and 2, with $e = 1$ being a reasonable compromise. We recommend setting $e = 1$, with sensitivity analysis at 0.5 and 1.5.

There has been considerable debate about the value of d since Ramsey's original formulation of the optimal growth rate approach. As mentioned earlier, Ramsey argues that it is ethically indefensible to use a positive value because this would discount future generations' well-being relative to the present one. However, Kenneth Arrow shows that weighting all generations' welfare equally results in very high rates of savings being required of the current (or even of every) generation.[61] He demonstrates that, under reasonable parameter values, the current generation could be required to save approximately two-thirds of its income! To avoid this result, a positive pure rate of time preference should be employed. Arrow suggests a figure of around 1 percent for d, which we use in the following calculations.

With an estimate of g = 2.3 percent, e = 1, and d = 1 percent, we obtain p_x = 3.3 percent. Sensitivity analysis with e ranging between 0.5 and 1.5 and with g varying between 2.0 and 2.5 percent implies p_x ranges from 2.0 to 4.8 percent or, rounding, between 2.0 and 5.0 percent. Thus, we recommend using a central estimate of p_x equal to 3.5 percent with sensitivity analysis at 2.0 and 5.0 percent.[62]

Criticisms of Calculation and Use of the Optimal Growth Rate

There are several criticisms of this approach and of the requisite parameter values. First, the estimate of g may be inaccurate. Using the national income accounts to measure the growth rate in real (aggregate) consumption expenditure per person may not accurately measure what economists mean by consumption. For example, this consumption measure includes purchases of consumer durables, which most analysts believe should be interpreted as investment. Also, it does not include the quantity and quality of public goods, which certainly affect consumers' welfare. An alternative plausible approach measures g as the average rate of growth of real per capita GDP, because GDP includes both private-sector consumption and goods produced in the public sector. During the 1947–1998 period, real GDP per capita grew at 2 percent per annum, which is slightly lower than our previous estimate of 2.3 percent.[63] Using this growth rate and e = 1 and d = 1 percent, gives p_x = 3.0 percent. But because GDP includes investment and net exports as well as consumption, we prefer the previous estimate.

Second, even if the growth rate in the past can be accurately measured, it is difficult to estimate the future long-run growth rate, g. Although the natural estimate is the recent historical growth rate, this varies over time. Splitting our data into two time periods shows that the average growth rate was 2.33 percent from 1947 to 1972 but 1.88 percent from 1972 to 1998.[64] The growth rate may have picked up again since 2001–2002.

Third, the parameter e relies on a social value judgment about intergenerational equality. It may be even more difficult to aggregate individual preferences about equality than to aggregate individual rates of time preference. Similarly, selecting a value for d also requires a value judgment.

The final criticism, which also applies to p_z, refers back to Harberger's argument. If p_x is less than the private marginal return on investment, society is underinvesting relative to the socially best outcome. If a public investment produces a one-period, real return greater than p_x, then society should make this investment because it improves social welfare, adopting the value judgments used in calculating p_x. However, if the return on an alternative private-sector project exceeds the return on the public project, then the private project would increase social welfare even more. This is, of course, only an issue if the public investment would actually crowd out the private investment, which, as discussed earlier, only would occur under somewhat special circumstances.

If the possibility that the return on a displaced private investment could have exceeded the return on public projects is an issue, using the shadow price of capital approach and then discounting consumption and consumption equivalents at p_x provides a solution. So, as in using p_z as the social discount rate, investment flows should be converted to consumption equivalents by the shadow price of capital before discounting at p_x. In doing this, θ must be recomputed by replacing p_z in equation (10.10) or (10.11) with p_x. When $p_x = 3.5$ replaces $p_z = 1.5$ in equation (10.11), and $r_z = 4.5$ percent, $f = 17$ percent, and $\delta = 10$ percent, then $\theta = 1.09$.[65] Given our recommended range for p_x of between 2 and 5 percent and for r_z of between 4 and 5 percent, θ can be as small as 1.0 and as large as 1.32. For sensitivity analysis, the smaller of these two values should be used with $p_x = 5$ percent and the larger value with $p_x = 2$ percent.

INTERGENERATIONAL DISCOUNTING

Reasons for Using a Time-Declining Discount Rate for Intergenerational Discounting

So far we have considered only constant (time-invariant) SDRs; thus, for example, the same discount rate is used to discount costs and benefits between years 51 and 50 as between years 1 and 0. There are at least four reasons to consider using a time-declining SDR (i.e., to use lower rates to discount costs and benefits that occur farther in the future than those that occur sooner). Most of these considerations become relevant when project effects cross generational lines. However, there is no obvious way to decide when a project is intragenerational or intergenerational. In many circumstances, those as yet unborn when a project is initiated will live to be affected by it, whether as beneficiaries, taxpayers, or both. Those alive bear some of the startup costs, but may not live to reap the benefits. Nonetheless, both the serious ethical dilemmas and the practical differences that occur when considering long-term projects do not begin before a span of about 50 years. For our purposes, we will define intragenerational projects as those whose main effects are contained within a 50-year horizon.[66] Projects with significant effects beyond 50 years are considered intergenerational.

The first reason to consider a time-declining SDR is based on empirical evidence that individuals are time inconsistent; they use lower discount rates for events that occur farther into the future.[67] Exhibit 10-1 presents evidence that individual MRTPs for saving lives now versus saving lives in the future decline as the time horizon extends farther into the future.[68]

David Laibson cites evidence from the psychology literature that individuals' discount functions are approximately hyperbolic; that is, they are characterized by relatively high discount rates over short time horizons and relatively low rates over long horizons.[69] He explains that individuals recognize that, if they cannot commit to saving, then on a day-to-day basis (using a high short-term discount rate) they will never save as much for the future as they know they should (using a low long-term discount rate). Recognizing their lack of self-control, individuals may commit themselves to savings plans with large penalties for early withdrawals, while using their available credit to otherwise maximize their current consumption. They may simultaneously save by purchasing an illiquid asset with a relatively low, after-tax real return (such as a government savings bond), make predetermined monthly mortgage payments, and borrow on a credit card at a very high real interest rate. These observed patterns of saving and borrowing simply reflect individuals' recognition of their lack of self-control and the time-declining discount rates that result from this. Borrowing on a credit card at a high interest rate reflects a high rate of discount for the near future, whereas purchasing a government savings bond or making monthly mortgage payments could

---

EXHIBIT 10-1

Maureen Cropper and colleagues have conducted surveys to measure how participants are willing to trade off lives saved today with lives saved in the future. In round numbers, this research suggests that people are indifferent between one life saved today and two lives saved in 5 years' time, three lives saved in 10 years' time, six lives saved in 25 years' time, eleven lives saved in 50 years' time, and forty-four lives saved in 100 years' time. More precisely, and expressing the results in terms of marginal rate of time preference (MRTP), the research found an implicit marginal rate of time preference of 16.8 percent over a 5-year horizon, 11.2 percent over a 10-year horizon, 7.4 percent over a 25-year horizon, 4.8 percent over a 50-year horizon, and 3.8 percent over a 100-year horizon. These results suggest that individual MRTPs are significantly greater than zero, but they decline as the time horizon extends farther into the future.

Source: Adapted from Maureen L. Cropper, Selma K. Aydede, and Paul R. Portney, "Rates of Time Preference for Saving Lives," *American Economic Review: Papers and Proceedings* 82(2) 1992, 469–472.

---

result if individuals applied low discount rates to the more distant future and, hence, had strong commitments to save for their retirements.

The second reason pertains to evaluating decisions with impacts that occur far in the future, such as environmental effects, including reforestation, efforts to mitigate global warming by greenhouse gas abatement, preserving biodiversity through the protection of unique ecosystems, and the storage of radioactive waste. Discounting at a time-constant discount rate can pose an ethical dilemma: The use of constant discount rates much in excess of 1 percent implies that it is not efficient for society to spend even a small amount today in order to avert a very costly environmental disaster, provided that the disaster occurs sufficiently far into the future. For example, if greenhouse gas buildup imposes a net cost of $1 trillion in 400 years' time (approximately 1/10th of current U.S. GDP), this has an *NPV* of less than $336 million today at a constant discount rate of 2 percent, and an *NPV* of less than $113,000 at a rate of 4 percent. Thus, CBA using a discount rate of more than 2 percent would result in the conclusion that we should do little greenhouse gas abatement today, even if the future effects on the climate are catastrophic.[70] Many economists and other persons are uncomfortable with the implication that it is not worth spending more than $113,000 today, or even $336 million, to avert a major disaster in 400 years. In contrast, with a time-declining SDR, the *NPV* may well imply that it is indeed worth averting the $1 trillion cost that will be incurred four centuries from now.

Even for less apocalyptic disasters, a large enough positive SDR gives negligible weight to costs and benefits that occur sufficiently far into the future.[71] Using a time-declining rate avoids having to choose between ignoring very long-term environmental or health consequences (with a time-invariant, non-zero SDR), and not discounting at all.

A third reason for using a time-declining SDR is that the values of current market rates of interest or marginal rates of time preference reflect the preferences of individuals currently alive, not those not yet born. Some economists argue that current individuals fail to account appropriately for the long-term impacts of their actions, or of the government's actions, on the welfare of future generations.[72] Those yet unborn do not have a direct voice in current markets, yet we may believe that they should have standing in our (current) CBAs.[73] Moreover, the standard compensation logic behind CBA fails when impacts are intergenerational. For example, the argument for discounting using the r_z is that the alternative to a particular public project is to invest in a marginal private sector project. If the public project yields a lower rate of return than the private project, then the future potential beneficiaries of the public project would be better off if society invested in the private project and gave them these proceeds instead. However, if those who are hurt are alive 400 years in the future, there is no plausible mechanism to "give them the cash instead." Even if the current generation set up a fund to compensate those who bear the costs of not reducing global warming, it is unlikely to be available in the far future—there are no viable 400-year private sector investments, so intervening generations would have the opportunity to rob the fund.

Unlike the use of market rates of interest, using the optimal growth rate method does permit an explicit consideration of the welfare of future generations. However, the most common social welfare function used with this method treats society as a single, representative individual whose well-being is equal to the discounted sum of the utility derived from present and future per capita consumption. This may make sense for evaluating 50-year investments; but it loses much of its relevance for evaluating 400-year or 10,000-year investments, such as for greenhouse gas abatement or the storage of radioactive waste.

The fourth reason for using a time-declining SDR is that the farther we look into the future, the greater is the inherent uncertainty as to the future growth rate of the economy and future market rates of interest. Allowing for this uncertainty means that lower and lower discount rates should be used to discount consumption flows that occur farther and farther in the future.[74]

To see why effective discount rates decline as they apply to flows of benefits or costs that occur farther out in time when there is uncertainty about future discount rates, consider the following example. Suppose a project delivers a single benefit of $1 billion in 400 years. Suppose further that there is a 50 percent chance that the appropriate (constant) discount rate over this period will be 7 percent and a 50 percent chance that it will be 1 percent. One might imagine that we should average these two rates to obtain the expected discount rate, 4 percent, and then use this average rate to compute the expected *NPV* of the future benefit as $1 billion $\times e^{-(0.04) \times 400}$, which is approximately $110. However, this is incorrect. The discount factors of $e^{-(0.07) \times 400}$ and $e^{-(0.01) \times 400}$ should be averaged, yielding an expected *NPV* equal to $1 billion $\times$ $[(0.5e^{-(0.07) \times 400}) + (0.5e^{-(0.01) \times 400})]$, which is approximately $9,157,800. This is equivalent to using a single, certain discount rate of approximately 1.2 percent. In effect, the larger discount rate almost completely discounts itself out of the average. This effect grows as time horizons become longer, resulting in a time-declining schedule of discount rates. In the distant future, only the very lowest possible rate matters; all the higher rates result in discount factors that approach zero. Note that this motivation for time-declining rates is due solely to uncertainty, and so it does not imply time inconsistency in social choices.

Numerical Values for Time-Declining Discount Rates

Time-declining discount rates can be used when discounting relies on either a market-based interest rate approach or on the optimal growth rate method. However, the schedule of rates will differ depending on which approach is used, just as the short-term rates based on each approach differ.

Based on research by Richard Newell and William Pizer,[75] *we suggest the following time-declining rate schedule based on the optimal growth rate model: 3.5 percent from year 0 to year 50, 2.5 percent from year 50 to year 100, 1.5 percent from year 100 to year 200, 0.5 percent from year 200 to year 300, and 0 percent thereafter.* For a single benefit in year 300, this schedule is equivalent to applying a single, constant rate of 1.67 percent. As an alternative, *we suggest the following time-declining schedule based on the social marginal rate of time preference: 1.5 percent from year 0 to year 50, 1.0 percent from year 50 to year 100, 0.5 percent from year 100 to year 200, and 0 percent thereafter.* For a single benefit in year 300, this schedule is equivalent to applying a single, constant rate of about 0.6 percent. These schedules allow the effects on far future generations to be given more weight than time-invariant discount rates. After a given period of time, all future generations are essentially treated alike.

To illustrate how the schedules would be used in practice, consider a project that has that a single benefit of $1 billion delivered in year 400, and an initial cost of $1 million today. Based on the optimal growth rate approach, the *NPV* for such a project would be $-\$1$ million $+ \$1$ billion $\times [(e^{-(0.035) \times 50}) \times (e^{-(0.025) \times (100-50)}) \times (e^{-(0.015) \times (200-100)}) \times (e^{-(0.005) \times (300-200)}) \times (e^{-(0) \times (400-300)})]$, which is approximately $5,737,000. Note that we discount at 0 percent from year 400 to 300; then we discount the year 300 value back to year 200 at 0.5 percent, take the resulting value in year 200 and discount it back to year 100 at 1.5 percent, and so on. In this example, this is equivalent to applying a single, constant rate of approximately 1.3 percent from year 400 to the present.

RECOMMENDED SOCIAL DISCOUNT RATES

There are many alternative approaches to discounting and many alternative potential candidates for the social discount rate. The choice among them can determine whether a government policy or project has a positive or negative net present value and, therefore, whether a project should be undertaken. The selection of a social discount rate and the procedure used in discounting depend on the specific circumstances surrounding the project.

There is wide agreement that investment flows should be treated differently from consumption flows and should be multiplied by the shadow price of capital before discounting. There is also some support for the view that market rates can serve as a basis for the SDR. If the shadow pricing approach is adopted, then the most appropriate market-based social discount rate is clearly one based on the social marginal rate of time preference, p_z. Even if the shadow price is not needed because domestic private sector investments seem unlikely to be very much affected by a public-sector project, then the most appropriate market-based SDR is still one based on p_z.

However, although opinions vary, we do not believe that market interest rates should serve as the basis for a parameter to represent the SDR because there are too many inconsistencies in observed individual consumer/saver behavior. Given observed individual intertemporal choices and the implied rates of individual time preference, there would be a wide range of possible discount rates and no obvious way to choose among them. For this reason, we prefer to specify a parameter for the SDR directly, based on an optimal growth rate model of intertemporal choice, using the expected growth rate in per capita consumption as well as explicit social values: p_x.

There are legitimate reasons for some disagreement about what to do for projects with long-term, intergenerational effects. However, we believe that the logic of explicitly incorporating uncertainty as to the future path of interest rates and growth rates is compelling. The key implication is that there are legitimate grounds for using a time-declining schedule of discount rates, especially for projects with large future (i.e., intergenerational) environmental or health effects.

Figures 10-5 and 10-6, which rely respectively on the optimal growth rate approach and the market-based interest rate approach, present flow charts that summarize our suggestions on how, in practice, to determine the most appropriate discounting method and rate. The choice between the two figures is not cut and dried. Although we prefer the optimal growth rate method and, hence, Figure 10-5, this is a judgment call. Others may have a preference for the market-based discount rates shown in Figure 10-6. Once a decision is made concerning which chart to use, there are two critical questions: Does the project have intergenerational costs or benefits that occur after 50 years time ($T > 50$), and is there a reason to believe that the project will crowd out private investment?

If the project does not have intergenerational impacts ($T < 50$) and does not crowd out private investment, then analysts can simply discount at our central estimate of either p_x = 3.5 percent or p_z = 1.5 percent (Box A), depending on whether Figure 10-5 or Figure 10-6 is being used. If the project does not have intergenerational impacts but there is a reason to believe that the project will crowd out private investment, then analysts should convert investment flows to consumption equivalents by multiplying them by our central estimate for θ in Box B and then discounting consumption equivalents and consumption flows at either 3.5 or 1.5 percent. Sensitivity analysis can be conducted using the lower and upper bounds for the discount rates and the shadow price of capital, which also appear in Box B. In practice, there will be few situations where shadow pricing will be necessary. Crowding out of private investment is likely only if the project is debt financed; the supply of foreign funds and savings are unresponsive to interest rates; and the project is large enough to affect bond yields. If a project-specific bond issue finances the project, then it is obviously debt financed. Otherwise, analysts should assume that it is tax financed and, as a result, is more likely to displace consumption than investment.

If the project has intergenerational impacts and there is no reason to believe that it will crowd out private investment, then we recommend using the time-declining scale of discount rates in Box C. The final situation pertains to projects that have intergenerational impacts and there is likely to be significant crowding out of private investment. In this case, we propose that analysts use a hybrid method: Box B for the first 50 years and then Box C for the remainder of the project. Even if there are likely to be significant investment effects in the far future ($T > 50$ years), the effect of uncertainty as to the return on investment implies that the expected value for r_z that applies after 100 or 200 years will converge to the expected value of the discount rate parameter that applies to the same period because both converge to their lowest possible values. In practice, this implies a shadow price of capital that is very close or equal to 1 for such long-term effects.

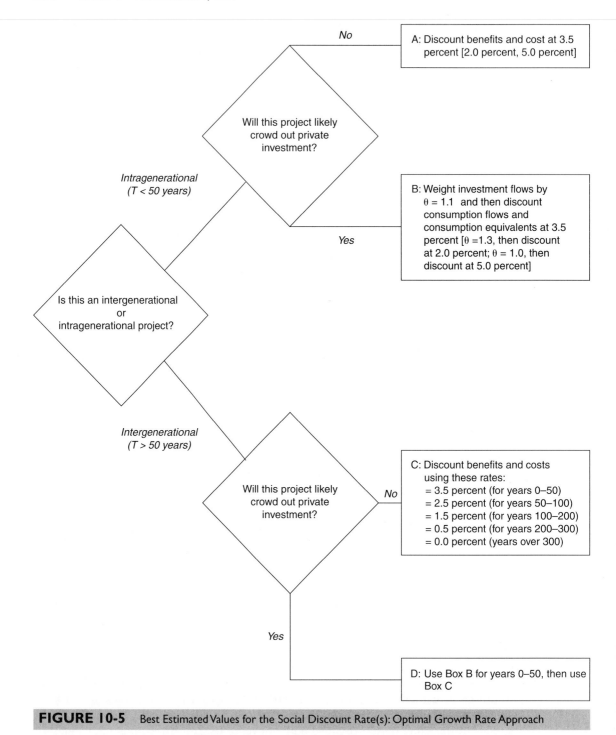

FIGURE 10-5   Best Estimated Values for the Social Discount Rate(s): Optimal Growth Rate Approach

Lower and upper bounds appear in brackets.
Source: Mark A. Moore, Anthony E. Boardman, Aidan R. Vining, David L. Weimer, and David H. Greenberg, "'Just Give Me a Number!' Practical Values for the Social Discount Rate," *Journal of Policy Analysis and Management* 23(4) 2004, 789–812.

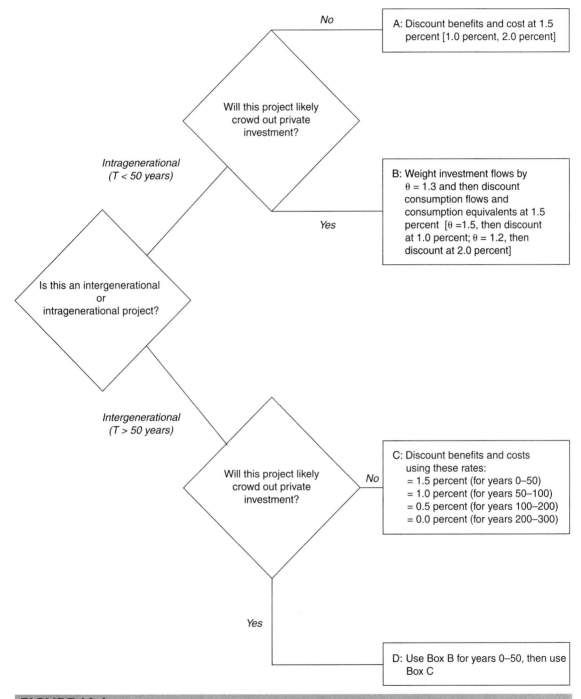

Lower and upper bounds appear in brackets.

THE SOCIAL DISCOUNT RATE IN ACTUAL PRACTICE

How do these proposed guidelines compare to actual practice? Current discounting practices in governments vary enormously. There is considerable evidence that many government agencies do not discount at all.[76] For example, a survey of 90 U.S. municipalities with populations over 100,000 found that only 43 percent use discounting in evaluating projects.[77] At the federal level, U.S. government agencies appear to have less choice over whether to discount but also appear to have considerable discretion over the discounting rate and procedure.[78] When governments do discount, they rarely use the shadow price of capital method. As indicated earlier, this method is difficult to implement and it is difficult to explain to noneconomists. Also, governments do not use time-varying discount rates. Thus, the issue is largely one of describing what (positive) constant discount rate practitioners use. This rate varies from country to country and often from department to department.

As we discuss in Chapter 1, spenders, guardians, and analysts tend to favor different discount rates. In general, guardians view government expenditures as crowding out private investment, or act as if they do; consequently, they tend to argue for a discount rate approximating the rate of return on private investment, a relatively high rate. In contrast, spenders view government as affecting consumption, and they tend to argue for a discount rate approximating the marginal rate of time preference, a relatively low rate. In most practical situations, the rate is prescribed by government review and monitoring agencies. Because such agencies tend to be staffed by guardians, the prescribed rates tend to be higher than social discount rates based on the theory presented in this chapter, but this is not always the case.

The prescribed rates in the U.S. federal government have tended to be fairly high, but they have been trending lower. For example, in the 1970s and 1980s, the Office of Management and Budget (OMB) required most agencies to use a real discount rate of 10 percent.[79] This rate was intended to approximate the opportunity cost of capital, measured as the real, marginal, before-tax rate of return on private investment. More recently, the OMB has revised this rate downward to 7 percent.[80] This new rate was based on low-yielding forms of capital (e.g., housing), as well as high-yielding corporate capital. The OMB advises agencies that wish to use either the consumption rate of interest with the shadow price of capital method or the optimal growth rate method to consult with the OMB prior to conducting their analyses. Even if discounting at the marginal rate of return on private investment were valid, our estimates suggest that the appropriate rate is only 4.5 percent, with sensitivity analysis at 4.0 and 5.0 percent.

Both the General Accounting Office (GAO) and the Congressional Budget Office (CBO) use a lower rate than the OMB. The CBO has estimated the real historical yield on U.S. government securities at 2 percent, and uses this rate plus or minus 2 percentage points. The GAO uses the average nominal yield on Treasury debt maturing between one year and the life of the project, less the forecast rate of inflation.[81] GAO uses the same rate for all applications, while the CBO and OMB have a number of exceptions.[82]

A recent proposal by the U.S. Panel on Cost-Effectiveness in Health and Medicine recommends the use of a 3 percent discount rate for cost-effectiveness studies, with sensitivity analysis at rates between 0 percent and 7 percent.[83]

Guidelines published by the U.S. Environmental Protection Agency recommend using p_z as the social discount rate and propose an estimate of p_z of 2 to 3 percent.[84]

They also suggest sometimes using the shadow price of capital, but because of their view that capital is relatively mobile and most environmental projects are likely to be marginal, they do not suggest doing this very often. However, correspondence with the EPA indicates that they have commonly annualized the capital costs of an environmental rule using the marginal rate of return on private investment and then discounted this flow using p_z. This is equivalent to using the shadow price of capital under the simple assumptions of equation (10.10).[85] Using our point estimates and equation (10.10) would estimate the shadow price of capital as equal to 3.00. In contrast, using the more sophisticated approach in equation (10.11) would estimate the shadow price of capital as equal to 1.33.

In 1976, the Federal Treasury Board Secretariat in Canada recommended the use of a real discount rate of 10 percent, with sensitivity analysis at 5 and 15 percent. In 1998, the Treasury Board revised its guidelines; it maintained the 10 percent rate, but narrowed sensitivity analysis to plus or minus 2 percent.[86] However, the Treasury Board sometimes allows much lower discount rates (0 to 3 percent) for health and environmental cost-benefit analyses, although this is not official policy. Provincial government guidelines in Canada have tended to follow the federal guidelines, but most currently use a lower rate.[87] The British Columbia Crown Corporations Secretariat currently recommends a real SDR of 8 percent.[88]

In 2003, the British Treasury issued recommendations for discounting that are similar to those in this chapter. The specific recommendation is for a discount rate of 3.5 percent, which is based on the optimal growth rate method. They also suggest using a time-declining discount rate for projects with effects that occur after 30 years. After 300 years, the recommended discount rate reaches a minimum of 1 percent.[89]

CONCLUSION

There has been considerable debate as to the appropriate method of discounting, as well as the specific estimate of the SDR. There is widespread agreement that the correct conceptual method of discounting is to shadow price investment flows and to discount the resulting consumption equivalents and consumption flows using a consumption-based social discount rate. The main disagreements center on the choice of the consumption-based SDR, the estimates of the requisite parameters, of the shadow price of capital, especially the rate of return on investment, and on how to deal with intergenerational issues. Inevitably, we have been forced to make several important judgment calls. Specifically, we believe that the most appropriate SDR is based on the optimal growth rate, p_x, although we also offer clear guidance on using a market-based measure, p_z, instead for those believe it is more appropriate. We also believe that both of these discount rates should be used in combination with the shadow price of capital under the rather limited circumstances when it is appropriate to do so. We suggest the use of time-declining discount rates in projects with significant intergenerational impacts. Others may make different judgment calls and arrive at different estimates.

Our discussion of the issues should have made it clear that analysts are unlikely ever to have complete confidence in whatever discounting procedure they use. Even in the case of the more simple discounting methods, choice of the appropriate social discount rate requires judgment. Taking account of the shadow price of capital demands that even more parameters that cannot be known with certainty be specified. It is almost always desirable, therefore, for analysts to test the sensitivity of their results to changes in the parameters used in discounting. Nonetheless, in conducting CBA, choices must be made. Our specific recommendations are summarized in Figure 10-5, with alternative recommendations provided in Figure 10-6 for market-based values. For most projects, those whose main impacts occur within 50 years and whose financing does not crowd out investment, we recommend a discount rate of 3.5 percent. With appropriate sensitivity analysis, we find that the range of likely values for the SDR is not that large—no matter which method one chooses, the estimates for the SDR vary between 1.0 and 5.0 percent for intragenerational projects and between 0 and 3.5 percent for intergenerational projects.

EXERCISES FOR CHAPTER 10

1. (Spreadsheet required.) The following table gives cost and benefit estimates in real dollars for dredging a navigable channel from an inland port to the open sea.

Year	Dredging and Patrol Costs ($)	Saving to Shippers ($)	Value of Pleasure Boating ($)
0	2,548,000	0	0
1	60,000	400,000	60,000
2	60,000	440,000	175,000
3	70,000	440,000	175,000
4	70,000	440,000	175,000
5	80,000	440,000	175,000
6	80,000	440,000	175,000
7	90,000	440,000	175,000

The channel would be navigable for seven years, after which silting would render it unnavigable. Local economists estimate that 75 percent of the savings to shippers would be directly invested by the firms or their shareholders, and the remaining 25 percent would be used by shareholders for consumption. They also determine that all government expenditures come at the expense of private investment. The social marginal rate of time preference is assumed to be 1.5 percent, the marginal rate of return on private investment is assumed to be 4.5 percent, and the shadow price of capital is assumed to be 1.3.

Assuming that the costs and benefits accrue at the end of the year they straddle and using the market-based interest rate approach, calculate the present value of net benefits of the project using each of the following methods.

a. Discount at the marginal rate of return on private investment, as suggested by the U.S. Office of Management and Budget.
b. Discount at the social marginal rate of time preference, as suggested by the U.S. Environmental Protection Agency.
c. Discount using the shadow price of capital method.
d. Discount using the shadow price of capital method. However, now assume that the social marginal rate of time preference is 2.0 percent, rather than 1.5 percent.
e. Discount using the shadow price of capital method. However, now assume that the shadow price of capital is 1.1, rather than 1.3. Again assume that the social marginal rate of time preference is 1.5 percent.

f. Discount using the shadow price of capital method. However, now assume that only 50 percent of the savings to shippers would be directly invested by the firms or their shareholders, rather than 75 percent. Again assume that the social marginal rate of time preference is 1.5 percent and that the shadow price of capital is 1.3.

2. An analyst for a municipal public housing agency explained the choice of a discount rate as follows: "Our agency funds its capital investments through nationally issued bonds. The effective interest rate that we pay on the bonds is the cost that the agency faces in shifting revenue from the future to the present. It is, therefore, the appropriate discount rate for the agency to use in evaluating alternative investments." Comment on the appropriateness of this discount rate.

3. Assume the following: Society faces a marginal excess tax burden of raising public revenue equal to METB; the shadow price of capital equals θ; public borrowing displaces private investment dollar for dollar; and public revenues raised through taxes displace consumption (but not investment). Consider a public project involving a large initial capital expenditure, C, followed by a stream of benefits that are entirely consumed, B.

    a. Discuss how you would apply the shadow price of capital method to the project if it is financed fully out of current taxes.

    b. Discuss how you would apply the shadow price of capital method to the project if it is financed fully by public borrowing, which is later repaid by taxes.

4. Assume a project will result in benefits of $1 trillion in 500 years by avoiding an environmental disaster that otherwise would occur at that time.

    a. Compute the present value of these benefits using a time-constant discount rate of 3.5.

    b. Compute the present value of these benefits using the following time-declining discount rate schedule: 3.5 percent, years 1–50; 2.5 percent, years, 51–100; 1.5 percent, years 101–200; 0.5 percent, years 201–300; and 0 thereafter.

Notes

1. This chapter draws on the first edition of this book; Anthony Boardman and David Greenberg, "Discounting and the Social Discount Rate," in Fred Thompson and Mark T. Green, eds., *Handbook of Public Finance* (New York: Marcel Dekker, 1998), 269–318, especially pp. 296–316; and Mark A. Moore, Anthony E. Boardman, Aidan R. Vining, David L. Weimer, and David H. Greenberg, "'Just Give Me a Number!' Practical Values for the Social Discount Rate," *Journal of Policy Analysis and Management* 23(4) 2004, 789–812. We would like to thank Mark Moore for his many contributions to this chapter.

2. Throughout this chapter we assume that impacts (costs and benefits) and discount rates are all measured in real dollars. See Chapter 6 for a discussion of the role of inflation discounting.

3. In practice, analysts usually do not convert net benefits to certainty equivalents or option prices. Specifically, they use expected values rather than option prices because the former can be estimated from observable behavior, while the latter requires contingent valuation surveys. Unless strong assumptions are made about individuals' utility functions, even the sign, let alone the magnitude, of the difference between expected values and option prices is usually theoretically uncertain, except in the case of uncertainty about income (see Chapter 8, and the references therein). It is important, however, both conceptually and in practice, to treat risk and discounting separately. Nonetheless, in order to compensate for risk, analysts sometimes discount expected net benefits using a higher rate than they would in the absence of risk. Unfortunately, this procedure generally results in an incorrect estimate of the *NPV*. For example, suppose that a project has a relatively large expected terminal cost that is subject to risk. Using a higher rate to account for this risk will reduce, rather than magnify, the present value of this cost, making a positive *NPV* more, rather than less, likely. In contrast, the certainty equivalent for a negative net benefit is a more negative net benefit. As this example illustrates, it is inappropriate to attempt to take account of risk by adjusting the discount rate.

For other reasons why doing this is problematic, see Coleman Bazelon and Kent Smetters, "Discounting Inside the Washington D.C. Beltway," *Journal of Economic Perspectives* 13(4) 1999, 213–228.

4. Robert C. Lind, "A Primer on the Major Issues Relating to the Discount Rate for Evaluating National Energy Projects," in Robert C. Lind, et al., *Discounting for Time and Risk in Energy Policy* (Washington, D.C.: Resources for the Future, 1982), 21–94 at p. 8.

5. Assume here that, in order to reveal your true preferences, there is no arbitrage opportunity; that is, you could not borrow or lend money. Arbitrage means that you can simultaneously buy something in one market and sell it in another market and thereby make a guaranteed profit. If interest rates were less than 20 percent and arbitrage were allowed, you could say that you would rather have the $1,200 next year and then immediately borrow between $1,000 and $1,200 from the bank. Thus, you would say you would prefer to have the $1,200 next year even though you would actually prefer to have $1,000 now.

6. Along an indifference curve,

$$dU = \frac{\partial U}{\partial C_1} dC_1 + \frac{\partial U}{\partial C_2} dC_2 = 0$$

7. Formally,

$$MRS \equiv -\frac{dC_2}{dC_1}\bigg|_{U=constant} = \frac{\partial U/\partial C_1}{\partial U/\partial C_2}$$

8. It would make no conceptual difference if the consumer received income in both periods.

9. The (absolute value of the) slope of the budget constraint exceeds 1, indicating that the consumer earns positive interest at rate i on the part of income saved this year.

10. To solve this problem formally we set up the following Lagrangian:

$$L = U(C_1, C_2) + \lambda[T - C_1 - \frac{C_2}{1+i}]$$

and then take derivatives with respect to C_1 and C_2:

$$L_{c_1} = \frac{\partial U}{\partial C_1} - \lambda = 0$$

$$L_{c_2} = \frac{\partial U}{\partial C_2} - \frac{\lambda}{1+i} = 0$$

Consequently,

$$\frac{\partial U/\partial C_1}{\partial U/\partial C_2} = 1 + i$$

Now, by definition,

$$MRS \equiv \frac{\partial U/\partial C_1}{\partial U/\partial C_2} = 1 + p$$

where p = marginal rate of time preference. Therefore, $i = p$ at the optimum.

11. Formally, the result holds as long as the problem has an interior solution. A very impatient person has an MRTP $> i$, which leads to a corner solution on the C_1 axis. For simplicity, we shall ignore this possibility.

12. At point Z, in Figure 10-2, the absolute value of the slope of the *CPF*, $(1 + r_z)$, exceeds the absolute value of the slope of the *SIC*, $(1 + p_z)$.

13. Frank P. Ramsey, "A Mathematical Theory of Saving," *Economic Journal* 38(152) 1928, 543–559.

14. See Frank Ramsey, "A Mathematical Theory of Saving"; Edmund Phelps, "The Golden Rule of Accumulation: A Fable for Growthmen," *American Economic Review* 51(4) 1961, 638–643; Stephen Marglin, "The Social Rate of Discount and the Optimal Rate of Investment," *Quarterly Journal of Economics* 77(1) 1963, 95–111; and Kenneth J. Arrow, "Intergenerational Equity and the Rate of Discount in Long-Term Social Investment," 1995, unpublished paper given to the IEA World Congress.

15. The values of these rates were obtained from Moore, Boardman, Vining, Weimer, and Greenberg, "'Just Give Me a Number!' Practical Values for the Social Discount Rate."

16. See Robert C. Lind, "Intergenerational Equity, Discounting, and the Role of Cost-Benefit Analysis in Evaluating Global Climate Change," *Energy Policy* 23(4–5) 1995, 379–389.

17. With a nominal interest rate n and an expected inflation rate of m during the year, $\$(1 + n)$ one year from now is expected to buy only as much as $\$(1 + n)/(1 + m)$ does today. The expected, real interest rate, r, is therefore defined by

$(1 + r) = (1 + n)/(1 + m)$. Rearranging, this converts a nominal interest rate, n, into an expected, real interest rate, r, when the expected inflation rate is m: $l = (n - m)/(1 + m)$. Notice that, with a modest rate of inflation, l is approximately equal to $n - m$.

18. Arnold C. Harberger, "The Discount Rate in Public Investment Evaluation," *Conference Proceedings of the Committee on the Economics of Water Resource Development* (Denver, CO: Western Agricultural Economics Research Council, Report No. 17, 1969).

19. See, for example, Robert E. Hall, "Intertemporal Substitution in Consumption," *Journal of Political Economy* 96(2) 1988, 339–357; and John Muellbauer and Ralph Lattimore, "The Consumption Function: A Theoretical and Empirical Overview," in M. H. Pesaran and M. R. Wickens, eds., *The Handbook of Applied Econometrics: Macroeconomics* (Cambridge, MA: Blackwell, 1995), 221–311.

20. Historical studies using U.S. data find this equity risk premium to be in the neighborhood of 6 to 7 percent. See R. Mehra and E. Prescott, "The Equity Premium: A Puzzle," *Journal of Monetary Economics* 15(2) 1985, 145–161. However, most researchers consider this to be too high, a result known as the equity premium puzzle. One problem is survivor bias, which results in a censored sample. A second problem is that the size of this premium is incompatible with the standard economic model of risk bearing. See N. Kocherlakota, "The Equity Premium: It's Still a Puzzle," *Journal of Economic Literature* 34(1) 1996, 42–71; and J. Y. Campbell, "Two Puzzles of Asset Pricing and Their Implications for Investors," *The American Economist* 47(1) 2003, 48–74.

21. See P. Dasgupta, K. Maler, and S. Barrett, "Intergenerational Equity, Social Discount Rates, and Global Warming," in P. Portney and J. Weyant, eds., *Discounting and Intergenerational Equity* (Washington, D.C.: Resources for the Future, 1999), 51–78.

22. K. J. Arrow and R. C. Lind, "Uncertainty and the Evaluation of Public Investment Decisions," *American Economic Review* 60(3) 1997, 364–378.

23. However, Klein argues that the government pays a lower rate on its debt because it enjoys the coercive power of taxation and money creation, thus guaranteeing that it can always pay its debt obligations. See M. Klein, "The Risk Premium for Evaluating Public Projects," *Oxford Review of Economic Policy* 13(4) 1997, 29–42.

24. C. J. Morrison and A. E. Schwartz, "State Infrastructure and Productive Performance," *American Economic Review* 86(5) 1991, 1095–1111.

25. One could argue that a potential alternative estimate is the after-tax return on equities, assuming that individuals save by holding risky equities. Campbell estimates that the average real return on U.S. stocks over the period 1947:2–1998:4 was 8.1 percent (J. Y. Campbell, "Two Puzzles of Asset Pricing and Their Implications for Investors"). Using a marginal personal tax rate of 30 percent, Shoven and Topper suggest the after-tax return on equities is about 5.7 percent. However, this estimate includes a risk premium which, as argued earlier, can result in incorrect *NPV* estimates. See J. B. Shoven and M. Topper, "The Cost of Capital in Canada, the United States and Japan," in J. B. Shoven and J. Whalley, eds., *Canada-U.S. Tax Comparisons* (Chicago, IL: University of Chicago Press, 1992), 217–235.

26. Unless otherwise indicated, all data are from the DRI Basic Economics macroeconomic database (formerly CITIBASE), viewed June 20, 2003.

27. J. B. Shoven and M. Topper, "The Cost of Capital in Canada, the United States and Japan." As high-income individuals do most of the personal saving, their rates are likely the most appropriate.

28. See D. Croushore, "The Livingston Survey: Still Useful After All These Years," *Federal Reserve Bank of Philadelphia Business Review* 1997, 1–12; and L. B. Thomas, "Survey Measures of Expected U.S. Inflation," *Journal of Economic Perspectives* 13(4) 1999, 125–144.

29. These data are available at the Federal Reserve Bank of Philadelphia's Web site: *www.phil.frb.org/econ/liv/index.html*. We use the average forecast for each June and December. We assume that the forecasters had the March and October Consumer Price Index (CPI) numbers available while making their June and December forecasts, respectively, and we use these and their CPI forecasts for the following June and December to calculate implicit one-year ahead inflation forecasts.

30. If you think you have only a short time to live, then you will value the present very highly because, quite literally, there may be no

tomorrow for you. Thus, it is reasonable to expect that older people have a higher MRTP rate than younger people. See Maureen L. Cropper, Sema K. Aydede, and Paul R. Portney, "Rates of Time Preference for Saving Lives." *American Economic Review* 82(2) (1992), 469–472, who found a positive relationship between age and the marginal rate of time preference but found no significant relationship between respondents' MRTP and their sex, education, marital status, or income.

31. From April 1971 through December 2001, the average nominal primary conventional mortgage rate was 9.79 percent. Using the CPI-U (All Items) inflation rate of 4.85 percent and the tax rate of 30 percent, and accounting for the tax deductibility of interest paid on mortgages, the real, after-tax return to paying down a mortgage averaged 1.91 percent. Adjusting for the CPI overstatement of inflation and rounding yields an estimate of 3 percent. Similar calculations for 2001 and 2000 give estimates of 3.3 and 2.2 percent, respectively.

32. An individual may have different marginal rates of time preference over different goods. For example, Jan Olsen suggests that it is possible that individual MRTPs for health differ from those for "ordinary consumption goods." See Jan Abel Olsen, "On What Basis Should Health be Discounted?" *Journal of Health Economics* 12(1) 1993, 39–53. Paul Stern and others have suggested that we might have a high MRTP for mainframe computers but a low MRTP for clean air, clean water, or biological diversity. Part of the reason for the different MRTPs may be due to the longevity of different goods: Computers have relatively short useful lives while environmental goods have long time horizons. See Paul C. Stern, "Blind Spots in Policy Analysis: What Economics Doesn't Say about Energy Use," *Journal of Policy Analysis and Management* 5(2) 1986, 200–227, especially pp. 207–209, for a discussion of differences in the implicit discount rates for different household appliances.

33. J. Warner and S. Pleeter. "The Personal Discount Rate: Evidence from Military Downsizing," *American Economic Review* 91(1) 2001, 33–53.

34. The real return to 10-year Treasuries was 3.4 percent in 2001 and 2.6 percent in 2000.

35. One might argue that the project should proceed as long as the beneficiaries as a class are no wealthier than those taxed to repay the government loan. This requires making explicit value judgments regarding the distribution of income before recommending that a project should go forward.

36. Increased government borrowing raises U.S. interest rates relative to those abroad, causing a financial capital inflow and the appreciation of the dollar. The appreciation in turn reduces net exports. So debt-financed increases in government spending reduce net exports, as well as crowd out investment and consumption.

37. See, among others, Robert C. Lind, "Reassessing the Government's Discount Rate Policy in Light of New Theory and Data in a World Economy with a High Degree of Capital Mobility," *Journal of Environmental Economics and Management* 18(2) 1990, S8–S28.

38. See Agnar Sandmo and Jacques H. Dreze, "Discount Rates for Public Investment in Closed and Open Economies," *Economica* 38(152) 1971, 395–412.

39. For example, see A. C. Harberger, "The Discount Rate in Public Investment Evaluation;" R. E. Hall, "Intertemporal Substitution in Consumption;" and J. Muellbauer and R. Lattimore, "The Consumption Function: A Theoretical and Empirical Overview."

40. Dynan and colleagues find that marginal propensities to save out of disposable income vary between 2.4 and 11 percent in the United States (K. E. Dynan, J. Skinner, and S. P. Zeldes, "Do the Rich Save More?" Federal Reserve Board, Financial and Economic Discussion Series, 2000). Souleles (2002) finds that the Reagan tax cuts of the 1980s had very strong effects on current consumption when enacted (rather than when announced), inducing marginal propensities to consume out of nondurables of between 0.6 and 0.9 (N. S. Souleles, "Consumer Response to the Reagan Tax Cuts," *Journal of Public Economics* 85(1) 2002, 99–120). Even predictable tax refunds are largely spent when received, indicating that consumption is very responsive to the actual, rather than the predictable, permanent level of income, contrary to standard economic theory. See N. S. Souleles, "The Response of Household Consumption to Income Tax Refunds," *American Economic Review* 89(4) 1999, 947–958.

41. For projects financed by borrowing in Canada, Jenkins suggests $a = .75, b = .05$ and $1 - a - b = .2,$

which implies WSOC = .75 × .045 + .05 × .015 + .2 × .037 = 4.2 percent, or rounding, 4 percent. Not surprisingly, given the relatively large value for *a*, this value is close to that for r_z. G. P. Jenkins, "The Measurement of Rates of Return and Taxation for Private Capital in Canada," in William A. Niskanen et al., eds., *Benefit Cost and Policy Analysis* (Chicago: Aldine, 1973), 211–245; G. P. Jenkins, *Capital in Canada: Its Social and Private Performance 1965–1974* (Discussion Paper No. 98, Economic Council of Canada, Ministry of Supply and Services, 1997); and G. P. Jenkins, "The Public Sector Discount Rate for Canada: Some Further Observations," *Canadian Public Policy* 7(3) 1981, 399–407. Burgess discusses the source of Jenkins' estimated weights and suggests that the parameter *a* is more likely to be in the range of 26 to 32 percent, *b* is more likely to be 10 to 13 percent, and 1 − *a* − *b* is more likely to be 55 to 64 percent. These estimates are based on an interest elasticity of the supply of foreign funding in the range of 7 to 10. Given our estimates of r_z, p_z, and *i*, this yields estimates of WSOC of 3.7 percent, again close to 4 percent. See F. D. Burgess, "The Social Discount Rate for Canada: Theory and Evidence," *Canadian Public Policy* 7(3) 1981, 383–394.

42. See R. H. Haveman, "The Opportunity Cost of Displaced Private Spending and the Social Discount Rate," *Water Resources Research* 5(5) 1969, 947–957.

43. This approach was first suggested by Otto Eckstein and was systematically developed by David Bradford. See Otto Eckstein, *Water Resource Development: The Economics of Project Evaluation* (Cambridge, MA: Harvard University Press, 1958); and David F. Bradford, "Constraints on Government Investment Opportunities and the Choice of Discount Rate," *American Economic Review* 65(5) 1975, 887–899. Also see the *Journal of Environmental Economics and Management* 18S(2) 1990.

44. Note that increments to investment are treated the same as displaced investments—they are also multiplied by θ. Thus, flows to investment are more beneficial than flows of consumption.

45. Proof of equation (10.11) is fairly straightforward. Understanding it clarifies the meaning of *f*. Suppose an investment of $1 yields a gross (before depreciation) return of ρ in the first period. Then, with a savings rate of *f*, *f*ρ is reinvested and (1 − *f*)ρ

is consumed. With depreciation of δ in this period, the total amount invested in the second period equals 1 + *f*ρ − δ. Similarly, in the second period the return is ρ(1 + *f*ρ − δ) of which *f*ρ(1 + *f*ρ − δ) is reinvested and (1 − *f*)ρ(1 + *f*ρ − δ) is consumed. With depreciation of δ(1 + *f*ρ − δ) in the second period, the total amount invested in the third period equals [1 + *f*ρ − δ] + [*f*ρ(1 + *f*ρ − δ)] − [δ(1 + *f*ρ − δ)] = (1 + *f*ρ − δ)². And so on. Consumption in period 1 is (1 − *f*)ρ, consumption in period 2 is (1 − *f*)ρ(1 + *f*ρ − δ), consumption in period 3 is (1 − *f*)ρ(1 + *f*ρ − δ)², and so forth. This consumption stream is a perpetuity [with annual benefits of (1 − *f*)ρ] that grows at a constant rate, *f*ρ − δ. Discounting this stream at p_z using the results in Chapter 6 gives:

$$\theta = \frac{\rho - f\rho}{p_z + \delta - f\rho}$$

In this formulation, r_z is the net return on capital after depreciation, that is,

$$\rho = r_z + \delta.$$

Substituting for ρ in the above equation yields equation (10.11). For more information see Randolph M. Lyon, "Federal Discount Policy, the Shadow Price of Capital, and Challenges for Reforms," *Journal of Environmental Economics and Management* 18(2) 1990, S29–S50, Appendix I.

46. C. R. Hulten and F. C. Wykoff, "The Measurement of Economic Depreciation" in R. Hulten, ed., *Depreciation, Inflation, and the Taxation of Income from Capital* (Washington, D.C.: Urban Institute Press, 1981), 81–125.

47. Fraumeni presents the Bureau of Economic Analysis' new depreciation rates, based primarily on Hulten and Wykoff's rates. Unfortunately, she does not provide an estimate of an economy-wide depreciation rate. See B. M. Fraumeni, "The Measurement of Depreciation in the U.S. National Income and Product Accounts," *Survey of Current Business* 77(7) 1997, 7–23.

48. R. C. Lind, "Reassessing the Government's Discount Rate Policy in Light of New Theory and Data in a World Economy with a High Degree of Capital Mobility."

49. U.S. Environmental Protection Agency, *Guidelines for Preparing Economic Analyses*

(Washington, D.C.: U.S. Government Printing Office, 2000), 43–46.

50. If the loans for the project were obtained from persons residing outside the community instead of local citizens, one might believe that benefits and costs accruing to these persons are irrelevant to its investment decisions and, therefore, ignore them in computing the project's net present value. Also, if there was the possibility of borrowing from abroad, then there will be less than complete crowding out of domestic private investment. Private investment may also be less than completely crowded out if there were unemployed resources in the local economy.

51. For a fascinating illustration of cost and benefit estimates that were politically influenced, see Steve H. Hanke and Richard A. Walker, "Benefit-Cost Analysis Reconsidered: An Evaluation of the Mid-State Project," *Water Resource Journal* 10(5) 1994, 324–329.

52. R. C. Lind, "Reassessing the Government's Discount Rate Policy in Light of New Theory and Data in a World Economy with a High Degree of Capital Mobility."

53. Laibson argues that individuals may have pre-committed themselves to saving a certain amount of their income in an illiquid asset, while borrowing for current consumption from ready sources of credit. However, they are still not equating their marginal rates of time preference to a single market rate. See D. Laibson, "Golden Eggs and Hyperbolic Discounting," *Quarterly Journal of Economics* 112(2) 1997, 443–477.

54. M. K. Cropper, S. K. Aydede, and P. R. Portney, "Rates of Time Preference for Saving Lives;" D. Laibson, "Golden Eggs and Hyperbolic Discounting;" G. Loewenstein and D. Prelec, "Anomalies in Intertemporal Choice: Evidence and an Interpretation," *Quarterly Journal of Economics* 107(2) 1992, 573–597.

55. G. Loewenstein and D. Prelec, "Anomalies in Intertemporal Choice: Evidence and an Interpretation."

56. J. Warner and S. Pleeter, "The Personal Discount Rate: Evidence from Military Downsizing."

57. Frank P. Ramsey, "A Mathematical Theory of Saving;" Otto Eckstein, *Water Resource Development: The Economics of Project Evaluation*; Edmund Phelps, "The Golden Rule of Accumulation: A Fable for Growthmen"; Stephen Marglin, "The Social Rate of Discount and the Optimal Rate of Investment;" Kenneth J. Arrow, "Intergenerational Equity and the Rate of Discount in Long-Term Social Investment"; P. Dasgupta, K. Maler, and S. Barrett, "Intergenerational Equity, Social Discount Rates, and Global Warming."

58. This value was obtained by regressing the natural logarithm of real per capita consumption on time. The standard error on the slope coefficient of 2.3 percent is 0.025 percent. Comparably, Prescott (p. 5) argues for a real growth rate of 2 percent because this is the secular growth rate of the U.S. economy in the twentieth century. See E. Prescott, "Prosperity and Depressions," *American Economic Review* 92(2) 2002, 1–15.

59. R. J. Brent, *Applied Cost-Benefit Analysis* (Brookfield, VT: Edward Elgar, 1994).

60. K. J. Arrow, W. R. Cline, K. G. Maler, M. Munasinghe, R. Squitieri, and J. E. Stiglitz, "Intertemporal Equity, Discounting and Economic Efficiency," in J. P. Bruce et al., eds., *Climate Change 1995* (Cambridge, UK: Cambridge University Press, 1995), 128–144.

61. Kenneth J. Arrow, "Intergenerational Equity and the Rate of Discount in Long-Term Social Investment."

62. Kula estimates the average annual growth rate in U.S. per capita consumption between 1946 and 1975 as 2.3 percent. He treats e as representing the preferences of average individuals and estimates it from an aggregate demand equation for food, arriving at 1.89. He views d as representing an average individual's expected annual mortality rate. He assumes this equals the average death rate in the population as a whole, which he estimates is 0.9 percent per year. Therefore, he estimates $p_x = (0.023)(1.89) + 0.009 = 5.2$ percent. See E. Kula, "Derivation of the Social Time Preference Rates for the United States and Canada," *Quarterly Journal of Economics* 99(4) 1984, 873–882. Cline, assuming the likely future world growth rate is 1 percent, $d = 0$, and $e = 1.5$, estimates $p_x = 1.5$ percent. See W. R. Cline, *The Economics of Global Warming* (Washington, D.C.: Institute for International Economics, 1992).

63. The estimated model (t-statistics in parentheses; $R^2 = .99$) is:

$$\ln(\text{real GDP/population}) = -30.60 + 0.02 \times \text{time.}$$
$$(44.7) \quad (58.9)$$

64. An F test rejected the hypothesis that these two coefficients are the same.

65. Cline proposes using a value of θ equal to 1.56 and then discounting using p_x measured at 1.5 percent for all CBAs, including greenhouse gas abatement projects. His estimate of θ uses $r_z = 8.0$ percent, assumes that all investments have 15-year lives, and that $f = 0.2$. See W. R. Cline, *The Economics of Global Warming*.

66. One rationale for this 50-year cutoff is that most equipment, structures, and buildings will not last much longer than 50 years. Depreciation rates appear to range between 3.4 and 13.3 percent per year, implying that between 80 percent and virtually everything has depreciated after 50 years. Thus, there are likely to be few public investments that are intergenerational in our sense. Another argument is that 50 years corresponds approximately to two generations—our generation and our children's—and that events beyond this time period truly belong to future generations. See C. R. Hulten and F. C. Wykoff, "The Measurement of Economic Depreciation"; and M. Nadir and I. Prucha, "Estimation of the Depreciation Rate of Physical and R&D Capital in the U.S. Total Manufacturing Sector," *Economic Inquiry* 34(1) 1996, 43–56. A third rationale is provided by Newell and Pizer, which we discuss later. R. G. Newell and W. A. Pizer, "Discounting the Distant Future: How Much do Uncertain Rates Increase Valuations?" *Journal of Environmental Economics and Management* 46(1) 2003, 52–71.

67. Put another way, the difference between the weights of successive periods in equation (10.1) is smaller for periods that are farther into the future; that is, we have decreasing timing aversion.

68. After reviewing the recent literature on counterexamples to constant discounting, George Loewenstein and Drazen Prelec conclude that "unlike the EU [expected utility] violations, which in many cases can only be demonstrated with a clever arrangement of multiple choice problems (e.g., the Allais paradox), the counterexamples to *DU* [constant discounting] are simple, robust, and bear directly on central aspects of economic behavior." See George Loewenstein and Drazen Prelec, "Anomalies in Intertemporal Choice: Evidence and an Interpretation," *Quarterly Journal of Economics*, 107(2) 1992, 573–597 at p. 574.

69. David Laibson, "Golden Eggs and Hyperbolic Discounting."

70. P. Portney and J. Weyant, eds., *Discounting and Intergenerational Equity* (Washington, D.C.: Resources for the Future, 1999).

71. With constant discounting, impacts that arise in year n are weighted by the present value factor $(1 + i)^{-n}$, which declines geometrically. Thus, impacts that occur far in the future have a low weight. For example, $1 in 100 years has an *NPV* of less than $0.01 using an SDR of more than 4 percent.

72. See, for example, Frank P. Ramsey, "A Mathematical Theory of Saving," and Edmund Phelps, "The Golden Rule of Accumulation: A Fable for Growthmen."

73. For a discussion of this issue, see Daniel W. Bromley, "Entitlements, Missing Markets, and Environmental Uncertainty," *Journal of Environmental Economics and Management* 17(2) 1989, 181–194. Note, however, the willingness of people to pass inheritances to their children and to pay to preserve certain areas gives indirect standing to future generations.

74. See R. G. Newell and W. A. Pizer, "Discounting the Distant Future: How Much Do Uncertain Rates Increase Valuations?"; and M. Weitzman, "Gamma Discounting," *American Economic Review* 91(1) 2001, 260–271.

75. Newell and Pizer ("Discounting the Distant Future: How Much do Uncertain Rates Increase Valuations?") follow an approach based on the historical behavior of interest rates. Their model captures the uncertainty in forecasting the rates that will prevail in the far future. They examine the U.S. government's real, long-term bond rate over the past 200 years and find the data do not clearly distinguish between a random-walk and a mean-reversion model. They prefer the random-walk version and use it to simulate the future path of the bond rate, from both a 4 percent and a 2 percent initial value. They generate thousands of different time paths and use these to construct expected discount factors. This results in a time-declining scale of effective discount rates. In an alternative approach, Weitzman ("Gamma Discounting") surveyed almost 2,200 economists, asked each to provide a single, real rate to use in discounting the costs and benefits of global climate change, and found that the frequency distribution of the respondents' rates approximated

a gamma distribution. His main finding is that even if every respondent believes in a constant discount rate, the widespread of opinion results in the SDR declining significantly over time. Based on the distribution of his respondents' preferred discount rates, Weitzman suggests a scale for SDRs that approaches zero after 200 years. Newell and Pizer derive rates that are generally higher than Weitzman's rates and fall more slowly, with the declining rate kicking in after about 50 years.

76. For a recent review of discounting in various U.S. government agencies, see Coleman Bazelon and Kent Smetters, "Discounting Inside the Washington D.C. Beltway."

77. Richard O. Zerbe Jr. and Dwight Dively, How Municipal Governments Set Their Discount Rate: Do They Get It Right? (manuscript, University of Washington, 1990).

78. Edward R. Morrison, "Judicial Review of Discount Rates Used in Regulatory Cost-Benefit Analysis," *The University of Chicago Law Review* 65(4) 1998, 1333–1363.

79. OMB (Office of Management and Budget, Circular A-94), 1972.

80. OMB, "Economic Analysis of Federal Regulations Under Executive Order 12866" (Office of Management and Budget: Washington, D.C.), 1996.

81. Using the U.S. government's 10-year, constant-maturity bond rate and the explicit 10-year ahead inflation forecasts in the Livingston survey, we calculate that the expected real return on long-term bonds has varied between 1.6 and 4.3 percent since 1991, with an average of 2.9 percent and a standard deviation of 0.67 percent. The latest 5-year moving average is 2.7 percent.

82. Both the OMB and CBO use private-sector rates for asset divestitures. If they did not, they would be using a lower discount rate than the private sector, implying that the *NPV* of assets is higher in the public sector than in the private sector.

Assuming no efficiency differences between public and private ownership, this would imply that the government should never divest any assets. See R. W. Hartman, "One Thousand Points of Light Seeking a Number: A Case Study of CBO's Search for a Discount Rate Policy," *Journal of Environmental Economics and Management* 18(2) 1990, S3–S7.

83. M. C. Weinstein, J. E. Siegel, M. R. Gold, M. S. Kamlet, and L. B. Russell, "Recommendations of the Panel on Cost-Effectiveness in Health and Medicine: Consensus Statement," *Journal of the American Medical Association* 276(15) 1996, 1253–1258.

84. U.S. Environmental Protection Agency, Guidelines for Preparing Economic Analyses.

85. See Jeffrey A. Kolb and Joel D. Scheraga, "Discounting the Benefits and Costs of Environmental Regulations," *Journal of Policy Analysis and Management* 9 (1990), 381–390.

86. See Treasury Board Secretariat, *Benefit-Cost Analysis Guide Regulatory Programs* (Ottawa, Ontario, March 1976), Chapter 11: Discounting. The rationale for this rate draws extensively on research by Glenn Jenkins, which was discussed in an earlier endnote. The 1998 Guidelines, which are still in "draft" form, are available at *www.tbs-sct.gc.ca/fin/sigs/revolving_funds/bcag/bca2_e.asp*.

87. See, for example, Verne W. Loose, ed., *Guidelines for Benefit-Cost Analysis*, Environment and Land Use Committee Secretariat (Victoria, BC: The Queen's Printer, June 1977).

88. See British Columbia Crown Corporations Secretariat, *Multiple Account Evaluation Guidelines* (Victoria, BC, 1993).

89. HM Treasury, *Green Book, Appraisal and Evaluation in Central Government: Treasury Guidance* (London: HM Treasury, 2003), Chapter 5 and Annex 6. Available at the Web site *www.hm-treasury.gov.uk/economic_data_and_tools/greenbook_index.cfm*.

CHAPTER 11

Valuing Impacts From Observed Behavior: Demonstrations

Throughout this book, we have emphasized that the key concept in valuing the positive and negative outcomes (impacts) of a policy is willingness-to-pay as measured by changes in social surplus. To estimate changes in social surplus, we need to know the shape of the relevant supply and demand curves. Earlier, we usually assumed that these were known. In practice, however, these curves are usually unknown. The analyst either has to estimate them in order to give precise measures of benefits and costs or find an alternative means of valuing policy impacts.

Analysts typically face a continuum of possibilities for estimation. At one end of this continuum are policy impacts on prices, quantities, or qualities of goods that are traded in well-functioning, competitive markets. At the other end are policy impacts on goods that are rarely traded in markets—impacts, for example, on health and safety, pollution levels, and access to scenic areas. In between are impacts on commodities that are traded in markets with important distortions such as monopoly power, information asymmetries, and externalities.

Where markets work well, analysts know at least one point on the demand and supply curves, represented by the observed intersection of market price and quantity exchanged, but still have to estimate these curves to measure either existing social surplus or changes in social surplus. Conceptually, estimation can be done using relatively standard econometric techniques, but only when suitable data are available.

As we have seen, however, the rationale for much CBA is that markets are nonexistent or imperfect. In these situations, the analyst may not have even one point on the appropriate demand or supply curve, which makes it particularly difficult to estimate policy impacts.

Nonetheless, as we show in this and the next four chapters, all is not lost! These chapters describe practical ways to value the impacts of a policy when estimates of the appropriate demand and supply curves are not readily available. In this chapter, we focus on estimating benefits and costs on the basis of *demonstrations* or *pilot programs*. (We use the two terms interchangeably; both remind us that the purpose of the project is to learn whether the program "works.")

The chapter first presents a brief discussion of using demonstration projects to obtain estimates of benefits and costs. It then explores alternative ways in which these demonstrations might be structured. The remainder of the chapter shows the value of demonstrations by describing their use in cost-benefit analyses of employment and training programs. The observed impacts of employment and training demonstrations have been used extensively in conducting CBAs. The chapter concludes by examining actual CBAs of employment and training demonstration programs that were targeted at welfare recipients. The chapter provides numerous illustrations of how concepts developed earlier in this book can be used in actual cost-benefit analyses.

WHY CONDUCT DEMONSTRATION PROJECTS?

In Chapter 1, we noted that the fourth basic step in conducting a CBA is to predict impacts over the life of a project. Demonstration projects can help do this. They provide a straightforward method for measuring impacts in the case of proposed programs that provide services to people—for example, health, education, training, employment, housing, and welfare programs. The method works by setting up a small-scale replica or demonstration of the proposed program. To understand why demonstration projects are almost exclusively limited to testing programs that provide people-oriented services, just try to think about how to test a proposed physical investment, such as a new dam, on a small-scale, pilot basis.

The idea behind demonstration projects is to see if the tested program works before it is adopted on a widespread basis. *Ex post* findings from the demonstration, which are based on observing program impacts, can be plugged into an *ex ante* analysis that predicts benefits and costs for the full-scale program. For example, parameters estimated from the Seattle-Denver negative income tax experiment, a prominent demonstration program, have been used to predict the costs and benefits of proposed changes in the U.S. welfare system.[1]

An advantage of conducting a CBA of a demonstration project is that if it turns out that certain aspects of the program being tested need adjustment, then this can be done before the program is implemented on a widespread basis. Even more importantly, if it turns out that the program is a bad idea because costs exceed benefits, then it can be scrapped before it is expanded and interest groups form to protect it.

Although the small scale of pilot projects offers important advantages, it also has potential disadvantages. First, the impacts of a small-scale demonstration program may not readily translate to a fully implemented large-scale program. For example, while it may be fairly easy to find jobs for graduates of a demonstration program that retrains unemployed workers as electricians if the program has only a few graduates, doing so may be far more difficult if large numbers of unemployed persons graduate from a full-scale program and seek employment in the same geographic area. Moreover, market-wide effects, such as those on the level of wages, may be missed by a small-scale demonstration.

More subtly, some policy innovations may cause changes in community attitudes and norms; these changes, in turn, may result in feedback effects that influence the innovation's success. Furthermore, program success may depend on information diffusion. For example, a training program that is available to all unemployed persons in a particular community will become well known to both the unemployed and employers. As a result, both the attitudes of the unemployed toward entering training and the decisions of employers concerning hiring the graduates of training programs could be affected. Such effects are unlikely to occur if only a subset of the unemployed is allowed to participate. Thus, it has been suggested that feedback effects and information diffusion will not occur unless the innovation is adopted on a large scale and, hence, will be missed by small-scale pilot projects.[2] However, there is virtually no evidence on how important such effects are in practice.

A second and related disadvantage of small-scale demonstration programs is uncertainty concerning their *external validity*. That is, there is no assurance that findings from the evaluation, even though valid for the group of persons who participated in the demonstration program, can be generalized to any other group. The reason for this is that personal and community characteristics interact in complex ways with the services provided by a demonstration program. As a result, the program may serve some persons more effectively than others. For example, findings for a training program for unemployed, male, blue-collar workers who live in a community with low unemployment may provide little information concerning how well the program would work for unemployed female welfare recipients who live in a community with high unemployment. For this reason, some demonstration programs are tested on a variety of different groups in different locations.

ALTERNATIVE EVALUATION DESIGNS

CBAs of pilot projects require comparisons between alternatives: The existing environment is compared to the proposed program being tested by the demonstration, and impact is measured as differences in outcomes between the two situations.[3] The term *internal validity* refers to whether this measured difference can be accurately attributed to the program being evaluated. Internal validity, in turn, depends on the particular way in which the comparison between the existing environment and the proposed program is made. There are numerous ways in which this comparison can be made. Researchers usually refer to the specific scheme used for making comparisons in order to measure impacts as an *evaluation design*.

Diagrams that represent five commonly used evaluation designs,[4] as well as brief summaries of the advantages and disadvantages of each of these designs, appear in Table 11-1. In these diagrams, the symbol O represents an outcome measurement point, X represents a treatment point, and R indicates that subjects were assigned randomly to treatment and control groups.

The evaluation designs that are listed in Table 11-1 are not the only ones that exist. There are numerous others. But these designs provide a good sampling of the major alternatives. So that we can make our discussion of them as concrete as possible, we assume that they all pertain to alternative ways in which a pilot program for training the unemployed might be evaluated. In this context, "being in the treatment group" means enrollment in the training program.

Design 1: Classical Experimental Design

Design 1 is a classical experimental design. The symbols indicate that unemployed persons are randomly allocated between a treatment group and a control (or comparison) group. Members of the treatment group can receive services from the pilot training program, while persons in the control group cannot. The way this might work in practice is that once the pilot program is put into place, unemployed persons are notified of its existence. Some of these persons apply to participate in it. A computer is used, in effect, to flip a fair coin: Heads the applicant is selected as a member of the treatment group

TABLE 11-1	Five Commonly Used Evaluation Designs		
Type	*Structure[1]*	*Major Advantages*	*Major Disadvantages*
Design 1: Comparison of net changes between treatment and true control groups	$R: O_1\ X\ O_2$ $R: O_3\quad O_4$	Random assignment guards against systematic differences between control and treatment groups so highest internal validity	Direct and ethical costs of random assignment; as with all evaluations of demonstrations, external validity may be limited
Design 2: Comparison of posttreatment outcomes between true control and treatment groups	$R:\ X\ O_2$ $R:\quad O_4$	Random assignment guards against systematic differences between control and treatment groups so high internal validity	Direct and ethical costs of random assignment; danger that a failure of randomization will not be detected
Design 3: Simple before/after comparison	$O_1\ X\ O_2$	Often feasible and relatively inexpensive; reasonable when factors other than treatment are unlikely to affect outcome	Does not control for other factors that may cause change
Design 4: Comparison of posttreatment outcomes between quasicontrol and treatment groups	$X\ O_1$ O_2	Allows for possibility of statistically controlling for factors other than treatment	Danger of sample selection bias caused by systematic differences between treatment and quasicontrol groups
Design 5: Comparison of net changes between treatment and quasicontrol group	$O_1\ X\ O_2$ $O_3\quad O_4$	Allows for possibility of statistically controlling for factors other than treatment; permits detection of measurable differences between treatment and quasicontrol groups	Danger of sample selection bias caused by systematic differences between treatment and quasicontrol group in terms of nonmeasurable differences

O — observation
X — treatment
R — random assignment
[1]Draws on notation introduced by Donald T. Campbell and Julian Stanley, *Experimental and Quasi-Experimental Designs for Research* (Chicago: Rand McNally College Publishing Company, 1963).

and, consequently, becomes eligible to participate in the program; tails the applicant becomes a member of the control group. Control group members are not eligible to participate in the program but can receive whatever other services are available for the unemployed.

The procedure just described for establishing treatment and control groups is called *random assignment*.[5] Random assignment evaluations of pilot projects of social programs—for instance, a training program—are often called *social experiments*.

To see how well the pilot program works, data on outcomes are collected for both the treatment group and the control group, both before the treatment is administered and after. Using the collected data, members of the experimental and control groups are compared. For example, the earnings of the two groups can be compared sometime after the training is completed to measure the size of the program's impact on earnings.[6]

Of the five design schemes summarized in Table 11-1, design 1 is the best for many types of evaluations. Its major advantage is the use of random assignment. Because of random assignment, the characteristics of people in the treatment and control groups should be similar, varying only by chance alone. As a result, random assignment helps assure that the evaluation has internal validity; that is, members of the experimental groups can be directly compared in terms of such outcomes as earnings, and any differences that are found between them can be reasonably attributed to the treatment.

Sometimes, however, random assignment may be impractical or infeasible.[7] One reason for this is the resources required to assign individuals randomly to treatment and control groups. Generally, however, these resource costs are quite small.

A second reason concerns the notion of experimenting on humans. For example, randomization implies that some persons—those assigned to the comparison group—will be denied services under the demonstration program. It is important to recognize, however, that if a program has only limited resources, some potential program participants will inevitably be denied services, and random assignment (which operates very much like a lottery) may be as fair a way to do this as any. A more serious ethical issue is raised by the possibility that some experimental treatments may actually harm some members of the treatment group. For example, as cost-benefit findings reported later in this chapter indicate, some training programs have been found to reduce the incomes of participants. However, this was not the intent of the program, and there was no way to know in advance that this result would occur. Not knowing the impacts of a social experiment in advance would seem to constitute an ethical justification for conducting the experiment.

Design 2: Classical Experimental Design Without Baseline Data

Design 2 is similar to design 1 in that random assignment is also used to allocate individuals between the treatment and control groups, and both are referred to as *experimental designs*. The difference between the two designs is that collection of pretreatment, baseline information on members of the treatment and control groups is not part of design 2 but is part of design 1. The problem with not collecting pretreatment information is that there is no way of checking whether the treatment and control groups are basically similar or dissimilar.

For the comparison between the two groups to measure program effects accurately, the groups should, of course, be as similar as possible. Yet, as previously mentioned, they could be dissimilar by chance alone. This is more likely if each group has only a few hundred members, as is sometimes the case in social experiments. It is also possible that those running an experiment fail to implement the random assignment process correctly. If information is available on pretreatment status—for example, on pretreatment earnings—then statistical adjustments can be made to make the comparison between the treatment and the control groups more valid. Hence, there is less certainty concerning internal validity with design 2 than design 1.

Nonetheless, design 2 may be more appropriate than design 1 when it is possible that the collection of pretreatment information predisposes the participants to certain relevant behaviors. For example, questions about knowledge of health risks may make the treatment group in a study of health education more prone to learning than the general public would be.

Design 3: Before and After Comparison

Design 3 is by far the worst of the five designs, relying as it does on a simple *before and after comparison* of the same group of individuals. For example, the earnings of a group of individuals that went through a training program are compared with their earnings before going through the program. The problem with this design is that there is no information on what would have happened without the program. Consequently, there is no way to ensure internal validity. For example, the average earnings of people going into a training program are likely to be very low if most of these people are unemployed at the time of entry. That, perhaps, is why they decided to go into the program in the first place. Even without the program, however, they might have found jobs eventually. If so, their average earnings would have gone up over time even if the program did not exist. With a before and after comparison, this increase in earnings would be incorrectly attributed to the program.

Before and after comparisons, however, do offer certain advantages. They provide a comparatively inexpensive way of conducting evaluations. Moreover, when valid information is not available for a control group, a before and after comparison may be the only feasible way of conducting an evaluation. Such a comparison is obviously most valid when nonprogram factors are not expected to affect the outcomes of interest (for example, earnings) or can be taken into account through statistical adjustments.

Design 4: Nonexperimental Comparison Without Baseline Data

Design 4 is based on a comparison of two different groups: one that has gone through a program and the other that has not. Unlike design 2, however, membership in the two groups is not determined by random assignment. For example, the comparison group could be made up of people who originally applied for training but ultimately decided not to participate. Because such a comparison group is not selected through random assignment, it is sometimes called a *quasicontrol group*. Use of a quasicontrol group may be necessary when obtaining a comparison group through random assignment seems to be costly, raises serious ethical issues, or would cause potentially important community effects to be ignored.

Unfortunately, with this design there is no means of controlling for those differences between the two groups that existed prior to the treatment and, hence, no way to ensure internal validity. Perhaps, for example, at the time of application for training, those who ultimately went through the program had been unemployed for a longer period of time than persons in the comparison group, suggesting that in the absence of training they would have fared worse in the job market than members of the comparison group. But if at the end of training it is observed that they actually did just as well as persons in the comparison group, this suggests the training had an effect: It pulled the trainees up even with the comparison group. However, with design 4, there is no way to know the difference in the length of unemployment prior to training. As a result, it would just be observed that, after training, members of the treatment group were doing no better than people in the comparison group. This finding is subject to a bias known as *sample selection bias* that results because systematic differences between the treatment and quasicontrol group are not, and indeed cannot be, taken into account. In this instance, sample selection bias is important because it could lead to the incorrect conclusion that the training made no difference.

Design 5: Nonexperimental Comparison With Baseline Data

Design 5 utilizes both a treatment group and a control group. In addition, both pretreatment and posttreatment data are collected. This provides information on how the treatment group differed from the comparison group prior to the training. This information can be used in a statistical analysis to control for pretreatment differences between the treatment and control groups. For this reason, design 5 offers greater opportunity to obtain internal validity than either designs 3 or 4.

Even so, because this design does not randomly assign individuals to the treatment and control groups, a major problem occurs if people in the treatment and the comparison groups differ from one another in ways that cannot be measured readily. Then it becomes very difficult to adjust statistically for differences between the two groups. Perhaps, for example, unemployed persons who enter training are more motivated than unemployed persons who do not. If so, they might receive higher earnings over time even without the training. If analysts cannot somehow take account of this difference—in motivation—in practice, sometimes they can, but often they cannot—then they may incorrectly conclude that higher posttraining earnings received by the trainees are due to the training when, in fact, they are really due to greater motivation on the part of the trainees. In the evaluation literature, such a situation creates a threat to internal validity that is known as the *selection problem.*[8]

The occurrence of selection problems can be greatly reduced by using design 1 or 2. The reason is that when random assignment is used, people assigned to the treatment group should not differ from members of the comparison group in terms of characteristics such as motivation except by chance alone. Because of this advantage, an increasing number of demonstration projects that embody experimental designs have been conducted since the early 1960s.[9] However, large numbers of demonstrations that utilize nonexperimental designs, such as designs 3, 4, and 5, also continue to be conducted.

CBAs OF DEMONSTRATION PROJECTS

Although numerous demonstrations have been conducted, formal CBAs have been carried out for only a minority of them. Often the evaluations of demonstrations focus on only one or two outcomes of interest. For example, in the housing or health areas, they might focus on whether the tested program could be administered effectively or whether housing or health status improved, and not attempt to measure other benefits and costs. In relatively rare instances, demonstrations have been used to estimate demand or supply relationships. Though these estimates can be used in CBAs, the demonstrations themselves were not subjected to CBA. Two especially important examples of such demonstrations are described in Exhibits 11-1 and 11-2.

How the consumption of medical care changes as a function of the cost of care to users is central to many public policy questions, especially those relating to universal health insurance. To address this question, the federal government funded a social experiment, the Rand Health Insurance Experiment, between 1974 and 1977. Analysis of the data from the six experimental sites by Willard Manning and colleagues suggests that the price elasticity of demand for health care services is in the range of –0.1 to –0.2.

Source: Adapted from Willard G. Manning, Joseph P. Newhouse, Naihua Duan, Emmett B. Keeler, Aileen Leibowitz, and Susan Marquis, "Health Insurance and the Demand for Medical Care: Evidence from a Randomized Experiment," *American Economic Review* 77(3) 1987, 251–277.

During the late 1960s and early 1970s, the U.S. government funded four income maintenance experiments. These experiments focused on how income transfers affected the supply of labor (equivalently the demand for leisure) of low-income persons. Data from these experiments were used to obtain estimates of wage and income elasticities. Based on averages of separate estimates from the numerous studies that have relied on data from these experiments, Gary Burtless derived a number of elasticity values from the studies of these experiments. The compensated wage elasticities are 0.09 for married men, 0.24 for married women, and 0.14 for single women. The uncompensated wage elasticities are −0.02 for married men, 0.17 for married women, and −0.04 for single women. The income elasticities are −0.11 for married men, −0.07 for married women, and −0.18 for single women.

Source: Adapted from Gary Burtless, "The Work Response to Guaranteed Income: A Survey of Experimental Evidence," in Alicia Munnell, ed., *Lessons from the Income Maintenance Experiments* (Boston: Federal Reserve Bank of Boston, 1986), 22–52.

CBAs OF EMPLOYMENT AND TRAINING DEMONSTRATIONS: AN INTRODUCTION

Almost all the demonstrations that have been subjected to CBA have tested programs that attempt to increase the employment or earnings of unemployed or low-skilled workers. In recent years, many of these demonstrations have focused on the welfare population. The services provided by these demonstration programs have varied considerably but have included job search assistance, remedial education, vocational training, subsidizing private-sector employers in exchange for hiring program participants, and the direct provision of public-sector jobs to participants. Although the individual programs that provide such services often differ greatly from one another, such programs are often referred to as *employment and training (E&T) programs*.[10]

E&T programs are often viewed as investments in the *human capital* of participants (i.e., attempts to improve their skills and abilities). Thus, the major economic rationale for funding them revolves around assertions that E&T programs help correct market or institutional failures that cause underinvestments in human capital. For example, low-income people may not have the resources to invest in certain kinds of training, such as classroom vocational training. Their access to private financing may be limited by a lack of collateral and a high risk of default. Moreover, public training may be justified as compensating for inadequacies in the public education system or as providing a second chance to those who prematurely terminate formal schooling because of imperfect foresight or a high subjective rate of time preference. In addition, E&T programs may help correct imperfect information among participants about human capital investment opportunities by guiding them into activities that yield the highest payoff for them.

A distinct rationale for E&T programs stems from a widely accepted value that, all else equal, it is better to receive income from employment than from transfer programs. To meet this goal, increasingly stringent requirements to participate in E&T programs have been imposed on welfare recipients since the early 1980s.

THE CBA FRAMEWORK IN THE EDUCATION AND TRAINING CONTEXT

The basic CBA accounting framework has been described in previous chapters. However, different policy areas have developed variations of the basic CBA framework that address issues specific to each area. The particular accounting framework that is used today in conducting most CBAs of E&T programs was originally developed during the late 1960s and refined in the early 1980s. A stylized version of this framework appears in Table 11-2. Although details concerning the specifics of the framework vary somewhat from one E&T CBA to another, depending upon the specific nature of the services provided, the table lists those benefits and costs that are typically measured.

This framework offers several advantages: It is readily understandable to policy makers; by displaying benefits and costs from the perspectives of both participants and nonparticipants, it suggests some of the distributional implications of the program being evaluated; and, possibly most important, because measures of each cost-benefit component listed can actually be obtained from demonstration data, it is operationally feasible. Indeed, despite shortcomings in the framework, it is difficult to find practical alternatives to it.

Table 11-2 presents the benefit and cost impact categories of a stylized E&T demonstration. Plus signs indicate anticipated sources of benefits and minus signs anticipated sources of costs from different perspectives. The first column (A) shows aggregate benefits and costs from the perspective of society as a whole. The remaining columns show the distribution of benefits and costs to the two groups that are typically relevant in assessing E&T programs: participants or clients served by the demonstration program (B); and nonparticipants, including taxpayers who pay for the program (C).

Benefits and costs to society are simply the algebraic sum of benefits and costs to participants and to nonparticipants because society is the sum of these two groups. Hence,

TABLE 11-2 Stylized Cost-Benefit Framework Showing the Impacts of E&T Demonstrations

	Society (A) (B + C)	Participant (B)	Nonparticipant (C)
Output produced by participant			
In-program output	+	0	+
Gross earnings	+	+	0
Fringe benefits	+	+	0
Participant work-related expenditures			
Tax payments	0	−	+
Expenditures on child care, transportation, etc.	−	−	0
Use of transfer programs by participants			
Welfare payments	0	−	+
Other transfer payments	0	−	+
Program operating costs	+	0	+
Use of support programs by participants			
Support services received by participants	−	0	−
Allowances received by participants	0	+	−
Program operating costs	−	0	−

the table implies that if a demonstration program causes transfer payments received by participants (e.g., unemployment compensation or welfare payment receipts) to decline, then this should be regarded as a savings or benefit to nonparticipant taxpayers, a cost to program participants (albeit one that may be offset by earnings), and neither a benefit nor a cost to society as a whole but simply income transferred from one segment of the population to another.

This approach is consistent with the standard one used in CBA. As we have seen, in standard CBA "a dollar is a dollar," no matter to whom it accrues. Thus, in Table 11-2, a dollar gained or lost by an E&T participant is treated identically to a dollar gained or lost by a nonparticipant. Consequently, if an E&T program caused the transfer dollars received by participants to fall, then this would be viewed as not affecting society as a whole because the loss to participants would be fully offset by benefits to nonparticipants in the form of reductions in government budgetary outlays.

Typically, however, E&T participants have much lower incomes, on average, than nonparticipants. For reasons that will be discussed in detail in Chapter 18, a case can sometimes be made for treating the gains and losses of low-income persons differently from those of higher-income persons. This is almost never done in CBAs of E&T demonstrations, however. Instead, as can be seen in Table 11-2, they simply lay out the results so that the distributional consequences of a particular program can be observed.

Table 11-2 divides the benefits and costs associated with E&T demonstrations into four major categories. The first two categories pertain to effects that result if a demonstration increases the work effort or productivity of participants—for example, by providing them work in a public-sector job where they perform useful services, providing them skill training, or helping them find private-sector employment through job search assistance. On the one hand, the value of the output they produce will rise, which in the private sector should be reflected by increases in earnings and fringe benefits. On the other hand, if hours at work rise, expenditures on child care and transportation will also increase. And if earnings rise, tax payments will increase. The third major cost-benefit category in Table 11-2 pertains to decreases in dependency on transfer payments that may result from an E&T program. Such reductions in dependency should cause both the amount of payments distributed under transfer programs and the cost of administering these programs to fall. The fourth major category refers to expenditures on support services for program participants. Obviously, such expenditures increase when a demonstration program is implemented. However, this increase will be partially offset because participants in the demonstration programs no longer need to obtain similar services from existing programs.

Three of the subcategories listed in Table 11-2 pertain to job-related expenditures and require clarification: participant expenditures on child care, transportation, and so forth; support services received by participants; and allowances received by participants. The first of these subcategories refers to total job-required outlays by E&T participants on such items as child care, transportation, and uniforms. The subcategory of support services pertains to the direct provision of such goods by a government agency, and the allowances subcategory refers to government reimbursement of job-required expenditures by participants. Table 11-2 reflects the philosophy that *all* program-induced increases in job-required expenditures should be treated identically, as resource costs to society engendered in producing goods and services. Of course, to the extent the government directly provides support services to participants, client outlays for this purpose will be smaller. In a CBA, this would be reflected by a smaller dollar amount appearing under the participant expenditures on job-related outlays and a larger dollar amount appearing under the subcategory of support services received by participants. Job-required expenditures are further discussed later in the chapter.

Benefits and costs that are sometimes referred to as *intangible effects* but are rarely, if ever, actually estimated in evaluations of E&T programs do not appear in Table 11-2. Examples of intangible effects include the values of leisure forgone and self-esteem from working. Almost by definition, intangible effects are difficult to measure, but they may be important. In the next section, we examine the implications of not measuring them.

CONCEPTUAL ISSUES IN CONDUCTING CBAs OF EDUCATION AND TRAINING DEMONSTRATIONS

We now turn to a number of limitations of the accounting framework illustrated in Table 11-2. As will be seen, these arise from the fact that the framework is not completely consistent with the theoretical concepts discussed in Chapters 3, 4, and 5. Because these limitations can result in incorrect policy conclusions, comparing some of the operational measures of benefits and costs typically used in conducting CBAs of E&T demonstrations with their conceptually correct counterparts appears useful. In doing this, it is helpful to examine measures of benefits and costs associated with E&T programs separately from the participant and the nonparticipant perspectives, keeping in mind that social benefits and costs are simply the algebraic sum of benefits received and costs incurred by these two groups.

The Participant Perspective

Two Alternative Measures   The standard E&T framework, as Table 11-2 suggests, estimates participant net benefits as net changes in the incomes of program clients—that is, as increases in earnings and fringe benefits minus increases in taxes, decreases in transfer payments, and increases in work-related expenditures that result from participation in the program. However, as Chapters 3 and 4 emphasize, the conceptually appropriate measure of participant net benefits is net changes in the surplus of program participants, not net changes in their incomes. As will be seen, the difference between these two measures can be substantial.

The extent to which the two measures diverge depends on the precise mechanism through which E&T programs influence earnings. For instance, E&T programs may either increase the hourly wage rates of participants (e.g., by imparting new skills) or increase the hours they work (e.g., by aiding in job search or increasing the obligations that must be met in exchange for transfer payments). Numerous E&T demonstrations have been found to increase hours worked. Meaningful impacts on wage rates are more rare but have occurred. In the discussion that follows, we compare the two alternative measures of net benefits from the perspective of several different hypothetical E&T participants, each of whom is assumed to respond differently to the program.

The first participant is represented in Figure 11-1. Curve S is the labor supply schedule of this participant, an individual who is assumed to have successfully participated in an E&T program that increased her market wage from W_0 to W_1.[11] As a result, the individual increases her hours of work from h_0 to h_1. In the diagram, area A represents the increase in both participant surplus and earnings that would have resulted from the wage increase even if the participant had not increased her hours. Area B represents an additional increase in both participant surplus and earnings,

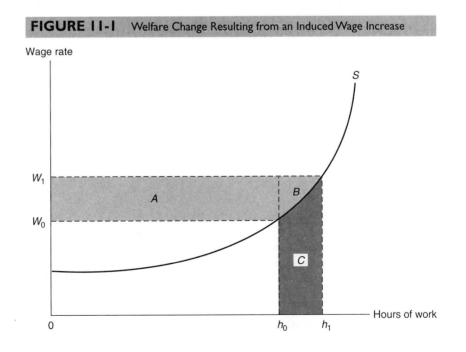

FIGURE 11-1   Welfare Change Resulting from an Induced Wage Increase

one resulting from the increase in hours that actually takes place. Finally, area C represents a further increase in earnings that results from the hours increase. However, this last increase in earnings is fully offset by the individual's loss of leisure.[12] Hence, no change in participant surplus is associated with it. Consequently, although areas A, B, and C are counted as benefits when using the net income change measure of E&T effects, only A and B are counted in the conceptually more correct net surplus change measure.

In Figure 11-1, the first E&T participant was assumed to be in equilibrium both before entering the program and upon completing the program; that is, it was assumed that at both points she was able to work the number of hours she desired to work at her market wage. Many E&T participants, however, are not in equilibrium prior to entering a program. Indeed, many persons participate in E&T specifically because they are unemployed.

Such a situation is assumed to face the second participant, an individual who is represented in Figure 11-2. In this figure, the individual has a market wage of W_0 prior to entering E&T but is able to obtain only h_0 hours of work instead of the desired h_1 hours. Assume now that, although participating in E&T does not affect the participant's market wage, it does permit him to increase his hours of work from h_0 to h_1. As a result of this hours increase, the participant enjoys an earnings increase equal to areas $A + B$ but a surplus increase equal to only area A. Thus, once again, the net income change measure of E&T benefits is larger than the conceptually more appropriate net surplus change measure.

Our findings for the first two E&T participants imply that while any earnings increases that result from wage increases should be fully credited to the program, only

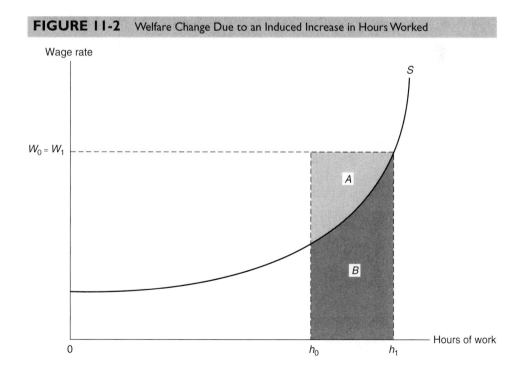

FIGURE 11-2　Welfare Change Due to an Induced Increase in Hours Worked

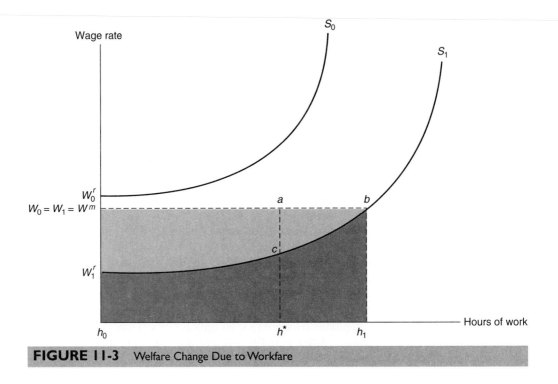

FIGURE 11-3 Welfare Change Due to Workfare

part of earnings increases resulting from hours increases should be credited. In Figure 11-3, we turn to a more complex situation facing a third E&T participant: a welfare recipient who, as a condition for receiving her welfare grant, is required to work at a public-sector job for h^* hours each month, where h^* is determined by dividing her grant amount by the minimum wage. Similar arrangements, which are often referred to as *workfare*, have frequently been used in administering welfare programs. The welfare recipient's market wage is assumed to equal W^m, the minimum wage, while curve S_0 represents her supply schedule in the absence of workfare. (Ignore curve S_1 for the moment.) Figure 11-3 implies that in the absence of workfare, W_0^r, the welfare recipient's reservation wage (i.e., the lowest wage at which she would be willing to work) would exceed her market wage. Thus, she would choose not to work.

Now imagine that the welfare recipient is enrolled in workfare in two distinct steps. In the first step, her welfare grant is withdrawn. This loss of income would cause her labor supply curve to shift to the right from S_0 to S_1. As a consequence, her reservation wage would fall from W_0^r to W_1^r, a value below the minimum wage. In the second step, she is offered the opportunity to work h^* hours at a public-sector workfare job at a wage of W^m. In other words, she is given the opportunity to earn back her welfare grant, which in the diagram corresponds to the rectangular area $W^m ah^* h_0$.[13] Because W^m exceeds W_1^r, the participant represented in Figure 11-3 would prefer workfare to not working at all.

If the welfare recipient accepts the workfare offer, then the net income change and net surplus change measures of program impacts have quite different implications. Assuming she has no opportunities to work in addition to h^*, her net income would be unchanged from what it was prior to the program; consequently, the measure based on changes in net income would imply that she is no worse off. However, the net surplus change measure does imply that she is worse off. Specifically, her net surplus would decline by an amount represented by the area $W_1^r ch^* h_0$, an amount equal to the value that the recipient places on her lost leisure.[14]

So far, the focus has been on benefits received by and costs incurred by welfare recipients while they are participating in workfare. Now let us consider a different situation: The benefits and costs associated with a participant move from welfare to a regular private-sector job. This is, of course, one of the major objectives of programs such as workfare, and Figure 11-3 implies that the program would in fact have the desired effect on the participant. Although in the absence of the workfare she would prefer not to work at all, given a choice between participating in workfare (point *a*) or working at a regular minimum-wage job (point *b*), the participant would select the latter. By restricting her hours to h^*, workfare causes the participant to be "off her labor supply curve." Only by finding a regular job can she work h_1 hours, the number of hours she would desire to work at the minimum wage. In actual practice, the participant might move directly from welfare to the job upon being confronted with the workfare requirement, or alternatively, she might first participate in workfare while seeking private-sector employment.

A comparison of the net income change measure of workfare's impact on a participant who moves directly to private-sector employment with the corresponding conceptually correct net surplus change measure yields an interesting finding. On the one hand, the net income change measure implies that the participant represented in Figure 11-3 enjoys a net gain. Her transfer payments fall from $W^m ah^* h_0$ to zero, but her earnings increase from zero to $W^m bh_1 h_0$, resulting in a net increase in income of $abh_1 h^*$. On the other hand, the participant suffers a net loss of surplus because her gain in surplus from working, area $W^m bW_1^r$, is exceeded by the value of her lost transfer payments, area $W^m ah^* h_0$. Thus, under the circumstances represented in Figure 11-3, the net income change measure suggests a conclusion that is the diametrical opposite from that implied by the conceptually more correct net surplus change measure.

In measuring the impacts of E&T programs from the participant perspective, three rules can be drawn from the preceding analyses of the three illustrative E&T participants. First, *the full value of reductions in transfer payments should be counted as a cost to E&T participants.* Second, *the full value of increases in earnings that result from wage rate increases should be counted as a benefit to E&T participants.* Third, *only part of the value of earnings increases that result from hours increases should be counted as a benefit to E&T participants; namely, the part that represents an increase in participant surplus should be counted, while the part that is offset by reductions in leisure should not.*

In conducting CBAs of E&T demonstrations, the first two of these rules are straightforward to implement. Implementing the third rule, however, requires an estimate of the percentage of earnings changes attributable to increases in hours that should be counted. A procedure that can be used to obtain such an estimate, which is illustrated later in the chapter, has been developed by one of the authors.[15]

Improvements in Self-Esteem   It is sometimes suggested that E&T programs can improve the self-esteem of E&T participants. For example, programs may impart skills that increase financial independence. If so, then this is a program benefit that should, in principle, be included in CBAs of E&T programs, although it is difficult to do so directly. However, to the extent an increase in the self-esteem of an E&T participant manifests itself as an increase in willingness-to-work (for example, because he or she is less concerned about rejection when seeking employment), the participant's labor supply curve will shift to the right. The resulting gain in surplus is represented graphically as the gap between the old and new supply curves below the market wage upon completion of training. Program benefits that are measured as increases in participant earnings will also be larger than if the curve does not shift. However, the increase in earnings will not correspond very well to the increase in surplus. Moreover, at most, only part of the benefits from an improvement in self-esteem is likely to be reflected by a shift in the labor supply curve. Indeed, it is easy to imagine E&T participants who enjoy increases in self-esteem as a result of participating in the program but whose willingness-to-work does not change.

Job-Required Expenditures   As discussed earlier, in the framework traditionally used in cost-benefit analyses of E&T programs, increases in job-related expenditures such as child care and transportation that result from program participation are counted as a social cost of the program, regardless of whether paid for by E&T participants or the government. As discussed next, however, this approach can sometimes result in double counting.

   For illustrative purposes, we focus on child care, although a similar analysis could be made for other work-related costs such as transportation. Panel (a) of Figure 11-4 pertains to an individual who participated in an E&T program that increased her wage from W_0 to W_1. The supply curve, S, indicates the hours the individual would work if she must pay for child care. The diagram implies that, as a result of the program-engendered wage increase, she would go from not working to working h_1 hours. Thus the program would engender an increase in earnings equal to area $W_1 a h_1 0$ and a smaller surplus gain equal to area $W_1 a W_r$. Panel (b) illustrates the E&T participant's

FIGURE 11-4(a)   Labor Market Effects of E&T Program

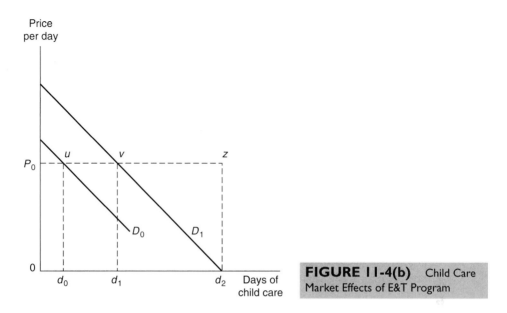

FIGURE 11-4(b) Child Care Market Effects of E&T Program

demand for child care. P_0 represents the market-set price for child care. As indicated in the figure, the demand curve for child care would shift out from D_0 to D_1 as a result of the wage increase and the increased hours worked resulting from the E&T.

As the reader may have noticed, Figure 11-4 is very similar to the diagrams of primary and secondary markets that appear in Chapter 5. This is hardly surprising. The direct effects of E&T programs typically occur in labor markets, while a complementary relationship exists between work effort and child care. Hence, the primary market is the labor market for E&T participants, while the market for child care is a secondary market.

As discussed in detail in Chapter 5, effects in undistorted secondary markets should usually be ignored if program benefits in primary markets are measured in terms of changes in surplus. Specifically, the individual represented in Figure 11-4 will presumably consider the child care expenses she will incur in determining the number of hours she would be willing to work at each wage rate. Thus, in using her labor supply curve to measure her surplus gain from participating in the E&T program, area $W_1 a W_r$, her child care expenditures are already fully taken into account. Consequently, her increase in expenditures in the secondary market represented in panel (b)—that is, area uvd_1d_0—should be ignored, as should the area between the two demand curves in panel (b). Not doing so will result in double counting.

As emphasized earlier, benefits to E&T participants are traditionally measured as changes in net income, rather than as changes in surplus. To obtain this measure, increases in expenditures on child care would, of course, be subtracted from earnings increases. As indicated in Figure 11-4(a), the increase in earnings overstates the gain in surplus resulting from the E&T program by an amount represented by area $W_r a h_1 0$. Subtracting the increase in day care expenditures, area uvd_1d_0, from the increase in earnings offsets this overstatement. However, area uvd_1d_0 could be either larger or smaller than area $W_r a h_1 0$. Thus, the net income measure could be either larger or smaller than the more appropriate net surplus measure.

We next consider benefits and costs if the government directly provides child care or reimburses individuals for their expenditures on child care. A rather natural way to examine such a policy is to compare the earnings increases that result from the government subsidizing child care with the government's cost. As will be seen, however, this approach is incorrect.

For illustrative purposes, we assume that child care is provided free to subsidized individuals, but the government pays the market price of P_0. As previously discussed, given a market wage of W_1, the demand curve for child care for the individual represented in Figure 11-4 would be D_1. Thus, if child care was provided to her free, she would consume d_2 units of child care.

Because the direct effects of the government's subsidy occur in the market for child care, it should now be viewed as the primary market for purposes of analysis, while the labor market should be viewed as the secondary market. Thus, although the government's provision of subsidized child care would shift the labor supply curve and this, in turn, would affect earnings,[16] these effects should be ignored. Instead, the effects of the policy on individuals are best examined by measuring surplus changes in the primary market. For example, the individual represented in Figure 11-4 would enjoy a surplus gain corresponding to area d_1vd_2. However, the cost to the government, which is represented by area d_1vzd_2, would be considerably greater, resulting in deadweight loss equal to area vd_2z.[17]

The Nonparticipant Perspective[18]

Several categories of benefits and costs accrue to nonparticipants: intangible benefits, benefits from in-program output, and costs resulting from the displacement of public-sector and private-sector workers.

Intangible Benefits Received by Nonparticipants The preceding section emphasized that in measuring the benefits and costs of E&T programs to participants it is changes in their surplus that should be estimated rather than changes in their money income. Thus, the effects on participant surplus of E&T-induced reductions in participant leisure time should be taken into account.

The same concept applies in measuring benefits and costs of E&T programs to nonparticipants. For example, if nonparticipants positively value the substitution of earnings for welfare payment in and of itself, then the increase in surplus they received will exceed any reductions in their tax obligations that might result from E&T programs targeted at welfare recipients. Thus, in principle, it is changes in the surplus of nonparticipants that result from E&T programs, rather than changes in their incomes, that should be measured. Given the practical difficulty of doing this, however, it has never been attempted. An approach that might be used for this purpose, contingent valuation, is taken up in Chapter 14.

Benefits from In-Program Output Some E&T programs involve the provision of public-sector jobs. Perhaps the best-known example of this is the Works Projects Administration (WPA), which operated in the United States during the Great Depression and was intended to absorb some of the massive number of workers who were unemployed during this period. More recently, the Comprehensive Employment and Training Act provided as many as 750,000 public-sector jobs for unemployed persons during the late 1970s. In still more recent years, as discussed earlier, welfare recipients in some states have been required to perform work at government and non-profit agencies in exchange for their payments.

How should the value to taxpayers of the in-program output produced by E&T participants be assigned to public-sector jobs? Ideally, this would be done by determining what taxpayers would be willing to pay for this output. Typically, this is infeasible, however, because the output is not purchased in market transactions. Consequently, an alternative approach is used that determines what the labor resources required to produce the output would have cost if purchased on the open market. Because agencies that "employ" E&T participants usually pay nothing for the services of these people, researchers use the wage rate that would have been paid to similar workers hired in the open market. Once an appropriate wage rate is determined, the basic calculation involves multiplying the number of hours E&T participants work by this wage and perhaps adjusting to account for differences between the average productivity of the E&T workers and workers hired in the open market.

This procedure can result in an estimate that either overstates or understates the true value of the in-program output produced by E&T participants. The reasons for this can be seen by examining a key assumption that underlies this valuation method: that the decisions of the public-sector agencies that employ E&T workers closely reflect the desires of taxpayers. More specifically, an analogy is drawn with the behavior of private-sector firms and consumers under perfect competition, and it is assumed that the amount that an agency would be willing to pay to employ an additional worker corresponds to the value that taxpayers would place on the additional output that the worker could potentially produce. Although this is not an appropriate place to assess the perfect competition analogy or discuss the extent to which bureaucratic behavior reflects taxpayer preferences, it should be obvious that a rather strong assumption is required to value output produced by E&T workers.[19]

The implications of this assumption can be explored by use of Figure 11-5, which depicts the demand curve for workers by a public-sector agency that might potentially be assigned E&T participants and the supply curve the agency faces in hiring workers in a competitive labor market. In using this diagram, we first examine a situation in which the assumption that bureaucratic behavior reflects taxpayer preferences is valid and then one where it is not.

In Figure 11-5, the horizontal line, S, represents the supply curve, which is set at the level of the market-determined wage, W, that must be paid to each regular worker hired by the agency; the downward-sloping line, D, represents the demand curve, which is assumed to slope downward as a result of diminishing returns and (as implied by the assumption about bureaucratic behavior) because the agency prioritizes its tasks so that, as its budget expands, successively less important services are performed. (Ignore curve D^* for the moment.) This demand curve reflects the willingness-to-pay for workers by the agency and, in keeping with the assumption concerning bureaucratic behavior, the area under this curve is presumed to measure the value to taxpayers of output produced by workers hired by the agency.

Figure 11-5 indicates that in the absence of E&T workers the agency would hire R regular workers; however, if P E&T participants were assigned to the agency, a total of $R + P$ workers would be employed. Thus, if the bureaucratic behavior assumption is valid, the value to taxpayers of the output added by the E&T workers would equal area A.

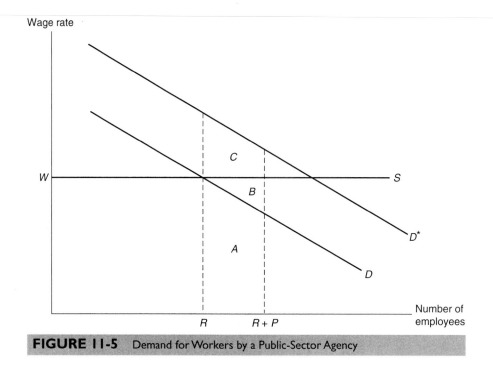

FIGURE 11-5 Demand for Workers by a Public-Sector Agency

Unfortunately, however, area *A* typically cannot be directly measured. The reason for this is that the output produced by public-sector agencies is rarely sold in market transactions and, consequently, the agency's demand curve, which is depicted in Figure 11-5, cannot actually be observed. However, even though government and nonprofit agencies that "employ" E&T participants pay nothing for the services of these people, the area under the supply curve between *R* and *R* + *P* can be valued by simply determining the wages that would have to be paid to similar workers hired on the open market to do the work performed by E&T participants. Consequently, it is the area under the supply curve—that is, area *A* plus area *B*—that is usually used in practice as the measure of the value of in-program participant output. As a glance at Figure 11-5 suggests, the size of the resulting overstatement of the value of the output produced by E&T participation, which is represented by area *B*, depends upon the slope of the agency demand curve.

So far, we have assumed that agency behavior simply reflects the value that taxpayers would place on the agency's output. Let us now look at one of the numerous possible situations where this is not the case. The specific example we examine is one in which the agency, perhaps because of budget constraints resulting from the public goods characteristics of whatever services it provides, produces less output than taxpayers collectively desire. These circumstances are represented in Figure 11-5 by two demand curves. As before, curve *D* indicates *agency* willingness-to-pay for workers, but the value that *taxpayers* place on the output produced by the agency is now represented by the area under demand curve *D**. Consequently, the value of the additional output produced by the *P* E&T participants now equals area *A* plus area *B* plus area *C*. Thus, under these circumstances, the measure based on the supply curve of the output produced by E&T workers, which as previously indicated equals area *A* plus area *B*, understates the true value by an area equal to *C*.

Costs from Public-Sector Labor Displacement   So far, our discussion has been based on the assumption that the E&T workers made available to a public-sector agency would simply be added to the regular workforce that the agency would hire in the absence of the program. However, the agency might instead substitute E&T workers for regular workers. In terms of Figure 11-5, this behavior on the part of the agency, which is usually referred to as *displacement,* would mean that agency employment would increase by less than the *P* number of workers provided by E&T. Indeed, with 100 percent displacement, the agency's workforce would remain at *R*, rather than increase to *R* + *P*. Consequently, at first blush, it would appear that displacement leads to overstatement of the value of output produced by E&T participants.

The issue is actually a bit more subtle and complex, however. If the displaced workers have a similar risk of joblessness as E&T participants, then increases in output produced by E&T participants assigned to public-sector agencies may be entirely offset by losses in the output formerly produced by those workers who are displaced. This need not be the case, however, if the E&T participants are exceptional in terms of lack of skills or if they face exceptional barriers to labor market access. Moving such persons directly into jobs under these circumstances will change the characteristics of the general pool of unemployed in ways that may allow a reduction in the net incidence of joblessness, especially if local labor market conditions are tight. Thus, to the extent that E&T participants are unskilled relative to those they replaced, the labor market consequences will differ from a simple one-for-one replacement.

Costs from Private-Sector Labor Displacement   A major objective of most E&T programs is to increase the unsubsidized private-sector employment of program participants. To the extent these efforts are successful, some participants undoubtedly end up in jobs that would otherwise have been held by nonparticipants. If, as a result, these nonparticipants become unemployed or accept lower-wage jobs, their earnings obviously fall. This earnings reduction, which is another type of displacement effect, is potentially a cost of E&T programs to nonparticipants. Because there is little research quantifying the magnitude of private-sector labor displacement, it has rarely been taken into account in CBAs of E&T programs.[20]

The failure to take account of private-sector displacement may not be very serious, however. CBA usually assumes that full employment is maintained. If it is, then it should be relatively easy for displaced nonparticipants to find alternative job opportunities and E&T programs will raise the feasible employment level. Nonetheless, if E&T programs add workers with a particular set of skills to the workforce, they may still depress the wages of workers with similar skills. Private-sector displacement is a more serious issue if unemployment is high. Even then, however, it is possible that E&T programs may impart skills that allow trainees to leave slack occupational labor markets for tight ones. If they do, then they will decrease the competition for job vacancies in the slack labor markets, making it easier for unemployed workers who remain in these markets to find jobs. To the extent this occurs, E&T programs will again raise feasible employment levels.

CHOOSING PREDICTION PARAMETERS

In using the cost-benefit framework illustrated in Table 11-2, it is necessary to take account of the fact that some benefits and costs of E&T programs are likely to extend beyond the period for which post-program data on outcomes are collected, which is typically only two or three years after participants leave the program. For example, as a result of having participated in an E&T demonstration, some individuals could potentially enjoy increased earnings but pay higher taxes, incur greater job-required expenses, and receive fewer transfer payments over the remainder of their working lives. These streams of future benefits and costs must be incorporated into the CBAs of the demonstrations. Doing this requires that three important parameters be specified: the social discount rate, the discounting time horizon, and the decay rate of program effects. The social discount rate was discussed in detail in Chapter 10. The other two parameters are discussed in turn next. Because E&T programs are typically funded through taxes, as indicated in Chapter 10, the shadow price of capital does not have to be used.

The Discounting Time Horizon

As described in Chapter 6, the time horizon is the period over which benefit and cost streams are estimated. In CBAs of E&T programs, benefits and costs beyond the specified time horizon are assumed equal to zero; that is, they are assumed to have zero horizon value. One procedure for determining the length of the time horizon in CBAs of E&T programs is to subtract the age of program participants at the time they entered the program from the age at which they are expected to retire from the workforce. Often, however, a shorter, somewhat arbitrarily selected time horizon—for example, five years—is used instead. Doing this is simply an acknowledgment on the part of analysts that because they do not possess crystal balls, uncertainty increases the further one attempts to extrapolate beyond the demonstration period. However, basing a CBA of an E&T program demonstration on a short time horizon will understate E&T benefits if the key potential benefit, earnings improvements, persists well beyond the time horizon.

This understatement of benefits relative to costs could be substantial. Table 11-3 shows the present discounted value of an improvement of $1 in annual earnings under alternative assumptions about time horizons over which the improvement persists and for the value of the discount rate. The figures in the table have two important implications. First, it is evident that the magnitude of benefit and cost estimates are quite

TABLE 11-3 The Sensitivity of a $1 Improvement in Annual Earnings to Alternative Time Horizons and Discount Rates

	Discount Rate	
Time Horizon	*3%*	*5%*
5 years	$4.58	$4.33
10 years	8.53	7.72
20 years	14.85	12.46
30 years	19.60	15.37

sensitive to the choice of the time horizon. For example, if a 5 percent discount rate and a five-year time horizon are used for extrapolation purposes, the present value of an improvement of $1 in earnings equals $4.33. But if a 5 percent discount rate and a 20-year time horizon are used instead, the present value equals $12.46, almost a three-fold increase. Second, the longer the time horizon that is used, the more sensitive are projections of benefits and costs to the choice of the discount rate. Hence, if a short time horizon is used, cost-benefit findings are less likely to be sensitive to the choice of a discount rate than if a long time horizon is used.

How long are program effects on earnings likely to last for actual E&T programs? While evidence on this topic is sketchy, a recent study that pooled findings from a large number of E&T evaluations indicates that program effects on earnings continue to exist for about six years for adult men and about four years for youth after they complete an E&T program, while program effects continue indefinitely for adult women.[21] However, results that are based on random assignment evaluations alone suggest that program earnings effects may last somewhat longer for adult men. Findings from a separate study that is based solely on random assignment evaluations of E&T programs targeted at female welfare recipients suggest that the effects of these programs on earnings continue for five to six years.[22]

Taken together, this evidence seems to suggest that, except for adult women participating in E&T programs, using fairly short time horizons in CBAs of these programs is probably appropriate. It is important to recognize, however, that these findings are based on averages for a variety of evaluated programs. The effects of a particular program could last for either a longer or a shorter period of time depending on its particular features.

The Decay Rate

A decay rate is necessary in extrapolating E&T effects that persist beyond the period over which post-program data on outcomes are collected in order to take account of the possibility that the size of these effects may change over time. For example, it is usually argued that programs that provide training or job placement for low-wage workers initially may give them a competitive advantage in the labor market, but this advantage may decay over time. In the case of training, however, one could alternatively argue that doors are opened on the job that allow participants to obtain additional training after leaving an E&T program and, consequently, the program's effects on earnings will grow over time.

Unfortunately, only limited empirical evidence exists as to whether the earnings effects of E&T programs tend to grow or decay over time, let alone the magnitude of the actual rate of decay or growth. However, one of the studies mentioned previously in discussing time horizons found that earnings effects for adult men, adult women, and youth who participated in E&T programs all initially grew after they completed training but only for a short period of time (perhaps a year or so). They then declined for the men and youth but remained constant for the women.[23] The other study indicated that the earnings effects of programs targeted at welfare recipients increased for two or three years and then begin declining until they disappeared altogether after five or six years.[24] It is again important to recognize that these patterns pertain to a "typical" program and may not hold for a particular program that is being subjected to a CBA.

Once values for the discount rate, time horizon, and decay rate are chosen, equations (6A.5) and (6A.7) in Appendix 6A can be used to compute present values. In using these formulas, care must be taken to use a negative value for g if it is determined that the effects of the E&T demonstration will decay over time and a positive value for g if it seems likely that these impacts will grow over time. For benefit and cost components that neither grow nor shrink over time, g should, of course, be set equal to zero.

A CASE STUDY: CBAs OF WORK/WELFARE DEMONSTRATIONS

Since the 1970s, many states have conducted demonstrations that had the objective of reducing dependency on transfer payments among welfare recipients by enhancing their employability. Similar to other E&T demonstrations, the specific components of each of these *welfare-to-work* programs varied but usually included one or more of the following: assessment of basic skills, structured job search, training and education, and subsidized employment in the public or private sector.

Many of the welfare-to-work demonstrations have been subjected to CBA. CBAs of a particular subset of demonstrations conducted during the 1980s, the Work/Welfare Demonstrations, exerted considerable influence on the Family Support Act of 1988, a major piece of welfare reform legislation. Much of this influence resulted from the fact that by 1988 many observers, particularly those in the policy-making community, had concluded on the basis of analyses of the Work/Welfare Demonstrations that welfare-to-work programs are cost-beneficial.[25] The Work/Welfare Demonstrations were targeted at participants in the Aid for Families with Dependent Children (AFDC) program, which at the time was the major cash welfare program in the United States. Using a similar framework and the classical experimental design denoted as design 1 earlier in the chapter, MDRC, a well-known nonprofit research firm, conducted the CBAs of each of these demonstrations.[26]

CBA Results

Table 11-4 presents summary results from MDRC's CBAs of the Work/Welfare Demonstrations. These estimates, which have been converted to 2003 dollar amounts using the U.S. Consumer Price Index, should be viewed as program impacts on a typical member of the treatment group in each of the listed demonstrations. They are reported separately for one-parent (AFDC-R) and two-parent (AFDC-U) households and, when available, for new AFDC applicants and prior AFDC recipients. Parentheses are used to indicate when benefits or costs are in the opposite direction from that intended by the demonstration programs—for example, when net remuneration from employment declines or amounts of transfer payments increase.

The first three columns in the table present estimated benefits and costs from the participant perspective and the next four from the nonparticipant perspective. Columns A and D, respectively, report total net gains (or losses) from these two perspectives, while columns B, C, E, F, and G provide information on the benefit and cost components that together account for these gains (or losses). For example, column B reports the estimated *net* gain by participants from employment under each demonstration program, that is, estimates of the sum of increases in earnings, fringe benefits, and any work-related allowances paid under the program less the sum of tax payments

TABLE 11-4 Summary of Cost-Benefit Estimates From MDRC Evaluations of Work/Welfare Demonstrations (in 2003 dollars)

	Participant Perspective			Nonparticipant Perspective				Net Social Gain (or Loss) (A + D)
	Net Present Value (A = B − C)	Net Gains from Employment	Loss in Transfer Payments	Net Present Value (D = E + F − G)	Value of In-Program Output	Tax-Transfer Gains	Program Service Costs	
	A	B	C	D	E	F	G	H
AFDC-R								
APPLICANTS ONLY								
San Diego EPP/EWEP:								
Job search only	$1,185	$2,434	$1,249	$830	($6)	$1,775	$939	$2,015
Job search/ CWEP	1,468	3,448	1,980	2,127	377	2,813	1,063	3,595
San Diego SWIM	(1,471)	1,906	3,377	2,731	301*	3,600	1,170	1,260
Virginia	2,000	2,995	995	1,176	72	1,550	446	3,176
West Virginia	(848)	(718)	130	686	956	44	314	(162)
RECIPIENTS ONLY								
San Diego SWIM	1,213	5,280	4,067	2,840	301*	4,324	1,785	4,053
Virginia	1,013	1,732	719	334	255	1,046	967	1,347
West Virginia	141	277	136	1,539	1,867	202	530	1,680
New Jersey	2,110	3,809	1,699	1,787	(15)	2,660	858	3,897
Maine	5,419	7,658	2,239	(713)	1,158	1,522	3,393	4,706
APPLICANTS AND RECIPIENTS								
Cook County:								
Job search only	(701)	243	944	794	1	1,005	212	93
Job search/ CWEP	(56)	521	577	607	168	703	264	551
Baltimore	3,067	3,420	353	130	688	905	1,463	3,197
Arkansas	(792)	723	1,515	1,665	35	1,908	278	872

(Continued)

303

TABLE 11-4 Continued

	Participant Perspective			Nonparticipant Perspective					
	Net Present Value (A = B − C)	Net Gains from Employment	Loss in Transfer Payments	Net Present Value (D = E + F − G)	Value of In-Program Output	Tax-Transfer Gains	Program Service Costs	Net Social Gain (or Loss) (A + D)
	A	B	C	D	E	F	G	H
AFDC-U								
APPLICANTS ONLY								
San Diego								
EPP/EWEP:								
Job Search only	($2,200)	$690	$2,890	$2,261	($9)	$3,269	$999	$61
Job search/ CWEP	(2,656)	237	2,893	2,600	651	3,186	1,237	(56)
San Diego SWIM	909	3,483	2,574	2,636	446*	3,294	1,104	3,545
RECIPIENTS ONLY								
San Diego SWIM	(1,540)	3,641	5,181	4,154	446*	5,421	1,713	2,614
APPLICANTS AND RECIPIENTS								
Baltimore	(2,174)	(3,557)	(1,383)	(3,274)	494	(2,821)	947	(5,448)

Notes: See text for detailed explanation of table.

Separate estimates of the value of in-program output for applicants and recipients not provided for San Diego SWIM.

( ): The parentheses indicate negative net gains or increases in transfer payment amounts changes that are contrary to expectations.

Sources: The following final reports on the individual Work/Welfare Demonstrations, all of which were published by MDRC, New York, NY: P. Auspos, G. Cave, and D. Long, *Maine: Final Report on the Training Opportunities in the Private Sector Program*, 1988; S. Freedman, J. Bryant, and G. Cave, *New Jersey: Final Report on the Grant Diversion Project*, 1988; D. Friedlander, G. Hoerz, J. Quint, and J. Riccio, *Arkansas: Final Report on the WORK Program in Two Counties*, 1985; D. Friedlander, G. Hoerz, D. Long, and J. Quint, *Maryland: Final Report on the Employment Initiatives Evaluation*, 1985; D. Friedlander, M. Erickson, G. Hamilton, and V. Knox, *West Virginia: Final Report on the Community Work Experience Demonstrations*, 1986; D. Friedlander, S. Freedman, G. Hamilton, and J. Quint, *Illinois: Final Report on Job Search and Work Experience in Cook County*, 1987; B. Goldman, D. Friedlander, and D. Long, *California: Final Report on the San Diego Job Search and Work Experience Demonstration*, 1986; G. Hamilton and D. Friedlander, *Final Report on the Saturation Work Initiative Model in San Diego*, 1989; J. Riccio, G. Cave, S. Freedman, and M. Price, *Virginia: Final Report on the Virginia Employment Services Program*, 1986.

and participant job-required expenditures on child care and transportation. Column C indicates changes in AFDC and other transfer benefits received by participants.

Column E presents MDRC's valuations of in-program output. Column F is the sum of tax increases paid by participants, reductions in transfer payments paid to participants, and reductions in transfer program operating costs, all of which may be viewed as benefits to nonparticipants. Column G shows the government's cost of operating the treatment programs. Finally, column H, which is computed by summing the benefit-cost components reported in columns B, C, E, F, and G, presents the overall CBA results.

As can be seen from column H, 16 of the 19 reported estimates indicate overall net gains and only three imply net losses. It is this preponderance of positive values that impressed the policy community. Nonetheless, most of the total net gains and losses for either participants and nonparticipants that are implied by columns A and D are not especially large; a majority are well under $2,000 per program participant in current dollars.

One of the most striking findings from Table 11-4 is that of the 19 reported sets of CBA estimates, 17 imply net gains for nonparticipants, but only 10 indicate net gains for participants. The reason for the nine instances of net losses among participants, which occur disproportionately among the two-parent AFDC-U households, is suggested by a comparison of columns B and C. Some of the demonstration treatments did not result in sufficiently large gains from employment to offset participant losses in transfer payments. Thus, as Table 11-4 implies, in eight of the nine instances, nonparticipants gained at the expense of participants. In one demonstration, that for Baltimore's AFDC-U population, both groups were apparently made worse off. Nine of the ten remaining sets of CBA estimates imply that the demonstration treatment made both participants and nonparticipants better off; the tenth, those for Maine, indicate that participants gained, while nonparticipants suffered losses.

Extrapolations of Benefits and Costs: The Baltimore Options Program

As pointed out earlier, some of the benefits and costs of E&T demonstrations may continue after the data collection period has ended. To incorporate these future benefit and cost streams into CBAs, assumptions have to be made concerning the social discount rate, the time horizon, and the decay rate. Thus, in obtaining the findings reported in Table 11-4, MDRC used a 5 percent discount rate and a five-year time horizon. For the decay rate, MDRC often selected several alternative values and examined whether its findings were sensitive to these alternatives. Given the absence of good evidence concerning decay rates at the time the evaluations were conducted, MDRC's strategy of examining the sensitivity of their findings to alternative rates was a good one.

The exact values used for this purpose varied among the studies but usually included a decay rate of zero, which implied no decay, and often also included a rate of infinity, which implied that no benefits or costs extended beyond the data collection period. In addition, the actual rate of decay that was observed during the post-program data collection period was sometimes used,[27] as was an annual rate of 22 percent, which was obtained from a 1980 national study of the then existing WIN program conducted by Ketron, Incorporated.[28] In no case did MDRC use a rate that implied that benefits or costs grew rather than declined over time. As discussed next, however, there is some evidence from MDRC's own data that benefits did grow over time in at least one of the Work/Welfare Demonstrations: the Baltimore Options program.

TABLE 11-5 Six Alternative Estimates of Benefits and Costs per Baltimore Options Program Treatment Group Member: Reported from Participant Perspective (in 2003 dollars)

	Lower Estimates		Middle Estimates		Upper Estimates	
	Original Estimates	Updated Estimates	Original Estimates	Updated Estimates	Original Estimates	Updated Estimates
Earnings and fringe benefits	$866	$2,252	$1,640	$3,327	$2,244	$3,565
Tax payments	–143	–304	–435	–474	–605	–512
Out-of-pocket work expenditures	–37	–44	–$43	–46	–43	–46
AFDC payments	–51	–92	–177	2	–261	22
Other transfer payments	–196	–307	–397	–372	–524	–375
Allowances and support services	335	388	375	413	375	413
Net gain	774	1,893	963	2,850	1,186	3,067

Notes: All estimates are based on a time horizon of five years. Lower estimates represent only observed program impacts and thus do not include estimates of future impacts; there is no extrapolation beyond the observation period. Middle estimates include estimates of future benefits and costs that are based on an assumed annual decay rate of 22 percent. Upper estimates include estimates of future benefits and costs that are based on an assumed zero decay rate. Original estimates are based on a demonstration period of about 1.5 years and an extrapolation period of about 3.5 years. Updated estimates are based on a demonstration period of about three years and an extrapolation period of about two years.
Source: Original estimates are from Table 6-7 of the Daniel Friedlander, Gregory Hoerz, David Long, and Janet Quint, Maryland: Final Report on the Employment Initiatives Evaluation (New York: MDRC, 1985). Updated estimates are from Table A.7 of Daniel Friedlander, Maryland: Supplementary Report on the Baltimore Options Program (New York: MDRC, 1987).

Table 11-5 presents cost-benefit findings for the Baltimore Options program. These particular results were selected because they could be obtained from two separate sets of published estimates: one that appeared in MDRC's 1985 final report for the Baltimore Options program,[29] and one from a 1987 supplemental report that updated the original estimates by obtaining information on the earnings and transfer receipts of members of the treatment and control groups for a longer post-program period and, hence, shortened the length of time over which extrapolation was required.[30] By comparing the two sets of estimates, one can obtain some sense of how sensitive the CBA results are to incorrect assumptions concerning the rate of decay.

The estimates appearing in Table 11-5 pertain to the participant perspective and are averaged over all members of the Baltimore Options AFDC-R treatment group. Three pairs of columns are displayed, one for each of three alternative assumptions that MDRC made concerning decay rates. The left column in each pair is taken from MDRC's originally published estimates and the right column from the updated estimates.

In Table 11-5, some variation is apparent across the three pairs of columns, but much greater differences occur within each pair. These differences between the original and updated estimates are attributable to the fact that at least during the extended data collection period, even an assumption of a zero decay rate for the earnings impact of the Baltimore Options program proved overly pessimistic. As it turned out, the earnings differences between the treatment and comparison groups in Baltimore continued to grow during the extended data collection period. This is one example of a *forecasting error,* a common CBA problem, which is discussed in some detail in Chapter 19.

Adjusting the Findings for Losses in Leisure

An analysis presented earlier in this chapter implies that if participants value the time they must relinquish in order to either participate in E&T activities or take paid employment— time that economists usually refer to as *leisure*—net gains for participants in E&T programs would be overstated (or, alternatively, net losses understated) by the results reported in the first column of Table 11-4. This possibility is explored in Table 11-6, which presents findings from a sensitivity analysis of the net social gains of a subset of the Work/Welfare Demonstrations that was conducted by one of the authors.[31] The first column in this table shows the unadjusted net gain estimates that are also reported in column H of Table 11-4. The second column reports net gain estimates that have been adjusted to reflect the costs associated with reductions in the leisure time of program participants.[32]

A comparison of the two columns in Table 11-6 indicates that the estimates of net social gains and losses are quite sensitive to adjustments that account for losses of leisure, with most of them becoming substantially smaller. Nevertheless, the adjusted estimates remain positive in value, which suggests the earlier conclusion that the programs listed in the table had positive impacts on society as a whole is robust to adjustments for lost leisure.

In assessing the findings reported in Table 11-6, two additional points should be kept in mind. First, the net social gain estimates are only adjusted for leisure that is lost through paid employment. The leisure of Work/Welfare participants was also reduced to the extent they participated in program activities, such as training and work experience. However, data on time spent in these activities are not available, and further adjustments to take account of these additional losses of leisure are not feasible.

Second, as pointed out earlier, it is likely that programs that reduce the leisure time of welfare recipients may, as a result, increase the utility of the nonrecipient

TABLE 11-6 Sensitivity of Findings from the Work/Welfare Demonstrations to Taking Account of the Value to Clients of Lost Leisure (in 2003 dollars)

	Unadjusted Net Social Gain	*Net Social Gain Adjusted for Lost Leisure*
AFDC-R		
APPLICANTS		
San Diego SWIM	$1,260	$348
Virginia	3,176	1,745
RECIPIENTS		
San Diego SWIM	4,053	1,527
Virginia	1,347	521
APPLICANTS AND RECIPIENTS		
Baltimore	3,197	2,381
Arkansas	872	527

Source: David H. Greenberg, "The Leisure Bias in Cost-Benefit Analyses of Employment and Training Programs," *Journal of Human Resources* 32(2) 1997, Table 4.

taxpayers who support the welfare system. The dollar value of this increase in utility is also not taken into account in Table 11-6. However, although most nonrecipient taxpayers, if asked, would probably express a desire to see welfare recipients employed, the appropriate CBA question is how much they are willing to pay for this. It is less obvious that the collective willingness-to-pay of nonrecipients for reductions in the leisure time of recipients is of large magnitude.

One additional finding from Table 11-6 of considerable interest is that once the adjustment for the loss of leisure associated with program-induced increases in work hours is made, the largest estimated net social gains are associated with the Baltimore program. Of the programs listed in Table 11-6, this program was the only one oriented toward the goal of increasing enrollee employment in better-paying jobs and, in fact, it had some success in accomplishing this. The other programs were more oriented toward increasing the hours worked by program participants, and their effects on earnings were almost entirely attributable to such increases.[33]

CONCLUSION

Demonstrations are a valuable source of information for applying CBA. Nonetheless, the analysis presented in this chapter suggests that CBAs of E&T demonstrations are more difficult both to conduct successfully and to interpret than they may first appear, even when the demonstrations utilize a classical experimental design. Nevertheless, they can provide useful insights. For example, MDRC's CBAs of the Work/Welfare Demonstrations suggest that the net social gains from the tested programs were generally positive but modest. However, some uncertainty exists concerning their exact values. On the one hand, they may be understated because of the relatively conservative assumptions concerning decay rates used in their computation. On the other hand, they would tend to be overstated because the value of reductions in the leisure time of demonstration participants is not taken into account in their estimation.

EXERCISES FOR CHAPTER 11

1. Using the scheme shown in Table 11-1, diagram the evaluation design used in each of the following demonstration programs.
   a. To evaluate a government training program that provides low-income, low-skilled, disadvantaged persons job-specific training, members of the target population are randomly assigned to either a treatment group that is eligible to receive services under the program or to a control group that is not. Data are collected on the earnings, welfare receipts, and so forth of both groups during the training period and for two years thereafter.
   b. To evaluate a government training program that provides low-income, low-skilled, disadvantaged persons job-specific training, members of the target population who live in the counties in the eastern half of a large industrial state are assigned to a treatment group that is eligible to receive services under the program, while members of the target population who live in the counties in the western half of the state are assigned to a quasicontrol group that is not. Information is collected on the earnings, welfare receipts, and so forth of both groups for one year prior to the beginning of training, during the training period, and for two years thereafter.

c. To evaluate a government training program that provides low-income, low-skilled, disadvantaged persons job-specific training, information is collected on the earnings, welfare receipts, and so forth of those persons who receive training. This information is collected for the year prior to the beginning of training, during the training period, and for two years thereafter.

2. Consider a government training program that provides low-skilled men job-specific training. To evaluate this program, members of the target population were randomly assigned to either a treatment group that was eligible to receive services under the program or to a control group that was not. Using this evaluation design, the following information was obtained:

   - Members of the treatment group were found to remain in the program an average of one year, during which time they received no earnings but were paid a tax-free stipend of $5,000 by the program to help them cover their living expenses. During the program year, the average annual earnings of members of the control group were $10,000, on which they paid taxes of $1,000. During the program year, the welfare and unemployment compensation benefits received by the two groups were virtually identical.
   - Program operating costs (not counting the stipend) and the cost of services provided by the program were $3,000 per trainee.
   - During the two years after leaving the program, the average annual earnings of members of the treatment group were $20,000, on which they paid taxes of $2,000. During the same period, the average annual earnings of members of the control group were $15,000, on which they paid taxes of $1,500.
   - During the two years after leaving the program, the average annual welfare payments and unemployment compensation benefits received by members of the treatment group were $250. During the same period, the average annual welfare payments and unemployment compensation benefits received by members of the control group were $1,250.

   a. Using a 5 percent discount rate, a zero decay rate, and a five-year time horizon, compute the present value of the net gain (or loss) from the program from the trainee, nonparticipant, and social perspectives. In doing this, ignore program impacts on leisure and assume that all benefits and costs accrue at the end of the year in which they occur.
   b. Once again ignoring program impacts on leisure, recompute the present value of the net gain (or loss) from the program from the trainee, nonparticipant, and social perspectives, assuming that at the end of the two-year follow-up period program impacts on earnings and transfer payments begin to decay at the rate of 20 percent each year.

3. Perhaps the most careful effort to measure the effects of compensatory preschool education was the Perry Preschool Project begun in Ypsilanti, Michigan, in 1962. Children, mostly three years old, were randomly assigned to treatment (58 children) and control (65 children) groups between 1962 and 1965. Children in the treatment group received two academic years of schooling before they entered the regular school system at about age five, while children in the control group did not. The project collected information on the children through age 19, an exceptionally long follow-up period. Using information generated by the study, analysts estimated that two years of preschool generated social net benefits (1988 dollars) of $13,124 at a discount rate of 5 percent. (For a more complete account, see W. Steven Barnett, "Benefits of Compensatory Preschool Education," *Journal of Human Resources* 27[2] 1992, 279–312.)

   a. Before seeing results from the project, what would be your main methodological concern about such a long follow-up period? What data would you look at to see if the problem exists?
   b. Benefit categories beyond the age of 19 included crime reduction, earnings increase, and reductions in welfare receipts. If you were designing the study, what data would you collect to help measure these benefits?

4. Five years ago a community college district established programs in ten new vocational fields. The district now wants to phase out those programs that are not performing successfully and retain those programs that are performing successfully. To determine which programs to drop and which to retain, the district decides to perform CBAs.
   a. What perspective or perspectives should be used in the studies? Are there any issues concerning standing?
   b. Using a stylized cost-benefit framework table, list the major benefits and costs that are relevant to the district's decision and indicate how each affects different pertinent groups, as well as society as a whole. Try to make your list as comprehensive and complete as possible, while avoiding double counting.
   c. What sort of evaluation design should the district use in conducting its CBAs? What are the advantages and disadvantages of this design? Is it practical?
   d. Returning to the list of benefits and costs that you developed in part b, indicate which of the benefits and costs on your list can be quantified in monetary terms. How would you treat those benefits and costs that cannot be monetized?
   e. What sort of data would be required to measure those benefits and costs that can be monetized? How might the required data be obtained?

Notes

1. David Greenberg, Donna Linksz, and Marvin B. Mandell, *Social Experimentation and Public Policymaking* (Washington, D.C.: The Urban Institute Press, 2003).
2. For a discussion, see Irwin Garfinkel, Charles F. Manski, and Charles Michalopoulos, "Micro Experiments and Macro Effects," in Charles F. Manski and Irwin Garfinkel, eds., *Evaluating Welfare and Training Programs* (Cambridge, MA: Harvard University Press, 1992), 25–75.
3. In practice, many of the services offered under a demonstration program may also be offered under the existing environment. For example, in the case of training programs, training of many types may already be available through community colleges and adult schools. Consequently, estimates of program effects on participants do not measure impacts of the receipt of service against the nonreceipt of services. Rather, such estimates usually pertain to the *incremental* effect of the demonstration program over the existing environment.
4. This method of diagraming evaluation designs was developed a number of years ago by Donald Campbell and Julian Stanley, *Experimental and Quasi-Experimental Designs for Research* (Chicago: Rand-McNally, 1963).
5. On randomization, see Leslie L. Roos Jr., Noralou P. Roos, and Barbara McKinley, "Implementing Randomization," *Policy Analysis* 3(4) 1977, 547–559; and Larry L. Orr, *Social*

Experiments: Evaluating Public Programs with Experimental Methods (Thousand Oaks, CA: Sage Publications, Inc., 1999).
6. Sometimes a problem occurs when some members of the two groups cannot be located for purposes of collecting post-program information on outcomes or refuse to provide the information. This problem, which can occur with all five of the sample designs listed in Table 11-1 and is known as *sample attrition,* can bias the impact estimates if those who can and cannot be located systematically differ from one another in terms of the post-program outcome measures. For example, those who can be located may have higher earnings, on average, than those who cannot be located.
7. For discussions of issues and problems that arise in conducting social experiments, see Gary Burtless, "The Case for Randomized Field Trials in Economic and Policy Research," *Journal of Economic Perspectives* 9(2) 1995, 63–84; James S. Heckman and Jeffrey A. Smith, "Assessing the Case for Social Experiments," *Journal of Economic Perspectives* 9(2) 1995, 85–110; and David H. Greenberg and Stephen Morris, "Large-Scale Social Experimentation in Britain: What Can and Cannot Be Learnt from the Employment Retention and Advancement Demonstration, *Evaluation* 11(2) 2005, 151–171.
8. The name stems from the fact that in the absence of random assignment people select themselves

to participate or not participate in a program on the basis of such unobservable characteristics as motivation. If appropriate statistical adjustments cannot be made to control for this—as the text indicates, sometimes this is possible, but sometimes it is not—then sample selection bias results. For further information on the selection problem and econometric techniques that are used to attempt to adjust for it, see William H. Greene, *Econometric Analysis,* 4th ed. (New York: Macmillan Publishing Company, 2000); and Christopher H. Achen, *Statistical Analysis of Quasi-Experiments* (Berkeley: University of California Press, 1986).

9. For a survey of the social experiments conducted between 1962 and 1996, see David Greenberg, Mark Shroder, and Matthew Onstott, "The Social Experiment Market," *Journal of Economic Perspectives* 13(3) 1999, 157–172. For two- to three-page summaries of each of the known 143 social experiments that were completed in the United States by the end of 1996, see David Greenberg and Mark Shroder, *The Digest of Social Experiments,* 3rd ed. (Washington, D.C.: The Urban Institute Press, 2004).

10. For summaries of findings from evaluations of E&T programs and methodological issues associated with these evaluations, see Robert J. LaLonde, "The Promise of Public Sector-Sponsored Training Programs," *Journal of Economic Perspectives* 9(2) 1997, 149–168; Daniel Friedlander, David H. Greenberg, and Philip K. Robins, "Evaluating Government Training Programs for the Economically Disadvantaged," *Journal of Economic Literature* 35(4) 1997, 1809-1855; James Heckman, Robert LaLonde, and Jeffrey Smith, "The Economics and Econometrics of Active Labor Market Programs," in Orley Ashenfelter and David Card, eds., *Handbook of Labor Economics, Volume 3A* (Amsterdam: North Holland, 1999), 1865–2097; and David H. Greenberg, Charles Michalopoulos, and Philip K. Robins, "A Meta-Analysis of Government Training Programs," *Industrial and Labor Relations Review* 57(1) 2003, 31–53. For summaries of evaluations of E&T programs specifically targeted at welfare recipients, see Judith M. Gueron and Edward Pauly, *From Welfare to Work* (New York: Russell Sage Foundation, 1991); and Karl Ashworth, Andreas Cebulla, David Greenberg, and Robert

Walker, "Meta-Evaluation: Discovering What Works Best in Welfare Provision," *Evaluation* 10(3) 2004, 193–216.

11. The supply curve in Figure 11-1 should be viewed as an equivalent variation supply curve—that is, it incorporates substitution, but not income, effects. For reasons discussed in Appendix 3A, this is the appropriate curve for measuring changes in worker surplus resulting from wage changes. However, as Exhibit 11-2 suggests, wage changes may engender substantial income, as well as substitution, effects. The implications of this possibility are mentioned in note 32.

12. The word *leisure,* as commonly used by economists and as used here, refers to all activities that take place outside the labor market. Many of these activities (e.g., child care, home repair, and education) may, of course, be quite productive.

13. Because the hours the recipient is required to work are computed by dividing her welfare grant by the minimum wage (i.e., $h^* = \text{grant}/W^m$), her grant equals $W^m h^*$, a value that in Figure 11-3 is represented by area $W^m a h^* h_0$.

14. Notice that because the supply curve first shifts from S_0 to S_1, and then, in response to this shift the participant adjusts the number of hours she works, the surplus loss is measured using S_1 rather than S_0.

15. David H. Greenberg, "The Leisure Bias in Cost-Benefit Analyses of Employment and Training Programs," *Journal of Human Resources* 32(2) 1997, 413–439.

16. Like Figures 11-1–11-3, the labor supply curve in Figure 11-4 should be viewed as an equivalent variation supply curve. The specific manner in which an uncompensated labor supply would shift in response to subsidized child care is complex. The reservation wage of nonworkers, W_r in Figure 11-4(a), will clearly fall as a result of subsidized child care. However, those who would work regardless of whether they receive a subsidy—for example, an individual at W_1 in Figure 11-4(a)—may actually work fewer hours as a result of the subsidy. This is due to the fact that the subsidy decreases their work-related expenditures and, hence, increases their discretionary income. The resulting income effect would tend to decrease hours of work. Hence, the earnings of these persons could actually fall as a result of the subsidy. Thus, the new uncompensated labor supply curve may be below and to the right of

the old supply curve at low market wage rates but above and to the left of the old supply curve at higher wage rates. (For a more detailed discussion, see Ronald G. Ehrenberg and Robert S. Smith, *Modern Labor Economics: Theory and Public Policy,* 7th ed. (Reading, MA: Addison-Wesley, 2000), Appendix 6A.

17. As mentioned earlier in the chapter, having as many able-bodied individuals work as possible is considered an important social goal by many U.S. citizens. Thus, even though subsidizing child care may be economically inefficient, it may still be justified if it helps meet this goal. Moreover, it is sometime argued that subsidies are needed to correct market failures in the market for child care that results in a lower quality of services than is socially optimal. For example, there may be information asymmetries because parents have difficulty in judging the quality of child care. In addition, viewing children as third parties, positive externalities may exist in the market for child care if parents are more concerned with convenience and price than with quality. See Suzanne W. Helburn and Barbara R. Bergmann, *America's Child Care Problem: The Way Out* (New York: Palgrave, 2002).

18. This section borrows heavily from David Greenberg, "Conceptual Issues in Cost-Benefit Analysis of Welfare-to-Work Programs," *Contemporary Policy Issues* 10(4) 1992, 51–63.

19. For a review of what bureaucrats actually maximize, see David L. Weimer and Aidan R. Vining, *Policy Analysis: Concepts and Practice,* 4th ed. (Upper Saddle River, NJ: Prentice Hall, 2005), 179–186.

20. For recent attempts to estimate the size of displacement effects, see Carl Davidson and Stephen A. Woodbury, "The Displacement Effect of Reemployment Bonus Programs," *Journal of Labor Economics* 11(4) 1993, 575–605; Richard Blundell, Monica Costa Dias, and J. Van Reenen, Evaluating the Employment Impact of a Mandatory Job Search Program: The New Deal for Young People in the UK, unpublished manuscript, London: University College London and Institute for Fiscal Studies, 2002; and Jeremy Lise, Shannon Seitz, and Jeffrey Smith, "Equilibrium Policy Experiments and the Evaluation of Social Programs," Working Paper 10283, Cambridge, MA: National Bureau of Economic Research, 2004.

21. David H. Greenberg, Charles Michalopoulous, and Philip K. Robins, "What Happens to the Effects of Government-Funded Training Programs Over Time?" *Journal of Human Resources* 39(1) 2004, 277–293.

22. David Greenberg, Karl Ashworth, Andreas Cebulla, and Robert Walker, "Do Welfare-to-Work Programmes Work for Long?" *Fiscal Studies* 25(1) 2004, 27–53.

23. See David H. Greenberg, Charles Michalopoulous, and Philip K. Robins, "What Happens to the Effects of Government-Funded Training Programs Over Time?" Greenberg, Michalopous, and Robins' findings for random assignment evaluations imply that the growth period may last well over a year. For a summary of the scant earlier evidence, see Friedlander, Greenberg, and Robins, "Evaluating Government Training Programs for the Disadvantaged," p. 1836.

24. David Greenberg, Karl Ashworth, Andreas Cebulla, and Robert Walker, "Do Welfare-to-Work Programmes Work for Long?"

25. For example, see David Greenberg, Donna Linksz, and Marvin B. Mandell, *Social Experimentation and Public Policymaking;* Ron Haskins, "Congress Writes a Law: Research and Welfare Reform," *Journal of Policy Analysis and Management* 10(4) 1991, 616–632; Erica Baum, "When the Witch Doctors Agree: The Family Support Act and Social Science Research," *Journal of Policy Analysis and Management* 10(4) 1991, 603–615; and Peter Szanton, "The Remarkable 'Quango': Knowledge, Politics, and Welfare Reform," *Journal of Policy Analysis and Management* 10(4) 1991, 590–602.

26. Summaries of each of the Work/Welfare Demonstrations, as well as more recent welfare-to-work demonstrations that have been evaluated using an experimental design, can be found in David Greenberg and Mark Shroder, *The Digest of Social Experiments.* Detailed descriptions of the Work/Welfare Demonstrations, as well as the CBA findings from these demonstrations, can be found in the following reports published by the MDRC, New York, NY: P. Auspos, G. Cave, and D. Long, *Maine: Final Report on the Training Opportunities in the Private Sector Program,* 1988; S. Freedman, J. Bryant, and G. Cave, *New Jersey: Final Report on the Grant Diversion Project,* 1988; D. Friedlander, G. Hoerz, J. Quint, and J. Riccio, *Arkansas: Final Report on the*

WORK Program in Two Counties, 1985;
D. Friedlander, G. Hoerz, D. Long, and J. Quint,
*Maryland: Final Report on the Employment
Initiatives Evaluation,* 1985; D. Friedlander,
M. Erickson, G. Hamilton, and V. Knox, *West
Virginia: Final Report on the Community Work
Experience Demonstrations,* 1986; D. Friedlander,
S. Freedman, G. Hamilton, and J. Quint, *Illinois:
Final Report on Job Search and Work Experience
in Cook County,* 1987; B. Goldman,
D. Friedlander, and D. Long, *California: Final
Report on the San Diego Job Search and Work
Experience Demonstration,* 1986; G. Hamilton
and D. Friedlander, *Final Report on the Saturation
Work Initiative Model in San Diego,* 1989; and
J. Riccio, G. Cave, S. Freedman, and M. Price,
*Virginia: Final Report on the Virginia
Employment Services Program,* 1986.

27. If the demonstration period were sufficiently
long, then the decay rate could be determined on
the basis of the pattern of changes in earnings
actually observed. Typically, however, this period
is only two or three years long, which is too short
a time to establish a clear pattern.

28. Ketron, Incorporated, *The Long-Term Impact of
WIN II: A Longitudinal Evaluation of the
Employment Experiences of Participants in the
Work Incentive Program* (Wayne, PA: Ketron,
1980).

29. Daniel Friedlander, Gregory Hoerz, David Long,
and Janet Quint, *Maryland: Final Report on the
Employment Initiatives Evaluation* (New York:
MDRC, 1985).

30. Daniel Friedlander, *Maryland: Supplemental
Report on the Baltimore Options Program* (New
York: MDRC, 1987).

31. David Greenberg, "The Leisure Bias in Cost-
Benefit Analyses of Employment and Training
Programs."

32. Greenberg reported several sets of adjusted estimates based on alternative assumptions. The second column of Table 11-6 is based on the most
conservative of these and, hence, differs the least
from the unadjusted estimates in the first column. In making the calculations appearing in the
second column of Table 11-6, Greenberg
assumed that the income effect is equal to zero.
However, Greenberg's analysis also indicates
that this assumption is unlikely to cause large
errors in the calculations.

33. Daniel Friedlander and Gary Burtless, *Five Years
After: The Long-Term Effects of Welfare-to-Work
Programs* (New York: Russell Sage Foundation,
1995).

CHAPTER 12

Valuing Impacts from Observed Behavior: Direct Estimation of Demand Curves

A key concept for valuing policy impacts is change in social surplus. As discussed in Chapters 3 and 4, changes in social surplus are represented by areas, often as triangles or trapezoids, bounded by supply and demand curves. Measurement of changes in social surplus is relatively straightforward when we know the shapes and positions of the supply and demand curves in the relevant primary market, before and after the policy change. In practice, however, these curves are usually not known. Analysts have to estimate them or find alternative ways to measure benefits and costs. In the previous chapter, we discuss how such information can be gathered from demonstrations. In this chapter, we discuss direct estimation of these curves.

We focus on estimating demand curves. The main reason is that, in practice, analysts are more interested in estimating changes in consumer surplus than changes in producer surplus. Many changes in producer surplus are either offset by changes in consumer surplus, and thereby constitute transfers, or are, in practice, negligible. There are two major exceptions. One pertains to unemployed labor, which we discuss in detail in Chapters 4 and 11. The second arises when the government intervenes in otherwise efficient markets for capital, foreign exchange, labor, and other productive assets. We discuss these issues in Chapter 16.

For goods traded in well-functioning markets, we can usually observe the market-clearing price. We may also observe the aggregate quantity bought and sold so that we have the point of intersection of the demand and supply curves. Combining price and quantity provides revenues (or expenditures depending on your perspective). The next section discusses the use of revenues as an estimate of (gross) benefits. It is appropriate in a few special situations.

When these situations do not apply, the analyst may need to estimate the market demand curve. In the following sections we consider three possible methods to estimate demand curves. These methods vary considerably in their accuracy. First, we suppose that we have only one observation on the demand curve but previous research provides an estimate of either the elasticity or slope of the demand curve. Second, we suppose that we have a few points on the demand curve. Third, we suppose we have many observations of prices and quantities from different regions or from different time periods. In the first two situations we will make simple extrapolations or will use the information to predict another point of relevance for policy evaluation. In the third situation we can apply standard econometric techniques to estimate the demand curve. Appendix 12A contains an introduction to multiple regression analysis and ordinary least squares estimation.

PROJECT REVENUES AS THE MEASURE OF (GROSS) CONSUMER BENEFITS

To private-sector producers of goods or services, project revenues are a natural measure of (gross) benefits, and they feature prominently in the computation of producer surplus. But, as shown in Chapter 4, revenues do not always equate to consumer surplus.

Of course, it is correct to treat revenues as benefits where changes in consumer surplus equal zero. Consider, for example, a publicly supported project that exports all of its output. The North East Coal Development Project, which we discuss in Chapter 6, provides an example. The primary beneficiaries (besides the Canadian federal government) were the mining and transportation companies. Their producer surplus increase is legitimately computed as the difference between their additional revenues and their additional costs, that is, as their incremental profits. However, as this project would supply coal to Japanese customers only, Table 6-5 does not include any consumer surplus benefits for Canadians. The consumer surplus would accrue to foreigners and, therefore, should not be counted in the CBA if the analyst takes a national perspective.

Another correct use of "revenues as benefits" occurs when the government sells a good in an undistorted market without affecting the market price. For example, a government may have surplus office equipment that it sells in sufficiently small quantities that the market price of office equipment does not change. The assumption of a negligible effect on price is more reasonable for goods traded in large, national markets than for goods traded in small, local markets. It is also more reasonable for homogeneous goods, such as surplus equipment, than for heterogeneous goods, such as land, which may differ in desirability from one parcel to another.

Unfortunately, the government often sells goods when markets are distorted or when the sale has an impact on the price of the good. For example, electricity may not be available to residents of a remote town unless the government sponsors the construction of an electric power transmission line. Here introduction of electricity effectively reduces the price from infinity to the user fee charged. In these situations, government or firm revenues are a poor measure of consumer benefits, and we should estimate the demand curve.

ESTIMATION KNOWING ONE POINT ON THE DEMAND CURVE AND ITS SLOPE OR ELASTICITY

Many municipalities charge annual fees for household refuse collection that do not depend on the quantity of refuse disposed of by households. In such communities, the marginal private cost (MPC) of an additional unit of garbage collected is effectively zero, whereas the marginal social cost (MSC) of collecting and disposing of it is shared equally among all households.[1] This divergence between MPC and MSC leads to free riding and a socially excessive amount of refuse disposal. Raising the MPC of refuse disposal would reduce the quantity of refuse disposed of by households and thereby reduce the social surplus loss from excess refuse disposal.

Imagine that you have been asked to measure the social benefits that would result if a town, Wasteville, which currently does not charge households by volume for refuse collection, imposes a fee of $1 for each 30-gallon container. That is, households would be charged $1 for each such container put at the curbside for emptying by the sanitation department. As a 30-gallon container holds about 20 pounds of waste, the new policy implies a price increase from zero to about $0.05/lb, assuming the containers are full.

From the sanitation department's records, you find that the current refuse disposal rate averages 2.60 pounds per person per day (lb/p/d) and the MSC of each ton of refuse collected is approximately $120 per ton, or $0.06/lb. (One ton equals 2,000 pounds in the United States.) This MSC is the sum of the marginal collection costs of $40 per ton and the tipping fee at the landfill of $80 per ton. Although the fee still leaves the MPC, the actual price, below the MSC, the socially optimal price, you expect it will produce a gain in social surplus by reducing the amount of waste generated.

To measure the social surplus gain, however, you require the demand curve for garbage collection and disposal. You know only one point on the demand curve: 2.60 lb/p/d of garbage at a price equal to zero. To progress any further, you must find a way of estimating the rest of the demand curve. Usually, demand curves are assumed to be linear or linear in logarithms. To begin, we assume the demand curve is linear.

Linear Demand Curve

A market demand curve for a good tells us how many units of the good consumers wish to purchase at each price. A linear functional form assumes that the relationship between the quantity demanded and the price is linear; that is, the demand curve can be written as:

$$q = \alpha_0 + \alpha_1 p \tag{12.1}$$

where q is the quantity demanded at price p, α_0 is the quantity that would be demanded when the price is zero (the intercept on the q axis), and α_1 indicates the change in the quantity demanded as a result of a one-unit increase in price (the slope). We expect demand curves to slope down, that is, $\alpha_1 < 0$.

For Wasteville, we measure q in terms of *quantity demanded per person* per day. Thus, we can assume $\alpha_0 = 2.60$ (the amount of refuse disposed of daily by each person at a price of zero). However, we do not know the slope, α_1, but we do know that other researchers have addressed this problem and have either estimated the slope or the price elasticity of demand.

Using a Slope Estimate   If you went to a research library or used the bibliography at the end of this book, you might turn up a study that would give you an empirically based estimate of the slope of the demand curve for refuse disposal. Indeed, Robin R. Jenkins conducted such a study.[2] Jenkins based her estimate on data from nine U.S. communities that employed a variety of refuse fees, ranging from zero in three communities to between $0.25 and $1.73 per 30- to 32-gallon container in the other six, over the period from 1980 to 1989. She estimated that each dollar increase in the price of a 30- to 32-gallon container reduced waste by 0.40 lb/p/d. Put another way, she

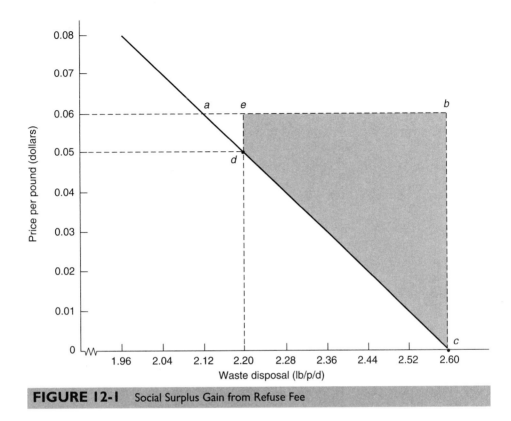

FIGURE 12-1   Social Surplus Gain from Refuse Fee

estimated $\alpha_1 = -0.40$ for those communities. Using this estimate leads to a prediction that if Wasteville imposed a fee of $1 per container ($0.05/lb), then residential waste disposal would fall by 0.40 lb/p/d from 2.60 lb/p/d to 2.20 lb/p/d.

Figure 12-1 shows the demand curve implied by Jenkins's slope estimate: $q = 2.60 - 0.4p$, drawn in the usual way with price on the vertical axis. This curve goes through the status quo point of 2.60 lb/p/d at zero dollars per pound (point *c*) and the predicted point of 2.20 lb/p/d at $0.05 per pound (point *d*).

We can use this curve to estimate the change in social surplus. Remembering that the socially optimal price is $0.06 per pound, the area of the triangle *abc*, $0.5(2.60 - 2.12)(0.06 - 0.00) = $0.0144 per pound per day (p/d), is the social surplus loss per person at a price of $0, and the area of the small triangle *aed*, $0.0004/p/d, is the social surplus loss per person at the price of $0.05/lb. Thus, the area of trapezoid *debc*, $0.0140/p/d, is the gain in social surplus per person that would result from the price increase from zero to $0.05/lb. If the population of Wasteville is 100,000 people, then the annual gain in social surplus from imposing a container fee of $1 is ($0.0140/p/d)(365 days)(100,000 persons) = $511,000. To obtain the net benefit of this policy we would have to subtract the administrative cost of collecting the fee and take into account gains due to reducing taxation, if any.

Usually, the equation for a demand curve is written with quantity as a function of price, as in equation (12.1). This is called an *ordinary demand curve*. However, demand curves are usually drawn with price on the vertical axis, as in Figure 12-1. Demand curves where price is a function of quantity are called *inverse demand curves.* Rearranging equation (12.1) gives the following inverse demand curve:

$$p = -\alpha_0/\alpha_1 + (1/\alpha_1)q \tag{12.2}$$

The slope of this curve equals $1/\alpha_1$. The intercept, $-\alpha_0/\alpha_1$, indicates the quantity that would be demanded if the price were zero; it is sometimes called the *choke price.* For the demand curve shown in Figure 12-1, the inverse demand curve is $p = 6.5 - 2.5q$, and the choke price is $6.50. We return to inverse demand curves later.

When using a slope or elasticity estimate from previous research, it is important to consider issues of *internal validity* and *external validity.* Internal validity involves the sort of evaluation design issues discussed in Chapter 11, as well as issues related to the proper use of econometric techniques, which we discuss later in this chapter. External validity concerns the appropriateness of using estimates derived from data collected at other times, in other places, and with different populations. Applying estimates to circumstances similar to those under which they were obtained has high external validity. Specifically, the closer Wasteville is in economic, policy, demographic, and geographic characteristics to the communities in Jenkins's sample, the more confident we can be in the accuracy of our estimated change in waste disposal following the introduction of a volumetric user fee in Wasteville. The fact that her estimate comes from the 1980s is of some concern because there has been time for other unmeasured variables, such as the level of environmental awareness or recycling infrastructure, to have changed.

Using an Elasticity Estimate   The preceding section assumes that the demand curve for garbage disposal in Wasteville is linear and that the analyst has a valid estimate of its slope. This section still assumes that the demand for garbage disposal in Wasteville is linear but now assumes that the analyst has an estimate of the price elasticity of demand. To estimate the benefits the analyst needs to determine the slope.

The price elasticity of demand, ϵ_d, measures the responsiveness of the quantity demanded to changes in price. For a linear demand curve, equation (12.1) or equation (12.2), the price elasticity of demand equals:

$$\epsilon_d = \alpha_1 p/q \tag{12.3}$$

The price elasticity of demand is *always* negative because $\alpha_1 < 0$, and p and $q > 0$. For a linear demand curve, the elasticity is nonconstant—it varies with both price and quantity.[3] Also, it *decreases* (become more negative) as the ordinary demand curve becomes steeper (α_1 becomes more negative). This is cumbersome. To simplify, we follow economists' usual practice of talking about an elasticity as if it were positive, in effect taking the absolute value. We say that the elasticity *increases* as the slope of the ordinary demand curve *increases,* and the more responsive quantity is to a change in price, the more elastic is demand. Noneconomists may find this a bit confusing at first, but everyone soon gets used to it.

Given an estimate of the price elasticity, we can use equation (12.3) to estimate the slope of an ordinary demand curve, α_1, if we also know the price and quantity at which the elasticity was estimated. Returning to our garbage example, suppose Jenkins has not provided an estimate of the slope but instead had reported an estimate of the price elasticity of demand for residential refuse disposal of -0.12, which had been estimated at the average price charged by those communities in her sample that had nonzero fees, \$0.81/container, and at the average residential waste disposed of by the communities in her sample, 2.62 lb/p/d.[4] Using this information, we can recover α_1 from equation (12.3) thus:

$$\alpha_1 = \epsilon_d q/p = (-0.12)(2.62)/(0.81) \cong -0.40$$

The general point is that construction of a linear demand curve to measure changes in social surplus requires either a direct estimate of the slope itself or an estimate of the price elasticity of demand and the price and quantity at which the elasticity was estimated.

Constant Elasticity Demand Curve

The market demand curve may not be linear. Economists have found that many goods have a *constant elasticity demand curve,* that is:

$$q = \beta_0 p^{\beta_1} \qquad\qquad (12.4)$$

where q denotes quantity demanded at price p, as before, and β_0 and β_1 are parameters. In order to interpret β_1 it is useful to take the natural logarithm, denoted by ln, of both sides of equation (12.4), which gives:

$$\ln q = \ln \beta_0 + \beta_1 \ln p \qquad\qquad (12.5)$$

We see immediately that the constant elasticity demand curve is linear in logarithms.[5] Furthermore, β_1, the slope of the linear in logarithm demand curve, equals ϵ_d, the price elasticity of demand.[6] As ϵ_d equals the slope of a linear curve, which is a constant, it follows that the price elasticity of demand is constant; hence the name of this demand curve—a constant elasticity demand curve.

With quantity on the vertical axis and price on the horizontal axis, the slope of the constant elasticity demand curve is not constant; specifically, it equals $\beta_1 q/p$.[7] Clearly, it varies with q and p. Because $\beta_1 < 0, q > 0$ and $p > 0$, the constant elasticity demand curve slopes downward (i.e., it has a negative slope). It is also asymptotic to both the price and quantity axes. That is, as price becomes infinite, the quantity demanded approaches zero, and as price approaches zero, the quantity demanded approaches infinity. However, because we are most often interested in the region of the demand curve where price is finite and greater than zero, and the estimates of elasticities are based on data in this range, these asymptotic extremes are usually not relevant to our analysis.

As an illustration of how to use a constant elasticity demand curve, consider the following situation. A community (not Wasteville) currently charges a refuse collection fee of \$0.05/lb and waste disposal is 2.25 lb/p/d. This status quo point is labeled point *a*

EXHIBIT 12-1

Erik Lichtenberg and David Zilberman wished to estimate the costs and benefits of government regulations that reduced pesticide use in agriculture. Their study covered three important crops: corn, cotton, and rice. There have been numerous empirical studies of price elasticities in agricultural markets. After reviewing this literature, they came up with "consensus values" for the elasticity of supply of 0.3 (corn), 0.5 (cotton), and 0.8 (rice), and for the elasticity of demand of –0.5 (corn), –0.41 (cotton), and –0.43 (rice). The supply and demand functions for all three crops were assumed to have constant elasticity forms.

Source: Adapted from Erik Lichtenberg and David Zilberman, "The Welfare Economics of Price Supports in U.S. Agriculture," *American Economic Review* 76(5) 1986, 1135–1141.

---

in Figure 12-2. We have been asked to estimate the change in consumer surplus that would result if the collection fee were raised to $0.08/lb, assuming that the demand for refuse collection and disposal has a constant elasticity functional form.

After some research we find an applicable study that reports an estimate of the price elasticity of demand of -0.15. Using this estimate of β_1 in equation (12.4), we first solve for β_0:

$$\beta_0 = (2.25)/(0.05)^{-0.15} \simeq 1.44$$

which gives $q = 1.44 \, p^{-0.15}$ as the underlying demand curve for our application.[8] Consequently, if fees were raised to $0.08/lb, waste disposal would fall to 2.10 lb/p/d.[9] This point is labeled as point b in Figure 12-2.[10]

The change in benefits resulting from an increase in the price from $0.05 to $0.08 is represented by the area *fbag* in Figure 12-2. This can be broken down into two areas, *bah*, the consumer surplus lost on the garbage that was previously disposed of but is no longer generated after the collection fee increase, and *fbhg*, the increase in fee payments on the remaining quantity. To estimate the former area, *bah*, we need to calculate the darkly shaded area under the demand curve and then subtract the rectangle *hadc*. In general, the area under a constant elasticity demand curve from quantity q_0 to quantity q_1 is given (exactly) by:

$$\text{Area} = \left(\frac{1}{\beta_0}\right)^{1/\beta_1}\left(\frac{q_1^\rho - q_0^\rho}{\rho}\right) \tag{12.6}$$

where $\rho = [1 + (1/\beta_1)]$.[11] Applying this formula to measure the area under the demand curve in Figure 12-2 where q ranges from 2.10 lb/p/d to 2.25 lb/p/d yields an area $0.0097/p/d. Subtracting area *hadc*, which measures the reduction in fee payments due to the reduction in quantity [($0.05/lb)(2.25 lb/p/d–2.10 lb/p/d) = $0.0075/p/d], gives an estimate of area *bah* equal to $0.0022/p/d.

We could approximate the area under the demand curve as a trapezoid given by a straight line between the status quo point (point a) and the predicted point (point b),

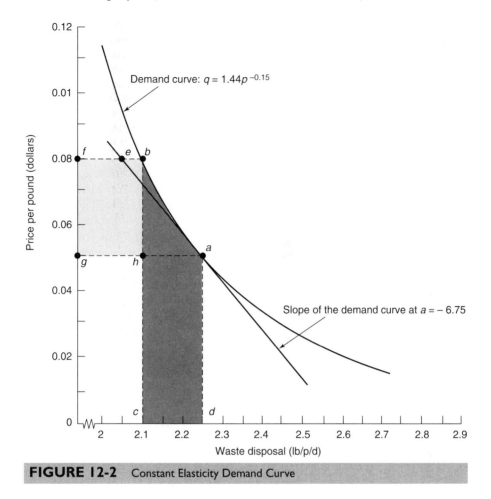

FIGURE 12-2 Constant Elasticity Demand Curve

and points *c* and *d*. This method would lead to an estimated area of $0.00975/p/d, a slight overestimation. In practice, imprecision in our empirical estimates of elasticities usually swamps the error resulting from linear approximation of areas. Thus, such approximations are usually reasonable.

Adding area *fbhg*, the increase in fee payments on the remaining quantity [($0.08 – $0.05)(2.10 lb/p/d) = $0.063/p/d], provides an estimate of overall loss in consumer surplus equal to $0.0652/p/d.[12] For a town with a population of 100,000, the consumer surplus lost annually would be $0.0652 × 365 × 100,000 = $2.38 million.

A complication arises when we wish to use an elasticity estimated from a constant elasticity functional form to predict the effect of raising a price from zero to some positive level. As the constant elasticity demand curve is inconsistent with an observation of zero price, there is no fully satisfactory way to make use of the elasticity estimate. We are forced to postulate some other functional form that goes through the status quo point (price equals zero) and use the constant elasticity estimate as a rough guide for specifying its parameters. This expediency should be thought of as an informed guess that can serve as the starting point for sensitivity analysis.

EXTRAPOLATING FROM A FEW OBSERVATIONS

Recent policy or other fortuitous changes (at least from the analyst's perspective) often provide a basis for predicting the impacts of future policy changes. For example, imagine that we wish to predict the effect of a fare increase on bus ridership. If the last increase of $0.25 resulted in 1,000 fewer riders per day, then it may be reasonable to assume that a further increase of $0.25 would have a similar effect. Here we are treating the observations as if they resulted from a simple before and after quasi-experimental design.

Two considerations are important in determining the appropriateness of extrapolating from the effects of a previous change. The first consideration concerns the assumed functional relationship between the outcome and the policy variable or, specifically, the functional form of the demand curve. Linear functional forms can produce very different predictions than constant elasticity functional forms, for instance. This is illustrated in Figure 12-3. Suppose that another municipality, Twopointsville, has been experimenting with waste disposal charges. When these residents were charged $0.01/lb for refuse, they disposed of 2.52 lb/p/d (point *a*), and when the fee was raised to $0.025/lb, they disposed of only 2.40 lb/p/d (point *b*). We would like to know how much waste disposal

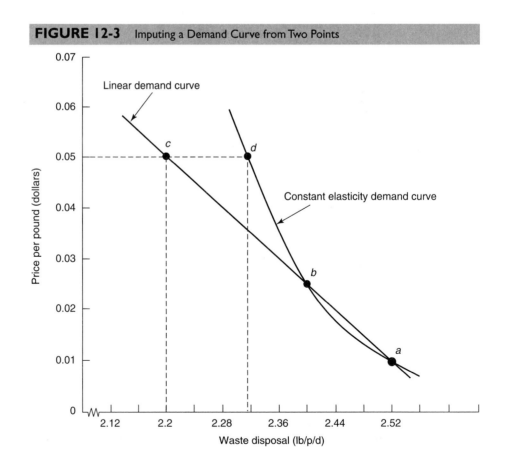

FIGURE 12-3   Imputing a Demand Curve from Two Points

would occur in Twopointsville if the fee were raised further to $0.05/lb. If we fitted a linear demand curve to the two known points (*a* and *b*), then we would predict that waste would fall by 0.20 lb/p/d to 2.20 lb/p/d (point *c*). If, instead, we fitted a constant elasticity demand curve to the two points, then we would predict that waste would fall by a smaller amount, 0.09 lb/p/d, to 2.31 lb/p/d (point *d*).[13] Note that each of these functional forms fits the two observed data points equally well—perfectly. In fact, there are an infinite number of curves that fit the two observed points perfectly.

Note also that Figure 12-3 illustrates an important point: *The further we extrapolate from past experience, the more sensitive are our predictions to assumptions about functional form.* In the absence of theoretical guidance or other empirical evidence, we have no basis for choosing between the two widely different predictions shown in Figure 12-3.

The second consideration concerns the validity of attributing the change in the outcome to the change in the policy variable. We are implicitly assuming that no other variable of relevance to the outcome changed during the time period under consideration. It is possible, for example, that the fall in bus ridership from *a* to *b* resulted in part from the opening of a major new highway. If this were the case, then it is unlikely that a similar further change in fare would produce as large a reduction in ridership as occurred after the earlier fare change.

One way to control for changes in other variables and to gain greater confidence about the appropriate functional form is to collect more observations and use econometric techniques to estimate key parameters.

ECONOMETRIC ESTIMATION WITH MANY OBSERVATIONS

If many observations of quantities demanded at different prices are available, then it may be possible to use econometric techniques to estimate demand curves or demand functions. The linear regression model typically serves as the starting point for such efforts. We assume here that the reader is familiar with the basic concepts of linear regression. Readers unfamiliar with these concepts, or desiring to review them, should read Appendix 12A. Readers requiring a fuller treatment should consult a basic econometrics text.[14]

Model Specification

The starting point for econometric estimation of demand functions is to specify the important explanatory (or independent) variables, such as price and income, that affect the quantity demanded and the functional form of the relationship.[15] For example, we may have theoretical reasons to believe that the demand for a particular good, *q*, is a function of the price of that good, *p*, income, *I*, and temperature, *T*:

$$q = f(p, I, T) \tag{12.7}$$

The functional form, represented by *f*, may be linear, linear in logarithms, or have some other form.

Sometimes the set of explanatory variables varies slightly. Returning to waste disposal, for example, a study by James Strathman, Anthony Rufolo, and Gerard Mildner assumes that the demand for waste disposal depends on the tipping fee, manufacturing income, and construction employment.[16] *Remember, however, the discussion in Chapter 5 that suggests we should* not *include the prices of substitutes or complements as explanatory variables.* With this exception, the model should include all variables that affect demand in theory. Even though we may not have a substantive interest in some of the explanatory variables, such as temperature or construction employment, they should be included to "control" for their effects on the dependent variable and thereby allow us to isolate the *independent effects* of the variables of interest, such as price and income.

In practice, the set of included explanatory variables is usually limited for three reasons. First, measures of variables may not be available at reasonable cost. For example, the demand for waste disposal may depend on attitudes toward recycling that we cannot measure without a costly specialized survey. Second, some variables may have relatively small effects. For example, temperature may have only a small effect on the demand for a good. Third, a variable may be excluded because it is too highly correlated with other explanatory variables—the problem of *multicollinearity,* which we discuss in Appendix 12A.

The seriousness of excluding a theoretically important variable depends on two factors. First, it depends on the degree to which the excluded variable is correlated with an included variable of interest—one whose coefficient we require for predicting policy effects.[17] The higher the correlation, the greater the bias in the estimated coefficient of the included variable.[18] Bias results because the estimated coefficient would incorporate part of the effect of the excluded variable with which it is correlated. Second, it depends on the true coefficient of the excluded variable if it were included. If this is very small, then the bias from excluding it is likely to be small.

After identifying the theoretically important and practically available variables, the next task is to specify the functional form of the model. As previously discussed, linear and constant elasticity forms are the most commonly used. Sometimes we have theoretical reasons for choosing between them; other times we simply see which fits the observed data better.

Assuming the model represented by equation (12.7) has a linear functional form gives the following model:

$$q = \alpha_0 + \alpha_1 p + \alpha_2 I + \alpha_3 T + \epsilon \tag{12.8}$$

where ϵ denotes an error term. This model can be estimated by *ordinary least squares* (OLS), assuming no simultaneity (i.e. identification) problem, which we discuss later.

A linear model may contain nonlinear functions of the explanatory variables. For example, by adding the square of temperature as an explanatory variable along with temperature itself, we allow for a nonlinear relationship between the quantity demanded and temperature. We can also allow for the possibility of different demand curves for different subgroups in our sample by introducing interaction terms. For example, if we have individual-level data and we suspect that men have a steeper demand curve than women, we could include a new variable that is the product of price and the dummy variable (or indicator variable) for gender (eg., "0" for men and "1" for women). We would then interpret the coefficient of price as the slope of the demand curve for men, and the sum of the coefficient of the price variable and the coefficient of the price-gender interaction variable as the slope of the demand curve for women. The general point is that we can have quite complicated functional forms within the basic linear specification that can be estimated by OLS.

Assuming the model represented by equation (12.7) has a constant elasticity functional form gives the following model:

$$q = \beta_0 p^{\beta_1} I^{\beta_2} T^{\beta_3} e^{\epsilon} \tag{12.9}$$

where the βs are parameters to be estimated, e is the base of the natural logarithm, and ϵ is the unobserved random error. Taking the natural logarithm of both sides of this equation gives:

$$\ln q = \ln \beta_0 + \beta_1 \ln p + \beta_2 \ln I + \beta_3 \ln T + \epsilon \tag{12.10}$$

This linear model can also be estimated by OLS with $\ln q$ as the dependent variable and $\ln p$, $\ln I$, and $\ln T$ as explanatory variables. The parameters, the βs, can be interpreted in the standard way, noting that the intercept is an estimate of $\ln \beta_0$ rather than β_0. The coefficient of the variable $\ln p$ is the price elasticity of demand, and the coefficient of the variable $\ln I$ is the income elasticity of demand.

Types of Data

Data availability is usually the limiting factor in estimating demand schedules. Researchers sometimes have sufficient resources to assemble their own data. More often, however, resource limitations force researchers to rely on *convenience samples,* that is, data that happen to be available at acceptable cost. These include previously published data, data collected by researchers for other purposes, and samples of administrative records or program clients. Nevertheless, it is worthwhile briefly reviewing the major considerations in the choice of data and their implications for demand function estimation.

Level of Aggregation   The first major consideration is the level of aggregation. Individual-level data measure the behavior of persons, families, households, or other consuming units. Aggregate-level data measure the combined (aggregate) behavior of groups of consumers, usually organized by geographic jurisdictions or demographic characteristics.

Consumer theory is based on models of individual utility maximization. Individual-level data are generally preferable because they provide a close congruence between theory and data. Furthermore, theoretically important variables, such as income, can often be measured directly with individual-level data. In contrast, when using aggregate-level data, a mean or median typically serves as the measure of income.

In using aggregate data, there is a risk of making serious errors about the effects of policy-relevant variables on demand. For example, suppose that we use individual-level data from different states to estimate the price elasticity of demand for each state.

Further suppose, as expected, each of these price elasticity estimates is negative. Now suppose that another less-fortunate researcher has only aggregate-level data that consist of one observation for each state (such as the average price and average quantity demanded in each state). He might hope that his estimated price elasticity is approximately a weighted average of the price elasticities of demand for each state and that his estimates of the effects of price changes are reasonably accurate. It is possible, however, that his estimated price elasticity is very different from the price elasticities that we estimate for each state. In fact, depending on the aggregate-level price and quantity observations, it could have the wrong sign.[19]

In practice, however, individual-level data are often not available. For example, in estimating the "demand" for criminal acts, an important theoretical variable is the "price," which depends on the perceived probability of arrest. We cannot directly observe the probability of arrest perceived by an individual, but we can assume that it is related to the objective (group) probability, which can be estimated as the fraction of crimes that result in arrest within a region or among a group of individuals.

Cross-Sectional Data versus Time Series Data   The second major consideration in selecting data concerns the choice between cross-sectional data and time series data. A cross section involves observations on a number of comparable units at the same point in time, whereas a time series involves making repeated observations on the same unit at several points in time. For example, if we wished to determine the price elasticity of demand for wine, we might take advantage of different excise tax rates across different states. Using observations for each of the 50 states for a particular year, we would regress per capita consumption of wine on after-tax retail prices and other explanatory variables, such as average state levels of income and education. Alternatively, if the real price of wine has varied over time, we might estimate a price elasticity by regressing national per capita consumption in each year on the real price of wine in each year and other variables, such as real per capita income in each year. Cross-sectional and time series data are prone to different types of econometric problems and yield coefficient estimates that have somewhat different interpretations.

Cross-sectional data generally provide estimates of long-run elasticities, whereas time series data usually provide estimates of short-run elasticities. In estimating elasticities from cross sections, we usually assume that the variations in demands across units reflect long-run adjustments to previous price changes. Thus, we obtain estimates of long-run elasticities. Only if we make our observations shortly after a major price change would we interpret the elasticity obtained from a cross-section as a short-run elasticity. In estimating elasticities from time series data, we observe responses to price changes occurring as frequently as the time unit of the observations. Thus, annual data provide estimates of annual elasticities, and monthly data provide estimates of monthly elasticities. For most goods, monthly elasticities would be interpreted as short run. Annual elasticities, however, may be either short run or long run, depending on the extent to which full adjustment to price changes requires changes in capital goods, location, and other factors that consumers alter gradually.

We would expect short-run price elasticities to be smaller in absolute value than long-run price elasticities because, by definition, there is less time for consumers to adjust to price changes. Indeed, based on a review of 120 empirical studies, Molly Espy found an average short-run price elasticity of demand for gasoline of –0.26 and an average long-run price elasticity of −0.58, and an average short-run income elasticity of 0.47 and an average long-run income elasticity of 0.88.[20] P. B. Goodwin reviewed 120 empirical studies and reported average elasticities of the demand for automobile "traffic" with respect to motor fuel prices were −0.16 in the short run and −0.33 in the long run.[21]

Cross-section and time series data tend to suffer different econometric problems. Cross sections, especially when they consist of units of different sizes, often have error terms with different variances—the *heteroscedasticity* problem. For example, the variance in the number of accidental deaths from fire is likely to be larger in larger cities, such as New York City, than in smaller cities, such as Utica, New York. If the variances of the error terms are unequal, then the OLS estimates of the coefficients are unbiased but their calculated standard errors are smaller than the true standard errors. That is, the reported precision of OLS estimates would be overly optimistic. If the relative sizes of the variances of the error terms were known, then estimating the model by *generalized least squares* (GLS) would give more precise estimates of the coefficients. Discussions of tests for detecting heteroscedasticity and for appropriate estimation procedures can be found in most econometrics texts.

Time series data also suffer from a common problem with the error term. Remember that the effects of excluded explanatory variables are incorporated into the error term. If an excluded variable tends to change gradually over time, then it may produce correlation between successive error terms. This is one example of the more general problem of *autocorrelation,* which often exists in one form or another in time series data. It has similar effects to heteroscedasticity: OLS coefficient estimates, though unbiased, are not as precise as reported. More precise estimates can be obtained by using GLS if the pattern of the autocorrelation is known. The most widely used test for autocorrelation is the Durbin-Watson statistic, which should always be a component of time series analysis. Again, discussions of methods for detecting autocorrelation and correcting for it can be found in econometrics texts.

It is also possible to pool cross-sectional and time series data, for example, by using data from each state for each of a number of years. Though modeling with pooled time series and cross-sectional data can be quite complex and cannot be discussed here, two points are worth noting. First, pooled data provide a rich source of information. Second, pooled data are vulnerable to the econometric problems encountered with both cross-sectional and time series data.

Identification

In a perfectly competitive market, price and quantity result from the simultaneous interaction of supply and demand. Changes in price and quantity can result from shifts in the supply curve, shifts in the demand curve, or both. In the absence of variables that affect only one side of the market, it may not be possible to estimate separately the supply and demand curves. Indeed, if quantity supplied and quantity demanded depended only on price, then the equation for both the demand curve and the supply curve would look identical. Determining whether we are estimating a demand curve or a supply curve is one example of the problem of *identification.* It occurs in multiple equation models in which some variables, such as price and quantity, are determined simultaneously. Such variables are called *endogenous variables.* In contrast, variables that are fixed or are determined outside of the model are called *exogenous variables.*

In order to identify a demand curve we need to have a variable that affects supply but not demand. Consider a competitive and unregulated market for wheat. If rainfall affects the supply of wheat but not the demand for wheat, then including rainfall in the supply equation but not in the demand equation identifies the demand equation. The reason is that changes in rainfall result in systematic shifts in supply but not demand, which will trace out the demand curve. Similarly, if income affects demand but not supply, then including income in the demand equation but not in the supply equation allows us to examine systematic shifts in the demand curve, which will trace out the supply curve. In general, a two-equation model will be identified if there is one exogenous variable that belongs in the first equation but not in the second equation, and another exogenous variable that belongs in the second equation but not in the first equation. By belong, we mean that it has a nonzero coefficient; by not belong, we mean that it has a zero coefficient. The zero coefficient conditions are most important. One cannot identify a model by excluding an exogenous variable from an equation that theoretically belongs in that equation.

Identification of demand curves tends to be less of a problem in the markets typically of interest to cost-benefit analysts than in markets generally. One reason is that CBA often deals with markets that are subject to exogenous government interventions. For example, the demand for cigarettes is probably easily identified in cross-sectional analysis because differences in state excise taxes shift the supply curve by a different amount in each state.

Another reason is that the identification problem does not arise in markets where the price is set exogenously. In some markets of interest to cost-benefit analysts, the government either provides the product or service, as is often the case with municipal waste disposal, or regulates the prices charged, as is the case with electricity. When government supplies a good or effectively sets price, there is no supply curve—price is exogenous and we avoid the identification problem.

Confidence Intervals

The standard errors of the estimated coefficients of a model can be used to construct confidence intervals for the coefficients. A 95 percent confidence interval is commonly interpreted as there being a 95 percent chance that the true value of the coefficient lies within the interval. Strictly speaking, this is an incorrect interpretation. The correct interpretation is that if we were to repeat our estimation procedure many times, with a new data sample for each repetition, the estimated confidence intervals would contain the true value of the coefficient in about 95 percent of the repetitions. Nevertheless, confidence intervals provide some guidance for sensitivity analysis. Most analysts would consider it reasonable to treat the ends of a 95 percent confidence interval as best and worst cases.

Prediction versus Hypothesis Testing

As a final topic on estimating demand functions, it is important to keep in mind the distinction between hypothesis testing and estimation. Social scientists are typically interested in testing hypotheses about one or more coefficients in a regression model. If the estimated coefficients are not statistically significantly different from zero, then social scientists do not reject the null hypothesis that the variables have no effect on the dependent variable. In other words, there is not a statistically convincing case that the variables have any effect.

As cost-benefit analysts, however, we have to make a prediction. For such purposes we should use the estimated value of the coefficient, even if it is not statistically significant from zero at conventional levels. Although we may not be very confident that the true value of the coefficient is not zero, the estimated coefficient may be our best estimate of the true value. If so, it will give the best predictions. Sensitivity analysis should reflect the imprecision of our estimate. If we were to use only the statistically significant coefficients from an estimated model, we would bias our prediction. Eliminating statistically insignificant variables and reestimating the model may or may not be appropriate, depending on the theoretical strength of their inclusion in the original model.

CONCLUSION

Estimating the net social benefits of a policy requires estimates of the change in social surplus. Changes in social surplus require knowledge of the appropriate market demand and supply curves. This chapter concerns estimation of these curves, focusing on demand curves.

Sometimes, project revenues can be used as a measure of (gross) benefits. This has relatively limited requirements: It requires the existence of a market for the primary outcome of the project and knowledge of expenditures in this market. However, project revenues are often an inappropriate measure of benefits and we may need to estimate consumer surplus. In these situations, we need to estimate the relevant market demand curve. Direct estimation of the demand curve is possible if we know at least one point on the demand curve, its functional form, and either its slope or the price elasticity of demand. In many practical situations we do not know the slope or the price elasticity of demand. We may be able to infer such information from a few observations. Preferably, there may be many observations and the analyst can use econometric techniques to estimate the demand curve. It is important to consider the advantages and potential limitations of these different estimation methods.

APPENDIX 12A

An Introduction to Multiple Regression Analysis

Linear regression provides a manageable way to examine statistically the effects of one or more explanatory variables on a variable of interest—the dependent variable.[1] Its use requires us to assume that the effects of the various explanatory variables on the dependent variable are additive. That is, the marginal effect of a unit change in any one of the explanatory variables on the dependent variable remains the same no matter what the values of the other explanatory variables are. We can express a linear regression model in mathematical form:

$$y = \beta_0 + \beta_1 x_1 + \beta_2 x_2 + \ldots + \beta_k x_k + \epsilon$$

where y is the dependent variable, $x_1, x_2, \ldots, x_k$ are k explanatory (or independent) variables, β_0, $\beta_1, \beta_2 \ldots, \beta_k$ are parameters (coefficients) to be estimated, and ϵ is an error term that incorporates the cumulative effect on y of all the factors not explicitly included in the model. The basic model assumes that the explanatory variables are nonrandom and are measured without error.

The intercept parameter, β_0, also called the *constant,* is the expected value of y if all of the explanatory variables equal zero. The other parameters, $\beta_1, \beta_2 \ldots, \beta_k$, which are called *slope* parameters, measure the marginal impact of an explanatory variable on the dependent variable. If, for instance, we were to increase x_1 by one unit while holding the values of the other explanatory variables constant, then y would change by an amount β_1.

Imagine that we set the values of all the explanatory variables except x_1 equal to zero. We could then plot y against x_1 in a two-dimensional graph. The equation $y = \beta_0 + \beta_1 x_1$ would represent the true regression line. The slope of this line is β_1; it measures the magnitude of the change in y that will result from a one-unit change in x_1,

other things being equal. The actual observations will not lie exactly on the line. The vertical deviation between an observed point and the line will equal the random error, represented in our model by ϵ. If the values of ϵ are small in absolute value, then the true regression line fits the data well in the sense that the actual observations are close to it.

Estimating the Parameters of the Model

The most commonly used procedure for fitting a line to the data is the method of ordinary least squares (OLS). When we have only one explanatory variable so we can plot our data on a two-dimensional graph, the OLS procedure picks the line for which the sum of squared vertical deviations from the estimated line to the observed data is smallest.

Suppose we denote the OLS estimates of the $k + 1$ parameters by "hats": $\hat{\beta}_0, \hat{\beta}_1, \ldots, \hat{\beta}_k$. For the ith observation $(y_i, x_{i1}, x_{i2}, \ldots, x_{ik})$, the predicted value of the dependent variable is:

$$\hat{y}_i = \hat{\beta}_0 + \hat{\beta}_1 x_{i1} + \hat{\beta}_2 x_{i2} + \ldots + \hat{\beta}_k x_{ik}$$
$$i = 1, \ldots, n$$

and the ith *prediction error* or *residual* is:

$$\hat{\epsilon}_i = y_i - \hat{y}_i \qquad i = 1, \ldots, n$$

Thus, the residual is the observed value of the dependent variable minus the value we would predict for the dependent variable based on our estimated parameters and the values of our explanatory variables. OLS selects the parameter estimates to minimize the sum of squares of these residuals.[2]

The square of the correlation between the actual and predicted values of the dependent variable, R^2, is commonly used as a measure of the goodness-of-fit of a regression. The R^2, which ranges between 0 and 1, measures the percentage of variation in the dependent variable that is explained by the estimated model. It can be used to help select between alternative model specifications when theory is ambiguous, or to test alternative theories.

Multicollinearity

As long as the number of observations in our sample exceeds the number of coefficients that we want to estimate, computer regression software packages will usually enable us to obtain the OLS estimates. However, when one explanatory variable can be written as a linear combination of the others, we have a case of *perfect multicollinearity*. A less severe but more common form of the problem occurs when the explanatory variables in the sample are highly correlated. This condition is called *multicollinearity*. If two or more variables are highly correlated, OLS has difficulty identifying the independent effect of each explanatory variable on the dependent variable. As a result, these parameter estimates are not very reliable or, in the extreme case, they cannot be estimated. When two explanatory variables are highly correlated, the sum of their estimated coefficients will be closer to the sum of their true coefficients than will either individual coefficient estimate be to its true value. Often, researchers respond to a multicollinarity problem by excluding one or more explanatory variables, though this may lead to biased estimates of some parameters. Two alternative ways to deal with multicollinearity problems include using ridge regression or combining collinear variables into indices using principal components analysis.[3]

Properties of OLS Estimators

The OLS estimator will generally have a number of very desirable properties. (Note: An *estimator* is the formula we use to calculate a particular parameter from the data. The resultant specific value is an estimate.) If all of the explanatory variables are uncorrelated with the error term, ϵ, and if the expected value of the error term is zero, then the OLS estimators will be *unbiased*. To understand what it means for an estimator to be unbiased, we must keep in mind that a particular estimate depends on the errors in the actual sample of data. If we were to select a new sample, then we would realize different errors and, hence, different coefficient estimates. When an estimator is unbiased, the average of our estimates across different samples will be very close to the true coefficient value. For example, if the price of gasoline had no true effect on the quantity of gasoline demanded, then we would almost certainly estimate its coefficient to be positive or negative rather than exactly zero. Repeating OLS on a large number of samples and averaging our estimates of the coefficient of gasoline price, however, would generally yield a result very close to zero. Indeed, by adding more and more samples, we could get the average as close to zero as we wanted.

The OLS estimator is also consistent, which means that its variance approaches zero as we increase the sample size.[4] Consequently, as the sample size increases, we become more confident about the accuracy of our estimates—the confidence intervals become narrower.

A problem arises, however, if an important variable is excluded from the estimation and that variable is correlated with an included variable. Suppose, for example, that the weather (temperature) affects the quantity demanded, that temperature is also correlated with gasoline price, but that temperature is excluded from the model. Now, the coefficient of gasoline price will reflect both the effect of gasoline price on quantity demanded and the indirect effect of temperature for which it serves as a proxy. Other things being equal, the stronger the true effect of temperature on quantity demanded, and the higher the absolute value of the correlation between gasoline price and temperature, the greater will be the bias in the coefficient of gasoline price. This problem cannot be solved by increasing the sample size.

Statistical Significance and Hypothesis Testing

It is often important to determine whether an estimate deviates enough from zero for us to conclude that the true value of the parameter is not zero. If we make the reasonable assumption that the error term for each observation can be treated as a draw from a normal distribution with constant variance, σ^2, then we can show that the OLS estimators will be distributed according to the normal distribution.[5] Specifically, we can interpret the particular numerical estimate of a coefficient, $\hat{\beta}$, as a draw from a random variable having a normal distribution centered around the true value of the coefficient, β, with variance, $\sigma_{\hat{\beta}}^2$, which depends on σ^2. (The OLS estimator is the random variable; the actual estimate based on the data is a particular realization of that random variable.) Because we want to know how likely it is that we would observe a coefficient estimate as large as we did if the true value of the coefficient were zero, we now suppose that the true value of the coefficient is zero (the null hypothesis) so that the distribution of our estimator is centered around zero. We then standardize our distribution to have a variance of one by dividing our coefficient estimate by its *estimated standard deviation*. The resultant statistic, called a *t* statistic, or *t* ratio, has a *Student's* t *distribution,* or *t* distribution.[6] The *statistical significance* of our coefficient estimate can be determined by comparing the *t* statistic to the critical values in a table of the *t* distribution, which can found in the appendix of almost any statistics text. For example, we might decide that we will reject the null hypothesis that the true value of the coefficient is zero if there is less than a 5 percent probability of observing a *t* ratio (in absolute value) as large as we did if the null hypothesis is true.[7] If the sample size is large we would reject this null hypothesis if the *t* statistic were larger in absolute value than 1.96.

The *t* distribution is tabulated by degrees of freedom. The OLS estimators have degrees of freedom equal to the total number of observations, denoted by *n,* minus the number of coefficients being estimated, $k + 1$. As the degrees of freedom increase, the Student's *t* distribution looks more like a standardized normal distribution.

Returning to our gasoline example, suppose that the analyst wants to test whether gasoline price has a statistically significant effect on gasoline demand at the 5 percent level of significance. She may specify a one-tailed alternative hypothesis test or a two-tailed alternative hypothesis test. For example, she may test the null hypothesis that the true coefficient value is greater than or equal to zero (the one-tailed alternative is that it is less than zero), which means that the *critical region* consists of the entire 5 percent in the negative tail. Alternatively, she may test the null hypothesis that the true coefficient value is equal to zero (the two-tailed alternative is that it is less than *or* greater than zero), which means that the critical region consists of the 2.5 percent in the negative tail and the 2.5 percent in the positive tail. Now suppose that the *t* statistic for the coefficient of gasoline price equals -1.84. Further suppose that the sample size was 122, and there was only one explanatory variable, so that only two parameters were estimated (the intercept and slope) and there were 120 degrees of freedom. The absolute values of the critical values of the *t* distribution with 120 degrees of freedom are 1.658 for the one-sided alternative and 1.98 for the two-sided alternative. Thus, at the 5 percent level of significance, the analyst would reject the null hypothesis if she had specified a one-sided alternative, but she would accept the null hypothesis if she had specified a two-sided alternative.

Most regression software saves us the trouble of looking up critical values in tables by directly calculating the probability under the null hypothesis of observing a *t* statistic as large as that estimated, assuming we want to test the null hypothesis that the true parameter equals zero against a two-sided alternative. To do this classical hypothesis test on the coefficient, we simply see if the reported probability is less than the maximum probability of falsely rejecting the null hypothesis that we are willing to accept. If it is smaller, then we reject the null hypothesis.

EXERCISES FOR CHAPTER 12

1. Consider the example presented in Figure 12-3. Imagine that the current price of waste disposal is $0.025/lb and the average waste disposal is 2.40 lb/p/d. As noted in the diagram, when the price was previously $0.01/lb, the average waste disposal was 2.52 lb/p/d. Assume that the marginal social cost of waste disposal is $0.06/lb, that marginal social costs are constant with respect to quantity, and that the town has a population of 100,000.

    a. Fitting a linear demand curve to the two observed points, calculate the annual net benefits of raising the price of waste disposal to $0.05/lb.

    b. Fitting a constant elasticity demand curve to the observed points, calculate the annual net benefits of raising the price of waste disposal to $0.05/lb.

2. (Regression software required.) An analyst was asked to predict the gross social benefits of building a public swimming pool in Dryville, which has a population of 70,230 people and a median household income of $31,500. The analyst identified 24 towns in the region that already had public swimming pools. He conducted a telephone interview with the recreation department in each town to find out what fee it charged per visit (Fee) and how many visits it had during the most recent summer season (Visits). In addition, he was able to find each town's population (Pop) and median household income (Income) in the most recent census. His data are as follows:

	Visits	Fee	Income	Pop
1	168,590	0	20,600	36,879
2	179,599	0	33,400	64,520
3	198,595	0	39,700	104,123
4	206,662	0	32,600	103,073
5	170,259	0	24,900	58,386
6	209,995	0.25	38,000	116,592
7	172,018	0.25	26,700	49,945
8	190,802	0.25	20,800	79,789
9	197,019	0.25	26,300	98,234
10	186,515	0.50	35,600	71,762
11	152,679	0.50	38,900	40,178
12	137,423	0.50	21,700	22,928
13	158,056	0.50	37,900	39,031
14	157,424	0.50	35,100	44,685
15	179,490	0.50	35,700	67,882
16	164,657	0.75	22,900	69,625
17	184,428	0.75	38,600	98,408
18	183,822	0.75	20,500	93,429
19	174,510	1.00	39,300	98,077
20	187,820	1.00	25,800	104,068
21	196,318	1.25	23,800	117,940
22	166,694	1.50	34,000	59,757
23	161,716	1.50	29,600	88,305
24	167,505	2.00	33,800	84,102

    a. Show how the analyst could use these data to predict the gross benefits of opening a public swimming pool in Dryville and allowing free admission.

    b. Predict gross benefits if admission is set at $1.00 and Dryville has marginal excess tax burden of 0.25. In answering this question, assume that the fees are used to reduce taxes that would otherwise have to be collected from the citizens of Dryville to pay for expenses incurred in operating the pool.

NOTES

1. More accurately, each household incurs a marginal private cost (MPC) of refuse disposal that is only $1/n$ of the marginal social costs (MSC); that is, $MPC = MSC/n$, where n is the number of households. The MPC approaches zero for large n.

2. Robin R. Jenkins, *The Economics of Solid Waste Reduction: The Impact of User Fees* (Brookfield, VT: Edward Elgar Publishing Company, 1993).

3. Formally, $\epsilon_d = \partial \ln q / \partial \ln p = (\partial q / \partial p)(p/q)$, where $\partial q / \partial p$ is the partial derivative of the quantity demanded with respect to price. For a linear demand curve, $\epsilon_d = (\partial q / \partial p)(p/q) = \alpha_1 p/q$.

4. Jenkins, *The Economics of Solid Waste Reduction: The Impact of User Fees*, pp. 88–90, 101.

5. Some economists call this functional form a *log-linear demand curve;* others call it a *log-log demand curve* or a *double-log* demand curve. In order to minimize potential confusion, we will not to use any of these terms, but will refer to the curve as linear in logarithms.

6. Because β_1 is the slope of the linear in logarithms demand curve, $\beta_1 = \partial \ln q / \partial \ln p$. By definition, the price elasticity of demand $\epsilon_d = \partial \ln q / \partial \ln p$. Consequently, $\epsilon_d = \beta_1$.

7. The slope is given by:

$$\partial q / \partial p = \beta_1 \beta_0 p^{\beta_1 - 1} = \beta_1 \beta_0 p^{\beta_1} p = \beta_1 q/p.$$

8. Note that our estimate of $\beta_0 = 1.44$ will generally differ from the original estimate of β_0 obtained by the researchers from whom we took our price elasticity estimate. This difference arises because we force the demand curve to pass through point a, our known data point, whereas the original, estimated equation probably will not pass through point a.

9. The demand curve is $q = 1.44\, p^{-0.15}$. If $p = 0.05$, then $q = 1.44(.05)^{-0.15} = 2.1$.

10. An alternate, slightly easier way to predict the reduction in the quantity of waste disposal uses the estimated elasticity to approximate the slope of the demand curve. At point a the slope of the demand curve is $(-0.15)(2.25)/(0.05) = -6.75$.

Therefore, a change in price from \$0.05/lb to \$0.08/lb would change the quantity of waste by approximately:

$$\Delta q = -6.75(0.05 - 0.08) = -0.20 \text{ lb/p/d}$$

which would lead us to predict that waste disposal would fall to 2.05 lb/p/d due to the price increase (point e in Figure 12-2).

The discrepancy in the predicted levels of waste disposal at the higher price results because of the difference between *point elasticities* and *arc elasticities*. The point elasticity is the exact elasticity at a particular point, while the arc elasticity is an approximate elasticity for a finite change. For small changes in price, the two methods give approximately the same reduction. But for large price changes, such as the 60 percent price change in this example, the two methods can differ substantially. If we are fairly confident in the estimated demand curve, then we should recover its formula and use the first method to predict changes in quantities. The second method is a linear approximation to the first method. The more curvature in the demand curve, the worse the approximation becomes.

11. The area is calculated by integrating the inverse demand curve from q_0 and q_1, that is, as $\int p\, dq = \int (q/\beta_0)^{1/\beta_1} dq$ with q_0 and q_1 as the limits of integration.

12. An easier way to estimate the change in consumer surplus (area *abfg*) is to integrate the demand curve between p_0 and p_1, that is, $\Delta CS = \int q\, dp = \int \beta_0 p^{\beta_1} dp$ with p_0 and p_1 as the limits of integration. For a constant elasticity demand curve, it can be shown that $\Delta CS = (p_1 q_1 - p_0 q_0)/(1 + \beta_1)$. Therefore, in this example $\Delta CS = (.08 \times 2.1 - .05 \times 2.25)/(1 - .15) = \$.0653$, which differs slightly from the number in the text due to rounding errors.

13. Solve for β_0 and β_1 as follows: $\beta_1 = \ln(q_0/q_1)/\ln(p_0/p_1) = -0.053$, and $\beta_0 = q_0/(p_0^{\beta_1}) = 1.97$.

14. For an excellent treatment of the econometric issues raised in this section, see William H. Greene,

Econometric Analysis, 5th ed. (New York: Macmillan, 2003).

15. Thus far, this chapter has focused on demand curves that relate quantity demanded to price. Other variables also affect demand. A demand function relates the quantity demanded to price and other variables. Because a demand function is more general than a demand curve, this section focuses on demand functions. Sometimes we use the term *demand schedule* to refer to demand curves or demand functions.

16. They estimated an elasticity of disposal demand with respect to tipping fees of −0.11 for communities in the region around Portland, Oregon, over a seven-year period; see James G. Strathman, Anthony M. Rufolo, and Gerard C.S. Mildner, "The Demand for Solid Waste Disposal," *Land Economics* 71(1) 1995, 57–64.

17. If the estimated regression equation contains more than one explanatory variable, then the bias in the coefficient of a particular variable depends on the *partial correlation* between that variable and the omitted variable, controlling for all other variables in the regression.

18. If an excluded variable is not correlated with an included variable, then excluding it will not bias the estimated coefficient of the included variable. However, the overall fit of the model, measured by its R^2, will be poorer, and the precision of the estimated coefficients will be lower.

19. See, for example, Henri Theil, *Principles of Econometrics* (New York: Wiley, 1971), 556–557.

20. Molly Espy, "Gasoline Demand Revisited: An International Meta-Analysis of Elasticities," *Energy Economics* 20(3) 1998, 273–295.

21. P. B. Goodwin, "A Review of New Demand Elasticities with Special Reference to Short and Long Run Effects of Price Changes," *Journal of Transport Economics and Policy* 26(2) 1992, 155–170 at pp. 158–159. See also Tae Moon Oum, W. G. Waters II, and Jong-Say Yong, "Concepts of Price Elasticities of Transport Demand and Recent Empirical Estimates," *Journal of Transport Economics and Policy* 26(2) 1992, 139–154.

APPENDIX NOTES

1. For clear introductions to regression analysis, see Eric A. Hanushek and John E. Jackson, *Statistical Methods for the Social Sciences* (New York: Academic Press, 1977); and Christopher H. Achen, *Interpreting and Using Regression* (Beverly Hills, CA: Sage Publications, 1982).

2. Formally, OLS minimizes $\sum_{i=1}^{n} \hat{\epsilon}_i^2$.

3. See Greene, *Econometric Analysis.* For an application of ridge regression, which presents both OLS and ridge regression estimates, see A. E. Boardman, S. Miller, and A. P. Schinnar, "Efficient Employment of Cohorts of Labor in the U.S. Economy: An Illustration of a Method," *Socio-Economic Planning Sciences* 13(6) 1979, 297–302.

4. The OLS estimators are also *efficient.* Here, efficiency means that among all estimators whose formulas are linear in the dependent variable,

the OLS estimator of a coefficient has the smallest variance. It therefore has the greatest "power" for rejecting the null hypothesis that a coefficient is zero.

5. The *central limit theorem* tells us that the distribution of the sum of independent random variables approaches the normal distribution as the number in the sum becomes large. The theorem applies for almost any starting distributions with finite variances. If we think of the error term as the sum of all the many factors excluded from our model and, furthermore, we believe that these excluded factors are not systematically related to one another or to the included variables, then the central limit theorem suggests that the distribution of the error terms will be at least approximately normal.

6. Student is the pseudonym of William Gosset, the quality control engineer at the Guiness Brewery in Dublin who originally derived the *t* distribution.

7. The probability we choose puts an upward bound on the probability of falsely rejecting the null hypothesis. Falsely rejecting the null hypothesis is referred to as Type I error. Failing to reject the null hypothesis when in fact the alternative hypothesis is true is referred to as Type II error. We usually set the probability of Type I error at some low level, such as 5 percent. Holding sample size constant, the lower we set the probability of a Type I error, the greater the probability of a Type II error.

CHAPTER 13

Valuing Impacts From Observed Behavior: Indirect Market Methods

Generally, estimation of changes in social surplus requires knowledge of entire demand and supply schedules. The previous chapter discusses direct estimation of demand and supply curves, focusing on the demand curve for the purpose of measuring consumer surplus. It assumes that there is a market demand curve for the good in question, such as garbage collection or gasoline, and we can observe some points along this demand curve. In many applications of CBA, however, the markets for certain "goods," such as human life or pollution, do not exist or are imperfect for reasons discussed in Chapter 3. In these situations it may be impossible or inappropriate to estimate the market demand (or supply) curve directly. In the past, such goods were treated as "intangible," and their impacts were excluded or analysts were restricted to qualitative CBA or multi-goal analysis. However, over the past 30 years, economists have devised methods to value these impacts, thus enabling analysts to conduct CBA.

In practice, the change in social surplus can often be estimated from knowledge of the impact of a policy (e.g., number of affected persons) and the marginal social benefit or the marginal social cost of one more unit of the affected good or service. In a perfect market, the market price equals both the marginal social cost and the marginal social benefit of an additional unit of a good or service. When a market does not exist or market failure leads to a divergence between market price and marginal social cost, analysts try to obtain estimates of what the market price would be if the relevant good were traded in a market where the demand curve measured marginal social benefits and the supply curve measured marginal social costs. As we discuss in Chapter 4, such an estimate is called a *shadow price.*

When a market for the good of interest does not exist, one of two major methods of estimating shadow prices can be used.[1] This chapter recognizes that although there may not be a market for the good or service of interest, its value (shadow price) may be reflected indirectly in markets for one or more other related goods. Through statistical analysis of these other markets, we can estimate the value of the nonmarketed good. The second way to estimate a shadow price is to use contingent valuation (survey) methods, which are discussed in the following chapter.

The indirect market methods discussed in this chapter are based on *observed behavior,* that is, *revealed preference.* Basing valuations on observed behavior is important because it means that people reveal their preferences without having to be asked. As we discuss in the following chapter, contingent valuation (survey) methods rely on stated preferences and are prone to a number of biases.

The chapter begins with a discussion of using information from private-sector markets to value publicly provided goods (the market analogy method). It then discusses estimation of shadow prices based on trade-offs, for example, the trade-off between time and wages to value leisure time or the trade-off between salaries and the risk of having a fatal accident to value a statistical life. Next, it discusses the intermediate good method, followed by the asset valuation method. All of these methods are subject to potential biases, including the omitted variables problem and self-selection bias. After discussing these problems, we turn to the hedonic price method, which attempts to overcome them. We then discuss the travel cost method and, finally, the defensive expenditures method. Some of these methods involve estimation of the whole demand or supply curve, whereas others provide only an estimate of the shadow price. This chapter focuses on methods of estimation. Chapter 15 presents and discusses specific estimates of the shadow prices.

MARKET ANALOGY METHOD

Governments supply many goods that are also provided by the private sector. For example, housing, campsites, university education, home care, and adoption services are often provided by both the public and private sectors. The government usually provides these services free or at significantly below market prices. However, it may be possible to estimate the demand curve for a government-provided good by using data on an analogous good that is produced by the private sector and sold in a well-functioning market.

In some situations, the private market may not be legal. For example, some countries have no legal private-sector adoption services. Nevertheless, analysts may turn to the *black market* to obtain an estimate of the value of such services.

Using the Market Price of or Expenditures on an Analogous Good

Consider, for example, a local government project that provides housing for 50 families. The local government may charge a nominal rent of $200 per month so that government revenue equals $10,000 per month. Clearly, using this expenditure would underestimate (gross) benefits. All families would be willing to pay $200 per month or more and, therefore, the benefits of this project would be larger than $10,000 per month.

Suppose that comparable units in the private sector charge rent of $500 per month. If we took this market price as the shadow price for the publicly provided units, then the estimated total monthly benefits of publicly provided housing would be $25,000 per month. *Using the market price would be an appropriate estimate of the value of the publicly provided good if it equals the average amount that users of the publicly provided good would be willing to pay.* In the case of government allocation at a lower-than-market price, however, there is no guarantee that those who receive the good value it as highly as do purchasers in the private market. Families willing to pay the market price, or more, for comparable housing might have already found housing in the private sector. Those who occupy public units typically have lower-than-average incomes and are likely to be willing to pay less than the market price, though more than the amount charged by government (i.e., somewhere between $200 and $500 per month).

The price of comparable private housing units might underestimate the value to families if the publicly provided housing were poorly targeted. Specifically, if the units were allocated to (moderately well-off) people who, in the absence of obtaining the publicly provided housing, would have purchased similar private-sector units at market prices, then the market price would be a lower bound for their willingness-to-pay. Ironically, from the CBA perspective, in the absence of market failures, the more poorly targeted public housing units are, the higher their benefits. Such ironies have led some people to suggest that benefits that accrue to low-income persons should be given greater weight than benefits that accrue to high-income persons, as we discuss in Chapter 18.

Using Information about an Analogous Private-Sector Good to Estimate the Demand Curve for a Publicly Provided Good

Suppose a municipal government wants to measure the gross benefits of a swimming pool that it owns and operates. Currently, the municipality does not charge an admission fee and the pool receives 300,000 visitors per year, shown as point *a* in Figure 13-1. In a comparable municipality, a privately operated swimming pool charges $5 for admission

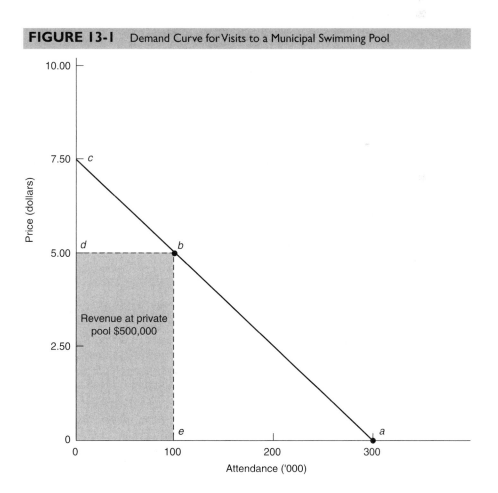

FIGURE 13-1   Demand Curve for Visits to a Municipal Swimming Pool

and receives 100,000 visitors per year (point *b*). Assuming a linear demand curve that passes through these two points, we can estimate the gross benefits of the municipal pool as ($7.5)(300,000)/2 = $1,125,000.

Using revenues at the private pool ($500,000) would underestimate the benefits of the public pool because it omits consumer surplus. It excludes the consumer surplus of those willing to pay more than the $5, the area of triangle *cbd*, as well as the consumer surplus of those willing to pay something less than $5, but more than $0, the area of triangle *bae*.

How reasonable is it to interpret the observed price and quantity at the private pool as a point on the demand curve for the municipal pool? The answer depends on the similarity of the two facilities and their markets. The pools should be similar in terms of features such as changing room facilities, hours of business, the friendliness of the staff, and levels of crowding, and the two communities should be similar in terms of population, income, and tastes. If these assumptions do not hold, then adjustments should be made.

THE TRADE-OFF METHOD

Economists may use the opportunity cost—the value of what one gives up to get something—as a measure of its value. For example, early studies used the after-tax wage as the value of travel time saved. The basic idea is that if you reduce your travel time by an hour then you can increase your income by the after-tax wage rate and vice versa. Put another way, people make trade-offs between time and money wages, and we can use the rate at which they make this trade-off to value time. Similarly the trade-off people are willing to make between changes in fatality risk and wages can be used to measure the value of a statistical life. For example, analysts can examine the trade-off people are willing to make between cash expenditures and increased safety from air bags, smoke detectors, or other risk-reducing goods and can use this information to impute the value of a statistical life.

One can think about these methods as special cases or extensions of the market analogy method. For example, the labor market, where people sell their time for wages, is an obvious analogous market for time saved. This section first discusses the value of time saved, then the value of a statistical life saved, and ends with a discussion of the problems with simple consumer purchase and wage-risk studies.

The Value of Time Saved, Including the Value of Travel Time Saved

This section concerns the value of time saved, whether that time would have been spent traveling, in a queue waiting for provision of a government service, or in some other way. In the absence of market imperfections, the social value of an additional hour of work equals that person's wage rate. All other things being equal, when people can choose the number of hours they work and there is no unemployment, the wage rate also equals the marginal value of their time. In other words, the value of an additional hour of leisure to the person enjoying it equals the wage rate. Thus, the value of a project that saves an hour for a person who earns $20 per hour, both to society and to that person, is $20.

Setting the value of time saved equal to the wage rate is relatively easy. However, serious problems exist in using the wage rate to value time saved by government projects.

First, wages ignore benefits. As benefits are a form of compensation for work, they should be added to wages.

Second, this method assumes that people do not work while they are traveling or standing in line. In practice, people can work and drive or fly at the same time. The notebook computer and the mobile phone facilitate working while flying or driving. If people work while they are traveling or waiting in line, then an hour of such time saved is worth less than the wage rate. Of course, this does not apply to truck drivers who are obviously working while they are driving. For them, it does make sense to value their time saved at their wage rate plus benefits.

Third, we must take account of taxes. Although it is reasonable to view the value to society of an hour saved for a person who is working at the before-tax wage rate plus benefits, when deciding whether to work, individuals consider the after-tax wage rate plus benefits. Thus, the time saved of people who are not working should be valued at the after-tax wage rate plus benefits.

Fourth, people are willing to pay different amounts to save an hour doing different things. For example, the value of travel time saved may be less than the value of an hour saved waiting in line. Some people like traveling, especially through spectacular scenery, such as along the highway from Banff to Jasper. These people derive consumption benefits from traveling and are willing to pay for the experience of traveling itself. (Consider, for example, the "busman's holiday.") In contrast, many people dislike waiting in line or in traffic jams and are willing to pay a lot to avoid it. Thus, the value of time saved depends on what one is doing. Because people generally do not dislike traveling, analysts value an hour of travel time saved for recreational travelers at a fraction (about 45 percent) of the *after-tax wage rate* plus benefits. In contrast, analysts value an hour of travel time saved for people who are working, such as truck drivers, at the *before-tax wage rate* plus benefits. (Estimates of the value of time saved are discussed in Chapter 15.)

Fifth, the wage rate may not be an appropriate shadow price for time saved because it assumes working hours are flexible: It ignores structural rigidities or market and government failures in the labor market. With an upward-sloping supply curve of labor, the more hours someone works, the more highly that person values leisure. In practice, however, a person may not be able to easily adjust the number of hours worked. For example, people who suffer from several weeks of unemployment or who involuntarily work overtime are "off their labor supply curve." Other structural rigidities result in unemployment. Minimum wages and the monopoly power of unions or other factors may distort the labor market. Consequently, everyone who wants to work at the market wage may not be able to find work at that wage. Indeed, for some people, such as retirees, no wage rate can be observed.

Finally, firms may not pay their employees the marginal social value of their output. For example, firms with market power may share their profits with employees in the form of higher-than-market wages. Of course, if an industry generated negative (positive) externalities, then the wage rate would exceed (be less than) the marginal social value of an hour saved.

Because of the serious nature of these problems, valuing time saved at the wage rate is only a first approximation to its social value. Later in this chapter, we present better methods for valuing time saved.

The Value of a Statistical Life

Valuing life is a highly contentious issue. Society often spends fortunes to rescue trapped miners or to give heart transplants to specific individuals. Yet it may not spend money to make obvious gains in mine safety or to reduce the risk of heart disease. In order to make efficient allocation of resources in the health care area or to determine the benefits of projects that save lives, analysts require a monetary value of a life saved.

Forgone Earnings Method   Early efforts by economists to value life followed a similar method to the one discussed earlier concerning the value of time. Specifically, if one accepts that a person's value to society for one hour equals that person's wage, then one might reason that the value of that person to society for the rest of his or her lifetime equals the present value of his or her future earnings. One would thus conclude that the value of a life saved equals that person's discounted future earnings. This is the *forgone earnings method* of valuing a life saved.[2] It is currently used by the courts in some U.S. states and in some other countries to award compensation in cases involving death due to negligence. On average, this method generates a higher value for saving the life of people with higher incomes than for people with lower incomes. It also generates higher values for younger people than for older people and for men than for women.

The forgone earnings method provides unsatisfactory estimates of the value of a life saved for reasons similar to those discussed previously concerning the value of time saved. It assumes full employment, although the method can be adjusted to reflect expected lifetime earnings given average employment expectations. It also assumes people are paid their marginal social product, although often they are not. The lives of full-time homemakers and volunteers who are not paid for their services are unreasonably valued at zero.

A fundamental problem with the forgone earnings method is that it ignores individuals' willingness-to-pay to reduce the risk of their own deaths. This point was made clearly by Thomas Schelling, who observed "[t]here is no reason to suppose that a person's future earnings . . . bear any particular relation to what he would pay to reduce some likelihood of his own death."[3] Schelling also distinguished between the deaths of identifiable individuals and *statistical deaths*. A safety improvement to a highway, for example, does not lead to the saving of the lives of a few individuals who can be identified *ex ante* but rather to the reduction in the risk of death (or injury) to all users of the highway. *In order to value the benefit of proposed safety improvements, analysts should ascertain how much people are willing to pay for reductions in their risk of death that are of the same magnitude as the reduced risk that would result from the proposed safety improvements.* Such reasoning has led to a series of consumer purchase and labor market studies that have attempted to compute the *value of a statistical life* (VSL).

Simple Consumer Purchase Studies   Suppose airbags were not standard in new cars, but for $300, you could purchase and install an airbag at the time you purchased your new car.[4] The airbag would increase your survival rate from use of the car from p to $p + \omega$. Would you buy the airbag? This problem is represented as a decision tree in Figure 13-2. If a person is indifferent between the two alternatives,

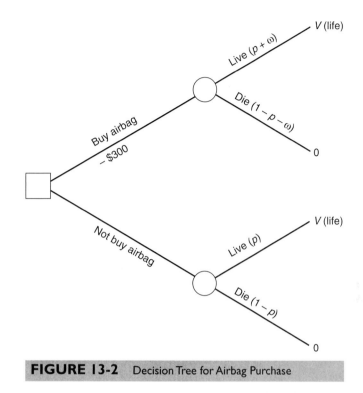

FIGURE 13-2 Decision Tree for Airbag Purchase

that is, is indifferent between spending the $300 and increasing the probability of surviving by ω (the upper-branch alternative) and not spending the $300 (the lower-branch alternative), then:

$$(p + \omega)V(\text{life}) - \$300 = pV(\text{life})$$
$$(p + \omega)V(\text{life}) - pV(\text{life}) = \$300$$
$$\omega V(\text{life}) = \$300$$
$$V(\text{life}) = \$300/\omega$$

Suppose $\omega = 1/10,000$; that is, if 10,000 people buy airbags, then one statistical life will be saved. Then, for a person who is indifferent:

$$V(\text{life}) = (\$300)/(1/10,000) = \$3 \text{ million}$$

This method has been applied not only to the purchase of airbags but also to the purchase of other safety-enhancing devices, such as smoke detectors and fire extinguishers.

Simple Labor Market Studies   Simple labor market studies examine the additional wage people require in compensation for exposing themselves to greater risk of death on the job (job fatality risk). Suppose, for example, one type of construction job has a 1/1,000 greater chance of fatal injury in a year than another type of construction job. Further suppose that the riskier job offers a salary that is

$3,500/year higher than the safer job. If workers are indifferent between these two types of job, then this implies:

$$(1/1,000)V(\text{life}) = \$3,500$$
$$V(\text{life}) = \$3.5 \text{ million}$$

In general, if $a is the amount workers are willing to accept in order to compensate for greater risk, and ω is the change in fatality risk, then the VSL is given by:

$$\text{VSL} = \frac{\$a}{\omega} \qquad\qquad\qquad \textbf{(13.1)}$$

Problems with Simple Consumer Purchase and Wage-Risk Studies

One problem with simple consumer purchase and wage-risk studies is that they assume workers have full information concerning the risks, that is, ω. For example, in addition to knowing that the chance of dying in a risky job is 1/1,000 higher than in the less risky job, workers have to know what this means. Evidence that we discuss in Chapter 14 suggests that people suffer from cognitive biases that limit their ability to make rational judgments in such situations. For example, some studies suggest that people overestimate the occurrence of low-probability "bad" events.[5] When people suffer from this cognitive bias, labor market studies overestimate the value of life. If workers underestimate the fatality risk of a job, then they will accept a lower risk premium to perform that job, and the VSL will be underestimated.

At the same time, however, people who are relatively less risk averse (more risk seeking) self-select into more risky jobs. The mean fatality risk in recent VSL studies ranges from between about 4 in 100,000 to 22 in 100,000. However, the average U.S. fatality rate for all occupations is about 4 in 100,000.[6] Consequently, risk-averse individuals may be underrepresented in wage-risk studies, which would cause such studies to underestimate the VSL.

A third problem is that researchers may not have an accurate measure of the difference in fatality risk faced by different workers or consumers, the ω. Many U.S. wage-risk studies use data from the Bureau of Labor Statistics, which are aggregated to the industry level. These data do not reflect the actual difference in risk faced by workers in different occupations within the same industry. For example, a coal miner and a secretary in a coal mining company have quite different fatality risks. Furthermore, ω may be based on currently inaccurate historical data. Suppose that in a consumer purchase study $a equals $800 and ω equals 0.0002 so that the VSL equals $4 million. Now suppose that there was one more death among 5,000 people, then ω would equal 0.0004 and the VSL would equal $2 million.

In general, people experience diminishing marginal utility for safety; that is, the value of additional amounts of safety declines as the level of safety increases. The relationship between the willingness-to-pay for increased safety and the level of safety (fatality risk) is probably convex. The willingness-to-pay for additional amounts of safety depends on both the base level of safety and the magnitude of the change in the level of safety. A validity problem arises if the level of risk in the consumer purchase or

---

EXHIBIT 13-1

Are estimates of the value of life that rely on wage premiums that workers receive for working in risky jobs systematically understated? Robert Frank and Cass Sunstein argue that they are understated by 18 to 75 percent *if* they are used to measure willingness-to-pay for government safety regulations that improve the safety of *all* workers. According to Frank and Sunstein, the reason is that workers who decide to take relatively safe jobs pay for their additional safety by bearing two costs: They lose the wage premium they would receive if they took a more dangerous job and they are lower down in the wage distribution and thus lose status. Both factors affect their willingness-to-pay for safety, although only the first is reflected in measures of the value of a statistical life that are based on wage premiums. However,

a safety regulation that is universally applied reduces risk for everyone without affecting economic position. Thus, workers would be willing to pay more for such a regulation than the amount reflected by wage premiums alone.

Thomas Kniesner and Kip Viscusi take issue with this conclusion for several reasons. They point out that estimates of wage premiums for workplace risk differences are fairly small, on the order of a few hundred dollars a year, and thus are unlikely to have much of an effect on economic status. Kniesner and Viscusi further argue that, even if wage premiums do positively influence status, these gains may be offset because relatively risky jobs are likely to affect feelings of well-being adversely insofar as, by definition, health and safety are lower in such jobs.

Source: Adapted from Robert H. Frank and Cass R. Sunstein, "Cost-Benefit Analysis and Relative Position," *University of Chicago Law Review* 68(2) 2001, 323–374; and Thomas J. Kniesner and W. Kip Viscusi, "Cost-Benefit Analysis: Why Relative Economic Position Does Not Matter," Working Paper 02–5, 2002, Washington, D.C.: AEI-Brookings Joint Center for Regulatory Studies.

---

wage-risk study used to obtain the VSL differs substantially from the level of risk applicable to where the policy is being applied.

Other problems with these methods are that they assume markets are efficient and that all other factors that influence prices or wages are held constant. In practice, wage differences may depend partially on the relative bargaining power of unions, on the different characteristics of the different jobs, or on different characteristics (skills) of workers in different jobs. For example, as Adam Smith noted, "[t]he wages of labour vary with the ease or hardship, the cleanliness or dirtiness, the honourableness or dishonourableness of employment."[7] The omitted variables issue, which is illustrated by Exhibit 13-1, is discussed in more detail later.

INTERMEDIATE GOOD METHOD

Some government projects produce intermediate goods, that is, goods that are used as inputs to some other *downstream* business. For example, a government irrigation project may provide water for farmers that is used in the production of avocados. If the intermediate good—water—is sold in a well-functioning market, it may be possible to directly estimate the market demand curve for water by using econometric methods. If it is not, we have to impute its value. The intermediate good method estimates the (gross) benefit of a project based on its *value added* to the downstream activity. Specifically, the value of the irrigation project can be measured by the increase in the incomes of avocado farmers. More generally, the annual benefit of a project equals the change in the annual incomes of the downstream businesses, thus:

Annual Benefit = Income (with the project) − Income (without the project)

The total benefit of a project can be computed by discounting these annual benefits over the project's life.

The intermediate good method can be used to value the benefits of education and training programs. Investment in the skills and abilities of human beings improves the stock of *human capital.* Much of the economic successes of Japan and Switzerland, for example, both of which are relatively poor in terms of physical natural resources, can be attributed to their investments in human capital. The intermediate good method measures the annual benefit of human capital programs by comparing the average incomes of those who have been enrolled in them and the average incomes of those who have not. The total benefit of the program is found by discounting the annual benefits over the years people work after graduation and multiplying by the number of participants.

One problem with this method is that it assumes that differences in income capture all the benefits of a project. Some intermediate goods, such as college education, may be partially "final" goods. That is, they may have consumption value in addition to having investment value. Some people may enjoy their college education so much that they would pay for it even if it had no impact on their expected earnings. People's willingness-to-pay for this consumption aspect should also be considered as a benefit of a college education. Because the intermediate good method does not include this benefit, it underestimates (overestimates) the value of goods that have positive (negative) consumption benefits. Other problems with the intermediate good method are discussed in Exhibit 13-2.

Care must be taken in application of the intermediate good method to avoid *double counting.* If the value of an intermediate good has been measured in some other way, then its contribution to the value of downstream production should not be counted as an additional benefit. For example, if the benefits of an irrigation project were estimated based on the estimated demand curve for water, then including the increased income of avocado farmers as an additional benefit would be double counting.

ASSET VALUATION METHOD

Government projects often affect the prices of assets such as land, housing, and stocks. The impacts are said to be *capitalized* into the market value of the assets. Observed increases (decreases) in asset values can often be used to estimate the benefits (costs) of projects. For example, returning to the irrigation project to provide water to avocado farms, if the farms are the only users of the irrigation water and if the market for farm land is undistorted, then the full value of the irrigation project will capitalize into the market value of avocado farms. Using the difference in the value of farms before and after the irrigation project is a relatively quick and easy way to estimate the benefits of a project.

A common application of the asset valuation method uses cross-sectional data on house prices to impute values of particular attributes of houses or of the environment, including negative externalities, such as noise or pollution.[8] For example, the

---

EXHIBIT 13-2

Many studies have used the intermediate good method to value the social benefits from education. These studies usually measure the social benefits from a college education, for example, as the difference in before-tax earnings of college graduates and those whose education stopped after graduating from high school. These studies usually also estimate the cost of education—tuition fees, tax revenues, donations, and earnings that are forgone while in college. Similar to the benefits from education, forgone earnings are estimated by comparing the before-tax earnings of those with a high school education and those who are in college.

These estimates of benefits and costs can be used to compute the rate of return to different additional amounts of education. For example, a recent summary found that the average rate of return to society from secondary schooling is 10 percent in developed countries, 18 percent in sub-Shaharan countries, and 11 to 13 percent in other developing countries. The estimated average rate of return to society from investments in higher education is 9 percent in developed countries and 11 to 12 percent in developing countries. The rate of return to private individuals is higher than these estimates because they capture the benefits whereas the cost is often subsidized by the government or donors.

Use of the intermediate good method to value the benefits of education is subject to several potentially important biases. First, the higher earnings of those with more education may be at least partially attributable to their greater ability or motivation rather than to their greater education. Second, at least part of the higher earnings of the more educated may not be attributable to education imparting greater skill but due instead to a "credentials" or a "signaling" effect. That is, employers who are willing to pay premium wages to hire more able employees, but who otherwise would be uncertain as to whom these workers are, use possession of a high school or college degree to identify them. Third, by focusing on earnings, the intermediate good method ignores other benefits from education such as better citizenship, greater fringe benefits, more pleasant working conditions, more responsibility, more flexibility, and so forth. The first two of these biases tend to cause estimates of educational benefits and rates of return to be overstated, whereas the third causes them to be understated.

Source: Adapted from George Psacharopoulos, "Returns to Investment in Education: A Global Update," *World Development* 22(9) 1994, 1325–1343.

---

difference in market price between a house with a view and a house with no view provides an estimate of how much households are willing to pay for a view. The difference between the average price of houses in a neighborhood with many parks and the average price of houses in neighborhoods with few parks provides an estimate of how much homeowners are willing to pay for parks.[9] Of course, similar to the other methods discussed earlier, this method assumes that houses are comparable in all other respects, and that no other factor affects differences in house prices. (Later we discuss how to control for such factors.)

Recently, *event studies* have become an important method for estimating the costs or benefits to shareholders of new programs, policies, or regulations that affect firms.[10] An event study examines changes in stock prices following some "event," such as the announcement of a new program or policy. The main advantage of using stock prices is that new information concerning policy changes is quickly and efficiently capitalized into stock prices. Changes in stock prices provide an unbiased estimate of the value of a policy change to shareholders. Also, stock price data are readily accessible in computer-readable form.

In an event study, researchers estimate the *abnormal return* to a security, which is the difference between the return to a security in the presence of an event and the return to the security in the absence of the event. Usually, researchers estimate daily abnormal returns during an *event window,* that is, for the period during which the event is assumed to affect stock prices—often a few days. Because the return to the security in the absence of the event is unobservable, it is inferred from changes in the prices of other stocks in the market, such as the Dow Jones Index or the FTSE 100.[11] The estimated daily abnormal returns during the event window can be aggregated to obtain the *cumulative abnormal return,* which measures the total return to shareholders that can be attributed to the event. Cumulative abnormal returns provide an estimate of the change in producer surplus due to some new policy.

PROBLEMS WITH SIMPLE VALUATION METHODS

The valuation methods discussed earlier in this chapter have several potential limitations, many of which were discussed earlier. This section focuses on the *omitted variable* problem and *self-selection* bias.

The Omitted Variable Problem

All of the methods discussed thus far in this chapter implicitly assume that all other explanatory variables are held constant, but this is unlikely in practice. Consider, for example, using the intermediate good method to value irrigation. Ideally, analysts would compare the incomes of farmers if the irrigation project were built with the incomes of the same farmers if the project were not built. In practice, if the project is built, analysts cannot directly observe what the farmers' incomes would have been if it had not been built. One way to infer what their incomes would have been without the project is to use the incomes of the same farmers before the project was built (a before and after design) or the incomes of similar farmers who did not benefit from an irrigation project (a non-experimental comparison group design). The before and after design is reasonable only if all other variables that affect farmers' incomes remain constant, such as weather conditions, crop choices, taxes, and subsidies. If these variables change then the incomes observed before the project are not good estimates of what incomes would have been if the project had not been implemented. Similarly, the comparison group design is appropriate only if the comparison group is similar in all important respects to the farmers with irrigation, except for the presence of irrigation.

As mentioned in Exhibit 13-2, salary differences between those with a college degree and those with a high school degree may depend on ability, intelligence, socioeconomic background and other factors in addition to college attendance. Similarly, in labor market studies of the value of life, differences in wages among jobs may depend on variations in status among jobs and the bargaining power of different unions in addition to fatality risk. In simple asset price studies, the price of a house typically depends on factors such as its distance from the central business district and size, as well as whether it has a view. Analysts should take account of all important explanatory variables. If a relevant explanatory variable is omitted from the model and if it is correlated with the included variable(s) of interest, then the estimated coefficients will be biased, as discussed in Chapter 12.

Self-Selection Bias

Another potential problem is self-selection bias. Risk-seeking people tend to self-select themselves for dangerous jobs. Because they like to take risks they may be willing to accept low salaries in quite risky jobs. Consequently, we may observe only a very small wage premium for dangerous jobs. Because risk seekers are not representative of society as a whole, the observed wage differential may underestimate the amount that average members of society would be willing to pay to reduce risks and, hence, may lead to underestimation of the value of a statistical life.

The self-selection problem arises whenever different people attach different values to particular attributes. As another example, suppose we want to use differences in house prices to estimate a shadow price for noise. People who are not adverse to noise, possibly because of hearing disabilities, naturally tend to move into noisy neighborhoods. As a result, the price differential between quiet houses and noisy houses may be quite small, which would lead to an underestimation of the shadow price of noise for the "average" person.

HEDONIC PRICING METHOD

The *hedonic pricing* method, sometimes called the *hedonic regression method,* offers a way to overcome the omitted variables problem and self-selection bias that arise in the relatively simple valuation methods discussed earlier. Most recent wage-risk studies for valuing a statistical life (also called labor market studies) apply the hedonic regression method.

Hedonic Regression

Suppose, for example, that scenic views can be scaled from 1 to 10 and that we want to estimate the benefits of improving the (quality) "level" of scenic view in an area by one unit. We could estimate the relationship between individual house prices and the level of their scenic views. But we know that the market value of houses depends on other factors, such as the size of the lot, which is probably correlated with the quality of scenic view. We also suspect that people who live in houses with good scenic views tend to value scenic views more than other people. Consequently, we would have an omitted variables problem and self-selection bias.

The hedonic pricing method attempts to overcome both of these types of problems.[12] It consists of two steps. The first estimates the effect of a marginally better scenic view on the value (price) of houses, a slope parameter in a regression model, while controlling for other variables that affect house prices. The second step estimates the willingness-to-pay for scenic views, after controlling for "tastes," which are proxied by income and other socioeconomic factors. From this information, we can calculate the change in consumer surplus resulting from projects that improve or worsen the views from some houses.

The hedonic pricing method can be used to value an attribute, or a change in an attribute, whenever its value is capitalized into the price of an asset, such as houses or salaries. The first step estimates the relationship between the price of an asset and all of the *attributes* (characteristics) that affect its value.[13] The price of a house, P, for example, depends on such attributes as the quality of its scenic view, *VIEW*, its distance from the central business district, *CBD*, its lot size, *SIZE*, and various characteristics of its neighborhood, *NBHD*, such as school quality. A model of the factors affecting house prices can be written as follows:

$$P = f(CBD, SIZE, VIEW, NBHD) \tag{13.2}$$

This equation is called a *hedonic price function* or *implicit price function*.[14] The change in the price of a house that results from a unit change in a particular attribute (i.e., the slope) is called the *hedonic price, implicit price,* or *rent differential* of the attribute. In a well-functioning market, the hedonic price can naturally be interpreted as the additional cost of purchasing a house that is marginally better in terms of a particular attribute. For example, the hedonic price of scenic views, which we denote as r_v, measures the additional cost of buying a house with a slightly better (higher-level) scenic view.[15] Sometimes hedonic prices are referred to as *marginal hedonic prices* or *marginal implicit prices*. Although these terms are technically more correct, we will not use them in order to make the explanation as easy to follow as possible.

Usually analysts assume the hedonic price function has a multiplicative functional form, which implies that house prices increase as the level of scenic view increases but at a decreasing rate. Assuming the hedonic pricing model represented in equation (13.2) has a multiplicative functional form, we can write:

$$P = \beta_0 CBD^{\beta_1} SIZE^{\beta_2} VIEW^{\beta_3} NBHD^{\beta_4} e^{\epsilon} \tag{13.3}$$

The parameters, $\beta_1, \beta_2, \beta_3,$ and β_4, are elasticities: They measure the proportional change in house prices that results from a proportional change in the associated attribute.[16] We expect $\beta_1 < 0$ because house prices decline with distance to the *CBD*, but $\beta_2, \beta_3,$ and $\beta_4 > 0$ because house prices increase as *SIZE, VIEW,* and *NBHD* increase.

The hedonic price of a particular attribute is the slope of equation (13.2) with respect to that attribute. In general, the hedonic price of an attribute may be a function of all of the variables in the hedonic price equation.[17] For the multiplicative model in equation (13.3), the hedonic price of scenic views, r_v, is:[18]

$$r_v = \beta_3 \frac{P}{VIEW} > 0 \tag{13.4}$$

In this model, the hedonic price of scenic views depends on the value of the parameter β_3, the price of the house, and the view from the house. Thus, it varies from one observation (house) to another. Note that plotting this hedonic price against the level of scenic view provides a downward-sloping curve, which implies that the implicit price of scenic views declines as the level of the view increases.

The preceding points are illustrated in Figure 13-3. The top panel shows an illustrative hedonic price function with house prices increasing as the level of scenic view increases, but at a decreasing rate. The slope of this curve, which equals the hedonic price of scenic views, decreases as the level of the scenic view increases. The bottom panel shows more precisely the relationship between the hedonic price of scenic views (the slope of the curve in the top panel) and the level of scenic view.

In a well-functioning market, utility-maximizing households will purchase houses so that their willingness-to-pay for a marginal increase in a particular

FIGURE 13-3 Hedonic Price Method

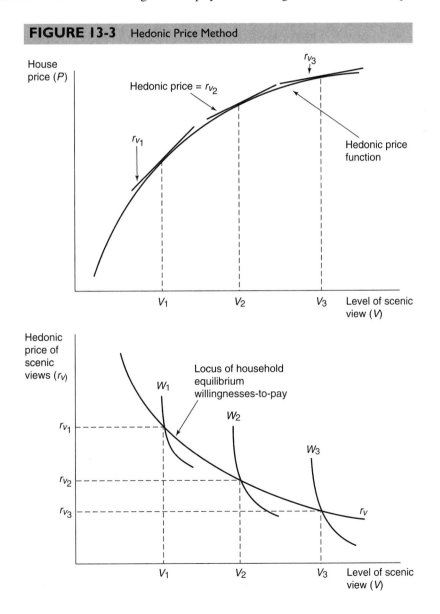

attribute equals its hedonic price. Consequently, in equilibrium, the hedonic price of an attribute can be interpreted as the willingness of households to pay for a marginal increase in that attribute. The graph of the hedonic price of scenic views, r_v, against the level of scenic view is shown in the lower panel of Figure 13-3. Assuming all households have identical incomes and tastes, this curve can be interpreted as a household inverse demand curve for scenic views.

Yet, households differ in their incomes and taste. Some are willing to pay a considerable amount of money for a scenic view; others are not. This brings us to the second step of the hedonic pricing method. To account for different incomes and tastes, analysts should estimate the following willingness-to-pay function (inverse demand curve) for scenic views:[19]

$$r_v = W(VIEW, Y, Z) \tag{13.5}$$

where r_v is estimated from equation (13.4), Y is household income, and Z is a vector of household characteristics that reflects tastes (e.g., socioeconomic background, race, age, and family size). Three willingness-to-pay functions, denoted W_1, W_2, and W_3, for three different types of households are drawn in the lower panel of Figure 13-3.[20] Equilibria occur where these functions intersect the r_v function. Thus, when incomes and socioeconomic characteristics differ, the r_v function is the locus of household equilibrium willingnesses-to-pay for scenic views.

Using the methods described in Chapter 4, it is straightforward to use equation (13.5) to calculate the change in consumer surplus to a household due to a change in the level of scenic view. These changes in individual household consumer surplus can be aggregated across all households to obtain the total change in consumer surplus.

Using Hedonic Models to Determine the VSL

The simple forms of consumer purchase and labor market studies to value life that we described previously may result in biased estimates due to omitted variables or self-selection problems. For example, labor market studies to value life that examine *fatality risk* (the risk of death) often omit potentially relevant variables such as *injury risk* (the risk of nonfatal injury). This problem may be reduced by using the hedonic pricing method. For example, a researcher might estimate the following nonlinear regression model to find the hedonic price of fatality risk:[21]

$$\ln(\text{wage rate}) = \beta_0 + \beta_1 \ln(\text{fatality risk}) + \beta_2 \ln(\text{injury risk}) + \beta_3 \ln(\text{job tenure})$$
$$+ \beta_4 \ln(\text{education}) + \beta_5 \ln(\text{age}) + \epsilon \tag{13.6}$$

The inclusion of injury risk, job tenure, education, and age in the regression model controls for variables that affect wages and would bias the estimated coefficient of β_1 if they were excluded. Using the procedure demonstrated in the preceding section, the analyst can convert the estimate of β_1 to a hedonic price of fatality risk and can then estimate individuals' willingness-to-pay to avoid fatal risks. Most of the empirical estimates of the value of life that are reported in Chapter 15 are obtained from labor market and consumer product studies that employ models similar to the one presented in equation (13.6).

EXHIBIT 13-3

Dean Uyeno, Stanley Hamilton, and Andrew Biggs used the hedonic pricing method to estimate the cost of airport noise in Vancouver, Canada. They estimated the following hedonic price equation:

$$\ln H = \beta_0 + \beta_1 \text{NEF} + \sum_{j=2}^{k} \beta_k \ln X_j + \epsilon$$

where $\ln H$ is the natural log of residential property value, NEF is a measure of noise level (ambient noise levels are in the NEF 15–25 range, "some" to "much" annoyance occurs in the NEF 25–40 range, and "considerable" annoyance occurs above NEFs of 40), the X_j are house characteristics ($j = 2, \ldots, k$), and ϵ is an error term.

Their results show that Vancouver International Airport generates noise costs that capitalize into residential house and condominium prices. The estimated coefficient of the noise variable implies that detached houses very close to the airport with NEFs of 40 are 9.75 percent cheaper than houses far from the airport with NEFs of 25. The estimated noise depreciation sensitivity is broadly consistent with previous studies, leading the authors to conclude that "the similarity of results spanning several decades and several Western countries would seem to suggest a broad and long-lived consensus on the issue (of the impact of airport noise on property values) ..." (p. 14). In aggregate, the social cost of noise from Vancouver International Airport amounts to about $15 million in 1987 Canadian dollars.

Source: Adapted from Dean Uyeno, Stanley W. Hamilton, and Andrew J.G. Biggs, "Density of Residential Land Use and the Impact of Airport Noise," *Journal of Transport Economics and Policy* 27(1) 1993, 3–18.

Problems with Hedonic Models

In theory, the hedonic pricing method can be used to determine the shadow price of many goods that are not traded in well-developed markets, such as externalities and public goods.[22] In practice, there are many potential problems, some of which were discussed earlier in the section on problems with simple consumer purchase and wage-risk studies and are not repeated here. First, people must know and understand the full implications of the externality or public good. For example, in order to use the hedonic pricing method to value pollution, families should know, prior to the purchase of their house, the level of pollution to which it is exposed and should also know the effect of different pollution levels on their health. In the case of hedonic wage-risk studies, workers must correctly perceive the actual risks. W. P. Jennings and A. Kinderman observe that the rate of occupational fatalities in most industries has fallen roughly 95 percent since 1920 and is now one-third of the rate of accidental deaths in the home.[23] They argue that "the current fatality rates are so low and their individual causes so often random that statistical attempts to measure how fatalities affect wages are unlikely to meet with success." Second, it is important that the hedonic equations, such as equation (13.3) or equation (13.6), include correctly measured variables, as opposed to more readily obtainable but incorrect proxies. For example, house values may depend on the quality of construction. As this variable is difficult to determine without inspection, the researcher may use the year of construction as a proxy for quality. In econometrics, this problem is referred to as the *errors in variables* problem. Third, if the hedonic pricing model is linear, then the hedonic price of each attribute is constant, which would make it impossible to estimate the inverse demand function, such as equation (13.5).[24] Fourth, the market should contain many different houses so that families can find an optimal "package," that is, a house with just the right combination of attributes. In other words, there should be sufficient variety so that families can find a house that permits them to reach an equilibrium. This would be a problem if, for example, a family wanted a small, pollution-free house, but all of the houses in pollution-free areas were large. Fifth, there may be multicollinearity problems in the data. To use the same example, if expensive houses were large and located mainly in areas free of pollution, but inexpensive houses were small and located mainly in polluted areas, it would be difficult to estimate separate hedonic prices for pollution and size. Sixth, the method assumes that market prices adjust immediately to changes in attributes and in all other factors that affect demand or supply.

TRAVEL COST METHOD[25]

Most applications of the travel cost method (TCM) have been to value recreational sites.[26] If the "market" for visits to a particular site is geographically extensive, then visitors from different origins bear different travel costs depending on their proximity to the site. The resulting differences in total cost, and the differences in the rates of visits that they induce, provide a basis for estimating a demand curve for the site.

Suppose that we want to estimate the value of a particular recreational site. We expect that the quantity of visits demanded by an individual, q, depends on its price, p, the price of substitutes, p_s, the person's income, Y, and variables that reflect the person's tastes, Z:

$$q = f(p, p_s, Y, Z) \tag{13.7}$$

The clever insight of the TCM is that although admission fees are usually the same for all persons (indeed, they are often zero), the total cost faced by each person varies because of differences in travel costs. Consequently, usage also varies, thereby allowing researchers to make inferences about the demand curve for the site.

The *full price* paid by visitors to a recreational site includes the opportunity cost of time spent traveling, the operating cost of vehicles used to travel, the cost of accommodations for overnight stays while traveling or visiting, parking fees at the site, and the cost of admission. The sum of all of these costs gives the total cost of a visit to the site. This total cost is used as an explanatory variable in place of the admission price in a model similar to equation (13.7).

Estimating such a model is conceptually straightforward. First, select a random sample of households within the market area of the site. These are the potential visitors. Second, survey these households to determine their numbers of visits to the site over some period of time, their costs involved in visiting the site, their costs of visiting substitute sites, their incomes, and their other characteristics that may affect their demand. Third, specify a functional form for the demand schedule and estimate it using the survey data. For an application of the TCM see Exhibit 13-4.

It is important to emphasize that when total cost replaces price in equation (13.7), this equation is not the usual demand curve that gives visits as a function of the price of admission. However, as we show next, such models can be used to

---

EXHIBIT 13-4

Kerry Smith and William Desvousges used the travel cost method to estimate the average household value of a trip to recreational sites along the Monongahela River and the average household value of improving water quality. Their estimates of travel costs assumed the marginal cost of operating an automobile was $0.08 per mile in 1976. For the time cost component of travel cost, they set the value of time equal to the wage rate in a person's particular occupation, which ranged from $2.75 per hour for female farmers to $7.89 per hour for male professional, technical, and kindred workers in 1977 dollars. Smith and Desvousges estimated many models including the following relatively simple travel cost model (*t*-statistics in parentheses):

$$\ln V = -3.928 - 0.051 TC + 0.00001 Y + 0.058 DO \qquad (R^2 = 0.225)$$
$$\qquad\quad (-3.075) \quad (-2.846) \qquad (1.109) \qquad (3.917)$$

where V is the number of site visits, Y denotes income and DO is the percent saturation of dissolved oxygen in the water. Based on this model, the authors estimated that the average annual value of improving the water quality from boatable to game fishing would be $7.16 in 1981 dollars (about $15 in 2004 dollars), and the average annual value of improving the water quality from boatable to swimming would be $28.86 in 1981 dollars (about $60 in 2004 dollars).

Source: Adapted from V. Kerry Smith and William H. Desvousges, *Measuring Water Quality Benefits* (Boston: Kluwer Nijhoff Publishing, 1986), especially pp. 270–271.

---

derive the usual market demand curve and to estimate the average willingness-to-pay for a visit.

Zonal Travel Cost Method

With the *zonal travel cost method*, researchers survey actual visitors at a site rather than potential visitors. This is often more feasible and less expensive than surveying potential visitors. Also, the level of analysis shifts from the individual (or household) to the area, or zone, of origin of visitors, hence the name *zonal travel cost method*.

The zonal TCM requires the analyst to specify the zones from which users of the site originate. Zones are easily formed by drawing concentric rings or iso-time lines around the site on a map. Ideally, households within a zone should face similar travel costs as well as have similar values of the other variables that would be included in an individual demand function, including similar prices of substitutes, similar incomes, and similar tastes. If residents from different regions within a zone have quite different travel costs, then the zones should be redrawn. In practice, analysts often use local government jurisdictions as the zones because they facilitate the collection of data.

Assuming a constant elasticity functional form leads to the following regression model:

$$\ln\left(\frac{V}{POP}\right) = \beta_0 + \beta_1 \ln \overline{p} + \beta_2 \ln \overline{p}_s + \beta_4 \overline{Y} + \beta_5 \overline{Z} + \epsilon \qquad \textbf{(13.8)}$$

where V is the number of visits from a zone per period; POP is the population of the zone; and $\bar{p}$, $\bar{p}_s$, $\bar{Y}$, and $\bar{Z}$ denote the average values of p, p_s, Y, and Z in each zone, respectively.

Note that the quantity demanded is expressed as a visit rate. An alternative specification is to estimate the quantity demanded in terms of the number of visits, V, but to include population, POP, on the right-hand side of the regression equation. Although both specifications are plausible, the specification in equation (13.8) is less likely to involve heteroscedasticity problems (which we discuss in Chapter 12) and is, therefore, more likely to be appropriately estimated by OLS.

Using estimates of the parameters of equation (13.8), it is possible to estimate the change in consumer surplus associated with a change in the admission price to a site, the total consumer surplus associated with the site at its current admission fee, and the average consumer surplus per visit to the site. We illustrate how to do this using an example for a hypothetical recreational wilderness area, using the basic data presented in Table 13-1. This illustration assumes there are only five relevant zones from which people travel to the recreational site. To avoid unnecessary complications, we assume that demand depends directly only on total price, not on income, the prices of substitutes, or any other variable.

In this example, the value of time for residents from different zones varies due to different income levels in different zones, as well as different travel times. Zone A is adjacent to the recreational area. Residents from zone A can, on average, pack up their equipment, drive to the site, park, and walk to the entrance in approximately one-half hour. Assuming the opportunity cost of their time is $9.40/hr and marginal vehicle operating costs are 15 cents/km, their total travel costs are $10 per round trip. Adding the admission fee of $10 per day yields a total cost of $20 per visit. Local residents make 15 visits each year, on average. Zone B is about 30 km away, requiring two hours of total travel time (including driving, parking, walking, and loading and unloading vehicles) for a round trip. Assuming the value of time for residents of zone B is $5.50/hr and they travel individually, total costs per visit are $30. Zone B residents make 13 visits per year on average. Zone C is about 90 km away, requiring two hours of total travel time in each direction. Assuming the value of their time is $10.35/hr on average, and that travel costs are shared between two people in each vehicle, total costs per person are approximately $65 per visit. Zone C residents make six visits per year on average. Zone D residents live on the other side of the metropolitan area and, on average, make three visits each year.

TABLE 13-1 Illustration of the Travel Cost Method

Zone	Travel Time (hours)	Travel Distance (km)	Average Total Cost per Person ($)	Average Number of Visits per Person	Consumer Surplus per Person	Consumer Surplus per Zone ($ thousands)	Trips per Zone (thousands)
A	0.5	2	20	15	525	5,250	150
B	1.0	30	30	13	390	3,900	130
C	2.0	90	65	6	75	1,500	120
D	3.0	140	80	3	15	150	30
E	3.5	150	90	1	0	0	10
Total						10,800	440

Assuming that their average wage rate is $8/hr and that two persons travel per vehicle, their per-person cost is $80 per visit. Zone E residents have to cross an international border. Though the distance is only slightly farther than from zone D, it takes almost one-half hour to get through customs and immigration. The average zone E wage is $8/hour. Assuming two persons per vehicle, the per-person cost is $90 per visit. On average, visitors from zone E make only one visit per year.

The data for average total cost per person (TC) and average visits per person (V) are represented graphically in Figure 13-4. The equation $TC = 95-5V$ fits the data for zones A through E perfectly. (In practice, ordinary least squares would be used to fit a line to data points that would not all lie exactly on the line.) This equation is the "representative" individual's inverse demand curve: It shows how much a typical visitor is willing to pay for a visit to the recreational area (specifically, $90 for the first visit, $85 for the second visit, . . . , $20 for the fifteenth visit).

Different individuals face different prices (costs) for their visits depending on their zone of origin. It is cheaper for those who live closer. Therefore, individuals' consumer surplus varies according to their zone of origin. The consumer surplus for a particular visit from a particular zone equals the difference between how much someone is willing to pay for that visit, given by the point on the "representative" individual's inverse

FIGURE 13-4 "Representative" Individual's Inverse Demand Curve for Visits to a Recreational Area

demand curve, and how much the person actually pays for a visit *from that zone.* As mentioned previously, "representative" visitors are willing to pay $90 for their first visit, $85 for the second, . . . $65 for their sixth. People from zone C actually pay only $65 for each visit. Consequently, their consumer surplus equals $25 for the first visit, $20 for the second visit, $15 for the third visit, $10 for the fourth visit, $5 for the fifth visit, and $0 for the sixth visit.

The total consumer surplus for someone from zone C is obtained by summing the consumer surpluses associated with each visit across all visits, which amounts to $75. This amount is represented by the area of the shaded triangle in Figure 13-4.[27] Similarly, the consumer surplus is $525 per person for residents of zone A, $390 for residents of zone B, $15 for residents of zone D, and $0 for residents of zone E. These amounts are presented in the sixth column of Table 13-1. Clearly, people who live closer to the recreational site enjoy more consumer surplus from it than people who live farther away.

From this information and knowledge of the populations of each zone, we can calculate the total consumer surplus per year and the average consumer surplus per visit for the site. Suppose zones A, B, D, and E have populations of 10,000 people, while zone C has a population of 20,000 people. The consumer surplus per zone is obtained by multiplying the consumer surplus per person in a zone by the population of that zone, as shown in the fifth column in Table 13-1. Adding across all zones yields the total annual consumer surplus for the site of $10.8 million. Adding admission fees of $4.4 million indicates that the annual (gross) benefit of the site to all visitors equals $15.2 million. If the government decided to use the site for some completely different purpose, such as logging, this would be a measure of the lost annual benefits.

The total number of visits to the recreational area is 440,000, as shown in the last column of Table 13-1. Dividing the total consumer surplus by the total number of visits gives an average consumer surplus per visit of $24.55. If we now add the admission fee of $10, then we obtain the *average demand price* per visit, which is the average maximum amount a visitor would pay for a visit to the site. In this example, the average demand price is $34.55.

Estimating the Market Demand Curve

It is possible to construct the usual inverse *market demand curve* from estimation of an equation similar to equation (13.8) where price is replaced with total cost. For illustrative purposes, we continue with the previous example where $TC = 95 - 5V$. Our purpose is to derive an equation in which the admission fee is a function of the *total* number of visits to the site. This curve can then be used to estimate total consumer surplus in the usual way. Unfortunately, because each point on the demand curve has to be estimated separately, precise computation is not straightforward.

To begin, we know two points on the market demand curve. At an admission price of $10, the current admission fee, there are 440,000 visits, represented by point c in Figure 13-5. Now consider how high admission fees can be raised until demand is choked off (equals zero). We know from the representative individual's inverse demand curve ($TC = 95 - 5V$) that the maximum willingness-to-pay (including all costs) is $95. Subtracting the travel cost of users from zone A (who have the lowest travel cost) implies that the maximum willingness-to-pay for admission is $95 - $10 = $85.

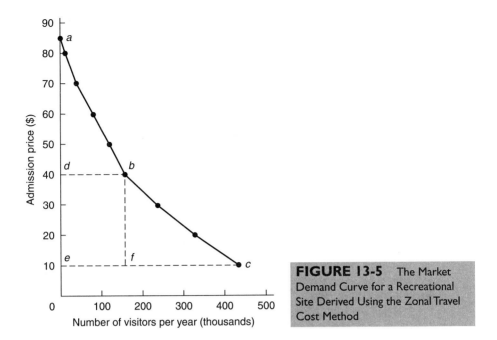

FIGURE 13-5 The Market Demand Curve for a Recreational Site Derived Using the Zonal Travel Cost Method

This is the intercept (choke price) of the inverse market demand curve and is represented by point *a* in Figure 13-5.

We can find other points on the market demand curve by assuming that the admission fee is increased or decreased and then predicting the visit rate from each zone at the new price. Suppose, for example, the admission fee were raised from $10 to $20, so that *TC* increased by $10 dollars. Given that the *individual* demand curve can be written as $V = 19 - 0.2TC$ (the inverse of $TC = 95 - 5V$), a $10 increase in *TC* would reduce the number of visits per person by two. Thus, if the admission price were $20, then the predicted number of visits would be 13 for zone A, 11 for zone B, 4 for zone C, 1 for zone D, and −1 for zone E. Because negative visits are not possible, we set the number of visits per person for zone E to zero. The total number of visits demanded at the new price is computed by multiplying the predicted visit rate for each zone by its population and summing these products ($13 \times 10,000 + 11 \times 10,000 + 4 \times 20,000 + 1 \times 10,000 = 330,000$). Thus, at a price of $20 we would expect 330,000 visits. This is a third point on the market demand curve.

Other points on the market demand curve can be obtained in the same way. With a sufficient number of points, the market demand curve can be sketched to any desired level of accuracy. The market demand curve in Figure 13-5 is computed on the basis of $10 price increments. The annual consumer surplus for the site is the area between the curve and the current admission fee from zero visits to 440,000 visits. Assuming for simplicity that the demand curve is linear between points *a* and *b*, and between points *b* and *c*, we estimate the annual consumer surplus of the site equals $12.6 million, and the annual (gross) benefit of the site is $17.0 million.[28] Due to the linear approximation and the relatively few points on the demand curve, we slightly overestimate the benefits.

Limitations of the TCM

The usefulness of the TCM is limited in a number of ways. One limitation is that the TCM provides an estimate of the willingness-to-pay for the entire site rather than for specific features of a site. As we often wish to value changes in specific features of a site (e.g., improvements in the hiking trails), the basic TCM does not provide the needed information. However, if the residents of zones can choose from among a number of alternative recreational sites with different attributes, then it may be possible to use the *hedonic travel cost method* to find attribute prices.[29] This method treats the total cost of visiting a particular site from a particular zone as a function of both the distance from that zone to the site and various attributes of the site. Its application raises a number of issues beyond those previously discussed in the context of the basic hedonic pricing model. Therefore, before attempting to apply the hedonic travel cost method, we recommend consulting other sources.[30]

Measuring the cost of a visit to the site may be difficult.[31] Perhaps the most obvious problem is the estimation of the opportunity cost of travel time, which we have previously discussed.[32] Even defining and measuring travel costs raises some difficult issues. Some analysts include the time spent at the site, as well as the time spent traveling to and from it, as components of total price. If people from different zones spend the same amount of time at the site, and if the opportunity cost of their time is similar, then it does not matter whether the time spent at the site is included or not—both the height of the demand curve and total price shift by the same amount for each consumer so that estimates of consumer surplus remain unchanged. If, however, people from different zones have different opportunity costs for their time, or if they spend different amounts of time at the site, then including the cost of time spent at the site would change the price facing persons from different zones by different amounts and, thereby, change the slope of the estimated demand curve.

Another problem arises because recreation often requires investment in fairly specialized equipment such as tents, sleeping bags, wet-weather gear, canoes, fishing rods, and even vehicles. The marginal cost of using such equipment should be included in total price. Yet, estimating the marginal cost of using capital goods is usually difficult. As with time spent at the site, however, these costs can be reasonably ignored if they are approximately constant for visitors from different zones.

Multiple-purpose trips also pose an analytical problem. People may visit the recreational site in the morning and, for example, go river rafting nearby in the afternoon. Sometimes analysts exclude visitors with multiple purposes from the data. Including visitors with multiple purposes is usually desirable if costs can be appropriately apportioned to the site being valued. If the apportionment is arbitrary, however, then it may be better to exclude multiple users.

A similar problem results because the journey itself may have value. The previous discussion assumes implicitly that the trip is undertaken exclusively to get to the recreation site and travel has no benefit per se. If the journey itself is part of the reason for the visit to the site, then the trip has multiple purposes. Therefore, part of the cost of the trip should be attributed to the journey, not the visit to the recreation site. Not doing so would lead to overestimation of site benefits.

A more fundamental problem is that the travel cost variable may be endogenous, not exogenous. One neighborhood characteristic some people consider when making their residential choices is its proximity to a recreational area. People who expect to make many visits to a recreational area may select a particular neighborhood (zone) partially on account of the low travel time from that neighborhood to the recreational area. If so, the number of trips to a particular recreational area and the price of these trips will be determined simultaneously. Under these circumstances equation (13.8) may not be identified, a problem which we discuss in Chapter 12.[33]

Another econometric problem is that the dependent variable in the estimated models is *truncated*. Truncation arises because the sample is drawn from only those who visit the site, not from the larger population that includes people who never visit the site. Application of ordinary least squares to the truncated sample would result in biased coefficients. However, there are more complicated estimation methods that overcome this problem.

There may also be an omitted variables problem. If the price of substitute recreational sites varies across zones or if tastes for recreation varies across zones, then the estimated coefficients may be biased if the model does not control for these variables. As previously discussed, bias results when an excluded variable is correlated with an included variable.

Finally, derivation of the market demand curve assumes that people respond to changes in price regardless of its composition. Thus, for example, people respond to, say, a $5 increase in the admission price in the same way as a $5 increase in travel cost. This presumes that people have a good understanding of the impact of changes in the prices of fuel, tires, and repairs on their marginal travel cost.

DEFENSIVE EXPENDITURES METHOD[34]

If you live in a smoggy city, then you will probably find that your windows often need cleaning. If you hire someone to clean your windows periodically, the cost of this action in response to the smog is termed a *defensive expenditure*—it is an amount spent to mitigate or even eliminate the effect of a negative externality. Suppose the city passes an ordinance that reduces the level of smog so that your windows do not get as dirty. You would now have to spend less on window cleaners. The reduction in defensive expenditures—the defensive expenditures avoided—has been suggested as a measure of the benefits of the city ordinance. Similarly, the costs of a policy change might be measured by the increase in defensive expenditures.

This method is an example of a broad class of *production function methods*. In these methods, the level of a public good or externality (e.g., smog) and other goods (window cleaners) are inputs to some production process (window cleaning). If the level of the public good or externality changes, then the levels of the other inputs can be changed in the opposite direction and still allow the quantity of output produced to remain the same. For example, when the negative externality of smog is reduced, less labor is required to produce the same number of clean windows. The change in expenditures on the substitute input (window cleaners) is used as a measure of the benefit of reduction of the public good or externality.

Suppose that the demand curve for clean windows is represented by the curve labeled D in Figure 13-6. Let S_0 represent the marginal cost of cleaning windows

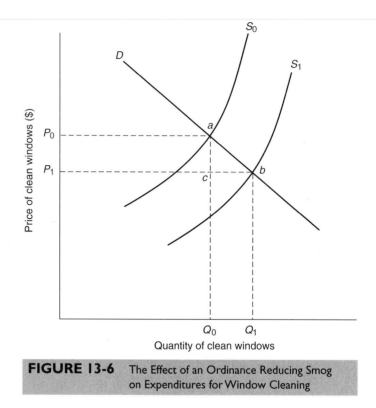

FIGURE 13-6 The Effect of an Ordinance Reducing Smog on Expenditures for Window Cleaning

initially, that is, prior to the new ordinance. The initial equilibrium price and quantity of clean windows are denoted by P_0 and Q_0, respectively. The effect of the new ordinance to restrict smog is to shift the marginal cost curve for clean windows down and to the right from S_0 to S_1: Because there is less smog, windows are easier to clean, so more windows can be cleaned for the same price. At the new equilibrium, the price of clean windows is P_1 and the quantity of clean windows is Q_1. The change in consumer surplus is represented by the area of the trapezoid P_0abP_1.

If households continued to consume the same quantity of clean windows after the price shift as they did before the price shift, Q_0, then the benefit of the ordinance would be represented by the rectangle P_0acP_1. This would be the amount by which consumers reduce their defensive expenditure. Consumers, however, would not maintain their consumption levels at Q_0, but would increase their consumption of clean windows to level Q_1. Individuals would spend area bQ_1Q_0c on the purchase of Q_1-Q_0 additional units of clean windows at a price of P_1. The net change in spending on window cleaning services equals the area of rectangle bQ_1Q_0c minus the area of rectangle P_0acP_1. This net change in spending may be quite small. Indeed, if the demand curve were a constant elasticity demand curve, with an elasticity equal to 1, there would be no change in total expenditure on window cleaning services at all. Yet there are obviously positive benefits to consumers. In general, *the reduced spending on defensive expenditures will underestimate the benefits of cleaner air or whatever benefit is being estimated.*[35]

There are at least four additional problems with the defensive expenditures method. First, it assumes implicitly that individuals quickly adjust to the new equilibrium. It may actually take some time for individuals to adjust their purchases and return to equilibrium. Second, a defensive expenditure may not remedy the entire damage so that reductions in this expenditure do not fully measure benefits. For example, expenditures on window cleaning do not "avoid" the whole problem of smog. Smog also leads to dirtier shirts and to health problems. Defensive expenditures avoided on these items should also be included. Exhibit 13-5 illustrates that there may be many categories of defensive expenditures. It examines the costs of groundwater degradation and includes

---

EXHIBIT 13-5

Charles W. Abdalla, Brian A. Roach, and Donald J. Epp measured the costs of groundwater degradation in the small Pennsylvania borough of Perkasie (population 7,877) using the defensive expenditures method. They conducted mail and telephone surveys to gather information from a sample of residents on the actions they took in response to trichloroethylene (TCE) contamination of one of the borough's wells between December 1987 and September 1989. They estimated the total costs to the community's residents, including both monetary costs and time expenditures, of each of five defensive actions:

Category of Cost	Cost Based on Value of Leisure Time Equal to Minimum Wage ($)[a]	Cost Based on Value of Leisure Time Equal to Individual Wage Rate ($)[a]
Increased Purchases of bottled water	11,100	11,100
New Purchases of bottled water	17,300	17,300
Home water treatment systems	4,700	4,700
Hauling water	12,500	34,000
Boiling water	15,600	64,100
Total	61,200	131,200

[a]*Costs in original rounded to nearest hundred dollars.*

Note that the costs of hauling and boiling water are very sensitive to the assumed opportunity cost of leisure. The researchers interpreted these total costs as a lower-bound estimate of the true cost of the contamination to residents because of the generally conservative nature of the defensive expenditures method.

A specific factor suggesting that these defensive expenditures represent a lower bound is that only 43 percent of residents were aware of the TCE contamination despite notification laws. Moreover, not all residents who knew about the contamination took defensive measures. Nevertheless, those who had more information about the contamination, those who perceived the cancer risk due to TCE to be higher, and those who had children between 3 and 17 years old in the household were generally more likely to take defensive action than other residents. Among those who took defensive action, having a child under 3 years of age seemed to be the most important factor influencing the intensity of the defensive actions taken.

Source: Adapted from Charles W. Abdalla, Brian A. Roach, and Donald J. Epp, "Valuing Environmental Quality Changes Using Averting Expenditures: An Application to Groundwater Contamination," *Land Economics* 68(2) 1992, 163–169.

five categories of costs, not just the cost of new purchases of bottled water. Third, the defensive expenditures may have benefits other than remedying damage. For example, the cleaning necessitated by the smog may result in cleaner windows than one would otherwise achieve. Fourth, not all of the defensive measures are purchased in markets. Some people clean their own windows, and reductions in their opportunity costs should also be included as benefits.

CONCLUSION

This chapter describes the major indirect market methods used in CBA for estimating shadow prices. Some methods are not discussed because we believe that they are too advanced for this book. Perhaps most notably, we have not discussed the use of random utility models or probabilistic choice models to estimate demand, an approach that is quite important in the transportation area.[36] Also, we do not discuss recent methods that estimate demand curves by combining survey data with data on observed behavior.[37] Nevertheless, the methods covered here provide a rich set of tools for practical valuation of impacts.

EXERCISES FOR CHAPTER 13

1. Child care services in a small midwestern city cost $30 per day per child. The high cost of these services is one reason why very few mothers who are on welfare work; given their low potential wages, virtually no welfare mothers are willing to pay these high costs. To combat this problem, the city establishes a new program: In exchange for their welfare benefits, a group of welfare recipients is required to provide child care for the children of other welfare recipients who obtain private-sector employment. The welfare mothers who use these child care services are required to pay a fee of $3 per day per child. These services prove very popular; 1,000 welfare children receive them each day and an additional 500 welfare children are on a waiting list. Do the mothers of the 1,000 children who receive services under the program value these services at $30,000 ($30 × 1,000) a day, $3,000 a day ($3 × 1,000), or at a value that is greater than $3,000 but less than $30,000? Explain.

2. A worker, who is typical in all respects, works for a wage of $30,000 per year in a perfectly safe occupation. Another typical worker does a job requiring exactly the same skills as the first worker, but in a risky occupation with a known death probability of 1 in 1,000 per year, and receives a wage of $36,000 per year. What value of a human life for workers with these characteristics should a cost-benefit analyst use?

3. (Spreadsheet software required.) Happy Valley is the only available camping area in Rural County. It is owned by the county, which allows free access to campers. Almost all visitors to Happy Valley come from the six towns in the county.

   Rural County is considering leasing Happy Valley for logging, which would require that it be closed to campers. Before approving the lease, the county executive would like to know the magnitude of annual benefits that campers would forgo if Happy Valley were to be closed to the public.

   An analyst for the county has collected data for a travel cost study to estimate the benefits of Happy Valley camping. On five randomly selected days, he recorded the license plates of vehicles parked overnight in the Happy Valley lot. (Because the camping season is 100 days, he assumed that this would constitute a 5 percent sample.) With cooperation from the state motor vehicle department, he was able to find the town of residence of the owner of each vehicle. He also observed a sample of vehicles from which he estimated that each vehicle carried 3.2 persons (1.6 adults), on average. The following table summarizes the data he collected.

Town	Miles from Happy Valley	Population (thousands)	Number of Vehicles in Sample	Estimated Number of Visitors for Season	Visit Rate (visits per 1,000 people)
A	22	50.1	146	3,893	77.7
B	34	34.9	85	2,267	65.0
C	48	15.6	22	587	37.6
D	56	89.9	180	4,800	53.4
E	88	98.3	73	1,947	19.8
F	94	60.4	25	666	11.0
Total				14,160	

In order to translate the distance traveled into an estimate of the cost campers faced in using Happy Valley, the analyst made the following assumptions. First, the average operating cost of vehicles is $0.12 per mile. Second, the average speed on county highways is 50 miles per hour. Third, the opportunity cost to adults of travel time is 40 percent of their wage rate; it is zero for children. Fourth, adult campers have the average county wage rate of $9.25 per hour.

The analyst has asked you to help him use this information to estimate the annual benefits accruing to Happy Valley campers. Specifically, assist with the following tasks.

a. Using the preceding information, calculate the travel cost of a vehicle visit (TC) from each of the towns.

b. For the six observations, regress visit rate (VR) on TC and a constant. If you do not have regression software available, plot the points and fit a line by sight. Find the slope of the fitted line.

c. You know that with the current free admission the number of camping visits demanded is 14,160. Find additional points on the demand curve by predicting the reduction in the number of campers from each town as price is increased by $5 increments until demand falls to zero. This is done in three steps at each price: First, use the coefficient of TC from the regression to predict a new VR for each town. Second, multiply the predicted VR of each town by its population to get a predicted number of visitors. Third, sum the visitors from each town to get the total number of predicted visits.

d. Estimate the area under the demand curve as the annual benefits to campers.

NOTES

1. When markets do exist but are imperfect due to government intervention, it is necessary to make adjustments to market prices in order to obtain the appropriate shadow prices. These methods are discussed in Chapter 16.

2. The *net output method* of valuing a life subtracts the value of a person's own consumption from his or her forgone earnings. It measures the benefit or cost the individual contributes to or imposes on the rest of society. The courts' use of this method to measure the loss to survivors of someone's death is somewhat arbitrary but perhaps reasonable. However, it is clearly inappropriate to use this method in CBA to value a

life saved. One reason is that the value of the person's own consumption should be counted because the individual is a member of society. Another reason is that it ignores the life cycle of earnings: Although a typical person's net output will be slightly positive over his or her entire lifetime, it will be negative for a retired person. For an overview of the net output method, see John J. Lawson, "The Value of Transport Safety," Final Report, Transport Canada Report No. 10569, 1989.

3. Thomas C. Schelling, "The Life You Save May Be Your Own," in Robert Dorfman and Nancy S. Dorfman, eds., *Economics of the Environment: Selected Readings,* 3rd ed. (New York: W. W. Norton, 1993), pp. 388–408 at p. 402.

4. This was the case until a few years ago. If you do not like thinking about airbags, you could think about smoke detectors or any other device one pays for voluntarily that reduces the probability of death.

5. W. Kip Viscusi, "Prospective Reference Theory: Toward an Explanation of the Paradoxes," *Journal of Risk and Uncertainty,* 2(3) 1989, 234–264. However, other studies suggest that people underestimate the probability of low-probability events, especially if they are in charge (e.g., driving a car) or when there are complex interdependent systems involved and the failure of one component causes failure in the whole system.

6. Jobs in finance, insurance, real estate, services, the retail trade, and the government all have fatality rates below 3 in 100,000 according to the U.S. Department of Labor, Bureau of Statistics, Census of Fatal Occupational Injuries, 2002.

7. Adam Smith, *The Wealth of Nations* (New York: Modern Press, 1776 reprinted 1937), p. 12.

8. See, for example, Jon P. Nelson, "Airports and Property Values: A Survey of Recent Evidence," *Journal of Transport Economics and Policy* 14(2) 1981, 37–52.

9. See T. D. Schroeder, "The Relationship of Local Public Park and Recreation Services to Residential Property Values," *Journal of Leisure Research* 14(3) 1982, 223–234.

10. See, for example, Anthony E. Boardman, Ruth Freedman, and Catherine Eckel, "The Price of Government Ownership: A Study of the Domtar Takeover," *Journal of Public Economics* 31(3) 1986, 269–285; John C. Ries,

"Windfall Profits and Vertical Relationships: Who Gained in the Japanese Auto Industry from VERs?" *Journal of Industrial Economics* 61(3) 1993, 259–276; Paul H. Malatesta and Rex Thompson, "Government Regulation and Structural Change in the Corporate Acquisitions Market: The Impact of the Williams Act," *Journal of Financial and Quantitative Analysis* 28(3) 1993, 363–379; Anthony Boardman, Ilan Vertinsky, and Diana Whistler, "Using Information Diffusion Models to Estimate the Impacts of Regulatory Events on Publicly Traded Firms," *Journal of Public Economics* 63(2) 1997, 283–300.

11. For a discussion of different ways to estimate what the return would have been in the absence of the event, see Stephen J. Brown and Jerold B. Warner, "Measuring Security Price Performance," *Journal of Financial Economics* 8(3) 1980, 205–258.

12. Sherwin Rosen developed the theory for estimating hedonic prices; see Sherwin Rosen, "Hedonic Prices and Implicit Markets: Product Differentiation in Pure Competition," *Journal of Political Economy* 82(1) 1974, 34–55.

13. The basic idea behind hedonic regression was introduced in Kelvin L. Lancaster, "A New Approach to Consumer Theory," *Journal of Political Economy* 74(1) 1966, 132–157.

14. In general, the hedonic price function can be written: $P = p(C_1, C_2, \ldots, C_k, N_1, \ldots, N_m)$, where C_i ($i = 1, \ldots, k$) denote k attributes of the house and N_j ($j = 1, \ldots, m$) denote m neighborhood characteristics.

15. Formally, $r_v = \dfrac{\partial P}{\partial VIEW}$.

16. As discussed in Chapter 12, in order to estimate the hedonic prices, analysts usually take the natural logarithms, ln, of both sides of equation (13.3) to obtain the hedonic regression model: $\ln P = \ln\beta_0 + \beta_1 \ln(CBD) + \beta_2 \ln(SIZE) + \beta_3 \ln(VIEW) + \beta_4 \ln(NBHD) + \epsilon$. The parameters of this model, which is linear in logarithms, may be estimated by ordinary least squares.

17. The hedonic price of C_i may be a function of all of the variables in the hedonic price function. Given the general hedonic price function presented in note 14, $\partial P/\partial C_i = f(C_1, \ldots, C_k, N_1, \ldots, N_m)$.

18. Formally, $r_v = \dfrac{\partial P}{\partial VIEW}$

    $= \beta_3 \beta_0 CBD^{\beta_1} SIZE^{\beta_2} VIEW^{\beta_3-1} NBHD^{\beta_4} e^{\epsilon}$

    $= \beta_3 \dfrac{P}{VIEW}$.

19. The functional form of this model may be linear, multiplicative, or have some other form.

20. These functions indicate households' willingness-to-pay holding household characteristics constant.

21. Many researchers estimate linear models of the following form:

    wage rate $= \beta_0 + \beta_1$fatality risk $+ \beta_2$injury risk $+ \beta_3$job tenure $+ \beta_4$education $+ \beta_5$age $+ \epsilon$

    If the dependent variable is the hourly wage rate, fatality risk is measured as the number of deaths per 10,000 workers and $\beta_1 = 0.3$, then researchers estimate the VSL $= 0.3 \times 2,000$ hours/yr $\times 10,000 = \$6$ million. However, linear hedonic models usually have identification problems as discussed below.

22. The seminal work on this topic, which actually preceded the formal development of the hedonic pricing method, is Ronald G. Ridker and John A. Henning, "The Determinants of Residential Property Values with Special Reference to Air Pollution," *Review of Economics and Statistics* 49(2) 1967, 246–257. For a review of studies that have attempted to use the hedonic method to estimate willingness-to-pay for reductions in particulate matter in air, see V. Kerry Smith and Ju-Chin Huang, "Can Markets Value Air Quality? A Meta-Analysis of Hedonic Property Value Models," *Journal of Political Economy* 103(1) 1995, 209–227. For an application to the value of life, see Paul Portney, "Housing Prices, Health Effects, and Valuing Reductions in Risk of Death," *Journal of Environmental Economics and Management* 8(1) 1981, 72–78.

23. W. P. Jennings and A. Kinderman, "The Value of a Life: New Evidence of the Relationship between Changes in Occupational Fatalities and Wages of Hourly Workers, 1992–1999," *The Journal of Risk and Insurance* 70(3) 2003, 549–561.

24. For a recent discussion concerning identification and estimation of hedonic models, see Ivar Ekeland, James J. Heckman, and Lars Nesheim, "Identification and Estimation of Hedonic Models," *Journal of Political Economy* 112(1) 2004, S60–S109.

25. This method is often referred to as the Clawson method, or the Knetsch-Clawson method. However, it is now attributed to Harold Hotelling; see Harold Hotelling, "Letter," *An Economic Study of the Monetary Evaluation of Recreation in the National Parks* (Washington, D.C.: National Park Service, 1949). For some of the earlier descriptions on this method see Marion Clawson, "Methods of Measuring the Demand for and Value of Outdoor Recreation," Reprint No. 10 (Washington, D.C.: Resources for the Future, 1959); Marion Clawson and Jack L. Knetsch, *Economics of Outdoor Recreation* (Baltimore: Johns Hopkins Press, 1966); and Jack L. Knetsch and Robert K. Davis, "Comparisons of Methods of Recreation Evaluation," in Allen V. Kneese and Stephen C. Smith, eds., *Water Research* (Baltimore: Johns Hopkins Press, 1966), 125–142.

26. For an interesting and novel application of the TCM, see Charles J. Cicchetti, A. Myrick Freeman III, Robert H. Haveman, and Jack L. Knetsch, "On the Economics of Mass Demonstrations: A Case Study of the November 1969 March on Washington," *American Economic Review* 61(4) 1971, 719–724.

27. Note that computing the area of the triangle using the formula ($95–$65)(6)/2 = $90 provides a slight overestimate of the consumer surplus, while using the formula ($90–$65)(6)/2 = $75 provides the correct answer. In effect, if we treat the intercept as $90 instead of $95, we obtain the correct answer. The problem arises because the number of visits is a discrete variable, while the equation for the inverse demand function is continuous.

28. Area *abc* ≈$3,600, area *dbfe* = $4,800, area *bcf* ≈ $4,200.

29. Gardner Brown Jr. and Robert Mendelsohn, "The Hedonic Travel Cost Model," *Review of Economics and Statistics* 66(3) 1984, 427–433.

30. For more detail, see Nancy G. Bockstael, Kenneth E. McConnell, and Ivar Strand, "Recreation," in J. B. Braden and C. D. Kolstad, eds., *Measuring the Demand for Environmental Quality* (Amsterdam: Elsevier, 1991), 227–270; and V. Kerry Smith and Yoshiaki Kaoru, "The Hedonic Travel Cost Model: A View From the Trenches," *Land Economics* 63(2) 1987, 179–192.

31. Alan Randall, "A Difficulty with the Travel Cost Method," *Land Economics* 70(1) 1994, 88–96.

32. See also John R. McKean, Donn M. Johnson, and Richard G. Walsh, "Valuing Time in Travel Cost Demand Analysis: An Empirical Investigation," *Land Economics* 71(1) 1995, 96–105.

33. Also, the travel cost variable may not be independent of the error term, thereby leading to ordinary least squares estimates that are biased and inconsistent.

34. This method is also referred to as the avoided cost method. For a review of the use of this method to measure groundwater values, see Charles Abdalla, "Groundwater Values from Avoidance Cost Studies: Implications for Policy and Future Research," *American Journal of Agricultural Economics* 76(5) 1994, 1062–1067.

35. The accuracy of using changes in defensive expenditures on a substitute to measure the benefits of changes in the levels of externalities or public goods depends on how these goods enter the individual's utility function and on the relationship between these goods and the market for the substitute. For more discussion of this issue, see Paul N. Courant and Richard Porter, "Averting Expenditure and the Cost of Pollution," *Journal of Environmental Economics and Management* 8(4) 1981, 321–329. Also see Winston Harrington and Paul Portney, "Valuing the Benefits of Health and Safety Regulation," *Journal of Urban Economics* 22(1) 1987, 101–112.

36. These models are also referred to as qualitative response models. See, for example, G. S. Maddala, *Limited-Dependent and Qualitative Variables in Econometrics* (Cambridge: Cambridge University Press, 1983); and Kenneth Train, *Qualitative Choice Analysis* (Cambridge, MA: MIT Press, 1986).

37. See, for example, David A. Hensher and Mark Bradley, "Using Stated Preference Response Data to Enrich Revealed Preference Data," *Marketing Letters* 4(2) 1993, 139–152.

CHAPTER 14

Contingent Valuation: Using Surveys to Elicit Information About Costs and Benefits

Economists generally are much more comfortable observing individuals' valuations of goods and services through their behavior in markets than eliciting their valuations through survey questionnaires. They prefer to observe purchasing decisions because these decisions directly reveal preferences, whereas surveys elicit statements about preferences. Nevertheless, for some public goods there are simply no, or very poor, market proxies or other means of inferring preferences from observations. In such circumstances, many analysts have concluded that there is no viable alternative to asking a sample of people about their valuations.

Questionnaires designed to elicit preferences are normally referred to as *contingent valuation* (CV) surveys,[1] or sometimes hypothetical valuation surveys, because respondents are not actually required to pay their valuations of goods.[2] The primary use of CV is to elicit people's willingness-to-pay for changes in quantities or qualities of goods. Many kinds of goods, including water quality at recreation sites, goose hunting, sports stadiums, and outdoor recreation, have been valued with CV surveys.[3] as have health outcomes.[4] Such agencies as the National Park Service and the U.S. Bureau of Reclamation use CV surveys to value recreation and wildlife opportunities. CV surveys are also used to value more complex and abstract goods, such as reductions in the volume of hazardous wastes, the value of archeological artifacts and sites, and the preservation of wetland ecosystems.[5] Valuing the use, or potential use, of goods with CV is relatively uncontroversial. Valuing passive use (nonuse) with CV is more controversial, both for the conceptual reasons discussed in Chapter 9 and the practical reasons related to gathering valid information from surveys discussed later in this chapter.

In spite of the controversy, the use of CV as a method for estimating costs and benefits is now widespread. Indeed, the federal courts have held that surveys of citizens' valuations have "rebuttable presumption" status in cases involving the assessment of damage to natural resources.[6] A blue-ribbon panel of social scientists convened by the National Oceanic and Atmospheric Administration (NOAA) further legitimized the use of CV by concluding that it could be the basis for estimating passive use values for inclusion in natural resource damage assessment cases.[7]

In this chapter we provide an overview of CV methods. We assess the major strengths and weakness of those methods most commonly used, emphasize the importance of informing respondents of how they would pay the costs of a project (the payment vehicle), review the major criticisms and problems related to CV use, discuss some of the survey issues most relevant to CV, and consider CV's accuracy. Finally, we present some heuristic checklists for analysts preparing or reviewing CV instruments.

OVERVIEW OF CONTINGENT VALUATION METHODS

The general approach of all CV methods is as follows. First, a sample of respondents from the population with standing is identified. Second, respondents are asked questions about their valuations of some good. Third, their responses provide information that enables analysts to estimate the respondents' willingness-to-pay (WTP) for the good. Fourth, the WTP amounts for the sample are extrapolated to the entire population. If, for instance, the respondents comprise a random sample of the population such that each member of the population had an equal chance of being in the sample, then the average WTP for the sample would simply be multiplied by the size of the population to arrive at the aggregate WTP.

As CV surveys are expensive to conduct, analysts may wish to extrapolate the results of existing surveys to different populations. However, the characteristics of these populations usually do not match those of the population previously sampled. For example, the populations may differ in terms of income, access to alternative goods, or other factors that may be relevant to their demands for the good. As discussed in Chapter 15, reasonable extrapolation requires that these differences be controlled for statistically.[8] Therefore, analysts increase the chances that their CV surveys will have use beyond their own CBAs by collecting and reporting information about the characteristics of their samples, including WTP amounts for subsets of the sample, even when such information is unnecessary for their own studies.

The remainder of this section introduces particular methods that are used to elicit WTP amounts from survey respondents. We first briefly sketch three methods that have been used at various times: the *open-ended willingness-to-pay* method, the *closed-ended iterative bidding* method, and the *contingent ranking* method. We then turn to the *dichotomous choice,* or *referendum,* method, which was advocated by the NOAA blue-ribbon panel as the method of choice in most circumstances.[9]

Direct Elicitation (Nonreferendum) Methods

Several CV methods ask questions about preferences directly. The open-ended willingness-to-pay method and the closed-ended iterative bidding method seek to elicit the WPT amounts for each respondent. The contingent ranking method seeks to elicit a preference profile over a set of alternatives for each respondent. These methods contrast with the dichotomous choice method, which is indirect in the sense that it relies on patterns of responses across a large number of respondents to make inferences about the preferences of respondents with particular characteristics.

Open-Ended Willingness-to-Pay Method   The earliest method to be used is the *open-ended willingness-to-pay* approach. Here respondents are simply asked to state their maximum WTP for the good, or policy, that is being valued.[10] The question might be formulated as follows: "What is the most that you would be prepared to pay in additional federal income taxes to guarantee that the Wildwood wilderness area will remain closed to development?" This method had dropped out of favor as analysts feared unrealistic responses because respondents needed some initial guidance on valuations.[11] Concerns that open-ended questions result in excessively large estimates of WTP seem unfounded; indeed, a more serious problem appears to be that respondents who have very low valuations of the good being valued often state a zero value.

Closed-Ended Iterative Bidding Method   In the *closed-ended iterative bidding* method, respondents are asked whether they would pay a specified amount for the good or policy that has been described. If respondents answer affirmatively, then the amount is incrementally increased. The procedure continues until the respondent expresses unwillingness to pay the amount specified. Similarly, if respondents answer negatively to the initial amount specified, the interviewer lowers the amount by increments until the respondent expresses a WTP.[12]

The initial question for determining WTP typically starts with something like the following: "Now suppose the costs to clean the Kristiansand Fjord were divided on [sic] all taxpayers in the whole of Norway by an extra tax in 1986. If this extra tax was 200 kronor for an average taxpayer, would you then be willing to support the proposal?"[13] In this CV survey the interviewer set the initial price at 200 kronor. If a respondent indicated a willingness-to-pay this initial price, then the interviewer raised the price by 200 kronor and asked the question again. The interviewer kept going until the respondent gave a negative answer. Similarly, if the initial response was negative, then the interviewer dropped the price by 200 kronor increments until the respondent gave a positive response. Although iterative bidding was at one time the most common method in use, it is rarely used now because of considerable evidence that its results are highly sensitive to the initially presented, or starting, value.

Contingent Ranking Method   In the *contingent ranking,* or *ranked choice,* method, respondents are asked to rank specific feasible combinations of quantities of the good being valued and monetary payments. For example, respondents choose on a continuum between a low level of water quality at a low tax-price and a high level of water quality at a high tax-price. The combinations are ranked from most preferred to least preferred.[14] The rankings provide a basis for estimating each respondent's WTP for various increments of quality. Contingent ranking implies an ordinal ranking procedure in contrast to the iterative bidding procedure, which requires cardinal evaluation. Typically, tasks that require only ordinal information processing, that is, a ranking rather than a precise specification of value, are considerably easier for respondents to perform.[15] This is a valuable attribute in the CV context where complex information must often be processed by respondents. Of course, unlike the open-ended WTP method or the closed-ended iterative bidding method, the WTP of interest must be inferred from ordinal rankings rather than directly elicited. Additionally, responses appear to be sensitive to the order in which alternatives are presented to respondents.

Dichotomous Choice (Referendum) Method

In the *dichotomous choice, binary choice,* or *referendum* method, respondents are asked whether they would be willing to pay a particular price to obtain a good or policy.[16] Each respondent receives one randomly drawn price. Respondents are then asked to state whether they would be willing to pay for the good or policy (e.g., closing the Wildwood wilderness area to development) at the offered price ("yes" means willing to pay and "no" means not willing to pay); in other words, they are made a binary "take it or leave it" offer of the sort that they face in many markets for private goods. The choice situation is also like that faced by referendum voters—hence the label referendum method. The dollar amounts, often referred to as *bid prices,* that are presented to respondents vary over a range selected by the analyst.[17] The probability of respondents accepting the offer can then be calculated for each bid price.[18]

Figure 14-1 shows the distribution of responses to bid prices in the form of a histogram. Specific bid prices are shown on the horizontal axis ranging from the lowest dollar price offered ($X = \$0$) to the highest price offered ($X = \$100$) in \$5 increments. The vertical axis measures the percentage of respondents who answer "yes" to the bid price offered to them. In this example, almost all of the respondents who are offered the specified outcome at $X = \$0$ state they would accept it. About 75 percent of respondents who are offered the outcome for \$30 indicate that they would accept it at this price. We can interpret the response frequencies as estimates of the probability that a randomly drawn member of the sample of respondents is willing to pay a specific amount. For example, the probability a randomly drawn respondent would pay at least \$30 for the specified outcome is about 0.75.

The fitted curve in Figure 14-1 may be viewed as the demand curve of a randomly drawn (i.e., average) member of the sample, while the histogram may be viewed as a rough approximation of this demand curve. The difference between the demand curve in Figure 14-1 and the more standard demand curve is that instead of the curve indicating the quantity of a good the individual would be willing to purchase at each price, the curve indicates the probability that the individual would be

FIGURE 14-1 Histogram of Dichotomous Choice Responses

Curve fitted to the histogram

willing to pay for the specified outcome at each price.[19] As in the case of a standard demand curve, the area under the curve in Figure 14-1 provides an estimate of the individual's willingness-to-pay.

If the values of X are evenly spread, then the histogram can be readily used to obtain a rough estimate of the average individual's willingness-to-pay by applying a simple formula:

$$\text{WTP} = v \sum_{k=0}^{N} [\text{Probability of acceptance at price } kv] \qquad \textbf{(14.1)}$$

where v is the interval between prices (i.e., the width of the individual bars in the histogram) and N is the number of values of X (i.e., the number of bars). In other words, the area covered by the bars (the approximate WTP for an average member of the sample) can be computed by simply summing the heights of the bars and multiplying by the bar width.

Analysts rarely work directly from the histogram of accepted bids. Better estimates can usually be made by estimating a statistical model for predicting the probability that an individual with specific characteristics will accept a particular bid price. The estimated model, often a logistic regression with bid price as one of the explanatory variables, allows the analyst to sketch the relationship between bid price and the probability of acceptance.[20] The area under this curve approximates the mean willingness-to-pay for these individuals.[21] It can be estimated through numerical methods.[22] The statistical model can also be used to estimate a probability-of-acceptance curve for each identified group within the sample. Therefore, it is possible to estimate a WTP for an average member of each of these groups as the area under each group's probability-of-acceptance curve. *To find the aggregate WTP for the entire population, one multiplies the mean for each group by the size of that group in the population with standing and then sums across groups.*[23]

Because this method only tells one whether a given respondent's valuation is greater or less than the offered amount, sample sizes have to be large in order to achieve reasonable levels of precision. For small samples, the true value of WTP may be considerably different from the observed value of WTP. On the other hand, "take it or leave it" questions are very easy for respondents to answer, and they are the closest approximation to market-like transactions.

Some analysts have now moved to *double dichotomous choice* (sometimes called *double bounded dichotomous choice*) rather than single elicitation questions to reduce the need for large samples. In this version of the method, depending on the answer to the first offer, a follow-up offer is made that is either double (if yes) or half (if no) the first offer. This provides considerably more information than the standard single-offer version. However, there is danger that the respondent's exposure to the first offer may affect the probability that he or she will accept the follow-up offer.[24] Recognizing that follow-up bids provide information to respondents that may change their perceptions of the likely price or quantity of the good being valued, Richard Carson and colleagues suggest several ways that this information might affect their responses to the second bids.[25] First, those who initially rejected bids may take the lower follow-up bid as an indication that the bid price is negotiable and reject bids that they previously would have accepted. Second, those who initially accepted bids may believe that there is some possibility that the good could be provided at the lower price and reject the higher second bid even though it is below their WTP. Third, in responding to the follow-up bid price, respondents may base their responses not on that price but on some weighted average of the two bid prices they encountered.[26] Whether the greater amount of information generated by the double dichotomous choice method is worth the risk of such response behaviors remains an open research question.

As we discuss in detail in a subsequent section of this chapter [see *the Strategic Response (Honesty) Problem*], a major advantage of a binary choice formulation is that it meets the necessary condition for incentive compatibility—the incentive for respondents to give truthful rather than strategic answers. The other methods we discuss are not incentive compatible. The possibility that the referendum method is incentive compatible is an important reason that it is the most commonly used CV method.

PAYMENT VEHICLE

Almost all CV exercises specify a *payment vehicle*, which describes how the respondent's costs of providing the good will be paid. Payment vehicles include taxes paid into a fund specifically earmarked for the good, increased utility bills, higher income or sales taxes, and higher product prices. Specifying a payment vehicle, along with reminders that payments come at the expense of expenditures on other goods, helps ensure that respondents perceive the questions as real economic choices. In order to increase the realism of CV surveys, researchers generally try to specify a payment vehicle that is as close as possible to the actual one that would be used were supply of the good to proceed.

The choice of payment vehicle can make a difference in the estimated WTP. In a recent study, for example, researchers found that respondents appeared to value watershed management plans differently depending on whether there was a guarantee that taxes imposed to pay for them would not be used for other purposes.[27] The presence or absence of such a guarantee also affected respondents' valuations of specific attributes of watershed plans.

There has been considerable debate in the CV literature as to whether differences in the WTP of respondents due to differences in payment vehicles should be treated as a bias. Kenneth Arrow and others argue that respondents are being asked to value all elements of a project, which include the method of payment; therefore, respondent preferences about payment methods do not imply bias.[28] Other analysts argue that if specific payment vehicles, such as taxes, introduce "protest" valuations, then such outliers should be excluded from the estimation of aggregate WTP. Protest bidders can sometimes be screened out by their answers to specific questions designed to identify them.

GENERIC SURVEY ISSUES

Before turning specifically to CV surveys, it is useful to consider briefly some issues relevant to all survey contexts. One issue concerns the trade-offs among methods for administering surveys. Another issue is the extent to which the procedures for identifying and reaching respondents leads to an appropriate sample from which to estimate the distribution of attitudes within the population with standing.

Survey Administration: In-Person, Telephone, Mail, and Internet

Currently, there are three major technologies for administering surveys: in-person interviews, telephone interviews, and mail questionnaires. Each has strengths and weaknesses, and each raises different methodological issues. None of the three procedures is unequivocally superior to the others. The Internet is now joining the list as one of the major technologies for administering surveys.

Table 14-1 summarizes the characteristics of the survey administration alternatives. In-person interviews involve interviewers meeting face-to-face with respondents. Especially relevant in the CV context, face-to-face interaction facilitates the provision of complex information to respondents through the presentation of maps, diagrams, photographs, and other visual aids by the interviewer. The interviewer can also clarify questions and provide additional information and otherwise interact directly with the respondent. This direct contact, however, also involves a high risk of interviewer bias, as respondents may react to the personal characteristics of the interviewer, perhaps slanting answers to gain the interviewer's approval. Unlike telephone interviews, which typically are conducted from a central location, in-person interviews are difficult to monitor. The greatest disadvantage, however, is that in-person interviews tend to be very expensive, especially for geographically disperse samples, because of the time spent traveling between interviews and the precautions that must be taken to ensure the security of the interviewers. As is the case with mail questionnaires, the capability for identifying a random sample of any population depends on the availability of lists of the individuals, families, or households that make up the population. In many locations, such as cities with guarded apartment buildings or suburbs with restricted-access housing developments, it may be difficult to reach respondents randomly selected to be in the sample.

Telephone interviews have become the most common method of administering CV surveys. Telephone interviews cost substantially less than in-person interviews, even with a large number of call-backs to reach persons who are not at home or who use answering

TABLE 14-1 Survey Administration Alternatives

	Cost per Completed Interview	Ease of Identifying and Reaching Respondents	Risk of Interviewer Bias	Maximum Complexity of Provided Information
In-Person	Very high—depends on questionnaire length and geographic spread	Medium—depends on availability of lists and access	High—personal presence, monitoring difficult	Very high—interactive communication and visual aids possible
Telephone	High—depends on questionnaire length and call-backs	Very high—random digit dialing	Medium—interviewer cues	Low—verbal communication limits complexity of content
Mail	Low—depends on number of follow-ups	High—depends on availability of appropriate lists	Low—uniform presentation	High—visual aids possible
Internet	Low—marginal costs very small	Low—"spamming" restrictions require panels of willing respondents	Low—uniform presentation	Very high—visual aids and interactive questions possible

machines. They also have the advantage of allowing researchers to draw reasonable random samples through random digit dialing, obviating the need for address lists in surveys of households. Unfortunately, verbal communication limits the complexity of information that can be provided. It also opens up the possibility of interviewer bias, as respondents react to voice cues and perceptions of the characteristics of the interviewer.

Several trends are making telephone interviews more costly and difficult to implement effectively. One trend is the greater prevalence of telemarketing, often masquerading as surveys. More people are refusing to participate in surveys to avoid unwanted telemarketing solicitations. Others use answering machines and caller identification to screen out calls from strangers. Another trend is the growing complexity of the telephone system, which makes it increasingly difficult to draw good random samples through random digit dialing. Households more often have multiple telephone lines, some of which are dedicated to facsimile machines or teenagers. Cellular telephones are breaking down area codes, making it more difficult to sample geographically. Dealing with these problems will likely raise the costs of telephone surveys in the future.

Mail questionnaires, which allow the provision of visual aids to respondents, have the advantage of very low cost. The ease of identifying samples depends on the availability of appropriate lists. Accurate lists also make it easy to identify a sample of respondents and contact them by mail, though response rates are typically low, often requiring multiple mailings to reach acceptable levels. As there are no interviewers, all respondents experience the same presentation, and therefore there is no interviewer bias.

As more U.S. adults become Internet users, the plausibility of using the Internet for conducting surveys increases. Internet surveys have several advantages over the other methods. Because interviewers are not needed, Internet surveys have extremely low marginal costs, perhaps even lower than mail surveys. Unlike mail surveys, the actual data collection can often be fully automated and implemented within a very short time frame, an advantage when the CV survey is intended to inform a pending decision. Like mail surveys, they avoid the risk of interviewer bias, and they allow for the provision of complex information. Indeed, one can imagine giving respondents access to large quantities of information through menus and other interactive devices. Unfortunately, drawing random samples of populations remains a barrier. Not all members of most populations of interest are currently Internet users. This is changing, but even when Internet use has become ubiquitous, sampling is complicated by restrictions on spamming, which prevents procedures analogous to random digit dialing in telephone surveys. Firms are beginning to develop databases of willing respondents, which may become sufficiently large and representative of populations of interest to allow scientifically valid CV studies to be administered through the Internet.[29]

Sample and Nonresponse Biases

The essence of survey research is eliciting information about a population from a small sample drawn from that population. As summarized in Table 14-1, survey administration alternatives differ in terms of the ease with which they facilitate identifying and reaching respondents. How to identify individuals to be sampled from target populations is the topic of *sample design*.[30] The extent to which valid responses are obtained from those identified determines whether the sample design will actually produce data adequate for making valid inferences.

In almost all cases, the sample is selected by a probability mechanism, which produces a *random sample*. In a random sample, each individual has a known probability of being drawn from the population. *Simple random samples* give each individual in the target population the same probability of being sampled. *Stratified samples* give members of particular groups within a population the same probability of being sampled. In either case, knowing the selection probabilities allows researchers to base inferences about the characteristics of the population on the characteristics of the sample.

If a given sample is appropriately selected and administered, then sample biases can be avoided. Advances in probability sampling techniques have been such that findings based on samples of approximately a thousand people can be representative of the entire population of the United States. However, approximately the same sample size may also be necessary for much smaller populations—essentially, for large populations the sample size needed to achieve any desired level of precision does not depend on the size of the population being sampled. Additionally, there is considerable evidence that the observed distributions of WTP in CV are skewed toward extreme values. For this reason, CV samples should be larger than samples drawn for many other purposes to obtain reliable estimates of population means. This is especially true for the dichotomous choice method.

For CV purposes, *the relevant target population is usually all individuals with standing who are affected by the policy.* Unfortunately, this heuristic begs the question of who is affected. For many projects it is apparent. But often it is not, especially in addressing environmental issues. In some contexts there is congruence between those who bear the cost of policies and those who are affected by them. In other contexts, however, these groups diverge, as when a state or province provides a wilderness area that is valued by people living in other jurisdictions. The greater such divergence, the more problematic it is to choose the correct population.[31]

Several major issues are involved in assessing who is affected. First, all those "users" directly affected by the project should be included. The term *users* is in quotes because we mean it in a specific way. Those who would directly utilize the good in question are, of course, users. But so are individuals who suffer direct negative impacts that they would pay to avoid. For example, nearby residents of a duck hunting reserve who dislike the noise are as much users as the duck hunters. Potential users should also be included. As discussed in Chapter 8, in situations involving uncertainty, the option price that an individual would be willing to pay for a good may differ from his or her expected surplus. So even people who never actually consume the good may value it.

Second, it is important for survey respondents to understand whether they are being asked to estimate WTP just for themselves or as a representative for their whole household. This distinction is important in extrapolating from the sample to the target population.

Third, an explicit decision should be made concerning the inclusion of passive use benefits. As discussed in Chapter 9, either users or nonusers may derive existence value from a project. Conceptually, existence value should be included as a component of benefits. For environmental goods, CV surveys that either sample nonusers or estimate existence values of users typically yield much higher aggregate WTP estimates than those that include only use benefits. However, there is considerable disagreement on the validity of using CV surveys to estimate nonuse benefits.

Fourth, the geographic *spread,* or *reach,* of the sample should be wide enough to capture all affected individuals. There is increasing recognition that decisions concerning the geographic definition of the relevant market can drive the outcomes of many CBAs, especially if nonusers are included.[32]

An important sampling question relates to the exclusion of responses. It has been suggested that three categories of respondents should be excluded in estimating WTP: first, respondents who reject the whole notion of placing a value on the good in question, or of paying for the good in a certain way (this has already been discussed); second, respondents who refuse to take the exercise seriously; and third, respondents who clearly demonstrate that they are incapable of understanding the survey.[33] In the direct elicitation methods, all three types of respondents are usually assumed to provide either zero valuations or extremely high valuations. Sometimes such respondents can be directly identified by their answers to specific questions intended to screen them from the sample. Respondents who provide extreme values are known as *outliers.* Outliers are normally handled in CV by simply eliminating valuations that are above some specified threshold or that are above a specified percentage of the respondent's gross or discretionary income.

An appropriate sampling design can usually eliminate most sample bias if it is fully executed. Yet, bias can still remain if some individuals do not respond to the survey. Nonresponse bias is a serious problem in almost all survey research. Nonresponse problems have grown over the last 20 years as the public has been asked to give time to more surveys and has become suspicious of the motives of many who claim to be survey researchers. If nonresponse is purely random, then it can be dealt with by increasing the sample size. Unfortunately, nonresponse is often not random.[34]

There are two major types of nonresponse problems: refusal to respond and unavailability to respond. In CV contexts, the primary approaches for dealing with

---

EXHIBIT 14-1

As part of a court case, the plaintiffs conducted a CV survey to estimate the natural resource damage caused by a mine. They surveyed residents of both the county (Eagle County) and the state (Colorado) in which the mine was located. Based on their surveys, they estimated past damages were $50.8 million and future expected damages would be between $15 and $45 million. The defendants sampled a much smaller group within Eagle County that they believed had been directly affected by pollution from the mine; they assumed that residents in the rest of Colorado did not bear costs from the mine. Although the per-unit values of both sides were similar (for example, on the value of a day's fishing), the defendants' estimate of total past and future expected damage was approximately $240,000, less than 1 percent of the plaintiffs' estimate. "The discrepancies in these respective aggregate estimates arise from the plaintiff's assumption that . . . there would be a much larger number of people experiencing gains with the restoration" (p. 605).

Source: Adapted from Raymond J. Kopp and V. Kerry Smith, "Benefit Estimation Goes to Court: The Case of Natural Resource Damage Assessments," *Journal of Policy Analysis and Management* 8(4) 1989, 593–612.

refusal to respond are to highlight the legitimacy of the exercise (e.g., by stressing government or university affiliations) or to offer various response incentives, such as donations to charities or entries into prize lotteries. Where unavailability biases the sample, researchers typically account for underrepresentation and overrepresentation in the sample when extrapolating to the target population.[35]

CONTINGENT VALUATION PROBLEMS AND ISSUES

This section discusses specific problems relevant to CV surveys. The subsequent section discusses more general survey problems that are relevant to CV. Surveying opinions is not an exact science. The science of CV surveys is even less exact. Some critics argue that CV has such serious weaknesses that it should be used only as a last resort. Other critics contend that it is so seriously flawed when used to value either complex goods or passive use impacts that it should not be used at all for these purposes.[36] It has been pointed out that the summation of average valuations over a broad range of projects to improve the environment would exhaust the budget of average individuals.[37]

Specific CV survey difficulties stem from several sources. First, CV inevitably raises questions that are more novel and complex than those raised in other survey situations. This poses problems of *hypotheticality* (we use this as a catchall word to cover problems of understanding, meaning, context, and familiarity). Hypotheticality appears to be more severe when respondents have not, and will not, consume the good in some way. That is, hypotheticality tends to be most severe in the valuation of passive use. Second, CV raises questions of *neutrality* in the presentation of information to respondents. Third, for certain methods, *judgmental biases* may arise in response to certain kinds of questions (including whether the question is framed as willingness-to-pay or as willingness-to-accept). Not all these problems necessarily create biases (i.e., a systematic tendency to overvalue or undervalue the goods in question), but all of them do raise questions about the validity and reliability of CV as a procedure. Some specific CV methods appear to be more prone to biases than others. Fourth, CV asks questions about WTP, raising the potential for biases related to *strategic behavior* (misstatements intended to influence some outcome) and the specified payment vehicle.

Hypotheticality, Meaning, and Context Problems

A major concern in CV design is whether respondents are truly able to understand and place into context the questions they are being asked and, consequently, whether they can accurately value the good in question. Issues relating to the valuation of the supply of many publicly provided goods are complex and highly contextual. CV questions can be contrasted to many other types of questions for which meaning is not an issue (eg., "For whom do you intend to vote in the next election?").

Questions of hypotheticality and meaning can be thought of as problems of specifying exactly what is the good in question. Understanding the good, or the policy that produces it, is difficult for respondents because they often are not familiar with either. When respondents are presented with questions about goods or projects that they do not understand, attitudes (and responses as expressed in the CV survey) are unlikely to correspond to the behavior that would occur if the project were actually implemented.[38] When a project (or the good itself) has multiple attributes, these all need to be explained to respondents: "Unless [an attribute is] specified explicitly (and comprehensively), evaluators must guess its value and, hence, what the offer really means. If they guess wrong, then they risk misrepresenting their values."[39]

This problem, however, has to be seen in context. Individuals also differentially value attributes of market goods: Some individuals may value a mountain bike mostly for prestige reasons and others for transportation purposes. The evidence also suggests that people find it somewhat difficult to value the attributes of new and unfamiliar products in market contexts.[40] As Richard Carson and his colleagues point out, "Many new products become available each year creating markets in which consumers regularly make purchase decisions . . . No standard microeconomics text has ever stated that prior experience is a precondition for rational decision making."[41]

Additional problems arise in CV if the perceptions of the good by respondents are not independent of the quality or quantity of the information provided. The possible information that could be provided when describing complex goods are unlimited. The quantity and quality of information, however, are limited in practice by the method of survey administration. Several commentators have emphasized that there is little evidence that hypotheticality per se introduces bias into CV.[42] But in the presence of hypotheticality certain kinds of bias may be more likely.

The potential for hypotheticality varies enormously across different CBA contexts. Unfortunately, CV is likely to be most useful in contexts in which goods are difficult to define, such as projects involving environmental impacts. When it is difficult to specify potential physical impacts, it is also likely to be difficult for respondents to understand what these impacts mean.

Hypotheticality and lack of realism can be reduced in a number of ways. *Clearly specifying the project and its impacts increases the likelihood of correspondence between attitudes and behavior; so too does providing explicit detail about the payment vehicle.* Visual aids such as photographs, maps, and diagrams often assist in understanding. One important class of visual aids useful in reducing hypotheticality is known as quality ladders. An example of a quality ladder is described in Exhibit 14-2. Quality ladders help respondents understand both what quality is under the status quo, and what particular increments of quality mean.

Baruch Fischhoff and Lita Furey have suggested a checklist for evaluating CV instruments in terms of the likelihood that respondents will understand the questions they are being asked.[43] It requires the analyst to assess the comprehensiveness of information with respect to the good, the specification of the payment vehicle, and the social context. In assessing the adequacy of information about the good, they stress the need to provide information on both substantive and formal components. The substantive aspect of the good deals with why someone might value it (basically its attributes), while the formal aspect of the good concerns how much they value it (once they understand its attributes).

In practice, *the only effective way to minimize hypotheticality and meaning problems in CV surveys is to devote extensive effort to developing detailed, clear, informative, and highly contextual materials and to pretest these materials extensively on typical respondents.*

Neutrality

While the previous section indicated that lack of clear meaning does not necessarily pose a bias problem, lack of neutrality is certain to do so. As CBA deals with increasingly

EXHIBIT 14-2

A "water quality ladder" has been used in several CBAs to help respondents understand how differing levels of toxins, dissolved solids, water clarity, and other factors affect water quality. In their CBA of water quality improvements to the Monongahela River, V. Kerry Smith and William Desvousges included a picture of a ladder with a 0-to-10 scale and the following interviewer instructions:

(*Interviewer: Read the following.*) Generally the better the water quality the better suited the water is for recreation activities and the more likely people will take part in outdoor recreation activities on or near the water. Here is a picture of a ladder that shows various levels of water quality. (*Interviewer: Give respondent water quality ladder.*)

The top of the ladder stands for the best possible quality of water. The bottom of the ladder stands for the worst possible water quality. On the ladder you can see the different levels of the quality of the water. For example: (*Interviewer: Point to each level—E, D, C, B, A—as you read the statements that follow*).

Level E (*Interviewer: Point.*) is so polluted that it has oil, raw sewage, and other things like trash in it; it has no plant or animal life and smells bad.

Water at level D is okay for boating but not fishing or swimming.

Level C shows where the water is clean enough so that gamefish like bass can live in it.

Level B shows where the water is clean enough so that people can swim in it safely.

And at level A, the quality of the water is so good that it would be possible to drink directly from it if you wanted to.

(*Interviewer: Now ask the respondent to use the ladder to rate the water quality in the Monongahela River on a scale of 0 to 10 and to indicate whether the ranking was for a particular site, and if so, to name it.*)

Source: Adapted from V. Kerry Smith and William H. Desvousges, *Measuring Water Quality Benefits* (Boston, MA: Kluwer Academic, 1986), 87.

controversial and complex topics, the neutrality of the CV questionnaire becomes an increasingly important issue. Neutrality has come to the fore as litigants in (especially environmental) court cases have conducted their own CV surveys.

Meaning and neutrality issues often intersect in ways that are extremely difficult to disentangle. For example, Daniel Hagen and colleagues surveyed 1,000 U.S. households by mail concerning the value of preserving the spotted owl.[44] Of the total, 409 questionnaires were returned. Some of the information that respondents were given included the following: " . . . a scientific committee concluded that logging should be banned on some forest lands to prevent the extinction of the Northern Spotted Owl . . ." and "a second group of independent scientists examined this study and agreed with these conclusions." The survey also included the comment that: "the well-being of the northern spotted owl reflects the well-being of the entire old-growth forest eco-system."

In a review of spotted owl CV studies in general, and the Hagen et al. study in particular, William McKillop criticized this framing of the issue. He argues that the survey did not include many relevant facts that respondents should have been told.[45] For example, the "committee of scientists" focused almost exclusively on old-growth habitat for spotted owls and largely ignored the fact that many are found in second-growth timber stands. Respondents were also not told that logging was already prohibited on considerable areas of old-growth timberland, and these acres were likely to increase in the course of normal national forest planning. In sum, McKillop argues that the spotted owl issue was not presented accurately or neutrally to respondents. He further argues that this issue is simply too complicated to be addressed by CV surveys.

There are no simple answers to the neutrality problem. But an inevitable conclusion is that one has to be especially cautious in interpreting the results of CV surveys that have been prepared by either parties to litigation or advocacy groups. At a practical level, *neutrality can best be ensured by pretesting the survey instrument with substantive experts who have "no axe to grind" in terms of the specific project that is being considered.* If neutral experts cannot be found, then pretesting with opposing advocates can be an alternative, perhaps enabling researchers to avoid the most serious challenges from those with positions not supported by the results.

Decision Making and Judgment Biases

Although it is reasonable to assume that individuals can make rational judgments about their valuations of goods in most market situations, evidence suggests that in certain circumstances they may not be able to do so readily. This is even more likely to occur in the context of CV surveys, because judgment rather than decision making is involved, and because there are not opportunities to learn from mistakes (we discuss the evidence on this issue later in the chapter).[46] More formally, in such circumstances, there is a tendency for individuals to behave as if they are not maximizing utility, especially with respect to choices involving uncertainty. In the context of functioning markets, these behaviors appear as decision-making biases that can result in irrational purchases (or lack of purchases). These decision-making errors can be thought of as a type of market failure.[47] In the context of CV, the term *judgment bias* rather than *decision-making bias* is applicable because the respondent is not actually purchasing the good in question.

Both decision-making and judgment biases appear to be most serious for activities or projects that would generate small changes in the probabilities of (already) low-probability events that have "catastrophic" costs if they occur (for example, activities that might cause a marginal change in the probability of a nuclear power plant accident).[48] As WTP depends on how likely respondents perceive such events will be, their perception of changes in probabilities is important in CV studies. Fortunately, researchers and analysts rarely rely solely on CV estimates in such contexts. For example, they can use value-of-life estimates derived from other methods in which these biases are less endemic (see Chapter 15).

Some of the major judgmental biases to which individuals are particularly prone include *availability bias,* whereby individuals estimate the probabilities of events by the ease with which occurrences can be recalled—more salient instances, such as those covered by the media, are more likely to be recalled; *representativeness,* or *conjunction bias,* whereby individuals judge the probabilities of events on the basis of their plausibility—people perceive the probability of an event as being higher as more detail is added, even though the detail is irrelevant; *optimism bias,* whereby people believe that they can beat the objective odds; *anchoring bias,* whereby individuals do not fully update their probability assessments as new information becomes available; *hindsight bias,* whereby individuals believe, after an event occurs, that it was more predictable than it actually was; *status quo bias,* whereby individuals stick with the status quo even when it is inexpensive to experiment or when the potential benefits from changing are large; and *probability assessment bias,* whereby people tend to overestimate small probabilities and underestimate large probabilities.[49]

Many of these violations of the expected utility hypothesis can be explained by the fact that, when dealing with complex information, people tend to use simplifying (non-utility-maximizing) heuristics, or "rules of thumb." Essentially, people frame problems consistently, but the framing does not correspond to maximization of expected utility.

One conceptual framework for explaining violations of the expected utility hypothesis is *prospect theory.*[50] Prospect theory, which is particularly relevant to CV issues, suggests that individuals deviate from expected utility maximization in several ways. They value gains and losses from a reference point rather than valuing net wealth. Moreover, people are risk averse toward gains and risk seeking toward losses (known as *loss aversion*)—a loss and a gain of the same size would leave a person with loss aversion worse off. This may stem from an *endowment effect,* whereby individuals have a greater psychological attachment to things they currently possess.[51]

Several of these effects can be summarized in a prospect theory value function, which is illustrated in Figure 14-2. In this figure, the vertical axis measures value and the horizontal axis measures losses and gains. The figure is drawn to show three things. First, people start from a reference point from which changes are measured as losses or gains.

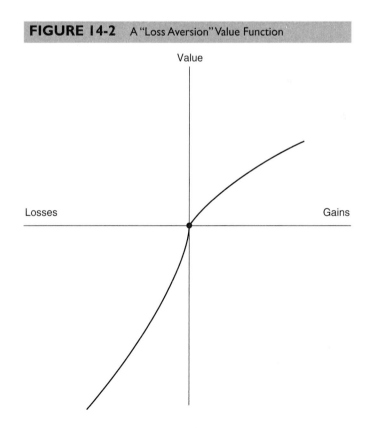

FIGURE 14-2   A "Loss Aversion" Value Function

Second, individuals are risk averse with respect to potential gains (i.e., they prefer a smaller certain gain over a larger probable gain, when the expected values of the two alternatives are the same). Individuals are also risk seeking with respect to potential losses (i.e., they prefer a larger probable loss to a smaller certain loss, when the expected values of the two alternatives are the same). This is represented in the figure by the concave gain function and the convex loss function. Third, losses loom larger than gains of equal size. This is represented in the figure as the loss function being steeper for losses than for gains from the reference point.

The biases suggested by prospect theory are particularly relevant to CV for a number of reasons. Anchoring via reference points is always a potential problem. Even if open-ended questions are used to eliminate starting point bias, payment vehicles and other descriptive detail may introduce anchoring indirectly. Furthermore, detailed descriptions may evoke availability bias. Finally, as we discuss later, CV questions can sometimes be plausibly framed as either involving gains or losses.

Empirical research suggests that the most serious judgment problems actually found in CV results relate to *noncommitment bias, order effects* (sometimes described as sequencing effects), *embedding effects* (sometimes described as whole/part effects or inclusiveness effects), and *starting point bias.*

Noncommitment Bias[52]   It is well recognized in the marketing literature that respondents to surveys tend to overstate their willingness to purchase a product that is described to them.[53] This may be a strategic response (an issue discussed later), but can also be thought of as either a form of anchoring bias (e.g., "this product must be valuable because they are asking me about it and describing it in such detail") in a context in which potential consumers do not engage in any learning. It is likely to be quite unconscious. The bias can flourish, of course, because the respondent does not actually have to commit money.

One set of experiments has attempted to test for noncommitment bias. The researchers conclude that "hypothetical WTP is consistently and significantly higher than the WTP that reflects real economic commitments."[54]

It is difficult to test for noncommitment bias when dealing with passive use values. One indirect way of testing for the bias is to introduce elements to the survey that encourage respondents to think more carefully about their income and their budget constraints. Michael Kemp and Christopher Maxwell have developed a "top-down disaggregation method" to do just this.[55] Top-down disaggregation attempts to mitigate noncommitment bias by raising awareness of budget constraints. After asking respondents to state initially their total WTP, they were questioned specifically about comparative valuations. For example, after respondents were asked about their WTP to avoid a specified oil spill, they were then asked about their valuations of environmental protection versus reduction in crime, homelessness, and other social problems. They were also asked about their valuations for different kinds of environmental protection (wilderness areas versus groundwater quality, rainforest protection, and other environmental goals). At the next level, they were asked to evaluate various kinds of wilderness area protection (reduction in harm from human-caused problems versus natural degradation and other destructive processes). At the end of this top-down disaggregation process, respondents were again asked their WTP. The result was WTP values several hundred times smaller than the WTP values from the initial open-ended questions.

In the more commonly used CV methods, it may be desirable to ask questions that require respondents to think more carefully about the budget constraints that they face.[56] For example, asking questions that encourage respondents to think about how much of their income is discretionary may help avoid noncommitment bias. The answers may also be useful in helping to assess whether the WTP values provided are subject to noncommitment bias.

Order Effects   George Tolley and Alan Randall found that survey respondents' statements of the value of improved visibility in the Grand Canyon were greatly affected by the order in which the issue was raised.[57] Other studies have also found important order, or sequence, effects. Consider, for example, a study that asked some respondents to value preserving seals and then whales, while others were asked to value preserving whales and then seals. Seal values were considerably lower when the seal question was asked after the whale question.[58]

These findings could be explainable in terms of either an income effect, a substitution effect, or a combination of both. The rationale for an income effect is as follows: If someone has expressed a positive WTP to pay for the first good in a sequence of goods, then that person has less income to spend on the second good in the sequence. Critics of CV, however, have observed that the steep declines in WTP as a good moves down in order cannot be fully explained by income effects because these should be relatively small.[59]

Substitution effects, such as between seals and whales, could be quite large, and consequently they can be important in CBA, especially in terms of assessing the aggregate impacts of projects. (That is, respondents may view one environmental improvement as a substitute for another quite different environmental improvement.) If people engage in extensive substitution, then the net aggregate benefits from a project may be smaller than predicted. For example, if a resident of Chicago agrees to contribute to a project that cleans the air in Chicago and is then offered a project that preserves visibility in the Grand Canyon, the value of the Grand Canyon project may be decreased because of the substitution effect.

The issue of whether substitution effects could account for much of the order inconsistency in CV surveys of passive use values is still undecided.[60] Critics argue that the phenomenon is explained neither by income nor by substitution effects, but it instead demonstrates that respondents cannot really understand these kinds of questions. Hence, they inevitably engage in judgment heuristics that usually cause them to overstate valuations. Thus, it is uncertain that income and substitution effects provide a complete explanation for order effects.[61]

Embedding Effects   A fundamental axiom in the standard economic description of preferences is that individuals value more of a good more highly than less of it. This is sometimes referred to as a *scope test*. If CV respondents' valuations are only slightly higher for large changes in the amount of the good offered than for small changes, then the validity of their responses becomes a concern. But research indicates that individuals often do not readily distinguish between small and large quantities in their valuations of a good when the different quantities are *embedded* in one another. For example, William H. Desvousges and colleagues found that different samples of respondents value 2,000 migratory birds approximately the same as 200,000 birds, and small oil spills much the same as much larger oil spills (given that these are different samples, it does not directly test whether given individuals prefer more to less).[62] Two additional examples of embedding are described in Exhibit 14-3. It is unlikely that declining marginal utility can explain all or even most of the absence of different valuations for different quantities of goods.

When dealing with passive use values, embedding is probably the most worrisome problem identified by critics of CV. It goes to the very heart of welfare economics. Critics argue that the empirical evidence suggests that in these contexts respondents are not actually expressing their valuations but instead are expressing broad moral attitudes to environmental issues—a "warm glow" or "moral satisfaction."[63] However, Carson and colleagues have argued that most studies that manifest embedding problems, or scope insensitivity, are poorly designed and executed, and they further argue that well-designed CV instruments do not manifest the problem.[64]

Starting Point Bias   Prospect theory identifies anchoring as a common behavioral response to being asked to make complex judgments. A problem arises in CV when starting values are presented to respondents. The iterative bidding method is particularly prone to this problem because this method provides respondents with a specific initial starting "price."[65] Consider, for example, the Kristiansand Fjord study mentioned earlier in the chapter. It was found that a range starting at 200 kronor and progressing to 2,000 kronor produced different valuations than a range starting at 0 kronor and progressing to 2,000 kronor, even when there were no bids between 0 and 200 kronor.[66]

The dichotomous choice question format is intended to eliminate starting point bias. It has been argued, however, that "responses to dichotomous choice questions are

---

EXHIBIT 14-3

Daniel Kahneman and Jack L. Knetsch report that residents of Toronto expressed a willingness to pay increased taxes to prevent a drop in fish stocks in all Ontario lakes that was only slightly larger than their expressed WTP to preserve fish stocks in a small area of the province. This is implausible.

The same researchers studied the impact of embedding. They did so by specifying a good: (1) very broadly to one sample of respondents (environmental services that included "preserving wilderness areas, protecting wildlife, providing parks, preparing for disasters, controlling air pollution, insuring water quality, and routine treatment and disposal of industrial wastes"; (2) considerably more narrowly to a second sample of respondents ("to improve preparedness for disasters" with a subsequent allocation to go to "the availability of equipment and trained personnel for rescue operations"), and (3) more narrowly still to a third sample ("improve the availability of equipment and trained personnel for rescue operations"). Respondents in each sample were asked to express their willingness to pay for their "good." The differences in WTP among the three samples were not large.

Source: Adapted from Daniel Kahneman and Jack L. Knetsch, "Valuing Public Goods: The Purchase of Moral Satisfaction," *Journal of Environmental Economics and Management* 22(1) 1992, 57–70. (For a critique of this study, see V. Kerry Smith, "Comment: Arbitrary Values, Good Causes, and Premature Verdicts," *Journal of Environmental Economics and Management* 22[1] 1992, 71–89.)

very strongly influenced by starting-point bias, because respondents are likely to take initial cues of resource value from the solicited contribution amount (e.g., assuming it to be his/her share of the needed contribution)."[67] Moreover, there is at least some empirical evidence to support the contention that the dichotomous choice method is subject to starting point bias,[68] although WTP estimated from dichotomous choice responses appears to be less affected by the provision of information about the total cost of providing a good or the size of the group receiving it than does WTP estimated from open-ended surveys.[69]

Hypotheticality Bias versus Judgment Bias   In the last resort it is almost impossible to disentangle hypotheticality issues from various forms of judgment bias in nonuse contexts because they are essentially two different sides of the same coin. Hence, the same approach is required to minimize both: an effort to present the project or good in question as concretely as possible, at the lowest level of disaggregation as possible, and with as much realism concerning budget constraints as possible. Neutrality problems also appear to be generic to CV. But this problem is less worrisome because it can be made reasonably transparent with good research protocols.

WTP versus WTA

Economic theory implies that if individuals behave rationally, and if markets are working efficiently, then in most circumstances it should make little difference whether respondents to a CV survey are asked their WTP for receiving a good or their willingness-to-accept (WTA) the loss of a comparable good.[70] Similarly, it should make little difference whether they are asked their WTP to prevent a loss or their WTA for a comparable loss.

As we have already discussed, considerable evidence suggests that individuals demand greater monetary compensation to give up things that they already possess than they are willing to pay to acquire the same exact item. In experiments that actually require people to trade goods for money, as well as in other contexts, it has been found that required WTA amounts range from a ratio of four to fifteen times greater than WTP amounts.[71] Similar differences have also been found in CV studies, even with a well-specified market good. There is some evidence that this difference between WTP and WTA is attributable to loss aversion.[72]

There is also considerable evidence, however, that as the subjects in experiments become more experienced, differences between WTP and WTA shrink considerably, usually as a result of decreases in WTA amounts.[73] Other experimental evidence suggests that for nonmarket goods with imperfect substitutes the divergence between WTP and WTA persists even with experience.[74] In any event, CV survey contexts, which are typically one-shot events for respondents, do not present opportunities for learning. Moreover, they often involve nonmarket goods with no close substitutes.

Some commentators have argued that stated preferences are preferences and that, if respondents are actually being asked to give up something, then the relevant formulation is WTA. But even in a context in which something is being given up, analysts still have to decide whether to treat WTA as involving a judgment bias problem that requires adjustments. In view of the fact that experiments show learning effects in some contexts and, as discussed later, WTP amounts are much closer to estimates derived from methods based on revealed preferences, the usual procedure is to use

WTP estimates.[75] This procedure is typically followed even in cases in which WTA questions fit the facts better than WTP questions—for example, as when the project involves the respondent giving up a good, such as a scenic view, that he or she currently consumes. The heuristic is, therefore, *that WTP question formats rather than WTA question formats should be used in CV in almost all cases.*

In thinking about WTP and WTA, one additional point should be kept in mind: We are concerned only about differences between the two *for the same individual.* The fact that different individuals have differing WTPs and WTAs is what makes markets work and presents no problem to CV.

The Strategic Response (Honesty) Problem

Will respondents answer honestly when asked about their WTP? It is frequently argued that respondents in CV surveys have incentives to behave *strategically,* that is, to misrepresent their true preferences in order to achieve a more desired outcome than would result if they honestly revealed their preferences. An analogy is often drawn between strategic behavior in CV studies and free riding in the provision of public goods.[76] The potential for strategic behavior in CV, however, is actually more varied than the free-riding characterization suggests.[77]

The Carson, Groves, and Machina Framework   Richard Carson, Theodore Groves, and Mark Machina assess the nature of strategic responses to CV questions likely to be encountered in use of the major CV methods.[78] They begin by making the point that we should not expect respondents' answers necessarily to be consistent with economic theory, and hence appropriate for inclusion in CBA, unless respondents believe that the survey is *consequential* in the sense that it could potentially influence some outcomes about which they care. In contrast, if respondents believe that the survey will have absolutely no influence on outcomes about which they care, then it is *inconsequential* and economic theory offers no predictions about the nature of responses.

They next note that the design of consequential CV surveys falls under the theory of *mechanism design,* which deals with the problem of creating rules for collective choice based on signals sent by individuals. Mechanisms that provide incentives for individuals to reveal their preferences truthfully are called *incentive compatible.*

One of the central theorems of mechanism design is that, in the absence of restrictions on the domain of preferences,[79] mechanisms involving more than binary signals will always be incentive compatible.[80] Mechanisms employing binary signals will not always be incentive compatible, but depending on the specific circumstances of choice, they may be (in other words, a binary signal is a necessary, but not necessarily sufficient, condition). More complex signals provide an opportunity for individuals to misstate their preferences in order to obtain a more desirable outcome.

As a brief illustration, return to the choice situation presented Chapter 2. Table 2-2 shows how the mechanism, pair-wise majority rule voting, could result in an intransitive social ordering. Consider a case in which the mechanism is being implemented by first putting X against Y in round one and then, in round two, Z against the winner of round one. Note that the signal sent by the voters in this situation is not binary—it consists of *two* binary signals, one for each round. If the voters send truthful signals about their preferences, then X beats Y in round one and Z beats X in round two, so that the mechanism selects Z as the social choice, which is voter 1's least preferred outcome. Anticipating this, voter 1 has an incentive to misrepresent his preferences by voting for Y in round one, so that Y would win and be put against Z in round 2 and win. This misrepresentation of preferences in round 1 would result in Y, an outcome more desirable to voter 1 than the one that resulted from sending a truthful signal about his preferences in round one. Once the voters reach round 2, it is as if they are facing a new choice situation in which they send only a binary signal. In this last round, there is no incentive to misrepresent preferences.

One immediate implication of this theorem is that continuous response formats, as used in the open-ended WTP method, or multiple response formats, as used in the contingent ranking method, will always be vulnerable to strategic responses that misstate true preferences.

Consider the open-ended WTP method. We can imagine two types of misrepresentation of preferences. First, assume that respondents perceive having to make payments that do not depend on their stated WTPs, that they have true WTPs above their anticipated payments, and that they anticipate that the likelihood of the good being provided depends on the aggregate of stated WTPs. They would then have an incentive to overstate their WTPs, so that the estimated aggregate WTP would be too high. The possibility of such overstatement was widely anticipated by economists. Yet at least in comparison with the dichotomous choice method, which, as we will discuss, can be incentive compatible, it does not appear that such overstatement is a major problem in the open-ended WTP method.[81] One explanation is that the assumptions that make overstatement a desirable strategy for respondents may not often hold. For example, respondents may fear that their shares of the cost of providing the good will be a positive function of their stated WTPs and, hence, state WTPs that are as small as possible. However, they may also believe that the likelihood of provision depends on the fraction of respondents who state WTPs at or above the average cost of provision, rather than on aggregate WTP. If both of these assumptions hold, then a strategic respondent with a true WTP above the anticipated cost would state a WTP that is only slightly above the anticipated cost—above anticipated cost to increase the chances of provision but as little above as possible to minimize cost share.

Second, now consider respondents with true WTPs that are less than the costs that they anticipate would be imposed on them if the good were to be provided. Assume that they believe that the likelihood of provision depends on aggregate WTP. As they do not want the good provided, they have an incentive to state the smallest possible WTP, usually set to zero for goods researchers believe to be desirable. These strategic responses in the open-ended WTP method should lead to many zeros, and few WTP amounts under the respondents' perceived costs of provision. The larger the fraction of respondents following this strategy, the greater will be the underestimation of aggregate WTP.

As it involves a binary response, the dichotomous choice method *may* be incentive compatible. Carson, Groves, and Machina note that incentive compatibility requires that payment for the good can be compelled and that the question deals only with a single issue. Table 14-2 summarizes the incentive properties of several circumstances in which the dichotomous choice method has been used.

Using the dichotomous choice method to elicit WTP for a new public (nonexcludeable) good that will be funded with coercive payments by respondents meets the

TABLE 14-2 Incentive Properties of Dichotomous Choice Questions Applied to Types of Goods

Type of Good	Incentive Property
New public good with coercive payment	Incentive compatible
New public good with voluntary payment	Not incentive compatible
Introduction of new private good	Not incentive compatible
Choice between two new public goods	Incentive compatible
Choice between an existing and an alternative private good	Incentive compatible, but choice does not reveal information about quantity demanded

Source: Adapted from Richard T. Carson, Theodore Groves, and Mark J. Machina, "Incentive and Informational Properties of Preference Questions," Plenary Address, European Association of Resource and Environmental Economists, Oslo, Norway, June 1999. Reprinted with authors' permission.

requirements for incentive compatibility. Respondents have no incentive to vote against their true preferences. Because CV is often the only way analysts can estimate WTP for public goods, this is reassuring. Incentive compatibility also holds for comparison between two mutually exclusive public goods with the same cost. As long as respondents place a positive value on both goods, they have no incentive to misstate their preferred good.

Incentive compatibility is lost in cases in which payment is voluntary because it introduces a second issue, whether to donate or to purchase, into the choice situation. In the case of a public good to be funded by contributions, respondents who place any positive value on the good have an incentive to accept bids above their WTPs to increase the chances that the good is provided because they do not actually have to make a donation in that amount.[82] Similarly, respondents who have any probability of actually wanting a new private (excludeable) good have an incentive to accept bids above their WTP to increase the chances that it will actually be provided because they can decline to purchase it if they decide that they do not want it. The problem is so severe for new private goods that dichotomous choice CV has largely been abandoned for this purpose.

Questions that ask respondents to choose between an existing private good and an alternative are incentive compatible about that choice as long as only potential users are surveyed. (The question will not be consequential for those who are not potential users.) Answers to the questions, however, do not reveal information about how much of the selected private good will actually be demanded. For example, a town may ask a sample of residents to choose between the existing skating rink, which is available only during daylight hours and has a small entrance fee, and a new skating rink with electric lighting, which would be available evenings and would have a higher entrance fee. The respondents have no incentive to misstate their true preferences over the choices, but the answers do not tell the town about how often residents will use the new facility.

Conclusion About the Importance of Strategic Responses The danger that strategic responses to CV questions will bias estimates of aggregate WTP cannot be assessed without considering both the elicitation method and the nature of the good being valued. The dichotomous choice method applied to the valuation of new public goods to be funded by taxes or other coercive payments can be designed to avoid strategic response bias. It is subject to an upward bias, however, if payments are voluntary. The open-ended WTP method will generally be subject to strategic response bias, most likely leading to aggregate WTP estimates that are too small if payments are coerced and too large if payments are voluntary.

HOW ACCURATE IS CONTINGENT VALUATION?

It is possible to test the accuracy of CV WTP estimates in a number of ways.[83] The first method is to compare CV values to those generated by other indirect methods. CV values have been found to be approximately the same as those derived from travel cost studies.[84] They have also been found to be reasonably similar to prices derived from hedonic price regressions[85] and to the market prices of substitutes.[86] Wesley Magat and W. Kip Viscusi tested whether respondents' WTP for risk reductions associated with an insecticide and toilet bowl cleaner were consistent with standard economic theory or subject to the kinds of judgment biases described earlier. In general, they did not find strong evidence of bias.[87]

The second type of comparison, one that is more common and more appropriate, is between respondents' CV statements and their actual behavior when they participate in an experiment that utilizes a simulated or constructed market for the good in question.[88] Results from studies that have used experimental techniques to examine CV accuracy typically suggest that CV valuations of WTP relying on open-ended and dichotomous choice methods approximate actual market transactions, although there is some tendency for overvaluation.[89] In assessing these experiments, it is useful to keep in mind that the simulated market only approximates the workings of a real market; for example, there is only one opportunity to buy the good. In addition, the experiments have only been conducted in contexts in which respondents clearly derive use value from the good. Richard Bishop and Thomas Heberlein have conducted a number of experiments along these lines. The example presented in Exhibit 14-4 is typical of these experiments.

John Loomis has investigated how consistent household CV valuations are over time. Though not a direct test of accuracy, his investigation is relevant because consistency is a prerequisite for accuracy. He surveyed both visitors and the general public's WTP for recreational, option, existence, and bequest values derived from Mono Lake in California. Identical surveys were administered to the same individuals eight or nine months apart. The results were virtually identical.[90]

Though the evidence tends to suggest that CV is plausible in use contexts, the jury is still out in terms of nonuse values, given the ordering, embedding, noncommitment, and starting point problems discussed previously. Obviously, given the nature of nonuse values, it is much more difficult to elicit WTP from observed behavior. Nonetheless, with sufficient cleverness researchers may be able to find ways to do so. For example, as noted in Chapter 9, voluntary contributions to environmental causes might serve as the basis for estimation. Market-like experiments might also be used.[91] For example, individuals who have expressed WTP for nonuse could be given the option of returning none, part, or all of the checks sent to them by experimenters (as described in Exhibit 14-4), thus testing noncommitment bias. Successfully implementing such experiments would be extremely difficult with current levels of knowledge and typically available resources, however.

EXHIBIT 14-4

A wildlife area in Wisconsin is periodically opened to hunting. Hunters require a special permit to participate in these hunts. The permits are issued free to the winners of a lottery. For the 1984 lottery, a large number of applications were received. As a result of the lottery, 150 permits to hunt were issued.

To measure WTA, half of these hunters also received a letter explaining the study and a check made out in their name. To cash these checks, the hunters had to relinquish their permits. The denominations of the checks, which ranged randomly from $18 to $518, corresponded to the dichotomous choice method described earlier. The other half of the hunters received a similar letter with a hypothetical payment offer drawn from the same range as the first half. They were asked if they would have been willing to give up their permits for the hypothetical amounts stated in their letters.

To measure WTP, 150 unsuccessful lottery participants were selected at random. Again,

75 received a letter explaining that a hunting permit was available if they paid the amount specified in the letter. The amounts covered the same range as described previously. The other 75 were asked the same question hypothetically. That is, they were asked the CV question rather than given the opportunity to reveal their preferences through purchases.

Looking first at WTP, the results indicated that the CV valuations ($35) were only slightly higher than those measured through revealed preference ($31), a difference that was not statistically significant. These results suggest that noncommitment bias was not a major problem in this context. But, consistent with the findings discussed earlier, WTA valuations were much higher than WTP valuations. Furthermore, the CV valuations ($420) were considerably higher than those actually revealed by check cashing ($153).

Source: Adapted from Richard C. Bishop and Thomas A. Heberlein, "The Contingent Valuation Method," in Rebecca L. Johnson and Gary V. Johnson, eds., *Economic Valuation of Natural Resources: Issues, Theory, and Application* (Boulder, CO: Westview Press, 1990), 81–104.

The Potential for Calibration

It has long been recognized in marketing research that it may be necessary to *calibrate* respondents' valuations of goods in various ways to obtain more accurate estimates of their WTP.[92] As noted earlier, noncommitment bias, which may also be interpreted as strategic response bias, is a well-recognized problem in marketing research when individuals are asked to express their valuations of market goods. Kenneth Arrow has concluded, "A hypothesis to be explored is that, if the results of CVs for nonuse values were suitably calibrated, they would provide useful and reliable estimates."[93] Testing Arrow's hypothesis may be one of the most valuable areas of future research on CV.

The Accuracy of Different CV Methods and Proneness to Biases

Richard Bishop and Thomas Heberlein have conducted experiments comparing the size of valuations from different elicitation formats (again, this is in a use context). They conclude that:

These experiments indicate that contingent values for willingness to pay may be somewhat high, but for open-ended and dichotomous choice questions the difference was not large enough to be statistically significant. . . . Bidding seems to introduce a substantial upward bias. . . . Contingent compensation demanded tended to produce excessive values when an open-ended question was asked and values that were biased substantially upward compared to values obtained from actual cash transactions when dichotomous choice questions were used.[94]

Other researchers have also addressed this issue. V. Kerry Smith and William Desvousges compared the valuations from several CV methods in their study of improvements in the quality of water in the Monongahela River. Their analysis suggests that starting point bias is important with iterative bidding: A low starting point ($25) generated lower valuations than other methods, while a high starting point ($125) produced valuations higher than other methods. Open-ended questions produced fairly similar valuations. Overall, mean valuations from different CV methods ranged from $7 to $36 for one water quality change, from $4 to $31 for another change, and from $11 to $51 for a third change.[95]

William Desvousges and his colleagues have compared open-ended question responses with dichotomous choice responses to the same questions. They found that in some contexts the differences in the mean WTP valuations were not statistically significant, but in other contexts they were. They also found the dichotomous choice method generated a considerable number of very high valuations.[96] This is consistent with the likely relative importance of strategic response bias discussed previously, as well as with the relatively lower precision of the dichotomous choice method relative to direct elicitation methods for given sample sizes.

HEURISTICS FOR THE DESIGN AND USE OF CV SURVEYS

Several experts in CV have suggested overall criteria for evaluating CV instruments. Ronald Cummings, David Brookshire, and William Schulze, for example, suggest five criteria for evaluating instruments. First, respondents should understand and be familiar with the good that is being valued. Second, respondents should have, or be given, experience in both valuation and the choice procedure. Third, there should be as little uncertainty as possible about the details of the project. All three of these concerns can best be addressed by attempting to reduce hypotheticality—for example, by employing quality ladders, by stressing realistically and concretely the substitution possibilities, and by presenting gains (benefits) in percentage terms as well as in absolute terms. Fourth, WTP rather than WTA should be used for valuation purposes. Fifth, attempts should be made to avoid anchoring and starting point bias.[97]

Heuristics for Using Estimates from Previous CV Studies

Because CV surveys are inevitably complex and expensive, many analysts are more concerned with using values derived from existing CV studies than they are in going out and doing CV surveys themselves. In an examination of alternative environmental regulatory policies for dealing with water pollution, Ralph Luken illustrates how existing CV estimates can be "plugged in" to a CBA. Specifically, he extrapolates previous CV valuations of benefits from the Monongahela River studies discussed earlier in this chapter. His analysis provides a useful example of how to use plug-in values, and is described more fully in Chapter 15.[98] He is careful to specify which studies and which specific estimates he is using, the specific assumptions he makes in the extrapolations, the quality changes that are involved, the distinction between use and any nonuse components, and any potential remaining biases. He also performs sensitivity analysis.

Environment Canada, in cooperation with several international organizations, has developed a database of CV and other studies that value environmental impacts.[99] In order to facilitate the use of findings from these studies in CBA, it provides an abstract for each study describing the study area and its population characteristics, the environmental asset being valued, the research methods employed, and the monetary values that were estimated. Access to the online database is by subscription.[100]

CONCLUSION

Contingent valuation is now relatively uncontroversial in contexts involving use values, although it may overestimate them. Its accuracy in nonuse contexts is more controversial, yet it is in this context where its potential usefulness is likely to be the greatest. Doubts about the accuracy of CV in nonuse contexts stem from the problems of hypotheticality and the attendant judgment biases that appear to flourish in the nonuse context. Strategic response bias, on the other hand, does not appear to be a major problem in the use of the dichotomous choice method to value public goods with coercive payments, and neutrality bias can be minimized by use of appropriate survey techniques. Probably the most important topics for future CV research are the directional biases in particular methods and the development of techniques that allow reliable calibration.

EXERCISES FOR CHAPTER 14

1. The construction of a dam that would provide hydroelectric power would result in the loss of two streams: one that is now used for sport fishing, and another that does not support game fish but is part of a wilderness area.
   a. Imagine that a contingent valuation method is used to estimate the social cost of the loss of each of these streams. Would you be equally confident in the two sets of estimates?
   b. Consider two general approaches to asking contingent valuation questions about the streams. The first approach attempts to elicit how much compensation people would require to give up the streams. The second approach attempts to elicit how much people would be willing to pay to keep the streams. Which approach would you recommend? Why?

2. A number of residents of Dullsville have complained to the mayor that the center of town looks shabby compared to the centers of many other nearby towns. At the mayor's request, the Parks Department has put together a proposal for converting the town square parking lot into a sitting park with flower displays—it modeled the design on a similar park in the neighboring town of Flowerville. The annualized cost of installing and maintaining the park,

and relocating parking to nearby Short Street, would be about $120,000. With about 40,000 households paying property taxes, the project would cost an average household about $3 per year.

   You have been asked to give advice about conducting a survey to measure the benefits of the project.

   a. The Parks Department proposes conducting a telephone survey. Does this seem like an appropriate survey vehicle?
   b. How might a random sample be drawn for a telephone survey?
   c. Write a statement that could be read by the interviewer to describe the project.
   d. Write questions to implement the open-ended WTP method.
   e. Propose a procedure for implementing the dichotomous choice method.

3. Consider a project that would involve purchasing marginal farmland that would then be allowed to return to wetlands capable of supporting migrant birds. Researchers designed a survey to implement the dichotomous choice method. They reported the following data.

Stated Price (annual payment in dollars)	Fraction of Respondents Accepting Stated Price (percent)
0	98
5	91
10	82
15	66
20	48
25	32
30	20
35	12
40	6
45	4
50	2

What is the mean willingness-to-pay for the sampled population?

NOTES

1. Most observers attribute the origins of CV to Robert K. David, "Recreation Planning as an Economic Problem," *Natural Resources Journal* 3(2) 1963, 239–249. Early applications include Ronald G. Ridker, *Economic Costs of Air Pollution: Studies in Measurement* (New York: Praeger, 1967); and Charles J. Cicchetti and V. Kerry Smith, "Congestion, Quality Deterioration, and Optimal Use: Wilderness Recreation in the Spanish Peaks Primitive Area," *Social Science Research* 2(1) 1973, 15–30.

2. The two "classic" CV overviews are Ronald G. Cummings, David S. Brookshire, and William D.

Schulze, *Valuing Environmental Goods: An Assessment of the Contingent Valuation Method* (Totowa, NJ: Rowman & Allanheld, 1986); and Robert C. Mitchell and Richard T. Carson, *Using Surveys to Value Public Goods: The Contingent Valuation Method* (Washington, D.C.: Resources for the Future, 1989). Some overviews include Richard C. Bishop and Thomas A. Heberlein, "The Contingent Valuation Method," in Rebecca L. Johnson and Gary V. Johnson, eds., *Economic Valuation of Natural Resources: Issues, Theory, and Application* (Boulder, CO: Westview Press, 1990), 81–104; Ian J. Bateman and Kenneth

G. Willis, eds., *Valuing Environmental Preferences: Theory and Practice of the Contingent Valuation Method in the U.S., EU, and Developing Countries* (Oxford and New York: Oxford University Press, 1999); Timothy C. Haab and Kenneth E. McConnell, *Valuing Environmental and Natural Resources: The Econometrics of Non-Market Valuation* (Cheltenham, UK: Edward Elgar Publishers, 2003).

3. William H. Desvousges, V. Kerry Smith, and Ann Fisher, "Option Price Estimates for Water Quality Improvements: A Contingent Valuation Study for the Monongahela River," *Journal of Environmental Economics and Management* 14(3) 1987, 248–267; and Richard C. Bishop and Thomas A. Heberlein, "Measuring Values of Extra-Market Goods: Are Indirect Measures Biased?" *American Journal of Agricultural Economics* 61(5) 1979, 926–930.

4. Alan Diener, Bernie O'Brien, and Amiram Gafni, "Health Care Contingent Valuation Studies: A Review and Classification of the Literature," *Health Economics* 7(4) 1998, 313–326.

5. For example, see Gretchen J. Burger, Application and Assessment of the Contingent Valuation Method for Federal Hazardous Waste Policy in the Washington, D.C. Area, Ph.D. dissertation, University of New Mexico, Albuquerque, 1984; David Maddison and S. Mourato, "Valuing Different Road Options for Stonehenge," *Conservation and Management of Archeological Sites* 4(4) 2001, 203–212; Peter C. Boxall, Jeffrey Englin, and Wiktor L. Adamowicz, "Valuing Aboriginal Artifacts: A Combined Revealed-Stated Preference Approach," *Journal of Environmental Economics and Management* 45(2) 2003, 213–230; Richard T. Woodward and Yong-Suhk Wui, "The Economic Value of Wetland Services: A Meta-Analysis," *Ecological Economics* 37(2) 2001, 257–270; and Bruce K. Johnson and John C. Whitehead, "Value of Public Goods from Sports Stadiums: The CVM Approach," *Contemporary Economic Policy* 18(1) 2000, 48–58.

6. Raymond J. Kopp, Paul R. Portney, and V. Kerry Smith, "The Economics of Natural Resource Damages after *Ohio v. U.S. Dept. of the Interior,*" *Environmental Law Reporter* 20(4) 1990, 10,127–10,131.

7. Kenneth Arrow, Robert Solow, Paul Portney, Edward Leamer, Roy Radner, and Howard Schuman, "Report of the NOAA Panel on Contingent Valuation," *Federal Register* 58(10) January 15, 1993, 4601–4614.

8. On this point, see Daniel McFadden and Gregory Leonard, "Issues in the Contingent Valuation of Environmental Goods: Methodologies for Data Collection and Analysis," in J. A. Hausman, ed., *Contingent Valuation: A Critical Assessment* (New York: North-Holland, 1993), 165–208.

9. Arrow et al., "Report of the NOAA Panel on Continent Valuation," p. 4608.

10. For an example of this approach, see J. C. Horvath, *Southeastern Economic Survey of Wildlife Recreation* (Atlanta, GA: Environmental Research Group, Georgia State University, 1974).

11. One compromise between the open-ended format and the provision of "guidance" that has been used in in-person interviews is the *payment card* with a range of prices. For example, in the Nestucca oil spill CV survey, respondents were asked to specify the maximum amount their households would pay for particular programs to prevent oil spills. They were then shown a payment card with dollar amounts ranging from $0 to $5,000 and asked to circle the amount closest to their evaluation. Robert Rowe, William D. Schulze, W. Douglas Shaw, David Schenk and Lauraine G. Chestnut, "Contingent Valuation of Natural Resource Damage Due to Nestucca Oil Spill," prepared for the Department of Wildlife, Ministry of the Environment, BC, and Environment Canada, by RCG/Hagler, Bailly Inc., June 1991.

12. For an example, see David Brookshire, Berry Ives, and William D. Schulze, "The Valuation of Aesthetic Preference," *Journal of Environmental Economics and Management* 3(4) 1976, 325–346.

13. James L. Regens, "Measuring Environmental Benefits with Contingent Markets," *Public Administration Review* 51(4) 1991, 345–352.

14. For an example, see V. Kerry Smith and William H. Desvousges, *Measuring Water Quality Benefits* (Boston, MA: Kluwer Nijhoff Publishing, 1986), Chapter 6.

15. Baruch Fischhoff and Louis A. Cox Jr., "Conceptual Framework for Regulatory Benefits Assessment," in Judith D. Bentkover, Vincent T. Covello, and Jeryl Mumpower, eds., *Benefits Assessment: The State of the Art* (Boston, MA: D. Reidel Publishing Co., 1986), 51–84.

16. For an example using this method, see John Loomis, *Integrated Public Lands Management* (New York: Columbia University Press, 1993), 276–279.

17. Selecting an appropriate set of bid prices is one of the most difficult tasks analysts face in applying the dichotomous choice method. The bid prices must be spaced sufficiently far apart so that they show a range of acceptance rates, ideally from about .85 to about .15. Simply spreading bid prices over a very wide range, however, is unsatisfactory because, for a given sample size, statistical efficiency in estimating willingness-to-pay from the pattern of acceptances is greater for fewer bid prices. These considerations suggest the importance of conducting pre-test surveys to determine an appropriate set of bid prices. (Of course, in any survey study, pre-tests are important for ensuring that respondents understand questions.) See Hans Nyquist, "Optimal Design of Discrete Response Experiments in Contingent Valuation," *Review of Economics and Statistics* 74(3) 1992, 559–563; and Barbara J. Kanninen, "Bias in Discrete Response Contingent Valuation," *Journal of Environmental Economics and Management* 28(1) 1995, 114–125.

18. For more detail on this method, see Bishop and Heberlein, "Measuring Values of Extra-Market Goods," 89–91. On the technical issues relating to interpreting the function as utility and how to deal with truncation, see W. Michael Hanemann, "Welfare Evaluations in Contingent Valuation Experiments with Discrete Responses," *American Journal of Agricultural Economics,* 66(3) 1984, 332–341.

19. The formula for computing the WTP of the average member of the sample can be derived more formally if some additional notation is introduced. (Note that this derivation involves approximating the expected value of WTP.) Assume that the offer prices are $0, v, 2v, 3v, \ldots Nv$, where v is the interval between prices, and Nv is the maximum price offered. For example, if the offer prices were 0, \$10, \$20, \$30, . . . , \$200, then $v = \$10$ and $N = 20$. Let $\mathbf{F}[X]$ be the fraction of respondents offered price X who accept the offer—this is the height of the bar in the histogram that sits above X. In order to calculate the expected value of WTP, we require the probability that each offer price is the *maximum* amount that a respondent would be willing to pay. We can approximate this for offer amount $\$kv$ with the expression: $\mathbf{F}[kv] - \mathbf{F}[(k + 1)v]$ for $k = 0, 1, \ldots, N - 1$ which is roughly the probability of a respondent accepting $\$kv$ minus the probability of accepting a larger offer price, $\$(k + 1)v$. The mean WTP (that is, the WTP of a randomly selected respondent) is then approximately the sum of the products of maximum payments times their probabilities:

$$E[WTP] = Nv\mathbf{F}[Nv] + (N - 1)v\{\mathbf{F}[(N - 1)v] \\ - \mathbf{F}[Nv]\} + (N - 2)v\{\mathbf{F}[(N - 2)v] - \mathbf{F}[(N - 1)]\} \\ + \ldots + 0\{\mathbf{F}[0] - \mathbf{F}[v]\}$$

Collecting terms yields the simple expression:

$$\mathbf{E}\,[WPT] = v\sum_{k=0}^{N} \mathbf{F}[kv]$$

20. For a thorough treatment of estimation issues, see W. Michael Hanemann and Barbara Kanninen, "The Statistical Analysis of Discrete Response CV Data," in Ian J. Bateman and Ken G. Willis, eds., *Valuing Environmental Preferences: Theory and Practice of the Contingent Valuation Method in the U.S., EC, and Developing Countries* (Oxford and New York: Oxford University Press, 1999), 302–441.

21. A complication arises because the statistical model usually assumes an infinite range for x. In practice, surveys use offer prices with a finite range, usually bounded from below at zero. Averaging over this finite range will miss some of the probability assumed by the statistical model. A correction to help account for this truncation bias involves rescaling the distribution to account for the missing areas in the tails of the distribution. See Kevin J. Boyle, Michael P. Welsh, and Richard C. Bishop, "Validation of Empirical Measures of Welfare Change: Comment," *Land Economics* 64(1) 1988, 94–98.

22. The area under the curve can be estimated through numerical integration. The procedure involves approximating the area with rectangles through the following steps. First, divide the range of X into equal segments of width n. Second, calculate the probability of acceptance at each of these points. Third, find the average acceptance value for adjacent pairs of points. Fourth, multiply each of these averages by n.

Fifth, sum all these products to get the estimate of the area. Any desired degree of accuracy can be obtained by choosing a sufficiently small value of n.

23. For an overview of the statistical issues in estimating aggregate WTP from such models, see Timothy Park, John B. Loomis, and Michael Creel, "Confidence Intervals for Evaluating Benefits Estimates from Dichotomous Choice Contingent Valuation Studies," *Land Economics* 67(1) 1991, 64–73.

24. Joseph A. Herriges and Jason F. Shogren, "Starting Point Bias in Dichotomous Choice Valuation with Follow-Up Questioning," *Journal of Environmental Economics and Management* 30(1) 1996, 112–131.

25. Richard T. Carson, Theodore Groves, and Mark J. Machina, "Incentive and Informational Properties of Preference Questions," Plenary Address, European Association of Resource and Environmental Economists, Oslo, Norway, June 1999.

26. Empirical work provides support for this weighted averaging explanation; see Anthony C. Burton, Katherine S. Carson, Susan M. Chilton, and W. George Hutchinson, "An Experimental Investigation of Explanations for Inconsistencies in Responses to Second Offers in Double Referenda," *Journal of Environmental Economics and Management* 46(3) 1996, 472–489.

27. Robert J. Johnston, Stephen K. Swallow, and Thomas F. Weaver, "Estimating Willingness to Pay and Resource Tradeoffs with Different Payment Mechanisms: An Evaluation of a Funding Guarantee for Watershed Management," *Journal of Environmental Economics and Management* 38(1) 1999, 97–120.

28. See "The Review Panel's Assessment," 180–204 and Kenneth Arrow, "Comments," 180–185, in Cummings, Brookshire, and Schulze, *Valuing Environmental Goods: An Assessment of the Contingent Valuation Method.*

29. See Robert P. Berrens, Alok K. Bohara, Hank Jenkins-Smith, Carol Silva, and David L. Weimer, "The Advent of Internet Surveys for Political Research: A Comparison of Telephone and Internet Samples," *Political Analysis* 11(1) 2003, 1–22; and Robert P. Berrens, Alok K. Bohara, Hank C. Jenkins-Smith, Carol L. Silva, and David L. Weimer, "Information and Effort in

Contingent Valuation Surveys: Application to Global Climate Change Using National Internet Samples," *Journal of Environmental Economics and Management* 47(2) 2004, 331–363.

30. For overviews, see Martin Frankel, "Sampling Theory," 21–67, and Seymour Sudman, "Applied Sampling," 145–194, in Peter H. Rossi, James D. Wright, and Andy B. Anderson, *Handbook of Survey Research.* For issues specifically relevant to CV, see Steven F. Edwards and Glen D. Anderson, "Overlooked Biases in Contingent Valuation Surveys: Some Considerations," *Land Economics* 63(2) 1987, 168–178.

31. Richard T. Carson, "Constructed Markets," in John B. Braden and Charles D. Kolstad, eds., *Measuring the Demand for Environmental Quality* (New York: Elsevier Science Publishers, 1991), 152.

32. For an example of an attempt to estimate the extent of a recreational market, see V. Kerry Smith and Raymond J. Kopp, "The Spatial Limits of the Travel Cost Recreational Demand Model," *Land Economics* 56(1) 1980, 64–72.

33. Desvousges, Smith, and Fisher, "Option Price Estimates for Water Quality Improvements."

34. F. L. Filion, "Estimating Bias Due to Nonresponse in Mail Surveys," *Public Opinion Quarterly* 39(4) 1975–1976, 482–492.

35. For a review, see John B. Loomis, "Expanding Contingent Value Sample Estimates to Aggregate Benefit Estimates: Current Practices and Proposed Solutions," *Land Economics* 63(4) 1987, 396–402.

36. The most comprehensive criticisms of CV can be found in Hausman, ed., *Contingent Valuation: A Critical Assessment.*

37. William D. Schulze, Ronald G. Cummings, and David S. Brookshire, *Methods Development in Measuring Benefits of Environmental Improvements, Vol. II* (Washington, D.C.: Report to U.S. EPA, 1983).

38. For an extensive discussion of the attitude-behavior nexus, see Mitchell and Carson, *Using Surveys to Value Public Goods: The Contingent Valuation Method,* 175–187.

39. Baruch Fischhoff and Lita Furey, "Measuring Values: A Conceptual Framework for Interpreting Transactions with Special Reference to Contingent Valuation of Visibility," *Journal of Risk and Uncertainty* 1(2) 1988, 147–184, at 179–180.

40. In marketing, the technique called *conjoint analysis* is used to elicit consumer valuations for

new, unfamiliar goods. For a review, see Daniel McFadden, "The Choice Theory Approach to Market Research," *Marketing Science* 5(4) 1986, 275–297.

41. Richard T. Carson, Nicholas E. Flores, and Norman F. Meade, "Contingent Valuation: Controversies and Evidence," *Environmental and Resource Economics* 19(2) 2001, 173–210, at 178.

42. For a discussion of this point, see Cummings, Brookshire, and Schulze, *Valuing Environmental Goods: An Assessment of the Contingent Valuation Method*, at 43, 253.

43. Fischhoff and Furey, "Measuring Values: A Conceptual Framework for Interpreting Transactions with Special Reference to Contingent Valuation of Visibility," Table 1, 156.

44. Daniel A. Hagen, James W. Vincent, and Patrick G. Welle, "The Benefits of Preserving Old-Growth Forests and the Northern Spotted Owl," *Contemporary Policy Issues* 10(2) 1992, 13–16. A second CV study of the spotted owl that can be critiqued on neutrality grounds is Jonathan Rubin, Gloria Heland, and John Loomis, "A Benefit-Cost Analysis of the Northern Spotted Owl: Results from a Contingent Valuation Survey," *Journal of Forestry* 89(12) 1991, 25–30.

45. William McKillop, "Use of Contingent Valuation in Northern Spotted Owls Studies: A Critique," *Journal of Forestry* 90(8) 1992, 36–37.

46. Ed Bukszar, "Does Overconfidence Lead to Poor Decisions? A Comparison of Decision Making and Judgment Under Uncertainty," paper presented at the Annual Conference of Judgment and Decision Making, Washington, D.C., November 7, 1993.

47. See David L. Weimer and Aidan R. Vining, *Policy Analysis: Concepts and Practice*, 4th ed. (Upper Saddle River, NJ: Pearson Prentice Hall, 2005), 121–122.

48. For a review of this issue, see Colin F. Camerer and Howard Kunreuther, "Decision Processes for Low Probability Events: Policy Implications," *Journal of Policy Analysis and Management* 8(4) 1989, 565–592.

49. For an extensive review of biases and the various theories behind them, see Camerer and Kunreuther, "Decision Processes for Low Probability Events: Policy Implications."

50. Daniel Kahneman and Amos Tversky, "Prospect Theory," *Econometrica* 47(2) 1979, 263–292. Many of the violations of expected utility

hypothesis that can be explained by prospect theory can also be explained by assuming people maximize expected utility but employ Bayesian updating of probabilities; see W. Kip Viscusi, "Prospective Reference Theory: Toward an Explanation of the Paradoxes," *Journal of Risk and Uncertainty* 2(3) 1989, 235–263.

51. Richard H. Thaler, "Towards a Positive Theory of Consumer Choice," *Journal of Economic Behavior and Organization* 1(1) 1980, 39–60. For some empirical evidence on loss aversion in housing markets, see David Genesove and Christopher Mayer, "Loss Aversion and Seller Behavior: Evidence from the Housing Market," *Quarterly Journal of Economics* 116(4) 2001, 1233–1260.

52. It may seem somewhat artificial to separate hypotheticality from noncommitment bias. However, as emphasized earlier, hypotheticality does not appear to generate upward or downward bias, whereas, as we will see, noncommitment does appear to bias valuations upward.

53. See, for example, Linda F. Jamieson and Frank M. Bass, "Adjusting Stated Intention Measures to Predict Trial Purchase of New Products: A Comparison of Models and Methods," *Journal of Marketing Research* 26(3) 1989, 336–345; and F. Thomas Juster, *Anticipations and Purchases* (Princeton, NJ: Princeton University Press, 1964).

54. Helen R. Neill, Ronald G. Cummings, Philip T. Ganderton, Glenn W. Harrison, and Thomas McGuckin, "Hypothetical Surveys and Economic Commitments," *Land Economics* 70(2) 1994, 145–154; and Kalle Seip and Jon Strand, "Willingness to Pay for Environmental Goods in Norway: A Contingent Valuation Study with Real Payment," *Environmental and Resource Economics* 2(1) 1992, 91–106.

55. For more detail, see Michael A. Kemp and Christopher Maxwell, "Exploring a Budget Context for Contingent Valuation Estimates," 217–265, in Hausman, ed., *Contingent Valuation: A Critical Assessment*.

56. I. J. Bateman and I. H. Langford, "Budget-Constrained, Temporal, and Question-Ordering Effects in Contingent Valuation Studies," *Environment and Planning A* 29(7) 1997, 1215–1228.

57. George Tolley and Alan Randall, "Establishing and Valuing the Effects of Improved Visibility in the Eastern United States," Report to the U.S. EPA, Washington, D.C., 1983.

58. Karl C. Samples and James R. Hollyer, "Contingent Valuation of Wildlife Resources in the Presence of Substitutes and Complements," in Rebecca L. Johnson and Gary V. Johnson, eds., *Economic Valuation of Natural Resources: Issues, Theory, and Application,* (Boulder, CO: Westview Press, 1990), 177–192.

59. See Peter A. Diamond, Jerry A. Hausman, Gregory K. Leonard, and Mike Denning, "Does Contingent Valuation Measure Preferences? Experimental Evidence," in Hausman, ed., *Contingent Valuation: A Critical Assessment,* 43–85.

60. See the heated argument between Peter Diamond and Richard Carson, in Hausman, ed., *Contingent Valuation: A Critical Assessment,* 87–89.

61. The case that these effects can adequately explain the empirical findings is made in Carson, Flores, and Meade, "Contingent Valuation: Controversies and Evidence," 186–189; see also Richard T. Carson, Nicholas E. Flores, and Michael Hanemann, "Sequencing and Valuing Public Goods," *Journal of Environmental Economics and Management* 36(3) 1998, 314–323.

62. William H. Desvousges, F. Reed Johnson, Richard W. Dunford, Sara P. Hudson, and K. Nicole Wilson, "Measuring Natural Resources Damages with Contingent Valuation: Tests of Validity and Reliability," in Hausman, ed., *Contingent Valuation: A Critical Assessment,* 91–159.

63. Daniel Kahneman and Jack L. Knetsch, "Valuing Public Goods: The Purchase of Moral Satisfaction," *Journal of Environmental Economics and Management* 22(1) 1992, 57–70, at 64–68.

64. Carson, Flores, and Meade, "Contingent Valuation: Controversies and Evidence," *Environmental and Resource Economics.*

65. Kevin J. Boyle, Richard C. Bishop, and Michael P. Walsh, "Starting Point Bias in Contingent Valuation Bidding Games," *Land Economics* 16(2) 1985, 188–194.

66. Regens, "Measuring Environmental Benefits with Contingent Markets," 347–348.

67. Walter J. Mead, "Review and Analysis of State-of-the-Art Contingent Valuation Studies," in Hausman, ed., *Contingent Valuation: A Critical Assessment,* 305–332.

68. See Trudy A. Cameron and D. D. Huppert, "Referendum Contingent Valuation Estimates: Sensitivity to the Assignment of Offered Values," *Journal of the American Statistical Association* 86(416) 1991, 910–918.

69. Alok K. Bohara, Michael McKee, Robert P. Berrens, Hank Jenkins-Smith, Carol L. Silva, and David S. Brookshire, "Effects of Total Cost and Group-Size Information on Willingness to Pay Responses: Open Ended vs. Dichotomous Choice," *Journal of Environmental Economics and Management* 35(2) 1998, 142–163.

70. But Michael Hanemann ("Willingness to Pay and Willingness to Accept: How Much Can They Differ?" *American Economic Review* 81[3] 1991, 635–647) points out that there is no reason why WTA should not be considerably larger than WTP in certain circumstances. For example, one cannot pay more than one's income year after year to save one's own life, but there may be no finite offer that could make one willingly give up one's life.

71. Jack Knetsch and J. S. Sinden, "Willingness to Pay and Compensation Demanded: Experimental Evidence of an Unexpected Disparity in Measures of Value," *Quarterly Journal of Economics* 99(3) 1984, 507–521; Shelby Gerking, Menno De Haan, and William Schulze, "The Marginal Value of Job Safety: A Contingent Valuation Study," *Journal of Risk and Uncertainty,* 1(2) 1988, 185–199; and Wesley Magat and W. Kip Viscusi, *Informational Approaches to Regulation* (Cambridge, MA.: MIT Press, 1992).

72. Timothy McDaniels, "Reference Points, Loss Aversion, and Contingent Values for Auto Safety," *Journal of Risk and Uncertainty* 5(2) 1992, 187–200.

73. Don L. Coursey, John J. Hovis, and William D. Schulze, "The Disparity between Willingness to Accept and Willingness to Pay Measures of Value," *Quarterly Journal of Economics,* 102(3) 1987, 679–690; Jason F. Shogren, Seung Y. Shin, Dermot J. Hayes, and James B. Kliebenstein, "Resolving the Differences in Willingness to Pay and Willingness to Accept," *American Economic Review* 84(1) 1994, 255–270; and Wiktor L. Adamovicz, Vinay Bhardwaj, and Bruce McNab, "Experiments on the Difference Between Willingness to Pay and Willingness to Accept," *Land Economics* 64(4) 1993, 416–427.

74. Shogren, Shin, Hayes, and Kliebenstein, "Resolving the Differences in Willingness to Pay and Willingness to Accept."

75. Arrow et al., "Report of the NOAA Panel on Continent Valuation," 4608.

76. On free riding in the provision of public goods, see R. Mark Isaac, James Walker, and Susan Thomas, "Divergent Evidence on Free Riding: An Experimental Examination of Possible Explanations," *Public Choice* 43(2) 1984, 113–149; Oliver Kim and Mark Walker, "The Free Rider Problem: Experimental Evidence," *Public Choice* 43(1) 1984, 3–24; G. Marwell and R. Ames, "Economists Free Ride, Does Anyone Else? Experiments on the Provision of Public Goods," *Journal of Public Economics* 15(3) 1981, 295–310; and Linda Goetz, T. F. Glover, and B. Biswas, "The Effects of Group Size and Income on Contributions to the Corporation for Public Broadcasting," *Public Choice* 77(2) 1993, 407–414.

77. Mitchell and Carson, *Using Surveys to Value Public Goods: The Contingent Valuation Method.*

78. Carson, Groves, and Machina, "Incentive and Informational Properties of Preference Questions."

79. On the domain of preferences, see the discussion of Arrow's Possibility Theorem in Chapter 2.

80. Alan Gibbard, "Manipulation of Voting Schemes: A General Result," *Econometrica* 41(4) 1973, 587–601; and Mark A. Satterthwaite, "Strategy-Proofness and Arrow's Conditions: Existence and Correspondence Theorems for Voting Procedures and Social Welfare Functions," *Journal of Economic Theory* 10(2) 1975, 187–217.

81. See Kevin J. Boyle, F. Reed Johnson, Daniel W. McCollum, William H. Desvousges, Richard W. Dunford, and Sara P. Hudson, "Valuing Public Goods: Discrete versus Continuous Contingent Valuation Responses," *Land Economics* 72(3) 1996, 381–396.

82. A number of studies have found a large divergence between WTP as expressed in contingent choice CV and actual donations. For a review, including a discussion of using follow-up questions on certainty of donation to adjust contingent donations, see Patricia A. Champ, Richard C. Bishop, Thomas C. Brown, and Daniel W. McCollum, "Using Donation Mechanisms to Value Nonuse Benefits from Public Goods," *Journal of Environmental Economics and Management* 33(2) 1997, 151–162.

83. For an overview of this issue and a listing of relevant studies, see V. K. Smith, "Nonmarket Valuation of Environmental Resources: An Interpretive Appraisal," *Land Economics* 69(1) 1993, 1–26, at 8–14, and Table 1.

84. See William K. Desvousges, V. Kerry Smith, and Matthew P. McGivney, "A Comparison of Alternative Approaches for Estimating Recreation and Related Benefits of Water Quality Improvements," Report to U.S. EPA, Research Triangle Institute, 1983; and Christine Sellar, John R. Stoll, and Jean-Paul Chavas, "Validation of Empirical Measures of Welfare Change: A Comparison of Nonmarket Techniques," *Land Economics* 61(2) 1985, 156–175. Smith and Desvousges, *Measuring Water Quality Benefits,* compare CV to "simple" travel cost methods.

85. David S. Brookshire, Mark A. Thayer, William D. Schulze, and Ralph C. d'Arge, "Valuing Public Goods: A Comparison of Survey and Hedonic Approaches," *American Economic Review* 72(1) 1982, 165–177.

86. Mark A. Thayer, "Contingent Valuation Techniques for Assessing Environmental Impacts: Further Evidence," *Journal of Environmental Economics and Management* 8(1) 1981, 27–44.

87. Magat and Viscusi, *Informational Approaches to Regulation,* Chapter 7.

88. For a listing of such studies, see Carson, "Constructed Markets," at 121–126.

89. Coursey, Hovis, and Schulze, "The Disparity Between Willingness to Accept and Willingness to Pay Measures of Value"; Mark Dickie, Ann Fisher, and Shelby Gerking, "Market Transactions and Hypothetical Demand Data: A Comparative Study," *Journal of the American Statistical Society* 82(398) 1987, 69–75.

90. John Loomis, "Test-Retest Reliability of the Contingent Valuation Method: A Comparison of General Population and Visitor Responses," *American Journal of Agricultural Economics* 71(1) 1989, 76–84.

91. For a discussion of this possibility, see Douglas M. Larson, "On Measuring Existence Value," *Land Economics* 69(3) 1993, 377–388.

92. An example of such calibration is Donald G. Morrison, "Purchase Intentions and Purchase Behavior," *Journal of Marketing,* 43(2), 1979,

65–74. "It is possible to improve prediction accuracy by measuring and using perceptions that affect and modify the relationship between stated intentions and trial purchase for new products," in Jamieson and Bass, "Adjusting Stated Intention Measures to Predict Trial Purchase of New Products," 344.

93. Kenneth Arrow, "Contingent Valuation of Nonuse Values: Observations and Questions," in Hausman, ed., *Contingent Valuation: A Critical Assessment,* 479–483.

94. Bishop and Heberlein, "The Contingent Valuation Method," 97.

95. Smith and Desvousges, *Measuring Water Quality Benefits,* Table 105, 271.

96. Desvousges, Johnson, Dunford, Hudson, and Wilson, "Measuring Natural Resources Damages with Contingent Valuation: Tests of Validity and Reliability."

97. Summarized from "Comparison Studies: What Is Accuracy," 71–109, and "reference operating conditions," Table 13-1, p. 230, in "Summary and Conclusions," 205–236 in Cummings, Brookshire, and Schulze, *Valuing Environmental Goods: An Assessment of the Contingent Valuation Method.*

98. Ralph A. Luken, *Efficiency in Environmental Regulation: A Benefit-Cost Analysis of Alternative Approaches* (Boston, MA: Kluwer Academic Publishers, 1990), 45–53.

99. Richard T. Carson, "Contingent Valuation: A User's Guide," *Environmental Science and Technology* 34(8) 2000, 1413–1418.

100. The database address is *www.evri.ec.gc.ca/evri/.*

CHAPTER 15

Shadow Prices from Secondary Sources

Policy analysts typically face time pressure and resource constraints. They naturally wish to do cost-benefit analysis as efficiently as possible and without getting into estimation issues beyond their competence. Anything that legitimately lowers the cost of doing CBA increases the likelihood that any particular CBA will be worth doing—in effect, it increases the chance that a CBA of doing a CBA will be positive.[1]

In order to evaluate existing or proposed policies and projects, analysts require credible measures of the social values of the impacts. As we see in Chapter 4, where these impacts occur in efficient markets, the value of these impacts can be estimated from changes in social surplus. Estimating social surplus requires knowledge of the appropriate demand and supply curves. When knowledge of these curves is not readily available, we may use the methods in Chapters 11 through 14 to value impacts. Most of these methods are expensive and time consuming. What else could the analyst do? Two situations are worth discussing in more depth.

In the first situation, the analyst believes that it is necessary to estimate the demand curve in order to measure consumer surplus. As we discuss in Chapter 12, this is relatively easy if we know one point on the demand curve and we have an estimate of its elasticity or slope at that point. Fortunately, economists have estimated price elasticities of demand, cross-elasticities, and income elasticities for a range of specific goods. Many elasticities have been summarized in survey articles.[2] Because these elasticities are based on the responses of people to similar price changes in the past, they provide an empirically grounded basis for predicting the responses to proposed price changes. For example, how consumers responded to a price increase for water in New Mexico can be reasonably used to estimate how they will respond to a similar price increase in Arizona. In addition to own-price elasticities, estimates of cross-price elasticities, which identify changes in the demand for a good that are likely to result from changes in the prices of other goods, though less often available, are frequently useful. For example, are transportation and various forms of communications (such as telecommuting and teleconferencing) complements or substitutes?[3] These cross-elasticities are important to transport planners and policy analysts who are estimating the costs and benefits of transport capital investments, assessing expected consumers' responses to price changes, or forecasting changes in demand for transportation. Existing estimates of income elasticities can also be useful, especially when policies have strong distributional effects. Elasticity estimates are scattered widely throughout the academic literature, usually in the topic-specific journals. Therefore, analysts often garner them from the relevant economic and policy journals on an ongoing basis and we will not discuss them further here.

In the second situation, analysts need to only predict the project's impacts and multiply them by the appropriate market prices or shadow prices. Many CBAs involve some impacts that can be valued at current market prices and other impacts that can be valued using shadow prices. Transportation and infrastructure project analyses, for example, often use current market prices for construction resources (materials, land, labor, and equipment) and ongoing operational costs (labor and maintenance materials), but require shadow prices for the value of lives saved, injuries avoided, crashes avoided, time saved, air quality changes, and noise level changes, to name only some. In order to obtain a shadow price, analysts might conduct their own valuation study using one of the methods discussed in Chapters 13 or 14. However, employing any of these methods is generally time consuming and resource intensive. The most straightforward, least-cost approach would be to use a previously estimated shadow price. Such estimates can be "plugged into" a cost benefit analysis. Consequently, we refer to such estimates as *plug-ins*.

More formally, using plug-ins in a CBA is known as *benefit transfer* or sometimes *information transfer*. The main purpose of this chapter is to survey the relevant literature and provide a "best estimate" for a number of frequently used shadow prices. It focuses on impacts that occur in many CBAs: the value of a statistical life (VSL), the cost of various kinds of injuries (including those resulting from road crashes), the cost of crime, and the value of time.[4] We also review per-unit values of recreational activities, the environment, and water and air pollution. Finally, we briefly discuss empirical estimates of the marginal excess tax burden. Many of these plug-ins are particularly useful in the evaluation of transportation projects, such as construction of new roads, better road lighting, altered speed limits, or new vehicle safety features. They are also applicable in a host of other areas including criminal justice, health, education, and training.

Most of the plug-ins discussed in this chapter are estimates of marginal values. For example, we provide estimates of the marginal social cost of one ton of particulate matter pollution or the value of one additional hour saved. The marginal value is usually the most useful value for policy purposes. However, some plug-ins can be thought of as average values. For example, the value of a life saved can be thought of as the average value in a population consisting of many people with different ages, incomes, and other characteristics.

In practice, marginal values are not likely to remain constant as output levels increase. For example, the value of time saved is likely to increase as the time stuck in traffic increases. Similarly, the marginal cost of pollution is likely to increase with the level of pollution. When marginal costs are increasing (or decreasing), it would be incorrect to estimate total costs by multiplying the output level by our plug-in estimate of the marginal cost.

The plug-ins are summarized in tables throughout this chapter. In order to facilitate comparability and for ease of use, plug-in values are usually expressed in 2002 U.S. dollars. The units of each impact are usually dollars per person or dollars per event. Other values are reported in terms of units produced, such as "per ton." We also report the relevant time unit, such as "per day" or "per year."

Different people have different opportunities and different preferences. Consequently, our plug-in values should be adjusted to take account of the preferences and characteristics of the affected population in a particular CBA. After discussing the plug-ins, we briefly address some of the information transfer issues related to adjusting plug-ins to different situations or to new CBAs.

During the past decade there have been an increasing number of *meta-analyses*.[5] These studies summarize the existing evidence about a particular topic, though they do not necessarily attempt to determine a best estimate. Their primary purpose is to explain why different studies obtain different estimates. For example, do certain estimation techniques provide larger estimated values than other estimation techniques or are valuations larger for some populations than for others? Answers to such questions assist benefit transfer. The usual approach in a meta-analysis is to estimate the statistical relationship between the plug-in estimate from each study and a number of characteristics of that study, such as the methodology employed (e.g., contingent valuation study), data source, and characteristics of the population (e.g., income).

THE VALUE OF A STATISTICAL LIFE

Researchers have used several techniques to estimate the value of life. These techniques either indirectly estimate the "price" people must be paid to be willing to take, or accept, the risk of a fatality by observing their behaviors in markets for commodities that embody this risk, as discussed in Chapter 13, or directly elicit these amounts with hypothetical survey questions, as discussed in Chapter 14. The most common and widely accepted market-based techniques are those that examine how much of a wage premium people working in risky jobs must be given to compensate them for the additional fatality risk. Our purpose here is not to revisit methodological issues, but to summarize the empirical estimates of the VSL.

The range in the VSL varies considerably among studies, sometimes between $0 and $30 million. Even when the outliers are discarded, the range is quite large. A number of important reviews were published around 1990.[6] Most of the reliable estimates of the VSL at that time ranged between $2 million and $3 million in 1990 dollars.[7] Recent estimates have been trending higher, even after adjusting for inflation. Here we briefly review three recent meta-analyses, one by Ted Miller, a second by Janusz Mrozek and Laura Taylor, and a third by W. Kip Viscusi and Joseph Aldy.[8]

The Miller Analysis of VSL Estimates

Ted Miller undertook a meta-analysis of 68 international studies of the VSL. He notes that studies that do not use occupational-specific mortality risk or that do not use variables to control for occupational differences tend to overestimate the VSL. Studies that use all mortality risk (from employment and all other sources) tend to underestimate the value of statistical life. Estimates of the VSL based on wage-risk studies and those based on contingent valuation studies are similar to one another but are significantly higher than those based on consumer behavior because consumers often underperceive the risks to which they are exposed. Miller estimates the VSL in the United States is $4.07 million in 2002 U.S. dollars, with a range of $3.7 to $5.1 million.

The Mrozek and Taylor Analysis of VSL Estimates

Janusz Mrozek and Laura Taylor undertook a meta-analysis of 33 international VSL studies. The mean VLS was roughly $6.4 million in 2002 U.S. dollars. The explanatory variables in their regression analyses include study design characteristics (model equation specifications, control of other risk factors), occupation (dummy variables for occupational attributes), and sample characteristics (blue collar workers, sex, unionized environment, and actual versus perceived risk levels). Also included are variables that reflected the sources of the wage and risk data. Basic regression results for their full dataset produce a mean VSL of $6 million U.S. dollars.

However, Mrozek and Taylor are suspect of VSL estimates from labor market studies that propose values in excess of $2.14 million to $3.2 million because they think that previous research has overlooked the importance of controlling for unobservable factors that occur at the industry level. To address this problem, Mrozek and Taylor include seven broad industry classification dummy variables in addition to the usual labor market covariates. These industry classification variables capture the effect of inter-industry wage differentials separately from the effect of occupational risks. For instance, a secretary working for an oil firm in an urban environment may earn a higher wage than a secretary in the same environment working for a nonprofit organization, even though their job risk profiles would be very similar. Imposing this adjustment on studies that did not do so originally yielded a predicted VSL of $2.77 million in 2002 U.S. dollars for the "average worker."

The Viscusi and Aldy Analysis of VSL Estimates

In their meta-analysis, W. Kip Viscusi and Joseph Aldy examine 49 wage-risk studies published over the past 30 years. More than half of the studies were specific to the U.S. labor market and the remaining studies were international. Roughly half of the U.S. labor market studies obtained estimates of the VSL that range between $5.18 million and $12.43 million (2002 U.S. dollars). The median value of these studies is near $7.25 million. Viscusi and Aldy have most confidence in studies whose estimates are near $5.5 million to $6.5 million dollars.

Viscusi and Aldy conducted a number of meta-analysis regressions, replicating the models used in previous meta-analyses. Their explanatory variables reflect whether the workplace was unionized, the level of education, income, the mean risk, the type of risk, and the type of study. They omitted studies that did not contain an income measure. Viscusi and Aldy used their regressions analyses to predict values of the VSL for each study. The mean predicted VSL for the U.S. population ranges between $5.7 million and $7.87 million. They also note that for most of the regression models the upper bound of the 95 percent confidence interval is roughly two times greater than the lower bound of the 95 percent confidence interval, or more.

Conclusion on the VSL

These three, well-conducted recent analyses reach quite different conclusions about the VSL. Mrozek and Taylor are lowest at $2.8 million; Miller is next with a best point estimate of $4.1 million with a range between $3.7 million and $5.1 million; and Viscusi and Aldy are highest with a mean predicted VSL for the U.S. population of between $5.7 million and $7.87 million. Many authors suggest figures at the lower end of this range for policy purposes, partially due to the methodological problems discussed in Chapters 13 and 14. In our opinion, the best point estimate of the VSL for policy purposes in the United States equals $4 million, with sensitivity analysis at $2 million and $6 million, as shown in Table 15-1.

TABLE 15-1 The Value of a Statistical Life, Injury Costs, and Crash Costs (in 2002 U.S. dollars)

Plug-In Category (Impact)	Shadow Price Value	Comments
Value of a Statistical Life (VSL)	Best point estimate $4.0 million (sensitivity analysis at $2.0 million to $6.0 million per life saved)	Based on Miller (2000), Mrozek and Taylor (2002), and Viscusi and Aldy (2003). Should adjust for risk level.
Value of a Life-Year (VLY)	$187,000 per person per year	Based on a VSL of $4 million, 40 years of life expectancy, and a discount rate of 3.5%.
Monetary Injury Costs 1. Eventually fatal 2. Hospitalized (nonfatal) 3. Nonhospitalized (nonfatal) 4. Average cost of an injury	1. $519,534 per injured person 2. $56,082 per injured person 3. $846 per injured person 4. $4,550 per injured person	Based on Rice, MacKenzie, and Associates (1989). Includes monetary costs only, not pain and suffering.
A. Motor vehicle injury B. Falls C. Firearm injuries D. Poisonings E. Fire injuries and burns F. Drownings and near drownings G. Other	A. $14,814 per injured person B. $4,973 per injured person C. $88,144 per injured person D. $8,250 per injured person E. $4,233 per injured person F. $106,450 per injured person G. $1,905 per injured person	
Cost of Work-Related Injuries A. Fatal injury	A. $3.2 million per injured worker	Based on Miller and Galbraith (1995). Includes quality of life losses.
B. Nonfatal injury	B. $59,052 per injured worker	
C. Nonfatal injury with compensation and work loss	C. $2,054 per injured worker	
D. Nonfatal injury with work loss, no compensation	D. $834 per injured worker	
E. Nonfatal injury, no work loss	E. $16,689 per injured worker	
F. Average injury cost G. Average motor vehicle work-related injury cost	F. $96,281 per injured worker G. $1,905 per injured worker	
Cost of Work-Related Injuries Value of one year of work impairment due to injury	$133,503 to $207,455 per year	Based on Dillingham, Miller, and Levy (1996).
Social Cost of Motor Vehicle Crash Injuries 1. Spinal cord	1. $2.9 M per victim ($1.02M–$4.39M for AIS 3–5)	Based on Zaloshnja, Miller, Romano, and Spicer (2004). All means are arithmetic and do not reflect the distribution of injury severity within each body region. M = million.
2. Brain	2. $1.2M per victim ($0.124M–$3.48M for AIS 1–5)	
3. Lower extremity	3. $0.46M per victim ($0.01M–$1.1M for AIS 1–5)	
4. Upper extremity	4. $0.15M per victim ($0.01M–$0.3M for AIS 1–3)	

(Continued)

TABLE 15-1 Continued

Plug-In Category (Impact)	Shadow Price Value	Comments
5. Trunk/abdomen	5. $0.28M per victim ($0.01M–$0.61M for AIS 1–5)	
6. Other face, head, or neck	6. $0.38M per victim ($0.01M–$1.08M for AIS 1–4)	
7. Minor external	7. $0.01M per victim	
8. Burn	8. $0.53M per victim ($0.07M–$0.89M for AIS 1–5)	
9. Average for fatal crash	9. $3.26M per victim (1.05 × VSL)	
Motor Vehicle Accident Costs		
1. PDO (Property damage only)	1. $2,625 per vehicle	Based on Blincoe et al. (2002). These figures reflect the per-person costs related to motor vehicle accidents of varying severity. AIS = Abbreviated Injury Scale.
2. AIS 1	2. $15,558 per injured person	
3. AIS 2	3. $163,625 per injured person	
4. AIS 3	4. $325,480 per injured person	
5. AIS 4	5. $757,837 per injured person	
6. AIS 5	6. $2,489,242 per injured person	
7. AIS 6 (Fatal)	7. $3,487,209 per fatality	

THE VALUE OF A LIFE-YEAR

The value of a life-year (VLY) is the constant annual amount which, taken over a person's remaining life span, has a discounted value equal to his or her VSL. We can think about the average VSL as the discounted value of the remaining life years of the average member of society. Thus, assuming the VLY is constant, it can be computed from an estimate of the average VSL, denoted $\widehat{VSL}$:

$$VLY = \frac{\widehat{VSL}}{A(T-a,r)} \quad \text{(15.1)}$$

where $A(T-a, r)$ is the annuity factor based on the expected number of remaining years of life $(T-a)$ and the appropriate discount rate (r). Thus, using an average VSL of $4 million, a discount rate of 3.5 percent, and a life expectancy of 40 years implies the VLY equals $187,309. This estimate is higher than many other estimates. For example, Eduard Zaloshnja, Ted Miller, Eduardo Romano, and Rebecca Spicer suggest the VLY equals $95,000 based on a VSL of $3.1 million.[9] Peter Abelson suggests the VLY for use by public agencies in Australia should be $79,700 in 2002 U.S. dollars ($108,000 in 2002 Australian dollars).[10]

Given the VLY one can now compute the VSL for a person aged a as the discounted sum of the value of the remaining life years; specifically,

$$VSL(a) = \sum_{t=0}^{T-a} \frac{VLY}{(1+r)^t} \quad \text{(15.2)}$$

where a is current age, T is the expected age at death and $T–a$ is life expectancy. According to this model, the VSL declines with age.[11]

There is some discussion in the literature about whether the VLY changes with age. Kevin Murphy and Robert Topel think it declines monotonically after about age 50.[12] However, it might increase with scarcity: If you expect you have only a few more years to live, you might be willing to pay more for an additional life year than when you were younger.[13]

A quality-adjusted life-year (QALY) weights the VLY by the quality of health during that year:

$$QALY_t = w_t VLY \qquad\qquad (15.3)$$

where the weight (w_t) equals 1 in perfect health, 0 in death, and something else in-between.[14] The purpose of a QALY is to account for the fact that not all years are lived with the same vigor and enthusiasm. Some years are spent in better health than others. For many ill people the weights decline over time as their condition becomes more severe. In order to compare one intervention or policy with another, analysts compute the discounted sum of future expected QALYs under each alternative, that is, VLY in equation (15.2) is replaced with $QALY_t$. We discuss QALYs in more depth in Chapter 17.

THE COST OF CRASHES AND THE COST OF INJURIES

Table 15-1 also summarizes five sets of estimates of the cost of injuries or the cost of crashes in the United States, again standardized to 2002 dollars. The first set is based on a major report prepared for Congress by Dorothy Rice, Ellen MacKenzie, and Associates.[15] It provides detailed estimates of the monetary costs of injuries from different causes and for three levels of severity. The second set, produced by Ted Miller and Maury Galbraith, focuses on the cost of occupational injuries.[16] The third set is based on a wage-risk study by Alan Dillingham, Ted Miller, and David Levy that estimates the value of an impaired work year.[17] The fourth set, produced by Eduard Zaloshnja, Ted Miller, Eduardo Romano, and Rebecca Spicer, focuses on motor vehicle crash injuries.[18] The fifth set is based on a report by Lawrence Blincoe et al. prepared for the National Highway Safety Administration.[19] It provides unit cost estimates for seven categories of motor vehicle crashes with varying levels of personal injury to occupants.

For relatively minor crashes, the cost of a motor vehicle crash per victim is higher than the cost of a personal injury because motor vehicle crashes typically engender additional costs, particularly property damage (vehicle) costs. However, for relatively severe crashes, the cost of pain and suffering from injury is the largest component of crash costs, often greater than half the total.

The Rice, McKenzie, and Associates' Estimates of the Cost of Injuries

Dorothy Rice, Ellen MacKenzie, and their associates focus on the direct monetary cost of injuries. Their estimates incorporate medical and rehabilitation costs and forgone earnings (including an imputed value for household labor). Because these estimates focus on monetary costs, they do not include pain and suffering and other dimensions of unhappiness that people would pay to avoid. Also, these estimates do not include property damage losses and other related social costs, such as court costs. Thus, the study leads to very conservative estimates of the social cost of injuries. However, the methodology and estimates are still widely cited in the literature.

The Miller and Galbraith Estimates of the Cost of Injuries

Ted Miller and Maury Galbraith estimate the cost of occupational injuries in the United States using a methodology similar to that of Rice, MacKenzie, and Associates. However, they include a measure of the willingness-to-pay to avoid the disutility associated with injury. Using incidences of injuries reported in the United States, predominantly through state worker's compensation systems, the authors use a top-down national accounting framework to estimate the cost of injury for all injuries, for fatal injuries, and for three subclasses of nonfatal injuries (compensable lost work, noncompensable lost work, and nonlost work). As the authors note, using a top-down accounting method is less accurate than using incidence-based bottom-up estimation techniques.

The estimated costs include the costs of medical and emergency services (hospital/home care, physician services, rehabilitation services, ancillary items, police, fire/paramedic response, and emergency transportation), wage and household work (lost wages, household work, and fringe benefits), administrative and legal costs (investigation, insurance processing, records keeping, limited litigation costs), workplace disruption (overtime pay, loss of specialized skills, recruitment and training associated with long-term disability) and quality of life (reduced quality of life to workers and their families who bear the nonmonetary losses associated with injury). Quality of life losses account for 43 percent of workplace injury costs, and the average cost per occupational injury is $16,689 (2002 U.S. dollars), but note the large range between specific injury categories as shown in Table 15-1.[20]

The Dillingham, Miller, and Levy Estimates of the Cost of Injuries

One problem with estimating the cost of injuries is that injuries come in a wide range of severities, affect different parts of the body, and cause different levels of pain and disability. Alan Dillingham, Ted Miller, and David Levy attempted to measure the cost of injuries through a wage-risk study, looking at the implied WTP in order to avoid one year of impairment to an individual's work life.

They estimate that individuals are willing to pay approximately $133,500 to $207,500 per year to avoid one year of impairment. However, there is no specific level of severity to which to apply this measure. One important assumption is that a work life shortened by a fatal injury is equivalent to one that is shortened by a nonfatal but permanent total disability. A specific advantage of their estimates is that they are transferable to nonwork-related injuries, allowing for the estimation of the WTP for safety improvements in other markets, such as recreational activities.

The Zaloshnja, Miller, Romano, and Spicer Estimates of the Cost of Crash Injuries

Eduard Zaloshnja, Ted Miller, Eduardo Romano, and Rebecca Spicer estimate the social cost of motor vehicle crash injuries for the year 2000, updating prior estimates made by Miller in 1993.[21] The main purpose of this study is to provide a relatively comprehensive estimate of the social cost of a large spectrum of body parts injured in motor vehicle crashes, such as the spinal cord or the brain. These cost estimates include medical and emergency services, household and workplace productivity losses, insurance and legal costs, property damage, and quality of life losses. Monetary costs are supplemented by the addition of the WTP to avoid pain and suffering for each type of injury, which is based on a VSL of $3.1 million (2002 U.S. dollars) and a VLY of $95,000.

Injuries to each body part are also broken down by level of severity, based on the most severe ("maximum") injury sustained by a person according to the Abbreviated Injury Scale (AIS) scale, sometimes referred to as the Maximum Abbreviated Injury Scale (MAIS). This scale ranges from one (minor) to six (fatal); see Table 15-2.[22] Following Miller, the pain and suffering or the lost quality of life for an injury of a

TABLE 15-2   AIS Classification System, Including Equivalent Proportion of VSL

AIS Code	Injury Severity	Fraction of VSL	Description of Common Injury
PDO	None	0.00	No injury
AIS 1	Minor	0.0020	Superficial abrasion or laceration of skin, sprain, first degree burn, head trauma with headache or dizziness but no other symptoms
AIS 2	Moderate	0.0155	Significant abrasion or laceration of skin, concussion with less than 15 minutes of lost consciousness, closedfracture with or without dislocation, digit crush/amputation
AIS 3	Serious	0.0575	Major nerve injury, multiple rib fracture without chest collapse, bruise of internal organ, hand/arm or foot crush/amputation
AIS 4	Severe	0.1875	Spleen rupture, leg crush/ amputation, concussion with loss of consciousness 15 minutes to 24 hours, chest wall perforation
AIS 5	Critical	0.7625	Permanent spinal cord injury, extensive burns (second or third degree), concussion with severe neurological signs
AIS 6	Fatal	1	Injuries which, if not immediately fatal, ultimately result in death

Source: Based on Stephan Hoffer, Frank Berardino, Jack Smith, and Stuart Rubin, *Economic Values for Evaluation of FAA Investment and Regulatory Decisions,* US DOT FAA-APO-98-8, Federal Aviation Administration, June 1998.

particular level of severity is expressed as a fraction of the WTP to avoid a fatal injury, less the lost human capital.[23] The particular fractions proposed by Miller for each level of severity are also shown in Table 15-2. This approach is not ideal because the fractions are somewhat arbitrary, but we are not aware of a better approach, and it has been adopted by many regulatory bodies.[24]

Table 15-1 presents the average cost of a motor vehicle crash injury to the spinal cord, brain, lower extremities, upper extremities, trunk/abdomen, and other head/face/neck, as well as minor external injuries, burns, and fatal injuries. It also reports in parentheses a range for each body part according to level of severity. For example, the average cost of a motor crash that causes a brain injury is $1.2 million, but it ranges from $124,000 for a brain injury of AIS 1 to $3.5 million for one of AIS 5. Injury costs range from approximately $10,000 for a minor injury to a leg or foot to $4.4 million to a critical injury (AIS level 5) to the spinal cord. Note that the cost of the latter injury exceeds the VSL by 5 percent.

The Blincoe and Colleagues Estimates of the Cost of Motor Vehicle Crashes

Lawrence Blincoe and his colleagues provide fully allocated costs for motor vehicle crashes. These comprehensive estimates include property damage, the costs of emergency and medical services, productivity losses, pain and suffering, and travel time delay to other motorists. Blincoe and his colleagues present estimates of the cost of a crash based on the maximum AIS to an injured person. At the lowest level (property damage only, PDO), there is no personal injury, but there is property damage, insurance administrative costs, and police costs. The figures that are shown in Table 15-1 are per (maximally) injured person, except for PDO (property damage only) crashes, which are per vehicle.

Transportation economists often distinguish between direct costs, indirect costs, and intangible costs. Direct costs include emergency treatment, initial medical costs (including physician, hospital, prescription costs, and ancillary costs, such as administration costs of processing medical payments to providers), rehabilitation costs, long-term care costs (if required), legal costs, and employer/workplace costs. Other direct costs are property damage to vehicles, cargo, and personal property. Indirect costs include productivity losses due to temporary and permanent disability and decreases in household productivity. Intangible costs relate to pain and suffering or lost quality of life. The individual components of crash costs for each level of severity appear in Table 15-3. These components may be applicable to other settings where injuries occur at similar severity levels.

Conclusion on the Cost of Injuries

The Rice, MacKenzie, and Associates study provides estimates of the monetary costs of a wide range of injuries. However, these estimates are not particularly useful as measures of social costs, especially for injuries that eventually prove fatal, as monetary costs are likely to be only a fraction of total social costs. If injury costs are underestimated, then the benefits of safety-enhancing road improvements are reduced relative to the benefits of time-saving road improvements. It may thus appear that it is better to be dead than to be stuck in traffic![25] This is usually not the case when the numbers are estimated correctly.

The Miller and Galbraith and the Dillingham, Miller, and Levy studies focus on the cost of work-related injuries, but the two studies focus on different measures.

TABLE 15-3 The Cost of Components of Crashes by Level of Severity (2002 U.S. dollars)

AIS Level	PDO	1	2	3	4	5	6 (Fatal)
Medical	0	2,466	16,186	48,163	136,018	344,390	22,888
Emergency	32	100	219	381	860	882	863
Market Productivity	0	1,812	25,915	74,018	110,259	454,451	616,725
Household Productivity	49	593	7,585	21,831	29,015	154,667	198,416
Insurance Admin	121	768	7,157	19,571	33,496	70,644	38,453
Workplace Costs	53	261	2,023	4,419	4,866	8,485	9,014
Legal Costs	0	156	5,160	16,375	34,894	82,722	105,803
QALYs	0	4,615	94,408	132,705	397,208	1,353,740	2,474,929
Property Damage	1,538	3,982	4,096	7,043	10,186	9,785	10,642
Travel Delay	832	805	876	974	1,035	9,476	9,476
Total	**2,625**	**15,558**	**163,625**	**325,480**	**757,837**	**2,489,242**	**3,487,209**

Source: Adapted from Lawrence J. Blincoe, Angela G. Seay, Eduard Zaloshnja, Ted R. Miller, Eduardo O. Romano, Stephen Luchter, and Rebecca S. Spicer, *The Economic Impact of Motor Vehicle Crashes 2000*, National Highway Traffic Safety Administration, U.S. Department of Transportation, May 2002, p. 9 and p. 62. Available at *www.nhtsa.dot.gov.*

The Zaloshnja and colleagues study provides comprehensive estimates of injuries sustained in a motor vehicle crash. Blincoe and colleagues adopt a similar methodology to measure the total social cost of an accident.

THE COST OF CRIME

Many criminal justice and training programs have reduction of crime as one of their goals. In order to estimate the aggregate benefits of crime reduction, it is necessary to estimate the number of crimes of each type that will be avoided during each time period and the social cost of each type of crime.[26] For the latter, it is often appropriate and easier to use estimates from secondary sources.[27] Table 15-4 provides evidence from two sources. Ted Miller and Mark Cohen estimate the victim costs of violent crimes, focusing on gunshots and cut/stab wounds, and Ted Miller, Mark Cohen, and Brian Wiersema estimate the social costs of crime in a report prepared for the National Justice Institute.[28] Both sets of estimates exclude criminal justice system costs and prevention costs.

The Miller and Cohen Estimate of the Cost of Intentional Gunshot and Cut/Stab Wounds

Ted Miller and Mark Cohen investigated the cost of intentional gunshot and cut/stab wounds. They estimate that gunshot wounds in the United States cost $149 billion per year (2002 U.S. dollars) and that cut/stab wounds add an additional $0.60 billion. Some wounds are self-inflicted (i.e., suicide and attempted suicide), but most are not. Miller and Cohen identify seven cost categories, including the cost of emergency response

TABLE 15-4   The Cost of Crime (in 2002 U.S. dollars)

Plug-In Category	Shadow Price Value	Comments
Victim Cost of Crime		
1. Gunshot – assault	1. $828,000 (199,000)	Based on Miller and Cohen (1997).
2. Gunshot – suicide	2. $2,252,000 (257,000)	Costs are per victim by intent and
3. Cut/Stab – assault	3. $163,000 (86,000)	include fatal or nonfatal injury
4. Cut/Stab – suicide	4. $125,000 (95,000)	(e.g. suicide attmepts), with the
		costs for survivors only in
		parentheses.
Monetary Cost of Crime		
Fatal Crimes		
DWI (drunk driver)	$3.75 million per incident	Based on Miller, Cohen, and
Arson	$3.23 million per incident	Wiersema (1996). Excludes
All other (rape, assault, etc.)	$3.47 million per incident	criminal justice system and
		prevention cost for potential
		victims.
Nonfatal Crimes		
Child abuse	$70,700 per incident	
Rape/sexual assault (excluding child abuse)	$102,600 per incident	
Other assault (or attempt)	$11,000 per incident	
Robbery (or attempt)	$9,400 per incident	
Drunk driving	$21,200 per incident	
Arson	$44,200 per incident	
Larceny (or attempt)	$400 per incident	
Burglary (or attempt)	$1,700 per incident	
Motor Vehicle Theft (or attempt)	$4,400 per incident	

and emergency services, medical care costs, mental health care costs, productivity losses at home and in the workplace, direct administrative costs including legal and court fees, costs of preventing future violence, and costs to individuals and family for pain and suffering (loss of quality of life). However, they do not include the cost of preventing future violence, which they liken to the cost of a burglar alarm, in their estimates. Nor do they include the costs of incarceration, sanctioning, and probation, which also contribute to the prevention of future violent events. Thus, Miller and Cohen focus on injury costs.

Examining the incidence of wound occurrence, the authors show that the peak age of occurrence is between 25 and 34 years of age for both assaults and suicide attempts and that it is roughly normally distributed across age. As shown in Table 15-4, gunshot crimes are more costly than cuts and stabbings. Suicide gunshot attempts are more costly than gunshot assaults because they are much more likely to result in death. Figures in parentheses reflect the victim's costs when the victim survives.

The Miller, Cohen, and Wiersema Estimates of the Cost of Crime

Ted Miller, Mark Cohen, and Brian Wiersema examine the consequences and cost of crime. They focus on victims' costs and ignore society's response to victimizations (which include multiple incidences to a single victim), including the real costs to the criminal justice system and other social costs, such as fear.[29] They examined rape, robbery, child abuse/neglect, assault, drunk driving (DWI), arson, larceny, burglary, and motor vehicle theft. They further examined the number of deaths resulting from these crimes and, if not fatal, whether there was injury.

Miller and colleagues include pain and suffering as well as direct costs. Direct costs include lost productivity, medical/emergency care, mental health care, police/fire services, social victim services, and property damage. The lost quality of life for a fatality was based on a VSL of $3.18 million (2002 U.S. dollars). For nonfatal consequences, intangible costs are based on jury awards to crime victims and burn victims. In the case of multiple incidents of crime occurring to single individuals, the intangible costs of a single incident were multiplied by the average number of victimizations per individual.

This study excludes criminal justice system costs and the cost of actions taken to reduce the risk of becoming a crime victim. These are two of the largest costs associated with criminal behavior. Other impacts omitted include expenses for processing insurance or welfare payments to totally disabled victims of crime, long-term effects on earnings resulting from psychological injury, and "second generation costs," which are described as crimes committed by persons who themselves are victims of crime. Some "second generation costs" are likely to be included implicitly, for example, property crime or assault that results from drug abuse (i.e., victimless drug offenses).

As is often the case in social cost estimates involving personal injury, the intangible costs are the largest component for all crime categories, except burglary, larceny, and motor vehicle theft where the likelihood of personal injury is low. The Miller, Cohen, and Wiersema costs are presented per criminal incident. These estimates are similar to those from other studies conducted in the past 25 years.

Conclusion on the Cost of Crime

As can be seen in Table 15-4, the cost of crime varies depending on the nature of the crime. Costs of intentional assault with a deadly weapon are the next highest after costs that arise due to death of a victim of criminal activity (intentional or accidental). The importance of intent is easily seen under the cost of all incidences of suicide and attempted suicide by gunshot. The survival rate is very low and the cost to survivors quite high relative to the other costs. The next highest cost estimates belong to victims of rape and childhood abuse, where psychological effects exact a high price on the quality of life. All other criminal activities cost relatively little in comparison to crimes with high personal injury rates.

THE VALUE OF TIME

Time is a valuable commodity; as the saying goes, "time is money." Time spent traveling, which individuals are generally willing to pay to avoid, is a cost. Change in travel time is an important component of many CBAs, most obviously those concerned with transportation. Though rarely a dominating cost or benefit, change in waiting time can be important in many nontransportation projects. For example, queuing time is an important cost component of policies that ration goods or affect access to services, such as motor vehicle registration, medical care, or social services.

Most of the empirical literature on the value of time has been concerned with estimating the value of travel time. This is normally referred to as the *value of travel time savings* (VTTS), reflecting the fact that many transportation projects save time. Recently some attention has been devoted to the value of time in other activities, recognizing that it may differ from the VTTS. For example, people usually experience considerably greater disutility from waiting time than from "pure" travel time.[30]

The VTTS captures several phenomenon that are all related but separate entities, including the benefits of travel time savings versus the benefits from reliability of those time savings (the variance of travel time savings).[31] Thus the VTTS is higher during congested periods, where there is more uncertainty, than under free-flow conditions.

One might think that time saved simply reflects time saved, but one should ask why drivers slow down as traffic flow increases or density increases.[32] Presumably drivers slow down because they want to prevent or reduce the risk of an accident. Thus, one can think of increases in travel time as reducing the *ex ante* cost of an accident. Another way to reduce one's expected private cost of an accident is to buy a larger, more sturdy car.

The large empirical literature on VTTS has been reviewed by several authors, mostly on a country-specific or regional basis. Typically, these have been commissioned by the relevant government and have led to the adoption of a standard VTTS for use in analysis in that country. For example, there have been reviews of the VTTS evidence in the United Kingdom, Canada, New Zealand, the Netherlands, the United States, and for developing countries.[33] In most cases, as we will discuss, VTTS is expressed as a proportion of the before-tax or after-tax wage rate. This allows analysts to readily estimate travel time costs using local wage rates, although one should adjust for income and other factors, as we discuss near the end of this chapter.

Table 15-5 contains estimates of the VTTS for road transportation, based primarily on literature reviews by William Waters, and by Markus von Wartburg and William Waters.[34] The latter study also presents estimates of the value time saved in other activities, such as walking and waiting, usually expressed as a multiple of the VTTS.

The Waters Estimates of VTTS

William G. Waters reviewed estimates of the VTTS from 56 empirical studies conducted between 1974 and 1990. These studies use revealed preference or contingent valuation methods. Revealed preference studies include a wide range of situations:

TABLE 15-5 The Value of Time

Plug-In Category	*Shadow Price Value*	*Comments*
VTTS for Road Transportation		
1. Nonwork travel time (commuting or leisure)	1. 50% of the average after-tax wage rate per hour saved	Based on Waters (1996) and von Wartburg and Waters (2004).
2. Work travel time	2. 100% of the before-tax wage rate (plus benefits) per hour saved	
Time in Other Activities		
1. Walking	1. 2 × VTTS	Common convention in
2. Waiting	2. 2.5 × VTTS	many jurisdictions
3. Congestion	3. 2 × VTTS	(von Wartburg and Waters, 2004).

route choice decisions in which there are different costs (e.g., toll roads versus nontoll roads), mode choice decisions (bus or car travel versus faster, but more costly, airline travel), speed choice decisions (in which faster speeds involve higher operating costs), and location choice decisions (hedonic methods that isolate the impact of commuting time on land values). Survey methods are also used to estimate VTTS because they allow researchers to gather data of direct relevance to determining willingness-to-pay.

As is the normal procedure in the VTTS literature, Waters presents the VTTS as a percentage of the after-tax hourly wage rate, rather than as a dollar figure. He found as much as a tenfold variation in estimates from the literature. As with other estimates described in this chapter, the studies cover a wide range of circumstances. Waters partitions these studies in a number of ways. He aggregates the 32 studies that focus on commuting trips (after eliminating some outliers) and calculates the mean value at 48 percent of the after-tax wage rate with a median of 40 percent. When using only the 15 North American automobile commuting studies, Waters calculates a mean of 59 percent (54 percent with the elimination of outliers) and a median of 42 percent. The 17 non–North American auto commuting studies generate a mean of 38 percent. Waters concludes that a shadow price of between 40 to 50 percent of the after-tax wage rate is the appropriate VTTS for auto commuting.

The von Wartburg and Waters Estimates of the VTTS and Time in Other Activities

In a recent examination of the literature, Markus von Wartburg and William Waters review recent advances in the study of the VTTS. They note that the establishment of toll roads is particularly useful for examining the components of VTTS (time saved and reduced variance in time saved). They also note that there is still considerable heterogeneity of results depending on the parameters of the study designs.

Von Wartburg and Waters recommend that the VTTS should be 50 percent of the average after-tax wage rate for nonwork trips. They also suggest that there should be no distinction based on the reason for these trips (i.e., vacation time saved and commuting time saved should be valued equally, even though some people enjoy travelling in cars on their vacations).[35] The VTTS for business trips should be valued at the gross (before-tax) wage plus labor-related overheads (e.g., employer-paid benefits); no other adjustments should be made for the socioeconomic characteristics of travelers.

They also suggest that travel time savings in congested traffic should be weighed at twice the uncongested (free-flow) rate.[36] Finally they recommend a weighing factor of two times the VTTS for time spent walking and two and one-half times for waiting time.[37] The authors state that these multipliers are in line with common convention.

THE VALUE OF RECREATION

The value of recreation is important for assessing damage to rural areas, whether this damage is caused by fire or development. The National Park Service, the Fish and Wildlife Service, the Bureau of Reclamation, and the Forest Service need this information to assess damage. This information is also helpful in assessing the benefits of new recreational opportunities and for determining whether to develop wilderness areas.

Studies that estimate the value of various kinds of recreation generally rely on the travel cost method or the contingent valuation method. Recreational facilities almost always provide both use benefits and nonuse benefits. Within the category of use benefits, we include rivalrous consumption (such as hunting), direct nonrivalrous consumption (such as hiking), and indirect nonrivalrous consumption (such as watching a movie about hiking in the wilderness). Within the category of nonuse benefits, which are discussed in more detail in Chapter 9, we include pure existence value (valuing the "natural order") and altruistic existence value (such as valuing other people's use or nonuse value of wilderness).

Reviews of the value of recreational activities have built upon one another over the past 20 years. An early review of 93 studies was conducted by Cindy Sorg and John Loomis in 1984.[38] Richard Walsh, Donn Johnson, and John McKean updated and extended this earlier study, incorporating studies that had been conducted through 1988.[39] In 2001 Randall Rosenberger and John Loomis merged the results of two more recent reviews.[40] This study focused on recreational activities that are of importance to the Forest Service. Most recently, Pam Kaval and John Loomis extended the survey; it now encompasses a study period from 1967 to 2003, covering 1239 observations from 593 individual studies.[41]

Kaval and Loomis report the mean net willingness-to-pay for 30 separate outdoor recreation activities, which are shown in Table 15-6. They report their findings by "activity day," which is the typical amount of time pursuing an activity within a 24-hour

TABLE 15-6 The Value of Recreational Activities (in 2002 U.S. dollars)

Backpacking	$48.20	Pleasure driving	$54.79
Bird watching	$27.39	(including sightseeing)	
Camping	$34.40	Rock climbing	$52.04
Cross-country skiing	$29.03	Scuba diving	$29.94
Downhill skiing	$30.98	Sightseeing	$34.08
Fishing	$43.63	Snorkeling	$28.04
Boating	$93.35	Snowmobiling	$33.57
(nonmotorized)		Swimming	$39.49
General recreation	$32.47	Visiting an environmental	$5.56
Going to the beach	$36.48	education center	
Hiking	$28.53	Visiting an arboretum	$12.52
Horseback riding	$16.76	Visiting an aquarium	$26.19
Hunting	$43.40	Waterskiing	$45.35
Motor boating	$42.80	Wildlife viewing	$39.19
Mountain biking	$68.25	Windsurfing	$365.84
Off-road vehicle	$21.20	*Average value of a*	*$44.07*
driving		*recreational day*	
Other recreation	$45.05		
Picnicking	$38.35		

All figures are per activity day.

Source: Based on Pam Kaval and John Loomis, Updated Outdoor Recreation Use Values with Emphasis on National Park Recreation, Final Report to National Park Service, Fort Collins, CO (Colorado State University, Department of Agricultural and Resource Economics: Fort Collins, CO, 2003).

period. This unit is easily converted to other visitation/participation units (e.g., recreation visitor days, trips, or seasons). Across all recreational activities, the average value of a recreational day is about $44.

THE VALUE OF NATURE (SPECIFIC SPECIES OR HABITATS)

Interest in the environment has increased considerably in recent years. At the same time, scientists have developed a better understanding of the relationship between the environment, human intervention, and human well-being.[42] However, valuing the environment is not easy. One reason is that each environmental area is generally used for multiple purposes—commercial (e.g., timber and fish), recreation, and other purposes. Consequently, there are potential problems of aggregation and double counting.

This section focuses on valuing aspects of nature and biodiversity. It concerns the value of specific species of flora and fauna and, more broadly, of habitats and ecosystems. Given the increasing interest in the environment, it is surprising that relatively few studies attempt to value such goods, at least relative to the number of studies that value recreation.[43]

Most studies that value elements of nature use the contingent valuation method. Estimates of value usually incorporate both option price (e.g., for bird watching, but possibly for hunting) and existence value. Value is usually measured in terms of dollars per household per year. The option price typically varies according to proximity. For example, Bateman et al. found that people living near the Norfolk Broads (a wetland site in England that covers three National Nature Reserves and offers opportunities for bird watching, sailing, and coarse fishing) were willing to pay £12 (about $23 in 2002 U.S. dollars), while people living elsewhere in the United Kingdom were willing to pay £4 (about $8 in 2002 U.S. dollars).[44] Recently, some authors have conducted longitudinal studies, which are particularly useful for examining the effects of changes in urban areas on ecosystem services and the value of those services.[45]

In 1993 David Pearce published one of the few literature surveys of the value of specific species and the value of ecosystem and biodiversity loss.[46] He summarizes earlier contingent valuation studies and reports the public's willingness-to-pay to preserve an endangered animal species or prized habitat on a per-person, per-year basis. As shown in Table 15-7, the willingness-to-pay to preserve a single species ranges from $1.50 to $65 per person per year. WTP to preserve habitats is higher, reaching almost $140 per person per year to preserve rivers against hydroelectric development. This figure is surprisingly high given that alternative sources of energy might have much higher environmental costs. More recently, Paulo Nunes and Jeroen van den Bergh survey various measures of biodiversity.[47] As shown in Table 15-7, they find that the existence value of different habitats ranges from $8 to $102 per household per year (2002 U.S. dollars).

THE VALUE OF WATER AND WATER QUALITY

Fresh water is a necessity and it is becoming increasingly scarce. As there generally is no well-established market for fresh water in most locations, analysts have to estimate its shadow price. Contingent valuation surveys, the market analogy method, the inter-

TABLE 15-7 The Value of Environmental Impacts (in 2002 U.S. dollars)

Plug-In Category	Shadow Price Value	Comments
Specific Species		
Bald Eagle	$15.92 per person per year	Based on Pearce (1993).
Whooping Crane	$1.54 per person per year	
Grizzly Bear	$23.75 per person per year	
Bighorn Sheep	$11.04 per person per year	
California Sea Otter	$10.40 per person per year	
Northern Elephant Seal	$10.40 per person per year	
Bottlenose Dolphin	$8.99 per person per year	
Blue Whale	$11.94 per person per year	
Humpback Whale	$64.51 per person per year	
Habitats		
Conservation of rivers against hydroelectric	$75.74 to $137.36 per person per year	Based on Pearce (1993).
Grand Canyon	$34.66 per person per year	
Colorado Wilderness	$11.94 to $27.22 per person per year	
Existence Value of Habitats		
Terrestrial	$27–$102 per household per year	Based on Nunes and van den Bergh (2001).
Coastal	$9–$52 per household per year	
Wetland	$8–$97 per household per year	
Water Quality Improvements		
1. From unusable to boatable	1. $8.50 to $59 per year per household	Based on Luken, Johnson, and Kibler (1992).
2. From boatable to rough fishing	2. $12.70 to $51 per year per household	
3. From rough fishing to game fishing	3. $16.90 to $42 per year per household	
4. From game fishing to superior game fishing	4. $20 to $35 per year per household	
5. From unusable to superior game fishing	5. $42 to $152 per year per household	
Water Values by Use		
Waste disposal	$3.46 ($1.15)	Based on Frederick, van den Berg, and Hanson (1996). Mean values with median values are in parentheses. Values are per acre-foot.
Recreation/fish and wildlife	$55.42 ($5.77)	
Navigation	$168.55 ($11.54)	
Hydropower	$28.86 ($24.24)	
Irrigation	$86.59 ($46.18)	
Industrial processing	$325.56 ($152.39)	
Thermoelectric power	$39.25 ($33.48)	
Domestic	$239.97 ($111.98)	

mediate good method, defensive expenditures, and the travel cost method have all been used to estimate the value of water of different quality levels or the benefits of improvements in water quality for various purposes.[48] We review a WTP study for water quality improvements for recreational purposes by Ralph Luken, Reed Johnson, and Virginia Kibler.[49] Also, we discuss a study by Kenneth Frederick, Tim van den Berg, and Jean Hanson that estimates the cost of water for different uses.[50]

The Luken, Johnson, and Kibler Estimates of the Value of Water Quality Improvements For Recreational Purposes

The fourth section in Table 15-7 summarizes annual household willingness-to-pay amounts for water quality improvements for recreational purposes by Ralph Luken, Reed Johnson, and Virginia Kibler. These authors drew on previous studies of the Monongahela River, near Pittsburgh. Luken, Johnson, and Kibler argue for 30 miles as an upper bound in defining the relevant markets for such recreational sites. They also recommend using visitation rates for households within this distance that range from 50 percent for sites with few substitutes to 10 percent for sites with numerous substitutes.

EXHIBIT 15-1

Ralph Luken wished to estimate the costs and benefits of (technology-based) water pollution standards introduced by the Clean Water Act of 1972. However, there were no existing estimates of WTP for improvements in the water quality of the rivers in question. Therefore, he utilized WTP estimates from existing studies as a basis for his estimates of the value of improvements in water quality.

He initially considered eight existing studies that might provide plug-in values. Five of the existing studies used the contingent valuation method, two studies used the travel cost method, and the eighth study was a user participation study. Luken eliminated five of the studies because their focus was not similar to the sites he was considering. These five stud-

ies dealt with water systems, such as those on a large western lake and a western river basin. His sites, in contrast, were generally eastern rivers with local recreation usage. Therefore he focused on three studies: one on the Charles River in Boston and two on the Monongahela River in Pennsylvania. The Monongahela studies estimated benefits for three levels of improvement in water quality (from boating to fishing, from fishing to swimming, and from boating to swimming), whereas the Charles River study only examined improvements in water quality from boating to swimming (i.e., the biggest "jump" in quality). The summarized values as annual WTP per household (1984 dollars) are as follows:

River	Water Quality Change		
	Boat-Fish	*Fish-Swim*	*Boat-Swim*
Monongahela (contingent valuation)	$25–40	$14–23	$40–64
Monongahela (travel cost)	$8	$10	$18
Charles (contingent valuation)	—	—	$74

(Continued)

(Continued)

Unfortunately, these benefit categories did not directly map into the benefit categories Luken was using, which covered five quality improvement levels: U = Unusable, B = Boatable, R = Rough fishing, G = Game fishing, and G^* = Superior game fishing. Luken assumed that the travel cost method provided lower-bound estimates (because they include only use valuations) and the contingent valuation estimates provided upper-bound estimates (as they include nonuse as well as use valuations). As shown next, he also included intrause estimates to reflect smaller benefit improvements. His plug-in values for water quality benefits (willingness-to-pay per household per year in $1984) follow:

Initial Water Quality	Final Water Quality	Lower Bound	Upper Bound
U	U	$1−3	$9−18
U	B	$5	$35
U	R	$15	$50
U	G	$20	$80
U	G*	$25	$90
B	B	$2−4	$8−15
B	R	$8	$30
B	G	$15	$50
B	G*	$20	$60
R	R	$3−5	$6−13
R	G	$10	$25
R	G*	$15	$35
G	G	$3−6	$5−10
G	G*	$12	$20

Although the purpose of this exhibit is to illustrate the use of secondary sources, it is interesting to note that in using these values, Luken generally found that costs exceed benefits.

Sources: Adapted from Frederick W. Gramlick, "The Demand for Clear Water: The Case of the Charles River," *National Tax Journal,* 30(2) 1977, 183–195; Ralph A. Luken, *Efficiency in Environmental Regulation* (Boston: Kluwer Academic Publishers, 1990), 45–50, 88–90; V. Kerry Smith and William H. Desvousges, *Measuring Water Quality Benefits* (Boston: Kluwer-Nijhoff Publishing, 1986); V. Kerry Smith, William H. Desvousges, and Ann Fisher, "A Comparison of Direct and Indirect Methods for Estimating Environmental Benefits," Working Paper No. 83–W32, Vanderbilt University, Nashville, TN, 1984.

The Frederick, van den Berg, and Hanson Study of the Value of Water

Frederick, van den Berg, and Hanson summarize plug-in values for different uses of water based on a survey of 41 earlier studies. The authors provide estimates of the cost of water in eight uses: waste disposal, recreation/fish and wildlife habitat, navigation, hydropower, irrigation, industrial processing, thermoelectric power generation, and domestic uses. Values are expressed in terms of dollars per acre-foot basis (one acre-foot equals 325,851 gallons, the volume of water required to cover one acre at a depth of one foot).

Water used for industrial processing and domestic use have the highest mean and median values. However, recreation/fish and wildlife habitat and irrigation account for nearly 80 percent of all the estimates and the highest values of any individual studies. We report both the median and mean values in Table 15-7 due to the lack of weighting in the final estimates. The authors point out that median values may be most applicable to national level assessment and likely reflect normal hydrologic conditions.

The authors note several caveats. Water quality is important in most uses, but is not reflected in the estimates. The timing of rainfall and levels of the water table play a large role in the cost of water, and values vary among regions (as water value is inversely related to availability). They also note that supply and demand conditions change over time (due to seasonal variation, technological changes, and meterological conditions), thereby affecting its value.

THE COST OF NOISE

The cost of noise is mostly relevant in the evaluation of transportation projects. The dominant method for estimating the cost of noise is the hedonic pricing method. Property values (usually those of private residences) are regressed on noise, structural characteristics of the houses (numbers of rooms, square footage), neighborhood characteristics (number of lots or broken windows per block), accessibility characteristics (to downtown or local waterfront), and other environmental characteristics (air pollution). It is important to control for air quality because it is correlated with noise pollution from automobiles.

Noise is measured in units of NEFs (ambient noise is in the 15–25 NEF range, "some" to "much" annoyance occurs in the 25–40 NEF range, and "considerable" annoyance occurs above 40 NEFs). One NEF is equal to a mean exposure over time to one decibel of noise.

The sensitivity of house prices to changes in noise level is measured by the noise depreciation sensitivity index (NDSI), which represents the percentage change in the value of a house that follows a unit increase in the noise level, measured in NEFs.[51] One way to obtain the NDSI is to specify a semi-log hedonic price function in which the price of a house (in logarithms) is a linear function of noise and various control variables. The NDSI equals the slope of this function with respect to noise multiplied by –100.[52]

Since Jon Nelson's survey in 1980, there have been several new studies and surveys.[53] Ian Bateman, Brett Day, Ian Lake, and Andrew Lovett recently conducted a review of the studies published after 1970.[54] Perhaps somewhat surprisingly, consensus estimates of the NDSI have remained fairly stable over several decades. As shown in Table 15-8, noise pollution has two primary sources—air traffic and road traffic. The best estimate of the NDSI for air traffic in the U.S. is 0.65 percent.[55] Recall that the NDSI measures the percentage change in house price for a change in ambient noise level of one NEF. In other words, if the noise level increases by one NEF, then the price of an affected house will decreases in value by 0.65 percent on average. Thus, houses adjacent to an airport with NEFs of 40 are priced 9.75 percent lower than houses farther from the airport with NEFs of 25. For roadway noise pollution, Bateman and his colleagues suggest that the NDSI is 0.64 percent.

TABLE 15-8 The Cost of Noise and Air Pollution (in 2002 U.S. dollars)

Plug-In Category	Shadow Price Value	Comments
Cost of Noise		
Airline noise pollution	0.65 percent reduction in value of property per NEF	Based on Schipper (1996) and Bateman, Day, Lake,
Roadway noise pollution	0.64 percent reduction in value of property per NEF	and Lovett (2001).
Cost of Noise		
1. Residential properties	1. 0.65 percent reduction in value per NEF	Based on Uyeno, Hamilton, and Biggs (1993).
2. Condominiums	2. 0.90 percent reduction in value per NEF	
3. Vacant land	3. 1.66 percent reduction in value per NEF	
Health Costs of Air Pollution		
Suspended particulates	$194 ($39) per microgram per m^3 per house	Based on Smith and Huang (1995). Mean (median) values.
Health Costs of Air Pollution		
1. PM_{10}	1. $26.5 to $74 ($42) per person per year (pp/yr) per microgram per m^3	Based on Krupnick's (1995) Monte Carlo simulations. Numbers in parentheses are
2. Lead	2. $5.6 to $17.5 ($10.4) pp/yr per .01 micrograms per m^3	central estimates directly computed from coefficient
3. SO_2	3. $1.38 to $24.8 ($11.3) pp/yr per microgram per m^3	estimates.
4. Ozone	4. $4.2 to $11.6 ($10.0) pp/yr per .01 parts per million	
Health Costs of Air Pollution from Motor Vehicles (LA Basin)		
1. VOCs	1. $3,700 per ton per year	Based on Small and Kazimi
2. NO_x	2. $13,400 per ton per year	(1995). Estimates reflect only
3. SO_x	3. $138,100 per ton per year	health care costs of pollutants
4. PM_{10}	4. $128,100 per ton per year	emitted by motor vehicles.
Cost of automobile	$0.03 per vmt	These numbers are upper
Cost of heavy-duty truck	$0.56 per vmt	bounds for urban areas.
Health Costs of Air Pollution (US)		
CO_x	$110 ($12) per ton per year	Based on McCubbin and
NO_x	$21,400 ($1,400) per ton per year	Delucchi (1999). Costs are
PM_{10}	$165,400 ($12,100) per ton per year	health care costs only due to
SO_x	$81,000 ($8,500) per ton per year	motor vehicle emissions. These
VOCs	$1,400 ($120) per ton per year	numbers are upper-bound
Ozone	$140 ($12) per ton per year	estimates per ton per year; lower bounds are in parentheses.
PM_{10}	$0.1614 per vmt	The per-ton estimates assume
Ozone	$0.0012 per vmt	1000 kilograms per metric ton.
CO	$0.0050 per vmt	
NO_x	$0.0037 per vmt	
Toxins	$0.0010 per vmt	The vmt estimates are based on
Total	*$0.1723 per vmt*	all vehicles.

TABLE 15-8 Continued

**Environmental Costs
of Air Pollution**

	Urban	Metropolitan Fringe	Rural	
SO_2	$127–$214[a]	$52–$124	$11–$28	Based on the Minnesota
PM_{10}	$5,067–$7,265	$2,247–$3,264	$636–$1,001	Public Utilities Commission,
CO	$1.20–$2.57	$0.86–$1.52	$0.24–$0.46	J. Jacobs, Chair (1996).
NO_x	$420–$1,106	$158–$301	$20–$115	Reflects environmental
Pb	$3,541–$4,383	$1,869–$2,257	$455–$507	costs only.
CO_2	$0.34–$3.51	$0.34–$3.51	$0.34–$3.51	

[a] *$/ton of emmission*
vmt = vehicle mile traveled

The estimated NDSIs discussed thus far pertain to residential properties. Dean Uyeno, Stan Hamilton, and Andrew Biggs recognize that the NDSI may differ according to land use.[56] They estimate a semi-log hedonic price function where the price of a house (in logarithms) is a linear function of noise (in NEFs) and other house quality characteristics. Using Canadian data, they estimate that the NDSI is 0.65 percent for detached houses with NEFs of 25 or higher (exactly the same as mentioned previously); they estimate it is 0.90 percent for condominiums and 1.66 percent for vacant land.

THE COST OF AIR POLLUTION

Air pollution results in both health and nonhealth costs. Health costs include the costs of premature death and the costs of morbidity (illness).[57] Nonhealth costs include environmental costs, such as those associated with rising sea levels, coastal erosion, river floods, deforestation, retarded plant growth, and reduced agricultural output. Other nonhealth costs include corrosion to buildings, cars, and materials (such as rubber), as well as loss of views.

Air pollutants are emitted from many sources, especially motor vehicles, industrial plants, and power plants.[58] Important pollutants are volatile organic compounds (VOCs), nitrogen oxides (NO_x), sulfur oxides (SO_x), carbon oxides (CO_x), chlorofluorocarbons (CFCs), and particulate matter of less than 10 microns in diameter (PM_{10}). VOCs combine with NO_x to produce ozone, which is a primary contributor to morbidity. Through chemical reactions SO_x, VOCs, and NO_x produce PM_{10}s, which cause both premature death and morbidity, especially respiratory diseases. The solution of SO_x and NO_x in cloud and rain droplets causes acid rain, which is known to damage pine and spruce forests and is thought to damage tobacco, wheat, and soya crops. Acid rain also damages buildings, increases the acidification of lakes, and affects fish populations.[59] CFCs cause significant depletion to the ozone layer, which increases exposure to ultraviolet radiation and can damage crops and cause skin cancer as well as cataracts. The accumulation of greenhouse gas (GHG) emissions (especially, carbon dioxide [CO_2], but also other gases including nitrous oxide [N_2O] and CFCs) causes global warming.[60]

Analysts estimate the cost of pollution using two main approaches. One is the hedonic property value method.[61] The more widely used approach is called the *dose response function* or *damage function* approach. A dose response function (or damage function) relates unit increases in a pollutant to various health effects, such as the probability of premature death and increases in different types of respiratory problems. These effects are then weighted by dollar valuations of the impacts, which are usually based on contingent valuation estimates of WTP. This approach excludes nonhealth costs, which may be reasonable if health costs are the much larger component.

We begin with a discussion of a meta-analysis by Kerry Smith and Ju-Chin Huang of 86 hedonic property value estimates based on 37 different studies conducted between 1967 and 1988.[62] We then present three sets of estimates of the health costs of pollutants based on dose response functions. Alan Krupnick provides estimates of the annual health costs per person attributable to PM_{10}, sulfur dioxide, lead, and ozone.[63] Kenneth Small and Camilla Kazimi report estimates of the annual health costs of adding one ton of various pollutants in the Los Angeles area.[64] Donald McCubbin and Mark Delucchi study the health costs of air pollution in the entire United States.[65] Finally, we discuss the environmental costs of air pollution as reflected in the recommendations of the Minnesota Public Utilities Commission, which drew heavily on a report by Triangle Economic Research, led by William Desvousges.[66]

The Smith and Huang Meta-Analysis

Each of the studies analyzed by Smith and Huang attempted to measure the impact of a one-unit change in total suspended particulates on the asset value of a typical house in one or more cities. The mean estimate is $194 per house per microgram per cubic meter (in 2002 dollars). However, Smith and Huang note that this value is substantially inflated due to a few outliers; the median value of the 86 estimates is only $39 per house per microgram per cubic meter. The variation in the estimates partially reflects the fact that they are for different cities, are estimated with different data, pertain to different time periods, and are based on different models and estimation techniques. Smith and Huang suggest that although the hedonic estimates partially reflect perceived health effects from pollution, they are probably more strongly influenced by "aesthetics, materials and soiling effects."[67] Indeed, they provide evidence which suggests that the dose response function approach results in much larger estimates of costs resulting from air pollution than does the hedonic property value approach.

The Krupnick Monte Carlo Estimates

Krupnick presents estimates of the costs of pollution on a per-particulate unit basis. These estimates include both morbidity and mortality costs, except for SO_2, which includes only mortality costs. With the exception of ozone, mortality costs dominate. The per-person per-year ranges reported in Table 15-8 may be viewed as 95 percent confidence intervals derived from Monte Carlo simulations, whereas the numbers in parentheses are point estimates directly computed from estimated coefficients.

The Small and Kazimi Estimates of the Health Care Costs of Pollutants from Vehicles

Estimates of the costs of pollution on a per-particulate unit basis are difficult to grasp intuitively and, for some purposes, may not provide a very convenient shadow price. Small and Kazimi present estimates of the annual health costs of adding one ton of various types of pollutants to the air and also compute the cost of polluting per vehicle mile traveled (vmt).

Small and Kazimi focus on health costs resulting from pollutants emitted by motor vehicles, costs that perhaps constitute the bulk of the costs engendered by air pollution in many urban areas. Their estimates imply that adding a ton of SO_x or PM_{10} to the air is much more costly than adding a ton of either VOCs or NO_x. Moreover, consistent with Krupnick's findings, Small and Kazimi indicate that most of the costs of air pollution result from premature death rather than from illness.

Small and Kazimi's estimates are based on an estimate of the VSL of about $5.9 million (in 2002 U.S. dollars). Earlier we suggested that a value about two-thirds as high may be more appropriate.[68] Use of a smaller value would cause the estimates of mortality costs to fall proportionately. Small and Kazimi's estimates are also based on an ambient PM_{10} concentration of 57.8 micrograms per cubic meter, computed from annual readings for downtown Los Angeles. The Los Angeles basin is especially conducive to chemical reactions that produce pollutants, and the area's mountain barriers are notorious for trapping pollutants. Comparable values for other cities in the United States would generally be smaller.

Small and Kazimi also estimate the pollution cost of driving one mile. Their baseline estimate is about 3 cents per vehicle mile traveled (vmt) for a typical automobile (or roughly 56 cents to 67 cents per gallon) and 59 cents per vmt for a heavy-duty diesel truck driven in Los Angeles.

The McCubbin and Delucchi Estimates of the Health Costs of Air Pollution from Motor Vehicles

Donald McCubbin and Mark Delucchi's approach is similar to that of Small and Kazimi, although they do not measure the effects of lead because this compound has been phased out of the U.S. gasoline market. McCubbin and Delucchi present ranges that depend on the value of a fatality in one of four categories (cancer, early imminent death, early death, and chronic death), the value of a single event of acute illness (headache, sore throat), the value of chronic illness, and the social discount rate. Table 15-8 contains their upper-bound estimates because the underlying values of mortality and morbidity (VSL nearly $4 million and values of chronic morbidity nearly $2 million) more closely match the current estimates of the VSL and the costs of injury presented earlier.[69] Their lower-bound estimates, which are substantially lower than their upper-bound estimates, are presented in parentheses.

The authors also present estimates per vehicle mile traveled (vmt). These range from 0.10 cents/vmt for toxins to 16.14 cents per vmt for particulates. The total cost of air pollution is 17.23 cents per vmt, indicating the dominant effect of particulate matter.

Minnesota Public Utilities Commission Study of Environmental Costs of Pollution

Thus far the discussion has focused on the costs of human morbidity and mortality and has ignored environmental effects. In 1996 the Minnesota Public Utilities Commission undertook a review of the costs of air pollution, focusing on environmental costs only, for the purpose of policy analysis of energy generation options. These estimates resulted from a consultative and somewhat politicized process during which estimates were provided by involved parties. However, the report's recommendations rely on a study led by William Desvousges.[70] The recommended estimates in dollars per ton of emission are presented at the bottom of Table 15-8. Their magnitudes are similar to those of a globally focused research study by Richard Tol and Thomas Downing.[71] These costs should be added to health costs to approximate the total social cost of pollution.

Conclusion on the Cost of Pollution

Pollution has health, environmental, and other costs. McCubbin and Delucchi and Small and Kazimi focus on health costs. Their estimates differ due to differences in methodology and differences in valuations of impacts, as well as due to the specific environmental and geographic qualities of the Los Angeles basin. However, these findings are fairly similar in value and they shed light on the magnitude of the difference between highly polluted areas and areas of better air quality. It is important to note that the cost estimates per vmt can be expected to fall by a significant amount as reductions in emissions due to the Clean Air Act Amendments (1990) take effect and older vehicles are taken off the road.

The Minnesota Public Utilities Commission undertook a study of pollution costs. These numbers should be added to health care costs in order to estimate the total costs of pollution. Even so, such an estimate is likely to underestimate pollution costs because some costs, such as the damage to buildings or cars and reduced quality of view, are still excluded.

THE COST OF TAXATION: MARGINAL EXCESS TAX BURDEN

Government projects often involve expenditures that have to be financed through taxes. As discussed in Chapter 4, taxes typically result in a deadweight loss: the marginal excess tax burden (METB). This loss, or "leakage," occurs whenever there is a behavioral response to a tax—for example, an excise tax on a good causes purchases to fall or a tax on earnings causes workers to reduce their work hours. The marginal social value of the lost consumption or lost work is the deadweight loss of the tax. Important manifestations of the deadweight loss include the inefficient substitution of leisure for work, of barter for legal trade, and the search for tax loopholes. METBs vary according to the type of tax. In general, METBs are greater when the taxed activity is more elastic. The METBs from income taxes are higher than the METBs from property taxes and sales taxes.

Quite a few studies provide estimates of METB for specific taxes and countries, usually by assuming "reasonable" values of key parameters and then simulating the efficiency costs. Table 15-9 provides a range of estimates for the United States for a number of important taxes: all taxes, income taxes, sales taxes, and property taxes. The ranges are

TABLE 15-9	Plug-Ins for the Marginal Excess Tax Burden per Dollar of Revenue	
1. All taxes	1. $0.33 to $0.46	Lower values generally drawn
2. Sales tax	2. $0.11 to $0.39	from Ballard, Shoven, and
3. Income tax	3. $0.31 to $0.65	Whalley (1985); higher values
4. Property tax	4. $0.17	from Jorgenson and Yun (1990);
		highest from Feldstein (1997).

derived from Charles Ballard, John Shoven, and John Whalley and from Dale Jorgenson and Kun-Young Yun, with the former generally obtaining lower estimates than the latter.[72] Ballard, Shoven, and Whalley estimate the METB for all taxes combined is 33 cents per dollar, assuming the uncompensated saving elasticity is 0.4 and the uncompensated labor supply elasticity is 0.15. Using similar assumptions, Jorgenson and Yun estimate that the METB for all taxes is 46 cents per dollar.

Martin Feldstein has argued that most estimates of the deadweight loss from income taxes are underestimates because they ignore the effect of tax avoidance on labor supply. In addition to supplying less labor, individuals consume more untaxed goods, such as fringe benefits and charitable donations. Feldstein estimates the METB ranges from approximately 32 cents per dollar to $3.76 per dollar (for high-income groups), with an average figure of 78 cents per dollar for a 10 percent increase in all marginal tax rates. He also emphasizes that income taxes are not the only taxes on labor supply and adds these other taxes to deadweight loss. In the United States, for example, the 15 percent Social Security payroll tax is an important part of most individuals' tax liability.[73] Elsewhere, Feldstein suggests that the METB is about 65 cents per dollar of revenue, and we use this figure for the upper bound for income taxes in Table 15-9.[74]

W. Erwin Diewert and Denis Lawrence provide estimates of the METB for different sectors in New Zealand.[75] Their estimated METBs for 1991 were $0.14 for general consumption taxation and $0.18 for labor taxation, which are lower than the values obtained for the United States. Not surprisingly, they find that the METB is positive for automobiles, implying that taxing automobiles has a benefit because it would reduce pollution and other negative externalities.

Which METB is relevant to CBA? With respect to federal projects in the United States, it is probably reasonable to view income taxes as the marginal tax source, suggesting that the appropriate METB would be about $0.40. With respect to local government projects, the marginal tax source is more reasonably viewed as the property tax, which has an METB of around $0.17.

TRANSFERRING AND ADJUSTING PLUG-IN VALUES

Most of the estimates discussed in this chapter are averages based on many studies. For example, the per-day values of recreational activities are drawn from almost six hundred articles. For the most part, the estimates discussed here are based on U.S. research (and, indeed, sometimes on specific regions within the United States). Differences in incomes, tastes, and other factors bring into question the appropriateness of using these estimates to analyze projects in other regions or other countries. Wherever possible, the plug-in values should be adjusted to reflect the particular characteristics of a specific application, whether that is a different country or a nonrepresentative region of the United States.[76] Here, we briefly review four sets of factors that one might consider as a basis for adjustment: (1) differences in socioeconomic and other personal characteristics of the population (e.g., income and age), (2) differences in physical and other characteristics of the jurisdiction (e.g., geographic characteristics), (3) differences in the characteristics of the project itself (e.g., project quality), and (4) temporal changes.

Income, Tastes, and Other Socioeconomic Factors

It is often important to make adjustments due to socioeconomic differences or preference differences among different populations. Perhaps the most important variable is income. Most of the goods discussed here, including safety and risk reduction (VSL), time, recreation, and the environment, are likely to be normal goods. People place higher values on them as their incomes rise. Some of them might be luxuries (i.e., people might be willing to spend a higher proportion of their incomes on these goods as their income increases).

Preferences may also differ from one region to another or from one occupational group to another. People who live near airports may object less than others to aircraft noise; people who live in polluted areas may not value changes in air quality as much as people who live in areas with better air quality; and people who work in dangerous jobs may have greater propensity for risk than the average worker. Such differences in preferences affect how much people are willing to pay for particular policy effects.

Adjusting the VSL for Income and Other Factors   The VSL rises with income. Thus, U.S. estimates should be adjusted before they are applied to other countries. Although one might suspect that health and safety is a luxury and thus has an income elasticity greater than 1, numerous researchers have estimated the income elasticity for the VSL and most obtain estimates of less than 1.[77] For example, Miller finds a range of income elasticity from 0.85 to 0.96, Mrozek and Taylor obtain estimates of 0.46 to 0.49, and Viscusi and Aldy find that it is between 0.52 and 0.61.[78]

Using the estimated VSL for the United States to obtain the VSL for some other country, such as Canada, requires two steps. The first step is to convert the U.S. estimate into Canadian dollars. At 2002 exchange rates, for example, one Canadian dollar was approximately equivalent to US$0.837. Consequently, US$4 million was equivalent to approximately C$4.8 million, where C$ represents Canadian dollars.[79] The second step is to adjust for income differences.

By definition, the income elasticity of the VSL, e_I, is given by:

$$e_I = \frac{\%\Delta \text{ VSL}}{\%\Delta I} \tag{15.4}$$

where $\%\Delta$ VSL represents the percentage change in VSL and $\%\Delta I$ represents the percentage change in income. Consequently, to convert a VSL based on U.S. data to an appropriate figure for Canada, we use the following formula:

$$V_{CAN} = V_{US} + e_I V_{US}(I_{CAN} - I_{US})/I_{US} \tag{15.5}$$

Adjusting for purchasing power, Canadian incomes are approximately 15 percent lower than U.S. incomes and have maintained this average difference over the past

30 years.[80] Setting $(I_{CAN} - I_{US})/I_{US} = -0.15$, the Canadian VSL equals C\$4.44 million if e_I equals 0.50, C\$4.26 million if e_I equals 0.75, and C\$4.08 million if e_I equals 1.00. It seems reasonable to pick the midrange and round to the nearest quarter of a million, thus giving a VSL for Canada in 2002 equal to C\$4.25 million. Further support for this estimate comes from examination of Canadian, Australian, and other non-U.S. VSL studies.[81]

Earlier we mentioned that, in theory, the willingness-to-pay to reduce fatality risk declines as the risk level decreases. Therefore, the VSL should be adjusted for fatality risk. Air carrier fatality rates are lower than motor vehicle fatality rates, which suggests that the VSL for air travel should be lower than the VSL for road travel, holding everything else constant. At the same time, road travel is approximately 20 times more risky than working on a per-hour basis.[82] This suggests that the VSL for improvements in road safety should be valued more than the VSL computed from wage-risk studies. However, there are two problems with adjusting the VSL for the level of fatality risk. First, estimated VSLs are based on different fatality risk levels than the fatality risk while traveling on a road. Second, contrary to theory, some estimated VSLs decline as risk increases.[83] More research is needed before adjusting the VSL for fatality risk.

A third potentially important factor is sense of control. M. W. Jones-Lee and colleagues found that the average WTP to reduce death on the London underground is 50 percent higher than on roads.[84] This difference may be due to many factors, including incorrect estimation of the risks, loss of sense of control, or the method of death (people may think that dying in an underground crash is more traumatic than dying in a car crash). The loss of sense of control may be associated with the feeling that when one gives up control to a train driver or pilot, then that person may not fully internalize the externality associated with one's own death.

Adjusting the VTTS for Income and Other Factors   W. G. Waters examined how estimates of the VTTS vary with income, time (year of study), country, and trip purpose (inter-urban versus commuting or "other").[85] He finds that VTTS increases with income but less than proportionately:

$$\text{VTTS}_Y = \left(\frac{Y}{\overline{Y}}\right)^{0.5} \overline{\text{VTTS}} \qquad (15.6)$$

where VTTS_Y is the VTTS of a traveler with income Y, $\overline{Y}$ is the average income level, and $\overline{\text{VTTS}}$ is the average VTTS. He suggests that a convenient rule of thumb for the relationship is a square root rule. For example, if income goes up fourfold from the average, the VTTS doubles. Using such a rule, the VTTS rises more slowly than does income; it is a normal good but not a luxury. Subsequently, von Wartburg and Waters suggest using an income elasticity of 0.75; that is, the exponent in equation (15.6) would be 0.75, rather than 0.5.[86]

The relationship between VTTS and other variables appears to be weak. Waters found that VTTS increases over time (drifting upward at one percentage point per year) and that inter-urban travel has a slightly higher value than trips for other purposes. von Wartburg and Waters suggest using a positive distance elasticity of 0.3.

Physical and Other Regional Characteristics

The second set of factors that may affect the transferability of plug-in values are the physical and other characteristics of a region. For example, the impact of air pollution varies widely geographically, depending on population density, climate, and topography. More people are affected in more densely populated areas. Other things held constant, greater precipitation in Vancouver than in Los Angeles means that the morbidity costs of NO_x or particulate matter are lower there.

The current level of consumption of a good in a region may also affect the value of changes in the amount of that good. In general, holding all other factors constant, people are willing to pay more (less) for safety-improving projects as the level of safety decreases (increases). Consequently, the VSL used in a project in a "high risk" area should be higher than the VSL used in a project in a "low risk" area, holding all other relevant factors constant.

Project Differences

The third set of factors pertains to the similarity between the policy under evaluation and the projects in the studies used to derive the plug-in values. For example, the value of water quality improvement obtained from studies involving small improvements in quality levels may not apply to a proposed policy that would involve a large change in the level of water quality. The magnitude of the error in the generalization depends on the degree of nonlinearity in the relationship between water quality improvements and willingness-to-pay. Additionally, there may be important differences in the price and availability of substitutes which, if not accounted for, can cause biases.[87] In sum, policies or projects under evaluation should ideally be similar to the projects in the studies used to derive the plug-in values in terms of the availability and quality of alternatives.

Temporal Changes

The final set of factors are those relating to the fact that valuations may change over time. Earlier we mentioned that the health costs per vmt are declining over time as heavily polluting vehicles are replaced. Technological change, as well as temporal changes in population characteristics or jurisdictional characteristics, may affect the plug-in estimates. For example, increasing incomes and declining supply of accessible recreational areas might increase the value of such activities, while increasing congestion at the sites might decrease the value of such activities. Updating original estimates using the composite CPI or the GDP deflator implies no change in the relative value of that activity.

CONCLUSION

By making use of the plug-in values presented in this chapter, analysts can apply CBA to a wider range of policies than would be feasible if all shadow prices had to be estimated firsthand. When analysts have the necessary resources, they can obtain their own estimates and check them against those reported here.

EXERCISES FOR CHAPTER 15

1. A 40-mile stretch of rural road with limited access is used primarily by regional commuters and business travelers to move between two major interstate highways. The legal speed limit on the road is currently 55 miles per hour (mph) and the estimated average speed is 61 mph. Traffic engineers predict that if the speed limit were raised to 65 mph and enforcement levels were kept constant, the average speed would rise to 70 mph.

   Currently, an average of 5,880 vehicles per day use the stretch of road. Approximately half are commuters and half are business travelers. Traffic engineers do not expect that a higher speed limit will attract more vehicles. Vehicles using the road carry, on average, 1.6 people. Traffic engineers predict that raising the speed limit on this stretch of road would result in an additional 52 vehicle crashes involving, on average, 0.1 fatalities annually. They also predict that operating costs would rise by an average of $0.002 per mile per vehicle.

   The average hourly wage in the county in which the majority of users of the road work is $18.30/hour.

   Estimate the annual net benefits of raising the speed limit on the road from 55 mph to 65 mph. In doing this, test the sensitivity of your estimate of annual net benefits to several alternative estimates of the value of time savings and the value of life that you have selected from the chapter.

2. Analysts estimate that the expansion of the capacity of the criminal courts in a city would require about 7,200 additional hours of juror time. The average wage rate in the county is $15/hour. A recent survey by the jury commissioner, however, found that the average wage for those who actually serve on juries under the present system, who are also currently employed, is only $9/hour. The survey also found that about one-third of those who actually serve on juries under the existing system do not hold jobs—for example, they are home-makers, retirees, or are unemployed.

   a. What shadow price should the analysts use for an hour of jury time?

   b. About one-fourth of the jurors do not receive wages from their employers while on jury duty. How does this affect your choice of the shadow price?

NOTES

1. This chapter draws upon Anthony E. Boardman, David H. Greenberg, Aidan R. Vining, and David L. Weimer, "Plug-In Shadow Price Estimates for Policy Analysis," *Annals of Regional Science* 31(3) 1997, 299–324; and Anming Zhang, Anthony E. Boardman, David Gillen and W. G. Waters II, *Towards Estimating the Social and Environmental Costs of Transportation in Canada: A Report for Transport Canada* (Vancouver, Canada: Centre for Transportation Studies, University of British Columbia, August 2004) also available on Transport Canada's Web site. We would like to thank Diane Forbes for research assistance in preparing this chapter.

2. For example, Tae Hoon Oum, W. G. Waters II, and Jong-Say Yong surveyed over 60 studies of own-price elasticities of transport demand, "Concepts of Price Elasticities of Transport Demand and Recent Empirical Estimates: An Interpretative Essay," *Journal of Transport Economics and Policy* 26(2) 1992, 139–154. A companion survey reviews empirical estimates of public transit and auto usage; see Philip Goodwin, "A Review of New Demand Elasticities with Special Reference to Short and Long Run Effects of Price Changes," *Journal of Transport Economics and Policy* 26(2) 1992, 155–169.

3. For example, one recent study suggests that transportation and communications are substi-tutes; see E. A. Selvanathan and Saroja Selvanathan, "The Demand for Transport and Communication in the United Kingdom and Australia," *Transportation Research–B* 28(1) 1994, 1–9.

4. For our purpose, *value and cost* can be used interchangeably, but we stick with common nomenclature—that is, we refer to "the value of (a lost) life" and "the cost of injury."

5. For example, on gasoline demand, see Molly Espey, "Explaining the Variation in Elasticity Estimates of Gasoline Demand in the United States: A Meta-Analysis," *Energy Journal* 17(3) 1996, 49–60.

6. Ted R. Miller, *Narrowing the Plausible Range Around the Value of Life* (Washington, D.C.: The Urban Institute, 1989); Ann Fisher, Lauraine G. Chestnut, and Daniel M. Violette, "The Value of Reducing Risks to Death: A Note on New Evidence," *Journal of Policy Analysis and Management* 8(1) 1989, 88–100; and W. Kip Viscusi, "The Value of Risks to Life and Health," *Journal of Economic Literature* 31(4) 1993, 1912–1946. See also Arianne de Blaeij, Raymond J. G. M. Florax, Piet Rietveld, and Erik Verhoef, "The Value of Statistical Life in Road Safety: A Meta-Analysis," *Accident Analysis and Prevention* 35, 2003, 973–986.

7. The mean VSL for the studies Miller reviews is $1.95 million (in 1990 dollars). Fisher, Chestnut, and Violette conclude that the most defensible estimate is between $1.6 million and $8.5 million, although they put more confidence in the lower end. The VSL in Viscussi's studies provide widely varying estimates of the VSL between $0.09 million and $5.10 million (in 1990 dollars). However, he argues that Scott Atkinson and Robert Halvorsen's analysis of the purchase of safety features on new automobiles provides the most reliable estimate—$4 million in 1990 dollars. See Scott E. Atkinson and Robert Halverson, "The Valuation of Risks to Life: Evidence from the Market for Automobiles," *Review of Economics and Statistics* 72(1) 1990, 332–340.

8. Ted R. Miller, "Variations Between Countries in Values of Statistical Life," *Journal of Transport Economics and Policy* 34(2) 2000, 169–188; Janusz R. Mrozek and Laura O. Taylor, "What Determines the Value of Life? A Meta-Analysis," *Journal of Policy Analysis and Management* 21(2) 2002, 253–270; and W. Kip Viscusi and Joseph Aldy, "The Value of Statistical Life: A Critical Review of Market Estimates Throughout the World," *Journal of Risk and Uncertainty* 27(1) 2003, 5–76.

9. Eduard Zaloshnja, Ted Miller, Eduardo Romano, and Rebecca Spicer, "Crash Costs by Body Part Injured, Fracture Involvement, and Threat to Life Severity, United States, 2000," *Accident Analysis and Prevention* 36(3) 2004, 415–427.

10. Peter Abelson, "The Value of Life and Health for Public Policy," *The Economic Record* 79(Special Issue) 2003, 2–13. This estimate is based on a VSL of $2.5 million, life expectancy of 40 years, and a discount rate of 3 percent.

11. For empirical evidence on this issue see Alan Krupnick, Anna Alberini, Maureen Cropper, Nathalie Simon, Bernie O'Brien, Ron Goeree, and Martin Heintzelman, "Age, Health and the Willingness to Pay for Mortality Risk Reductions: A Contingent Valuation Survey of Ontario Residents," *Journal of Risk and Uncertainty* 24(2) 2002, 161–186; and Anna Alberini, Maureen Cropper, Alan Krupnick, and Nathalie Simon, "Does the Value of a Statistical Life Vary with Age and Health Status? Evidence from the United States and Canada," Discussion Paper 02-19, 2002, Washington, D.C.: Resources for the Future.

12. See Kevin Murphy and Robert Topel, "Diminishing Returns? The Costs and Benefits of Improving Health," *Biology and Medicine* 46(3) 2003, S108–S128.

13. Although empirical studies of parents' willingness-to-pay to avoid deaths of their children are not available, a recent study of parents' willingness to trade off days of their own illness with days of illness of their children at least suggests a higher value of life for children. Dickie and Messman find that parents place a higher value on avoiding illness days for their children than themselves. The trade-off is at a rate of more than two-to-one for children of 5 years of age, but declines exponentially to approximately one-to-one for offspring of 21 years or older. Mark Dickie and Victoria L. Messman, "Parental Altruism and the Value of Avoiding Acute Illness: Are Kids Worth More than Parents?" *Journal of Environmental Economics and Management* 48(3) 2004, 1146–1174.

14. As we discuss in Chapter 17, the weights can be determined in a variety of ways including, for example, the standard gamble method, time trade-off value measurements, or estimated by physicians. Scores on indirect utility assessment instruments, such as the Health Utilities Index

Mark 2 and 3, the EuroQol, and the Short-Form 6-D, can also be used as weights. For more discussion of these topics see Carlo A. Marra, Outcome Measures in Economic Evaluations of Rheumatoid Arthritis, unpublished Ph.D. dissertation, University of British Columbia, 2004.

15. Dorothy P. Rice, Ellen J. MacKenzie, and Associates, *Costs of Injury in the United States: A Report to Congress* (San Francisco, CA: Institute for Health and Aging, University of California and Injury Prevention Center, The Johns Hopkins University, 1989)

16. Ted R. Miller and Maury Galbraith, "Estimating the Costs of Occupational Injury in the United States," *Accident Analysis and Prevention* 27(6) 1995, 741–747.

17. Alan E. Dillingham, Ted Miller, and David T. Levy, "A More General and Unified Measure for Valuing Labour Market Risk," *Applied Economics* 28 1996, 537–542.

18. Zaloshnja, Miller, Romano, and Spicer, "Crash Costs by Body Part Injured, Fracture Involvement, and Threat to Life Severity, United States, 2000."

19. Lawrence J. Blincoe, Angela G. Seay, Eduard Zaloshnja, Ted R. Miller, Eduardo O. Romano, Stephen Luchter, and Rebecca S. Spicer, *The Economic Impact of Motor Vehicle Crashes 2000*, National Highway Traffic Safety Administration, U.S. Department of Transportation. Available at *http://www.nhtsa.dot.gov*.

20. Note the high cost of motor vehicle crashes that cause workplace injuries. Although they account for only 3 percent of workplace injuries, they represent 6 percent of total costs, nearly six times the average cost of $96,281. This is partly explained by the high rate of fatalities from these crashes and by litigation with nonemployees over crashes involving multiple vehicles.

21. Ted R. Miller, "Costs and Functional Consequences of U.S. Roadway Crashes," *Accident Analysis and Prevention* 25(5) 1993, 593–607.

22. Technically there is an AIS 0, but we ignore this level because it is very similar to property damage only (PDO).

23. Ted Miller, "Costs and Functional Consequences of U.S. Roadway Crashes."

24. The Federal Aviation Authority, the Office of the Secretary of Transportation for the Department of Transportation, American Road & Transportation Builders Association, and the Texas Transportation Institute commonly use these fraction of VSL figures to determine the WTP for avoiding an injury caused by an accident.

25. Ascribed by Miller, *Narrowing the Plausible Range Around the Value of Life*, 1989, p. 605, to Ezra Hauer (no cite).

26. For an excellent example see David A. Long, Charles D. Mallar, and Craig V. Thornton, "Evaluating the Benefits and Costs of the Jobs Corps," *Journal of Policy Analysis and Management* 1(1) 1981, 55–76.

27. For estimates of the costs and benefits of criminal justice programs based on available research on effectiveness, see Steve Aos, Polly Phipps, Robert Barnoski, and Roxanne Lieb, *The Comparative Costs and Benefits of Programs to Reduce Crime, Version 4.0*, Washington State Institute for Public Policy (*www.wsipp.wa.gov*), May 2001.

28. Ted R. Miller and Mark Cohen, "Costs of Gunshot and Cut/Stab Wounds in the United States, with some Canadian Comparisons," *Accident Analysis and Prevention* 29(3) 1997, 329–341; and Ted R. Miller, Mark Cohen, and Brian Wiersema, *Victim Costs and Consequences: A New Look*, NCJ 155282, National Institute of Justice, Washington, D.C., 1996.

29. Note that their estimates are affected by underreporting of some crimes, particularly those of family violence to spouses and children and for knife and gunshot assaults.

30. Herbert Mohring, John Schroeter, and Paitoon Wiboonchutikula, "The Values of Waiting Time, Travel Time, and a Seat on a Bus," *Rand Journal of Economics* 18(1) 1987, 40–56.

31. Markus von Wartburg and William G. Waters II, "Congestion Externalities and the Value of Travel Time Savings," Chapter 2 in Anming Zhang, Anthony E. Boardman, David Gillen, and William G. Waters II, *Towards Estimating the Social and Environmental Costs of Transport in Canada: A Report for Transport Canada* (Vancouver, Canada: Centre for Transportation Studies, University of British Columbia, 2004). von Wartburg and Waters note that although reliability in travel time is a significant component of the VTTS, there is not enough information to provide a good point estimate

at this time. The value of reliability (VOR) has been estimated between 50 to 140 percent of the wage rate, a variation larger than for recent estimates of VTTS. See Terence C. Lam and Kenneth A. Small, "The Value of Time and Reliability: Measured from a Value Pricing Experiment," *Transportation Research Part E* 37(2–3) 2001, 231–251; Kenneth A. Small, Clifford Winston, and Jia Yan, "Uncovering the Distribution of Motorists' Preferences for Travel Time and Reliability: Implication for Road Pricing," Working paper (2002); and David Brownstone and Kenneth A. Small, "Valuing Time and Reliability: Assessing the Evidence from Road Pricing Demonstrations," Working paper, University of California, Irvine, 2003.

32. The relationship between speed and flow and between speed and density has been well documented. For example, see Anthony E. Boardman and Lester B. Lave, "Highway Congestion and Congestion Tolls," *Journal of Urban Economics* 4(3) 1977, 340–359.

33. United Kingdom: C. Sharp, "Developments in Transport Policy: The Value of Time Savings and of Accident Prevention," *Journal of Transport Economics and Policy* 22(2) 1988, 235–238; Mark Wardman, "The Value of Travel Time: A Review of British Evidence,"*Journal of Transport Economics and Policy* 32(3) 1998, 285–316; Canada: J. J. Lawson, *The Value of Passenger Travel Time for Use in Economic Evaluation of Transport Investments* (Ottawa, Ontario: Transport Canada, 1989); New Zealand: Ted Miller, "The Value of Time and the Benefit of Time Saving," presented to the National Roads Board, New Zealand, and the Federal Highway Administration, U.S. Dept. of Transportation (Washington, D.C.: Urban Institute, 1989); The Netherlands: H. F. Gunn and C. Rohr, "The 1985–1996 Dutch Value of Time Studies," paper presented at PTRC International Conference on the Value of Time, Wokingham, UK, 1996; Norway: Farideh Ramjerdi, Lars Rand, and Kjartan Saelensminde, *The Norwegian Value of Time Study: Some Preliminary Results* (Oslo: Institute of Transport Economics); United States: Texas Transportation Institute, "Value of Time and Discomfort Costs, Progress Report on Literature Review and Assessment of Procedures and Data," Technical Memorandum for NCHRP, pp.7–12; Miller (this note);

Developing countries: John Bates and Stephen Glaister, "The Valuation of Time Savings for Urban Transport Appraisal for Developing Countries: A Review," Report prepared for the World Bank, 1990.

34. William G. Waters II, "Values of Travel Time Savings in Road Transportation Project Evaluation," in David A. Hensher, Jenny King, and Tae Hoon Oum, eds., *World Transport Research: Proceedings of the 7th World Conference on Transport Research,* vol. 3 (New York: Elsevier, 1996).

35. Richard G. Walsh, Larry D. Sanders, and John R. McKean, "The Consumptive Value of Travel Time on Recreation Trips," *Journal of Travel Research* 29(1) 1990, 17–24. These authors found that travelers express a positive WTP for up to three hours of scenic driving in the Rockies on weekends.

36. Other researchers have shown that the VTTS under congestion varies significantly under different conditions, with smaller values for slowed traffic to a roughly threefold increase in valuation under stop-and-go driving conditions. See David A. Hensher, "The Valuation of Commuter Travel Time Savings for Car Drivers: Evaluation Alternative Model Specifications," *Transportation* 28(2) 2001, 101–118.

37. See also Mark Wardman, "A Review of British Evidence on Time and Service Quality Valuations," *Transportation Research Part E* 37(2) 2001, 107–128.

38. Cindy F. Sorg and John B. Loomis, *Empirical Estimates of Amenity Forest Values: A Comparative Review*, General Technical Report RM-107 (Fort Collins, CO: Rocky Mountain Forest and Range Experiment Station, Forest Service, USDA, 1984).

39. Richard G. Walsh, Donn M. Johnson, and John R. McKean, "Benefit Transfer of Outdoor Recreation Demand Studies, 1968–1988," *Water Resources Research* 29(3) 1992, 707–713.

40. Randall Rosenberger and John B. Loomis, *Benefit Transfer of Outdoor Recreation Use Values: A Technical Report Supporting the Forest Services Strategic Plan* (2000 Revision). General Technical Report RMRS-GTR-72 (Fort Collins, CO: Rocky Mountain Research Station, 2001). This report was based on Doug MacNair, *1993 RPA Recreation Values Database,* RPA Program Contract 43-4568-3-1191 (Washington, D.C.:

USDA Forest Service, 1993) and John Loomis, Randall S. Rosenberger, and Ram Shrestha, *Updated Estimate of Recreation Values for the RPA Program by Assessment Region and Use of Meta-Analysis for Recreation Benefit Transfer,* Final Report RJVA 28-JV7-962 (Fort Collins, CO: Colorado State University, Department of Agricultural and Resource Economics, 1999).

41. Pam Kaval and John Loomis, *Updated Outdoor Recreation Use Values with Emphasis on National Park Recreation*, Final Report to National Park Service, Fort Collins, CO (Colorado State University, Department of Agricultural and Resource Economics: Fort Collins, CO, 2003).

42. See, for example, the reports produced by the Millennniun Ecosystem Assessment (*www.millenniumassessment.org/en/index.aspx*).

43. Two literature surveys appeared recently. See Paulo A. L. D. Nunes and Jeroen C. J. M. van den Bergh, "Economic Valuation of Biodiversity: Sense or Nonsense?" *Ecological Economics* 39(2) 2001, 203–222; and R. Kerry Turner, Jouni Paavola, Philip Cooper, Stephen Farber, Valma Jessamy, and Stavros Georgiou, "Valuing Nature: Lessons Learned and Future Research Directions," *Ecological Economics* 43(3) 2003, 492–510. The former article defines biodiversity, discusses the various components of biodiversity, and summarizes the valuation of those components. The latter article presents some useful frameworks for categorizing valuation studies.

44. I. J. Bateman, K. G. Willis, G. D. Garrod, P. Doktor, I. Langford, and R. K. Turner, "Recreation and Environmental Preservation Value of the Norfolk Broads: A Contingent Valuation Study," Report to the National Rivers Authority, Environmental Appraisal Group, University of East Anglia, 1992.

45. See, for example, Urs P. Kreuter, Heather G. Harris, Marty D. Matlock, and Ronald E. Lacey, "Change in Ecosystem Service Values in the San Antonio Area, Texas," *Ecological Economics* 39(3) 2001, 333–346.

46. David W. Pearce, *Economic Values and the Natural World* (London: Earthscan, 1993).

47. Paulo A. L. D. Nunes and Jeroen C. J. M. van den Bergh, "Economic Valuation of Biodiversity: Sense or Nonsense?"

48. For a contingent valuation survey example, see Jeffrey L. Jordan and Abdelmoneim H. Elnagheeb, "Willingness to Pay for Improvements in Water Drinking Quality," *Water Resources Research* 29(2) 1993, 237–245.

Charles W. Abdalla, Brian A. Roach, and Donald J. Epp, "Valuing Environmental Quality Changes Using Averting Expenditures: An Application to Groundwater Contamination," *Land Economics* 68(2) 1992, 163–169, use both the market analogy method (observations of bottled water expenditures) and defensive expenditures (expenditures incurred in boiling or hauling water or installation of household treatment systems). A study that estimates the benefits of water quality improvements on river segments using the travel cost method is V. Kerry Smith and William H. Desvousges, *Measuring Water Quality Benefits* (Boston, MA: Kluwer-Nijhoff Publishing, 1986).

49. Ralph Luken, F. Johnson, and V. Kibler, "Benefits and Costs of Pulp and Paper Effluent Controls Under the Clean Water Act," *Water Resources Research* 28(3) 1992, 665–674.

50. Kenneth D. Frederick, Tim van den Berg, and Jean Hanson, "Economic Values of Freshwater in the United States," Discussion Paper 97–03 (Resources for the Future: Washington, D.C., 1996).

51. Specifically, NSDI = D/property value × 100 where D = reduction in property value from noise exposure / difference in noise exposure $((\partial H/\partial NEF) \times 100/H)$. In contrast, the hedonic price of noise or marginal implicit price of noise is the slope of the function relating house prices, H, to noise level $(\partial H/\partial NEF)$.

52. Specifically, $NDSI = -100 \dfrac{\partial \ln H}{\partial NEF}$. In contrast, the hedonic price of noise or marginal implicit price of noise is the slope of the function relating house prices, H, to noise level, that is, $\dfrac{\partial H}{\partial NEF}$.

53. Jon P. Nelson, "Airports and Property Values: A Survey of Recent Evidence," *Journal of Transport Economics and Policy* 14(1) 1980, 37–52.

54. Ian Bateman, Brett Day, Iain Lake, and Andrew Lovett, "The Effect of Road Traffic on Residential Property Values: A Literature Review and Hedonic Pricing Study," Report to the Scottish Executive Development Department (Scottish Executive: Edinburgh, 2001).

55. See Y. J. J. Schipper, On the Valuation of Aircraft Noise: A Meta-Analysis, unpublished paper, Titenberg Institute, Free University of Amsterdam, 1996.

56. Dean Uyeno, Stanley Hamilton, and Andrew J. G. Biggs, "Density of Residential Land Use and the Impact of Airport Noise," *Journal of Transport Economics and Policy* 27(1) 1993, 3–18.

57. Dallas Burtraw, Alan Krupnick, Erin Mausur, David Austin, and Deirdre Farrell, "Costs and Benefits of Reducing Air Pollutants Related to Acid Rain," *Contemporary Economic Policy* 16(4) 1998, 379–400.

58. For more on the sources of emissions in the United States, Germany, and the United Kingdom, see David W. Pearce and R. Kerry Turner, *Economics of Natural Resources and the Environment* (Baltimore: The Johns Hopkins University Press, 1990), 192. Also see Alan J. Krupnick and Paul R. Portney, "Controlling Urban Air Pollution: A Benefit-Cost Assessment," *Science* 252(26) 1991, 522–528.

59. Pearce and Turner, *Economics of Natural Resources and the Environment.*

60. Thomas C. Schelling, "Some Economics of Global Warming," *American Economic Review* 82(1) 1992, 1–14 and Intergovernmental Panel on Climate Change, *Climate Change 2001: Synthesis Report* (Cambridge: Cambridge University Press, 2001).

61. For a recent example see Kenneth Y. Chay and Michael Greenstone, "Does Air Quality Matter? Evidence from the Housing Market," *Journal of Political Economy* 113(2) 2005, 376–424.

62. Kerry Smith and Ju-Chin Huang, "Can Markets Value Air Quality? A Meta-Analysis of Hedonic Property Value Models," *Journal of Political Economy* 103(1) 1995, 209–227.

63. Alan Krupnick, "The Implementation and Enforcement of the Clean Air Act Amendments of 1990," Testimony before the Subcommittees on Oversight and Investigations and on Health and the Environment of the Committee on Commerce, U.S. House of Representatives, Thursday, November 9, 1995.

64. Kenneth Small and Camilla Kazimi, "On the Costs of Air Pollution From Motor Vehicles," *Journal of Transport Economics and Policy* 29(1) 1995, 7–32.

65. Donald R. McCubbin and Mark A. Delucchi, "The Health Costs of Motor-Vehicle-Related Air Pollution," *Journal of Transportation Economics and Policy* 33(3) 1999, 253–286.

66. The study by Triangle Economic Research was submitted by the Northern States Power Company and is not cited in the record of the "*Order Establishing Environmental Cost Values*" issued by the Minnesota Public Utilities Commission, 1996. See Minnesota Public Utilities Commission, "*Order Establishing Environmental Cost Values,*" Docket No. E-999/CI-93-583, In the Matter of the Quantification of Environmental Costs Pursuant to Laws of Minnesota 1993, Chapter 356, Section 3, December 16, 1996. Available at *www.me3.org/projects/costs/pucorderfull.html.*

67. Smith and Huang, "Can Markets Value Air Quality?" p. 223.

68. Indeed, Alan Krupnick and Paul Portney, "Controlling Urban Air Pollution," argue that smaller value of life estimates than those found in the literature should be used in estimating the costs of air pollution because air pollution mainly results in the premature deaths of older persons, that is, persons with considerably shorter life expectancies than average members of the population.

69. See also Inge Mayeres, Sara Ochelen, and Stef Proost, "The Marginal External Costs of Urban Transport," *Transportation Research Part D* (2) 1996, 111–130. This study of air pollution in Brussels finds values of $111,430, $18,484, $3,951, and $127,530 per ton for PM_{10}, No_x, VOCs, and SO_2, respectively.

70. The study by Triangle Economic Research was noted as being state of the art, and was referred to frequently as influencing the estimates.

71. Richard S. J. Tol and Thomas E. Downing, *The Marginal Costs of Climate Changing Emissions* (Amsterdam: Institute for Environmental Studies, Vrije Universiteit, 2000). See also Richard S. J. Tol, Thomas E. Downing, Samuel Frankhauser, Richard G. Richels, and Joel B. Smith, "Progress in Estimating the Marginal Costs of Greenhouse Gas Emissions," Working Paper SCG-4, Centre for Marine and Climate Research, Hamburg University, 15 January 2001.

72. Charles L. Ballard, John B. Shoven, and John Whalley, "General Equilibrium Computations of the Marginal Welfare Costs of Taxes in the United States," *American Economic Review* 75(1)

1985, 128–138; Charles L. Ballard, John B. Shoven, and John Whalley, "The Total Welfare Cost of the United States Tax System: A General Equilibrium Approach," *National Tax Journal* 38(2) 1985, 125–140; and Dale W. Jorgenson and Kun-Young Yun, "Tax Reform and U.S. Economic Growth," *Journal of Political Economy* 98(5) 1990, S151–S193. Other studies that provide U.S. estimates include Edgar K. Browning, "On the Marginal Welfare Cost of Taxation," *American Economic Review* 77(1) 1987, 11–23; and Charles E. Stuart, "Welfare Costs per Dollar of Additional Tax Revenue in the United States," *American Economic Review* 74(3) 1984, 452–462. Estimates for Sweden are Charles. E. Stuart, "Swedish Tax Rates, Labor Supply, and Tax Revenues," *Journal of Political Economy* 89(5) 1981, 1020–1038; and Ingemar Hansson and Charles E. Stuart, "Tax Revenue and the Marginal Cost of Public Funds in Sweden," *Journal of Public Economics* 27(3) 1985, 331–353. For Canada: see Harry F. Campbell, "Deadweight Loss and Commodity Taxation in Canada," *Canadian Journal of Economics* 8(3) 1975, 441–446; for Australia: see Harry F. Campbell and K. Bond, "The Costs of Public Funds in Australia," *Economic Record* 73 1997, 28–40; and Harry F. Campbell, "Deadweight Loss and the Cost of Public Funds in Australia," *Agenda* 4(2) 1997, 231–236.

73. Martin Feldstein, "Tax Avoidance and the Deadweight Loss of the Income Tax," *The Review of Economics and Statistics* 81(4) 1999, 674–680.

74. Martin Feldstein, "How Big Should Government Be?" *National Tax Journal* 50(2) 1997, 197–213.

75. W. Erwin Diewert and Denis Lawrence, "The Deadweight Costs of Taxation in New Zealand," *Canadian Journal of Economics* 29(Part 2) 1996, S658–S673.

76. For further discussion of these issues, see Kevin J. Boyle and John C. Bergstrom, "Benefit Transfer Studies: Myths, Pragmatism and Idealism," *Water Resources Research* 28(3) 1992, 657–663; William H. Desvousges, Michael C. Naughton, and George R Parsons, "Benefit Transfer: Conceptual Problems in Estimating Water Quality Benefits Using Existing Studies," *Water Resources Research* 28(3) 1992, 675–683; Kenneth E. McConnell, "Model Building and Judgment: Implications for Benefit Transfers with Travel Cost Models," *Water Resources*

Research 28(3) 1992, 695–700; John B. Loomis "The Evolution of a More Rigorous Approach to Benefit Transfer: Benefit Function Estimation," *Water Resources Research* 28(3) 1992, 701–705; and Mark Downing and Teofilo Ozuna Jr. "Testing the Reliability of the Benefit Function Transfer Approach," *Journal of Environmental Economics and Management* 30(3) 1996, 316–322.

77. In Brad J. Bowland and John C. Beghin, "Robust Estimates of Value of a Statistical Life for Developing Economies: An Application to Pollution and Mortality in Santiago," *Journal of Policy Modelling* 23(4) 2001, 385–396, the authors find a median income elasticity of 1.95, and a range of income elasticity from 1.7 to 2.3.

78. Ted R. Miller, "Variations Between Countries in Values of Statistical Life," *Journal of Transport Economics and Policy* 34(2) 2000, 169–188; W. Kip Viscusi and Joseph Aldy, "The Value of Statistical Life: A Critical Review of Market Estimates Throughout the World," *Journal of Risk and Uncertainty* 27(1) 2003, 5–76; and Janusz R. Mrozek and Laura O. Taylor, "What Determines the Value of Life? A Meta-Analysis," *Journal of Policy Analysis and Management* 21(2) 2002, 253–270.

79. See PACIFIC Exchange Rate Service, University of British Columbia at *http://fx.sauder.ubc.ca/*.

80. Over the past 45 years Canadian incomes have varied between 80 and 90 percent of U.S. incomes according to the Centre for the Study of Living Standards, Table 3 at *www.csls.ca/data/ipt11.pdf*.

81. For more discussion see Anthony E. Boardman and Steve Yong, "The Value of Statistical Life," Chapter 3 in Anming Zhang, Anthony E. Boardman, David Gillen, and William G. Waters II, *Towards Estimating the Social and Environmental Costs of Transport in Canada: A Report for Transport Canada*.

82. See Anthony E. Boardman and Steve Yong, "The Value of Statistical Life," p. 185.

83. See, for example, Mrozek and Taylor, "What Determines the Value of Life? A Meta-Analysis." However, de Blaeij, Florax, Rietveld, and Verhoef, "The Value of Statistical Life in Road Safety: Meta-Analysis," find WTP declines as the risk level declines.

84. M. W. Jones-Lee, G. Loomes, S. Jones, P. Rowlatt, M.. Spackman, and S. Jones, "Valuation of Deaths from Air Pollution," *NERA and CASPAR,* report

prepared for the Department of the Environment, Transport and the Regions and the Department of Trade and Industry, London, 1998.

85. W. G. Waters II, "The Value of Travel Time Savings and the Link with Income: Implications for Public Project Evaluation," *International Journal of Transport Economics* 12(3) 1994, 243–253.

86. von Wartburg and Waters, "Congestion Externalities."

87. Stephanie Kirchhoff, Bonnie G. Colbey, and Jeffrey T. LaFrance, "Evaluating the Performance of Benefit Transfer: An Empirical Inquiry," *Journal of Environmental Economics and Management* 33(1) 1997, 75–93.

CHAPTER 16

Shadow Prices: Applications to Developing Countries[1]

Why does this book contain a separate chapter on cost-benefit analysis in developing countries? CBA in developing countries has much in common with CBA in industrialized countries. For the most part, therefore, the other chapters in the book are applicable to both. The major distinguishing characteristic of CBA in developing countries is the greater emphasis on adjusting the market prices of project outputs and inputs so that they more accurately reflect their value to society. Doing so obviously is important for those who actually will apply CBA in developing countries. However, examining CBA in developing countries provides insight into shadow pricing even for those who apply it only in developed countries.

The reason for the emphasis on shadow pricing in developing countries is that analysts in this field argue that markets in developing countries are much more distorted than in developed countries. They suggest, for example, that labor markets are segmented and labor mobility is limited by systems of land tenure; that official exchange rates do not accurately reflect the value of the national currency; that the prices of goods exchanged in international markets are distorted by trade taxes, import controls, and high tariffs; and that credit markets are divided between formal and informal sectors. Consequently, the experts advocate that shadow prices, which are often called *accounting prices,* be used instead of market prices in conducting CBAs in developing countries. Just like shadow price adjustments used in industrialized countries for CBA, accounting prices may incorporate adjustments for market failures such as monopoly and externalities. Particular emphasis, however, is placed on adjustments for taxes (especially tariffs), subsidies, and quotas that affect the market prices of imports and exports.

Surprisingly, perhaps, there is not only agreement among the experts on using shadow prices, but also on the basic methods to use in determining the values of these shadow prices. Nonetheless, considerable variation remains in the details of how these methods are applied in practice. These methods, which received much of their impetus from international organizations involved in the funding of projects in developing countries, were developed in the early 1970s by the United Nations Industrial Development Organization[2] and by I. M. D. Little and J. A. Mirrlees.[3] The ideas contained in these two publications were then synthesized by Lyn Squire and Herman G. van der Tak,[4] two employees of the World Bank. Squire and van der Tak especially emphasized the concepts developed by Little and Mirrlees. As a consequence, the resulting approach toward shadow pricing, which with some modification continues to enjoy wide acceptance, is sometimes called the *LMST accounting price method.*

This chapter describes the LMST method and discusses some of the key issues it raises. Because use of the method involves a large number of details and involves issues that can only be treated very briefly in the space available for this chapter, readers who plan to use this method in a CBA are advised to consult sources that provide more detailed information.[5]

THE LMST METHODOLOGY

The LMST methodology makes a basic distinction between tradeable goods and nontradeable goods. *Tradeable goods* include consumption goods and productive factors that are exported or imported, as well as products for which there might potentially be an international market—for example, close substitutes of the goods that are traded internationally. Thus, traded goods affect, or potentially can affect, a nation's balance of payments. *Nontradeable goods* include all other consumption goods and productive factors such as local transportation, electricity, services, and (most importantly) local labor. The key to the LMST project evaluation approach is in using *world prices,* the prices at which goods are actually bought and sold internationally, to shadow price all project inputs and outputs that are classified as tradeable.[6] Nontradeable goods are often produced with inputs that are tradeable so that world prices can also be used to value them. Even the labor for a project may be drawn from other sectors of the economy where it was previously producing tradeable goods so that world prices can once more be used.[7]

The rationale for using world prices is not that free trade prevails or that world prices are undistorted—although they are less distorted than the domestic market prices in many developing countries and are probably less distorted today than they were when the LMST methodology was initially developed—but that they more accurately reflect the opportunities that are available to a country and these opportunities should be recognized in evaluating projects. For example, if a project input has to be imported, it is reasonable to value it at its import price. Similarly, if project output is to be exported, it is reasonable to value it on the basis of its export price because this indicates what it would contribute to the nation's foreign exchange. Thus, the methodology is based on the principle of *trade opportunity costs.*

To see the rationale for using world prices to value project outputs and inputs more clearly, consider a developing country that is conducting a CBA of a proposal to build a steel plant with government funds. Although the country currently has a high tariff on imported steel, it nonetheless is dependent on steel produced in other countries. Because the tariff is incorporated into the domestic market price of steel, it can be viewed as a transfer between domestic steel buyers and the government. However, world prices do not incorporate tariffs. Thus, the world price for an export is often considerably lower than its market price. Consequently, a CBA that is based on domestic market prices could indicate that the steel plant project should proceed, when, in fact, the real resource cost of importing steel (that is, the cost net of the tariff) is smaller than the resource cost of producing it domestically. Similarly, if a project uses a locally produced (but potentially importable) input that has an artificially inflated price because of high tariffs or import quotas, the potential to purchase the input more cheaply on the world market should be recognized in determining the project's cost.

As a third example, consider a project to increase the production and foreign sales of an agricultural crop. In some developing countries, national policies keep the domestic market prices of some agricultural crops artificially low. When this occurs, a crop production project might not pass the cost-benefit test if domestic market prices are used, but could if the analysis is based instead on world prices. Thus, the LMST method argues that the values of imports and exports on the world market should be the basis for decisions about domestic projects.

ILLUSTRATIONS OF THE LMST METHOD IN PRACTICE

To describe how shadow pricing is done in practice, we discuss three illustrations: an import, an export, and a nontradeable good (electricity).[8] All three examples are assumed to pertain to a project being considered in a small, developing country. For simplicity, it is also assumed that the amounts of imports and exports involved would not be large enough to affect world prices. This last assumption, which is sometimes called the "small country assumption," is the one usually made in conducting CBAs of projects in developing countries and is realistic except when a project will substantially affect a country's export of a good and the country has a large share of the world market for that good.[9]

Shadow pricing in all three cases involves multiplying each market price by an *accounting price ratio* (APR). An APR can be defined as follows:

$$\text{The accounting price ratio for good } i = \frac{\text{accounting price of good } i}{\text{market price of good } i}$$

$$= \frac{\text{shadow price of good } i}{\text{market price of good } i} \qquad \textbf{(16.1)}$$

Because the accounting price of a good or a productive factor is essentially synonymous with its shadow price, multiplying a market price of a good by its accounting price ratio converts it to its shadow price. That is,

shadow price for good i = accounting price ratio for good i × market price for good i

The ways in which accounting price ratios are obtained in practice are described as we work through the examples.

An Import

Determination of the accounting price for an import that is being used as an input to our hypothetical project (or, alternatively, an output from the project that substitutes for a good that otherwise would have to be imported) is shown in Table 16.1. The *CIF price* of a unit of the good on the world market, that is, the cost of the item (C) plus insurance (I) and freight expenses to the port of destination (F), is US$40. This $40 price is sometimes called a *border price* because it corresponds to the amount of foreign currency needed to pay for the good at the border. To translate the $40 amount into the local currency, pesos, it would be multiplied by the country's

TABLE 16-1 Accounting Price for Imported Good

Item	Dollars (U.S. $)	Market Value (Pesos)	APR	Accounting Value (Pesos)
CIF price	40	80	1.00	80
Tariff	—	10	0.00	—
Transport	—	8	0.50	4
Distribution	—	5	0.80	4
All components	—	103	0.85	88

Exchange rate: 2 pesos = US$1
Source: Adapted from Terry A. Powers, "An Overview of the Little-Mirrlees/Squire-van der Tak Accounting Price System," in Terry A. Powers, ed., *Estimating Accounting Prices for Project Appraisal* (Washington, D.C.: Inter-American Development Bank, 1981), Table 1-1.

exchange rate. In the example, a dollar is assumed to equal 2 pesos. Thus, the $40 CIF price is equivalent to 80 pesos. Because the 80 peso price is already a world price, its shadow price is also 80 pesos. Hence, the accounting price ratio equals 1.

As just indicated, an exchange rate is needed to translate foreign currency such as dollars into the local currency. Usually, the official exchange rate is used for this purpose. However, as the existence of black markets in currency exchange in many developing countries attests, a nation's official exchange rate may not accurately reflect the actual value of its currency. This would occur, for example, if the official exchange rate is that a dollar is convertible into 2 pesos, but a dollar can, on average, actually be used to purchase domestic output worth 3 pesos. This latter value is called the *shadow exchange rate.* In practice, the official, rather than the shadow, exchange rate, is normally used in determining accounting prices because it is more easily obtained. This choice is not very important for CBA, however. In conducting a CBA using the LMST method, *all* project benefits and costs must be expressed in accounting prices. As just seen, some, such as imports, already are. As discussed later, others, such as nontradeables, must be converted into accounting prices. As a result, all benefits and costs are commensurable. Moreover, each is the multiplicative product of its value in dollars (or some other foreign currency) and a constant that equals whatever exchange rate is being used. Consequently, the choice between the official and the shadow exchange rates affects the absolute size of benefits and costs—the shadow rate is usually larger than the official rate—but not their relative size. Thus, the choice neither determines whether net benefits are positive or negative nor the relative ranking of projects.[10]

As indicated in Table 16.1, in addition to its CIF price of 80 pesos, the domestic market price of the import also reflects a tariff of 10 pesos, local transportation costs of 8 pesos, and distribution costs of 5 pesos. Thus, a unit of the import would cost 103 pesos in the local market. However, only part of these additions to the market price reflect real resource costs to the economy. For example, the revenue from a tariff is simply a transfer between buyers and the government. Thus, its accounting price ratio is set equal to zero. Transportation and distribution do involve the use of real resources, but in this example, their accounting price ratios are less than 1. Consequently, their shadow or accounting prices are less than their market prices. (The reasons for this divergence will be discussed later.) Hence, the shadow price of the import equals 88 pesos (80 + 4 + 4), considerably less than its market price of 103 pesos. The import's overall accounting price ratio is, therefore, less than 1 (0.85 = 88/103), which is typically the case for imports.

An Export

Table 16-2 describes the determination of the shadow price of an export that is produced by the project (or, alternatively, a project input that otherwise would have been exported). The price of the export at the port of origin, before insurance and freight charges to its ultimate destination are added (its so-called *free on board [FOB] price)*, is assumed to equal $100 or 200 pesos. Because the $100 is the amount of foreign currency received at the border, it is the border price for an export. The FOB price includes the cost of producing a unit of the good (148 pesos), as well as an export tax (50 pesos) and transportation costs to the port of origin (2 pesos). Only half the transportation costs are assumed to reflect real resource costs to the economy (the APR equals 0.5). The export tax is a transfer between foreign purchasers and the domestic government, but because foreigners typically would not be given standing in evaluating the project, the tax amount would be included in the shadow price. Therefore, if the good were produced by the project and exported, its shadow price would equal 199 pesos (148 + 50 + 1). Thus, the overall accounting price ratio for the export is slightly less than 1 (0.99 = 199/200).

It may be useful to point out that by shadow pricing the export, it is valued on the basis of each unit's contribution to the nation's foreign exchange. Thus, for example, although a tax on an export increases its shadow price, possibly decreasing sales, a subsidy on an export, perhaps, to encourage sales, decreases its shadow price.

Now, imagine that rather than a product for export, the good in question is a project input, one that would be exported if the project were not undertaken. Under these circumstances, the shadow price must include the additional costs incurred by diverting the good to domestic use, as well as revenue forgone and costs saved by not exporting the product. Thus, the net effects of not exporting the good must be determined. The revenue forgone is the 200 peso FOB price, while the cost saved is the 1 peso of transportation cost to the port of origin. The additional costs incurred by diverting the good to the project include local transportation costs of 4 pesos and distribution costs of 10 pesos. As previously discussed, because only part of these additional costs reflect real resource costs to the economy, they must be adjusted to their shadow price equivalents by multiplying them by their accounting price ratios. Thus, the shadow price of the export when it is diverted to domestic use is 209 pesos (200 − 1 + 2 + 8).

TABLE 16-2 Accounting Price for Export

Item	U.S. Dollars (U.S. $)	Market Value (pesos)	APR	Accounting Value (pesos)
FOB price	100	200	—	—
Export tax	25	50	1.0	50
Transport for export	1	2	0.5	1
Factory gate price	74	148	1.0	148
Transport for Domestic sale	—	4	0.5	2
Distribution in Domestic market	—	10	0.8	8

Exchange rate: 2 pesos = U.S. $1
Source: Adapted from Terry A. Powers, "An Overview of the Little-Mirrlees/Squire-van der Tak Accounting Price System," in Terry A. Powers, ed., *Estimating Accounting Prices for Project Appraisal* (Washington, D.C.: Inter-American Development Bank, 1981), Table 1-2.

A practical problem arises when project inputs are potential exports, such as the case just described, and also when project outputs are substituted for potential imports. The problem involves selecting the appropriate world price to use in shadow pricing because often there will be several alternative world prices that are candidates because similar products may vary along different dimensions such as quality and ease of access. Obviously, a CBA that selects an export price from the low end or an import price from the high end of such a range is more likely to show that net benefits are positive than one that selects from the opposite end of the range. One reasonable approach is simply to use a value from the middle of the range if the good cannot be priced in terms of its specific characteristics.

A Nontradeable

Table 16-3 lists the costs of the various inputs needed to produce the additional electricity required by the project. These inputs would presumably be diverted by the project from other uses and, thus, represent opportunity costs associated with the project. The electricity itself is assumed to be produced domestically and, hence, is an example of a nontraded good. However, for CBA purposes, it must be made commensurable with traded goods, which, as already discussed, are valued in terms of their world prices.

TABLE 16-3   Accounting Price for Electricity Value at Marginal Cost of Supply (in thousands of pesos)

Item	Cost in Domestic Prices	APR	Cost in Accounting Prices
Capital costs	**3,000**	0.89[c]	**2,678**
Thermal generating unit (CIF)	1,800	1.00	1,800
Building and site construction	1,200	0.73	878
Imported materials (CIF)	500	1.00	500
Labor	250	0.60[a]	150
Industry taxes and tariffs	200	0.00	0
Other expenses	250	0.91	228
Imported materials (CIF)	180	1.00	180
Labor	40	0.60[a]	24
Other expenses	30	0.80[b]	24
Annual operating costs	**1,000**	0.83[c]	**831**
Fuel oil (CIF)	800	1.00	800
Maintenance	40	0.78	31
Parts (CIF)	15	1.00	15
Labor	20	0.60[a]	12
Other	5	0.80[b]	4
Taxes and tariffs	160	0.00	0

[a] *The accounting price ratio of labor is discussed later; here it is assumed to equal 0.6 for purposes of the example.*
[b] *The standard conversion factor (SCF), which is assumed to have a value of 0.8 for purposes of the example, is used to convert the domestic value to its accounting price.*
[c] *Rounded to two significant digits.*
Source: Adapted from Terry A. Powers, "An Overview of the Little-Mirrlees/Squire-van der Tak Accounting Price System," in Terry A. Powers, ed., *Estimating Accounting Prices for Project Appraisal* (Washington, D.C.: Inter-American Development Bank, 1981), Table 1-3.

To make tradeable and nontradeable goods commensurable, the LMST approach involves determining the equivalent value of nontradeables in world prices. To do this, it exploits the fact that the production of nontradeables involves inputs that are tradeable. As the table indicates, many of the inputs required to produce the needed electricity—for example, the material required to construct the generating plant—are tradeable. Thus, using the LMST method to shadow price a nontraded good involves breaking down the cost of the good into its traded, nontraded, and labor components. The non-traded components can then be further broken down into *their* traded, nontraded, and labor components, and so forth. These components and subcomponents are listed in the table. By multiplying each of these components and subcomponents by their accounting price ratio, the opportunity cost of supplying an additional amount of a nontraded good to the project can be evaluated in terms of the tradeable goods required to produce the additional amount. Although this example pertains to electricity, a similar procedure would be used in the case of other nontraded goods such as the transport and distribution costs items listed in Tables 16-1 and 16-2.

The different accounting price ratios listed in Table 16.3 are derived by several different methods. As previously indicated, the accounting price ratio of a tradeable component that is expressed in CIF prices (for example, imported materials) is 100, although the ratio for a domestic transfer (for example, tariffs on tradeables and taxes on non-tradeables) is zero. The accounting price ratio for domestic labor is complex to derive and will be discussed in some detail later. Those for nontradeable components are simply weighted averages of the APRs of their components, where the weights are the cost of each component expressed in shadow prices as a fraction of total cost. Sometimes these weighted averages are derived from calculations made by the project evaluators. For example, the APR for annual operating costs of 0.83, which is listed in Table 16-3, is computed as follows: 1.0 (800/1000) + 0.78(40/1000) + 0(160/1000). However, the weighted accounting price ratios that are used to obtain shadow pricing for fairly small subcomponents (for example, other maintenance expenses) are often *conversion factors* (CFs), which are obtained from previous studies and pertain to entire industries or national economic sectors, such as the electricity and gas industry, rather than to one specific input, such as the fuel oil used to produce the electricity needed by the project.

Except for pertaining to a broader segment of the economy, conversion factors are similar to APRs that are developed for a specific project evaluation. Like project-specific APRs, they are weighted averages of their components. Because conversion factors can be plugged into more than one CBA, they are obviously another example of a shadow price that is obtained from secondary sources, the topic covered in Chapter 15. Because the use of conversion factors saves time for evaluators, the extent to which they are used in a particular CBA depends on the resources available for the study and the accuracy required. In practice, the role of conversion factors is often of considerable importance.

A technique called *semi-input-output (SIO) analysis* is often used to derive conversion factors. SIO analysis utilizes national input-output tables, national censuses, household expenditure surveys, and other national data, such as information on tariffs, quotas, and subsidies. SIO analysis is particularly difficult to conduct if input-output tables are not already available, because then the analyst must piece together the equivalent information. Using the available data, an SIO table is constructed that divides the economy into as many productive sectors as the data allow (for example, corn and corn products, fishing, mining, hotels, electricity and gas, real estate, etc.). Often fifty or more productive sectors are listed. Part of the output produced in each sector will be directly consumed, and part will be used as inputs in the other sectors. The table indicates the percentage contribution of the output produced in each sector to the total market value of the output produced in all the other sectors. In addition, primary factor inputs such as labor, capital, foreign exchange, and taxes and subsidies are also listed, and their percentage contributions to the total market value of the output produced in each of the productive sectors is also indicated. Deriving conversion factors from the table constructed for SIO analysis essentially involves solving a set of simultaneous equations using matrix algebra.[11] In doing this, SIO analysis consistently treats interdependence between different sectors of the economy; for example, coal may be used to produce electricity and electricity may be used in mining coal.

In addition to being used to obtain CFs for individual industries, SIO can be used to obtain CFs for skilled and unskilled labor and aggregate CFs. One such aggregate CF is the *consumption conversion factor* (CCF), which is a weighted average of accounting price ratios for a nationally representative market basket of goods. The CCF plays several roles in shadow pricing that are mentioned later. Another aggregate CF is the *standard conversion factor* (SCF), which is the ratio of the value of all production at accounting prices to the value of all production at market prices. In other words, the SCF is the weighted average of the CFs for the productive sectors of the economy, where the weights are the contribution that each sector makes to total national output. The SCF is used in computing the shadow prices of minor components of nontraded goods when more specific CFs are not available.

Although nowadays the SCF is usually derived by actually computing a weighted average of the CFs for the productive sectors of an economy, it is instructive to examine briefly the following formula, which has been used in the past to obtain a crude approximation of the SCF:

$$\text{SCF} = (M + X)/[M(1 + T_m - S_m) + X(1 - T_x + S_x)] \tag{16.2}$$

where M is the total value of imports in market prices, X is the total value of exports in market prices, T_m is the total effective tariff rate on imports, T_x is the total effective tax rate on exports, S_m is the total effective subsidy rate on imports, and S_x is the total effective subsidy rate on exports. The numerator of this expression values imports and exports at their market prices, while the denominator values them at their world prices. The expression is only a crude approximation because it ignores nontraded goods in the economy and because it assumes that distortions in domestic market prices are entirely due to tariffs and import taxes and subsidies (thereby ignoring other distortions such as taxes on nontraded goods and import quotas, monopoly power, and externalities). What is interesting about the expression is that it implies that tariffs and export subsidies cause market prices to be larger than world prices, while taxes on exports and import subsidies have the opposite effect. As the former are usually more important in developing countries than the latter, the SCF, most CFs for specific sectors of the economy, and most APRs for specific goods have values that are less than 1.[12] For example, Steve Curry and John Weiss examined separate studies of 13 different countries and find that estimates of the SCF range between 0.59 and 0.96, with an average value of about 0.8.[13]

SHADOW PRICING WHEN GOODS ARE IN FIXED SUPPLY

As previously indicated, the LMST approach normally relies on the shadow prices of inputs required to produce a good to convert its market price to a shadow price. An important exception to this procedure occurs when the supply of a good is fixed, however. This could happen, for example, if there is a quota on imports or the government exercises a monopoly over providing a particular good or service and has run out of funds needed to supply more.

A situation in which supply is fixed is illustrated in Figure 16-1, which pertains to the electricity that would be required for our project. The production of electricity is often characterized as having constant marginal costs up to a capacity level. Consistent with this, the supply curve in the figure is perfectly elastic to Q_1 and then becomes completely inelastic when the nation's generating capacity is exhausted. Say that D_a represents the demand curve for electricity without the project and D_a' represents the demand curve with the project. Under these circumstances, the fixed supply of electricity is not binding. As a result, the project would not affect the current consumers of electricity. However, it would require that additional inputs be used to produce the additional electricity needed by the project. Consequently, the method outlined earlier for deriving the shadow cost of the electricity used on the project would be appropriate.

FIGURE 16-1   Shadow Pricing when Electricity Is Completely Elastic and Inelastic

Now assume that without the project the demand curve for electricity is D_b and with the project it is D_b'. Thus, the project would increase the market price of electricity from P_1 to P_2 and reduce the consumption of electricity by current consumers from Q_1 to Q_2. Because of the price increase, current consumers lose surplus, while the producers of electricity gain surplus. As explained in Chapter 4, these changes in surplus can be appropriately taken into account in determining the cost of electricity to the project by simply using the average of the old and new prices, $(P_1 + P_2)/2$, as the market price. Thus, measured in market prices, the cost of electricity for the project would equal $[(P_1 + P_2)/2](Q_1-Q_2)$.

To use the LMST method, however, this cost must be converted to its shadow price equivalent. In doing this, account must be taken of the fact that when the supply of electricity is fixed the opportunity cost of diverting some electricity from current consumers to the project is not additional inputs but the consumption forgone by current consumers. One way of doing this is to ask what consumers would purchase with $[(P_1 + P_2)/2](Q_1-Q_2)$ of additional income and then determine the shadow prices of each of these goods using the techniques discussed earlier. Of course, it is highly unlikely that the specific items that consumers would purchase would actually be known. Thus, in practice, $[(P_1 + P_2)/2](Q_1-Q_2)$ would probably be converted to its shadow price equivalent by multiplying it by the consumption conversion factor, which as previously mentioned is a weighted average of accounting price ratios for a nationally representative market basket of goods.

THE SHADOW PRICE OF LABOR

A project in any country will use labor. In developing countries, increasing the employment of unskilled workers may, in fact, be an important part of the motivation for initiating many projects. Even when it is not, labor is still likely to be a major nontradeable input used in the project. Hence, shadow pricing the cost of employing workers is of critical importance in conducting CBA in developing counties. Shadow pricing labor raises some difficult special issues, however.

Like any input used in a project, labor has an accounting price ratio:

$$\text{Accounting price ratio of type } j \text{ labor} = \frac{\text{shadow wage of type } j \text{ labor}}{\text{the market wage of type } j \text{ labor}} \quad \textbf{(16.3)}$$

This expression implies that different types of labor (for example, skilled and unskilled workers) may have different accounting price ratios. It also indicates that to determine the shadow price of labor it is first necessary to determine labor's market wage. Doing this is fairly straightforward when skilled workers who are employed at a nation's business establishments are hired to work on a project, but it is not so apparent when the project hires unskilled workers. We discuss the easier case first.

If a nation's labor markets for skilled workers are functioning reasonably well— for example, unemployment among such workers is not high—then, as seen in Chapter 4, the wage at which they are hired by a project provides a reasonable approximation of their market wage. Consequently, the project wage provides a reasonable approximation of their productivity elsewhere and, hence, represents the social opportunity cost (expressed in domestic prices) of hiring them for the project.[14] If a conversion factor is available for skilled workers, then the shadow wage can be obtained by multiplying it by the project wage. Alternatively, but less satisfactorily, the project wage can be multiplied by sector-specific conversion factors to convert it to its foreign exchange equivalent. For example, if carpenters are hired, then the project wage for carpenters can be multiplied by the conversion factor for the construction industry. Still less satisfactory if neither a conversion factor for skilled workers nor an appropriate sector-specific conversion factor is available, then an estimate of the standard conversion factor can be used.

A special case occurs when a developing country does not have sufficient workers with the skills demanded by the project being evaluated and the required workers must be hired from abroad. These foreign workers would typically not be given standing. Nonetheless, they would spend some of their earnings within the country, while sending or taking the remainder out of the country. Thus, to determine the shadow cost of hiring foreign labor, the fraction of earnings sent abroad would have to be estimated. As these earnings would be a direct loss of foreign exchange, they would have an accounting price ratio of 1. In principle, the value of each item purchased within the country should be multiplied by its APR. Because the information to do this would probably not be available in practice, however, all earnings that remain in the country would probably be multiplied by the economy-wide consumption conversion factor (CCF).[15] Hence, the shadow wage for foreign workers, SW_f, would be computed as follows:

$$SW_f = [h + (1 - h)(\text{CCF})](PW) \qquad (16.4)$$

where PW is the project wage, h is the fraction of the project wage sent or taken home, and $(1 - h)$ is the fraction spent domestically.

A substantial fraction of the unskilled workers for a project in a developing country are ultimately likely to be drawn from the countryside. This will be true not only of projects in rural areas, but also of projects in cities, even if the workers who are directly hired by the project currently reside in urban areas. The reason is that as employment increases in urban areas in developing countries, workers in rural areas are induced to migrate to the areas where employment has increased.

Why this migration occurs is suggested by a well-known model developed by John Harris and Michael Todaro.[16] Their model is based on two observations about developing countries: Unemployment is often very high in urban areas and earnings are typically considerably higher in urban than in rural areas. Although Harris and Todaro do not explain the reasons for the higher urban wages, they could be due to minimum wages that are enforced in urban areas but not rural areas, unions, decisions by foreign corporations that are under pressure in their home countries to pay wages that exceed subsistence levels, or a belief on the part of employers that higher wages result in higher productivity because higher paid workers are healthier, less likely to leave the firm, and more motivated.[17] The key point for purposes of the Harris-Todaro model is that urban wages are above their equilibrium level and, consequently, result in urban unemployment.[18] Rural wages, in contrast, are at their equilibrium level and, consequently, lower than urban wages.

Harris and Todaro suggest that because of the higher urban wages workers will migrate from the countryside to the cities, even though some of them will not be able to find jobs. More specifically, they postulate that the probability that a rural worker will obtain employment upon migrating to a city equals $(L - U)/L$, where L is the size of the workforce in the city, U is the number of unemployed persons, and $E = (L - U)$ is the number of employed workers. Therefore, the model implies that workers will have an incentive to migrate from the countryside to the city as long as:

$$RW < UW(E/L) \tag{16.5}$$

where RW is the rural wage, UW is the urban wage, and $UW(E/L)$ is the wage that migrating workers will receive on average [in other words, $UW(E/L)$ is their expected wage]. Thus, according to the model, rural-urban migration will cease when:

$$RW = UW(E/L) \tag{16.6}$$

Two important implications of this model are that even when there is no incentive for further migration urban unemployment may continue to be high and urban wages may continue to exceed rural wages.

We now use the Harris-Todaro model to examine the effects of locating a new project in a city. Assume that prior to initiating the project the equilibrium condition specified in equation (16.6) is being met. Now assume that ΔE unskilled workers are hired to work on the project. If ΔE is fairly small relative to the size of the workforce, then wage rates are unlikely to be affected. Moreover, urban wage rates may also be unaffected because they are already above their equilibrium level. However, because of the increase in the number of available urban jobs, the expected urban wage facing rural workers will increase to $UW[(E + \Delta E)/L]$, inducing some rural workers to migrate. Consequently, the equilibrium can only be reestablished if:

$$E/L = (E + \Delta E)/(L + \Delta L) \tag{16.7}$$

where ΔL is the number of workers added to the urban labor force.

There are two things to notice here. First, if there are no changes in urban wage rates, then current residents of the city who are presently outside the labor force (that is, not already employed or seeking employment) will not be induced to join it, except perhaps by the increase in the number of available jobs. Therefore, many, if not most, of the workers added to the urban labor force will be migrants from rural areas. Second, according to the model, the number of migrants is likely to exceed the number jobs created by the project. This can be seen by first rearranging the terms in equation (16.7) to obtain:

$$L + \Delta L = L(E + \Delta E)/E \tag{16.8}$$

and then by subtracting $L = L(E)/E$ from equation (16.8) and rearranging the terms to obtain:

$$L + \Delta L - L = L(E + \Delta E)/E - L(E)/E$$

or

$$\Delta L/\Delta E = L/E \tag{16.9}$$

Because the urban labor force consists of both workers and the unemployed (that is, $L = E + U$), the ratio L/E must exceed 1 and, thus, as equation (16.9) implies, so will the ratio $\Delta L/\Delta E$.

The implications of this simple model can be illustrated with an example. If the urban wage is 50 percent higher than the rural wage (that is, if $RW(L/E) = 1.5RW = UW$), then equation (16.6) implies that E/L equals 0.67. Hence, one-third of the urban workforce will be unemployed. Moreover, equation (16.9) implies that for each job created by a project, 1.5 persons will enter the urban labor force (that is, $\Delta L = \Delta E (L/E) = 1(3/2) = 1.5$). For reasons already stressed, many, if not most, of these persons are likely to be rural migrants.

Because most of the unskilled workers added to the workforce as a result of a government project would probably be drawn from the countryside, the output that is forgone is production in rural areas. If the project is located in a rural area, then rural-urban migration is not a consideration, and the shadow wage would be obtained by simply multiplying the rural wage by the most appropriate conversion factor that is available. (Some of the possible conversion factors that might be used were listed earlier when the shadow wage of skilled workers was discussed.) However, if the project is located in an urban area, then account must be taken of the number of workers who would leave the countryside for each job created. According to the Harris-Todaro model, if *all* the workers added to the workforce as a result of the project are rural migrants, then this can be accomplished by multiplying the product of the rural wage and the conversion factor by the ratio, L/E. Notice, however, that equation 16.6 indicates that $RW(L/E) = UW$. In other words, the Harris-Todaro model implies that an *upper-bound* estimate of the shadow wage rate for evaluating projects in urban areas can be obtained by multiplying the urban wage rate by the appropriate conversion factor.[19]

The product of the urban wage rate and the conversion factor should be viewed as an upper bound because fewer than L/E rural workers may migrate in response to each job created by an urban project. First, as previously mentioned, some urban residents may be induced into the labor force as jobs are created by the project. Second, the actual number of migrants could be less if workers are risk averse or there are monetary or psychic costs associated with migrating. Third, if the project is sufficiently large, then the migration of rural workers could cause rural wages to rise, thereby reducing the ultimate number of migrants. If fewer than L/E workers migrate, then the appropriate market wage to use in determining the shadow wage rate would be less than the urban wage. Thus, Caroline Dinwiddy and Francis Teal demonstrate that, under a wide variety of assumptions, the appropriate market wage to use is likely to fall somewhere between the rural and the urban market wage.[20] Consequently, *if large numbers of unskilled workers will be employed on an urban project in a developing country, and there are wide differences between rural and urban wages, a sensitivity test should be conducted in determining the shadow wage rate by first using the rural market wage and then using the urban wage.*

While urban wage rates for unskilled workers can be obtained from survey data—for example, the average manufacturing wage can be used[21]—many rural workers produce home-grown crops. Hence, the wage rate of these workers is more difficult to ascertain. One way to construct an estimate of the rural market wage is to first determine how a typical rural worker who is likely to be affected by the project being evaluated allocates his or her productive time and then estimate the value of the worker's output. For instance, suppose that the typical worker is employed on a cacao plantation for half the year and receives a daily wage of 40 pesos and food and transportation valued at 10 pesos a day, for a total of 50 pesos. Because the worker is only needed at the plantation for six months, he or she works at home during the remainder of the year, growing corn for three months and bananas for the remaining three months. Although the corn and bananas are mostly grown for home consumption, if they were brought to the local market they could be sold for 910 pesos and 1,365 pesos, respectively. Dividing market value of corn and bananas by the 91 days during which the work to grow each was performed suggests that the worker earned a daily market wage of 10 pesos from growing corn and a daily market wage of 15 pesos from growing bananas. Given this information, the worker's daily wage can be computed as a weighted average of his or her daily return from each endeavor, where the weights are the fraction of time he or she devoted to each activity. That is:[22]

$$RW = .5(50) + .25(10) + .25(15) = 31.25 \text{ pesos} \qquad \textbf{(16.10)}$$

In principle, at least two additional factors should be taken into account in determining the shadow wage rate of rural, unskilled workers, although in practice they rarely are because of the lack of adequate information.

First, it is possible that moving to the city requires the worker to work longer hours, places the worker under greater stress, and results in a less satisfactory lifestyle. If so, then the shadow wage rate should, in principle, be adjusted upward to account for the resulting loss of utility.

Second, many rural workers live in large extended families. If a project induces a rural worker to migrate to the city, then the effects on the remaining family members should, in principle, be taken into account. The remaining family members lose the migrating worker's output, of course, but they gain because the worker no longer consumes the income available to the family. These two amounts are not necessarily entirely offsetting; it is possible that the gain exceeds the loss. This would occur, for example, if the family shares its income (the total value of the output produced by all family members) equally among its members. Under these circumstances, each family member's consumption level would be equal to the average value of the output produced by the family. The family member's contribution to family output, however, would correspond to his or her marginal product. Because rural families typically produce much of their output at home on a fixed amount of land, it is likely that the family would be producing on the declining segment of its marginal product curve. If so, the value of a family member's marginal product will be smaller than the value of the output that he or she consumes. Thus, if a family member is induced by a project to migrate in such circumstances, the consumption levels of the remaining family members will increase.

EXHIBIT 16-1

In 1974 the World Bank led an international effort to eradicate onchocerciasis (river blindness) in West Africa. The project, which extended over more than two decades and covered 11 countries, used insecticides to kill the blackfly, the carrier of the parasite that causes onchocerciasis. The benefits of the program stem from the reduction in the number of cases of river blindness. A cost-benefit analysis of a similar program in a developed country would likely have measured benefits by monetizing the morbidity and mortality effects with shadow prices. However, estimating the necessary shadow prices in these very poor countries was impractical. Instead, the cost-benefit analysis of the project conducted by the World Bank in 1995 measured benefits in terms of the value of increased agricultural output resulting from increased labor and land. As the average person who develops blindness lives with it for 8 years and dies 12 years prematurely, each avoided case adds about 20 years of productive life. Assuming that these years are employed in agriculture, the percentage increase in the rural labor supply resulting from the project was projected and multiplied by an estimated output elasticity of labor of 0.66 to obtain the predicted percentage increase in agricultural output. The increase in agricultural output was in turn valued using an accounting price, the agricultural value-added, which is estimated by the World Bank. A similar procedure was used to value the additional agricultural land made available through eradication. Overall, the project offered net positive benefits, even when assuming labor force participation rates and land utilization rates of only 70 percent.

Source: Adapted from Aehyung Kim and Bruce Benton, "Cost-Benefit Analysis of the Onchocerciasis Control Program," World Bank Technical Paper Number 282, May 1995.

ADDITIONAL TOPICS

As previously mentioned, with the exception of using world prices to shadow price benefits and costs, conducting CBAs in developing countries is similar to CBA in industrialized countries. However, the literature concerning CBA in developing countries has evolved somewhat separately from the main body of CBA literature. As a result, there are a few additional topics that are treated somewhat differently in the former than in the latter. In this section, we briefly review these topics. The discussion is brief because these differences are mainly conceptual in nature; they appear to have had little effect on the actual conduct of CBA.

Discounting

The points discussed in Chapters 6 and 10 concerning discounting are equally applicable to CBA in developing and industrialized countries. Chapter 10, however, presumed that funding for a public-sector project would displace private-sector investment, private-sector consumption, or both. The literature on developing countries often considers another possibility: Governments in some developing countries are extremely reluctant or unable to borrow addition funds or increase tax revenues. In other words, government expenditures in some developing countries cannot, or will not, be increased even if such an increase would greatly benefit the public. By the same token, they cannot or will not be decreased even if the funds could be better used in the private sector. Given a fixed public-sector budget, a new project can be funded only if the funds are diverted from a current government project or program.[23] Therefore, the opportunity cost of undertaking a project is not forgone private sector investment or consumption, but forgone public-sector investment, which results in a lower amount of some other government output or services being available

We are skeptical that a government's budget would ever really be fixed, at least over the long run. Nonetheless, if this were the case, then private-sector interest rates would not be relevant to government investment decisions. Consequently, a discount rate would have to be obtained by conducting CBAs of current government projects and determining their internal rates of return. The social discount rate could then be selected from among the positive internal rates of return at the lower end of the range, as funding for projects at this end of the range is among the more marginal of current public expenditures. Thus, existing projects with low internal rates of return are the best candidates for displacement by new projects that can reap a higher rate of return.

If government budgets are reasonably flexible, then the social discount rate is related to observed private-sector interest rates. The practical problems in doing this, however, are considerably more formidable in developing than in developed countries because of the high degree of fragmentation in domestic lending markets in developing countries. For example, Karla Hoff and Joseph Stiglitz cite evidence that lending rates in the informal economy in some developing countries are up to six times higher than rates in the formal sector and that within the informal sector in many developing countries there is considerable variation in rates.[24]

Social Accounting in Project Evaluation

The literature on CBA in developing countries suggests that public expenditures have three somewhat conflicting goals: (1) increasing economic efficiency (that is, maximizing net economic worth), (2) encouraging economic growth, and (3) redistributing income from the rich to the poor. In the literature, a sharp distinction is made between CBAs that focus solely on the first goal, economic efficiency, and analyses that attempt to assess the contribution of projects to all three goals. This chapter has so far discussed only CBA. The second type of anaysis is sometimes called *social project appraisal.*

In the LMST approach, social project appraisal is based on the following general framework:

$$SB = NPV - (C)(CCF) + (C)(W/\theta) \tag{16.11}$$

where *SB* is the total social benefit from a project, *NPV* is the net present value of benefits as they are usually estimated in CBA using appropriate accounting prices, *C* is the present value of the net change in private sector consumption resulting from the project and is measured in domestic market prices, *CCF* is the economy-wide consumption conversion factor, θ is the shadow price of capital as it is defined in Chapter 10, and *W* is a *distributional weight* parameter with a value that is greater than 1 if the change in consumption disproportionately accrues to persons with below-average incomes and a value smaller than 1 if the consumption change disproportionately accrues to persons with above-average incomes. The value of W would be 1 if the per capita consumption of all income groups changed by the same amount. Methods for obtaining values for the parameter, W, are described in Chapter 18.

The first term on the right-hand side of equation (16.11), NPV, reflects only the first of the goals listed above: economic efficiency. Most actual CBAs in developing, as well as in industrialized countries, simply stop at this point, thereby implicitly setting the second and third terms equal to zero. The second and third terms are meant to incorporate the other two goals: economic growth and income redistribution. For example, it is often suggested that savings rates are especially low in developing countries and result in insufficient investment to sustain economic growth. Thus, the second term, $(C)(CCF)$, is subtracted from the first to reflect the notion that an increase in consumption has less social value than an equal increase in investment. In other words, the intent is to bias choices among projects toward those that do the most to increase investment. Because the benefits and costs that comprise the NPV estimate are all measured in shadow prices, but C is measured in domestic market prices, the consumption conversion factor is used to make the two terms commensurable. The third term in equation (16.11) tends to offset the second, as factoring out C to obtain $C(W/\theta - CCF)$ indicates, implying that while a reduction in investment is a social cost, an increase in consumption is a social benefit. The ratio, W/θ, indicates that this benefit increases as a greater part of the increase in consumption accrues to persons with incomes below the national average (that is, as W becomes larger) but decreases as the amount of forgone investment becomes greater (that is, as θ becomes larger).[25]

To get some flavor for how use of the framework summarized by equation (16.11) might affect a CBA in practice, consider a project that increases the per capita consumption of higher income groups more than lower income groups, so that $W = 0.5$. Chapter 10 suggests that a reasonable value for θ is 1.1. Finally, Steve Curry and John Weiss have assembled 14 different estimates of the value of CCF from 12 studies of different developing countries.[26] These estimates range between 0.74 and 1.12, but all but four are between 0.79 and 0.94. For illustrative purposes, we assume that CCF = 0.85. Given these values, $(W/\theta - CCF) = (0.45 - 0.85) = -0.40$. This implies that a one peso increase in consumption as a result of a government project is around 40 percent as valuable as a one peso increase in investment. Notice, however, that if the consumption from the project is spread more evenly across income groups, it is conceivable that $(W/\theta - CCF)$ will have a positive value, implying that an increase in consumption has greater social value than a similar increase in investment. This would occur, for example, if $W = 1$.

Although the LMST framework for social project appraisal addresses important issues, it is somewhat ad hoc. In our view, the method that is described in Chapter 10 for incorporating the shadow price of capital into social discounting, which results in a direct adjustment of the NPV estimate, provides a more appropriate way of taking account of the opportunity cost of consuming project output, rather than investing it. The use of the parameter, W, in equation (16.11) represents one particular approach to taking account of the possibility that an increase in the consumption of low-income persons is of greater social value than an equal increase in the consumption of higher-income persons. Alternative, and perhaps preferable, approaches that can be used to do this are described in some detail in Chapter 18, where we discuss distributional weighting. These alternative approaches also directly adjust the net present value estimate.

Value of a Statistical Life in the Absence of Country-Specific Studies

CBAs of policies with impacts on longevity and mortality require estimates of the value of a statistical life. As indicated in Chapter 15, a large number of studies in developed countries have estimated the value of life using a variety of empirical methods. Thus, analysts working in developed countries, especially the United States, can refer to several meta-analyses to borrow shadow prices for the value of life. Analysts working in developing countries, however, are much less likely to be able to find even a single country-specific study let alone a relevant meta-analysis. Is there any way to link the wealth of information from studies conducted in developed countries to the problem of valuing life in developing countries?

One possible approach is to take advantage of estimates of the elasticity of the value of a statistical life with respect to income that have been made in meta-analyses.[27] Consider, for example, the meta-analysis conducted by W. Kip Viscusi and Joseph E. Aldy.[28] They regressed the natural log of the statistical value of life on the natural log of mean study income, mean study risk, and a number of other variables describing 46 studies from 10 countries in a variety of model specifications. Based on their regressions, they estimate the income elasticity of the value of a statistical life to be between 0.5 and 0.6, with a 95 percent confidence interval from approximately 0.2 to 0.8. Lacking any country-specific studies as a source for the value of a statistical life, an analyst might employ the following method: First, start with an estimate of the value of a statistical life for the United States or some other developed country for which there have been a large number of value-of-life studies. Second, assuming that differences in per capita income are the most meaningful differences between the United States and the developing country, use the income elasticity to relate the difference in per capita income to a difference in the value of life.

Algebraically, the procedure finds the value of a statistical life in the developing country, VSL_d, as follows:

$$VSL_d = VSL_{US} - \frac{VSL_{US}(I_{US} - I_d)\epsilon}{I_{US}} \tag{16.12}$$

where VSL_{US} is the value of a statistical life for the United States, I_{US} is the per capita income in the United States, I_d is the per capita income in the developing country, and ε is the elasticity of the value of life with respect to income. For example, imagine that you were asked to do a CBA of a project to reduce the vulnerability of the Three Gorges Dam in China to earthquakes. One benefit would be the reduction in mortality risk. To employ equation (16.12) to find a value of life to monetize this benefit, one could start with the per capita income in the United States in 2002, which was $35,400, and the per capita income in China in 2002, which was $960. If we take the value of a statistical life in the United States to be $4 million and the income elasticity to be 0.6, then equation (16.12) provides an estimate of $1.7 million.

The estimates derived from this approach should be viewed as highly speculative for several reasons. First, because the sample of studies used to estimate the income elasticity consists disproportionately of richer countries, the assumption that the income elasticity is actually constant over the wide range of per capita incomes is questionable. Second, countries like the United States and China differ in many respects beside per capita income. Some of these differences might be accounted for in the sorts of equations estimated by Viscusi and Aldy. For example, their equations include a variable for the mean risk in the study countries. If the mean value of the risk experienced by the population was much higher in China than in the United States, then their models would call for reductions in the predicted value of life for China.[29] Other differences, such as those related to cultural perceptions of risk, are not taken into account in the models and, therefore, cannot be addressed within the context of the meta-analyses.

IS THE LMST METHOD ACTUALLY USED FOR PROJECT EVALUATION?

Not surprisingly, international organizations such as the World Bank make regular use of the shadow pricing procedures discussed in this chapter in conducting CBA. However, the governments of many developing countries do not. Some time ago, the World Bank surveyed 27 developing countries about the project evaluations that they conduct.[30] All but three of these countries had one or more offices with specific responsibility for project evaluation. None of these offices conducted social project appraisals; that is, their formal analyses were concerned solely with whether the evaluated projects increased economic efficiency. However, some of the offices were not using appropriate methods to determine this. Although information was not available for several of the surveyed countries, only eight of the countries surveyed were found to use shadow pricing regularly in conducting project evaluations. In fact, seven of the remaining countries not only failed to shadow price, they also did not discount benefits and costs.

CONCLUSION

A large fraction of economic activity in developing countries typically occurs outside of efficient markets. Consequently, the application of CBA in developing countries requires extensive use of shadow prices. The LMST accounting price method is the most commonly used framework for determining a consistent set of shadow prices. Implementing it often requires considerable skill in working with available information. Finding appropriate shadow prices for unskilled labor poses a particularly difficult problem. Thus, although the principles of CBA are readily transferable to developing countries, their application requires familiarity with a variety of complex shadow pricing issues.

EXERCISES FOR CHAPTER 16

1. A developing country is considering building a steel plant in its largest city. The estimated construction costs of this plant in domestic prices are listed in the following table.
   a. Compute the weighted accounting price ratio for the imported materials that would be used in constructing the plant.
   b. Compute the total construction cost of the plant in accounting prices.

Accounting Price for Steel Plant Construction (in Thousands of Dubyas)			
Item	Cost in Domestic Prices	APR	Cost in Accounting Prices
Imported materials			
CIF price	500		
Taxes and tariffs	100		
Transportation	50	0.60	
Distribution	20	0.80	
Local materials	600	0.90	
Labor			
Skilled	300	0.95	
Unskilled	800	0.55	
Capital costs			
Equipment	250	0.75	
Other	100	0.90	

2. A certain developing country currently imports all its wheat but is considering funding an irrigation project that would allow domestic farmers to grow and sell wheat. The domestically grown wheat would be sold in competitive markets at an estimated price of 15 dubyas per bushel. The wheat the nation currently imports has a CIF price of US$3 per bushel. The official exchange rate is 4 dubyas per dollar. The nation's tariff on imported wheat is 2 dubyas per bushel. Transportation and distribution charges from the port to a typical market are 2 dubyas and 1 dubya per bushel, respectively. The accounting price ratio has been estimated to be 0.6 for transportation and 0.8 for distribution.
   a. Calculate the market price of imported wheat.
   b. Calculated the shadow price of imported wheat.
   c. Should the irrigation project proceed?
3. Assume that a typical unskilled rural worker in a developing country would be paid 2 dubyas a week if he migrates to the city and finds a job. However, the unemployment rate for unskilled workers is 40 percent in the city.
   a. What does the Harris-Todaro model predict the worker's rural wage is?
   b. Assume now that the government is considering funding a project in the city that would use substantial numbers of unskilled workers. Using your answer to part a, suggest a reasonable upper-bound and lower-bound estimate of the market wage rate for unskilled workers that the government might use in conducting a CBA of the proposed project.
4. (Spreadsheet recommended.) Assuming that the elasticity of the value of a statistical life with respect to income is between 0.4 and 0.8 and that the value of a statistical life in the United States is between $2 million and $6 million, generate ranges of value of a statistical life for the following countries: Republic of Korea, Brazil, and Poland. Data on per capita income can be found at the following World Bank site: *www.worldbank.org/ data/countrydata/countrydata.html*.

NOTES

1. We are indebted to Tim Gindling for suggestions on this chapter.

2. *United Nations Industrial Development Organization, Guidelines for Project Evaluation* (New York: United Nations, 1972).

3. I. M. D. Little and J. A. Mirrlees, *Project Appraisal and Planning for Developing Countries* (London: Heinemann Educational 1974).

4. Lyn Squire and Herman van der Tak, *Economic Analysis of Projects* (Baltimore: John Hopkins Press, 1975).

5. An excellent concise summary of the approach can be found in Terry A. Powers, "An Overview of the Little-Mirrlees/Squire-van der Tak Accounting Price System," in Terry A. Powers, ed., *Estimating Accounting Prices for Project Appraisal* (Washington, D.C.: Inter-American Development Bank, 1981), 1–59. Recent book-length treatments include Caroline Dinwiddy and Francis Teal, *Principles of Cost-Benefit Analysis for Developing Countries* (Cambridge, UK: Cambridge University Press, 1996); Robert J. Brent, *Cost-Benefit Analysis for Developing Countries* (Cheltenham, UK: Edward Elgar Publishing, 1998); and Steve Curry and John Weiss, *Project Analysis in Developing Countries* (London: Macmillan, 1993). The book by Curry and Weiss provides a particularly clear exposition of how to use the approach in practice. The Dinwiddy and Teal book focuses on the economic principles that underlie the approach.

6. There is an alternative to this approach, which is known as the UNIDO approach and is based on the United Nations Industrial Development Organization's 1972 guidelines. Instead of using world prices to shadow price project inputs and outputs, it uses domestic prices to do this. In practice, the major focus of the LMST method is in adjusting nontradeables to world prices, whereas the major focus of the UNIDO approach is in adjusting tradeables to domestic prices. CBA can be conducted using either approach and, as demonstrated by Curry and Weiss, *Project Analysis in Developing Countries,* Chapter 6, the two approaches will produce similar results if equivalent assumptions are made in conducting analyses under them. Because the LMST method is more widely used than the UNIDO approach, we focus on it in this chapter.

7. What is the world price? The purchasing power parity (PPP) theory predicts that "the nominal exchange rate between two currencies should be equal to the ratio of aggregate price levels between the two countries, so that a unit of currency of one country will have the same purchasing power in a foreign country" (Alan M. Taylor and Mark P. Taylor, "The Purchasing Power Parity Debate," *Journal of Economic Perspectives* 18(4) 2004, 135–158 at 135). The PPP theory suggests that the world price can be measured in any free-floating currency. However, the PPP appears not to hold fully in the short run, so the choice of a currency for the world price may make a difference. The best strategy is probably to choose a widely traded currency such as the U.S. dollar.

8. These examples are all adapted from Terry A. Powers, "An Overview of the Little-Mirrlees/Squire-van der Tak Accounting Price System," 20–28.

9. If a project increases a country's exports of a good, and the increase reduces the world price for the good, then a CBA must not only take account of the benefits to the country from the increased sales of the product but also the cost that results because previous exports of the product must now be sold at a lower price.

10. For a detailed discussion, see Dinwiddy and Teal, *Principles of Cost-Benefit Analysis for Developing Countries,* 128–131; or Curry and Weiss, *Project Analysis in Developing Countries,* 130–137.

11. For an introduction into using the semi-input-output approach to derive conversion factors, see Curry and Weiss, *Project Analysis in Developing Countries,* Chapter 11. For a detailed description of methods for computing conversion factors either directly with input-output tables or using the semi-input-output approach, as well as four studies in which these methods are used to compute conversion factors for developing countries, see Terry A. Powers, ed., *Estimating Prices for Project Appraisal.*

12. The major exceptions usually occur among APRs for goods that are exported.

13. Curry and Weiss, *Project Analysis in Developing Countries,* 264–266.

14. This will not be the case, of course, if labor markets are highly distorted by union contracts, government wage controls, or for other reasons. Under these circumstances, the method described in Chapter 4 for determining the opportunity cost of hiring the unemployed to work on a project may have to be used.

15. Because the spending patterns of domestic and foreign workers are likely to differ, a CCF that is specific to foreign workers should ideally be used. Such a CCF is unlikely to be available, however. Thus, the CCF for the overall population would probably be used in practice.

16. John. R. Harris and Michael. P. Todaro, "Migration, Unemployment, and Development, *American Economic Review* 60(1) 1970, 126–142. This model is quite simple, making no attempt to capture all important labor market phenomena in developing countries, yet it provides some very useful insights.

17. See Dinwiddy and Teal, *Principles of Cost-Benefit Analysis for Developing Countries,* 145–147 and 151. Higher living costs could also contribute to higher urban wages but, unlike the factors listed in the text, would not induce workers to migrate from rural to urban areas.

18. The urban wage is still equal to the marginal product of labor because urban employers hire workers until the point where the marginal product of labor equals the marginal cost of hiring an additional worker.

19. The conclusion that the urban wage should be used was also reached by Christopher J. Heady ("Shadow Wages and Induced Migration," *Oxford Economic Papers* 33[1] 1981, 108–121) on the basis of a model that incorporated more general and complex assumptions than the Harris-Todaro model. However, Heady also discussed certain circumstances under which a lower wage, but one that is probably higher than the rural wage, should be used.

20. Dinwiddy and Teal, *Principles of Cost-Benefit Analysis for Developing Countries,* Chapter 9.

21. This particular measure is suggested by Heady, "Shadow Wages and Induced Migration."

22. If the rural market wage rate is being used to determine the shadow wage rate and a conversion factor exists for each crop, then the shadow wage can be directly computed by multiplying each of the terms in equation (16.10) by its conversion factor.

23. Little and Mirrlees, *Project Appraisal and Planning for Developing Countries,* in particular, emphasize this possibility. The alternative possibility that is often also mentioned in the CBA literature on developing countries is that government investment will be funded through foreign borrowing. This latter possibility is discussed in Chapter 10.

24. Karla Hoff and Joseph E. Stiglitz, "Imperfect Information and Rural Credit Markets: Puzzles and Policy Perspectives," *World Bank Economic Review* 4(3) 1990, 329–351.

25. In the framework represented in equation (16.11), the *NPV* would not be estimated by using the shadow price of capital method described in Chapter 10. Instead, the shadow price is incorporated into the third term of the equation.

26. Curry and Weiss, *Project Analysis in Developing Countries,* Table 11-5.

27. The elasticity of the value of a statistical life with respect to income is the percentage change in the value of a statistical life that results from a percentage change in income. Algebraically, it can be written as $\epsilon = (\Delta VSL/VSL)/(\Delta I/I)$ where VSL is the value of a statistical life, ΔVSL is the change in the value of a statistical life, I is income, and ΔI is the change in income.

28. W. Kip Viscusi and Joseph E. Aldy, "The Value of a Statistical Life: A Critical Review of Market Estimates Throughout the World," *Journal of Risk and Uncertainty* 17(1) 2003, 5–76.

29. Viscusi and Aldy estimate negative coefficients for the mean risk. See "The Value of a Statistical Life: A Critical Review of Market Estimates Throughout the World," Table 8, 41–42.

30. The findings are reported in Lyn Squire, "Project Evaluation in Theory and Practice," in Hollis Chenery and T. N. Srinivasan, eds., *Handbook of Development Economics,* Volume II, (Amsterdam: North Holland, 1989), 1126–1127.

CHAPTER 17

Cost-Effectiveness Analysis

Cost-effectiveness analysis (CEA) is a widely used alternative to CBA, especially in areas such as health and defense policy. Analysts seeking efficient policies but facing constraints that prevent them from doing CBA may find it useful. In particular, CEA circumvents three common constraints. First, analysts may be unwilling or unable to monetize the most important policy impact. Relatedly, clients may not want monetization. This constraint arises frequently in the evaluation of alternative health policies; for example, many people are willing to predict the numbers of lives saved by alternative public health programs but are unwilling to place a dollar value on a life saved. Second, analysts may recognize that a particular effectiveness measure does not capture all of the social benefits of each alternative, and some of these other social benefits are difficult to monetize. In using CBA, analysts face the burden of monetizing all impacts. If the effectiveness measure captures most of the benefits, then it may be reasonable to use CEA to avoid the burden of conducting a CBA. Third, analysts may be dealing with intermediate goods whose linkage to preferences is not clear. For example, the exact contribution of different types of weapon systems to overall national defense is often unclear. In such situations, CBA is not possible, but CEA may give useful information concerning the relative efficiency of alternatives.

CEA compares (mutually exclusive) alternatives in terms of the ratio of their costs and a single quantified, but not monetized, effectiveness measure. For example, alternative highway safety programs may each involve different costs and numbers of lives saved. The cost-effectiveness ratios of the programs would be expressed as dollars per life saved, and the program that costs the least per life saved would be assessed as the most efficient. In many circumstances such an assessment is valid; in other circumstances, however, the assessment would not be valid because cost-effectiveness ratios ignore scale effects, ranking policies that produce small impacts at a relatively low cost per unit above policies that produce much larger impacts at a somewhat higher cost per unit. Consequently, care must be taken in interpreting cost-effectiveness ratios as measures of efficiency.

In some applications, especially in health policy, it may be possible to construct an outcome measure that serves as a direct proxy for changes in individuals' utilities. In such applications, CEA is referred to as cost-utility analysis (CUA). For example, the benefit measure may be quality-adjusted life-years, which combines both the number of additional years of life and the quality of life during those years. If a CUA employs a perfect proxy for changes in utility, then use of the marginal utility of money would enable the analyst to move directly to CBA; this would not be the case for a CEA that excludes some dimension of utility, such as quality of life.

The presentation that follows addresses the following questions: How should cost-effectiveness ratios be computed and used to compare policy alternatives? How should costs and excluded benefits be handled? How should sensitivity analysis be conducted? How can health outcome measures be made proxies for utilities? How reliable are league tables for comparing large numbers of policies?

COST-EFFECTIVENESS RATIOS AND POLICY CHOICE

CEA involves computing cost-effectiveness ratios and using these ratios to choose policies that promote efficiency. These apparently simple tasks typically involve several complications. The analyst must choose an appropriate basis from which to compute the effects and costs of alternatives. Once cost-effectiveness ratios for alternative policies have been specified, the analyst must also take account of relevant resource constraints in choosing among them.

Cost-Effectiveness Ratios: Incremental Costs and Benefits

As CEA does not monetize benefits, it inevitably involves two different metrics: Costs are measured in dollars, whereas effectiveness may be measured in units such as lives saved, tons of carbon monoxide reduced, or children vaccinated. Because noncommensurate metrics cannot be added, it is impossible to obtain a single measure of net social benefits from the two metrics. However, it is possible to compute the ratio of the two measures, which can be used as a basis for ranking alternative policies. Obviously, the ratio can be expressed in two ways: either as a *cost-effectiveness ratio* (CE ratio), computed by dividing the costs of an alternative by the measure of its effectiveness, or as an *effectiveness-cost ratio* (EC ratio), computed by dividing the effectiveness measure of an alternative by its costs. The discussion that follows focuses on the cost-effectiveness ratio, which is by far the more commonly used ratio.

Costs and effectiveness are always measured *incrementally*. Consider two policies, labeled i and j. The cost-effectiveness ratio of policy i relative to policy j, CE_{ij}, is given by the following formula:

$$CE_{ij} = \frac{C_i - C_j}{E_i - E_j} \tag{17.1}$$

where C_i is the cost of alternative i, C_j is the cost of alternative j, E_i is the number of effectiveness units produced by alternative i, and E_j is the number of effectiveness units produced by alternative j. The simplest application of the formula occurs when a single policy, i, is being assessed as an addition to the status quo, j, and both the cost and effectiveness of i can be expressed as increments to the status quo, $C_i = C + C_j$ and $E_i = E + E_j$. The cost-effectiveness ratio then becomes C/E. For example, imagine that in addition to the highway safety program already in place, it is possible to add an additional program that would cost \$2 million more than the current program and avoid an additional 4 fatalities. The cost-effectiveness ratio would then be

($2 million)/(4 avoided fatalities), or $500,000 per avoided fatality. By itself, this ratio does not indicate whether the program is efficient. Rather, it indicates that the program should be adopted before other safety programs that avoid the same number of fatalities and cost more than $500,000 per avoided fatality.

The application of the cost-effectiveness ratio becomes more complicated when choosing among multiple policy alternatives. As an illustration, consider alternatives for improving student achievement scores. Imagine that a school currently assigns 30 students per classroom at a total marginal cost per classroom of $60,000 and achieves an average achievement score of 60. Label this alternative S_{30}. Alternatively, the school could reduce class size to 25 students (S_{25}), 20 students (S_{20}), or 15 students (S_{15}). Obviously, these are mutually exclusive alternatives because there can only be one class size. Imagine that an alternative to reducing class size below 30 students is to enhance 30-student classrooms with computer support (S_c). The costs and effects of each of these alternatives are displayed in the columns of Table 17-1, which are labeled C and E, respectively. The third column, labeled C/E, presents the ratio of costs to effects. It can be thought of as the incremental cost-effectiveness ratio where the comparison alternative, S_j, is no schooling, with zero costs and zero effectiveness. This ratio is referred to as the *average cost-effectiveness ratio.* Not surprisingly, relative to no schooling, a 30-student classroom offers the smallest cost-effectiveness ratio of $33 (per student) per point increase in average test.

No schooling, however, is not a realistic alternative. Rather, the current classroom size of 30 students should be thought of as the status quo policy and, therefore, the starting point for comparisons. The column labeled S_j makes clear the alternative used as the basis for calculating the *incremental cost-effectiveness ratio, $\Delta C/\Delta E$,* shown in the last column. It is appropriate to compare the reduced class size of 25 (S_{25}) as well as the computerized classroom (S_c) to the status quo. Further reductions in class size, however, are more appropriately assessed relative to the previous reduction, so that S_{20} is assessed relative to S_{25} and S_{15} is assessed relative to S_{20}. Note that the smallest incremental cost-effectiveness ratio arises in moving from S_{30} to S_{25}. The next smallest incremental cost-effectiveness ratio results from moving from S_{30} to S_c, suggesting that S_c should be selected over S_{20} if the decision maker wants to achieve a higher average test score than that provided by S_{25}. Yet a comparison of S_{20} and S_c in terms of costs and effects in the first two columns of Table 17-1 makes clear that this would be an incorrect choice because S_{20} and S_c have the same total cost but S_{20} offers a larger gain in average test score. S_{20} *strictly dominates* S_c; thus it would never make sense to choose S_c over S_{20}.

TABLE 17-1 Working with Cost-Effectiveness Ratios

	C (dollars per student)	E (average test score)	C/E (relative to no schooling)	S_j (basis for comparison)	ΔC (relative to S_j)	ΔE (relative to S_j)	$\Delta C/\Delta E$ (incremental cost-effectiveness ratio)
S_{30}	2000	60	33.3	—	—	—	—
S_{25}	2400	68	35.3	S_{30}	400	8	50
S_{20}	3000	74	40.5	S_{25}	600	6	100
S_{15}	4000	76	52.6	S_{20}	1000	2	500
S_c	3000	72	41.7	S_{30}	1000	12	83.3

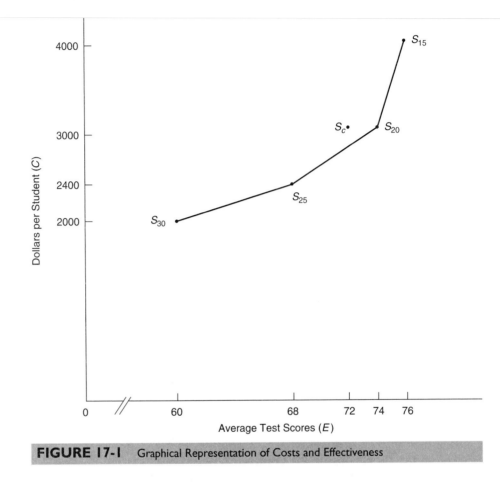

The dominance of S_{20} over S_c is shown graphically in Figure 17-1, which plots the cost of each alternative on the vertical axis and its effect on the horizontal axis. Holding cost constant, one should always prefer an alternative that has a larger effect. In other words, one would always like to make possible moves due east—S_{20} is due east of S_c and therefore should always be preferred. In addition, holding effect constant, one should also prefer an alternative with a smaller cost. In other words, one should always want to make possible moves due south because they give the same effect at lower cost.

The lines shown connecting S_{30} to S_{25} to S_{20} to S_{15}, which have slopes equal to their incremental cost-effectiveness ratios, map out a frontier of the best possible outcomes—those that push as far to the southeast as possible. Points to the northwest of this frontier are subject to what is called *extended dominance.*[1] For example, if S_c costs a few dollars less, then it no longer is strictly dominated by S_{20}. Yet as long as it still falls to the northwest of the frontier, it will be subject to extended dominance. *The first step in comparing alternatives using cost-effectiveness ratios should always be to remove from further consideration all alternatives that are dominated, either strictly or by extension.* Plotting costs and effects as in Figure 17-1 facilitates the identification of dominated alternatives.

Frontiers like the one shown in Figure 17-1 narrow the set of alternatives to consider, but in the absence of information about the decision maker's preferences there is no way to select a particular alternative on the frontier. In contract, CBA leads to a specific choice.[2] In the example presented in Table 17-1, assigning a shadow price to average test scores enables the analyst to estimate the net benefits of each alternative. One can easily verify that, if an average test score point is valued at $50 or less, then S_{30} should be chosen. If the shadow price of a point is between $50 and $100, then S_{25} should be selected. If the shadow price is between $100 and $500, then S_{20} should be selected. Only if the shadow price is over $500 should S_{15} be selected. No shadow price exists at which S_c should be selected because S_{20} has larger net benefits for any positive shadow price.

CEA Where Scale Problems Are Irrelevant: Identical Program Budgets or Identical Program Effectiveness

In general, absent additional information about preferences or the context of the decision problem, cost-effectiveness ratios do not provide a clear basis for choosing among alternatives. The reason is that ratios do not take into account the different scales of projects, a reason discussed in Chapter 2 for avoiding benefit-cost ratios. The major exception arises when one alternative clearly dominates all others.

Dominance is immediately apparent, and scale is not a problem, if all of the alternatives have the same cost. Table 17-2 compares three alternative projects for saving lives. The only costs are budgetary costs (in millions of dollars), and the effectiveness criterion is the number of lives saved. The cost-effectiveness ratio reveals the average cost per life saved. Of course, in this simple example one does not even have to compute cost-effectiveness ratios: By "eye-balling" the table, one can easily observe that alternative C saves the most lives. Computing the cost-effectiveness ratio simply confirms this. It does not matter whether the ratio is calculated as cost per life saved or as lives saved per (million) dollars. Because all alternatives involve the same level of expenditure, they can be thought of as different ways of spending a *fixed budget*. In this case, CEA corresponds to a simple effectiveness maximization problem (maximize lives saved).

Similarly, scale is not a problem if the level of effectiveness is constant across all alternatives. Obviously, the alternative that offers the lowest cost dominates the others because it provides the same level of outcome at a lower cost. Situations in which the level of effectiveness is constant across alternatives can be thought of as different ways of achieving a *fixed effectiveness*. In this case, CEA corresponds to a simple cost-minimization problem (minimize dollars).

TABLE 17-2 Cost-Effectiveness Analysis with Fixed (Identical) Costs

	Alternatives		
Cost and Effectiveness	*A*	*B*	*C*
Cost measure (budget cost)	$10M	$10M	$10M
Effectiveness measure (number of lives saved)	5	10	15
CE ratio (cost per life saved)	$2.0M	$1.0M	$0.67M[a]
EC ratio (lives saved per million dollars)	0.5 life	1.0 life	1.5 lives[a]

[a] *CE ratio or EC ratio of the most cost-effective alternative.*

In the fixed budget and fixed effectiveness cases, dominance is readily apparent. It is possible, however, that one alternative can dominate another even if they have neither the same cost nor the same effectiveness, as long as it is superior on both dimensions. Clearly, dominated alternatives should not be selected. If an alternative dominates all others, then it should be selected.[3]

Imposing Constraints to Deal with Scale Differences

Scale differences among alternatives may distort choice as illustrated in Table 17-3. If we used a cost-effectiveness ratio, then we would choose alternative A. Yet if we look more closely at alternative B, we see that it would save a large number of lives at the relatively low "price" per life saved of $0.5 million which is much less than the shadow prices reviewed in Chapter 15. It is, therefore, likely that a CBA would show that alternative B has larger net social benefits. Given that CEA was probably proposed in the first place because an analyst, client, or decision maker was unwilling to monetize lives saved, how can CEA be used sensibly as a decision rule without monetizing lives saved?

Before answering this question, it is helpful to remind ourselves that if we could replicate project A in 49 other locations (50 in total), the total cost would be $50 million and 200 lives would be saved. This alternative, which we will call project C, would dominate project B. However, project C is not feasible. If it were feasible, then it should have been included in Table 17-3 as one of the alternatives in an *exhaustive* (i.e., complete) set of mutually exclusive alternatives.

In order to use CEA for decision making, a common practice is to impose a constraint, either a minimum acceptable level of effectiveness, denoted $\overline{E}$, or a maximum acceptable cost, denoted $\overline{C}$.

If we impose a minimum level of effectiveness, we may either minimize costs, C_i, or the cost-effectiveness ratio, CE_i. Thus, we could select the project that meets a minimum level of effectiveness at the lowest cost:

$$\text{Minimize } C_i$$
$$\text{Subject to } E_i \geq \overline{E} \qquad\qquad (17.2)$$

In this specification, the decision maker is acting as if he or she does not value additional units of effectiveness. This might apply, for example, to alternative ways of ensuring that children receive minimum amounts of fluoride to protect their teeth. It might also apply to some national defense activities, such as sea lift capability. Even in these examples,

TABLE 17-3 The Problem with the CE Ratio When Scale Differs

Cost and Effectiveness	Alternatives	
	A	B
Cost measure (budget cost)	$1M	$100M
Effectiveness measure (number of lives saved)	4	200
CE ratio (cost per life saved)	$250,000[a]	$500,000
EC ratio (lives saved per million dollars)	4.0 lives[a]	2.0 lives

[a] *CE ratio or EC ratio of the most cost-effective alternative.*

however, additional units of effectiveness above $\overline{E}$ are probably worth something to decision makers. Alternatively, we could select the most cost-effective alternative that satisfies the effectiveness constraint:

$$\text{Minimize } CE_i$$
$$\text{Subject to } E_i \geq \overline{E} \qquad \qquad \textbf{(17.3)}$$

This rule generally leads to higher levels of effectiveness and higher costs than the first rule.

If we specified a maximum budgetary cost, $\overline{C}$, then we might select the project that yields the largest number of units of effectiveness, subject to the budget constraint:

$$\text{Maximize } E_i$$
$$\text{Subject to } C_i \leq \overline{C} \qquad \qquad \textbf{(17.4)}$$

The problem with this rule is that it ignores incremental cost savings. In other words, cost savings beyond $\overline{C}$ are not valued. Alternatively, we could select the project that most cost-effectively meets the imposed budget constraint:

$$\text{Minimize } CE_i$$
$$\text{Subject to } C_i \leq \overline{C} \qquad \qquad \textbf{(17.5)}$$

This rule places some weight on incremental cost savings and is more likely to result in the selection of a project with less than the maximum cost.

An Illustration of the Different CE Rules

Imagine that each of the ten mutually exclusive and exhaustive projects shown in Table 17-4 are intended to save lives. The expected number of lives saved for each project is given in column 2, and the expected budgetary cost in millions of dollars for each project is in column 3. Dominated projects can be eliminated from the choice set at the outset to simplify the analysis: Project D can be eliminated because it is dominated by project C, and projects C and F can be eliminated because they are dominated by project A.

The cost-effectiveness ratio (cost per life saved) appears in column 4. The projects can be ranked from most cost-effective to least cost-effective using this ratio. Project E is the most cost-effective alternative with an average cost per life saved of $2.0 million. The next most cost-effective alternative is project B, followed by J, then I and A, which have equal cost-effectiveness, then G, and then H.

Note, however, that Project E saves the fewest lives. Project B saves twice as many lives as project E and costs only $24 million more. Which project is better? This question illustrates the problem of different scales. Preferably, we would like the option of performing project E 2.2 (or more) times, but this option is not feasible because the list of projects was constructed to be exhaustive.

Suppose the decision maker is willing to specify that she wants to adopt only projects that save at least 50 lives. Which alternative that satisfies this constraint is preferable? The least costly of the acceptable alternatives is project H, whereas the most cost-effective acceptable alternative is project A. Note that project A costs $50 million more

TABLE 17-4   Cost-Effectiveness Analysis with Constraints

| | | | | $E \geq 50$ | | $C \leq 250$ | |
| | | | | | | | |
Projects (1)	Lives Saved (2)	Budget Cost ($M) (3)	CE Ratio (cost per life saved) ($M/life saved) (4)	Budget Cost of Projects That Save at Least 50 Lives (5)	CE Ratio of Projects That Save at Least 50 Lives (6)	Lives Saved of Projects That Cost No More than $250M (7)	CE Ratio of Projects That Cost No More than $250M (8)
A	100	250	2.5	250	2.5[a]	100[a]	2.5
B	20	44	2.2	—	—	20	2.2
C	100	300	3.0	300	3.0	—	—
D	50	300	6.0	300	6.0	—	—
E	10	20	2.0[a]	—	—	10	2.0[a]
F	100	900	9.0	900	9.0	—	—
G	60	210	3.5	210	3.5	60	3.5
H	50	200	4.0	200[a]	4.0	50	4.0
I	40	100	2.5	—	—	40	2.5
J	45	110	2.4	—	—	45	2.4

[a] *CE ratio, budget cost, or effectiveness of the most preferred alternative*

than project H, but it saves 50 more lives. The incremental cost-effectiveness ratio of project A relative to project H is $1 million per life saved, on average, which is very low. Indeed, spending the additional $50 million would be even more cost-effective than project E. However, the choice depends on the decision maker's willingness to trade additional lives saved for additional budgetary cost. Even though CEA is often proposed as a way of avoiding monetization of an important benefit category, analysts or decision makers must often make trade-offs between costs and a nonmonetized benefit to rank alternatives. In doing so, they implicitly consider the value of an additional saved life.

The same type of problem arises if a budget constraint is imposed. Suppose, for example, the decision maker indicates that she cannot spend more than $250 million. Subject to this constraint, project A saves the most lives, but project E is the most cost-effective. Again, to choose between projects A and E, the decision maker must consider trade-offs between additional lives saved and additional budgetary costs.

Sensitivity Analysis: The Problem of Ratios

We rarely predict either costs or effects of policy alternatives with great certainty. Conveying the level of uncertainty in projected cost-effectiveness ratios provides important information to decision makers. The methods of sensitivity analysis for CBA presented in Chapter 7—partial sensitivity analysis, worst- and best-case analysis, and Monte Carlo simulations—can also be applied to CEA. The problem posed by ratios, however, makes Monte Carlo simulations particularly attractive in cost-effectiveness analysis.

If we were to add or subtract normally distributed random variables, then the resulting random variable would also be normally distributed. In contrast, dividing one normally distributed random variable by another does not produce a normally distributed ratio. More generally, the ratio of any two random variables generally does not have the same distribution as either of the random variables that make it up.

Figure 17-2 illustrates this property of cost-effectiveness ratios. The cost of the project is estimated to be $20 million with a standard deviation of $2 million. The number

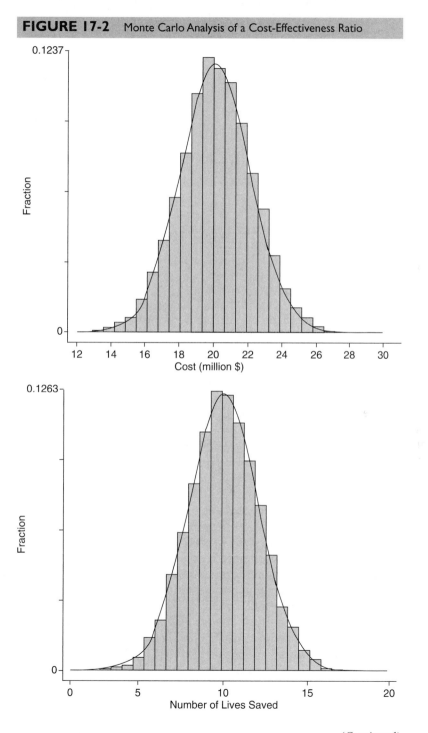

FIGURE 17-2 Monte Carlo Analysis of a Cost-Effectiveness Ratio

(Continued)

FIGURE 17-2   (Continued)

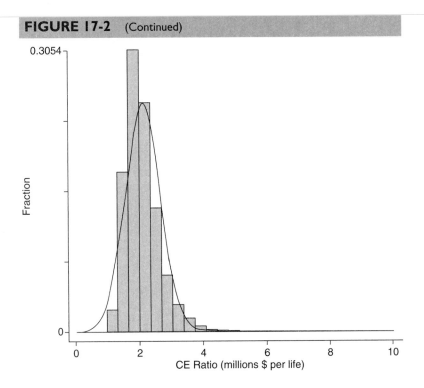

of lives saved is estimated to be 20 with a standard deviation of 2. The estimates might be based on data from similar projects that have been implemented elsewhere, in which case the standard deviations might be a by-product of the estimations, or the estimates might be constructed from shadow prices and elasticities, in which case the standard deviations would be based on their ranges. The Monte Carlo simulation presented in the table assumes that cost and lives saved are each normally distributed. The simulation involves generating 10,000 pairs of values of cost and lives saved based on draws from their respective normal distributions. The top two histograms show the resulting distributions of draws for costs and lives saved separately, with theoretical normal distributions superimposed to show that they are approximately normal. The simulation next computes a cost-effectiveness ratio for each pair of costs and lives saved. The distribution of the resulting 10,000 cost-effectiveness ratios is displayed in the histogram at the bottom of the figure. Note that the distribution of cost-effectiveness ratios does not correspond nearly as closely to the normal distribution, again superimposed on the histogram, as did the variables used to construct it. It is considerably skewed with a longer tail to the right of the mean of $2.1 million per life saved. In other words, the most likely outcome is a cost-effectiveness ratio slightly below the mean but with some probability of substantially larger ratios. The distribution of the ratios can also be used to provide other information, such as the probability of the ratio being above, say, $3 million (5.6 percent).

Note that the skew shown in the figure would be even more dramatic if the distribution of effectiveness were spread more evenly over some range rather than having a central mode like the normal distribution. Also note that one could compare the distributions of cost-effectiveness ratios for two alternatives by superimposing their Monte Carlo distributions. A thicker left-hand tail, showing a higher probability of lower CE ratios, would tend to favor that alternative. To make a more systematic comparison, one would construct a cumulative distribution for each alternative and, if one cumulative distribution lay consistently to the right of the other, select it as *stochastically dominant*. That is, it would consistently offer higher probabilities of achieving more desirable outcomes.

OMITTED COSTS AND BENEFITS

As should be clear from the previous chapters, CBA seeks to include *all* social costs and benefits. For CEA to be an appropriate guide for the more efficient allocation of resources, given its inherent limitations, it too should seek to be as comprehensive as possible in measuring valued impacts. Most fundamentally, it should be based on social costs and take account of social benefits not captured in the effectiveness measure.

Measurement of Costs

The measurement of costs in actual CEA studies varies enormously. In the health care area, costs might include only the costs of treatment, perhaps even just the costs of medication. More broadly, costs might include other treatment costs, such as doctors' time or hospitalization expenses. This is important, for example, in assessing drugs for schizophrenia, which may be expensive but may reduce the time patients spend in hospitals, which may be even more expensive. Costs might also include waiting time or time lost from work, which are borne by patients or employers—effects on members of society that would be included in CBA.

If CEA is to be a guide to the more efficient use of resources, then it should include all social costs. Costs that are constant across all alternatives can be omitted without changing the CE rankings of the alternatives under consideration. Their exclusion, however, generally changes the magnitude of the computed CE ratios, which may be relevant in using these context-specific CE ratios as a basis for making general comparisons across types of alternatives.[4]

In practice, when CEA is conducted for a particular government agency, costs are often measured as that agency's budgetary costs.[5] In the regulatory area, for example, analysts might measure only the agency's cost of enforcing compliance. From an efficiency perspective, the costs should also include firms' costs of complying with the regulations. Of course, even when looking at agency costs, the guiding principle should be opportunity cost.

Omitted Benefits: Technical versus Allocative Efficiency

CEA almost invariably omits impacts that would be included in CBA. CEA considers only one measure of effectiveness. In practice, however, projects often have multiple benefits. For example, regulations that save lives almost always also reduce injuries or illnesses. Similarly, new drugs may effectively cure a disease and also have fewer harmful side effects than current drugs. To measure allocative efficiency, all costs and benefits should be taken into consideration. One way to get closer to doing this—that is, to reach a "halfway house" between standard CEA and CBA—is to compute the following *adjusted CE* ratio:

$$CE^* = \frac{\text{Social Cost} - \text{Other Social Benefits}}{\text{Effectiveness}} \qquad (17.6)$$

If the numerator can be fully valued and monetized, then this adjusted CE ratio incorporates all the impacts that would be included in a CBA. The omission of a particular category of social cost or benefit from the numerator could very well alter the ranking of alternatives, however. The danger of obtaining an arbitrary ranking increases as alternatives become less similar in terms of the inputs they require and the various impacts they produce. Moreover, the transparency of CEA is also reduced because costs may no longer have a simple interpretation, such as budgetary dollars. For these reasons, moving all the way to CBA with extensive sensitivity analysis is often a better analytical strategy than expanding the scope of measured costs and benefits within a CEA framework.

It is important to emphasize that in CEA a weak link may exist between the measure of effectiveness and things that individuals value. It is quite reasonable to presume that individuals would be willing to pay for incremental units of "lives saved," an often used measure of effectiveness. But now consider the "number of addicts treated." This intermediate output may or may not be a good proxy for the final consumption good that individuals value, such as reductions in street crime. Analysts cannot avoid estimating the value of final consumption goods when doing CBA, even if they must rely on shadow prices from secondary sources. However, in CEA they may not make an explicit connection between the effectiveness measure used and benefits that individuals value. When analysts use an intermediate output as a measure of effectiveness, they should establish a link between the effectiveness measure and a final consumption good or at least show that the intermediate output indeed has some value.[6]

COST-UTILITY ANALYSIS

The most common use of *cost-utility analysis* occurs in the evaluation of health policies. In CUA the incremental costs of alternative policies are compared to the health changes, usually measured in *quality-adjusted life-years* (QALYs) or *disability-adjusted life-years* (DALYs), that they produce.[7] CUA is most useful when alternative programs or treatments embody a trade-off between quality of life (morbidity) and length of life (mortality). It can be thought of as a form of CEA that employs a more complex effectiveness measure that more directly corresponds to changes in utilities. All of the previous discussion about cost-effectiveness ratios and decision rules thus applies. The rationale for looking specifically at CUA is that considerable analytical effort has gone into the measurement of QALYs, which not only serve as a common effectiveness measure in CEA but also can be directly monetized for CBA through application of a shadow price for life years.

The Meaning of Life—Quality-Adjusted Life-Years, That Is!

QALYs involve two distinct dimensions: quality and quantity. The analyst must decide how to define, measure, and combine these dimensions. Consider, for example, the effects of three mutually exclusive prenatal programs. Under the status quo, no babies with a particular condition are born alive. Prenatal alternative A will result in five babies being born alive per year, but with permanent, serious disabilities. Prenatal alternative B will result in only two live births, but with only low levels of disability. Before we can compare the costs of these alternatives to their effectiveness, we first have to make quantity and quality commensurate.

The general form of the problem is shown in Table 17-5. The columns show additional years of life ranging from a low of Y_1 to a high of Y_5. The rows show health status ranging from the worst (health state H_1) to the best (health state H_5). For simplicity, assume that alternatives A and B and the status quo involve the same costs and that there is no uncertainty about the longevities and health statuses they will yield. Suppose that the status quo (denoted SQ) gives Y_1H_1 (the fewest years of life in the worst health status), while alternative A achieves Y_3H_3 and alternative B achieves Y_4H_2. Clearly, the status quo is dominated, but how should we choose between alternatives A and B? In order to make the comparison, alternatives A and B must be expressed in a common metric.

Before discussing the various methods for putting health statuses into a common metric, QALYs, a prior question of relevance must be asked: Whose preferences should be the basis for assessing health-related quality of life (HRQoL)? Researchers have used three groups of people as respondents to questions designed to elicit valuations of health statuses: medical experts, patients who have experience with similar statuses, and the general population.

Medical experts typically bring to the valuation exercise relevant experience and knowledge, especially with respect to the physical implications of various health statuses. They also are likely to be sophisticated respondents who can answer more complex questions. Nonetheless, their medically informed assessments may not be consistent with the holistic assessments made by patients or the general public.

The appropriate choice between patients and the general public as respondents is not clear. Some commonly made arguments in favor of patients as respondents include: Patients are likely to be more knowledgeable than the general public about what it is like to experience illnesses and disabilities; researchers need not provide as much description about health statuses to patients as respondents from the general public in order to obtain informed valuations; and, in some circumstances, the general public may be biased against certain conditions, such as those that result from risky behavior or unhealthy lifestyles. Commonly made arguments in favor of the general public as respondents include: the preferences of the general public are most relevant in making decisions concerning the allocation of scarce resources through public policy; patients may overstate their HRQoL relative to the general public because of

TABLE 17-5 The Basic QALY Format

Health Status (H)	Additional Years of Life (Y)				
	Y_1	Y_2	Y_3	Y_4	Y_5
H_1	$Y_1H_1{}^{SQ}$	Y_2H_1	Y_3H_1	Y_4H_1	Y_5H_1
H_2	Y_1H_2	Y_2H_2	Y_3H_2	$Y_4H_2{}^{B}$	Y_5H_2
H_3	Y_1H_3	Y_2H_3	$Y_3H_3{}^{A}$	Y_4H_3	Y_5H_3
H_4	Y_1H_4	Y_2H_4	Y_3H_4	Y_4H_4	Y_5H_4
H_5	Y_1H_5	Y_2H_5	Y_3H_5	Y_4H_5	Y_5H_5

cognitive dissonance or psychological adaption or actual adaptation to their conditions; and the general public is less likely than patients to offer strategic responses to influence public policy.[8]

Although valuations based on patients and the general public tend to provide similar rankings of health statuses, and no systematic differences related to demographic characteristics other than health status appear to exist,[9] patients tend to place higher valuations on conditions that they are experiencing.[10] The difference implies an asymmetry in the valuation of losses and gains: The loss in utility from moving from perfect health to some impaired condition is greater than the gain in utility in moving from the same impaired condition back to perfect health. It can be explained either as a consequence of loss aversion (discussed in Chapter 14) or costly adjustments to changes in health status.[11] If the policy being analyzed just involves gains in the HRQoL, then patients would be the appropriate group to survey. In contrast, if it involves just losses, the general public should be surveyed. The choice between patients and the general public is not clear, however, when policies involve both gains and losses in HRQoL.

The basic approach for constructing QALYs involves assessing HRQoL for different health statuses. The HRQoL is usually measured on a scale in which the value 1 is assigned to perfect health and the value 0 to death. The HRQoL measures can then be used to weight life-years to produce QALYs. Researchers have used four approaches, three direct and one indirect, to assess HRQoL: the health rating method, the time trade-off method, the standard gamble method, and the health index method.[12]

Health Rating Method Generally, researchers derive a *health rating* (HR) from questionnaires or interviews with health experts, potential subjects of treatment, or the general public. They present scales with well-defined endpoints to respondents, typically with death assigned a value of 0 and perfect health a value of 1. Intermediate health states are described in detail to the respondents, who are then asked to locate each state between the end points, 0 and 1. For example, if three intermediate health states described to an individual correspond to "seriously disabled," "moderately disabled," and "minimally disabled," then an individual might assign values of 0.15, 0.45, and 0.90 to these states, respectively.

Respondents often have difficulty assigning numerical values to the various health states, however. An alternative version of the health rating method uses a bisection process to obviate the need for respondents to provide numerical values. It provides respondents with a list of health states from which they are asked to find the one that falls midway between the end points on a visual display, such as a thermometer scale.[13] The respondents are then asked to find the health state that falls midway between the initially placed health state and the upper and lower endpoints, respectively. The process continues until respondents have placed the various health states on the scale. It yields an interval scale for HRQoL, but one without a clear basis in revealed preferences that usually provide the preferred basis for assessing utilities.

The Time Trade-Off Method In the *time trade-off* (TTO) method, respondents are asked to compare different combinations of length and quality of life.[14] The typical comparison is between a longer life of lower health status and a shorter life with a higher health status. Figure 17-3 illustrates such a comparison. The horizontal axis measures additional years of life (Y) and the vertical axis measures health status (H). Respondents might be asked to compare some status quo point, say R, representing health status H_2

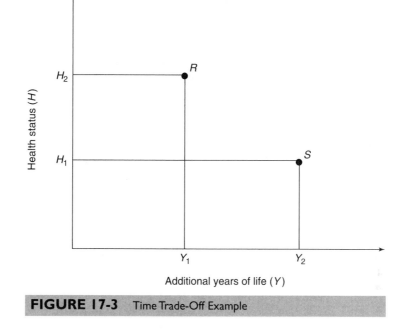

FIGURE 17-3   Time Trade-Off Example

and additional years of life Y_1, with an alternative point, say S, representing health status H_1 and additional years of life Y_2. If a respondent is indifferent between the two points, then he or she is willing to give up $H_2 - H_1$ units of health quality in return for $Y_2 - Y_1$ additional years of life. Assuming that health status H_2 is perfect health and assigning it a utility of 1, the utility assigned to H_1 is then Y_1/Y_2.

For example, imagine that one wanted to assign a utility to the health status of twice-weekly severe lower back pain that prevented strenuous physical activity. The severity and consequences of the back pain would be carefully described to a number of respondents. Then each would be asked to compare living 10 additional years with the back pain to living some number of years in perfect health. If a respondent were indifferent between living 10 years with the back pain and 9 years in perfect health, then the analyst would assign a utility of 9/10 for the health state of back pain. Thus, in comparing medical interventions, an additional year of life with back pain would be valued at 0.9 instead of at 1 for an additional year in perfect health.

A complication arises if a person views the health status being valued as worse than death. In such cases, respondents are asked to compare immediate death as one alternative with t_1 additional years of life in the extremely undesirable health status followed by t_2 years in full health as the other. Holding the total of t_1 and t_2 constant, the values that make the respondent indifferent between the alternatives would assign a utility to the extremely undesirable health status of $-t_2/t_1$. The resulting negative value is consistent with the health status being valued as worse than death, which is assigned a utility of 0.

In order for the TTO values to be valid utilities, a strong assumption must be met: Individuals must be willing to give up constant proportions of their remaining life years to attain an improvement in health status no matter how many additional life years remain. For example, if a person expecting to live 10 years with a disability were willing to give up 5 years to attain perfect health, then when the person has only 8 years of expected life, he or she should also be willing to give up 4 of the 8 remaining years to obtain perfect health. The assumption of constant proportional time trade-off implies that the person has a zero marginal rate of time preference. A particularly serious violation of the constant proportions assumption occurs when a person's preferences for life years in some health status exhibit *maximum endurable time* (MET): There is a limit to the number of years people want to live with the health status.[15] The stringency of the constant proportions assumption suggests caution in interpreting TTO values as utilities. Nonetheless, the TTO method continues to be used to place relative values on health statuses for the construction of QALYs.

The Standard Gamble Method   In the *standard gamble* (SG) approach, respondents are presented with a decision tree like those described in Chapter 7.[16] Respondents are offered a choice between two alternatives. Alternative A has two possible outcomes: either a return to normal health for n additional years (occurring with probability p) or immediate death (occurring with probability $1 - p$). Alternative A might be an operation that has probability $1 - p$ of failure (death), but which, if successful, will return the patient to normal health for n years. Alternative B guarantees the patient n additional years with a specified level of health impairment. This choice is shown in Figure 17-4. The probability p is varied until a respondent is indifferent between alternatives A and B. When using a health status index ranging from 0 (death) to 1 (normal health for n years), the p at which a respondent is indifferent can be interpreted as that respondent's utility from alternative B.

For example, consider again the assignment of a utility to the health status of twice-weekly severe lower back pain that prevented strenuous physical activity. There are two approaches to finding the probability of perfect health that would make the respondent indifferent between the gamble and the back pain. First, we could simply ask the respondent to state the probability. Second, we could offer an initial probability, and then raise or lower it until the respondent expresses indifference. The former

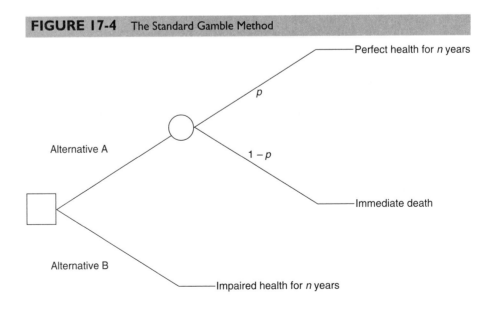

FIGURE 17-4   The Standard Gamble Method

approach might falter with respondents who are not used to thinking in terms of probabilities. To avoid this problem, it may be desirable to engage the respondent in some valuations of other health statuses before turning to the one of interest. The latter approach risks the sort of starting point bias that was discussed in connection with contingent valuation in Chapter 14. Starting points should be varied across respondents to allow for the possibility of detecting any starting point bias. Imagine that the method used reveals that the respondent is indifferent between the back pain for certain and a gamble with a probability of perfect health of 0.95 and a probability of death of 0.05. The SG method would assign a utility to the health status of lower back pain of 0.95.

The SG method assumes that individuals make choices consistent with the expected utility hypothesis. To the extent that they do follow the expected utility hypothesis, then the utilities resulting from the SG method are valid utilities. Deviations from the expected utility hypothesis, such as the judgmental biases discussed in Chapter 14, challenge the validity of the utilities derived from the SG method. Of particular relevance, people may show risk aversion in comparing certain and uncertain outcomes, suggesting that the SG method probably overestimates the utilities of health statuses presented as certain alternatives. Although direct comparisons of the TTO and SG methods generally conclude that they provide similar utilities at least in terms of ordinal rankings,[17] a majority of studies find that the SG method yields higher values.[18]

Health Index Method Clinicians have developed a variety of scales to assess variations in health, whether in relationship to particular diseases, injuries, or mental states, or to health in general. The *health index* (HI) method uses one of the direct methods (HR, TTO, or SG) to assign utilities to points on the health scales, which can then be used to construct QALYs in a variety of applications. The HI method provides utility weights that can be applied to standard health scales, thus offering analysts utilities akin to the shadow prices discussed in Chapter 15.

A widely used HI method evolved out of a health classification system introduced by George Torrance and colleagues[19] and further developed by the McMaster University's Centre for Health Economics and Policy Analysis. Heath Utilities, Inc., currently offers several copyrighted versions to researchers.[20] Its Health Utility Index Mark 3, for instance, is comprised of eight attributes: vision, hearing, speech, ambulation, dexterity, emotion, cognition, and pain. Each attribute has clearly defined levels. For example, the levels for pain are "free of pain and discomfort," "mild to moderate pain that prevents no activities," "moderate pain that prevents a few activities," "moderate to severe pain that prevents some activities," and "severe pain that prevents most activities." With either five or six levels for each attribute, this classification system defines 972,000 different health statuses.[21] Standardized questionnaires enable researchers to assess health outcomes for individuals or population samples. Health Utilities, Inc., provides tables derived from general population surveys and multi-attribute utility scaling that convert responses into utilities for each of the attributes. For example, a researcher seeking a utility based only on the attribute of pain would find that Health Utilities assigns a value of 0.48 for "moderate to severe pain that prevents some activities." For constructing an overall utility that takes account of all eight dimensions, the tabulated utility for the same level of pain would be 0.77, which along with the utilities for the levels of the other attributes would be combined into a single value using a multiplicative formula.

The most widely used index of general health status is the Short Form Health Survey (SF-36), which was originally developed by researchers at the RAND Corporation as part of the Medical Outcomes Study.[22] Constructed to conform to psychometric standards for making group comparisons, the SF-36 uses 35 items to construct eight scales: physical functioning, role limitation due to physical problems, bodily pain, general health, vitality, social function, role limitation due to emotional problems, and mental health. The first four of these scales combine to form a summary measure of physical health, and the latter four combine to form a summary measure of mental health. The SF-36 is licensed through Quality Metric, Inc.,[23] and has been made available in many languages through the International Quality of Life Assessment Project.[24]

Efforts are underway to create a mapping from scales derived from the SF-36 to utilities. For example, John Brazier and his colleagues have created a simplified version of the SF-36, the SF-6D, which reduces the number of scales (dimensions) from eight to six by excluding the general health scale and combining the physical and emotional role limitations into a single index.[25] Each of the six dimensions has five or six levels of response, enabling them to define 18,000 different health statuses. The researchers next selected 49 representative health statuses and employed the SG method in interviews with a general population sample of UK respondents. They next estimated econometric models with utilities as the dependent variable and the various levels on the six dimensions as explanatory variables. The coefficients estimated for the various levels can then be used to assign utilities to any one of the possible health statuses.[26] Researchers who can classify outcomes in terms of the SF-6D scale can thus obtain utilities for these outcomes. Of course, the utilities are based on the preferences of the UK general public and might not be appropriate in other national contexts. In the future, however, the estimates are likely to be replicated for other populations.

Other health status indexes have been created and related to population preferences. For example, European researchers organized as the EuroQol association have developed the EQ-5D index to supplement existing indexes.[27] Utilities have been assigned to EQ-5D health status through general population surveys using the TTO method.[28] Researchers have begun to compare the utilities and the sensitivity of these utilities to changes in health statuses across the various health indexes. For example, a recent comparison of EQ-5D and SF-6D utilities for liver transplant patients found that the SF-6D does not describe health statuses at the lower end of the utility scale well but is more sensitive than EQ-5D in detecting small changes toward the top of the scale.[29] A comparison of the HUI Mark 3, the SF-6D, and the EQ-5D for patients with rheumatological conditions suggested broad agreement, but it also showed a number of specific differences that make the particular choice of index potentially relevant to constructing QALYs.[30]

QALYs: Caveats and an Extensions

The construction of QALYs using health status utilities requires a strong assumption: The utility of being in a particular health status is proportional to the time spent in that status. For example, consider a person who has an expected life of Y years in health status H. The number of QALYs accruing to this person would be $YU(H)$, the product of the number of years in the health status and the utility of the health status, $U(H)$.

EXHIBIT 17-1

Researchers recently conduced a study comparing various utility elicitation methods for gastroesophageal reflux disease with heartburn. Samples of patients with a history of heartburn were recruited in Germany and Sweden. After asking respondents about the severity of their heartburn in a typical week, the researchers administered the EQ-5D health index and then applied the health rating (HR), time trade-off (TTO), and standard gamble (SG) methods. For example, the SG alternatives were presented as follows:

Alternative 1 is that you know for certain that you will live for another 10 years in your current health state. During these 10 years, your heartburn as well as symptoms of any other health problems that you may have will be exactly as you have experienced them over the last 12 months. After these 10 years you will die.

Alternative 2 is that there is a treatment that either is successful or fails. If the treatment is successful, you will recover perfect health and remain perfectly healthy during 10 years, that is, the same period of time as in alternative 1. Perfect health

means that you are free from all health problems, that is, you are free from heartburn as well as symptoms of any other health problems that you may have. After these 10 years you will die. If treatment fails, you will die immediately. (p. 43)

After giving respondents randomly assigned starting points of either 0.95 or 0.70 for the probability of success, probabilities were raised or lowered until the respondent was indifferent between the alternatives. Over one-third of respondents were unwilling to accept any risk of death for the chance of perfect health (or accept any reduction of years in the TTO method). The mean values from the SG method were 0.92, 0.88, and 0.86 for mild, moderate, and severe heartburn, respectively. The TTO values for the three levels of severity were 0.90, 0.87, and 0.85. In contrast to these relatively high utilities, the HR method produced utilities of 0.75, 0.67, and 0.49, while the EQ-5D based utilities were 0.78, 0.67, and 0.49. Thus, the SG and TTO methods showed much smaller losses in utility from chronic heartburn than the HR or the EQ-5D methods.

Source: Adapted from Bernt Kartman, Gudrun Gatz, and Magnus Johannesson, "Health State Utilities in Gastroesophageal Reflux Disease Patients with Heartburn: A Study in Germany and Sweden," *Medical Decision Making* 24(1) 2004, 40–52.

A number of conceptual issues about how to measure utilities remain.[31] A particularly important issue is discounting for time. From a CBA perspective, it is problematic to discount costs but not to discount health years. The reason is that if costs but not QALYs were discounted, the cost-effectiveness ratio of a policy that involved the accrual of costs and QALYs over substantial periods of time would improve if we delayed the health expenditure until the following year.[32] As discussed in Chapter 10, the basic idea that individuals have positive discount rates relating to additional years is widely accepted, but considerable controversy over the theory, measurement, and level of the appropriate discount rate exists.[33]

The use of QALYs is not limited to CEA, but can also be used in CBA. The basic procedure would be to monetize QALYs using a value of a life-year. For example, imagine that a public health intervention would save 10 QALYs this year and 20 QALYs next year. If the analyst values a life-year (VLY) at $200,000, then the benefits in the first year of the intervention would be $2 million and the benefits in the second year would be $4 million. These yearly benefits would then be discounted to produce a present value of benefits. As noted in Chapter 15, however, moving from the value of a statistical life (VSL) to a VLY is especially controversial as it implies a VSL that is lower for older people with shorter life expectancies.

THE USE OF LEAGUE TABLES

CEA usually compares mutually exclusive projects. By definition, this means that the alternative projects address the same problems, for example, alternative methods of breast cancer screening. Yet CEA has been used to make rankings *across* policies that have the same broad purpose (e.g., saving lives) but are not necessarily mutually exclusive. *League tables* rank multiple CEAs that share the same cost-effectiveness measure. Tammy Tengs and her colleagues, for example, have developed a league table of 587 interventions intended to avert premature death (i.e., to save lives).[34] They found that, on average, the United States spent about $433,500 per life saved or $41,600 per year of life saved (in 1999 dollars). They also asked the question: How many lives would be saved if the same investment were focused on the most cost-effective interventions? They conclude that an additional 60,200 lives could be saved, or about twice as many lives as under the status quo allocation. In a similar study, John Morrall III, updating an earlier review he conducted, assessed the cost-effectiveness of 76 regulations issued by the U.S. federal government between 1967 and 2001. He found that the cost-effectiveness ratios differed by six orders of magnitude and that regulations aimed at reducing safety and cardiovascular risks have been much more cost-effective than regulations aimed at reducing cancer risks.[35]

How useful are league tables? Comparisons of mutually exclusive projects inherently control for some of the differences in the measurement of cost and effectiveness. There can be no such presumption when comparing studies across different authors, using different data, and somewhat different methodologies. Different studies may measure costs differently, they may omit different costs, and they may differ considerably in scale. These problems apply even more so to CUA league tables because different methodologies

---

EXHIBIT 17-2

The Cost-Utility Registry, a project sponsored by the Harvard School of Public Health, provides a comprehensive listing of cost-effectiveness studies in the health area. The first phase of the project covered 228 studies published between 1976 and 1997 that produced over 600 cost-utility ratios for health-related interventions. The second phase of the project is adding studies published between 1998 and 2001. This comprehensive database supports an extensive league table ranking interventions in terms of dollars per QALY.

The project also provides a catalog of preference scores (utilities) that have been used in various studies. Analysts with insufficient resources to conduct their own surveys for assigning utilities to health statuses may be able to borrow plausible values from the catalog. Analysts planning to conduct surveys may find it useful to review studies that used similar methods.

Source: Adapted from CEA Registry, Harvard School of Public Health, *www.hsph.harvard.edu/cearegistry/*.

are used to calculate QALYs and, as discussed earlier, these methodologies do not necessarily produce similar results. Therefore, Karen Gerard's caution on the use of league tables is appropriate:

> [A]s more and more studies were read in the course of the investigation, it became striking how many not only placed their results in some standard QALY league table ... but also purported to present their results as "favourable." It is unlikely to be the case that all of these studies can have "favourable" results.[36]

Other critics have noted the absence of information on uncertainty in most league tables.[37] Thus, caution is warranted in using league tables as guides for policy choice.

CONCLUSION: WHEN IS CEA CLOSE TO CBA?

CEA measures technical efficiency, not allocative efficiency. It can rank alternative policies is terms of technical efficiency but cannot indicate whether something is worth doing. CEA is closest to CBA when all social costs are measured, when the effectiveness measure captures all of the social benefits, and when alternative projects are of similar scales. Under these circumstances the most cost-effective alternative is the most allocatively efficient alternative. However, this does not necessarily imply that it should be adopted because it may not be worth doing. Unless we can monetize units of effectiveness, we cannot answer the latter question.

When significant nonbudgetary social costs or other categories of benefits exist, CEA is not close to CBA. Analysts have three options. First, they can try to incorporate significant nonbudgetary social costs and other categories of benefits into an adjusted cost-effectiveness measure, such as is done in the construction of QALYs. Second, if they can also monetize effectiveness, then they should do CBA. Third, they can move to a more qualitative evaluation method such as multigoal analysis.

EXERCISES FOR CHAPTER 17

1. A public health department is considering five alternative programs to encourage parents to have their preschool children vaccinated against a communicable disease. The following table shows the cost and number of vaccinations predicted for each program.

Program	Cost ($)	Number of Vaccinations
A	20,000	2,000
B	44,000	4,000
C	72,000	6,000
D	112,000	8,000
E	150,000	10,000

   a. Ignoring issues of scale, which program is most cost-effective?
   b. Assuming that the public health department wishes to vaccinate at least 5,000 children, which program is most cost-effective?

c. If the health department believes that each vaccination provides social benefits equal to $20, then which program should it adopt?

2. Analysts wish to evaluate alternative surgical procedures for spinal cord injuries. The procedures have various probabilities of yielding the following results.

Full recovery (FR)—the patient regains full mobility and suffers no chronic pain.

Full functional recovery (FFR)—the patient regains full mobility but suffers chronic pain that will make it uncomfortable to sit for periods of longer than about an hour and will interfere with sleeping two nights per week, on average.

Partial functional recovery (PFR)—the patient regains only restricted movement that will limit mobility to slow-paced walking and will make it difficult to lift objects weighing more than a few pounds. Chronic pain is similar to that suffered under full functional recovery.

Paraplegia (P)—the patient completely loses use of legs and would, therefore, require a wheelchair or other prosthetic for mobility and suffers chronic pain that interferes with sleeping four nights per week, on average. Aside from loss of the use of his or her legs, the patient would regain control of other lower body functions.

a. Describe how you would construct a quality-of-life index for these surgical outcomes by offering gambles to respondents. Test your procedure on a classmate, friend, or other willing person.

b. Assume that the index you construct on the basis of your sample of one respondent is representative of the population of patients. Use the index to measure the effectiveness of each of three alternative surgical procedures with the following distributions of outcomes.

	Surgical Procedures		
	A	B	C
FR	0.10	0.50	0.40
FFR	0.70	0.20	0.45
PFR	0.15	0.20	0.10
P	0.05	0.10	0.05

c. Imagine that the surgical procedures involved different life expectancies for the various outcomes. Discuss how you might revise your measure of effectiveness to take account of these differences.

3. Two alternative mosquito control programs have been proposed to reduce the health risks of West Nile disease in a state over the next five years. The costs and effectiveness of each program in each of the next five years are provided in the following table.

	Alternative A		Alternative B	
	QALYs Saved	Incremental Cost (millions of dollars)	QALYs Saved	Incremental Cost (millions of dollars)
Year 1	1.0	3.8	0.5	1.0
Year 2	0.5	0.0	0.5	1.0
Year 3	0.3	0.0	0.5	1.0
Year 4	0.1	0.0	0.5	1.0

a. Calculate CE ratios for each program without discounting.
b. Calculate CE ratios discounting cost but not effectiveness assuming a discount rate of 4 percent.
c. Calculate CE ratios discounting both costs and effectiveness at 4 percent.
d. (Spreadsheet required.) Assume that the uncertainty range for each of the yearly effectiveness estimates is plus or minus 20 percent and the uncertainty in each of the yearly cost estimates is 10 percent. Assuming uniform distributions of errors, produce Monte Carlo distributions of CE ratios for each program and compare them.

NOTES

1. See Alan M. Garber, "Advances in Cost-Effectiveness Analysis," in Anthony J. Culyer and Joseph P. Newhouse, eds., *Handbook of Health Economics* 1A (New York: Elsevier, 2000), 181–221 at 193–194.

2. Economists have attempted to determine the circumstances under which CEA is consistent with the assumptions of welfare economics that underlie CBA. Overall, strong assumptions are required for consistency. For overviews, see Werner B. F. Brouwer and Marc A. Koopmanshap, "On the Economic Foundations of CEA: Ladies and Gentlemen, Take Your Positions!" *Journal of Health Economics* 19(4) 2000, 439–459; and Paul Dolan and Richard Edlin, "Is It Really Possible to Build a Bridge Between Cost-Benefit Analysis and Cost-Effectiveness Analysis?" *Journal of Health Economics* 21(5) 2002, 827–843.

3. Dominant alternatives tend to be rare, but they can occur. For an example, see Russell D. Hall, Jack Hirsh, David L. Sackett, and Greg L. Stoddart, "Cost-Effectiveness of Primary and Secondary Prevention of Fatal Pulmonary Embolism in High-Risk Surgical Patients," *Canadian Medical Association Journal* 127(10) 1982, 990–995.

4. Christopher J. L. Murray, David B. Evans, Arnab Acharya, and Rob M. P. M. Baltussen, "Development of WHO Guidelines on Generalized Cost-Effectiveness Analysis," *Health Economics* 9(3) 2000, 235–251.

5. Karen Gerard found that approximately 90 percent of the health studies she reviewed only looked at direct budgetary costs; see Karen Gerard, "Cost-Utility in Practice: A Policy Maker's Guide to the State of the Art," *Health Policy* 21(3) 1992, 249–279 at 263.

6. See Michael Drummond, Greg L. Stoddart, and George W. Torrance, *Methods for the Economic Evaluations of Health Care Programmes* (Oxford, UK: Oxford University Press, 1987), at especially 76.

7. DALYs were developed primarily to quantify the mortality and morbidity burdens of various diseases in populations. See Christopher J. L. Murray and Arnab K. Acharya, "Understanding DALYs," *Journal of Health Economics* 16(6) 1997, 703–730. For a critique, see Sudhir Anand and Kara Hanson, "Disability-Adjusted Life Years: A Critical Assessment," *Journal of Health Economics* 16(6) 1997, 685–702.

8. These arguments are taken from Peter A. Ubel, Jeff Richardson, and Paul Menzel, "Societal Value, the Person Trade-Off, and the Dilemma of Whose Values to Measure for Cost-Effectiveness Analysis," *Health Economics* 9(2) 2000, 127–136 at 128.

9. David L. Sackett and George W. Torrance, "The Utility of Different Health States as Perceived by the General Public," *Journal of Chronic Diseases* 31(11) 1978, 697–704; and Debra Froberg and Robert L. Kane, "Methodology for Measuring Health-State Preferences—IV: Progress and a Research Agenda," *Journal of Clinical Epidemiology* 42(7) 1989, 775–685.

10. Paul Dolan, "The Measurement of Health-Related Quality of Life for Use in Resource Allocation in Health Care," in Anthony J. Culyer and Joseph P. Newhouse, eds., *Handbook of Health Economics* 1B (New York: Elsevier, 2000), 1723–1760 at 1738–1739 and 1748.

11. Rajiv Sharma, Miron Stano, and Mitchell Haas, "Adjusting to Changes in Health: Implications for Cost-Effectiveness Analysis," *Journal of Health Economics* 23(2) 2004, 335–351.

12. In addition to these methods, which attempt to elicit individual valuations of health states, the *person trade-off* (PTO) method seeks to assess societal values for different distributions of health outcomes. For example, if respondents were indifferent between a policy that would move five people from extremely poor health to moderate health and an alternative that would move fifteen people from moderate health to perfect health, then the social value of the effect of the first policy is three times that of the effect of the second. See Erik Nord, Jose Luis Pinto, Jeff Richardson, Paul Menzel, and Peter Ubel, "Incorporating Societal Concerns for Fairness in Numerical Valuations of Health Programs, *Health Economics* 8(1) 1999, 25–39.

13. For an overview of this and the other methods for assessing HRQoL, see Dolan, "The Measurement of Health-Related Quality of Life for Use in Resource Allocation in Health Care."

14. The TTO method was first proposed by G. W. Torrance, W. H. Thomas, and D. L. Sackett, "A Utility Measurement Method for Evaluation of Health Care Programs," *Health Services Research* 7(2) 1972, 118–133.

15. Paul Dolan and Peep Stalmeier, "The Validity of Time Trade-Off Values in Calculating QALYs: Constant Proportional Time Trade-Off versus the Proportional Heuristic," *Journal of Health Economics* 22(3) 2003, 445–458.

16. The general SG method was introduced by John von Neumann and Oskar Morgenstern, *Theory of Games and Economic Behavior* (Princeton, NJ: Princeton University Press, 1944).

17. See, for example, J. L. Read, R. J. Quinn, D. M. Berrick, H. V. Fineberg, and M. L. Weinstein, "Preferences for Health Outcomes: Comparisons of Assessment Methods," *Medical Decision Making* 4(3) 1984, 315–329; and George W. Torrance, "Social Preferences for Health States: An Empirical Evaluation of Three Measurement Techniques," *Socio-Economic Planning* 10(2) 1976, 129–136.

18. See, for example, Han Bleichrodt and Magnus Johannesson, "Standard Gamble, Time Trade-Off and Rating Scale: Experimental Results on Ranking Properties of QALYs," *Journal of Health Economics* 16(2) 1997, 155–175.

19. George W. Torrance, Michael H. Boyle, and Sargent P. Horwood, "Application of Multi-Attribute Utility Theory to Measure Social Preferences for Health Status," *Operations Research* 30(6) 1982, 1043–1069.

20. Additional information, including a bibliography of studies that have used the health utilities indices, can be found at, *www.healthutilities.com*.

21. John Horsman, William Furlong, David Feeny, and George Torrance, "The Health Utilities Index (HUI®): Concepts, Measurement Properties, and Applications," *Health Quality and Life Outcomes* 1(1) 2003, 54–67.

22. John E. Ware Jr. and Cathy D. Sherbourne, "The MOS 36-Item Short Form Health Survey: I. Conceptual Framework and Item Selection," *Medical Care* 30(6) 1992, 473–483.

23. See *www.qualitymetric.com/products/descriptions/sflicenses.shtml* for additional information.

24. John E. Ware Jr. and Barbara Gandek, "Overview of the SF-36 Health Survey Instrument and the International Quality of Life Assessment (IQOLA) Project," *Journal of Clinical Epidemiology* 51(11) 1998, 903–912.

25. John Brazier, Jennifer Roberts, and Mark Deverill, "The Estimation of a Preference-Based Measure of Health from the SF-36," *Journal of Health Eocnomics* 21(2) 2002, 271–292; and John Brazier, Tim Usherwood, Rosemary Harper, and Kate Thomas, "Deriving a Preference-Based Single Index from the UK SF-36 Health Survey," *Journal of Clinical Epidemiology* 51(11) 1998, 1115–1128.

26. John Brazier, Jennifer Roberts, and Mark Deverill, "The Estimation of a Preference-Based Measure of Health from the SF-36," Tables 5 and 6.

27. Richard Books and EuroQol Group, "EuroQol: The Current State of Play," *Health Policy* 37(1) 1996, 53–72. For current information about EuroQol and the EQ-5D index, see *www.euroqol.org/*.

28. See, for example, Paul Dolan, "Modelling Valuations for Health States: The Effect of Duration," *Health Policy* 38(3), 189–203.

29. Louise Longworth and Stirling Bryan, "An Empirical Comparison of EQ-5D and SF-6D in Liver Transplant Patients," *Health Economics* 12(12) 2003, 1061–1067.

30. Barbara Conner-Spady and Maria E. Suarez-Almazor, "Variation in the Estimation of Quality Adjusted Life-Years by Different Preference-Based Instruments," *Medical Care* 41(7) 2003, 791–801.

31. For more on the debate over how well different methods get at utility, see A. J. Culyer and Adam Wagstaff, "QALYs versus HYEs," *Journal of Health Economics* 11(3) 1993, 311–323; and Amiram Gafni, Stephen Birch, and Abraham Mehrez, "Economics, Health and Health Economics: HYEs versus QALYs," same issue, 325–329.

32. Emmett B. Keeler and Shan Cretin, "Discounting of Life-Saving and Other Nonmonetary Effects," *Management Science* 29(3) 1983, 300–306. However, this is not a paradox per se because, as we have shown, a CE ratio never tells us whether a project has positive social value and hence, should be implemented—whether this year or next year.

33. Amiram Gafni, "Time in Health: Can We Measure Individuals' 'Pure Time Preference'?" *Medical Decision Making* 15(1) 1995, 31–37; Donald A. Redelmeier, Daniel N. Heller, and Milton C. Weinstein, "Time Preference in Medical Economics: Science or Religion?" *Medical Decision Making* 13(3) 1993, 301–303; and Magnus Johannesson, Joseph Pliskin, and Milton C. Weinstein, "A Note on QALYs, Time Trade-off and Discounting," *Medical Decision Making* 14(2) 1994, 188–193.

34. Tammy O. Tengs, Miriam E. Adams, Joseph S. Pliskin, Dana Gelb-Safran, Joanna E. Seigel, Michael C. Weinstein, and John D. Graham, "Five-Hundred Life-Saving Interventions and Their Cost-Effectiveness," *Risk Analysis* 15(3) 1995, 369–390. For more on their methodology and policy implications, see Tammy O. Tengs and John D. Graham, "The Opportunity Costs of Haphazard Social Investment in Life-Saving," in Robert W. Hahn, ed., *Risks, Costs, and Lives Saved: Getting Better Results from Regulation* (New York and Oxford: Oxford University Press; Washington, D.C.: The AEI Press, 1996).

35. John F. Morrall III, "Saving Lives: A Review of the Record," *Journal of Risk and Uncertainty* 27(3) 2003, 221–237.

36. Gerard, "Cost-Utility in Practice," 274.

37. Josephine Mauskopf, Frans Rutten, and Warren Schonfeld, "Cost-Effectiveness League Tables: Valuable Guidance for Decision Makers?" *Pharmacoeconomics* 21(14) 2003, 991–1000.

CHAPTER 18

Distributionally Weighted Cost-Benefit Analysis

Government policies, programs, and projects typically affect individuals differently. Thus, in conducting CBAs, analysts often report benefits and costs for separate categories of people. The relevant classification of individuals into groups for this purpose depends on the specific policy under evaluation. Some examples include consumers versus producers versus taxpayers, program participants versus nonparticipants, citizens (of a nation or a state or a city) versus noncitizens, and high-income groups versus low-income groups. For reasons discussed in the chapter, the most common form of distributionally weighted CBA involves high-income versus low-income groups.

Once individuals are divided into categories, the first issue that must be decided is whether each group will be given standing in the CBA.[1] For example, in conducting a CBA of U.S. regulatory policy on acid rain, a decision must be made as to whether to give standing to Canadians affected by acid rain resulting from manufacturing in the United States.

Given a decision on standing, costs and benefits may be reported separately for each group with standing. The usefulness of doing this is illustrated by the following example, in which it is assumed that the government is considering proposals from three different companies for developing and operating an oil pipeline. The benefits and costs associated with each proposal may be presented in two ways. Table 18-1 breaks them down into their component parts; Table 18-2 indicates how three different groups would be affected by each proposal. Table 18-2 indicates that both producer surplus and government surplus would result from each proposal but that a third party composed of individuals who live near the pipeline would be worse off under all three proposals. (There is no consumer surplus in this illustration because it is assumed that the price of oil would be unaffected by the pipeline.) Table 18-2 also indicates that, although net social benefits would be similar under the proposals from Company A and B, there is a trade-off between them because the government would receive greater tax revenues under Company A's proposal, but residents would be better off under the proposal from Company B. Thus, Table 18-2 provides richer information than Table 18-1. But how is this information to be utilized in making a decision concerning the three proposals?

Throughout this book, we have emphasized use of the Kaldor-Hicks potential compensation test in reaching such decisions. In using this test, benefits and costs are simply summed across all groups that have standing to determine whether total

TABLE 18-1 Social Cost-Benefit Analysis of Alternative Pipeline Proposals

	Company A	*Company B*	*Company C*
Social benefits			
Revenues	4.00	4.00	4.00
Total benefits	4.00	4.00	4.00
Social costs			
Construction cost	1.88	1.98	2.36
Operating costs	1.20	1.25	1.50
Environmental cost of construction	0.20	0.20	0.20
Expected subsequent environmental costs	0.29	0.13	0.08
Total costs	3.57	3.56	4.14
Net social benefits	0.43	0.44	−0.14

TABLE 18-2 Social Cost-Benefit Analysis of Alternative Pipeline Proposals (Net Benefits to Each Affected Group)

	Company A	*Company B*	*Company C*
COMPANY			
Benefits			
Revenues	4.00	4.00	4.00
Costs			
Construction cost	1.88	1.98	2.36
Operating costs	1.20	1.25	1.50
Taxes	0.24	0.20	0.05
Expected firm environmental costs	0.18	0.08	0.05
Costs	3.50	3.51	3.96
Expected profit	**0.50**	**0.49**	**0.04**
RESIDENTS' COSTS			
Environmental cost of construction	0.20	0.20	0.20
Expected subsequent environmental costs	0.15	0.07	0.04
Less compensation received	−0.04	−0.02	−0.01
Cost to residents	**0.31**	**0.25**	**0.23**
GOVERNMENT REVENUES (TAXES)	**0.24**	**0.20**	**0.05**
Net social benefits	**0.43**	**0.44**	**−0.14**

benefits are larger than total costs and, hence, whether the policy should be adopted. Thus, this test examines benefits and costs from the perspective of society as a whole. Indeed, an implicit result of using the Kaldor-Hicks potential compensation test is that, with standing, it does not matter who receives the benefits from a government program or who pays the costs ("a dollar is a dollar regardless of who receives or pays it"), as long as there is a net gain to society as a whole—in other words, as long as the program is efficient in terms of potential Pareto improvement. Consistent use of the Kaldor-Hicks test means that information on how benefits and costs are distributed among groups is ignored in decision making. Thus, regardless of whether Table 18-1 or 18-2 is used to make a decision, the decision would be in favor of Company B's proposal.

In making actual policy decisions, however, the way in which benefits and costs are distributed among various groups is important. Quite often, this consideration can have an influence over whether a policy is politically acceptable. For example, effects on local residents may have more influence than the same amount of funds added to government revenue. Hence, a dollar received or expended by a member of one group may not be treated as equal to a dollar received or expended by a member of another group.

In this chapter, we focus on the role of the distribution of benefits and costs among groups in using CBA for decision making.[2] We first examine the economic rationale for treating dollars received or expended by various groups differently in CBA. We then consider approaches for doing this in practice.

DISTRIBUTIONAL JUSTIFICATIONS FOR INCOME TRANSFER PROGRAMS

The rationale suggested by economists for treating dollars received or expended by various groups differently in CBA is mainly limited to situations in which low-income persons are helped (or hurt) by a program more than other persons.[3] Political decision makers may treat dollars received or expended by various other groups differently, even if their income levels are similar. They may, for example, be influenced by differences among groups in voting behavior or campaign contributions. Economists, however, typically argue for treating dollars received or expended by various groups similarly unless they differ in terms of income or wealth.[4] Consequently, in the remainder of this chapter, we focus on CBAs of policies that have differential effects on groups that differ by income—for example, projects that are located in underdeveloped regions or programs that are targeted at disadvantaged persons.

To illustrate such policies, consider a program that taxes high-income persons in order to provide income transfers to low-income persons. The tax component of this program is illustrated in Figure 18-1. For purposes of discussion, assume that the market represented in this graph is for a luxury good, such as yachts, that is purchased only by the rich. In the absence of the tax, equilibrium in this market would occur at a price of P_1 and a quantity of Q_1. If an excise tax of t is levied against each unit of output, then the supply curve would shift up by this amount as suppliers attempt to pass along to consumers the additional cost the tax imposes upon them.

Using the approach implied by the Kaldor-Hicks rule, a distributional analysis of the costs and benefits associated with this tax would look like this:

	Benefits	*Costs*
Producers		$C + D$
Consumers		$A + B$
Transfer recipients	$A + C$	
Society		$B + D$

FIGURE 18-1 An Excise Tax on a Luxury Good

Source: Adapted from Arnold C. Harberger, "On the Use of Distributional Weights in Social Cost-Benefit Analysis," *Journal of Political Economy* 86(2) 1978, S87–S120; Figure 1, p. S89.

Thus, a deadweight loss equal to areas $B + D$ would result from the tax. In addition to this deadweight loss, two off-graph social costs also result from our transfer program:

1. Administering both the tax and the transfer parts of the program requires the use of social resources.
2. Some of those receiving the transfer will probably work less or stop working entirely, thereby reducing the goods and services available to society. In fact, there is considerable evidence that this is exactly what occurs under existing welfare programs.[5] Only part of this loss would be offset by the gains in leisure to transfer recipients (see Chapter 11). The remaining residual is a second source of deadweight loss.

It should be obvious that this program does not pass the Kaldor-Hicks test. It must instead be justified on distributional grounds. In other words, one would have to argue that giving a low-income person a dollar warrants taking more than a dollar away from a higher-income person. Apparently, this distributional argument has some force because programs such as AFDC and food stamps, which transfer income from higher-income to lower-income persons, do in fact exist. Hence, it appears that society is willing to sacrifice some efficiency in order to provide assistance to low-income persons.

The importance of this for CBA analysis is that it implies that, in practice, a dollar of benefits received or a dollar of costs incurred by a low-income individual is sometimes given greater weight in assessing government programs than a dollar of benefits received or a dollar of costs incurred by a higher-income individual. How can this be justified?

THE CASE FOR TREATING LOW- AND HIGH-INCOME GROUPS DIFFERENTLY IN CBA

The economics literature contains at least three arguments for giving dollars received or paid by low-income persons greater weight in CBA than dollars received or paid by higher-income persons:

1. Income has diminishing marginal utility.
2. The income distribution should be more equal.
3. The "one person, one vote" principle should apply.

We discuss each of these arguments in turn.

Diminishing Marginal Utility of Income

The first argument is based on the standard assumption in economics that each additional dollar an individual receives provides less utility than the preceding dollar. A corollary of this assumption is that a dollar received or a dollar of cost incurred by a high-income person has less of an impact on his or her utility than it would on a low-income person's utility. For that reason, the argument suggests, it should count less in a CBA.[6]

This argument can be summarized algebraically as follows:

$$\Delta u_l / \Delta y_l > \Delta u_h / \Delta y_h \tag{18.1}$$

where $\Delta u_i / \Delta y_i$ is the marginal private utility of income of individual i, l indicates a low-income person, and h a high-income person.

Income Distribution Should Be More Equal

The second argument for giving dollars received or paid by the poor greater weight in CBA than dollars received or paid by the rich is premised on the assertion that the current income distribution is less equal than it should be and social welfare would be higher if it were more equal.[7] There are several possible bases for such an assertion. The first is that a highly unequal distribution of income may result in civil disorder, crime, and riots. More equality in income may reduce these threats to the general social welfare. Second, it can be argued that some minimum threshold of income exists that is so low that no one can (or, to preserve human dignity, should have to) live below it. This suggests that the income distribution be made more equal by truncating it at the minimum threshold through income floors. Third, some relatively well-off persons may receive utility if the circumstances facing the worse-off members of society at the bottom of the income distribution improve. Certain types of charitable giving, such as contributions to the Salvation Army, provide evidence for the existence of this form of altruism. Finally, it is possible that some persons value greater income equality in and of itself.[8]

If for any of these reasons society prefers greater income equality than currently exists, then a dollar increase in the income of a low-income person would result in a larger increase in the welfare of society as a whole than would a dollar increase in the income of a high-income person. Note that this would still be true even if the marginal utility of income was not diminishing and, consequently, a dollar increase in the income of high- and low-income persons resulted in equal increases in the utilities of these persons. Each of the justifications listed in the previous paragraph suggests that society as a whole (or at least some relatively well-off members of society) becomes better off if those at the bottom of the income distribution gain relative to those in the rest of the distribution. Thus, the first and second arguments are distinct from one another.

Stated algebraically, the second argument implies that:

$$\Delta SW/\Delta y_l > \Delta SW/\Delta y_h, \text{ even if } \Delta u_1/\Delta y_l = \Delta u_h/\Delta y_h \qquad \textbf{(18.2)}$$

where ΔSW refers to the change in aggregate social welfare and $\Delta SW/\Delta y_i$ is the marginal effect on social welfare of a change in income that is received by individual i.[9]

This argument confronts the Kaldor-Hicks test quite directly. It implies that some projects or programs that fail the Kaldor-Hicks test should nonetheless be adopted if they redistribute income in a way that makes the income distribution more equal. In other words, the argument suggests that some programs that are inefficient should be undertaken if they increase income equality sufficiently. This also implies that some projects that make the income distribution less equal should not be undertaken, even though the Kaldor-Hicks test implies that they are efficient.

The "One Person, One Vote" Principle

This argument begins by noting that the benefits and costs of government programs to consumers are appropriately measured as changes in consumer surplus. Then it goes on to point out that because high-income persons have more income to spend than low-income persons, the measured impacts of policies on their consumer surplus will typically be larger and, hence, will be of greater consequence in a CBA based strictly on the Kaldor-Hicks rule.

This is illustrated by Figure 18-2, which compares the demand schedules of a typical high-income consumer and a typical low-income consumer for a good. If the good is a *normal good,* that is, if demand for the good increases as income increases, then the demand schedule of the high-income consumer will be to the right of that of

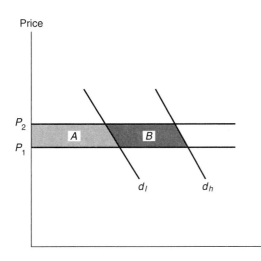

FIGURE 18-2   Changes in Consumer Surplus for High- and Low-Income Consumers

the low-income consumer, as the diagram shows. If a government policy increases the price of the good, say from P_1 to P_2, both consumers will bear the cost of that increase in the form of a loss in consumer surplus. However, the loss suffered by the high-income consumer (areas $A + B$) will be greater than the loss borne by the low-income consumer (area A alone). As a result, a CBA will give more weight to the impact of the policy on the high-income consumer than on the low-income consumer.

The final part of the argument suggests that in a democracy low-income persons should have as much influence over decisions on whether to undertake public projects as high-income persons. In other words, it is argued that "since the principle of 'one person, one vote' is deeply embedded in the concept of democracy," measures of changes in consumer surplus for different persons should be adjusted to what they would be if everyone had the same income.[10] For example, we would count the impact of the price change on the low-income person represented in the diagram at about double what we would count the impact on the high-income person, in effect, equalizing the "votes" of the two individuals.[11]

DISTRIBUTIONAL WEIGHTS

In principle, various groups can be treated differently in a CBA by using *distributional weights*. Distributional weights are just numbers—such as 1, 2, or 1.5—that are intended to reflect the value placed on each dollar paid out or received by each group. Table 18-3 compares standard and distributionally weighted CBA for two projects affecting two income groups. In standard CBA, as shown in the upper panel of the table, both groups receive an equal weight of 1. In distributionally weighted CBA, Group B (the higher-income group) is given a value of 1, while Group A (the lower-income group) is given a value of 3, implying that a dollar received by a member of the low-income group is valued in the CBA at three times that of a dollar received by a member of the high-income group. Given this weighting, as shown in the lower panel, project selection switches from Project I to Project II.

TABLE 18-3   Standard versus Distributionally Weighted CBA

1. Standard CBA

	Net Benefits		
	---	---	---
Projects	**Group A**	**Group B**	**Aggregate Net Social Benefits**
I	10	50	60
II	20	30	50
Weights	1	1	Selection: Project I

2. Distributionally Weighted CBA

	Net Benefits		
	---	---	---
Projects	**Group A**	**Group B**	**Aggregate Net Social Benefits**
I	$10 \times 3 = 30$	50	80
II	$20 \times 3 = 60$	30	90
Weights	3	1	Selection: Project II

Proposed mergers that appear likely to result in price increases are not allowed in the United States, but they are permitted in Canada if the potential gains in efficiency are deemed sufficient. Viewed somewhat differently, mergers are permitted in Canada if potential gains in producer surplus seem to offset potential losses in consumer surplus resulting from price increases, but such mergers are not permitted in the United States. Thomas Ross and Ralph Winter point out that this is equivalent to giving producer and consumer surplus equal distributional weights in Canada, but giving consumer surplus a greater weight than producer surplus in the United States. Indeed, producer surplus is, in effect, given a weight of zero in the United States. One rationale for the U.S. approach might be that producers (e.g., corporative stockholders) tend to be wealthier than consumers, but Ross and Winter argue that this need not always be the case (e.g., consider the markets for luxury goods) and, even if it is, distributional weights should be based on the actual wealth or income of individuals, not on whether they happen to be classified as "producers" or "consumers" in the case of a particular merger.

Source: Adapted from Thomas W. Ross and Ralph A. Winter, "The Efficiency Defense in Merger Law: Economic Foundations and Recent Canadian Developments," paper in progress (Vancouver, B.C.: University of British Columbia, 2004).

More formally, distributional weights can be incorporated into a CBA through a slight modification of the net present value (*NPV*) formula:

$$NPV = \sum_{j=1}^{m} \left[W_j \sum_{t=0}^{\infty} \frac{b_{t,j} - c_{t,j}}{(1+r)^t} \right] \tag{18.3}$$

where W_j is the distributional weight for group j, $b_{t,j}$ are the benefits received by group j in period t, $c_{t,j}$ are the costs imposed on group j in period t, m is the number of groups, and r is the social discount rate.

The idea behind this formula is simple. The persons affected by the government policy are divided into as many groups as seems appropriate. Each group is then given a distributional weight. The *NPV* for each group is then computed and multiplied by its weight. These weighted *NPV*s are then added together to obtain an overall *NPV*. Note that in CBAs that rely strictly on the Kaldor-Hicks rule, W_j is implicitly set equal to 1 for all groups. On the other hand, W_j is set to 0 for any group that is not given standing.

DETERMINING DISTRIBUTIONAL WEIGHTS

The obvious difficulty with implementing this approach is determining appropriate weight for each group. The weights should, of course, be consistent with the rationale for using them. However, of the three arguments for using weights presented earlier, only the one based on the one person, one vote principle suggests an approach that could potentially be used in practice for valuing the weights of various groups, and even in this case, the information requirements are substantial. Among the required information is the average income level of each relevant group, an estimate of the *income elasticity of demand* for each good affected by the government policy being evaluated (i.e., the percentage change in the quantity demanded of each good that results from a 1 percent increase in income), and an estimate of the market demand curve for each affected good. Given this information, the consumer surplus of the average member of each group can then be computed. These estimates can, in turn, be used to derive distributional weights for each group that are consistent with the one person, one vote principle.[12]

To develop weights that are consistent with the remaining two arguments, information is needed on $\Delta u/\Delta y$ (the marginal private utility of income) and $\Delta SW/\Delta y$ (the marginal effect on social welfare of a change in income) for a typical member of each group of interest. For example, a set of distributional weights could be developed that is consistent with the diminishing marginal utility of income argument if we knew that a $100 increase in income increased the utility of rich people by two units and the utility of poor people by three units by simply computing weights on the basis of the ratio of the marginal utility values. Thus, W_j would be set equal to 1 for rich persons and to 1.5 for poor persons. Similarly, a set of distributional weights that is consistent with the argument that the income distribution should be more equal could be developed if we knew that a $100 increase in the income of a typical poor person increased social welfare by two units, but the same increase in the income of a typical rich person increased social welfare by only one unit.

Unfortunately, such information is not available, nor is there any known way to obtain it. First, utility is a subjective concept that defies cardinal measurement.[13] Indeed, many economists eschew any explicit interpersonal comparisons of utility for this reason. But in the absence of interpersonal comparisons of utility, it is not possible to develop a system of relative distributional weights that is consistent with

---

EXHIBIT 18-2

Whether a dollar of benefits or costs is valued higher in poor developing countries than in a richer developed countries has important implications for international environmental agreements. For example, in the absence of weighting, the per capita benefits of an agreement to reduce global climate change by restricting emissions of fossil fuel would be smaller in a poor country than in a rich country. One reason for this is that when based on willingness-to-pay, the value of a statistical life is smaller in the poor country simply because of differences in ability to pay. Without weighting, the per capita dollar costs of restricting emissions in a poor country (for example, job losses) would also be smaller than in a rich country. A recent analysis by Christian Azar, which uses a cost-benefit framework, found that, as compared to a situation in which weighting is not used, the use of weighting greatly reduces emissions that rich countries should be allowed relative to those that poor countries should be permitted.

Source: Adapted from Christian Azar, "Weight Factors in Cost-Benefit Analysis of Climate Change," *Environmental and Resource Economics* 13(3) 1999, 249–268.

the diminishing marginal utility of income argument. Second, no general consensus among members of society exists concerning the specific relationship between a given change in the income levels of individuals and social welfare, except that most persons would, perhaps, agree that the relation is positive and its magnitude is larger for low-income than for high-income persons. Without such a consensus, however, it is not possible to develop distributional weights that are consistent with the greater income equality argument.[14]

POLITICALLY DETERMINED WEIGHTS

Given these problems in deriving distributional weights, how can distributional issues be handled in CBA? One possibility is to use contingent valuation techniques to determine distributional weights. Distributional weights, after all, can be viewed as a type of shadow price—an effort to measure benefits and costs in terms of their true social value. To the best of our knowledge, however, no attempt has been made to do this. If such an attempt were made, it would be subject to the limitations of contingent valuation described in Chapter 14.

Another approach is to derive distributional weights on the basis of revealed political behavior.[15] For example, Otto Eckstein suggested that marginal income tax rates might be used to determine weights for different income classes.[16] For instance, families with annual incomes between $15,000 and $30,000 face a marginal tax rate of 15 percent under the U.S. income tax, whereas families with incomes over $30,000 face a marginal tax rate of between 28 and 33 percent. One might infer that in establishing these tax rates society, or at least Congress, felt that at the margin taxing away 15 cents from a low-income person was as painful as taxing away around 30 cents from a higher-income person. Taking this one step farther, one could infer that the political process has implied that dollars paid out or received by moderate-income families under a government program should be weighted twice as heavily as dollars paid out or received by families at the top of the income distribution.

Although weighting schemes based on tax rates have been used in CBA, such schemes raise serious issues.[17] One problem is that tax rates do not reflect only what Congress thinks the relative value of a dollar to different income groups should be. For example, Congress may be worried about setting tax rates too high because of concern that high rates will create work and investment disincentives. In addition, Congress may use the progressive federal income tax to offset the fact that other taxes, such as state sales taxes, tend to be regressive. Indeed, it might be better to base weighting schemes on the total tax system than on the federal income tax alone.

An alternative to using marginal tax rates to derive distributional weights is to use public expenditure decisions instead.[18] To illustrate, consider two projects, A and B. If project A has a higher *NPV* than project B—that is, $NPV^A > NPV^B$—yet project A is rejected and B is undertaken, then this suggests that decision makers must have viewed project B as at least as desirable as project A on nonefficiency grounds. One possible explanation is that project B provides greater net gains to low-income persons than does project A (that is, $NPV_l^A < NPV_l^B$), while higher-income persons would be better off under project A ($NPV_h^A > NPV_h^B$).

If these conditions hold and the values of NPV_l^A, NPV_l^B, NPV_h^A, and NPV_h^B are known, then it is possible to obtain distributional weights by solving the following two simultaneous equations for W_l and W_h:[19]

$$W_l NPV_l^A + W_h NPV_h^A = NPV^A$$

$$W_l NPV_l^B + W_h NPV_h^B = NPV^A \qquad \text{(18.4)}$$

The second equation is based on the premise that, because decision makers selected project B over project A even though NPV^A was actually larger than NPV^B, they must have implicitly used a set of weights that allowed them to treat project B *as if* it had an *NPV* that was *at least as* high as NPV^A. The weights are derived by treating the two projects as if, once weighted, they were of exactly equal value in the eyes of the decision makers.

The estimates of W_l and W_h should provide a reasonable approximation of the implicit weights that decision makers used in deciding between the two projects. Unfortunately, however, the estimates may reflect factors other than only the concern of decision makers over the trade-off between efficiency and distributional equity. Considerations related to electoral prospects, for example, may have been more important in making the decision. Moreover, if different projects were used in obtaining the weights, the estimated weights would probably differ.

A final approach to estimating weights is to use experiments with real resources to test preferences for redistribution. One type of experimental game places subjects behind a "veil of ignorance" where they have to decide the rules for allocating goods before they have any knowledge as to their share. Their ignorance is presumed to help produce "impartial reasoning" about their preferences for distributional weights. In one set of such experiments, most subjects preferred allocations that provided everyone with at least a minimum level of income, suggesting that they favored at least minimal redistribution.[20] Another type of experimental game that can be used to get a sense of distributional weights are *dictator games*. In this type of game, the first player unilaterally decides on the split of a fixed pie between the first player and a second player. Although allocations vary widely, depending on specific game contexts, the evidence suggests that fairness matters, but that it is complex: "Apparently, a player does not care about the other's welfare per se, but desires some kind of equity in the context of this particular interaction."[21]

A PRAGMATIC APPROACH TO WEIGHTING

Given the enormous practical problems with obtaining a defensible set of distributional weights, we suggest that their use be limited to only those CBAs where distributional issues are of central concern (for example, CBAs of programs targeted at disadvantaged groups or at impoverished areas within countries, states, or cities) or CBAs of policies that explicitly treat different income groups differently (for example, a CBA of a plan to store radioactive waste in a low income area). Even then, it may be possible to use an approach that highlights the importance of the distributional implications associated with the policy being analyzed without requiring that any particular set of distributional weights be selected as the "correct" set.

To illustrate the particular approach that we suggest using to do this, we return to the Work/Welfare Initiative Demonstrations first described in Chapter 11. As indicated there, these demonstrations were run in a randomized experimental setting during the 1980s to determine the impacts of various combinations of job search, education, training, and subsidized jobs for AFDC recipients. Because these experimental programs were targeted at welfare recipients—an especially disadvantaged low-income group—both their distributional effects and their effects on economic efficiency are relevant. Thus, CBAs of the Work/Welfare Initiative Demonstrations should take both types of effects into account.

Displaying Unweighted Cost and Benefit Estimates

The first step in taking account of both the efficiency and distributional effects of the Work/Welfare Initiative Demonstrations is simply to display unweighted program impacts on society as a whole, as well as on pertinent subgroups. This is accomplished in the first three columns in Table 18-4, which simply duplicate the total net present value estimates for the Work/Welfare Initiative Demonstrations that were originally reported in Table 11-4.[22] Column 1 reports these estimates from the perspective of program participants, column 2 from the perspective of nonparticipants, and column 3 (which is computed by summing the first two columns) from the perspective of society as a whole.

None of the estimates reported in the first three columns of Table 18-4 are weighted. *Even when distributional weighting is used, unweighted estimates of benefits and costs for society as a whole should always be provided in CBAs. In addition, whenever distributional considerations are important, benefit and cost estimates for relevant subgroups should also be provided* if it is feasible to do so.

The unweighted *NPV* estimates reported in the first three columns of Table 18-4 have two especially important implications. First, they indicate that almost all the Work/Welfare Demonstration programs pass the Kaldor-Hicks test. Specifically, 16 of the 19 unweighted *NPV* estimates for society as a whole, which appear in column 3, are positive. Second, in 6 of the 16 cases that pass the Kaldor-Hicks test, program participants were apparently made worse off by the tested program, while nonparticipants—a group who, on average, enjoys substantially higher incomes than participants—were made better off. In these instances, a trade-off occurs between economic efficiency and distributional considerations. (A similar trade-off would also arise if a program failed the Kaldor-Hicks test, but participants were made better off. However, this situation did not arise in any of the Work/Welfare Demonstrations, but as shown earlier, it does in the case of income transfer programs.) *It is only when a policy or program change results in a trade-off between efficiency and equality in the income or wealth distribution that distributional weighting is relevant. It is not needed in the case of a "win-win change" (i.e., both efficiency and progressivity improve) or a "lose-lose change" (both efficiency and progressivity decline).*[23] Table 18-4 displays ten win-win changes and three lose-lose changes, as well as the six trade-off changes.

Conducting Sensitivity Tests

Column 4 tests whether the estimates reported in column 3 of Table 18.4 are sensitive to the choice of distributional weights. Thus, in contrast to the unweighted figures appearing in column 3, which are based on the assumption that society values the gains and losses of AFDC recipients and nonrecipients equally, those appearing in column 4 assume that

TABLE 18-4 Sensitivity of the Work/Welfare Initiative Demonstration Estimates to the Use of Distributional Weights (in 2003 dollars)

	NPV from Participant Perspective (1)	NPV from Nonparticipant Perspective (2)	Unweighted Social NPV [Col 1 + Col 2] (3)	NPV If Participant Distributional Weight = 2 [2 × Col 1 + Col 2] (4)	Estimates of Internal Weights for Participants [Col 2/Col 1] (5)
AFDC-R					
Applicants Only					
San Diego					
EPP/EWEP					
Job search only	$1,185	$830	$2,015	$3,200	NA
Job search/CWEP	1,468	2,127	3,595	5,063	NA
San Diego SWIM	(1,471)	2,731	1,260	(211)	1.86
Virginia	2,000	1,176	3,176	5,176	NA
West Virginia	(848)	686	(162)	(1,010)	NA
Recipients Only					
San Diego SWIM	1,213	2,840	4,053	5,266	NA
Virginia	1,013	334	1,347	2,360	NA
West Virginia	141	1,539	1,680	1,821	NA
New Jersey	2,110	1,787	3,897	6,007	NA
Maine	5,419	(713)	4,706	10,125	NA
Applicants and Recipients					
Cook County					
Job search only	(701)	794	93	(608)	1.13
Job search/CWEP	(56)	606	551	494	10.80
Baltimore	3,067	130	3,197	6,264	NA
Arkansas	(792)	1,665	872	81	2.10
AFDC-U					
Applicants Only					
San Diego					
EPP/EWEP:					
Job search only	(2,200)	2,261	61	(2,139)	1.03
Job search/CWEP	(2,656)	2,600	(56)	(2,712)	NA
San Diego SWIM	909	2,636	3,544	4,454	NA
Recipients Only					
San Diego SWIM	(1,540)	4,154	2,614	1,074	2.70
Applicants and Recipients					
Baltimore	(2,174)	(3,274)	(5,448)	(7,622)	NA

NA: Not Applicable
( ): The parentheses indicate negative net gains or increases in transfer payment amounts.
Source for columns 1–3: Table 11.4.

the gains and losses of AFDC recipients are valued by society at twice those of nonrecipients. In other words, participants are given a distributional weight of 2 and nonparticipants a weight of 1. Although these weights are obviously arbitrary—as previously stressed, we do not know the actual relative values that society places on dollars received and paid out by participants and nonparticipants—in our judgment, it seems likely that they overstate society's generosity toward AFDC recipients and thus test whether the net social gain and loss estimates are sensitive to a rather extreme assumption.

A comparison of columns 3 and 4 indicates that this assumption causes ten of these estimates to become larger and nine smaller. More importantly, however, only three change sign. Although all three of these sign changes are from positive to negative, thereby turning a net gain into net loss, in two cases the originally estimated net gain was well under $100. Hence, it appears that conclusions concerning whether most of the Work/Welfare Initiative Demonstrations listed in the table were cost-beneficial to society are not very sensitive to the choice of distributional weights.

Computing Internal Weights

Column 5 in Table 18-4 is based on the computation of *internal weights,* an alternative to the approach used in column 4 for distributional weighting. This scheme works best if there are just two pertinent groups, one of which is relatively disadvantaged (e.g., participants in the Work/Welfare Demonstrations) and the other relatively advantaged (e.g., nonparticipants in the demonstrations).

Internal distributional weights are derived by first setting the weight for the advantaged group equal to unity and then computing the weight for the disadvantaged group by dividing the estimated *NPV* for the advantaged group by the estimated *NPV* for the disadvantaged group. The idea is similar to that behind the computation of internal rates of return. Instead of somehow selecting weights, one finds the weights at which the program being analyzed would just break even; in other words, the weights at which the *NPV* for society as a whole would equal zero. Viewed a bit differently, the internal weight for the disadvantaged group indicates the dollars of costs incurred by the advantaged group per dollar of benefits received by the disadvantaged group if the former is made worse off by the program and the latter better off, or the dollars of benefits received by the advantaged group per dollar of costs incurred by the disadvantaged group if the former is made better off and the latter worse off.

In Table 18-4, we compute internal weights for Work/Welfare Demonstration participants by dividing column 2 by column 1. We do this, however, only when the program results in a trade-off between efficiency and distribution (that is, when column 1 and column 3 are of the opposite sign). In the case of win-win or lose-lose changes (i.e., when columns 1 and 3 are both positive or both negative), a trade-off between efficiency and distribution does not exist and, consequently, distributional weighting is not germane. As trade-off changes occurred in only six instances in the Work/Welfare Demonstration estimates, only six internal weights for program participants appear in column 5.

Each of these six values indicates the weight at which a demonstration program would just break even. Thus, if the "true" weight for participants is larger than their internal weight, programs with positive unweighted (or standard) social *NPV*s would fail to break even once their distributional implications were taken into account, and programs with negative unweighted social *NPV*s would more than break even. However, because the "true" weight for participants is unknown, policy makers would have to make a judgmental decision as to whether dollars of benefits or costs to participants should be given a higher or lower value than that implied by the computed internal weights. Indeed, a major advantage of internal weighting is that it makes the trade-off between efficiency and distribution explicit for policy makers.

For example, in all six of the cases for which internal weights are computed in Table 18-4, program participants were worse off under the demonstration programs, but the unweighted (standard) social *NPV* estimate was positive. Thus, all six programs pass the Kaldor-Hicks test, even though they make the distribution of income less equal. If policy makers believed that dollars lost to participants in the Work/Welfare Demonstrations should be valued at, say, 25 percent more than dollars gained by non-participants, then this would imply that two of these six programs failed to break even and, hence, should be discontinued even though they passed the Kaldor-Hicks test. If they instead valued dollars lost to participants at three times more than dollars gained by nonparticipants, then this would imply that five of the six programs failed to break even. Thus, they would conclude that five of the programs that passed the Kaldor-Hicks test actually had a negative payoff once their adverse effects on the income distribution were taken into account. But is a weight for participants as high as 3 plausible? We consider this issue next.

Obtaining Upper-Bound Values for Distributional Weights

It was pointed out earlier in this chapter that pure transfer programs inevitably fail the Kaldor-Hicks test because each dollar of transfer benefits costs nonrecipients more than a dollar. However, it has been argued that transfer programs can be used as a standard to which other types of programs that redistribute income can be compared.[24] Specifically, the argument suggests that if a nontransfer program makes the disadvantaged better off but results in a loss of efficiency, then it should not be accepted if a transfer program that results in a smaller loss in efficiency can potentially be used instead. By the same token, if a nontransfer program makes the disadvantaged worse off but results in gains in efficiency, then it should be accepted if there is a transfer program that can potentially compensate the disadvantaged for their losses without fully offsetting the gains in efficiency from the nontransfer program.

This approach requires that internal weights that are derived similarly to the six values that appear in the last column of Table 18-4 be obtained for transfer programs. This has been done by Edward Gramlich, who estimates that it costs taxpayers approximately $1.50 to $2.00 to transfer a dollar to a recipient under a transfer program.[25] As Gramlich suggests, although these estimates should be considered rough and tentative, if one accepts them as being of the right order of magnitude, then it can be argued that distributional weights for the disadvantaged should never be set above one and a half to two times the weight for the advantaged.

Consider, for example, a nontransfer program that has a negative unweighted net present value, although it makes the poor better off. More specifically, assume the program costs the advantaged $2.50 for every dollar of benefits received by the disadvantaged. Gramlich's estimates imply that every dollar received by the disadvantaged under a transfer program would cost the advantaged only $1.50 to $2.00. Thus, in principle, the transfer program could be used instead to make the disadvantaged just as well off as under the nontransfer program but at a lower cost to the advantaged. Thus, not only does the nontransfer program have a negative unweighted social *NPV*, it is inferior to a simple transfer program for redistributing income to the disadvantaged.

Now consider a different program that provides the advantaged $2.50 of benefits for every dollar of costs incurred by the disadvantaged. Under these circumstances, each dollar lost under the program by the disadvantaged could, in principle, be reimbursed through a transfer program at a cost to the advantaged of only $1.50 to $2.00. Hence, this program not only has a positive unweighted social *NPV,* the disadvantaged also can be compensated for their losses without completely offsetting the gains in efficiency from the program.

The argument just presented implies that distributional weights assigned to the disadvantaged should not exceed 1.5 or 2 in value if the value for the advantaged is set to 1. Larger weights would imply acceptance of inefficient programs that are also inferior to simple transfer programs for redistributing income and rejection of efficient programs that allow the advantaged to enjoy net gains even when the disadvantaged could be fully compensated through income transfers for losses they suffer. Thus, the argument suggests that the two programs in Table 18-4 that have internal weights well in excess of 2 should definitely be accepted, while the two that have internal weights that are close to 2 should probably also be accepted, even though all four programs have adverse effects on the income distribution.

Note, however, that this argument is very similar in spirit to the one underlying the Kaldor-Hicks rule. Both are based on the *potential* use of transfer payments to compensate losers under a policy, while leaving winners better off than they would be in the absence of the policy. Nothing, however, requires that these income transfers actually be made.

CONCLUSION

This chapter focuses on the use of distributional weighting to take account of the fact that many policies have divergent impacts on different income groups. Given the absence of generally accepted sets of distributional weights, we suggest that the use of distributional weights should be limited to policies that meet both of the following conditions: (1) they are targeted at the disadvantaged or treat the advantaged and the disadvantaged differently, and (2) they result in reductions in overall social efficiency but make low-income persons better off, or they increase social efficiency but make low-income persons worse off.

There may, in fact, be relatively few policies that meet both of these conditions. Those policies that do might be subjected to sensitivity tests based on a plausible range of weights. Or alternatively, internal weights might be computed, thereby providing policy makers with information on which to base their choice of distributional weights. In either case, however, a cogent argument can be made for not allowing the distributional weights for low-income groups to be set much more than 50 to 100 percent above those for higher-income groups.

EXERCISES FOR CHAPTER 18

1. A city is about to build a new sanitation plant. It is considering two sites, one located in a moderately well-to-do neighborhood and the other in a low-income neighborhood. Indeed, most of the residents in the latter neighborhood live below the poverty line. The city's sanitation engineer is adamant that "the city needs the new plant and it has to go somewhere." However, he is indifferent as to which neighborhood it is located in. The plant would

operate at the same cost and as efficiently in either neighborhood, and about as many people would be affected by the air pollution emitted by the plant. The city hires an economist to study the two sites. The economist finds that the plant would cause a considerably larger fall in average property values in the well-to-do neighborhood than in the low-income neighborhood, given the more expensive homes that are located in the former. Consistent with this, a contingent valuation study that the economist conducts finds that willingness-to-pay to avoid the sanitation plant is substantially higher in the well-to-do neighborhood than in the low-income neighborhood.

The residents of the poor neighborhood strongly prefer that the plant be built in the well-to-do neighborhood. In the face of the economist's findings, what sort of arguments might they make?

2. Cost-benefit analyses have been conducted for six proposed projects. None of these projects are mutually exclusive, and the agency has a sufficient budget to fund those that will make society better off. The following findings from the CBAs are summarized in millions of dollars:

	Net Social Benefits	Net Group I Benefits	Net Group II Benefits
Project A	$2	$2	$0
Project B	6	8	−2
Project C	4	12	−8
Project D	−1	−3	2
Project E	−2	−1	−1
Project F	−2	4	−6

Group I consists of households with annual incomes over $15,000, whereas Group II consists of households with annual incomes under $15,000.

a. According to the net benefit rule, which of these projects should be funded?
b. For which of the projects might distributional considerations be an issue?
c. Compute internal distributional weights for the projects you selected in part b. Using these weights, indicate the circumstances under which each project might actually be undertaken.
d. Recompute social net benefits for the six projects using a distributional weight of 1 for Group I and a distributional weight of 2 for Group II. Using these weight-adjusted net social benefit estimates, indicate the circumstances under which each project might actually be undertaken. In doing this, assume that the distributional weight for Group II is an upper bound—that is, it probably overstates society's true generosity toward low-income households.

Notes

1. For a further discussion of standing in CBA, see Chapter 2.
2. For a more general discussion of the role of distributional considerations in assessing policy initiatives, see Alphonse G. Holtmann, "Beyond Efficiency: Economics and Distributional Analysis," in David L. Weimer, ed., *Policy* *Analysis and Economics* (Boston, MA: Kluwer Academic Publishing, 1991), 45–64.
3. It would be better to distinguish among the persons or families affected by government programs in terms of their wealth (i.e., the value of their stock of assets), rather than in terms of their income (the observed flow of payments

they receive in exchange for the labor, capital, and land that they provide the production process). For example, two households may have similar incomes, but if one owns a house and the other does not, their standard of living may be quite different. However, income normally is used instead of wealth in categorizing individuals or families because it is more readily measured.

4. As discussed in Chapter 16, however, an exception sometimes occurs in the case of less-developed countries. Because of the paucity of funds for investment in such countries, some economists argue that each dollar of increase or reduction in savings that results from a project should count more heavily in conducting a CBA of the project than each dollar of increase or reduction in consumption. In principle, however, the relative importance of savings and consumption can be taken into account by using the shadow price of capital approach to discounting, which is described in Chapter 10.

5. See Robert Moffitt, "Incentive Effects of the U.S. Welfare System: A Review," *Journal of Economic Literature* 30(1) 1992, 1–61, and the references cited therein.

6. Martin Feldstein's discussion of technical issues in computing distributional weights is premised on this argument. See Martin S. Feldstein, "Distributional Equity and the Optimal Structure of Public Prices," *The American Economic Review* 62(1) 1972, 32–36.

7. Arnold Harberger's classical examination of distributional weighting ("On the Use of Distributional Weights in Social Cost-Benefit Analysis") can be viewed as a critical assessment of whether this assertion provides a basis for conducting distributionally weighted CBA.

8. These points are discussed in greater detail by Aidan R. Vining and David L. Weimer, "Welfare Economics as the Foundation for Public Policy Analysis: Incomplete and Flawed but Nevertheless Desirable," *The Journal of Socio-Economics* 21(1) 1992, 25–37. John Rawls, *A Theory of Justice* (Cambridge, MA: Harvard University Press, 1971), and others have provided a more philosophical basis than the reasons listed here for greater income equality.

9. The first two arguments can be derived more formally by specifying a social welfare function. To illustrate, we specify a very simple social welfare function in which individual utility depends upon

income, total social welfare depends upon a linear combination of individual utilities, and the possibility of interdependent utility (i.e., one person's utility being affected by the gains or losses of others) is ignored:

$$SW = f[u_1(y_1) \ldots, u_i(y_i) \ldots, u_n(y_n)]$$

where n is the total number of individuals in society. Totally differentiating the social welfare function yields the following expression:

$$dSW = \sum_{i=1}^{n} [(\partial SW/\partial u_i)(\partial u_i/\partial y_i) \, dy_i]$$

where dy_i represents the change in income resulting from a government policy. The first argument implies that $\partial u_l/\partial y_l > \partial u_h/\partial y_h$, while the second argument implies that $\partial SW/\partial u_l > \partial SW/\partial u_h$. Thus, together the two arguments imply that $(\partial SW/\partial u_l)(\partial u_l/\partial y_l) > (\partial SW/\partial u_h)(\partial u_h/\partial y_h)$.

10. D. W. Pearce, *Cost-Benefit Analysis,* 2nd ed. (New York: St. Martin's Press, 1983), 64–66.

11. From the perspective of social choice theory, this is a somewhat naive view of democracy. See William H. Riker, *Liberalism Against Populism* (San Francisco: Freeman, 1982).

12. For an illustration of how this might be done in practice, see Pearce, *Cost-Benefit Analysis,* p. 71.

13. For a brief overview, see Amartya Sen, *On Ethics and Economics* (New York: Basil Blackwell, 1987). For a more detailed discussion, see Robert Cooter and Peter Rappoport, "Were the Ordinalists Wrong About Welfare Economics?" *Journal of Economic Literature* 22(2) 1984, 507–530.

14. In principle, as implied by note 9, a set of weights that is consistent with both the diminishing marginal utility of income and the greater income equality arguments could be derived by simply setting them equal to $(\partial SW/\partial u)(\partial u/\partial y)$ for the average member of each group of interest and then dividing the resulting values for each group by the value for the highest income group. However, finding values for $(\partial SW/\partial u)(\partial u/\partial y)$ is subject to the same informational problems mentioned in the text. Moreover, the term itself was derived in note 9 by first arbitrarily specifying a simple social welfare function that did not allow for interdependencies in utility and in which social welfare depends upon a linear

combination of individual utilities. As noted in the text, general agreement on the form of the social welfare function does not exist. For example, utilities are probably interdependent and the social welfare function could very well be nonlinear.

15. Shlomo Yitzhaki has developed a method for deriving distributional weights from inequality indices commonly used by economists such as the Gini coefficient. He argues that doing this is appropriate because inequality indices are explicitly or implicitly based on a set of axioms concerning distribution and, hence, "by choosing an inequality measure the economist implicitly assumes distributional weights" (p. 326). Thus, Yitzhaki relies on the behavior of economists, rather than that of politicians. See Shlomo Yitzhaki, "Cost-Benefit Analysis and the Distributional Consequences of Government Projects," *National Tax Journal* 56(2) 2003, 319–336.

16. Otto Eckstein, "A Survey of the Theory of Public Expenditure Criteria," in James M. Buchanan, ed., *Public Finances: Needs, Sources and Utilization* (Princeton, NJ: Princeton University Press, 1961), 439–494.

17. For example, see Robert H. Haveman, *Water Resource Investment and the Public Interest* (Nashville, TN: Vanderbilt University, 1965); and V. C. Nwaneri, "Equity in Cost-Benefit Analysis: A Case Study of the Third London Airport," *Journal of Transport Economics and Policy* 4(3) 1970, 235–254.

18. This approach was first developed by Burton A. Weisbrod, "Income Redistribution Effects and Benefit-Cost Analysis," in S. B. Chase, ed., *Problems in Public Expenditure Analysis* (Washington, D.C.: The Brookings Institution, 1968), 177–208.

19. The empirical analysis in Weisbrod's 1968 paper is actually somewhat more complex than suggested in the text. For example, Weisbrod analyzed four water resource projects considered by the U.S. Corps of Engineers. Of these projects, the one with the highest estimated *NPV* was rejected, whereas the other three were accepted. Thus, Weisbrod used four equations to estimate weights for four separate subgroups (rich whites, poor whites, rich nonwhites, and poor nonwhites).

20. Norman Frohlich, Joe A. Oppenheimer, and Cheryl L. Eavey, "Choices of Principles of Distributive Justice in Experimental Groups," *American Journal of Political Science* 31(3) 1987, 606–636.

21. Colin Camerer and Richard H. Thaler, "Ultimatums, Dictators and Manners," *Journal of Economic Perspectives* 9(2) 1995, 209–219.

22. Table 11.4 also provides estimates of the individual benefit and cost components of the various Work/Welfare Demonstrations.

23. Shlomo Yitzhaki coined the terms "win-win reforms," "trade-off reforms," and "lose-lose reforms" to distinguish among the three types of reforms described in the text. See Shlomo Yitzhaki, "Cost-Benefit Analysis and the Distributional Consequences of Government Projects."

24. This argument was apparently first made by Arnold C. Harberger, "On the Use of Distributional Weights in Social Cost-Benefit Analysis," *Journal of Political Economy* 86(2) 1978, S87–S120.

25. Edward M. Gramlich *A Guide to Benefit-Cost Analysis,* 2nd ed. (Englewood Cliffs, NJ: Prentice Hall, 1990), 123–127. Gramlich bases his conclusion on his own "simple analysis" and on findings from a general equilibrium computer simulation conducted by Edgar Browning and William Johnson ("The Trade-Off between Equality and Efficiency," *Journal of Political Economy* 92[2] 1984, 175–203). Both analyses are examples of attempts to compute the marginal excess burden associated with taxes, which is discussed in Chapter 15.

CHAPTER 19

How Accurate is CBA?

Chapter 1 emphasized that CBA can be useful as a public-sector decision-making tool. In practice, its usefulness depends on its accuracy. One way to examine the accuracy of CBA is to perform analyses of the same project at different times and to compare the results. We suggested in Chapter 1 that *ex ante/ex post* comparisons and *ex ante/in medias res* comparisons are most valuable for learning about the accuracy of CBA. However, that discussion provided few details. We now return to this subject in more detail.[1]

An *ex ante* CBA is performed when the decision is made about whether to proceed with a proposed project. We refer to this time as year 0 or $t = 0$. An *ex post* analysis is performed after all the impacts of the implemented project have been realized. This may take many years, even centuries. Suppose that all impacts have occurred by year T; then an *ex post* analysis is one performed in year t, where $t \geq T$. Although an *ex post* analysis is conducted too late to influence a decision about this particular project, it offers insight into similar projects. An *in medias res* analysis is performed in some year t, where $0 < t < T$. An *in medias res* analysis may provide information about similar projects or about whether to continue or to terminate a particular project if not yet completed. Both *in medias res* and *ex post* analyses are performed in the same way as EA analysis but use data actually revealed from the project. As time passes, there is usually less uncertainty about impacts, and therefore, it is possible to obtain more accurate estimates of the actual *NPV* of the project.

Accuracy of CBA depends on how well the analyst performs the nine steps presented in Chapter 1. Each step is subject to errors. The most important ones for analysts and decision makers relate to specifying the impact categories, predicting the impacts, valuing the impacts and, for *in medias res* or *ex post* studies, incurring measurement error. Difficulties associated with the other steps, while they occur frequently enough, should be avoidable by analysts with a good training in the concepts of CBA. In this chapter, then, we consider only omission errors, forecasting errors, valuation errors, and measurement errors.

In general, these errors decline as CBAs are performed later, but they never reach zero. Thus, CBAs performed toward the end of a project are more accurate than those performed earlier, but even later studies contain errors. This chapter illustrates these errors in CBA by providing a detailed example of the highway project discussed in Chapter 1. This project has been the subject of three separate CBAs performed at different times—one *ex ante,* one *in medias res,* and one *ex post.*

The estimates of net benefits differ considerably across the studies. Contrary to what might have been expected, the largest source of the difference was not errors in forecasts or differences in evaluation of intangible benefits but major differences in declared and actual construction costs of the project. Thus, the largest errors arose from what most analysts would have thought were the most reliable figures entered into the CBA.

SOURCES OF ERRORS IN CBA STUDIES

Errors in CBA studies may arise for many reasons. They may result from the manager's bureaucratic lens, as we discussed in Chapter 1.[2] Some errors in CBA studies appear to be disingenuous or strategic, that is, resulting from self-interest. There is considerable evidence that managers systematically overestimate benefits and underestimate costs; see, for example, Exhibit 19-1.[3] Strategic bias of this sort is widespread among managers and does not appear to be limited to the public sector.[4] For example, Nancy Ryan found that nuclear power projects experienced "awe-inspiring" cost overruns, some attributable to strategic underestimation of costs.[5]

When CBAs are performed by independent analysts, as was the case for our highway example, one would not expect to encounter strategic bias. Consequently, this section focuses on other potential causes of errors.

Omission Errors

Analysts may exclude some impact category completely because they think it is too unlikely to occur. This problem is quite likely where a project is highly technical and there are genuine disagreements about the physical impacts. For example, much uncertainty surrounds the fundamental scientific relationships concerning global warming.[6] The scientific literature pertaining to many environmental issues, from dioxins to the marbled murrelet, is sparse or controversial. Analysts may find themselves in the middle of a "battle of the experts," not knowing with certainty the impacts of various policy alternatives. For our highway example, we would be surprised if there were significant problems of this sort.

EXHIBIT 19-1

Political and bureaucratic actors not only directly underestimate costs and overestimate benefits of their favored alternative, they also overestimate the costs and underestimate the benefits of alternatives they do not favor. John Kain documents the use of such "straw men" alternatives by Houston's regional transit authority in its consideration of a new urban light rail system. He shows how it made its preferred rail alternative appear better by "goldplating" the all-bus alternatives. For example, it overestimated the capital costs of the bus-way alternatives in one report by 70 percent.

Source: Adapted from John F. Kain, "The Use of Straw Men in the Economic Evaluation of Rail Transport Projects," *American Economic Review: Papers and Proceedings* 82(2) 1992, 487–493.

Double counting is the converse of omission and, consequently, can be considered in this section. One way analysts double count benefits is by including benefits that arise in both the primary and secondary markets, for example, including both time saved and increases in house prices. As discussed in Chapter 5, benefits (or costs) in secondary markets should not be included when prices equal social marginal costs.

Although omission errors may be present in a CBA conducted at any time, we expect these errors to decline over a project's life time. Undoubtedly, as a project progresses, more knowledge comes to light concerning the actual impact categories. Thus, omission errors are likely to be less frequent in CBAs performed later.

Forecasting Errors

Forecasting errors in CBA can arise from inherent difficulties (due, for example, to the difficulty of predicting technological change), cognitive biases, changing project specifications, and for strategic reasons. Forecasting beyond a few months is often inaccurate whatever the context.[7] The difficulty of accurate forecasting generally increases as projects are more complex, unique, farther in the future, and involve unknown cause-and-effect relationships.[8]

The impacts of some government projects are relatively easy to predict because they are of low complexity, are not unique, and are easily comparable to previous projects. Small road improvements, for example, typically fall into this category. In contrast, major projects such as the Big Dig, a large multi-tunnel construction

---

EXHIBIT 19-2

Steven Popper, Robert Lempert, and Steven Bankes are sufficiently concerned about forecasting errors resulting from uncertainty in the case of long-term, complex projects that they are attempting to develop an alternative to cost-benefit analysis. As discussed in Chapter 7, when there is uncertainty about which of several contingencies will be realized, one approach in CBA is to compare alternative policies by first estimating the benefits and costs of each under each contingency, then estimating the expected value for each alternative policy by using predicted probabilities of each contingency being realized, and finally selecting the alternative with the largest net expected values. Popper, Lempert, and Bankes suggest, in contrast to selecting the most optimal policy in terms of its net expected value, which under some contingencies may result in outcomes that are unsatisfactory, choosing a policy that yields "satisfactory" outcomes under all possible contingencies, even if this policy has a smaller expected value than another alternative. One reason they promote their approach is that they believe that under many circumstances the probabilities for each contingency cannot be accurately forecast. Thus, they suggest computing what the probability of each possible contingency being realized would have to be to justify selecting one policy alternative over another and then letting policy makers assess whether the actual probabilities are larger or smaller than these estimates.

Source: Adapted from Steven W. Popper, Robert J. Lempert, and Steven C. Bankes, "Shaping the Future," *Scientific American* 292(4) 2005, 66, 6p.

project in Boston, are complex, not easily compared to previous projects, and have impacts that extend far into the future (for example, unanticipated leaks in the Big Dig tunnels).

Unknown cause-and-effect relationships frequently arise when there is uncertainty concerning fundamental scientific relationships, as discussed previously. They also arise when a government attempts a new project and analysts cannot be certain how affected individuals will respond. Evidence suggests, for example, that some individuals tend to react to new rules and regulations with "offsetting behavior," which attenuates the anticipated benefits of risk-reducing regulations.[9]

In the presence of uncertainty, both people affected by policies and analysts of policies are potentially subject to cognitive biases. Evidence suggests that people systematically underweight low-probability "bad" events and overweight low-probability "good" events.[10] People who live on flood plains buy too many lottery tickets and not enough flood insurance! Analysts and decision makers are not immune from such biases. Indeed, there is a large amount of literature is available concerning the importance of cognitive perceptions on decision making and information processing. Charles Schwenk provides a summary of the effect of cognitive biases on decision making, which one can reasonably assume also pertains to forecasting.[11] The main conclusion of this literature is that cognitive biases may lead analysts to make severe and systematic errors of forecast and judgment, with an overall tendency toward overoptimism.

Forecasting errors also arise due to changing project specifications. Large and complex projects are invariably modified when underway, often as a result of irresistible "evolutionary" adaptation by front-line employees.[12] Sometimes these changes are quite substantial. For example, changing regulatory requirements contributed significantly to construction cost overruns of nuclear power plants.[13] When projects are later modified, *ex ante/ex post* comparisons may, in effect, compare "apples and oranges."

There is a tendency to assume that forecasting errors do not arise in *ex post* analysis because all impacts have been realized. But the analyst must still compare what did happen to what would have happened in the absence of the project—the counterfactual. While analysts may know what did happen (subject to measurement error), they must estimate what would have happened if the project had not been implemented. In general, though, *ex post* forecasting error is likely to be smaller than *ex ante* forecasting error.

Valuation Errors

Accurate monetary estimates of the social value (i.e., shadow prices) of some impacts are scarce, as discussed in Chapter 15. Until recently, even estimates of the value of such important categories as time saved and lives saved varied widely; many previous estimates were inaccurate. Valuation problems can be much greater in some CBA contexts than in others. For example, as discussed in Chapter 16, obtaining appropriate shadow prices is particularly difficult for projects in developing countries.[14]

Valuation errors also arise due to unanticipated relative price changes. (In a way, this is a forecasting error rather than a valuation error.) This type of error can have significant impacts, especially on large infrastructure development projects.

Measurement Errors

There is a tendency to assume that once an impact has occurred, all uncertainty associated with the impact is removed. But, in practice, impacts are often observed, recorded, or interpreted inaccurately. For example, although there were new traffic safety laws and vehicle safety improvement during the 1990s, vehicle crashes per capita remained relatively stable. David Grabowski and Michael Morrisey have demonstrated that in assessing benefits from these improvements in automobile safety, it is important to take account of the fact that the price of gasoline declined over the same period, resulting in more vehicle miles traveled and more fatalities.[15]

The extent of problems resulting from measurement errors depends largely on the quality of the measurement equipment (technology) and on the ability of statistical or econometric methods to make inferences in the presence of measurement errors (methodology). These problems have received little specific attention within the CBA literature. One possible explanation is that they are perceived as being of relatively little importance compared to other problems. Another reason is that current statistical methods for handling measurement error are complex, have stringent data requirements, or require strong underlying assumptions.

THE DISTRIBUTION OF NET BENEFITS OVER TIME

Different types of error have different impacts on estimated net benefits. Furthermore, these errors have different impacts at different times. This section examines how the distribution of net benefits changes over time.

Suppose NB_t denotes the present value (in year 0 dollars) of the net benefits of a project at time t. NB_t is a random variable with a probability density function, $f_t(NB_t; \mu_t, \sigma_t)$, where μ_t is the mean and σ_t is the standard deviation. *Ex ante*, the distribution of the present value of net benefits, NB_0, typically has quite a large variance. Over time some impacts are realized—nature "rolls the dice" on some impact variable, for example, the initial volume of traffic. Consequently, the distribution of NB_t changes over time. The mean of the distribution, μ_t, may increase or decrease relative to the *ex ante* mean, μ_0. It may sometimes be above NB_T, the actual net benefits of the project, and sometimes below NB_T, but it will tend to approach NB_T over time. In contrast, the variance monotonically decreases over time, although it never equals zero.

These changes in the distribution of NB_t over time are represented graphically in Figure 19-1. Here, the present value of net benefits has an approximate normal distribution, which is a reasonable assumption for any project with many impacts. As t increases, the distribution of NB_t changes, its mean tends to move closer to NB_T, and its variance decreases. As t approaches T, NB_t converges toward NB_T, which is represented by the vertical line in Figure 19-1.

Now consider the effects on omission, forecasting, valuation, and measurement errors when we vary the time a CBA is conducted. Omission errors will certainly decline over time as more is known about the project. Similarly, forecasting errors are likely to be reduced or eliminated as impacts are realized. Of course, as mentioned earlier, even an *ex post* study may contain some forecasting errors due to the problem associated with predicting the counter-factual events. Valuation errors are also likely to decline over the life of a project due to methodological improvements in valuing impacts.

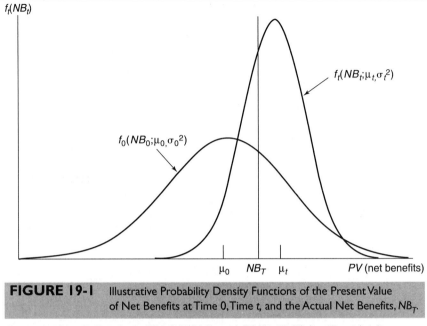

$f_t(NB_t)$

$f_t(NB_t;\mu_t,\sigma_t^2)$

$f_0(NB_0;\mu_0,\sigma_0^2)$

μ_0 NB_T μ_t PV (net benefits)

FIGURE 19-1   Illustrative Probability Density Functions of the Present Value of Net Benefits at Time 0, Time t, and the Actual Net Benefits, NB_T.

Source: Anthony E. Boardman, Wendy L. Mallery, and Aidan R. Vining, "Learning from *Ex Ante/Ex Post* Cost-Benefit Comparisons: The Coquihalla Highway Example," *Socio-Economic Planning Sciences* 28(2) 1994, 69–84. Reprinted with kind permission from Elsevier Science Ltd, The Boulevard, Langford Lane, Kidlington OX5 19GB, UK.

While measurement errors may not change over time, this type of error is likely to be relatively small. Thus, in aggregate, as t increases, the variance of the estimate of the present value of net benefits will decrease. It will never equal zero: Uncertainty is reduced but never completely resolved.

Whether estimates of the present value of net benefits are consistently above or below NB_T, that is, whether estimators are systematically positively or negatively biased, depends on whether omission, forecasting, valuation, or measurement errors are systematically biased (as well as on the size of these biases relative to other errors). Obtaining and comparing estimates of net benefits at different times provides clues about the magnitude of the different types of errors in a CBA and about the presence of systematic biases. With such knowledge, analysts may be able to provide better information about the precision of their estimates in similar situations.

SUMMARY OF THE CBAs OF THE COQUIHALLA HIGHWAY

The Coquihalla Highway is a four-lane toll road, which improves access to the interior of British Columbia (B.C.) from Vancouver; see Figure 19-2. Alternate routes are generally two-lane, with occasional sections of passing lanes. Congestion and safety concerns on alternate routes were important factors in the decision to build the highway. Construction was performed in three phases. Phase I, which extends for 115 kilometers from Hope to Merritt, was completed in 1986. Phase II, which extends for another 80 kilometers from

FIGURE 19-2 Map of the Coquihalla Highway and Nearby Routes

Source: Anthony E. Boardman, Wendy L. Mallery, and Aidan R. Vining, "Learning from *Ex Ante/Ex Post* Cost-Benefit Comparisons: The Coquihalla Highway Example," *Socio-Economic Planning Sciences* 28(2) 1994, 69–84. Reprinted with kind permission from Elsevier Science, Ltd., The Boulevard, Langford Lane, Kidlington OX5 19GB, UK.

Merritt to Kamloops, was completed in 1987. Phase III, which extends for 108 kilometers east from Merritt to Peachland (near Kelowna), was completed in 1990.

Three CBAs of the Coquihalla Highway are summarized in Table 19-1.[16] All were performed by independent analysts from the perspective of 1984, when the initial decision was made, but using the information available at the time the CBA was conducted. Each study took a global perspective; that is, everyone had standing, including foreigners. All three studies assumed there would be tolls at the levels that were implemented initially. All CBAs were compared to the status quo (no new highway in this region) alternative. Furthermore, all used a 7.5 percent real social discount rate with a discounting period of 20 years, the assumed life of the project. Benefits and costs were expressed as present values in 1984 Canadian dollars. It is important to note that the *ex ante* study was performed on the first two phases only, whereas the other two studies were performed on all three phases.

TABLE 19-1   Three CBAs of the Coquihalla Highway

	Waters and Meyers Phases I and II Ex Ante	Mallery Phases I, II, and III In Medias Res	Boardman, Mallery, and Vining Phases I, II, and III Ex Post
PROJECT BENEFITS:			
Time and operating savings	$290.7	$417.6	$900.3
Safety benefits	36.5	51.5	203.1
Reduced congestion on alternative routes	14.1	29.7	56.6
Terminal value after 20 years	53.3	140.6	147.8
Total Benefits	$394.6	$639.4	$1,307.8
PROJECT COSTS:			
Construction	$338.4	$702.6	$837.2
Toll collection	8.4	8.4	8.4
Maintenance and snow removal	7.6	56.6	67.9
Total Costs	$354.4	$767.6	$913.5
NET BENEFITS	$40.2	($128.2)	$394.3

Note: All figures are present values expressed in millions of 1984 Canadian dollars, discounted at 7.5 percent, assuming a project life of 20 years.
Source: Anthony E. Boardman, Wendy L. Mallery, and Aidan R. Vining, "Learning from Ex Ante/Ex Post Cost-Benefit Comparisons: The Coquihalla Highway Example," Socio-Economic Planning Sciences 28(2) 1994, 69–84, Table 2, p. 77. Reprinted with kind permission from Elsevier Science, Ltd., The Boulevard, Langford Lane, Kidlington OX5 19GB, UK.

The first CBA was conducted by W. Waters and Shane Meyers (henceforth WM) in 1986.[17] This is essentially an *ex ante* study, although Phase I was just opening at that time. The authors used "information and forecasts developed before the highway was built as this is more relevant to assessing the original decision to build the highway."[18] The impact categories, which are listed in Table 19-1, are self-explanatory. Because the CBAs were performed from the global perspective, there is no impact category for toll revenues, which are transfers. WM calculated the present value of the net benefit of the project to be $40.2 million in 1984 dollars.

The second study was conducted by Wendy L. Mallery (hereafter MLY) in late 1987.[19] At that time, Phases I and II had been completed, but Phase III had not. MLY had access to actual traffic data (for sixteen months for Phase I and for one month for Phase II) and published estimates of actual construction costs. Thus, MLY's study is an early *in medias res* CBA.

The most recent study by Anthony Boardman, Wendy Mallery, and Aidan Vining (hereafter BMV) was completed in 1993, although some impacts were estimated earlier.[20] Despite the fact that this study was conducted before the end of the project's life, we will treat it as an *ex post* study.

ANALYSIS OF THE DIFFERENCES AMONG THE CBAs

This section discusses the different types of errors that occurred in the Coquihalla Highway CBAs and the reasons for these errors. Because the sources of many errors are unobservable, it is often impossible to disentangle the degree to which errors result from each source, for example, from optimism bias or from strategic bias.

Omissions

It could be argued that there were omission errors in all three studies. No study considered the opportunity cost of the land occupied by the highway. This land was owned by the provincial government. Even analysts have a tendency to treat publicly owned land as "free," which, of course, is incorrect. In fact, the land did not have a high opportunity cost, so excluding it did not have a large impact on the *NPV*s.

There is considerable controversy over the highway's environmental impacts. Though there is no separate impact category for environmental damage in any of the studies, the cost of constructing underpasses, which allow animals to safely cross underneath the highway, careful timing of construction activity, and special efforts to repair any encroachment of rivers were included in construction costs. All studies assumed implicitly that, after taking these actions, environmental impacts would be negligible. Environmentalists, however, contend the actual environmental impacts (e.g., wild animal road kills, wildlife and fish habitat destruction) are quite large.

None of the CBAs includes benefits associated with regional development. Such indirect, local benefits are generally viewed in CBA as transfers from other areas, rather than real benefits. Yet, analysis of indirect effects becomes complicated in the presence of *network externalities*. Since the construction of the highway, there has been an unexpected economic boom in Kelowna. These positive network externalities or agglomeration effects may be partially attributable to the highway.[21] If so, it would be legitimate to treat part of the regional development benefits as real benefits.

Forecasting Differences

Traffic Volume Data on the Coquihalla and Other Routes Estimates of traffic volume are likely to be the most crucial forecast in a highway CBA because they directly affect many of the benefit categories. Traffic levels are difficult to predict. Furthermore, they may change over the life of the project as potential consumers "learn" about the advantages and disadvantages of the highway and alternative routes, as population distributions change, and as consumer tastes change.

WM obtained aggregate annual traffic forecasts by applying traffic growth patterns around the time of their study to a British Columbia Ministry of Transportation forecast for 1986 and allowing for an EXPO 86 traffic bulge. They then disaggregated the data into different origin-destination groups for three categories of vehicles (trucks, passenger vehicles—work, and passenger vehicles—leisure). For each group, they estimated the proportion of diverted, undiverted, and generated traffic.[22] Price-sensitive diversion rates were used to account for the impacts of tolls on the Coquihalla Highway.

MLY used actual Coquihalla traffic counts from May 1986 (when Phase I opened) to September 1987 (when Phase II opened). For subsequent years, MLY produced three different *NPV*s, assuming a 1, 3, and 5 percent annual traffic growth. The 3 percent rate is used in Table 19-1. Under this assumption, total vehicle traffic (at the toll booth) in the years 2000 and 2005 was projected to be 2.85 million and 3.65 million, respectively. MLY estimated the annual average daily traffic allocations on alternative routes for 1984–1987 based on actual average summer daily traffic counts.[23] This historical information was used to estimate a diversion rate of 30 percent for Highway 3 traffic to the Coquihalla after the completion of Phase III.

BMV draw on four sources of data: (1) Toll booth receipts for the years 1986–1990, which were broken out by the following vehicle classes: motorcycles; passenger vehicles; and trucks with two axles, three axles, four to five axles, or six axles or more:[24] (2) perusal of April 1991 traffic counts at the Coquihalla toll booth and on the Okanagan Connector (Phase III), which shows that completion of Phase III increased Coquihalla traffic by about 40 percent; (3) counters on all alternative routes for 1985–1989 (the summer traffic counts for each highway section were then adjusted to account for seasonality: Summer traffic was 1.25 to 1.9 times the annual average daily traffic); and (4) Ministry of Transportation origin-destination surveys, which suggested 90 percent of passenger vehicles were leisure travelers, while 10 percent were business travelers. Based on these data, and assuming a 5 percent annual growth rate (after completion of Phase III), BMV project annual Coquihalla traffic volumes of 4.03 million and 5.14 million vehicles for the years 2000 and 2005, respectively.

It is impossible to determine the accuracy of the traffic volume forecasts of WM's *ex ante* study because they did not present them, nor did they specify the growth rate. Backward induction suggests that WM only slightly overestimated initial use but seriously underestimated future traffic volumes. MLY used actual data for the initial year and then estimated a growth rate of 3 percent, while actual growth has been about 5 percent. She predicted that the opening of Phase III would increase the traffic base by 20 percent, but it actually increased by around twice as much. BMV's *ex post* study projections for the years 2000 and 2005 are 41 percent higher than MLY's estimates.

Time and Distance Savings on the Coquihalla   One would expect that time and distance savings per trip would not vary by much among the studies. In fact, they did vary, as shown in Tables 19-2 and 19-3. Differences in distance are due to changes in the final design as well as the use of different data to measure distance. Differences in time saved are due to differences in distance saved and different assumptions about the speeds traveled on different routes.

TABLE 19-2 Distance Saved per Coquihalla Trip (Kilometers)			
Trip	*Waters and Meyers Ex Ante*	*Mallery In Medias Res*	*Boardman, Mallery, and Vining Ex Post*
Phase I: Hope to Merritt	N/A[a]	87	112
Phases I and II: Hope to Kamloops	72	83	107
Phases I and III: Hope to Peachland	N/A	77	53

[a]*N/A = Not available or not applicable.*
Source: Anthony E. Boardman, Wendy L. Mallery, and Aidan R. Vining, "Learning from *Ex Ante/Ex Post* Cost-Benefit Comparisons: The Coquihalla Highway Example," *Socio-Economic Planning Sciences* 28(2) 1994, 69–84, Table 3A, p. 79. Reprinted with kind permission from Elsevier Science, Ltd., The Boulevard, Langford Lane, Kidlington OX5 19GB, UK.

	Waters and Meyers Ex Ante	Mallery In Medias Res	Boardman, Mallery, and Vining Ex Post
TABLE 19-3 Time Saved per Coquihalla Trip (Minutes)			
Trip			
Phase I: Hope to Merritt	N/A[a]	102	108
Phases I and II: Hope to Kamloops	72	89	120
Phases I and III: Hope to Peachland	N/A	100	79

[a]*N/A = Not available or not applicable.*
Source: Anthony E. Boardman, Wendy L. Mallery, and Aidan R. Vining, "Learning from *Ex Ante/Ex Post* Cost-Benefit Comparisons: The Coquihalla Highway Example," *Socio-Economic Planning Sciences* 28(2) 1994, 69–84, Table 3B, p. 79. Reprinted with kind permission from Elsevier Science, Ltd., The Boulevard, Langford Lane, Kidlington OX5 19GB, UK.

Reduced Congestion on Alternative Routes   WM estimated that, due to the Coquihalla, through traffic on the old routes would save 20 minutes during congested periods. They assumed local traffic would save less, proportional to the number of cars diverted to the new highway. MLY also used the 20-minute saving. BMV followed a different approach, assuming users of alternative routes would save 2 kph in 1986 and 5 kph from 1987 onward.

Accident Rates   WM calculated safety benefits resulting from both reduced distance traveled and from traveling on a safer highway. To estimate safety benefits from reduced distances, they multiplied the predicted 130 million vehicle-kilometers saved by the accident rates for fatal, injury, and property-damage-only accidents on two-lane highways determined by Radnor Pacquette and Paul Wright.[25] To estimate benefits resulting from a safer road, they multiplied the estimated 313 million vehicle-kilometers traveled on the Coquihalla by one-third of the accident rate—their estimate of the accident rate reduction due to using a four-lane divided highway versus the existing highway. MLY followed a similar approach but, for benefits due to a safer road, she used the higher accident rate reductions implied by Pacquette and Wright, which ranged from 35 to 50 percent, depending on the severity of accident. BMV obtained accident rate data by severity from the ministry.

The Coquihalla Highway does save lives. The fatal accident rate of the Coquihalla is about 50 percent lower than on alternate routes, a higher reduction than WM assumed but similar to MLY's estimate. Furthermore, actual fatal accident rates on all routes in British Columbia are higher than WM or MLY assumed. Consequently, more lives are saved due to reduced distance driving than either WM or MLY predicted. Relative to other routes, the Coquihalla has a lower injury rate but higher property-damage-only rate. Nonetheless, because both of these types of accident rates are also higher in British Columbia than anticipated, the shorter Coquihalla generates much higher safety benefits than projected.[26]

Valuation Differences

Value of Vehicle Operating Cost Savings and Value of Time Saved   The three studies were similar in terms of how they valued time savings. Specifically, each assumed that business travelers value an hour of their time at the average gross wage for British Columbia hourly and salaried employees, whereas leisure travelers value their time at 25 percent of this rate. Each of the studies also made similar assumptions about the number of passengers in each vehicle. Based on a perusal of estimates from the ministry, BMV assumed 2.2 passengers per leisure vehicle and 1.2 passengers per business vehicle. As far as we know, the other studies used similar estimates.

The studies differed, however, in the estimated gross wage rates and in the vehicle operating costs. Consider, for example, the estimates pertaining to a trip from Hope to Kamloops. WM estimated vehicle operating cost savings per Coquihalla trip at $7.00 for automobiles and $33.50 for large trucks. Estimated time savings were $8.00, $14.40, and $16.80 per trip for leisure vehicles, business vehicles, and trucks, respectively. MLY calculated vehicle operating cost savings at $9.66 per automobile trip and at $46.73 per truck trip. Time savings were calculated as $6.58 per leisure trip, $20.25 per business-auto trip, and $22.35 per truck trip.[27] BMV's estimates were considerably higher. Based largely on data provided by Trimac Consulting Services, BMV estimated time *and* vehicle operating cost savings at $27.50 per leisure trip, $46.80 per business trip, and $86.50 for a five-axle semi-trailer trip in 1987 Canadian dollars.[28]

Value of Safety Benefits   WM valued fatalities, injuries, and property-damage-only accidents at $500,000, $11,000, and $2,000, respectively. MLY used slightly higher valuations: Saved fatalities, injuries, and property-damage-only accidents were valued at $550,000, $12,000, and $2,000, respectively. Since 1984 there has been considerable research on this topic. As discussed in Chapter 15, current valuations are considerably higher than was thought appropriate in 1984. Based on the most recent research at the time of their study, BMV used $2.2 million (1984 Canadian dollars) for the value of an avoided fatality.

Terminal Value   As discussed in Chapter 6, with a discounting period of 20 years, the terminal value conceptually equals the present value of the net benefits of the project from the 21st year to infinity. The obvious difficulty is in making projections that far into the future. Future costs, for example, will depend critically on the actual depreciation rate of the highway, which is partially endogenous insofar as it varies with use.

The method used in all three studies was to base the terminal value on the initial construction cost. WM assumed the terminal value in the 21st year was 75 percent of the initial construction costs. MLY used 85 percent of initial construction costs, due partially to the high proportion of Coquihalla construction costs, such as rock cutting and sand blasting, that needed to be done only once. BMV used 75 percent.

Estimation/Measurement Differences

Maintenance Expenses   At the time of the *ex ante* study, the Maintenance Services Branch estimated the cost of annual maintenance and snow removal ranged between $2,500 and $7,500 per lane-kilometer. WM selected a number near the low end of this range but interpreted the figures as per kilometer rather than per lane-kilometer, resulting in an estimate of $2,600 per kilometer. In contrast, MLY estimated $7,000 per lane-kilometer for Phase I, and $5,000 per lane-kilometer for Phases II and III. Because the highway was 80 percent a four-lane highway and 20 percent a six-lane highway, MLY's maintenance and snow removal estimates are far higher than WM's estimates. BMV made a largely unsuccessful attempt to isolate actual maintenance expenses. One problem was that the ministry maintained appropriate data by district, not by highway. To complicate matters, in 1988 the ministry privatized highway maintenance. The two major contractors for the Coquihalla were reluctant to reveal their costs because they were bidding on new tenders. They did admit, however, that, due to poor quality control in construction, ditch cleaning costs were larger than expected and some older sections of the highway already required resurfacing. Ultimately, BMV used an estimate of $6,000 per lane-kilometer, the average of the two figures used by MLY. There was one difference, however, stemming from the record-breaking snowstorms over the 1990–1991 winter. To account for the "once in 10, 20, or 50 year" snowstorms that can severely affect the Coquihalla, maintenance and snow removal costs were arbitrarily increased in each of two, randomly chosen years. Overall, this approach is not entirely satisfactory, but it highlights that, like *ex ante* analyses, *ex post* analyses can suffer from prediction error.

Construction Costs WM performed their study after Phase I was completed. Consequently, forecasting construction costs was not an issue, but they still encountered measurement problems. Based on the best available estimates, WM estimated the present value of construction costs for Phases I and II were equal to $338.1 million (in 1984 dollars).

Soon after completion of the highway, rumors circulated of higher costs. On November 7, 1987, the *Vancouver Sun* published estimates of undiscounted total costs of $570 million for Phases I and II and $270 million for Phase III. MLY discounted these estimates to obtain construction costs of $507.9 million for Phases I and II and $194.7 million for Phase III. BMV's construction cost estimates are based on the MacKay Commission, a commission of inquiry that was formed when it became publicly known that the Coquihalla had cost much more than originally anticipated.[29] MacKay concluded that "differences between costs and estimates of the Coquihalla Highway . . . are due to . . . lack of proper budgeting, monitoring cost-control and reporting systems" (p. xi), and observed "[t]he current method of reporting highway capital spending . . . by individual contracts, by Electoral Districts, and on an annual basis . . . has served to disguise the true cost of major projects" (p. xi). MacKay also commented that "The Ministry's cost reporting system for capital works is fragmented and inconsistent" (p. xx). Based on the MacKay Commission report, BMV estimated that the present value of construction costs of the Coquihalla was $837 million, which is $135 million higher than MLY. The difference between BMV's estimate and the estimates in the earlier studies is probably mostly due to strategic biases.

During BMV's enquiries on actual construction costs, one ministry official estimated that MacKay's total Coquihalla construction cost figures were "out" (underestimated) by as much as 300 percent. Uncertainties undoubtedly remain even after the events. Doubling construction costs would be a rough way of accounting for work that was hidden or lost in general accounts and for increases in indirect ministry overhead costs due to the Coquihalla.

CONCLUSIONS ARISING FROM THE COMPARISONS

Did the *Ex Ante* and *In Medias Res* Analyses Have Overall Predictive Capability?

Contrasting an *ex post* analysis with earlier CBAs of the same project provides an opportunity to assess the predictive capability of earlier analyses. This is a critical element in determining the value of *ex ante* CBAs. The *NPV* estimates of $40 million and –$128 million for the earlier studies are significantly lower than the *NPV* of $394 million for the *ex post* study. Given that total costs were under $1 billion, the overall order of magnitude of error in estimation is disconcertingly large.

Furthermore, the aggregate differences understate actual differences in the earlier studies for two reasons. First, some benefits and costs erred in the same direction, thereby tending to cancel each other. For example, the *ex post* study had higher construction costs but also had higher time and operating savings benefits than the previous studies. Second, some errors offset one another within an impact category. For example, concerning safety benefits, the Coquihalla accident rate was higher than predicted, but highway ridership and accident rates elsewhere were also higher than forecast.

One comparison study alone cannot tell us everything about the general accuracy of CBA. Are such aggregate prediction errors prevalent in other CBAs? If they are, it is troubling. One might argue that this particular project raises more problems than is typical, but we think not. This project is *relatively* straightforward; after all, it is a highway, not a high-tech, mega project. Another possibility is that the cost underestimation problem (partly due to regional rather than project-specific budgeting) is specific to "wild and woolly" British Columbia. Again, we do not think so. Several non-British Columbia bureaucratic readers acknowledge that their agencies routinely hide project budget items in other accounts.

Other Lessons from this Comparison Study

This exercise is somewhat humbling. One lesson is that *ex ante* CBA is difficult to do precisely. Accuracy depends on omission, forecasting, valuation, and measurement errors (as well as other types of errors). In this study, there are examples of all four types of errors. As noted previously, some errors cancel out. Often, however, errors compound one another. For example, estimation of *ex ante* travel benefits requires estimates of both total time saved and the valuation of time. In turn, time saved depends on both the estimated number of vehicles and time saved per vehicle. When two or more terms with error are multiplied, the error in the resulting product can be quite large.

At least in other contexts, economists tend to anticipate forecasting errors, especially those associated with benefits. In this example, however, there were also large differences in measurement error (e.g., construction costs) and valuation (e.g., value of safety benefits, including life). The *ex ante* CBA relied on announced estimates of total costs and did not attempt to reanalyze cost estimates. Although independent estimates of project costs are not easy to obtain, the *ex ante*/*ex post* comparison highlights the importance of not passively accepting announced cost estimates of projects. Analysts should attempt to generate at least rough independent estimates.

Of course, research on the value of life is independent of construction of the Coquihalla. We expect that future estimates of the value of life and of other impact categories to use in CBA will be more accurate. In general, valuation errors are less likely to occur as CBA matures and progresses technically.

Despite the difficulty of identifying the source of errors in *ex ante* studies, we found evidence of a variety of sources. Uniqueness and cognitive biases played a part. The highway is liable to extreme amounts of snow. The actual maintenance costs were underestimated. Other forecasting errors, for example, underestimation of the usage levels, are inherent and unavoidable. Project specifications also changed. Strategic biases by bureaucrats and politicians probably accounted partially for the low cost estimates in the *ex ante* study. And there were analysts' procedural errors; for example, WM erred in using maintenance costs per kilometer, rather than maintenance costs per lane-kilometer.

In conclusion, the main lesson illustrated here is the importance of periodically conducting *ex ante/ex post* comparisons. This may seem trivial, but it is almost totally ignored in the cost-benefit analysis literature. If *ex ante* studies were mandatory, should one in ten be subject to *in medias res* or *ex post* follow-up and comparison to the *ex ante* analysis? If so, this chapter provides a template for how to do such comparisons.

NOTES

1. The chapter draws upon Anthony E. Boardman, Wendy L. Mallery, and Aidan R. Vining, "Learning from Ex Ante/Ex Post Cost-Benefit Comparisons: The Coquihalla Highway Example," *Socio-Economic Planning Sciences* 28(2) 1994, 69–84.

2. See also Anthony Boardman, Aidan Vining, and W. G. Waters II, "Costs and Benefits Through Bureaucratic Lenses: Example of a Highway Project," *Journal of Policy Analysis and Management* 12(3) 1993, 532–555.

3. For example, see Bent Flyvbjerg, Mette K. Skamris Holm, and Soren L. Buhl, "How (In)accurate Are Demand Forecasts in Public Works Projects? The Case of Transportation," *Journal of the American Planning Association* 71(2) 2005, 131–146; and, by the same authors, "Cost Underestimation in Public Works Projects: Error or Lie?" *Journal of the American Planning Association* 68(3) 2002, 279–295.

4. This bias has been found in a wide range of corporations by Stephen W. Pruitt and Lawrence J. Gitman, "Capital Budgeting Forecast Biases: Evidence from the Fortune 500," *Financial Management* 16(1) 1987, 46–51.

5. Nancy E. Ryan, "Policy Formation in a Politically Charged Atmosphere: An Empirical Study of Rate-Base Determination for Recently Completed Nuclear Power Plants," paper presented at the 14th Annual APPAM Research Conference, 1992, at p. 3.

6. William E. Colglazier, "Scientific Uncertainties, Public Policy, and Global Warming: How Sure Is Sure Enough?" *Policy Studies Journal* 19(2) 1991, 61–72; P. K. Rao, *The Economics of Global Climatic Change* (Armonk, NY: M.E. Sharpe, 2000); John Houghton, *Global Warming: The Complete Briefing,* 2nd ed. (New York:

Cambridge University Press, 1997); and Robert Mendelsohn, *The Greening of Global Warming,* (Washington, D.C.: American Enterprise Institute for Public Policy Research, 1999).

7. For reviews see, for example, Spyros Makridakis, "The Art and Science of Forecasting: An Assessment and Future Directions," *International Journal of Forecasting* 2(1) 1986, 15–39; Kenneth F. Wallis, "Macroeconomic Forecasting: A Survey," *Economic Journal* 99(1) 1989, 28–61; and K. Holden, D. A. Peel, and J. L. Thompson, *Economic Forecasting: An Introduction* (Cambridge: Cambridge University Press, 1990).

8. Jeffrey L. Pressman and Aaron Wildavsky, *Implementation* (Berkeley: University of California Press, 1973).

9. Robert S. Chirinko and Edward P. Harper Jr., "Buckle Up or Slow Down? New Estimates of Offsetting Behavior and Their Implications for Automobile Safety Regulation," *Journal of Policy Analysis and Management* 12(2) 1993, 270–296. Also see Darren Grant and Stephen M. Rutner, "The Effect of Bicycle Helmet Legislation on Bicycling Fatalities," *Journal of Policy Analysis and Management* 23(3) 2004, 595–611 at p. 606.

10. Howard Kunreuther, Ralph Ginsberg, L. Miller, Philip Sagi, Paul Slovic, B. Borkan, and N. Katz, *Disaster Insurance Protection: Public Policy Lessons* (New York: John Wiley, 1978); and Colin F. Camerer and Howard Kunreuther, "Decision Processes for Low Probability Events: Policy Implications," *Journal of Policy Analysis and Management* 8(4) 1989, 565–592.

11. Charles R. Schwenk, "The Cognitive Perspective on Strategic Decision Making," *Journal of Management Studies* 25(1) 1988, 41–55.

See also J. E. Russo and P. J. Schoemaker, "Managing Overconfidence," *Sloan Management Review* 33(2) 1992, 7–17.

12. E. Hutchins, "Organizing Work by Adaption," *Organization Science,* 2(1) (1991), 14–39.

13. Oak Ridge National Laboratory, *Prudence Issues Affecting the U.S. Electric Utility Industry,* Oak Ridge, TN, 1987.

14. I. M. D. Little and J. A. Mirrlees, "Project Appraisal and Planning Twenty Years On," *Proceedings of the World Bank Annual Conference on Development Economics* Stanley Fischer, Dennis de Tray and Shekhar Shah (eds.) (New York: The World Bank, 1990), 351–391.

15. David C. Grabowski and Michael A. Morrisey, "Gasoline Prices and Motor Vehicle Fatalities," *Journal of Policy Analysis and Management* 23(3) 2004, 575–593.

16. For various reasons the summary benefit and cost figures of the *ex ante* CBA in Table 19-1 are not exactly the same as those presented in Table 1-3.

17. W. G. Waters II and Shane J. Meyers, "Benefit-Cost Analysis of a Toll Highway—British Columbia's Coquihalla," *Journal of the Transportation Research Forum* 28(1) 1987, 435–443.

18. Ibid.

19. Wendy L. Mallery, "A Cost-Benefit Analysis of the Coquihalla Highway," course paper for J. M. Munro, Simon Fraser University, December 1987.

20. Boardman, Mallery, and Vining, "Learning from Ex Ante/Ex Post Cost-Benefit Comparisons." Using a similar approach, Winston Harrington, Richard D. Morgenstern, and Peter Nelson ("On the Accuracy of Regulatory Cost Estimates," *Journal of Policy Analysis and Management* 19[2] 2000, 297–322) compared *ex ante* cost estimates of the direct cost of regulations with *ex post* estimates of the same regulations and found that the former were overestimated much more often than they were underestimated.

21. A positive network externality arises where the utility one person derives from the consumption of a good increases with the number of other people consuming the good. For example, the benefit of having a telephone increases with the number of other people who have telephones that are connected to the same network; see Michael A. Katz and Carl Shapiro, "Network Externalities, Competition and Compatibility," *American Economic Review* 75(3) 1985, 424–440. In the context of regional development, positive externalities may arise when a region reaches a critical mass, or agglomeration, in terms of the nature, depth, and breadth of its economic activity. Michael Porter uses the related concept of clustering to explain the comparative advantage of nations in international competitiveness; see Michael E. Porter, *The Comparative Advantage of Nations* (New York: The Free Press, 1990).

22. Diverted traffic refers to traffic that would have gone on the old routes but now travels on the Coquihalla. Undiverted traffic refers to traffic that continues on the old routes despite the existence of the Coquihalla. Generated traffic refers to traffic that would not have made the trip by road at all without the Coquihalla but now does so because the effective price is lower. These travelers may have gone by air or train or done something completely different.

23. These numbers were then adjusted by the estimated ratio of average summer to average annual traffic.

24. Total traffic data were obtained for 1986 to 1990. Traffic data by vehicle class were obtained for the period April 1987 to March 1991 and estimated for 1986 and part of 1987. The traffic data thus cover three full years of Phase II operation from Hope to Kamloops and a few months of Phase III operation from Hope to Peachland.

25. Radnor J. Pacquette and Paul H. Wright, *Highway Engineering* (New York: Wiley & Sons, 1979), at p. 73.

26. MLY based her projections on Pacquette and Wright (p. 73), who estimated the accident rates on a divided highway are 0.0155, 0.168, and 0.304 (per million vehicle-kilometers) for fatalities, injuries, and property damage only, respectively.

27. MLY used the average April 1986 gross wage for all B.C. industries for hourly and salaried employees, from the Statistics Canada publication, *Monthly Employment Earnings and Hours,* as the business hourly wage.

28. Trimac Consulting Services Limited, *Operating Costs of Trucks in Canada,* 1986 and 1988 editions, prepared for the Motor Carrier Branch, Surface Transport Administration, Transport Canada (Ottawa, Ontario: Minister of Supply and Services, 1986, 1988).

29. Douglas L. MacKay, Commissioner, *Report of the Commission Inquiry into the Coquihalla and Related Highway Projects,* Province of British Columbia, December 1987.

A Selected Cost-Benefit Analysis Bibliography

This bibliography provides representative CBA studies in a number of substantive areas. Instructors who adopt this book as a text can obtain a more comprehensive bibliography from the publisher's Web site. Others may obtain an electronic copy by emailing Aidan Vining at vining@sfu.ca.

Table of Contents

1. Agriculture

Adams, R., B. McCarl, K. Segerson, C. Rosenwieg, K. Bryant, B. Dixon, R. Connor, R. Evenson, and D. Ojima, "Economic Effects of Climate Change on U.S. Agriculture," in R. Mendelsohn and J. Neumann, eds., *The Impact of Climate Change on the United States Economy* (Cambridge: Cambridge University Press, 2004), 18–54.

Alston, J., "The Effects of the CAP on International Trade in Poultry Meat," *European Review of Agricultural Economics* 13(2) 1986, 217–231.

Bonnieux, F., P. Rainelli, and D. Vermersch, "Estimating the Supply of Environmental Benefits by Agriculture: A French Case Study," *Environmental and Resource Economics* 11(2) 1998, 135–153.

Borcherding, T., and G. W. Dorosch, *The Egg Marketing Board: A Case Study of Monopoly and Its Social Cost* (Vancouver, B.C.: The Fraser Institute, 1981).

Bower, J., and D. Didychuck, "Estimation of Market Benefits of Agricultural Land Retention in Eastern Canada," *Agricultural and Resource Economics Review* 23(2) 1994, 218–255.

Brouwer, R., and L. Slangen, "Contingent Valuation of the Public Benefits of Agricultural Wildlife Management: The Case of Dutch Peat Meadow Land," *European Review of Agricultural Economics* 25(1) 1998, 53–72.

Graham, J. D., C. A. Webber, and R. J. MacGregor, "A Regional Analysis of Direct Government Assistance Programs in Canada and Their Impacts on the Beef and Hog Sectors," *Canadian Journal of Agricultural Economics* 36(4) 1988, 915–928.

Henze, A., and J. Zeddies, "EC Programmes, Economic Effects and Cost Benefit Considerations on Adjustments in EC Agriculture," *European Review of Agricultural Economics* 15(2/3) 1988, 191–210.

Klein, K. K., and F. P. Jetter, "Economic Benefits From the Alberta Warble Control Program," *Canadian Journal of Agricultural Economics* 35(2) 1987, 289–303.

Krystynak, R. H. E., "An Economic Assessment of 2,4-D in Canada: The Case of Grain," *Canadian Farm Economics* 18(1) 1983, 7–30.

Kuik, O., J. Helming, C. Dorland, and F. Spaninks, "The Economic Benefits to Agriculture of a Reduction of Low-Level Ozone Pollution in the Netherlands," *European Review of Agricultural Economics* 27(1) 2000, 75–90.

McLeod, P. B., E. J. Roberts, and G. J. Syme, "Willingness to Pay for Continued Government Service Provisions: The Case of Agriculture Protection Services," *Journal of Environmental Management* 40(1) 1994, 1–16.

Norton, G. W., V. G. Ganoza, and C. Pomereda, "Potential Benefits of Agricultural Research and Extension in Peru," *American Journal of Agricultural Economics* 69(2) 1987, 247–257.

Parks, P. K. and I. W. Hardie, "Least-Cost Forest Carbon Reserves: Cost-Effective Subsidies to Convert Marginal Agricultural Land to Forests," *Land Economics* 71(1) 1995, 122–136.

Reichelderfer, K. H., "Externalities and the Returns to Agricultural Research: Discussion," *American Journal of Agricultural Economics* 71(2) 1989, 464–465.

Sampson, J. A., and C. D. Gerrard, "Government Interventions and the Production of Wheat in Saskatchewan and North Dakota: An Empirical Analysis," *Canadian Journal of Agricultural Economics* 35(1) 1987, 1–20.

Spash, C. L, "Assessing the Economic Benefits to Agriculture from Air Pollution Control," *Journal of Economic Surveys* 11(1) 1997, 47–70.

Ulrich, A., W. H. Furtan, and A. Schmitz, "The Cost of a Licensing System Regulation: An Example From Canadian Prairie Agriculture," *Journal of Political Economy* 95(1) 1987, 160–178.

van Kooten, G., C., W. P. Weisensel, and E. de Jong, "Estimating the Costs of Soil Erosion in Saskatchewan," *Canadian Journal of Agricultural Economics* 37(1) 1989, 63–75.

Whitehead, J., T. Hoban, and W. Clifford, "Willingness to Pay for Agricultural Research and Extension Programs," *Journal of Agricultural and Applied Economics* 33(1) 2001, 91–101.

2. Air Pollution

Adams, R. M., D. M. Adams, J. M. Callaway, C. Chang, and B. A. McCarl, "Sequestering Carbon on Agricultural Land: Social Cost and Impacts on Timber Markets," *Contemporary Policy Issues* 11(1) 1993, 76–87.

Adams, R. M., J. M. Callaway, and B. A. McCarl, "Pollution, Agriculture, and Social Welfare: The Case of Acid Deposition," *Canadian Journal of Agricultural Economics* 34(1) 1986, 3–19.

Adams, R. M., T. D. Crocker, and N. Thanavibulchai, "An Economic Assessment of Air Pollution Damages to Selected Annual Crops in Southern California," *Journal of Environmental Economics and Management* 9(1) 1982, 42–58.

Adams, R. M., S. A. Hamilton, and B. A. McCarl, "The Benefits of Pollution Control: The Case of Ozone and U.S. Agriculture," *American Journal of Agricultural Economics* 68(4) 1986, 886–893.

Adams, R. M., and B. A. McCarl, "Assessing the Benefits of Alternative Ozone Standards on Agriculture: The Role on Response Information," *Journal of Environmental Economics and Management* 12(3) 1985, 264–276.

Anderson, R. C., and B. Ostro, "Benefits Analysis and Air Quality Standard," *Natural Resources Journal* 3(3) 1983, 566–575.

Bailey, M. J., "Risks, Costs and Benefits of Fluorocarbon Regulation," *American Economic Review Papers and Proceedings* 72(2) 1982, 247–250.

Bayless, M., "Measuring the Benefits of Air Quality Improvement: A Hedonic Salary Approach," *Journal of Environmental Economics and Management* 9(1) 1982, 81–99.

Brady, G. L., B. T. Bower, and H. A. Lakhani, "Estimates of the National Benefits and Costs of Improving Ambient Air Quality," *Journal of Environmental Management* 16(3) 1983, 191–210.

Brown, D., and M. Smith, "Crop Substitution in the Estimation of Economic Benefits Due to Ozone Reduction," *Journal of Environmental Economics and Management* 11(3) 1984, 347–360.

Butraw, D., R. Bharvirkar, and M. McGuiness, "Uncertainty and the Net Benefits of Emissions Reductions of Nitrous Oxides from Electricity Generation," *Land Economics* 79(3) 2003, 382–401.

Butraw, D., A. Krupnik, E. Mansur, D. Austin, and D. Farrell, "Costs and Benefits of Reducing Acid Rain Pollutants Related to Acid Rain," *Contemporary Economic Policy* 16(4) 1998, 379–400.

Cline, W. R., *The Economics of Global Warming* (Washington, D.C.: Institute for International Economics, 1992).

Crocker, T. D., and J. L. Regans, "Acid Deposition Controls — A Benefit-Cost Analysis: Its Prospects and Limits," *Environment Science and Technology* 19(2) 1985, 112–116.

Farber, S., and A. Rambaldi, "Willingness to Pay for Air Quality: The Case of Outdoor Exercise," *Contemporary Policy Issues* 11(4) 1993, 19–30.

Fraas, A., and A. McGartland, "Alternative Fuels for Pollution Control: An Empirical Evaluation of Benefits and Costs," *Contemporary Policy Issues* 8(1) 1990, 62–74.

Freeman, A. M., III, "On Estimating Air Pollution Control Benefits from Land Value Studies," *Journal of Environmental Economics and Management* 1(1) 1974, 74–83.

Garcia, P., B. L. Dixon, J. W. Mjelde, and R. M. Adams, "Measuring the Benefits of Environmental Change Using a Duality Approach: The Case of Ozone Air Pollutants," *Journal of Environmental Economics and Management* 13(1) 1986, 69–80.

Gerking, S., and W. Schulze, "What Do We Know About Benefits of Reduced Mortality from Air Pollution Control?" *American Economic Review* 71(2) 1981, 228–234.

Giannias, D. A., "Consumer Benefit From Air Quality Improvements," *Applied Economics* 21(8) 1989, 1099–1108.

Haigh, J. A., D. Harrison Jr., and A. Nichols, "Benefit-Cost Analysis of Environmental Regulation: Case Studies of Hazardous Air Pollutants," *Harvard Environmental Law Review* 8(2) 1984, 395–434.

Hubbard, T., "Using Inspection and Maintenance Programs to Regulate Vehicle Emissions," *Contemporary Economic Policy* 15(2) 1997, 52–62.

Joyce, T. J., M. Grossman, and F. Goldman, "An Assessment of the Benefits of Air Pollution Control: The Case of Infant Health," *Journal of Urban Economics* 25(1) 1989, 32–51.

Kim, C., T. Phipps, and L. Anselin, "Measuring the Benefits of Air Quality Improvements: A Spatial Hedonic Approach," *Journal of Environmental Economics and Management* 45(1) 2003, 24–39.

Kopp, R. J., and A. J. Krupnick, "Agriculture Policy and the Benefits of Ozone Control," *American Journal of Agricultural Economics* 69(5) 1987, 956–962.

Krewitt, W., M. Holland, A. Trukenmuller, T. Heck, and R. Friedrich, "Comparing Costs and Environmental Benefits of Strategies to Combat Acidification and Ozone in Europe," *Environmental Economics and Policy Studies* 2(4) 1999, 249–266.

Krupnick, A. J., "Costs of Alternative Policies for the Control of Nitrogen Dioxide in Baltimore," *Journal of Environmental Economics and Management* 13(2) 1986, 189–197.

Krupnick, A. J., and M. A. Walls, "The Cost-Effectiveness of Methanol for Reducing Motor Vehicle Emissions and Urban Ozone," *Journal of Policy Analysis and Management* 11(3) 1992, 373–396.

Kumar, S., and D. Rao, "Valuing the Benefits of Air Pollution Abatement Using a Health Production Function," *Environmental and Resource Economics* 20(2) 2001, 91–102.

Maddison, D., "A Cost-Benefit Analysis of Slowing Climate Change," *Energy Policy* 23(2/3) 1995, 337–346.

McCorriston, S., and I. M. Sheldon, "The Welfare Implications of Nitrogen Limitation Policies," *Journal of Agricultural Economics* 40(2) 1989, 143–151.

Mendelsohn, R., "An Economic Analysis of Air Pollution from Coal Fired Plants," *Journal of Environmental Economics and Management* 7(1) 1980, 30–43.

Navrud, S., "Valuing Health Impacts from Air Pollution in Europe," *Environmental and Resource Economics* 20(4) 2001, 305–329.

Nelson, J. P., "Residential Choice, Hedonic Prices, and the Demand for Urban Air Quality," *Journal of Urban Economics* 5(3) 1978, 357–369.

Parks, P. K., and I. W. Hardie, "Least-Cost Forest Carbon Reserves: Cost-Effective Subsidies to Convert Marginal Agricultural Land to Forests," *Land Economics* 71(1) 1995, 122–136.

Perl, L. J., and F. C. Dunbar, "Cost Effectiveness and Cost-Benefit Analysis of Air Quality Regulations," *American Economic Review* 72(2) 1982, 208–213.

Regens, J. L., and R. W. Rycroft, *The Acid Rain Controversy* (Pittsburgh, PA: University of Pittsburgh Press, 1988).

Rowe, R. D., R. C. d'Arge, and D. S. Brookshire, "An Experiment on the Economic Value of Visibility," *Journal of Environmental Economics and Management* 7(1) 1980, 1–19.

Schulze, W. D., and D. S. Brookshire, et al., "The Economic Benefits of Preserving Visibility in National Parklands of the Southwest," *Natural Resources Journal* 23(1) 1983, 149–173.

Schwing, R. C., B. W. Southwark, C. R. von Buseck, and C. J. Jackson, "Benefit-Cost Analysis of Automobile Emission Reductions," *Journal of Environmental Economics and Management* 7(1) 1980, 44–64.

Smith, V. K., and J. Huang, "Can Markets Value Air Quality? A Meta-Analysis of Hedonic Property Value Models," *Journal of Political Economy* 103(3) 1995, 209–227.

Thomas, V., "Evaluating Pollution Control: The Case of Sao Paulo, Brazil," *Journal of Development Economics* 19(1 and 2) 1985, 133–146.

Young, D., and S. Aidun, "Ozone and Wheat Farming in Alberta: A Micro-Study of the Effects of Environmental Change," *Canadian Journal of Agricultural Economics* 41(1) 1993, 27–43.

3. Crime and Drug Abuse (Including Alcohol)

Anderson, D. A, "The Aggregate Burden of Crime," *Journal of Law and Economics* 42(2) 1999, 611–642.

Cartwright, W., Cost-Benefit and Cost-Effectiveness Analysis of Drug Abuse Treatment Services," *Evaluation Review* 22(5) 1998, 609–636.

Cartwright, W., Cost-Benefit Analysis of Drug Treatment Services: A Review of the Literature," *The Journal of Mental Health Policy and Economics* 3(1) 2000, 11–26.

Cartwright, W., "Cocaine Medications, Cocaine Consumption and Societal Costs," *Pharmacoeconomics* 18(4) 2000, 406–413.

Coate, D., and M. Grossman, "Effects of Alcoholic Beverage Prices and Legal Drinking Ages on Youth Alcohol Use," *Journal of Law and Economics* 31(1) 1988, 145–171.

Cohen, M. A., "Pain, Suffering, and Jury Awards: A Study of the Cost of Crime to Victims," *Law and Society Review* 22(3) 1988, 537–555.

Cook, P., and G. Tauchen, "The Effect of Liquor Taxes on Heavy Drinking," *Bell Journal of Economics* 13(2) 1982, 255–285.

Crew, R., and R. Hart Jr., Assessing the Value of Police Pursuit," *Policing: An International Journal of Police Strategies and Management* 22(1) 1999, 58–73.

French, M., "Economic Evaluation of Alcohol Treatment Services," *Evaluation and Program Planning* 23(1) 2000, 27–39.

French, M., H. Salome, and M. Carney, "Using the DATCAP and ASI to Estimate the Costs and Benefits of Residential Addiction Treatment in the State of Washington," *Social Science & Medicine* 55(12) 2002, 2267–2282.

Grant, M. M., and A. W. Williams, eds., *Economics and Alcohol Consumption and Controls* (New York: Gardner Press, 1983).

Greenwood, P., ed., *Intervention Strategies for Chronic Juvenile Offenders* (New York: Greenwood Press, 1988).

Gutzwiller, F., and T. Steffen, eds., *Cost-Benefit Analysis of Heroin Maintenance Treatment* (Basel and New York: Karger, 2000).

Hakim, S., and Y. Shachmurove, "Social Cost Benefit Analysis of Commercial and Residential Burgler and Fire Alarms,"*Journal of Policy Modeling* 18(1) 1996, 49–67.

Kenkel, D. S., "Drinking, Driving, and Deterrence: The Effectiveness and Social Costs of Alternative Policies," *Journal of Law and Economics* 36(2) 1993, 3877–3914.

Kimbrough, J., "School-Based Strategies for Delinquency Prevention," in P. Greenwood, ed., *Intervention Strategies for Chronic Juvenile Offenders* (New York: Greenwood Press, 1987), 193–206.

Lee, D. R., "Policing Cost, Evasion Cost, and the Optimal Speed Limit," *Southern Economic Journal* 52(1) 1985, 34–45.

Levy, D., and N. Sheflin, "New Evidence on Controlling Alcohol Use Through Price," *Journal of Studies on Alcohol* 44(6) 1983, 929–937.

Lipsey, M., "Is Delinquency Prevention a Cost-Effective Strategy? A California Perspective," *Journal of Research in Crime and Delinquency* 21(4) 1984, 279–302.

Martin, S., C. Butzin, C. Saum, and J. Inciardi, "Three-Year Outcomes of Therapeutic Community Treatment for Drug-Involved Delaware from Prison to Work Release to Aftercare," *The Prison Journal* 79(3) 1999, 294–320.

Miller, T. R., M. A. Cohen, and B. Wiersema, *Crime in the United States: Victim Costs and Consequences* (Washington, D.C.: Final Report to the National Institute of Justice, 1995).

Plotnick, R., and L. Deppman, "Using Benefit-Cost Analysis to Child Abuse Prevention and Intervention Programs," *Child Welfare* 78(3) 1999, 381–407.

Pogue, T. F., and L. G. Sgontz, "Taxing to Control Social Costs: The Case of Alcohol," *American Economic Review* 79(1) 1989, 235–243.

Robertson, A., P. Grimes, and K. Rogers, "A Short-Run Cost-Benefit Analysis of Community-Based Interventions for Juvenile Offenders," *Crime & Delinquency* 47(2) 2001, 265–285.

Saffer, H., and M. Grossman, "Drinking Age Laws and Highway Mortality Rates: Cause and Effect," *Economic Inquiry* 25(3) 1987, 403–418.

Shanahan, M., and R. Donato, "Counting the Cost: Estimating the Economic Benefit of Pedophile Treatment Programs," *Child Abuse & Neglect* 25(4) 2000, 541–556.

Welsh, B., and D. Farrington, "Value for Money? A Review of the Costs and Benefits of Situational Crime Prevention," *British Journal of Criminology* 39(3) 1999, 345–368.

Welsh, B., and D. Farrington, "Correctional Intervention Programs and Cost-Benefit Analysis," *Criminal Justice and Behavior* 27(1) 2000, 115–133.

Wilson, S., and M. Lipsey, "Wilderness Challenge Programs for Delinquent Youth: A Meta-Analysis of Outcome Evaluations," *Evaluation and Program Planning* 23(1), 2000, 112.

4. Culture, Sports, and Entertainment

Baade, R. "An Analysis of the Economic Rationale for Public Subsidization of Sports Stadiums," *Annals of Regional Science* 22(2) 1988, 37–48.

Bille, T. "A Contingent Valuation Study of the Royal Theatre in Copenhagen," in S. Navrud and R. Ready, eds., *Valuing Cultural Heritage* (Cheltenham, UK: Edward Elgar, 2002), 200–237.

Boxall, P., J. Englin, and W. Adamowicz, "The Contribution of Aboriginal Rock Paintings to Wilderness Recreation Values in North America," in S. Navrud and R. Ready, eds., *Valuing Cultural Heritage* (Cheltenham, UK: Edward Elgar, 2002), 105–117.

Boxall, P., J. Englin, and W. Adamowicz, "Valuing Aboriginal Artifacts: A Combined Revealed-Stated Preference Approach," *Journal of Environmental Economics and Management* 45(2) 2003, 213–1230.

Finn, A., S. McFadyn, and C. Hoskins, "Valuing the Canadian Broadcasting Corporation," *Journal of Cultural Economics* 27(3–4) 2003, 177–192.

Fleisher, A., and D. Felsenstein, "Cost-Benefit Analysis Using Economic Surpluses: A Case Study of a Televised Event," *Journal of Cultural Economics* 26(2) 2002, 139–156.

Garrod, G., K. Willis, H. Bjarnadottir, and P. Cockbain "The Non-Priced Benefits of Renovating Historic Buildings: A Case Study of Newcastle's Grainger Town," *Cities* 13(6) 1996, 420–430,

Haener, M., D. Dosman, W. Adamowicz, and P. Boxall, "Can Stated Preference Methods be Used to Value Attributes of Subsistence Hunting by Aboriginal Peoples? A Case Study in Northern Saskatchewan,"

American Journal of Agricultural Economics 83(3) 2001, 1334–1340.

Hamilton, B., and P. Kahn, "Baltimore's Camden Yards Ballparks," in R. Noll and A. Zimbalist, eds., *Sports, Jobs and Taxes* (Washington, D.C.: Brookings Institution Press, 1997), 245–281.

Holt, G., D. Elliot, and A. Moore, "Placing a Value on Public Library Services," *Public Libraries* 38(2) 1999, 98–108.

Irani, D., "Public Subsidies to Stadiums: Do the Costs Outweigh the Benefits?" *Public Finance Review* 25(2) 1997, 238–254.

Johnson, B., and J. Whitehead, "Value of Public Goods from Sports Stadiums: The CVM Approach," *Contemporary Economic Policy* 18(1) 2000, 48–58.

Maddison, D., and S. Mourato, "Valuing Different Road Options for Stonehenge," *Conservation and Management of Archaeological Sites* 4(4) 2001, 203–12.

Martin, F. "Determining the Size of Museum Subsidies," *Journal of Cultural Economics* 18(4) 1994, 255–270.

Morey, E., K. Rossman, L. Chesnut, and S. Ragland, "Valuing Reduced Acid Rain Deposition Injuries to Cultural Resources: Marble Monuments in Washington, D.C." in S. Navrud and R. Ready, eds., *Valuing Cultural Heritage* (Cheltenham, UK: Edward Elgar, 2002), 159–183.

Navrud, S., and J. Strand, "Social Costs and Benefits of Preserving and Restoring the Nidaros Cathedral," in S. Navrud and R. Ready, eds., *Valuing Cultural Heritage* (Cheltenham, UK: Edward Elgar, 2002), 31–39.

Noll, R., and A. Zimbalist, eds., *Sports, Jobs and Taxes* (Washington, D.C.: Brookings Institution Press, 1997).

Noonan, D., "Contingent Valuation and Cultural Resources: A Meta-Analytic Review of the Literature," *Journal of Cultural Economics* 27(3–4) 2003, 159–176.

Papandrea, F., "Willingness to Pay for Domestic Television Programming," *Journal of Cultural Economics* 23(3) 1999, 147–164.

Rolfe, J., and J. Windle, "Valuing the Protection of Aboriginal Cultural Heritage Sites," *The Economic Record* 79 (Special Issue) 2003, 85–95.

Sanz, J., L. Herrero, and A. Bedate, "Contingent Valuation and Semiparametric Methods: A Case Study of the National Museum of Sculpture in Valladolid, Spain," *Journal of Cultural Economics* 27(3–4) 2003, 241–57.

Schwer, R., and R. Daneshvary, "Willingness to Pay for Public Television and the Advent of Look-Alike Cable-Television Channels—A Case Study," *Journal of Media Economics* 8(3) 1995, 95–109.

Thompson, E., M. Berger, G. Blomquist, and S. Allen, "Valuing the Arts: A Contingent Valuation Approach," *Journal of Cultural Economics* 26(2) 2002, 87–113.

Throsby, D., "Determining the Value of Cultural Goods: How Much (or How Little) Does Contingent Valuation Tell Us?" *Journal of Cultural Economics* 27(3–4) 2003, 275–285.

Whitehead, J., and S. Finney, "Willingness to Pay for Submerged Maritime Cultural Resources," *Journal of Cultural Economics* 27(3–4) 2003, 231–240.

Zimmerman, D., "Subsidizing Stadiums: Who Benefits, Who Pays?" in R. Noll and A. Zimbalist, eds., *Sports, Jobs and Taxes* (Washington, D.C.: Brookings Institution Press, 1997).

5. Education and Employment/Training Programs

Arulampalam, W., and A. Booth, "Learning and Earning: Do Multiple Training Events Pay? A Decade of Evidence from a Cohort of Young British Males," *Economica* 68(271) 2001, 379–400.

Ashenfelter, O., "Estimating the Effects of Training Programs on Earnings," *Review of Economics and Statistics* 60(1) 1978, 47–57.

Barnett, W. S., "Benefits of Compensatory Preschool Education," *Journal of Human Resources* 27(2) 1992, 279–312.

Bas, D., "Cost-Effectiveness of Training in Developing Countries," *International Labour Review* 127(3) 1988, 355–369.

Bloom, H. S., L. Orr, S. H. Bell, G. Cave, F. Doolittle, W. Lin, and J. M. Bos, "The Benefits and Costs of JTPA Title II-A Programs: Key Findings from the National Job Training Partnership Act Study," *Journal of Human Resources* 32(3) 1997, 549–576.

Borus, M. E., "Assessing the Impact of Training Programs," in E. Ginzberg, ed., *Employing the Unemployed* (New York: Basic Books, 1980), 25–40.

Cohn, E., and W. W. Hughes Jr., "A Benefit-Cost Analysis of Investment in College Education in the United States: 1969–1985," *Economics of Education Review* 13(2) 1997, 109–123.

Cooper, S. T., and E. Cohn, "Internal Rates of Return to College Education in the United States by Sex and Race," *Journal of Education Finance* 23(1) 1997, 101–133.

Garces, E., Thomas, D., and J. Currie, "Longer-Term Effects of Head Start," *American Economic Review* 92(4) 2002, 999–1013.

Gill, A., and D. Leigh, "Do the Returns to Community Colleges Differ Between Academic and Vocational Programs?" *Journal of Human Resources* 38(1) 2003, 134–155.

Greenberg, D., and U. Appenzeller, *Cost Analysis Step by Step: A How-to-Guide for Planners and Providers of Welfare-to-Work and Employment and Training Programs* (New York: Manpower Demonstration Research Corporation, 1998).

Greenberg, D., K Ashworth, A. Cebulla, and R. Walker, "Do Welfare-To-Work Programmes Work for Long?" *Fiscal Studies* 25(1) 2004, 27–53.

Greenberg, D., C. Michaloupoulos, and P. K. Robins, "What Happens to the Effects of Government-Funded Training Programs Over Time," *Journal of Human Resources* 39(1) 2004, 277–293.

Gueron, J. M., *Reforming Welfare With Work* (New York: The Ford Foundation, 1987).

Haveman, R. H., "The Dutch Social Employment Program," in J. L. Palmer, ed., *Creating Jobs: Public Employment Programs and Wage Subsidies* (Washington, D.C.: The Brookings Institution, 1978), 241–269.

Kemper, P., and P. Moss, "Economic Efficiency of Public Employment Programs," in J. L. Palmer, ed., *Creating Jobs: Public Employment Programs and Wage Subsidies* (Washington, D.C.: The Brookings Institution, 1978), 277–312.

Lalonde, R., and R. Maynard, "How Precise Are Evaluations of Employment and Training Programs: Evidence From a Field Experiment," *Evaluation Review* 11(4) 1987, 428–451.

Lane, J., and T. Berry, "A Multi-State Analysis of the Targeted Jobs Tax Credit Programme," *Applied Economics* 21(1) 1989, 85–94.

Long, D. A., C. D. Mallar, and C. V. D. Thornton, "Evaluating the Benefits and Costs of the Job Corps," *Journal of Policy Analysis and Management* 1(1) 1981, 55–76.

Nicaise, I., "Giving Fish or Teaching to Fish: A Cost-Benefit Analysis of Belgium Employment Training Programs for Minimum Income Recipients," *Public Finance and Management* 2(2) 2002, 272–293.

Psacharopoulos, G., "Returns to Education: A Global Update," *World Development* 22(9) 1994, 1325–1343.

Reynolds, A., J. Temple, D. Robertson, and E. Mann, "Age 21 Cost-Benefit Analysis of the Title 1 Chicago Child-Parent Centers," *Educational Evaluation and Policy Analysis* 24(4) 2002, 267–303.

Sakellariou, C., "Rates of Return to Investments in Formal and Technical/Vocational Education in Singapore," *Education Economics* 11(1) 2003, 73–87.

Vawda, A., P. Mook, J. Price Gettinger, and H. Patrinos, "Economic Analysis of World Bank Education Projects and Project Outcomes," *International Journal of Educational Development* 23(6), 2003, 645–661.

Woodbury, S. A., and R. G. Spiegelman, "Bonuses to Workers and Employers to Reduce Unemployment: Randomized Trials in Illinois," *American Economic Review* 77(4) 1987, 513–530.

Zuidema, T., "Cost-Benefit Analysis in a Situation of Unemployment: Calculating the Decline in Unemployment as a Result of the Realization of a Government Project," *Public Finance Quarterly* 15(1) 1987, 105–115.

6. Energy and Energy Conservation

Anand, S., and B. Nalebuff, "Issues in the Application of Cost-Benefit Analysis to Energy Projects in Developing Countries," *Oxford Economic Papers* 39(1) 1987, 190–222.

Boyd, R., K. Krutilla, and W. K. Viscusi, "Energy Taxation as a Policy Instrument to Reduce CO_2 Emissions: A Net Benefit Analysis," *Journal of Environmental Economics and Management* 29(1) 1995, 1–24.

Burkhart, L. A., "Conservation Program Cost-Benefit Analysis—Choosing Among Options," *Public Utilities Fortnightly* 125(7) 1990, 41–44.

Burwell, C. C., and D. L. Phung, "On the Energy Cost-Effectiveness of Electric Home Heating," *Public Utilities Fortnightly* 113(6) 1984, 26–31.

Caves, D. W., L. R. Christensen, P. E. Schoech, and W. E. Hendricks, "A Comparison of Different Methodologies in a Case Study of Residential Time-of-Use Electricity Pricing," *Journal of Econometrics* 26(1,2) 1984, 17–35.

Chao, H., and A. S. Manne, "An Integrated Analysis of U.S. Oil Stockpiling Policies," in J. L. Plummer, ed., *Energy Vulnerability* (Cambridge, MA: Ballinger Publishing Co., 1982), 59–82.

Cicchetti, C. J., "The Trans Alaska Pipeline: A Benefit-Cost Analysis of Alternatives," in R. H. Havemann,
et al., eds., *Benefit-Cost and Policy Analysis, 1973* (Chicago: Aldine Publishing, 1974), 110–143.

Dixon, J. A., "Selected Policy Options for Fuelwood Production and Use in the Philippines," from materials prepared by E. L. Hyman in J. A. Dixon and M. M. Hufschmidt, eds., *Economic Valuation Techniques for the Environment* (Baltimore and London: The Johns Hopkins University Press, 1986), 163–177.

Frieden, B., and L. Baker, "The Market Needs Help: The Disappointing Record of Home Energy Conservation," *Journal of Policy Analysis and Management* 2(3) 1983, 432–448.

Friedman, L., and K. Hausker, "Residential Energy Consumption: Models of Consumer Behavior and Their Implications for Rate Design," *Journal of Consumer Policy* 11(3) 1988, 287–313.

Hartman, R. S., "An Analysis of Department of Energy Residential Appliance Efficiency Standards," *The Energy Journal* 2(2) 1981, 49–70.

Hausman, J. A., and P. Joskow, "Evaluating the Costs and Benefits of Appliance Efficiency Standards," *American Economic Review* 72(2) 1982, 220–225.

Horwich, G., H. Jenkins-Smith, and D. L. Weimer, "The International Energy Agency's Mandatory Oil-Sharing Agreement: Tests of Efficiency, Equity and Practicality," in G. Horwich and D. Weimer, eds., *Responding to International Oil Crisis* (Washington, D.C.: American Enterprise Institute, 1988), 104–133.

Horwich, G., and D. L. Weimer, *Oil Price Shocks, Market Response and Contingency Planning* (Washington, D.C.: American Enterprise Institute, 1984).

Kalt, J. P., "The Costs and Benefits of Federal Regulation of Coal Strip Mining," *Natural Resources Journal* 23(4) 1983, 893–915.

Khazzoom, J. D., "Economic Implications of Mandated Efficiency Standards for Household Appliances," *Energy Journal* 4(1) 1980, 27–40.

Levinson, M., "Alcohol Fuels Revisited: The Costs and Benefits of Energy Independence in Brazil," *Journal of Developing Areas* 21(3) 1987, 243–257.

MacAvoy, P. W., "The Regulation-Induced Shortage of Natural Gas," *Journal of Law and Economics* 12(1) 1971, 167–200.

Morrison, W., and R. Mendelsohn, "The Impact of Global Warming on U.S. Energy Expenditures," in R. Mendelsohn and J. E. Neumann, eds., *The Impact of Climate Change on the United States Economy* (Cambridge: Cambridge University Press, 2004), 209–236.

Rosenfeld, A., C. Atkinson, J. Koomey, A. Maier, R. Mowris, and L. Price, "Conserved Energy Supply Curves for U.S. Buildings," *Contemporary Policy Issues* 11(1) 1993, 45–68.

Rowe, R., M. G. Shelby, J. B. Epel, and A. Michelsen, "Using Oxygenated Fuels to Mitigate Carbon Monoxide Air Pollution: The Case of Denver," *Contemporary Policy Issues* 8(1) 1990, 39–53.

Sexton, R. J., and T. A. Sexton, "Theoretical and Methodological Perspectives on Consumer Response to Electricity Information," *Journal of Consumer Affairs* 21(2) 1987, 238–257.

Trane, K. E., "Incentives for Energy Conservation in the Commercial and Industrial Sectors," *The Energy Journal* 9(3) 1988, 113–128.

Walls, M. A., "Welfare Costs of an Oil Import Fee," *Contemporary Policy Issues* 8(2) 1990, 176–189.

Wenders, J. T., and R. A. Lyman, "An Analysis of the Benefits and Costs of Seasonal-Time-of-Day Electricity Rates," in M. A. Crew, ed., *Problems in Public Utility Economics Regulation* (Lexington, MA: D.C. Heath, 1979), 73–91.

Wenders, J. T., and R. A. Lyman, "Determining the Optimal Penetration of Time-of-Day Electricity Tariffs," *Electric Ratemaking* 1 1982, 15–20.

7. Forestry

Anderson, F. J., "Ontario Reforestation Policy: Benefits and Costs," *Canadian Public Policy* 5(3) 1979, 336–347.

Hagen, D. A., J. W. Vincent, and P. G. Welle, "The Benefits of Preserving Old-Growth Forests and the Northern Spotted Owl," *Contemporary Policy Issues* 10(2) 1992, 13–26.

Hyde, W. F., R. G. Boyd, and B. L. Daniels, "The Impacts of Public Interventions: An Examination of the Forestry Sector," *Journal of Policy Analysis and Management* 7(1) 1987, 40–61.

Newcomb, K., "An Economic Justification for Rural Afforestation: The Case of Ethiopia," *Annals of Regional Science* 21(3) 1987, 80–99.

Rosenthal, D. H., and T. C. Brown, "Comparability of Market Prices and Consumer Surplus for Resource Allocation Decisions," *Journal of Forestry* 83(2) 1985, 105–109.

Rubin, J., G. Helland, and J. Loomis, "A Benefit-Cost Analysis of the Northern Spotted Owl: Results from a Contingent Valuation Survey," *Journal of Forestry* 89(12) 1991, 25–30.

Songhen, B. L., and R. Mendelsohn, "The Impacts of Climate Change on the U.S. Timber Market," in R. Mendelsohn and J. E. Neumann, eds., *The Impact of Climate Change on the United States Economy* (Cambridge: Cambridge University Press, 2004), 94–132.

Stone, M., and R. Reid, "Opportunity Costs of Spotted Owl Management Options for British Columbia," *Canadian Public Policy* 23(2) 1997, 69–82.

8. Hazardous Waste (Including Nuclear Power and Waste)

Gamble, H. B., and R. H. Downing, "Effects of Nuclear Power Plants on Residential Property Values," *Journal of Regional Science* 22(4) 1982, 457–478.

Grossman, P. Z., and E. S. Cassedy, "Cost-Benefit Analysis of Nuclear Waste Disposal: Accounting for Safeguards," *Science, Technology and Human Values* 10(1) 1985, 47–54.

Hageman, R. K., "Nuclear Waste Disposal: Potential Property Value Impacts," *Natural Resources Journal* 21(4) 1981, 789–810.

Nelson, J. P., "Three Mile Island and Residential Property Values: Empirical Analysis and Policy Implications," *Land Economics* 57(3) 1981, 363–372.

O'Donnell, E. P., and J. J. Mauro, "A Cost-Benefit Comparison of Nuclear and Non-Nuclear Health and Safety Protective Measures and Regulation," *Nuclear Safety* 20(5) 1979, 525–540.

Payne, B. A., S. J. Olshansky, and T. E. Segel, "The Effects on Property Values of Proximity to a Site Contaminated with Radioactive Waste," *Natural Resources Journal* 27(3) 1987, 579–590.

Sengupta, M., "The Choice Between Coal and Nuclear Power in India: A Cost-Benefit Approach," *Journal of Energy and Development* 2(1) 1986, 85–92.

Smith, V. K., and W. H. Desvousges, "The Value of Avoiding a LULU: Hazardous Waste Disposal Sites," *Review of Economics and Statistics* 68(2) 1986, 293–299.

9. Health and Health Regulation

Albritton, R. B., "Cost-Benefits of Measles Eradication: Effects of a Federal Intervention," *Policy Analysis* 4(1) 1978, 1–22.

Bartel, A., and P. Taubman, "Some Economic and Demographic Consequences of Mental Illness," *Journal of Labor Economics* 4(2) 1986, 243–256.

Bartel, A. P., and L. G. Thomas, "Direct and Indirect Effects of Regulation: A New Look at OSHA's Impact," *Journal of Law and Economics* 28(1) 1985, 1–25.

Berger, M. C., et al., "Valuing Changes in Health Risks: A Comparison of Alternative Measures," *Southern Economic Journal* 53(4) 1987, 967–984.

Birch, S., and C. Donaldson, "Applications of Cost-Benefit Analysis to Health Care: Departure from Welfare Economic Theory," *Journal of Health Economics* 6(3) 1987, 211–225.

Boyle, M. H., G. W. Torrance, J. C. Sinclair, and S. P. Horwood, "Economic Evaluation of Neonatal Intensive Care of Very-Low-Birth-Weight Infants," *New England Journal of Medicine* 308(22) 1983, 1330–1337.

Brown, R. A., and C. H. Green, "Threats to Health and Safety: Perceived Risk and Willingness-to-Pay," *Social Science and Medicine* 15(2) part D, 1981, 67–75.

Bunker, J. P., B. A. Barnes, and F. Mosteller, eds., *Costs, Risks and Benefits of Surgery* (New York: Oxford University Press, 1977).

Butler, J. R., and D. P. Doessel, "Measuring Benefits in Health: A Clarification," *Scottish Journal of Political Economy* 28(2) 1981, 196–205.

Buxton, M. J., and R. R. West, "Cost-Benefit Analysis of Long-Term Haemodialysis for Chronic Renal Failure," *British Medical Journal* 2(5967) 1975, 376–379.

Cauley, S. D., "The Time Price of Medical Care," *Review of Economics and Statistics* 69(1) 1987, 59–66.

Chernickovsky, D., and I. Zmora, "A Hedonic Prices Approach to Hospitalization Costs: The Case of Israel," *Journal of Health Economics* 5(2) 1986, 179–191.

Churchill, D. N., B. C. Lemon, and G. W. Torrance, "A Cost-Effectiveness Analysis of Continuous Ambulatory Peritoneal Dialysis and Hospital Hemodialysis," *Medical Decision Making* 4(4) 1984, 489–500.

Clarke, P., "Cost-Benefit Analysis and Mammographic Screening: A Travel Cost Approach," *Journal of Health Economics* 17(6) 1998, 767–787.

Cummings, J., and F. Weaver, "Cost Effectiveness of Home Care," *Clinics in Geriatric Medicine* 7(4) 1991, 865–874.

Cummings, J., and F. Weaver, et al., "Cost Effectiveness and Hospital-Based Home Care," in J. Romeis and R. Coe, eds., *Quality and Cost Containment in Care of the Elderly* (New York: Springer Publishing Company, 1991), 159–174.

Dardis, R., S. Aaronson, and Y. Lin, "Cost-Benefit Analysis of Flammability Standards," *American Journal of Agricultural Economics* 60(4) 1978, 695–700.

Devaney, B., L. Bilheimer, and J. Schore, "Medicaid Costs and Birth Outcomes: The Effects of Prenatal WIC Participation and the Use of Prenatal Care," *Journal of Policy Analysis and Management* 11(4) 1992, 573–592.

Dewees, D. N., and R. J. Daniels, "The Costs of Protecting Occupational Health: The Asbestos Case," *Journal of Human Resources* 21(3) 1986, 381–396.

Disbrow, D., "The Costs and Benefits of Nutrition Services: A Literature Review," *Journal of American Dietetic Association* 89(4) 1989, supplements.

Evans, R. G., and G. C. Robinson, "Surgical Day Care: Measurements of the Economic Payoff," *Canadian Medical Association Journal* 123(9) 1980, 873–880.

Fisher, G. W., "Willingness-to-Pay for Probabilistic Improvements in Functional Health Status: A Psychological Perspective," in S. Mushkin and D. W. Dunlop, eds., *Health: What Is It Worth? Measures of Health Benefits* (New York: Pergammon Press, 1979), 167–200.

Ginsberg, G., S. Sham, and B. Lev, "Cost-Benefit Analysis of Risperidone and Clozapine in the Treatment of Schizophrenia in Israel," *Pharmaco-economics* 13(7) 1998, 231–241.

Ginsberg, G. M., and D. Shouval, "Cost-Benefit Analysis of a Nationwide Neonatal Inoculation Programme against Hepatitis B in an Area of Intermediate Endemicity," *Journal of Epidemiology and Community Health* 46(6) 1992, 587–594.

Goldman, F., and M. Grossman, "The Demand for Pediatric Care: A Hedonic Approach," *Journal of Political Economy* 86(2) part 1, 1978, 259–280.

Goodwin, P. J., R. Feld, W. K. Evans, and J. Pater, "Cost-Effectiveness of Cancer Chemotherapy: An Economic Evaluation of a Randomized Trial in Small-Cell Lung Cancer," *Journal of Clinical Oncology* 6(10) 1988, 1537–1547.

Grannemann, T. W., R. S. Brown, and M. V. Pauly, "Estimating Hospital Costs: A Multiple Output Analysis," *Journal of Health Economics* 5(2) 1986, 107–127.

Hagard, S., and F. A. Carter, "Preventing the Birth of Infants with Down's Syndrome: A Cost-Benefit Analysis," *British Medical Journal* 1(6012) 1976, 753–756.

Hagard S., F. Carter, and R. G. Milne, "Screening for Spina Bifida: A Cost-Benefit Analysis," *British Journal of Social and Preventive Medicine* 30(1) 1976, 40–53.

Harrington, W., and P. R. Portney, "Valuing the Benefits of Health and Safety Regulation," *Journal of Urban Economics* 22(1) 1987, 101–112.

Hartunian, N. S., C. N. Smart, and M. S. Thompson, "The Incidence and Economic Costs of Cancer, Motor Vehicle Injuries, Coronary Heart Disease and Stroke: A Comparative Analysis," *American Journal of Public Health* 70(12) 1980, 1249–1260.

Hellinger, F. J., "Cost-Benefit Analysis of Health Care: Past Applications and Future Prospects," *Inquiry* 17(3) 1980, 204–215.

Hull, R., J. Hirsh, D. L. Sackett, and G. L. Stoddart, "Cost-Effectiveness of Clinical Diagnosis, Venography and Noninvasive Testing in Patients with Symptomatic Deep-Vein Thrombosis," *New England Journal of Medicine* 304(26) 1981, 1561–1567.

Jerrell, J. M., and T. Hu, "Cost-Effectiveness of Intensive Clinical and Case Management Compared with an Existing System of Care," *Inquiry* 26(2) 1989, 224–234.

Johnson, L. L., *Cost-Benefit Analysis and Voluntary Safety Standards for Consumer Products* (Santa Monica, CA: Rand Corporation, 1982).

Joyce, T. J., M. Grossman, and F. Goldman, "An Assessment of the Benefits of Air Pollution Control: The Case of Infant Health," *Journal of Urban Economics* 25(1) 1989, 32–51.

Kutner, N. G., "Cost-Benefit Issues in U.S. National Health Legislation: The Case of the End-Stage Renal Disease Program," *Social Problems* 30(1) 1982, 51–64.

Levin, H. V., "A Benefit Cost Analysis of Nutritional Programs for Anemia Reduction," *World Bank Research Observer* 1(2) 1986, 219–245.

Logan, A. G., B. J. Milne, C. Achber, W. P. Campbell, and R. B. Haynes, "Cost-Effectiveness of Worksite Hypertension Programme," *Hypertension* 3(2) 1981, 211–218.

Ludbrook, A., "A Cost-Effectiveness Analysis of the Treatment of Chronic Renal Failure," *Applied Economics* 13(3) 1981, 337–350.

Mauskopf, J. A., C. J. Bradley, and M. J. French, "Benefit-Cost Analysis of Hepatitis B Vaccine Program for Occupationally Exposed Workers," *Journal of Occupational Medicine* 33(6) 1991, 691–698.

Neuhauser, D., and A. M. Lewicki, "What Do We Gain from the Sixth Stool Guaiac?" *New England Journal of Medicine* 293(5) 1975, 226–228.

Paterson, M. L., "Cost-Benefit Evaluation of a New Technology for Treatment of Peptic Ulcer Disease," *Managerial and Decision Economics* 4(1) 1983, 50–62.

Rosser, R., and P. Kind, "A Scale of Valuations of States of Illness: Is There a Social Consensus?" *International Journal of Epidemiology* 7(4) 1978, 347–358.

Ruchlin, H. S., et al., "The Efficacy of Second-Opinion Consultation Programs: A Cost-Benefit Perspective," *Medical Care* 20(1) 1982, 3–20.

Schoenbaum, S. C., et al., "Benefit-Cost Analysis of Rubella Vaccination Policy," *New England Journal of Medicine* 294(6) 1976, 306–310.

Schoenbaum, S. C., et al., "The Swine-Influenza Decision," *New England Journal of Medicine* 295(14) 1977, 759–785.

Shukla, R. K., "ALL-RN Model of Nursing Care Delivery: A Cost-Benefit Evaluation," *Inquiry* 20(2) 1983, 173–184.

Stilwell, J. A., "Benefits and Costs of the Schools' BCG Vaccination Programme," *British Medical Journal* 1(6016) 1976, 1002–1004.

Strange, P. V., and A. T. Sumner, "Predictive Treatment Costs and Life Expectancy for End Stage Renal Disease," *New England Journal of Medicine* 298(7) 1978, 372–378.

Torrance, G. W., "Measurement of Health State Utilities for Economic Appraisal: A Review," *Journal of Health Economics* 5(1) 1986, 1–30.

Warner, K. E., and R. C. Hutton, "Cost-Benefit and Cost-Effectiveness Analysis in Health Care: Growth and Composition of the Literature," *Medical Care* 18(11) 1980, 1069–1084.

Weisbrod, B. A., "Costs and Benefits of Medical Research: A Case Study of Poliomyelitis," *Journal of Political Economy* 79(3) 1971, 527–544.

Weisbrod, B. A., "Benefit-Cost Analysis of a Controlled Experiment: Treating the Mentally Ill," *Journal of Human Resources* 16(4) 1981, 523–548.

Williams, A. H., "The Costs and Benefits of Surgery," in J. S. P. Lumley and J. L. Craven, eds., *Surgical Review I* (London: Butterworths, 1978).

Williams, A. H., "Economics of Coronary Artery Bypass Grafting," *British Medical Journal* 291(2) 1985, 326–329.

Windle, R., and M. Dresner, "Mandatory Child Safety Seats in Air Transport: Do They Save Lives?" *Transportation Research Forum* 31(2) 1991, 309–316.

Zeckhauser, R., "Measuring Risks and Benefits of Food Safety Decisions," *Vanderbilt Law Review* 38(3) 1985, 539–569.

10. Industry Regulation (Not Professional or Safety)

Anderson, J. E., "The Relative Inefficiency of Quotas," *American Economic Review* 17(1) 1985, 178–190.

Bailey, E. E., D. R. Graham, and D. Kaplan, *Deregulating the Airlines* (Cambridge, MA: MIT Press, 1985).

Barnekov, C. C., and A. N. Kleit, "The Efficiency Effects of Railroad Deregulation in the United States," *International Journal of Transport Economics* 17(1) 1990, 21–38.

Barth, J. R., J. J. Cordes, and A. M. J. Yezer, "Benefits and Costs of Legal Restrictions on Personal Loan Markets," *Journal of Law and Economics* 29(2) 1986, 357–380.

Beck, R., C. Hoskins, and G. Mumey, "The Social Welfare Loss from Egg and Poultry Marketing Boards, Revisited," *Canadian Journal of Agricultural Economics* 42(2) 1994, 149–158.

Benston, G. J., "An Appraisal of the Costs and Benefits of Government-Required Disclosure: SEC and FTC Requirements," *Law and Contemporary Problems* 41(3) 1977, 30–62.

Bogen, K. D., "The Costs of Price Regulation: Lessons From Railroad Deregulation," *Rand Journal of Economics* 18(3) 1987, 408–416.

Boorstein, R., and R. C. Feenstra, "Quality Upgrading and Its Welfare Cost in U.S. Steel Imports, 1969–74," in Elhanam Helpman and Assaf Razin, eds., *International Trade and Trade Policy* (Cambridge, MA: The MIT Press, 1991), 167–186.

Boyer, K., "The Costs of Price Regulation: Lessons from Railroad Deregulation," *Rand Journal of Economics* 18(3) 1987, 408–416.

de Melo, J., and D. Tarr, "Welfare Costs of U.S. Quotas in Textiles, Steel and Autos," *The Review of Economics and Statistics* 72(3) 1990, 489–497.

DeVany, A. S., W. Gram, T. Saving, and C. W. Smithson, "The Impact of Input Regulation: The Case of Costs and Input Use," *Journal of Law and Economics* 25(2) 1982, 367–382.

Dinopoulos, E., and M. E. Kreinin, "Effects of the U.S.-Japan Auto VER on European Prices and on U.S. Welfare," *The Review of Economics and Statistics* 70(3) 1983, 484–491.

Feenstra, R. C., "How Costly is Protectionism?" *Journal of Economic Perspectives* 6(3) 1992, 159–178.

Felton, J. R., "Costs and Benefits of Motor Truck Regulation," *Quarterly Review of Economics and Business* 18(2) 1980, 7–20.

Gomez-Ibanez, J., R. Leone, and S. O'Connell, "Restraining Auto Imports: Does Anyone Win?" *Journal of Policy Analysis and Management* 2(2) 1983, 196–219.

Gray, W., "The Cost of Regulation: OSHA, EPA and the Productivity Slowdown," *American Economic Review* 77(5) 1987, 998–1012.

Guash, J. L. and R. W. Hahn, "The Costs and Benefits of Regulation: Implications for Developing Countries," *The World Bank Research Observer* 14(1) 1999, 137–158.

Hahn, R. W., and J. A. Hird, "The Costs and Benefits of Regulation: Review and Synthesis," *Yale Journal of Regulation* 8(1) 1991, 233–278.

Hazilla, M., and R. Kop, "Social Cost of Environmental Quality Regulations: A General Equilibrium Analysis," *Journal of Political Economy* 98(4) 1990, 853–873.

Hufbauer, G. C., and K. A. Elliott, *Measuring the Cost of Protection in the United States* (Washington, D.C.: Institute for International Economics, 1994).

Ippolito, R. A., "The Effect of Price Regulation in the Automobile Insurance Industry," *Journal of Law and Economics* 23(1) 1979, 55–90.

Len, G. M., A. Schnitz, and R. D. Knutsen, "Gains and Losses of Sugar Program Policy Options," *American Journal of Agricultural Economics* 69(5) 1987, 591–608.

Moore, T. G., "U.S. Airline Deregulation: Its Effects on Passengers, Capital and Labor," *Journal of Law and Economics* 29(1) 1986, 1–2.

Morrison, S., and C. Winston, *The Economic Effects of Airline Deregulation* (Washington, D.C.: The Brookings Institution, 1986).

Mynemi, G., J. Dorfman, and G. C. Ames, "Welfare Impacts of the Canada-U.S. Softwood Lumber Trade Dispute: Beggar Thy Consumer Trade Policy," *Canadian Journal of Agricultural Economics* 42(3) 1994, 261–271.

Olsen, E. O., "An Economic Analysis of Rent Control in New York City," *Journal of Political Economy* 80(6) 1972, 1081–1110.

Peltzman, S., "The Effect of FTC Advertising Regulation," *Journal of Law and Economics* 24(3) 1981, 403–448.

Schmitz, A., and T. G. Schmitz, "Supply Management: The Past and Future," *Canadian Journal of Agricultural Economics* 42(2) 1994, 125–148.

Schneider, L., B. Klein, and K. M. Murphy, "Governmental Regulation of Cigarette Health Information," *Journal of Law and Economics* 24(3) 1981, 575–612.

Sloan, F. A., and B. Steinwald, "Effects of Regulation on Hospital Costs," *Journal of Law and Economics* 23(1) 1980, 81–110.

Smith, A., and A. J. Venables, "Counting the Cost of Voluntary Restraints in the European Car Market," in E. Helpman and A. Razin, eds., *International Trade and Trade Policy* (Cambridge, MA: The MIT Press, 1991), 187–220.

Smith, J. K., "An Analysis of State Regulations Governing Liquor Store Licensees," *Journal of Law and Economics* 25(2) 1982, 301–319.

Smith, R. L., II, "Franchise Regulation: An Economic Analysis of State Restrictions on Automobile Distribution," *Journal of Law and Economics* 25(1) 1982, 125–157.

Treda, I., and J. Whalley, "Global Effects of Developed Country Trade Restrictions on Textiles and Apparel," *The Economic Journal* 100(403) 1990, 1190–1205.

Winston, C., "Welfare Effects of ICC Regulation Revisited," *Bell Journal of Economics* 12(1) 1981, 232–244.

Winston, C., T. M. Corsi, C. M. Grimm, and C. A. Evans, *The Economic Effects of Surface Rate Deregulation* (Washington, D.C.: The Brookings Institution, 1990).

11. Noise Pollution

Alexandre, A., J. Barde, and D. W. Pearce, "Practical Determination of a Charge for Noise Pollution," *Journal of Transport Economics and Policy* 14(2) 1980, 205–220.

Brons, M., "Railroad Noise: Economic Valuation and Policy," *Transportation Research-D* 8(3) 2003, 169–184.

Epsey, M., and H. Lopez, "The Impact of Airport Noise and Proximity on Residential Property Values," *Growth and Change* 31(3) 2000, 409–419.

Gautrin, J. F., "An Evaluation of the Impact of Aircraft Noise on Property Values with a Simple Model of Urban Land Rent," *Land Economics* 51(1) 1975, 80–86.

Harrison, D., Jr., "The Problem of Aircraft Noise," in T. C. Schelling, ed., *Incentives for Environmental Protection* (Cambridge, MA: The MIT Press, 1983), 43–69.

Langley, J. C., Jr., "Adverse Impacts of the Washington Beltway on Residential Property Values," *Land Economics* 52(1) 1976, 54–65.

Mayeres, I., S. Ochelen, and S. Proost, "The Marginal External Costs of Urban Transport," *Transportation Research-D* 1(2) 1996, 111–130.

Mieszkowski, P., and A. M. Saper, "An Estimate of the Effects of Airport Noise on Property Values," *Journal of Urban Economics* 5(4) 1978, 425–440.

Morrell, P., and C. Lu, "Aircraft Noise Social Cost and Charge Mechanisms—A Case Study of Amsterdam Airport Schiphol," *Transportation Research-D* 5(4) 2000, 305–320.

Nelson, J. P., "Airports and Property Values," *Journal of Transport Economics and Policy* 14(1) 1980, 37–52.

Nelson, J. P., "Highway Noise and Property Values: A Survey of Recent Evidence," *Journal of Transport Economics and Policy* 16(2) 1982, 117–138.

Nero, G, and J. Black, "A Critical Examination of an Airport Noise Mitigation Scheme and an Aircraft Noise Charge: The Case of Capacity Expansion and Externalities at Sydney (Kingford Smith) Airport," *Transportation Research-D* 5(6) 2000, 433–461.

O'Byrne, P. H., J. P. Nelson, and J. J. Seneca, "Housing Values, Census Estimates, Disequilibrium, and the Environmental Cost of Airport Noise: A Case Study of Atlanta," *Journal of Environmental Economics and Management* 12(2) 1985, 169–178.

Pearce, D. W., "Noise Valuation," in D. W. Pearce, ed., *The Valuation of Social Cost* (London: George Allen, 1978), 31–53.

Pennington, G., N. Topham, and R. Ward, "Aircraft Noise and Residential Property Values Adjacent to Manchester International Airport," *Journal of Transport Economics and Policy* 24(3) 1990, 49–59.

Whitbread, M., "Measuring the Costs of Noise Nuisance from Aircraft," *Journal of Transport Economics and Policy* 12(2) 1978, 202–208.

Wilhelmsson, M., "The Impact of Traffic Noise on the Values of Single-Family Houses," *Journal of Environmental Planning and Management* 43(6) 2000, 799–815.

12. Parks, Lakes, Rivers, Open Space, and Other Recreation

Bateman, I., and I. Langford, "Non-Users" Willingness to Pay for a National Park: An Application and

Critique of the Contingent Valuation Method," *Regional Studies* 31(6) 1997, 571–582.

Beasley, S. D., W. G. Workman, and N. A. Williams, "Estimating Amenity Values of Urban Fringe Farmland: A Contingent Valuation Approach: Note," *Growth and Change* 17(4) 1986, 70–78.

Breffle, W., E. Morey, and T. Lodder, "Using Contingent Valuation to Estimate a Neighborhood's Willingness to Pay to Preserve Undeveloped Urban Land," *Urban Studies* 35(4) 1998, 715–728.

Brookshire, D. S., B. Ives, and W. D. Schultze, "The Valuation of Aesthetic Preferences," *Journal of Environmental Economics and Management* 3(4) 1976, 325–346.

Burt, O. R., and D. Brewer, "Estimation of Net Social Benefits from Outdoor Recreation," *Econometrica* 39(5) 1971, 813–827.

Caulkins, P. P., R. C. Bishop, and N. Bouwes Sr., "The Travel Cost Model for Lake Recreation: A Comparison of Two Methods for Incorporating Site Quality and Substitution Effects," *American Journal of Agricultural Economics* 68(2) 1986, 291–297.

Clawson, M., and J. L. Knetsch, *Economics of Outdoor Recreation* (Baltimore: Johns Hopkins University Press, 1966).

Darling, A. H., "Measuring Benefits Generated by Urban Water Parks," *Land Economics* 49(1) 1973, 22–34.

Daubert, J. T., and R. A. Young, "Recreational Demands for Maintaining Instream Flows: A Contingent Valuation Approach," *American Journal of Agricultural Economics* 63(4) 1981, 666–684.

Dwyer, J. F., H. W. Schroeder, J. J. Louviere, and D. H. Anderson, "Urbanites Willingness to Pay for Trees and Forests in Recreation Areas," *Journal of Arboriculture* 15(10) 1989, 247–252.

Fix, P., and J. Loomis, "Comparing the Economic Value of Mountain Biking Estimated Using Revealed and Stated Preference," *Journal of Environmental Planning and Management* 41(2), 1998, 227–236.

Gum, R. L., and E. W. Martin, "Problems and Solutions in Estimating the Demand for and Value of Rural Outdoor Recreation," *American Journal of Agricultural Economics* 57(4) 1975, 558–566.

Hanley, N. D., "Valuing Rural Recreation Benefits: An Empirical Comparison of Two Approaches," *Journal of Agricultural Economics* 40(3) 1989, 361–374.

Hanley, N. D., R. Wright, and G. Koop, "Modelling Recreation Demand Using Choice Experiments: Climbing in Scotland," *Environmental and Resource Economics* 22(3) 2002, 449–466.

Harris, B. S., and A. D. Meister, "The Use of Recreation Analysis in Resource Management: A Case Study," *Journal of Environmental Management* 16(2) 1983, 117–124.

Irwin, E., "The Effects of Open Space on Residential Property Values," *Land Economics* 78(4) 2002, 465–480.

Lindsay, G., and G. Knapp, "Willingness to Pay for Urban Greenway Projects," *Journal of the American Planning Association* 65(3) 1999, 44–51.

Loomis, J. B., "Balancing Public Trust Resources of Mono Lake and L.A.'s Water Right: An Economic Approach," *Water Resources Research* 23(8) 1987, 1449–1456.

Loomis, J. B., C. S. Sorg, and D. M. Donnelly, "Evaluating Regional Demand Models for Estimating Recreation Use and Economic Benefits: A Case Study," *Water Resources Research* 22(4) 1986, 431–438.

McConnell, K. E., "Congestion and Willingness to Pay: A Case Study of Beach Use," *Land Economics* 53(2) 1977, 185–195.

Menz, F. C., and J. K. Mullin, "Expected Encounters and Willingness to Pay for Outdoor Recreation," *Land Economics* 57(1) 1981, 33–40.

Raybould, M., and T. Mules, "A Cost-Benefit Study of the Protection of the Northern Beaches of Australia's Gold Coast," *Tourism Economics* 5(2) 1999, 121–139.

Richer J., Willingness to Pay for Desert Protection, *Contemporary Economic Policy* 13(4) 1995, 93–104.

Schroeder, T. D., "The Relationship of Local Public Park and Recreation Services to Residential Property Values," *Journal of Leisure Research* 14(3) 1982, 223–234.

Schulze, W. D., and D. S. Brookshire, "The Economic Benefits of Preserving Visibility in the National Parklands of the Southwest," *Natural Resources Journal* 23(1) 1983, 124–133.

Walker, J. L., "Tall Trees, People, and Politics: The Opportunity Costs of the Redwood National Park," *Contemporary Policy Issues* 0(5) 1984, 22–29.

Willis, K. G., and J. F. Benson, "A Comparison of User Benefits and Costs of Nature Conservation at Three Nature Reserves," *Regional Studies* 22(5) 1988, 417–428.

Willis, K. G., and G. D. Garrod, "Valuing Landscape: A Contingent Valuation Approach," *Journal of Environmental Management* 37(1) 1993, 1–22.

13. Professional Regulation

Begun, J. W., *Professionalism and the Public Interest: Price and Quality in Optometry* (Cambridge, MA: MIT Press, 1981).

Benham, L., "The Effect of Advertising on the Price of Eyeglasses," *Journal of Law and Economics* 15(2) 1972, 337–352.

Caroll, S. L., and R. J. Gaston, "Occupational Restrictions and Quality of Service Received: Some Evidence," *Southern Economic Journal* 47(4) 1981, 959–976.

Feldman, R., and J. W. Begun, "The Effects of Advertising Restrictions: Lessons from Optometry," *Journal of Human Resources* 13(supplement) 1978, 248–262.

Feldman, R., and J. W. Begun, "The Welfare Cost of Quality Changes Due to Professional Regulation," *The Journal of Industrial Economics* 34(1) 1985, 17–33.

Haas-Wilson, D., "The Effect of Commercial Practice Restrictions: The Case of Optometry," *Journal of Law and Economics* 29(1) 1986, 165–186.

Leffer, K. B., "Physician Licensure: Competition and Monopoly in American Medicine," *Journal of Law and Economics* 21(1) 1978, 165–186.

Shepard, L., "Licensing Restrictions and the Cost of Dental Care," *Journal of Law and Economics* 21(1) 1978, 187–201.

White, W. D. "The Impact of Occupational Licensure of Clinical Laboratory Personnel," *Journal of Human Resources* 8(4) 1978, 91–102.

White, W. D., *Public Health and Private Gain: The Economics of Licensing Clinical Laboratory Personnel* (Chicago: Maaroufa Press Inc., 1979).

14. Public Works (Nontransit)

Blackorby, C., G. Donaldson, R. Picard, and M. Slade, "Expo 1986: An Economic Impact Analysis," in R. C. Allen and G. Rosenblath, eds., *Restraining the Economy: Social Credit Economic Policies for B.C. in the Eighties* (Vancouver: New Star Books, 1986), 254–278.

Conrad, K., and H. Seitz, "The Economic Benefits of Public Infrastructure," *Applied Economics* 26(4) 1994, 303–311.

Graves, S. C., M. Horwitch, and E. H. Bowman, "Deep-Draft Dredging of U.S. Coal Ports: A Cost-Benefit Analysis," *Policy Sciences* 17(2) 1985, 153–178.

Muller, R. A., "Some Economics of the Grand Canal," *Canadian Public Policy* 14(2) 1988, 162–174.

Shaffer, M., "The Benefits and Costs of Two B.C. Hydro Construction Projects," in R. C. Allen and G. Rosenblath, eds., *Restraining the Economy* (Vancouver: New Star Books, 1986), 279–296.

Viscencio-Brambila, H., and S. Fuller, "Estimated Effects of Deepened U.S. Gulf Ports on Export-Grain Flow Pattern and Logistics Costs," *Logistics and Transportation Review* 23(2) 1987, 139–154.

Yochum, G. R., and V. B. Agarwal, "Economic Impact of Port on a Regional Economy: Note," *Growth and Change* 18(3) 1987, 74–87.

15. R&D

Bozeman, B., and A. N. Link, "Tax Incentives for R&D: A Critical Evaluation," *Research Policy* 13(1) 1984, 21–31.

Fox, G., "Is the United States Really Underinvesting in Agricultural Research?" *American Journal of Agricultural Economics* 67(4) 1985, 806–812.

Griliches, Z., "Research Cost and Social Returns: Hybrid Corn and Related Innovations," *Journal of Political Economy* 66(1) 1958, 419–431.

Mansfield, E., and L. Switzer, "How Effective Are Canada's Direct Tax Incentives for R&D?" *Canadian Public Policy* 11(2) 1985, 241–246.

Nagy, J. G., and W. H. Furtan, "Economic Costs and Returns From Crop Development Research: The Case of Rapeseed Breeding in Canada," *Canadian Journal of Agricultural Economics* 26(1) 1978, 1–14.

Nelson, R., "Government Support of Technical Progress—Lessons from History," *Journal of Policy Analysis and Management* 2(4) 1983, 499–514.

Norton, G. W., and J. S. Davis, "Evaluating Returns to Agricultural Research: A Review," *American Journal of Agricultural Economics* 63(4) 1981, 685–699.

Norton, G. W., V. G. Ganoza, and C. Pomereda, "Potential Benefits of Agricultural Research and Extension in Peru," *American Journal of Agricultural Economics* 69(2) 1987, 247–257.

Stranahan, H. A., and J. S. Shonkwiler, "Evaluating the Returns to Postharvest Research in the Florida Citrus-Processing Subsector," *American Journal of Agricultural Economics* 68(1) 1986, 88–94.

Terleckyj, N., "Direct and Indirect Effects of Industrial Research and Development on the Productivity Growth of Industries," in J. W. Kendrick and B. Vaccara, eds., *New Developments in Productivity Measurements* (Chicago: Chicago University Press for NBER, 1980), 359–377.

Widmer, L. R., G. Fox, and G. L. Brinkman, "The Rate of Return to Agricultural Research in a Small Country: The Case of Beef Cattle Research in Canada," *Canadian Journal of Agricultural Economics* 36(1) 1988, 23–35.

Zentner, R. P., "Returns to Public Investment in Canadian Wheat and Rapeseed Research," in K. K. Klein and W. H. Furtan, eds., *Economics of Agricultural Research in Canada* (Calgary: The University of Calgary Press, 1983), 169–188.

16. Recreational and Commercial Fisheries

Anderson, D. M., S. A. Shankle, M. J. Scott, D. A. Neitzel, and J. C. Chatters, "Valuing Effects of Climate Change and Fishery Enhancement on Chinook Salmon," *Contemporary Policy Issues* 11(4) 1993, 82–94.

Anderson, L. G., "The Demand Curve for Recreation Fishing with an Application to Stock Enhancement Activities," *Land Economics* 59(3) 1983, 279–286.

Cauvin, D., "The Valuation of Recreational Fisheries," *Canadian Journal of Fishing and Aquatic Sciences* 37(8) 1980, 1321–1327.

Hufschmidt, M. M., and J. A. Dixon, "Valuation of Losses of Marine Produce Resources Caused by Coastal Development of Tokyo Bay," adapted from materials prepared by Y. Hanayama and I. Sano in J. A. Dixon and M. M. Hufschmidt, eds., *Economic Valuation Techniques for the Environment* (Baltimore and London: The Johns Hopkins University Press, 1986), 102–120.

Layman, R. C., J. R. Boyce, and K. R. Kriddle, "Economic Valuation of the Chinook Salmon Sport Fishery of the Gulkana River, Alaska, Under Current and Alternative Management Plans," *Land Economics* 72(1) 1996, 113–128.

Loomis, J. B., C. Sorg, and D. Donnelly, "Economic Losses to Recreational Fisheries Due to Small-Head Hydro-Power Development: A Case Study of the Henry's Fork in Idaho," *Journal of Environmental Management* 22(1) 1986, 85–94.

Markowski, M., A. Knapp, J. E. Neumann, and J. Gates, "The Economic Impact of Climate Change on the U.S. Commercial Fishing Industry," in R. Mendelsohn and J. Neumann, eds., *The Impact of Climate Change on the United States Economy* (Cambridge: Cambridge University Press, 2004), 237–264.

McConnell, K. E., "Values of Marine Recreational Fishing: Measurement and Impact of Measurement," *American Journal of Agricultural Economics* 61(5) 1979, 921–925.

McConnell, K. E., and V. Duff, "Estimating Net Benefits of Recreational Fishing," *Journal of Environmental Economics and Management* 2(3) 1976, 224–230.

McConnell, K. E., and I. Strand, "Measuring the Cost of Time in Recreation Demand Analysis: An Application to Sportfishing," *American Journal of Agricultural Economics* 63(1) 1981, 153–156.

Meyer, P. A., "Publicly Vested Values for Fish and Wildlife: Criteria in Economic Welfare and Interface with the Law," *Land Economics* 55(2) 1979, 223–235.

Russell, C. S., and W. J. Vaughan, "The National Recreational Fishing Benefits of Water Pollution Control," *Journal of Environmental Economics and Management* 9(3) 1982, 328–354.

Samples, K. C., and R. C. Bishop, "Estimating the Value of Variations in Anglers' Success Rates: An Application of the Multiple-Site Travel Cost Method," *Marine Resource Economics* 2(1) 1985, 55–74.

Schwindt, R., A. Vining, and S. Globerman, "Net Loss: A Cost-Benefit Analysis of the Canadian Pacific Salmon Fishery," *Journal of Policy Analysis and Management* 19(1) 2000, 23–45.

Sorg, C., et al., "The Net Economic Value of Cold and Warm Water Fishing in Idaho," Resource Bulletin, Rocky Mountain Forest and Range Experiment Station, U.S. Forest Service, Fort Collins, Colorado, 1985.

Vaughan, W. J., and C. S. Russell, "Valuing a Fishing Day: An Application of a Systematic Varying Parameter Model," *Land Economics* 58(4) 1982, 450–463.

17. Redistribution Programs and Costs

Ballard, C., "The Marginal Efficiency Cost of Redistribution," *American Economic Review* 78(5) 1988, 1019–1033.

Browning, E. K., "On the Marginal Welfare Costs of Taxation," *American Economic Review* 77(1) 1987, 11–23.

Browning, E., T. Gromberg, and L. Liu, "Alternative Measures of the Marginal Cost of Public Funds," *Economic Inquiry* 38(4) 2000, 591–599.

Caniglia, A. S., "The Economic Evaluation of Food Stamps: An Intertemporal Analysis with Nonlinear Budget Constraints," *Public Finance Quarterly* 16(1) 1988, 3–30.

Creedy, J., "Measuring Welfare Changes and the Excess Burden of Taxation," *Bulletin of Economic Research* 52(1) 2000, 1–47.

Gramlich, E., and M. Wolkoff, "A Procedure for Evaluating Income Distribution Policies," *Journal of Human Resources* 14(3) 1979, 319–350.

Hu, S. T., and N. L. Knaub, "Effects of Cash and In-Kind Welfare on Family Expenditures," *Policy Analysis* 2(1) 1976, 71–92.

Jorgenson, D. W., and K. Yun, "The Excess Burden of Taxation in the United States," *Journal of Accounting, Auditing, and Finance* 6(4) 1991, 487–508.

Knaub, N. L., "The Impact of Food Stamps and Cash Welfare on Food Expenditures, 1971–1975," *Policy Analysis* 7(2) 1981, 169–182.

Lermer, G., and W. T. Stanbury, "The Cost of Redistributing Income by Means of Direct Regulation," *Canadian Journal of Economics* 28(1) 1985, 190–207.

Lewis, H. G., and R. J. Morrison, *Income Transfer Analysis* (Washington, D.C.: The Urban Institute, 1989).

Mead, L. W., "The Potential for Work Enforcement: A Study of WIN," *Journal of Policy Analysis and Management* 7(2) 1988, 264–288.

Moffitt, R. A., and K. C. Kehrer, "The Effect of Tax and Transfer Programs on Labor Supply," *Research in Labor Economics* 4 1981, 103–150.

Tullock, G., *Economics of Income Redistribution* (Hingham, MA: Kluwer Boston, 1983).

Slemrod, J., and S. Yitzhaki, "Integrating Expenditure and Tax Decisions: The Marginal Cost of Funds and the Marginal Benefits of Projects," *National Tax Journal* 54(2) 2001, 189–202.

18. Transportation/Transit (Including Safety)

Alexander, D. A., "Motor Carrier Deregulation and Highway Safety: An Empirical Analysis," *Southern Economic Journal* 59(1) 1992, 28–36.

Beggs, S., S. Cardell, and J. Housman, "Assessing the Potential Demand for Electric Cars," *Journal of Econometrics* 17(1) 1981, 1–20.

Blomquist, G., "Economics of Safety and Seat Belt Use," *Journal of Safety Research* 9(4) 1977, 179–189.

Brems, H., "Light Rail Transit: Cost and Output," *Journal of Urban Economics* 7(1) 1980, 20–30.

Brent, R. J., "Imputing Weights Behind Past Railway Closure Decisions Within a Cost-Benefit Framework," *Applied Economics* 7(2) 1979, 157–170.

Chalk, A. J., "Market Forces and Commercial Aircraft Safety," *The Journal of Industrial Economics* 36(1) 1987, 61–80.

Claybrook, J., and D. Bollier, "The Hidden Benefits of Regulation: Disclosing the Auto Safety Payoff," *Yale Journal of Regulation* 3(1) 1985, 87–132.

Clotfelter, C., and J. Hahn, "Assessing the 55 MPH Speed Limit," *Policy Sciences* 9(3) 1978, 281–294.

Conybeare, J. A. C., "Evaluation of Automobile Safety Regulations: The Case of Compulsory Seat Belt Legislation in Australia," *Policy Sciences* 12(1) 1980, 27–39.

Crandall, R. W., and J. D. Graham, "Automobile Safety Regulation and Offsetting Behaviour: Some New Empirical Estimates," *American Economic Review Papers and Proceedings* 74(2) 1984, 328–331.

Crandall, R. C., H. W. Gruenspecht, T. E. Keeler, and L. B. Lave, *Regulating the Automobile* (Washington, D.C.: The Brookings Institution, 1986).

Davidson, B. R., "A Benefit-Cost Analysis of the New South Wales Railway System," *Australian Economic History Review* 22(2) 1982, 127–150.

de Rus, G., and V. Inglada, "Cost-Benefit Analysis of the High-Speed Train in Spain," *Annals of Regional Science* 31(3) 1997, 175–188.

Dodgson, J. S., "Benefits of Changes in Urban Public Transport Subsidies in Major Australian Cities," *Economic Record,* 62(177) 1986, 224–235.

Dodgson, J. S., and N. Topham, "Benefit-Cost Rules for Urban Transit Subsidies: An Integration of Allocational, Distributional and Public Finance Issues," *Journal of Transport Economics and Policy* 21(1) 1987, 57–71.

Forester, T., R. McNown, and L. Singell, "A Cost-Benefit Analysis of the 55 MPH Speed Limit," *Southern Economic Journal* 50(3) 1984, 631–641.

Gardner, B. M., and R. O. Goss, "Lifeboats vs. Inflatable Liferafts: A Comparison of Costs and Benefits," in R. O. Gross, ed., *Advances in Maritime Economics* (Cambridge, MA: Cambridge University Press, 1977), 247–287.

Gomez-Ibanez, J. A., and G. R. Fauth, "Downtown Auto Restraint Policies: The Costs and Benefits for Boston," *Journal of Transport Economics and Policy* 14(2) 1980, 155–168.

Goodman, A. C., "Willingness to Pay for Car Efficiency: A Hedonic Price Approach," *Journal of Transport Economics and Policy* 17(3) 1983, 247–266.

Gross, R. O. and A. H. Vanags, "The Costs and Benefits of Navigational Aids in Port Approaches," in R. O. Gross, ed., *Advances in Maritime Economics* (Cambridge, MA: Cambridge University Press, 1977), 213–256.

Graham, J. D., and S. Garber, "Evaluating the Effects of Automobile Safety Regulation," *Journal of Policy Analysis and Management* 2(2) 1984, 206–224.

Graves, S. C., M. Horwitch, and E. Bowman, "Deep-Draft Dredging of U.S. Coal Ports: A Cost-Benefit Analysis," *Policy Sciences* 17(2) 1984, 153–178.

Greene, D., and K. G. Duleep, "Costs and Benefits of Automotive Fuel Economy Improvement: A Partial Analysis," *Transportation Research-A* 27(3) 1993, 217–235.

Hanke, S. H., and R. A. Walker, "Benefit-Cost Analysis Reconsidered: An Evaluation of the Mid-State Project," *Water Resources Research* 10(5) 1974, 898–908.

Hansen, B., and K. Tourk, "The Suez Canal Project to Accommodate Super-Tankers," *Journal of Transport Economics and Policy* 8(2) 1974, 103–121.

Hartunian, N., C. N. Smart, T. R. Willemain, and P. Zander, "The Economics of Safety Deregulation: Lives and Dollars Lost Due to Repeal of Motorcycle Helmet Laws," *Journal of Health Politics, Policy and Law* 8(1) 1981, 76–98.

Hettich, W., "The Political Economy of Benefit-Cost Analysis: Evaluating STOL Air Transport for Canada," *Canadian Public Policy* 9(4) 1983, 478–498.

Horowitz, A. J., "Assessing Transportation User Benefits With Maximum Trip Lengths," *Transportation Planning and Technology* 6(3) 1980, 175–182.

Jara-Diaz, S. R., "On the Relation Between Users' Benefits and the Economic Effects of Transportation Activities," *Journal of Regional Science* 26(2) 1986, 379–391.

Jara-Diaz, S. R., and T. L. Friezz, "Measuring the Benefits Derived from a Transportation Investment," *Transportation Research-B* 16(1) 1982, 57–77.

Jonah, B. A., and J. L. Lawson, "The Effectiveness of the Canadian Mandatory Seat Belt Use Laws," *Accident Analysis and Prevention* 16(5/6) 1984, 433–450.

Jones-Lee, M. W., M. Hammerton, and P. R. Philips, "The Value of Safety: Results of a National Sample Survey," *Economic Journal* 95(377) 1985, 49–72.

Joray, P. A., and P. A. Kochanowski, "Inter-Urban Rail Passenger Service — Social Benefits of Retaining the South Shore Railroad (Chicago)," *Logistics and Transportation Review* 14(1) 1978, 81–89.

Kamerud, D. B., "The 55 MPH Speed Limit: Costs, Benefits, and Implied Trade-Offs," *Transportation Research–A* 17(1) 1983, 51–64.

Kamerud, D. B., "Benefits and Costs of the 55 MPH Speed Limit: New Estimates and Their Implications," *Journal of Policy Analysis and Management* 7(2) 1988, 341–352.

Kanemoto, Y., "Cost-Benefit Analysis and the Second Best Land Use for Transportation," *Journal of Urban Economics* 4(4) 1977, 483–503.

Kanemoto, Y., "General Equilibrium Analysis of the Benefits of Large Transportation Improvements," *Regional Science and Urban Economics* 15(3) 1985, 343–363.

Keeler, T. E., "Public Policy and Productivity in the Trucking Industry: Some Evidence on the Effects of Highway Investments, Deregulation, and the 55 MPH Speed Limit," *American Economic Review* 76(2) 1986, 153–158.

Kim, J., and D. S. West, "The Edmonton LRT: An Appropriate Choice?" *Canadian Public Policy* 17(2) 1991, 173–182.

Krupnick, A. J., and M. A. Walls, *The Cost-Effectiveness of Methanol for Reducing Motor Vehicle Emissions and Urban Ozone Levels* (Washington, D.C.: Resources for the Future, 1990).

Lave, C. A., "Speeding, Coordination, and the 55 MPH Limit," *American Economic Review* 75(5) 1985, 1159–1164.

Lave, L. B., and W. E. Weber, "Benefit-Cost Analysis of Auto Safety Features," *Applied Economics* 2(4) 1970, 265–275.

Loeb, P. D., "The Efficacy and Cost-Effectiveness of Motor Vehicle Inspection Using Cross-Sectional Data — An Econometric Analysis," *Southern Economic Journal* 52(2) 1985, 500–509.

Loeb, P. D., and B. Gilad, "The Efficacy and Cost-Effectiveness of Motor Vehicle Inspection: A State Specific Analysis Using Time Series Data," *Journal of Transport Economics and Policy* 18(2) 1984, 145–164.

Mackie, P. J., and D. Simon, "Do Road Projects Benefit Industry? A Case Study of the Humber Bridge," *Journal of Transport Economics and Policy* 20(3) 1986, 377–384.

Mohring, H., "Maximizing, Measuring and Not Double Counting Transportation Improvement Benefits: A Primer on Closed- and Open-Economy Cost-Benefit Analysis," *Transportation Research–B* 27(6) 1993, 413–424.

Muller, A., "Evaluation of the Costs and Benefits of Motorcycle Helmet Laws," *American Journal of Public Health* 70(6) 1980, 586–592.

Nelson, D. E., T. D. Peterson, T. L. Chorba, O. J. Devine, and J. Sacks, "Cost Savings Associated with Increased Safety Belt Use in Iowa, 1987–1988," *Accident Analysis and Prevention* 25(5) 1993, 521–528.

Obeng, K., "Fare Subsidies to Achieve Pareto Optimality: A Benefit-Cost Approach," *Logistics and Transportation Review* 19(4) 1983, 367–384.

Obeng, K., "The Economics of Bus Transit Operation," *Logistics and Transportation Review* 20(1) 1984, 45–65.

Olson, D. D., "A Benefit-Cost Analysis of Improving Alaska's Dalton Highway," *Logistics and Transportation Review* 22(2) 1986, 141–157.

Orr, L. D., "Incentives and Efficiency in Automobile Safety Regulation," *Quarterly Review of Economics and Business* 22(3) 1982, 43–65.

Peaker, A., "The Economics of VTOL Aircraft," *Journal of Transport Economics and Policy* 8(1) 1974, 48–57.

Peltzman, S., "The Effect of Automobile Safety Regulation," *Journal of Political Economy* 83(4) 1975, 677–725.

Sagner, J. S., "Benefit/Cost Analysis: Efficiency-Equity Issues in Transportation," *Logistics and Transportation Review* 16(4) 1980, 339–388.

Sawicki, D. S., "Break-Even B-C Analysis of Alternative Express Transit Systems," *Journal of Transport Economics and Policy* 8(3) 1974, 274–293.

Schwing, R. C., B. Southwark, C. von Buseck, and C. J. Jackson, "Benefit-Cost Analysis of Automobile Emission Reductions," *Journal of Environmental Economics and Management* 7(1) 1980, 44–64.

Small, K. A., "Estimating Air Pollution Costs of Transport Modes," *Journal of Transportation Economics* 11(2) 1977, 109–132.

St. Seidenfus, H., "European Ports in the Context of the World Economy and the European Economy: Changes in Sea Transport," *International Journal of Transportation Economics* 14(2) 1987, 133–138.

Swoveland, C., "Benefit-Cost Analysis of a Proposed Runway Extension," *Management Science* 27(2) 1981, 155–173.

Talley, W. K., and E. E. Anderson, "An Urban Transit Firm Providing Transit, Paratransit and Contracted-Out Services: A Cost Analysis," *Journal of Transport Economics and Policy* 20(3) 1986, 353–368.

Taylor, S., and R. Wright, "An Economic Evaluation of Calgary's North-East Light Rail Transit System," *Logistics and Transportation Review* 19(4) 1983, 351–365.

Viscencio-Brambila, H., and S. Fuller, "Estimated Effects of Deepened U.S. Gulf Ports on Export-Grain Flow Pattern and Logistics Costs," *Logistics and Transportation Review* 23(2) 1987, 139–154.

Vitaliano, D. F., "An Economic Assessment of the Social Costs of Highway Salting and the Efficiency of Substituting a New De-Icing Material," *Journal of Policy Analysis and Management* 11(3) 1992, 397–418.

Viton, P. A., "On the Economics of Rapid-Transit Operations," *Transportation Research–A* 14(4) 1980, 243–253.

Wabe, S., and O. Coles, "The Short and Long Run Cost of Bus Transport in Urban Areas," *Journal of Transport Economics and Policy* 9(2) 1975, 127–140.

Walters, A. A., "The Benefits of Minibuses: The Case of Kuala Lumpur," *Journal of Transport Economics and Policy* 13(3) 1979, 320–334.

Waters, W. G., II, and Shane J. Meyers, "Benefit-Cost Analysis of a Toll Highway: British Columbia's Coquihalla," *Journal of the Transportation Research Forum* 28(1) 1987, 434–443.

Watson, G. S., P. L. Zador, and A. Wilks, "The Repeal of Helmet Use Laws and Increased Motorcyclist Mortality in the United States, 1975–1978," *American Journal of Public Health* 70(6) 1980, 579–585.

Wheaton, W. C., "Residential Decentralization Land Rents and the Benefits of Urban Transportation Investment," *American Economic Review* 67(2) 1977, 136–143.

Woolley, P. K., "C-B Analysis of the Concorde Project," *Journal of Transport Economics and Policy* 6(3) 1972, 225–239.

19. Waste Disposal

Bingham, T. M., "Allocative and Distributive Effects of a Disposal Charge on Product Packaging," in D. Pearce and I. Walter, eds., *Resource Conservation: Social and Economic Dimensions of Recycling* (London: Macmillan, 1977).

Dewees, D. N., and M. J. Hare, "Economic Analysis of Packaging Waste Reduction," *Canadian Public Policy* 24(4) 1998, 453–470.

Dinan, T. M., "Economic Efficiency Effects of Alternative Policies for Reducing Waste Disposal"

Journal of Environmental Economics and Management 25(3) 1993, 242–256.

Ibenholt, K., and H. Lindhejm, "Costs and Benefits of Recycling Liquid Board Containers," *Journal of Consumer Policy* 26(3) 2003, 301–326.

Jenkins, R. R., *The Economics of Solid Waste Reduction: The Impact of User Fees* (Brookfield, VT: Edward Elgar Publishing Company, 1993).

Judge, R., and A. Becker, "Motivating Recycling: A Marginal Cost Analysis," *Contemporary Policy Issues* 11(3) 1993, 58–68.

Palmer, K., H. Sigman, and M. Walls, "The Cost of Reducing Municipal Solid Waste," *Journal of Environmental Economics and Management* 33(2) 1997, 128–150.

Porter, R. C., "A Social Benefit-Cost Analysis of Mandatory Deposits on Beverage Containers," *Journal of Environmental Economics and Management* 5(4) 1978, 351–375.

Rose, D., "National Beverage Container Deposit Legislation: A Cost-Benefit Analysis," *Journal of Environmental Systems* 12(1) 1982, 71–84.

Strathman, J. G., A. M. Rufolo, and G. C. S. Mildner, "The Demand for Solid Waste Disposal," *Land Economics* 71(1) 1995, 57–64.

20. Water

Boyle, K., G. L. Poe, and J. C. Bergstrom, "What Do We Know About Groundwater Values? Preliminary Implications from a Meta Analysis of Contingent-Valuation Studies," *American Journal of Agricultural Economics* 76(5) 1994, 1055–1061.

Crouter, J. P., "Hedonic Estimation Applied to a Water Rights Market," *Land Economics* 63(3) 1987, 259–271.

Decooke, B. G., J. W. Buckley, and S. J. Wright, "Great Lakes Diversions Preliminary Assessment of Economic Impacts," *Canadian Water Resources Journal* 9(1) 1984, 1–15.

Gibbons, D. C., *The Economic Value of Water* (Washington, D.C.: Resources for the Future, 1986).

Hurd, B., J. M. Callaway, J. B. Smith, and P. Kirshen, "Economic Effects of Climate Change on US Water Resources," in R. Mendelsohn and J. Neumann, eds., *The Impact of Climate Change on the United States Economy* (Cambridge: Cambridge University Press, 2004), 133–177.

Kanazawa, M., "Pricing Subsidies and Economic Efficiency: The U.S. Bureau of Reclamation," *Journal of Law and Economics* 36(1) 1993, 205–234.

Kulshreshtha, S. N., et al., "Economic Impacts of Irrigation Development in Alberta Upon the Provincial and Canadian Economy," *Canadian Water Resources Journal* 10(2) 1985, 1–10.

MacRae, D., Jr., and D. Whittington, "Assessing Preferences in Cost-Benefit Analysis: Reflections on Rural Water Supply Evaluation in Haiti," *Journal of Policy Analysis and Management* 7(2) 1988, 246–263.

McGuckin, J. T., and R. A. Young, "On the Economics of Desalination of Brackish Household Water Supplies," *Journal of Environmental Economics and Management* 8(1) 1981, 79–91.

Renzetti, S., "Evaluating the Welfare Effects of Reforming Municipal Water Prices," *Journal of Environmental Economics and Management* 22(2) 1992, 147–163.

21. Water Pollution

Ashworth, J., J. Papps, and D. J. Storey, "Assessing the Impact Upon the British Chlor-Alkali Industry of the EEC Directive on Discharges of Mercury into Waterways," *Land Economics* 63(1) 1987, 72–78.

Beck, M. B., and B. A. Finney, "Operational Water Quality Management: Problem Context and Evaluation of a Model for River Quality," *Water Resources Research* 23(11) 1987, 2030–2042.

Bockstael, N. E., W. M. Hanemann, and C. L. Kling, "Estimating the Value of Water Quality Improvements in a Recreational Demand Framework," *Water Resources Research* 23(5) 1987, 951–960.

Cohen, M. A., "The Costs and Benefits of Oil Spill Prevention and Enforcement," *Journal of Environmental Economics and Management* 13(2) 1986, 167–188.

Dasgupta, A. K., and M. N. Murty, "Economic Evaluation of Water Pollution Abatement: A Case Study of Paper and Pulp Industry in India," *India Economic Review* 20(2) 1985, 231–267.

Desvousges, W. H., V. K. Smith, and A. Fisher, "Option Price Estimates for Water Quality Improvements: A Contingent Valuation Study for the Monongahela River," *Journal of Environmental Economics and Management* 14(3) 1987, 248–267.

Farber, S., and B. Griner, "Valuing Watershed Quality Improvements Using Conjoint Analysis," *Ecological Economics* 34(1) 2000, 63–76.

Feenberg, D., and E. S. Mills, *Measuring the Benefits of Water Pollution Abatement* (New York: Academic Press, 1980).

Gardner, R. L., and R. A. Young, "An Economic Evaluation of the Colorado River Basin Salinity Control Program," *Western Journal of Agricultural Economics* 10(1) 1985, 1–12.

Greenley, D. A., R. G. Walsh, and R. A. Young, "Option Value: Empirical Evidence From a Case Study of Recreation of Water Quality," *Quarterly Journal of Economics* 96(1) 1981, 657–673.

Grigalunas, T. A., et al., "Estimating the Cost of Oil Spills: Lessons from the Amoco Cadiz Incident," *Marine Resource Economics* 2(3) 1986, 239–262.

Harris, B. S., "Contingent Valuation of Water Pollution Control," *Journal of Environmental Management* 19(3) 1984, 199–208.

Hufschmidt, M. M., "Systematic Analysis of Water Pollution Control Options in a Suburban Region of Beijing, China," from a report prepared by F. Guowei, Z. Lansheng, C. Shengtong, and N. Guisheng in J. A. Dixon and M. M. Hufschmidt, eds., *Economic Valuation Techniques for the Environment* (Baltimore and London: The Johns Hopkins University Press, 1986), 178–192.

Hufschmidt, M. M., "The Nam Pong Water Resources Project in Thailand," from a paper prepared by R. Srivardhana in J. A. Dixon and M. M. Hufschmidt, eds., *Economic Valuation Techniques for the Environment* (Baltimore and London: The Johns Hopkins University Press, 1986), 141–162.

Kitabatake, Y., "Welfare Costs of Eutrophication-Caused Production Losses: A Case of Aquaculture in Lake Kasumigaura," *Journal of Environmental Economics and Management* 9(3) 1982, 199–212.

Lichtengerg, E., and D. Zilberman, "Efficient Regulation of Environmental Health Risks: The Case of Groundwater Contamination in California," *Recherche Economics* 39(4) 1985, 540–549.

Mitchell, R. C., and R. T. Carson, "Option Value: Empirical Evidence from a Case Study of Recreation of Water Quality, Comment," *Quarterly Journal of Economics* 100(1) 1985, 291–294.

Montgomery, M., and M. Needelman, "The Welfare Effects of Toxic Contamination in Freshwater Fish," *Land Economics* 73(2) 1997, 211–223.

Peshin, H. M., and E. P. Seskin, eds., *Cost-Benefit Analysis and Water Pollution Policy* (Washington, D.C.: The Urban Institute, 1975).

Raucher, R. L., "A Conceptual Framework for Measuring the Benefits of Ground Water Protection," *Water Resources Research* 19(2) 1983, 320–326.

Raucher, R. L., "The Benefits and Costs of Policies Related to Ground Water Contamination," *Land Economics* 62(1) 1986, 33–45.

Russell, C. S., and W. J. Vaughan, "The National Recreational Fishing Benefits of Water Pollution Control," *Journal of Environmental Economics and Management* 9(3) 1982, 328–354.

Smith, V. K., and W. H. Desvousges, "The Generalized Travel Cost Model and Water Quality Benefits: A Reconsideration," *Southern Economic Journal* 52(2) 1985, 371–381.

Smith, V. K., and W. H. Desvousges, *Measuring Water Quality Benefits* (Boston, MA: Kluwer Nijhoff Publishing, 1986).

Sutherland, R. J., "A Regional Approach to Estimating Recreation Benefits of Improved Water Quality," *Journal of Environmental Economics and Management* 9(3) 1982, 229–247.

Sutherland, R. J., and R. G. Walsh, "Effects of Distance on the Preservation Value of Water Quality," *Land Economics* 61(3) 1985, 281–291.

22. Wilderness/Wetlands/Wildlife

Batie, S. S., and C. C. Mabbs-Zeno, "Opportunity Costs of Preserving Coastal Wetlands: A Case Study of a Recreational Housing Development," *Land Economics* 61(1) 1985, 1–9.

Batie, S. S., and L. A. Shabman, "Estimating the Economic Value of Wetlands: Principles, Method, and Limitations," *Coastal Zone Management Journal* 10(3) 1982, 255–278.

Brouwer, R., and L. Slangen, "Contingent Valuation of the Public Benefits of Agricultural Wildlife Management: The Case of Dutch Peat Meadow Land," *European Review of Agricultural Economics* 25(1) 1998, 53–72.

Carson, R., L. Wilks, and D. Imber, "Valuing the Preservation of Australia's Kakadu Conservation Zone," *Oxford Economic Papers* 46(5) 1994, 727–749.

Chambers, C., and J. Whitehead, "A Contingent Valuation Estimate of the Benefits of Wolves in Minnesota," *Environmental and Resource Economics* 26(2) 2003, 249–268.

Clayton, C., and R. Mendelsohn, "The Value of Watchable Wildlife: A Case Study of McNeil River," *Journal of Environmental Management* 39(2) 1993, 101–106.

Cicia, G., E. Ercole, and D. Marino, "Costs and Benefits of Preserving Farm Animal Genetic

Resources from Extinction: CVM and Bio-Economic Models for Valuing a Conservation Program for the Italian Pentro Horse," *Ecological Economics* 45(3) 2003, 249–459.

Danielson, L. E., and J. A. Leitch, "Private vs. Public Economics of Prairie Wetland Allocation," *Journal of Environmental Economics and Management* 13(1) 1986, 81–92.

Farber, S. C., "The Value of Costal Wetlands for Protection of Property Against Hurricane Wind Damage," *Journal of Environmental Economics and Management* 14(2) 1987, 143–151.

Guldin, R. W., "Wilderness Costs in New England," *Journal of Forestry* 78(9) 1980, 548–552.

Guldin, R. W., "Predicting Costs of Eastern National Forest Wildernesses," *Journal of Leisure Research* 13(2) 1981, 112–128.

Hanley, N., D. MacMillan, R. Wright, C. Bullock, I. Simpson, D. Parsisson, and B. Crabtree, "Contingent Valuation vs. Choice Experiments: Estimating the Benefits of Environmentally Sensitive Areas in Scotland," *Journal of Agricultural Economics* 49(1) 1998, 1–15.

Hyde, W. F., "Developments versus Preservation in Public Resource Management: A Case Study from the Timber-Wilderness Controversy," *Journal of Environmental Management* 16(4) 1983, 347–355.

Lakhani, H., "Benefit-Cost Analysis: Substituting Iron for Lead Shot in Waterfowl Hunting in Maryland," *Journal of Environmental Management* 14(3) 1982, 201–208.

Loomis, J. B., and R. G. Walsh, "Assessing Wildlife and Environmental Values in Cost-Benefit Analysis: State of the Art," *Journal of Environmental Management* 22(2) 1986, 125–131.

Lynne, G. D., P. Conroy, and F. Prochaska, "Economic Valuation of Marsh Areas for Marine Production Processes," *Journal of Environmental Economics and Management* 8(2) 1981, 175–186.

Mahan, B., S. Polasky, and R. Adams, "Valuing Urban Wetlands: A Property Price Approach," *Land Economics* 76(1) 2000, 100–113.

Oglethorpe, D., and D. Miliadou, "Economic Valuation of the Non-Use Attributes of a Wetland: A Case-Study of Lake Kerkina," *Journal of Environmental Planning and Management* 43(6) 2000, 755–767.

Peterson, G. L., and A. Randall, *Valuation of Wildland Benefits* (Boulder, CO: Westview, 1984).

Sathirathai, S., and E. Barbier, "Valuing Mangrove Conservation in Southern Thailand," *Contemporary Economic Policy* 19(2) 2001, 109–122.

Simpson, R. D., R. A. Sedjo, and J. W. Reid, "Valuing Biodiversity for Use in Pharmaceutical Research," *Journal of Political Economy* 104(1) 1996, 163–185.

Woodward, R., and Y.-S. Wui, "The Economic Value of Wetland Services: A Meta-Analysis," *Ecological Economics* 37(2) 2001, 257–270.

Name Index

Subject Index